THE MACMILLAN DICTIONARY OF

SYNONYMS & ANTONYMS

EDITED BY
LAURENCE URDANG

MACMILLAN

First published 1978 by the New American Library Inc.

Revised editions first published in Great Britain as
The Pan Dictionary of Synonyms and Antonyms 1980 and 1991 by Pan Books

This edition published 1995 by Macmillan Reference Books
an imprint of Macmillan Publishers Ltd
25 Eccleston Place, London SW1W 9NF
and Basingstoke

Associated companies throughout the world

ISBN 0-333-63408-X

5 7 9 8 6

A CIP catalogue record for this book is available from
the British Library.

Printed and bound in Great Britain by
Mackays of Chatham PLC, Chatham, Kent

Introduction

A synonym is a word that has a meaning similar to that of another word. This dictionary gives a list of synonyms for common words in English. It can be used when you cannot think of a word to express your exact meaning, or when you want to add variety to your speech or writing.

how to use this book

Look up the word for which you want to find a synonym, as in a normal dictionary; all the entries are in alphabetical order. Each entry indicates the part of speech of the word – noun, verb, etc. – followed by the list of synonyms. Where the word has more than one meaning, different meanings are numbered, and an example of the use of the word is given. For example:

angle *n.* 1 corner, edge; branch, fork *A triangle has three angles.*
2 viewpoint, point of view, position, standpoint: *Let's look at this question from a different angle.*

The first meaning has the synonyms *corner, edge, . . .* and an example of the use of the meaning is given. The second meaning has the synonyms *viewpoint, point of view, . . .* with a different example. Sometimes more than one example is given to explain the use of the word in more detail.

Not all the words given in the list of synonyms have exactly the same meaning: in fact there are no such things as exact synonyms; words are never completely substitutable for each other. For example:

dislike *vb.* disapprove of; hate, detest, loathe.

The words *hate, detest, loathe* are stronger than *disapprove of,* and this difference is shown by dividing the groups by a semicolon. Furthermore, the synonyms given may also combine with other words in different ways. For example:

favour ... *vb.*   prefer, support, want to: *We favour going to Germany for our holiday.*

The words *prefer, support* can replace favour, but if *want to* is chosen, the sentence has to be rephrased to give something like *We want to go to Germany for our holiday.* The list of synonyms given should therefore be used with care. If you are in doubt, check first how the word is used by asking someone or by looking it up in a good dictionary.

antonyms

An antonym is a word that has a meaning opposite to that of another word. At the end of many entries there is a list of antonyms, shown after the word ANT. Where there is more than one part of speech, the part of speech that the antonyms refer to is given. Similarly, when there is more than one numbered meaning, the number of the meaning referred to in the list of antonyms is shown in brackets. For example:

attack *vb.*   **1** assault, set upon, assail, charge, storm: *The army attacked the fort, and it was soon captured.*   **2** criticize, blame, abuse: *The newspapers attacked the local council for refusing to collect the rubbish.*   *n.*   assault, charge, onslaught, encounter: *The robber was accused of an armed attack outside the bank.* ANT. *vb.* **(1)** withdraw, retreat. **(2)** praise, endorse. *n.* withdrawal, retreat.

The antonyms *withdraw, retreat* refer to the first meaning of the verb part of the entry: *assault, set upon* . . . ; the antonyms *praise, endorse* to the second meaning of the verb part of the entry; and *withdrawal, retreat* to the noun part of the entry. Occasionally, the same list of synonyms may refer to more than one numbered part of the entry or more than one part of speech, and this is also shown.

levels of usage

Some words are used informally, that is they are used widely in conversation but would not be used in writing a formal letter or composition. This is shown by placing the word *Informal* before the list of synonyms. For example:

cranky *adj. Informal:*   eccentric, odd, strange, peculiar.

This means that the word *cranky* is informal. The label *Slang* is used in a similar way, to show words that are very informal and are to be used in fewer contexts than informal words. They are not suitable for use in most kinds of writing. If you are uncertain about how to use a particular word, look it up in a dictionary.

Some of the words that are given in the list of synonyms itself may also be either informal or slang. In this case the label is put in front of the particular word in brackets. For example:

mislead *vb.*   deceive, delude, (*informal*) take in; trick

cross-references

Occasionally a cross-reference is used to show that the list of synonyms of a word is in a different part of the book. For example:

lethal *see* **fatal.**

This means that a list of synonyms for the word *lethal* is given at the entry *fatal*.

list of abbreviations

adj.	adjective	*n.*	noun
adj. phr.	adjectival phrase	*n. phr.*	noun phrase
adv.	adverb	*pl.*	plural
adv. phr.	adverbial phrase	*prep.*	preposition
ANT.	antonym	*prep. phr.*	prepositional phrase
conj.	conjunction	*v.*	verb
foll.	followed	*vb. phr.*	phrasal verb

a

abandon *vb.* 1 leave, quit; desert, forsake *The captain was the last to abandon the sinking ship.* 2 give up, surrender *The castaways never abandoned hope that they would be found.* *adv. phr.* **with abandon** freely, unrestrainedly, without restraint, control, inhibition, *or* constraint *Whenever his parents were not at home, he behaved with wild abandon.* ANT. join, engage, unite, embrace, retain.

abandoned *adj.* wicked, depraved, evil; immoral *Her abandoned behaviour caused a lot of trouble.* ANT. righteous, virtuous.

abbey *n.* church, minster; priory, monastery, friary, nunnery.

abbot *n.* prior, monk, friar.

abbreviate *vb.* shorten, abridge, cut, reduce, condense *They abbreviated the long novel for publication as a paperback.* ANT. lengthen, extend, augment.

abbreviation *n.* cut, shortening, abridgement, condensation: *The abbreviation for 'United Kingdom' is 'UK'.*

abdicate *vb.* give up, relinquish, resign, renounce.

ability *n.* capability, skill, competence; power *Does the child have the ability to look after himself?*

able *adj.* 1 capable, qualified, fit, competent *Some people are able to write well.* 2 talented, skilled, clever, skilful *She is an able mathematician.* ANT. unable, incompetent; incapable.

abnormal *adj.* unusual, uncommon, odd, peculiar, queer; strange, weird *They thought he was abnormal because he put salt on his grapefruit.* ANT. normal, average, usual.

abolish *vb.* end, obliterate, erase, put out, eliminate *Slavery has been abolished in almost every nation.* ANT. establish; keep, retain.

abominable *adj.* hateful, loathsome, bad, terrible, awful, nasty, unpleasant *They lived in abominable conditions of poverty.* ANT. admirable, fine, noble.

about *prep.* 1 concerning, relating to, involving *The book was about pirates.* 2 near, close to, around, almost, approximately *The blouse is about my size.* *adv.* 1 nearby, around, close by *There's a ghost about at midnight!* 2 nearly, almost *It is about four o'clock.*

above *prep.* over, higher than, superior to *His house was above hers on the hill. The admiral is above the lieutenant in every navy.* ANT. below, under, beneath.

abreast *adv.* alongside, beside, side by side *The boys walked down the street three abreast.*

abridge *vb.* shorten, cut, abbreviate, abstract *Many of the dictionar-*

ies we use today have been abridged from larger books. ANT. expand, extend, increase.

abroad *adv.* 1 overseas *She studied abroad last year.* 2 publicly, widely, at large; in all directions, in all places *The news was made known abroad that they were to be married.* ANT. (2) privately, secretly.

abrupt *adj.* 1 sudden, hasty *He came to an abrupt stop at the door.* 2 short, curt, blunt, brusque, rude, hasty *When I asked where she had been, she became very abrupt and asked me to leave.* 3 steep, precipitous, sudden *The road made an abrupt descent to the valley.* ANT. (1, 3) gradual.

abscess *n.* sore, inflammation, boil *The doctor said he should have that abscess lanced.*

absence *n.* want, need, lack *The absence of any affection made him yearn for his family.* ANT. presence, existence.

absent *adj.* 1 away, not present, off, out *I was absent from school on Monday.* 2 missing, lacking, nonexistent *Common sense was clearly absent from their decision.* ANT. present.

absent-minded *adj.* forgetful; inattentive, day-dreaming, wool-gathering, preoccupied *He is getting so absent-minded that he nearly went out without his shoes.* ANT. alert, attentive, observant; aware.

absolute *adj.* 1 positive, certain, sure, definite *The court had absolute proof that he had committed the crime.* 2 total, complete, unlimited, limitless, unrestricted, arbitrary; tyrannical, dictatorial *The dictator assumed absolute power.* ANT. partial, limited, fragmentary, incomplete.

absolutely *adv.* definitely, positively, really, doubtlessly *If she goes to the party, I absolutely refuse to go!* ANT. doubtfully, questionably.

absolve *vb.* acquit, exonerate, excuse, forgive, pardon, clear, free from blame *or* responsibility (for), cleanse, discharge. ANT. involve, blame; accuse, charge.

absorb *vb.* 1 consume, occupy, engage *The film absorbed their attention completely.* 2 suck up, sop up, take in *or* up *A sponge absorbs water.* ANT. (2) leak, drain.

abstain *vb.* do without, give up, deny oneself, renounce *We abstain from drinking spirits in our house.*

abstract *adj.* theoretical, hypothetical; unreal *The concept of number is abstract.* ANT. concrete, real, substantial.

absurd *adj.* foolish, ridiculous, preposterous, laughable, silly *The belief that the earth is flat is regarded today as absurd.* ANT. sensible, sound, reasonable.

abundance *n.* plenty, copiousness, ampleness, profusion *There is an abundance of water in our reservoirs this year.* ANT. scarcity, want, dearth, absence.

abundant *adj.* plentiful, abounding, copious, profuse, ample: *An abundant harvest means that there will be enough food for everyone.* ANT. scarce, scant, absent, rare, uncommon, insufficient.

abuse *vb.* 1 misuse, misapply, misemploy *The king abused his power by making the people pay high taxes.* 2 mistreat, maltreat, hurt, harm, injure *It was cruel of the children to abuse their kitten by keeping it in a cage.* 3 insult, malign, revile *The politicians abused each other in the election campaign.* *n.* misuse, mistreatment, maltreatment *The puppy suffered the boys' abuse without whimpering.*

accelerate *vb.* speed up, quicken, hasten *We shall miss the boat if you don't accelerate.* ANT. slow down.

accent *n.* 1 stress, accentuation *The accent in the word 'college' comes on the first syllable.* 2 emphasis, importance, weight *The preacher put the accent on discipline in his sermon.* *vb.* stress, emphasize, accentuate *You must try to accent the better qualities in your personality.*

accept *vb.* 1 receive, take *She accepted the gift with thanks.* 2 admit, allow, consent to *He accepts criticism from anyone but his father.* ANT. (1, 2) refuse, reject, ignore.

access *n.* approach, entrance; way, passage *The only access to the wine cellar is through the dining room.*

accessory *n.* addition, extra, supplement *She added some pretty accessories to dress up her hat.*

accident *n.* mishap, misadventure, misfortune, mischance, disaster, calamity, catastrophe *Three men were knocked unconscious in the accident at the factory.* *n. phr.* by accident unintentionally, accidentally *I spilt the sugar by accident.*

acclaim *vb.* praise, applaud; welcome *The soldiers were acclaimed by all as returning heroes.*

accommodate *vb.* 1 aid, assist, help *The neighbours accommodated us with lodging after the fire.* 2 provide for, serve; hold *Are you sure that this bus can accommodate any more people?*

accompany *vb.* escort, go with, join, attend *Two of my friends accompanied me on the trip.* ANT. abandon, leave, forsake.

accomplice *n.* confederate, accessory, assistant, associate, partner (in crime) *The police accused the bank teller of being the robber's accomplice.*

accomplish *vb.* do, complete, achieve, fulfil, perform, finish *It is disappointing not to accomplish all one sets out to do.* ANT. fail.

accord *vb.* 1 agree, correspond, concur *The description that the witness gave of the attack accorded with that of the victim.* 2 award, grant, reward with, give *When the sergeant was killed in action, he was accorded an officer's burial.* *n.* agreement, concord; pact, treaty *The governments reached accord regarding offshore fishing rights.* ANT. *n.* disagreement, difference, quarrel.

account *n.* 1 explanation, report, description, recital, history *John gave an account of what had happened to him over the weekend.* 2 story, tale, anecdote, narration, narrative *We were frightened by the old man's strange account of the cave.* 3 record, balance sheet, ledger, book *According to the store's account, we owe them £52.*

vb. explain, give an explanation *or* reason for, make *or* give excuses for *The teacher asked Maria to account for her absence from school.*

accumulate *vb.* gather, store up, amass, save (up), pile up *If we accumulate enough coupons, we can get a free radio.*

accurate *adj.* precise, correct, exact, right, true *Was that an accurate description of what happened?* ANT. inaccurate, inexact, mistaken, wrong.

accuse *vb.* blame, charge, incriminate: *An innocent man was accused of the crime.* ANT. absolve, clear, discharge, acquit.

accustomed (to) *adj.* used to, in the habit of, wont to *I was accustomed to seeing you at choir practice.*

ache *vb.* hurt; be sore; throb, sting *My back still aches from lifting that box.*

achieve *vb.* **1** do, perform, complete, accomplish, reach, realize *Only after much hard work are most of us able to achieve our goals.* **2** attain, gain, acquire, secure, procure *The candidate achieved victory in the election after a hard campaign.* ANT. fail.

acid *adj.* **1** sour, tart, vinegary *Lemons have an acid taste.* **2** sardonic, sarcastic, bitter, biting *Because of his acid wit, few people would associate with him.* ANT. **(1)** sweet, bland, mild.

acknowledge *vb.* **1** agree to, admit, allow, concede, accept, grant *After a fierce battle, the general finally acknowledged defeat.* **2** accept, receive, express thanks *or* gratitude for, thank for *The prizewinner gratefully acknowledged the award.* ANT. deny, refuse, reject.

acquaintance *n.* associate, colleague, companion: *He's not really a close friend, just an acquaintance.*

acquire *vb.* obtain, procure, secure, get, gain, appropriate *When did you acquire that collection of rare books?* ANT. lose, forfeit.

acquit *vb.* excuse, forgive, exonerate, discharge, find not guilty *After a long trial, the accused was acquitted.* ANT. condemn, sentence.

act *n.* **1** deed, achievement, action, accomplishment, feat, exploit *He received a medal for an act of bravery.* **2** law, decree, statute, judgement *Parliament voted on the crime-prevention act.* **3** performance, routine, skit *We saw the balancing act at the circus.* **4** show, pretence *She wasn't really crying, it was just an act.* *vb.* **1** do, operate, function *The crowbar acts as a lever.* **2** perform, play, impersonate *She acts the part of the vampire in the film.*

action *n.* **1** movement *His actions are not graceful.* **2** battle, fight, fighting, combat *He saw action on the western front.*

active *adj.* **1** energetic, vigorous, agile *He's eighty but still active.* **2** busy, occupied, engaged, committed *Mrs Robinson is active in many charitable organizations.* ANT. **(1)** lazy, lethargic, inactive. **(2)** apathetic.

activity *n.* action, motion, movement *I thought I saw some activity at the deserted house last night.*

actor *n.* actress, performer, entertainer, player; star *This is a play requiring only three actors.*

actual *adj.* real, true, genuine, certain *We saw an actual crime in the process of being committed.* ANT. unreal, pretended, fake, bogus, false.

actually *adv.* really, in fact, truly *I never actually saw the ghost with my own eyes.*

acute *adj.* 1 severe, piercing, intense *I have an acute pain in my toe.* 2 sharp, keen, quick, perceptive, discerning, intelligent *A human's eyesight is not as acute as that of an eagle.* ANT. (2) insensitive, dull, blind, deaf.

adapt *vb.* conform, suit, modify, adjust, fit *Some people find it hard to adapt to city life.*

add *vb.* 1 combine, put together, join, unite *Add this painting to your collection.* 2 total *Adding the numbers in this column gives exactly 312.* ANT. subtract, remove, withdraw.

additional *adj.* new, extra, further, supplementary *I had something additional to tell you, but I forgot it.*

address *n.* 1 location; residence, home, dwelling, place; office *We have moved to a new address.* 2 speech, lecture, oration, presentation *The president's address lasted three hours.* *vb.* 1 speak to, talk to *Don't ever address me in that way in public.* 2 apply oneself to, concentrate on, pay attention to *You should address yourself to the problem in hand and avoid rambling.*

adequate *adj.* sufficient, enough; satisfactory, fit, suitable *There isn't adequate food for all these people. His playing isn't adequate for the philharmonic.* ANT. inadequate, insufficient.

adhere *vb.* 1 cling, stick, hold; cleave *The new tape will adhere to anything.* 2 be attached, be faithful, be devoted *She adheres to the ideas she had as a child.* ANT. (1) separate, loosen.

adherent *n.* supporter, follower *The new religions are gaining adherents.* ANT. defector, renegade, drop-out.

adjacent *adj.* near, next (to), close (to), neighbouring, nearby *It is noisy in the buildings adjacent to the railway tracks.* ANT. apart, separate, distant.

adjoining *adj.* next (to), near (to), touching, bordering *Is the adjoining house vacant?* ANT. separate, distant, remote.

adjourn *vb.* suspend, postpone, put off; defer, delay *The meeting was adjourned till the next day.* ANT. assemble, convene, begin.

adjust *vb.* 1 set, regulate; change, alter; repair, fix *I adjusted the clock so that it would be on time.* 2 arrange, adapt, settle *We adjusted our spending to our income.* 3 adapt, acclimatize; accustom oneself, get used to *Betty quickly adjusted to her new school.*

adjustable *adj.* adaptable, variable, changeable; flexible, pliable *This piano stool is adjustable. I have an adjustable schedule and can meet you any time.*

administer *vb.* 1 manage, direct, supervise, oversee; rule, govern; conduct, control, superintend; administrate *The general manager* *administers the work schedules in the company.* **2** dispense, mete out, deal out, give out, distribute *The magistrate administers justice in a court.* **3** give, provide, contribute, distribute *The doctor administered the vaccine to the villagers.*

administration *n.* **1** management, direction, conduct, supervision *The new administration will emphasize safety.* **2** government *Will the new administration lower taxes?*

admirable *adj.* excellent, fine, worthy, praiseworthy *Bill did an admirable job of reorganizing the team.* **ANT.** contemptible, despicable, sorry.

admiration *n.* wonder, awe, pleasure, approval, esteem *We all have a great deal of admiration for Susan's charity works.* **ANT.** contempt, disdain, disrespect.

admire *vb.* revere, esteem, venerate; like; honour, praise *I admire the way you got rid of that nasty customer.* **ANT.** dislike, loathe, detest, hate.

admissible *adj.* permissible, lawful; proper, fair, just *I am not sure that such evidence is admissible in court.*

admission *n.* **1** entrance, access, admittance; ticket, pass *The authorities charged for admission to the hockey game.* **2** confession, acknowledgment *Her admission of guilt resulted in a suspension of two days from school.*

admit *vb.* **1** confess, acknowledge, own *Bob admits that he ate all the cake.* **2** let in, allow to enter *When we paid the entrance charge, we were admitted into the stadium.* **ANT.** (1) deny. (2) obstruct, reject.

admittance *n.* entrance, access, admission *The sign read 'Admittance to Authorized Personnel Only'.*

admonish *vb.* **1** warn, caution, advise against *The teacher admonished Jimmy to stop talking in class.* **2** scold, reprimand, rebuke, censure, reprove *Afterwards the teacher had to admonish him for making faces.* **ANT.** praise, commend, extol.

ado *n.* fuss, trouble, bother, to-do, bustle, flurry, activity, commotion, stir, excitement, upset, hubbub, confusion, tumult, turmoil *There was entirely too much ado about such a trifling matter.* **ANT.** quietness, composure, tranquillity.

adolescent *adj.* teenage, young, youthful; immature *Why do so many adults act in such an adolescent way?* *n.* teenager, youth, young person *Many adolescents have difficulties growing into adults.* **ANT.** *adj.* adult, grown; mature.

adopt *vb.* **1** foster, take in, take care of *The family adopted a little girl.* **2** take up, choose, select *The director adopted the committee's plans.*

adorable *adj.* delightful, lovely, charming, wonderful *Penny's father gave her an adorable puppy for Christmas.*

adore *vb.* love, idolize, worship, revere, venerate; respect, honour, esteem *It is gratifying to see the way the children just adore the new teacher.* **ANT.** hate, despise, loathe.

adorn *vb.* decorate, ornament, beautify, enhance, embellish *The elephants were adorned with the most luxurious trappings.* ANT. strip, bare, denude.

adrift *adj.* 1 drifting, floating, afloat *The mutineers set the captain and the officers adrift in the South Pacific.* 2 aimless, purposeless *David was adrift for a while after losing his job.*

adroit *adj.* skilful, clever, adept, dexterous, ingenious, expert *It is a pleasure to watch the adroit hands of such a craftsman.* ANT. clumsy, awkward, graceless.

adult *adj.* mature, developed, full-grown; of age *'Please act in a more adult way,' the teacher reminded her pupils.* *n.* man, woman, grown-up *This ticket admits one adult and one child.* ANT. *adj.* immature, infantile.

adulterate *vb.* contaminate, defile, pollute, debase *The medicine was adulterated by the addition of an improper substance.*

advance *vb.* 1 proceed, progress, move, bring, *or* go forward *The armies advanced towards one another.* 2 further, promote *These treaties will advance the cause of peace.* *n.* progress, advancement, forward movement; improvement, promotion *Progress in many industries has been brought about by advances in technology.* ANT. *vb.* (1) retreat, withdraw, flee. (2) retard, obstruct. *n.* decline, deterioration; retreat, withdrawal.

advantage *n.* 1 benefit, gain, profit *Driving a car has some advantages over travelling by train.* 2 favour, help, (*informal*) edge *Because of his height, Mark has the advantage in the long jump.* ANT. (1) disadvantage, drawback. (2) obstacle, hindrance.

adventure *n.* exploit, experience; event, undertaking, incident *The captain told us of an adventure he had had in Tahiti.*

adventurous *adj.* daring, bold, brave; enterprising *It was very adventurous for women to speak their minds in those days.*

adversary *n.* opponent, antagonist, foe, enemy, contestant *For many years we fought this noble adversary.* ANT. friend, ally.

adverse *adj.* 1 unlucky, unfortunate, unfavourable *Adverse business conditions made him decide to close the shop.* 2 contrary, opposite, opposing, opposed *Adverse winds delayed the plane by two hours.* ANT. (1) beneficial, favourable.

adversity *n.* trouble, misfortune; distress, calamity, disaster, catastrophe *Having lost all her children, that poor woman has suffered enough adversity in her lifetime.* ANT. fortune; happiness, benefit.

advertise *vb.* publicize, (*informal*) plug; make known, propagate *If you don't advertise, how will people know whose sweet to buy?*

advertisement *n.* commercial, poster, billboard; brochure, bill, handbill *The advertisements in every medium are sometimes too much to bear.*

advice *n.* 1 counsel, recommendation, guidance, suggestion *Take my advice and finish school before starting to work.* 2 caution, admonition, warning *The policeman's advice is to walk only on well-lit streets at night.*

advisable *adj.* prudent, sensible, wise; proper, suitable, fit, fitting *Do you think it advisable for the entire class to watch surgery on television?* ANT. inadvisable, ill-considered, imprudent.

advise *vb.* 1 counsel, recommend, suggest *Her father advised her to go out with friends of her own age.* 2 inform, notify, acquaint *The premier was advised of the treachery of the generals.*

advocate *vb.* support, recommend, defend, argue for, plead for *The ecologists advocate preservation of forests.* *n.* supporter, promoter, upholder *Advocates of spelling reform in English have a long fight ahead of them.* ANT. *vb.* oppose, withstand, resist. *n.* opponent, foe, adversary.

affair *n.* business, concern; matter, thing *She is always interfering in other people's affairs.*

affect *vb.* 1 influence, determine, modify, alter, change *A change in the speed limit affects everyone's driving habits.* 2 impress, stir, move, touch *The death of Jennie's kitten affected her deeply.*

affected *adj.* false, sham, pretended, fake, *(informal)* phoney *He is so affected that I cannot spend any time with him.*

affection *n.* liking, fondness, attachment, friendliness, warmth, tenderness *The teacher's affection for her students showed in her many acts of kindness.* ANT. dislike, aversion, antipathy.

affectionate *adj.* fond, tender, attached, warm, loving *Suzy's new puppy is so affectionate!* ANT. cold, distant, unfeeling.

affirm *vb.* 1 declare, state, assert *The defendant affirmed that he was at home on the night of the murder.* 2 confirm, establish, ratify *Parliament affirmed the minister's plans.* ANT. (1) deny, contradict, repudiate, disclaim.

afflict *vb.* hurt, trouble, distress; disturb, torment, harass *It is hard to imagine the troubles that have afflicted that poor family.*

affliction *n.* 1 trouble, distress, grief, misfortune *Poverty is the affliction of millions of people.* 2 pain, suffering, misery; illness, sickness, ailment *In his old age, headaches became a serious affliction.* ANT. (1) benefit, gain. (2) relief, comfort.

affluent *adj.* rich, wealthy, prosperous, well-to-do, well-off *Affluent people are less affected by tax increases.*

afford *vb.* 1 be able to pay for; spare, manage, support *I cannot afford a more expensive car.* 2 provide, give, accord *At last, the chairman afforded me an opportunity to speak.*

afraid *adj.* frightened, fearful, scared, terrified *Liza was afraid to go into the cave alone.* ANT. courageous, bold, daring.

against *prep.* opposed to, in opposition to, in disagreement with, versus, at odds with, adverse to, hostile to, con *In the Second World War, it was the Allies against the Axis. The Tories often vote against Labour.* ANT. for, in favour of, pro, in support of, with.

age *n.* era, time, period, epoch *The last ice age ended about 20,000 years ago.* *n. phr.* **of age** mature, grown-up *When you become of age, you will have the right to vote.* *vb.* 1 grow old, get on; decline

My grandmother began to age in her early seventies. 2 mature, develop, ripen *I think this wine has aged long enough.*

aged *adj.* old, elderly, ancient *That aged gentleman is almost a hundred years old.* ANT. young, youthful.

agent *n.* 1 representative, delegate, deputy; operator *John is an agent for a plastics firm.* 2 instrument, means, cause *The sun is an agent in the growth of plants.*

aggravate *vb.* 1 intensify, worsen, heighten *His illness was aggravated by the lack of heat in the room.* 2 *Informal:* irritate, exasperate, annoy *'Stop aggravating your sister!' shouted Jean.* ANT. (1) ease, relieve, soothe.

aggressive *adj.* 1 attacking, pugnacious, ready to fight, offensive *Her aggressive manner irritated so many people that no one wanted to spend time with her.* 2 assertive, vigorous, energetic, enterprising, determined *We need an aggressive chairman, not one who is too shy to act for us.* ANT. (1) peaceful, friendly, amicable. (2) passive, shy, timid, withdrawn.

agile *adj.* active, nimble, graceful, lively, spry *An agile dancer, Marie had studied ballet for many years.* ANT. clumsy, awkward, inept.

agitate *vb.* 1 stir up, excite, disturb *Her speech on equal rights for women agitated some in the crowd.* 2 shake (up), jar *Agitate the bottle to stir up the sediment from the bottom.* ANT. calm, soothe.

agitated *adj.* 1 nervous, jumpy, jittery, ill-at-ease, restless, restive *George was so agitated about the state of his business that he had to take a holiday.* 2 upset, disturbed, perturbed, ruffled, shaken, in a dither, *Informal* in a tizzy, *slang* all shook up *The news of the child's disappearance had everyone very agitated.* ANT. calm, tranquil, at ease.

agony *n.* pain, suffering, torment, torture *After his accident, Peter was in agony from his broken ankle.*

agree *vb.* 1 settle, concur, harmonize, unite *The members of the committee could not agree on where the party should be held.* 2 assent, consent, yield, concede *He agreed to leave the room so that his parents could talk in private.* ANT. (1) differ, disagree, argue. (2) refuse.

agreeable *adj.* friendly, cooperative, pleasing, pleasant *I like being with George because he is so agreeable.* ANT. disagreeable, quarrelsome, contentious, touchy.

agreement *n.* 1 treaty, pact; deal, bargain, contract, understanding, arrangement *An agreement was reached between the union and the company.* 2 settlement, accord, harmony, concord *There was basic agreement on the terms of the pension contribution.* ANT. disagreement, discord, misunderstanding.

agriculture *n.* farming, husbandry *Agriculture is no longer the mainstay of the economy of industrialized nations.*

aid *vb.* help, assist, support, back *Unless you all aid me, I cannot win.* *n.* help, assistance, support, backing *Without his aid I* *couldn't have climbed to the top of the mountain.* ANT. *vb.* impede, obstruct, hinder. *n.* obstacle, hindrance.

ailing *adj.* sick, ill, unwell *The ailing old man felt that he would not live much longer.* ANT. well, hearty, hale.

ailment *n.* sickness, illness, affliction, disease *Donald's ailment turned out to be indigestion from too much ice cream.*

aim *vb.* 1 point, direct *Aim a little below the bull's-eye when firing a rifle at a target.* 2 try *or* strive for *Some of us aim at perfection, but only a few ever achieve it.* *n.* 1 purpose, goal, target, object, objective *My aim in life is to be a really good doctor.* 2 direction, sight, sighting *His aim was so poor that he missed the target completely.*

aimless *adj.* purposeless, pointless, directionless, adrift *This aimless wandering will only leave us hopelessly lost.*

air *n.* 1 atmosphere *The envelope of air is kept close to earth by gravity.* 2 manner, appearance, character, look, attitude *He has an air about him that gives everyone the impression that he thinks he's just wonderful.* *vb.* 1 ventilate *We really ought to air the room to get rid of the smell.* 2 display, publicize, expose, reveal *The headmaster gave the students the chance to air their complaints against the teacher.* ANT. *vb.* (2) hide, conceal, cover up.

aisle *n.* passage, opening; corridor; path *The aisle between the rows of seats in the cinema was very narrow.*

alarm *n.* 1 fright, fear, dismay *They greeted the news of the accident with alarm.* 2 siren, bell, gong *The fire alarm could be heard far away.* *vb.* frighten, scare, terrify, startle *The nurse was alarmed by Jane's temperature.* ANT. *vb.* calm, soothe, comfort.

alarming *adj.* frightening, disturbing, shocking, appalling, daunting *The warders show an alarming lack of sympathy for the prisoners.*

album *n.* book, scrapbook, notebook; collection, record *I have kept all the press cuttings of your interviews in my family album.*

alcohol *n.* spirits, intoxicants, (strong) drink, liquor *People who drink alcohol ought not to drive cars.*

alert *adj.* 1 watchful, attentive, wide-awake, vigilant, keen, observant *The alert watchman gave the alarm when he found the broken window.* 2 quick, lively, active, spirited, bright *Dick's alert mind understood at once where the error was in the calculation.* *n.* alarm, warning *When they smelled smoke, they sounded the alert.* ANT. *adj.* listless, dulled, sluggish, lethargic.

alien *n.* foreigner, immigrant; stranger *In some countries, aliens become eligible for citizenship after one year.* *adj.* foreign, strange; non-native *The spacemen landed on an alien planet.* ANT. *adj.* familiar, commonplace, accustomed.

alight *vb.* disembark, descend from, get down, get out, get off; detrain, deplane *Sally was alighting from the train just as we arrived to meet her.* ANT. board, embark.

alike *adj.* the same, identical; similar *I don't think the brothers look alike at all.*

alive *adj.* **1** live, living, existing, breathing *There is hardly anyone still alive who can remember that battle.* **2** lively, animated, vivacious, sprightly *Margot is alive with the sheer joy of youth.* ANT. (1) dead. (2) moribund, inactive.

allay *vb.* quiet, soothe, calm, lessen, lighten, soften, moderate *Mother's anxiety was allayed when we phoned to say we were safe.* ANT. arouse, worsen, intensify.

allege *vb.* declare, affirm, state, assert *The boy whom the police officer alleged to be the thief was innocent.* ANT. deny, refute, contradict.

allegiance *n.* loyalty, faithfulness, duty, obligation *He owes his allegiance to the country where he was born.* ANT. disloyalty, treachery, infidelity.

alley *n.* lane, alleyway, way; path, footpath *The back door of the shop opens onto an alley.*

alliance *n.* **1** agreement, treaty, pact; union, league *The Triple Alliance was between Germany, Austria-Hungary and Italy.* **2** association, connection, combination; affinity, correspondence *The alliance between biology and psychology is well established.*

allot *vb.* distribute, divide, deal out *Each child was allotted a fair share of dessert.*

allow *vb.* **1** permit, let *My mother won't allow me to go out until my cold is better.* **2** grant, let have, concede *Allow me one more chance to prove I can run faster than Jim.* **3** set aside or apart, provide for *We didn't allow enough time to drive to the station and missed the train.* ANT. (1) forbid, prohibit.

allowance *n.* amount, contribution; money *How much of an allowance ought a small boy to receive?*

all right *adv. phr.* satisfactory, fine, acceptable *Informal* OK, okay *The astronauts signalled that everything was all right.*

ally *n.* associate, friend, partner *Britain and America were allies against Germany in the Second World War.* *vb.* **1** associate, join, unite *The countries were allied by the treaty.* **2** unite, unify, combine, connect, join *If we ally ourselves with them, we could be much stronger than if we remain alone.* ANT. *n.* enemy, foe, adversary.

almost *adv.* nearly, just about *Almost every house was recently painted.*

alone *adj.* isolated, solitary; deserted *Robinson Crusoe was alone until he found Friday.* *adv.* solo, solitarily; solely, exclusively *She sang alone at the concert.* ANT. *adv.* accompanied, together.

aloof *adj.* distant, uninvolved, uninterested, withdrawn, cool, unfriendly; disdainful *Her aloof attitude won her few friends.* ANT. friendly, outgoing, cordial, warm.

aloud *adv.* audibly, out loud; articulately, clearly, plainly, distinctly *I would be embarrassed to say aloud what I was thinking.*

already *adv.* **1** now, by this time, before now *If he left at noon, he should be here already.* **2** yet *Is he already here?*

also *adv.* too, as well, besides, furthermore, moreover, further *They stole not only the chairs but the table also.*

alter *vb.* change, modify; vary; adjust *The doorways have been altered to allow wheelchairs to pass through.* ANT. keep, preserve, maintain.

alteration *n.* change, modification, difference, adjustment *After the dressmaker made the alterations, the dress fitted perfectly.* ANT. preservation, maintenance.

alternate *vb.* substitute, interchange, rotate *In order to be fair, the teacher alternated the children at the head of the line.* *adj.* successive, consecutive, in rotation *The guards stood watch outside the palace for alternate hours.*

alternative *n.* choice, selection, option; possibility *In 'The Lady or the Tiger', the hero is given a difficult set of alternatives.*

although *conj.* even though, though, even if, in spite of (the fact that), despite, notwithstanding *Although Gillian wished very much to go, she had to stay home and study.*

altitude *n.* height, elevation *Our plane was flying at an altitude of 37,000 feet.* ANT. depth, deepness, profundity.

altogether *adv.* entirely, completely, wholly, quite *He was altogether too rude to his father.* *n. phr.* **in the altogether** *Informal:* nude, naked, stripped *After the night football game, the whole team went swimming in the altogether.*

always *adv.* **1** for ever, everlastingly, eternally, forevermore *I shall love you always.* **2** forever, continuously, constantly, perpetually *Jennie is always trying to make an impression on the teacher.* ANT. (1) never. (2) rarely.

amateur *n.* novice, nonprofessional, beginner, tiro *When it came to repairing watches, Jimmy was obviously an amateur.* *adj.* unprofessional, nonprofessional *The amateur theatre group put on an excellent performance.* ANT. professional.

amaze *vb.* astonish, astound, surprise, stun, dumbfound *The magician's tricks truly amazed the audience.* ANT. bore, tire, weary.

amazement *n.* astonishment, wonder, surprise, bewilderment *Much to his amazement, David was selected to receive first prize.*

ambassador *n.* diplomat, envoy, representative; minister *When we were stranded in Rome, the British ambassador himself saw that we got help.*

ambiguous *adj.* unclear, uncertain, vague, deceptive *When asked if he had broken the vase, Paul gave an ambiguous reply.* ANT. clear, unmistakable, certain.

ambition *n.* drive, initiative; eagerness, enthusiasm *Her ambition to become a doctor made Sara study hard.*

ambitious *adj.* aspiring, zealous, (*informal*) pushing, (*informal*) high-flying *Roger is so ambitious that his supervisor thinks her job might be in danger.*

ambush *vb.* ensnare, trap, lure, trick; lie in wait for *Twelve o'clock struck and the thugs knew it was time to ambush the patrol.* *n.*

trap, snare, lure, pitfall *The highwaymen planned the ambush of the mail coach.*

amend *vb.* improve, better *We prefer the amended version of the agreement.* ANT. worsen.

amiable *adj.* friendly, amicable, good-natured, outgoing, agreeable, kindhearted, kind, pleasant *Dan's amiable manner has won him many friends.* ANT. disagreeable, ill-tempered, cross, touchy.

amid *prep.* amidst, surrounded by, among, amongst, in the midde of *It was difficult to find the flowers amid all the weeds.*

amiss *adv.* improperly, wrongly, astray, awry *We knew that something had gone amiss when Barbara didn't come to school for three days.* *adj.* improper, wrong, faulty *Something is amiss in the wiring of this house—the lights always flicker.* ANT. *adv.* properly, correctly, rightly. *adj.* right, correct.

among *prep.* amid, in the middle *or* midst of, surrounded by *Among the crowd I could pick out my parents.*

amorous *adj.* loving, affectionate, amatory *That man kept giving Anne such amorous looks that she was embarrassed.*

amount *n.* quantity, measure *There was only a small amount of sugar in the box.* *vb.* add up, total, come to *At the last count, those opposed to the plan amounted to less than a majority.*

ample *adj.* abundant, plentiful, generous, liberal *There was ample food for everyone.* 1 spacious, roomy, capacious, large *This room is ample enough to hold all the people you invited.* ANT. (1) insufficient, inadequate. (2) cramped, confined.

amplify *vb.* enlarge, extend, broaden, develop, expand *Asked to amplify his remarks, the speaker gave many more examples.* ANT. restrict, confine, narrow, shorten, condense.

amuse *vb.* entertain, please, interest, divert *Oscar's parents hired a clown to amuse the children at his birthday party.* ANT. bore, tire.

amusement *n.* entertainment, pastime; diversion; enjoyment, recreation, pleasure *We used to play cards for amusement before we had television.* ANT. boredom, tedium.

amusing *adj.* entertaining, diverting, pleasing, pleasant; funny, comical *Harvey helped to pass the time by telling amusing stories.* ANT. boring, tiring, tedious.

analyse *vb.* examine, investigate, study, scrutinize; explain *In the laboratory we analysed each specimen.*

analysis *n.* examination, investigation, study *The analysis of the blood sample shows that you are healthy.*

ancestor *n.* forefather; predecessor *What would our ancestors think if they were alive today?*

ancestral *adj.* inherited, hereditary *George went to live in his family's ancestral home.*

ancestry *n.* lineage, descent, line, family, house *Chauncy's ancestry is royal.* ANT. posterity, descendants.

anchor *n.* stay, mooring *The anchor was thrown overboard as the ship docked.* *vb.* 1 moor, berth, tie up *The ship anchored off-*

shore. **2** fasten, tie, secure, attach, fix *We anchored the rope to the rock.* ANT. *vb.* **(1)** set sail. **(2)** loosen, free, detach.

ancient *adj.* antique, old, aged, old-fashioned, primitive *There are said to be ancient cities buried beneath the sands of the Sahara.* ANT. new, fresh, recent, current.

anecdote *n.* story, tale, narrative, account *The old man used to tell us anecdotes about his sailing days.*

angel *n.* seraph, cherub, archangel *Hark! the herald angels sing!* ANT. devil, demon.

anger *n.* fury, rage, indignation, wrath; displeasure, exasperation *We felt anger at the unfair way that Sue had been treated.* *vb.* enrage, infuriate, arouse, nettle, exasperate, inflame, madden *Jean's mother was angered at her refusal to help with the housework.*

angle *n.* **1** corner, edge; branch, fork *A triangle has three sides and three angles.* **2** viewpoint, point of view, position, standpoint *Let's look at this question from a different angle.*

angry *adj.* furious, mad, inflamed, irate *Mother became angry when I told her I had not gone to school.* ANT. happy, content, peaceful, tranquil.

anguish *n.* pain, suffering, misery, distress, torment, agony *The anguish of losing her kitten was more than she could bear.*

animal *n.* creature, beast *To assert your freedom, you do not have to behave like an animal.*

animate *vb.* enliven, vitalize, invigorate, stimulate *Her animated conversation made Amy a welcome guest at parties.* *adj.* alive, lively, vital, vigorous *Rocks are not animate beings, but mice are.* ANT. *adj.* inanimate, dead.

annex *vb.* add, attach, join, append *Poland was sometimes annexed to Russia, sometimes to Germany.*

annexe *n.* extension, wing *Professor Newley's office is in the annexe, not the main building.*

announce *vb.* proclaim, declare, report, publish, publicize *Have they announced the names of the prizewinners?* ANT. suppress, stifle; censor.

announcement *n.* notice, declaration, report, statement, message *The announcement of the winners' names appeared in the newspaper.*

annoy *vb.* bother, irritate, irk, pester, harass, disturb *Every time he tried to read his book, the children annoyed him.* ANT. comfort, soothe, please.

annual *adj.* yearly, every year, once a year *The annual dues continue to increase.*

annul *vb.* cancel, repeal, invalidate, revoke *My credit card was annulled because I failed to pay the bill.*

answer *n.* reply, response; retort, rejoinder *His answer to her question was a nod.* *vb.* reply, respond *She answered him with a shake of the head.* ANT. *n.* question, query, inquiry. *vb.* ask, question, inquire.

antagonism *n.* hostility, enmity, opposition, conflict, animosity *The* *antagonism between the competitors caused them to insult each other constantly.* ANT. friendliness, geniality, cordiality.

antagonist *n.*   adversary, opponent, rival; enemy, foe *Philbert may well lose the fight as his antagonist is far stronger.* ANT. friend, ally.

anticipate *vb.*   1 expect, foresee, forecast *Because we had anticipated our parents' permission, we got ready to go.*   2 forestall, provide against, prevent *He anticipated the attack by altering his route home.*

anthology *n.*   collection, treasury, garland *Have you read this anthology of romantic poetry?*

antiquated *adj.*   old-fashioned, out-of-date, out-moded, dated, passé *He enjoys driving that antiquated car even though he can afford a new one.*

antique *n.*   objet d'art, rarity, curio *The auctioneer sold the antiques to the collector for a huge sum.*   *adj.*   old, ancient, early; antiquated, old-fashioned, out-of-date *They sold the antique furniture at the auction.*   ANT. *adj.* new, fresh, recent.

anxiety *n.*   uneasiness, distress, worry, foreboding, apprehension *I cannot tell you the anxiety we felt when you failed to come home for dinner.*   ANT. peacefulness, placidity, calmness, tranquillity.

anxious *adj.*   worried, troubled, concerned, uneasy, apprehensive *After midnight, I became anxious for your safety.*   ANT. calm, composed.

anyway *adv.*   anyhow, nevertheless, in any event, in any case *Anyway, I couldn't forgive you for the way you treated Kathy.*

apathetic *adj.*   indifferent, unconcerned; uncaring, unsympathetic *We found people to be totally apathetic towards our campaign for the protection of the housefly.*   ANT. interested, concerned; excited.

apologetic *adj.*   regretful, sorry *Arthur was terribly apologetic about not having come to the wedding.*   ANT. unrepentant; stubborn, obstinate.

apology *n.*   explanation, plea; excuse, justification *I accept your apology for stepping on my toe.*

appal *vb.*   horrify, shock, dismay; frighten *We were appalled at the poverty and hunger we saw in Africa.*   ANT. please, edify, comfort.

appalling *adj.*   awful, frightful, shocking, dreadful *The people in those slums live in the most appalling conditions.*

apparatus *n.*   machinery, equipment, materials; mechanism, device.

apparel *n.*   clothing, clothes, attire, garb, garments, robes, dress *They refused him entrance at the club because his apparel was not appropriate.*

apparent *adj.*   1 plain, evident, clear, obvious; transparent *When we found the book in Cora's desk, it was apparent who had taken it.*   2 seeming *Although the grey mare had been the apparent winner of the race, the photo showed the real winner to be the brown one.*   ANT. (2) real, actual.

appeal *n.*   1 request, plea, petition, entreaty *The annual appeal for contributions resulted in huge donations this year.*   2 attractiveness, glamour, charm *The cartoon has much more appeal than the main feature film.* *vb.* 1 request, plead, petition, entreat, beseech *The charity appealed to the millionaire for financial support.* 2 attract, interest; captivate, fascinate *Frankly, that colour doesn't appeal to me at all.* ANT. *vb.* (2) repel, repulse.

appealing *adj.* attractive, fascinating, interesting, captivating *The request for contributions is accompanied by an appealing photograph of a little puppy.*

appear *vb.* 1 seem, look *Although that person may appear wise, he is really very stupid.* 2 emerge; arise; turn up, arrive *Just when we were sure he wouldn't come, he appeared.* ANT. (2) disappear, vanish, evaporate.

appearance *n.* 1 look, condition, expression; attitude, bearing *From his appearance, I'd say he hasn't slept for days.* 2 arrival, presence *Her appearance at the party wearing a long dress was a surprise to us all.* ANT. (2) departure, going; disappearance, vanishing.

append *vb.* add, attach, supplement *The notes are appended to the ends of the chapters.*

appetite *n.* hunger, craving, thirst, desire *These people have demonstrated some very unusual appetites.*

applaud *vb.* praise, approve of, acclaim *We applaud your efforts to establish an architectural review committee.* ANT. disapprove of, criticize, condemn, denounce.

appliance *n.* apparatus, machine; instrument, device, contrivance *The tin opener is an essential appliance in any kitchen.*

applicable *adj.* usable, fitting, suitable, proper, fit, appropriate, suited *The statement you made about boys is simply not applicable to girls.* ANT. inapplicable, inappropriate.

application *n.* 1 use, utilization, employment; relevance, value *The professor's ideas had application in the field of technology.* 2 form, request; statement, paper *She filled in an application for a new job.*

apply *vb.* use, utilize, employ, make use of, put to use *The techniques used for training horses do not apply to training dogs.* ANT. neglect, ignore.

appoint *vb.* assign, nominate, name, designate, elect, establish, place *Victor has been appointed to the committee by its chairman.* ANT. dismiss, discharge, (*informal*) fire.

appointment *n.* 1 engagement, meeting *I made two appointments for ten o'clock, so please change one of them.* 2 selection, choice; installation *Her appointment as head of the school board was widely applauded.* ANT. (2) dismissal, discharge.

appreciate *vb.* 1 prize, value, acknowledge; thank, be grateful for *What child really appreciates what his parents do for him?* 2 recognize, understand *I don't think that Martin fully appreciates the dangers of swimming alone.* ANT. (1) take for granted; scorn, depreciate, undervalue.

apprehend *vb.* 1 arrest, catch, seize, capture *The police apprehended the burglar while he was trying to pick the lock on the door.* 2 understand, perceive, grasp *He had difficulty apprehending all that the company director said in his statement.*

apprehension *n.* 1 uneasiness, worry, fear, fearfulness, misgiving, dread, anxiety *When the police officer asked to speak to his father, Philip was filled with apprehension.* 2 arrest, capture, seizure *The apprehension of the fugitive at the top of the tower was dramatic.* ANT. (1) composure, self-assuredness, confidence.

apprehensive *adj.* troubled, worried, uneasy, fearful *One cannot blame parents for being apprehensive about their children's safety.* ANT. calm, composed.

apprentice *n.* learner, beginner; amateur; recruit *In former times, an apprentice to a carpenter trained for ten years.* ANT. master, professional.

approach *vb.* come near, draw near, progress *There was a storm approaching as we set sail.* ANT. recede, go away.

appropriate *adj.* fitting, proper, suitable *Her blue jeans were not appropriate clothing for school.* *vb.* take possession of, seize; take up *The treasurer appropriated the society's funds for his own personal use.* ANT. *adj.* inappropriate, unfit, inapt.

approve (of) *vb.* 1 praise, commend; favour, support; appreciate *I approve neither of borrowing nor of lending money.* 2 authorize, sanction, endorse, confirm *The committee approved plans for an increase in teachers' salaries.* ANT. (2) disapprove, oppose.

approximate *adj.* rough, loose, inexact, imprecise; close *Give me an approximate idea of the number of people who attended the rally.* ANT. exact, precise; perfect.

apt *adj.* 1 proper, suitable, fitting, appropriate, fit, suited *Before dinner, the speaker offered some apt comments on the undernourished peoples of the world.* 2 likely, disposed, liable, prone, inclined *If you criticize him, he's apt to tell you to jump in the lake!* ANT. (1) unfit, ill-becoming, unsuitable. (2) unlikely.

aptitude *n.* gift, talent, knack, faculty; ability *Edmund's remarkable musical aptitude did not go unnoticed at the conservatory.*

architect *n.* designer, planner; draughtsman *The architect of this town plan will be presenting it next week.*

ardent *adj.* passionate, fervent, intense *Elizabeth has an ardent desire to become a stage designer.* ANT. cold, unemotional, unfeeling; feeble.

arduous *adj.* hard, difficult, laborious, strained, burdensome *Working in a mine was the most arduous job I have ever had.* ANT. easy.

area *n.* 1 district, region, locality *James lives in a new area of the town.* 2 part, section *Tony kicked the ball into the goal area.* 3 expanse, space; range, field *The area covered by the sky is enormous.*

arena *n.* ground, field, pitch *The teams ran out into the arena at the start of the games.*

argue *vb.* 1 debate, discuss *We argued for an increase in time for* *lunch, and we won.* 2 dispute, disagree *My parents never argued about what they wanted to do.* ANT. (2) agree, concur.

argument *n.* 1 quarrel, dispute, controversy; disagreement *There was a big argument at the restaurant about whether chocolate ice cream was more fattening than vanilla.* 2 reason, ground, grounds, proof *José's argument was that Cuba was still better off under Castro than it had been under Batista.* ANT. (1) agreement, harmony, accord.

arise *vb.* emerge, originate, appear, spring up *The problem arose when the students refused to do their homework.*

aristocrat *n.* nobleman, noble, peer, lord *The aristocrats were once very cruel to the peasants.* ANT. commoner, peasant.

arm *n.* forearm *Anne held her handbag over her arm.* *vb.* provide, supply, furnish, fit out *The Navy will be armed with new types of missiles.*

arouse *vb.* awaken, stir, activate, animate, excite, stimulate, fire *His strange behaviour in the bank aroused suspicion.* ANT. calm, settle, soothe; dull.

arrange *vb.* 1 place, order, put in order, group, distribute; array *Before we arranged the furniture in the bedroom, we laid down the rug.* 2 organize, plan, prepare *The travel agent arranged all of my hotel reservations.* ANT. (1) disarrange, disturb, disorder.

arrangement *n.* 1 order, grouping, array, display *The arrangement of the paintings in the gallery was haphazard.* 2 Usually, **arrangements.** preparation(s), plan(s), scheme(s) *William made arrangements for us to take the Orient-Express to Paris.*

array *vb.* 1 clothe, dress, attire; adorn *Penny came into the room arrayed in her best clothes.* 2 arrange, order, line up, distribute *The soldiers were arrayed along the front line in full battle dress.* *n.* 1 order, arrangement, line up *The troops are in battle array.* 2 display, arrangement, exhibit *The array of diamonds in the jeweller's window took her breath away.* ANT. *n.* (1) disarray, disorder, disorganization.

arrest *vb.* 1 take into custody, seize, apprehend, catch, capture, take prisoner *The police arrested the burglar as he was trying to escape through the window.* 2 stop, restrain, curb, delay, hinder, slow *We arrested the growth of the plant by withholding water.* 3 attract, engage, capture *A small scratch near the lock arrested the detective's attention.* *n.* 1 seizure, capture, detention, custody, apprehension *The arrest of the judge was reported on the front page.* 2 restraint, obstruction, delay, hindrance; halt, stoppage *Any arrest in the development of a child can have serious results.* *n. phr.* **under arrest** in custody, imprisoned, incarcerated *The Queen placed Sir Walter Raleigh under arrest.* ANT. *vb.* (1) release, free. (2) activate, encourage, stimulate.

arrival *n.* coming, advent; appearance *The teenagers eagerly awaited the arrival of their favourite rock star.* ANT. departure, going, leaving.

arrive *vb.* 1 come, reach *We arrived in Rome at six-thirty in the* *morning. He arrived at the right decision.* 2 *Informal:* succeed, attain success *Donald finally felt he had arrived when they presented him with the medal.* ANT. (1) leave, depart.

arrogance *n.* insolence, pride, haughtiness *Donald had the arrogance to tell the teacher he knew more than she did.* ANT. humility, humbleness, modesty.

arrogant *adj.* proud, haughty, insolent; scornful *Young man, your arrogant attitude won't endear you to people around here!* ANT. humble, modest.

art *n.* skill, aptitude, craft, dexterity, ingenuity *The art of whittling seems to be lost.*

artful *adj.* tricky, cunning, clever, deceitful *The fugitive tried an artful ruse by doubling back through the wood.* ANT. artless, simple, naïve.

article *n.* 1 thing, object, item, commodity *'Articles for sale' said the notice in the shop window.* 2 essay, commentary; review; column *Phil writes a weekly article for the local paper.*

artificial *adj.* 1 unnatural, synthetic, man-made, manufactured, unreal *Can't you tell artificial flowers from real ones?* 2 false, pretended, unnatural, feigned, fake, faked, fraudulent *Betty's sympathy for my problem was entirely artificial—she really didn't care.* ANT. real, genuine, authentic.

artist *n.* painter, sculptor; creator, composer *Do you believe that artists ought to be supported by their governments?*

artistic *adj.* imaginative, creative; tasteful *One can count on Mrs Baskerville for an artistic flower arrangement every time.* ANT. tasteless, dull, flat.

artless *adj.* simple, naive, innocent, natural, open, frank, honest, sincere; candid, truthful *Andrea's artless attempt to help her friend only embroiled her more deeply in the murder investigation.* ANT. artful.

ascend *vb.* rise, mount, climb *or* go upward *The balloon ascended gently over the city, wafting us across the Thames.* ANT. descend, go down.

ascent *n.* rise, climb; slope, incline, gradient *The ascent of Mont Blanc is seldom easy, but we tried it during a storm.* ANT. descent, fall.

ashamed *adj.* embarrassed, shamefaced, abashed, humiliated *You ought to be really ashamed for talking to your mother that way!* ANT. proud; self-respecting.

ask *vb.* 1 question, inquire (of), seek information (from), put a question (to) *Della asked people on the street if they knew where the bus stopped.* 2 demand, request, charge, expect *Alan complained that the shop was asking too much for the pair of sandals.* 3 invite, call in *Marie asked all of her friends to her party.* ANT. (1) answer, reply.

asleep *adj.* sleeping; inactive, resting, dormant *I was asleep when the burglar entered and heard nothing.* ANT. awake, alert.

aspect *n.* **1** look, appearance *The gloomy aspect of the mountains through the fog depressed the hikers.* **2** point of view, viewpoint, attitude, view, outlook *If you look at the problem from another aspect, you might understand what I mean.* **3** phase, side, part, feature *But I haven't considered that aspect of the situation.*

aspire *vb.* yearn, wish, hope, want, desire *Little Roderick aspires to be just like his father when he grows up.*

assail *vb.* attack, assault, set upon *The minute we stepped out the door, we were assailed by reporters and cameramen.*

assault *n.* attack, onslaught *The cavalry could not withstand the assault of the trained mountain troops.* *vb.* attack, assail; rape *The woman told the police that the tall man had assaulted her.*

assemble *vb.* **1** meet, convene, collect, gather *The class assembled in the hall to listen to the teacher.* **2** put together, connect, manufacture *The manager told us that they could assemble an entire car in thirty minutes.* **ANT.** (1) scatter, disperse. (2) disassemble, undo.

assembly *n.* parliament, legislature, congress, council *The measure was voted on by the assembly at yesterday's session.*

assent (to) *vb.* agree (to), consent(to); allow, concede, accede *When Janet asked her father if she could go on the summer camp, he assented.* *n.* consent, agreement, approval, permission *I'll have to ask the headmaster's assent if I want to go on holiday during term.* **ANT.** *vb.* refuse, dissent; disapprove. *n.* refusal; disapproval, opposition.

assert *vb.* **1** declare, state, affirm *The judge asserted that the suspect had been in jail at the time of the murder.* **2** insist (on), emphasize, claim, support, uphold, maintain *These days, women are very firm about asserting their rights.* **ANT.** (1) deny, contradict. (2) decline, reject.

assertion *n.* declaration, statement, affirmation *Her assertion that you were with her at the time of the murder is totally false.* **ANT.** denial, contradiction.

assess *vb.* estimate, evaluate, appraise; value *I don't know how to assess the accuracy of her statement.*

assign *vb.* **1** appoint, designate *The minister assigned an expert to the new post.* **2** give, distribute, allot, apportion *The English teachers always assign too much homework.* **3** fix, pinpoint, arrange *Please don't assign Friday as the day for the meeting because I want to leave early.*

assignment *n.* responsibility, job, task, charge, duty *The reporter was given the assignment to write about the airline merger.*

assimilate *vb.* absorb, digest, take in; incorporate, embody *This complicated book on nuclear physics is difficult to assimilate.*

assist *vb.* aid, help, support, back *I promised to assist you in any way I could.* **ANT.** hinder, obstruct, impede, thwart.

assistance *n.* help, aid, support *He needs all the assistance he can get.* **ANT.** obstruction, interference.

assistant *n.* helper, supporter, aide *The supervisor has turned over his less important tasks to an assistant.*

associate (with) *vb.* 1 connect, relate, link *I notice that cream always seems to be associated with jelly in your mind.* 2 join, ally, team up; keep company, go around *Jim's father didn't think he associated with the right sort of people.* *n.* colleague, fellow-worker, partner, ally; companion; accomplice *Greg's associate in the deal provided all of the money.* ANT. *vb.* dissociate, disassociate, disconnect.

association *n.* 1 society, organization, club, union, group *Some joined the association in order to meet people with common interests.* 2 friendship, companionship *My mother disapproves of my continued association with you because she thinks you're a bad influence.*

assorted *adj.* various, varied, miscellaneous *This is our most popular product, a box of assorted chocolates.* ANT. same, alike.

assortment *n.* mixture, variety, collection; ragbag, conglomeration *A very strange assortment of people came aboard the ship at New York.*

assume *vb.* 1 suppose, presume, postulate *I assume that you will arrive an hour before the party.* 2 take on, undertake *At the age of sixteen he had to assume responsibility for his sister's care.* 3 pretend, affect, feign; acquire *Although Ezra was really very upset, his face assumed a calm expression.*

assumption *n.* supposition, presumption; guess, theory, conjecture, postulate *Your assumption that I had died in the accident was evidently incorrect.*

assurance *n.* 1 pledge, guarantee, warranty, promise, oath *Despite the assurance Pedro had given the teacher, he continued to miss school.* 2 confidence, self-confidence, self-reliance; courage, boldness *Dr Gorman examines his patients with an assurance that comes with years of experience.*

assure *vb.* pledge, promise, warrant, guarantee *My solicitor assured me that the deed was valid.* ANT. deny, equivocate.

astonish *vb.* surprise, amaze, astound; startle, shock, stupefy, stun *We were astonished at the brazen attitude of the shop assistant.* ANT. bore, tire.

astonishment *n.* surprise, amazement, wonder; bewilderment *The wonders we saw during our dive at the reef filled us with astonishment.*

astound *vb.* surprise, astonish, shock, amaze, stun, stagger, (*informal*) floor, flabbergast *We were astounded to learn that Shirley had given birth to quadruplets.*

astute *adj.* perceptive, shrewd, keen *Benjamin is an extremely astute observer of the financial world.* ANT. slow, dull, dim-witted.

atmosphere *n.* 1 air, wind; climate *The atmosphere in many of our cities is not very clean.* 2 mood, feeling, tone, character; impression, sense *As the play reached its climax, you could feel the atmosphere of foreboding in the theatre.*

atrocious *adj.* awful, terrible, abominable, horrible, horrid, horrifying, ghastly, unspeakable *They did the most atrocious things to prisoners during the war.*

attach *vb.* **1** fasten, affix, fix, connect *The panel was attached to the wall with nails.* **2** bind, tie *Carolyn is attached to her father.* ANT. (1) detach, unfasten, loosen, loose.

attachment *n.* **1** devotion, regard, affection, fondness, liking *Dennis showed a close attachment to his teacher.* **2** accessory, addition; extension *Tom's father bought a new set of attachments for his skis.* ANT. (1) detachment.

attack *vb.* **1** assault, set upon, assail, charge, storm *The army attacked the fort, and it was soon captured.* **2** criticize, blame, abuse *The newspapers attacked the local council for refusing to collect the rubbish.* *n.* assault, charge, onslaught, encounter *The robber was accused of an armed attack outside the bank.* ANT. *vb.* (1) withdraw, retreat. (2) praise, endorse. *n.* withdrawal, retreat.

attain *vb.* accomplish, reach, achieve, gain, win, obtain, secure, procure, acquire, get *Nicole attained the highest honours in school.*

attainment *n.* achievement, accomplishment, success *We are here to honour Professor Dweeb for his many attainments in the field of carpology.* ANT. failure.

attempt *vb.* try, seek *The football team attempted to win every game.* *n.* try, effort, undertaking, endeavour, trial *After three attempts, Jonathan finally jumped over the fence.* ANT. *vb.* achieve, accomplish. *n.* achievement, accomplishment.

attend *vb.* **1** go to, frequent, be present at *The entire family attends church.* **2** care for, serve, tend, wait on, minister to *The waitress attended to our order first.*

attendant *n.* servant, waiter, valet, footman *The movie star has three attendants with him at all times.*

attention *n.* observation, heed, alertness, care, consideration *The class turned their attention to the teacher.* ANT. inattention, absent-mindedness, preoccupation.

attentive *adj.* **1** observant, alert, heedful *Unless you agree to be more attentive when I speak, I shall ask you to leave.* **2** thoughtful, kind, polite, considerate, courteous *Michael was always a very attentive father and husband.* ANT. inattentive, absent-minded, preoccupied.

attire *vb.* dress, clothe, apparel *The beggar was attired in rags.* *n.* dress, clothing, clothes, apparel *Blue jeans are not appropriate attire for a dinner dance.*

attitude *n.* view, regard, position, manner, disposition, demeanour *I don't like your unfriendly attitude towards old people.*

attract *vb.* draw, invite, win; fascinate, captivate *You are not likely to attract much of a following by being so unpleasant.* ANT. repel, repulse.

attraction *n.* **1** allure, captivation, draw; (*informal*) pull *Mademoiselle Fifi was the main attraction at the Palazzo Theatre for years.*

2 tendency; affinity *I cannot understand the attraction those two feel for one another.*

attractive *adj.* appealing, alluring, pleasing, charming *Henry behaves differently when an attractive girl enters the shop.* ANT. unattractive, plain, ugly.

attribute *vb.* assign, credit, ascribe *She attributed her nervousness to the importance of the interview.* *n.* characteristic, quality, property *One of Beth's chief attributes is her patience.*

audible *adj.* distinct; perceptible, discernible *There is an audible squeak in the engine that disappears when I bring it to the garage.* ANT. inaudible; imperceptible; indistinct.

audience *n.* spectators, viewers; hearers; turn-out, patrons *The audience was so enthusiastic that they demanded another encore.*

austere *adj.* **1** stern, severe, hard, harsh, firm, strict, stiff, inflexible *The austere look on the teacher's face told the children that he would tolerate no nonsense.* **2** plain, simple, unadorned, severe *For the first few years, the lives of the emigrants were very austere.* ANT. (1) lenient, permissive, soft. (2) luxurious, fancy, opulent.

austerity *n.* severity, harshness, strictness *Few survived the austerity of frontier life in America in the early 1800s.* ANT. comfort, luxury.

authentic *adj.* **1** genuine, real *Unless it is at least a hundred years old, it isn't an authentic antique.* **2** true, reliable, trustworthy, accurate, authoritative *The witness testified that the signature on the wall was authentic.* ANT. fake, bogus; imitation, counterfeit.

authenticate *vb.* verify, validate, certify, warrant, guarantee *The museum's curator authenticated the painting as a genuine Vermeer.*

author *n.* writer, creator, originator; (of a play) playwright, dramatist; (of a poem) poet; (of a novel) novelist; (of a musical composition) composer; (of words to a song) lyricist, songwriter; (of a biography) biographer *She received the award as the author of the best work of the year in that classification.*

authority *n.* **1** jurisdiction, authorization; permission, sanction, approval *You have no right to go into that room without the proper authority.* **2** command, rule, order, control, power *The library is under the authority of the librarian.*

authorize *vb.* **1** empower; commission, charge, entrust *She wasn't authorized to use that typewriter.* **2** allow, permit, sanction, approve *The committee authorized the purchase of new playground equipment.* ANT. (2) prohibit, forbid.

automatic *adj.* **1** self-moving, self-regulating; programmed *The spinning cycle on this washing machine is automatic.* **2** uncontrolled, uncontrollable, involuntary, unconscious *The circulation of the blood is automatic.* ANT. (1) manual, hand-operated. (2) deliberate, intentional.

auxiliary *adj.* secondary, supplementary, supporting, subordinate *We shall have to find some auxiliary method, as using dynamite is too dangerous.*

avail *vb.* benefit, help, serve; profit *Dishonesty avails us naught.* *n.*

help, benefit, use, advantage, profit *Attempts to persuade them to stay were to no avail.*

available *adj.* obtainable, accessible, at hand, ready, handy *Is room service available at that hotel?* ANT. unavailable, unobtainable.

average *adj.* normal, common, typical, ordinary *I never understood why 'C' was considered an average mark for school work.* *n.* mean; median *Prices rose by an average of ten per cent last year.* ANT. *adj.* atypical, abnormal.

aversion *n.* dislike, distaste; abhorrence, disgust, loathing, hatred *He has an aversion to eating oysters.* ANT. liking, affinity, attraction.

avoid *vb.* elude, evade, dodge; shun *The murderer avoided capture for two years.* ANT. meet, confront, encounter, face.

await *vb.* wait for, expect, anticipate *We were awaiting word on the outcome of the competition.*

awake *vb.* wake up, arouse *He awoke his children very early the day they went on holiday.* *adj.* **1** conscious, not asleep; up and about *The young boys stayed awake and told each other stories for hours.* **2** aware (of); vigilant, attentive, alert; lively *Those who are in high positions in society must be awake to the problems of pride.*

award *vb.* bestow, give *She was awarded first prize in the essay contest. The father was awarded custody of the children.* *n.* prize, reward, payment, medal *An award will be given to the employee who offers the best idea.*

aware *adj.* conscious, informed, mindful *Before agreeing to buy something one must be aware of the price.* ANT. unaware, unconscious.

awe *n.* respect, wonder, fear, admiration *You have no idea the great awe with which nurses regard doctors.* ANT. scorn, contempt.

awesome *adj.* awe-inspiring, moving, overwhelming, formidable *The stage settings for the opera were awesome.*

awful *adj.* dreadful, terrible, abominable, bad, poor, unpleasant *We saw an awful play last night. Losing your wedding ring is an awful thing to have happen.* ANT. wonderful, delightful.

awkward *adj.* **1** clumsy, graceless, unskilful, sloppy, ungraceful, ungainly, crude *In an awkward attempt to reach the sugar, Eve spilled the milk.* **2** inconvenient, unwieldy, unmanageable *From that awkward position, I was unable to turn the bolt.* ANT. **(1)** graceful, deft, elegant, skilled, skilful.

b

baby *n.*   **1** toddler, suckling, child *When she was a little baby Alexandra could recite the alphabet.*   **2** youngest *Bill, at thirty-two, is the baby of the family.*

back *adj.*   rear, hind *The back door was open so I went in.*   *vb.* support, help, assist; endorse, ratify, stand by, approve; finance *The investors agreed to back the new company with £1 million.*   *vb. phr.* **back out** withdraw, retreat, escape *Nigel backed out of the deal when he realized he wasn't going to make any profit.*

backbone *n.*   **1** spine *The backbone is part of the skeleton.*   **2** determination, persistence, resolution, courage, tenacity *To be a leading politician you have to have a lot of backbone.*

backer *n.*   supporter, sponsor, patron, angel *If we don't get a backer for our show, it will never be produced.*

background *n.*   **1** context, setting; framework, perspective; circumstances *Let me tell you the background to this problem.*   **2** training, experience, education, knowledge, qualifications *At only 18, Peter doesn't have the background needed for this job.*   *prep. phr.* **in the background** unobtrusive, inconspicuous *Millie always kept her personal feelings in the background.*

backward *adj.*   **1** rearward *Looking over her shoulder, Suzanne gave him a final, backward glance.*   **2** slow, underdeveloped, retarded *Some of the students were backward in their physical skills.*   ANT. *adv.* forward. *adj.* (1) forward. (2) advanced; precocious.

bad *adj.*   **1** evil, immoral, wicked, corrupt, sinful, depraved *The people considered the dictator to be a totally bad man.*   **2** rotten, contaminated, spoiled, tainted *Eight people were poisoned by the bad meat at that restaurant.*   **3** harmful, injurious; unfavourable *Eating too many sweets is bad for your teeth.*   **4** poor, defective, inferior, imperfect, substandard, faulty *The picture tube is bad in this TV set.*   **5** improper, inappropriate, unsuited, unsuitable *The paintings by amateurs are usually bad examples of art.*   **6** upset, sorry *We all feel bad when a pet dies.*   **7** sick, ill, out of sorts; suffering *I felt bad after eating all that chocolate.*   **8** disagreeable, unpleasant, uncomfortable *Because of the storm, we had a bad crossing from Dover.*   **9** cross, nasty, unpleasant, unfriendly, irritable, disagreeable, short-tempered *When Sam heard about who was coming for dinner, it put him into a bad mood for the rest of the day.*   ANT. good.

badge *n.*   symbol, emblem, crest, decoration; star; shield; medal *He was presented with the badge of honour—an enamelled pin showing crossed swords.*

baffle *vb.* mystify, puzzle, confuse, frustrate, bewilder *I was completely baffled as to why she was paying so much attention to me.* ANT. enlighten, inform.

bag *n.* basket, carrier bag; handbag; purse; case; sack *My neighbour helped me carry in my bags of groceries.*

baggage *see* **luggage.**

bait *n.* lure, enticement *Many fishermen use worms for bait.* *vb.*
1 lure, entice, entrap, captivate, ensnare *Enid baited her boyfriend with her good cooking.* 2 tease, torment, worry, pester, badger, heckle *The audience baited the politician by asking him about his record.*

bake *vb.* 1 cook; toast, dry, roast *We baked some cakes in the oven.*
2 harden, temper *The sun baked their skins as they lay on the beach.*

balance *n.* equilibrium *The acrobat was able to keep his balance easily on the wire.* *vb.* 1 weigh, evaluate, compare *When you balance the advantages against the disadvantages, I'd say we ought to go.* 2 offset, counterbalance, make up for *My reasons for staying balance my reasons for going, so I don't know what to do.*

balk *vb.* hesitate, stop *He gave us moral support but balked at making a cash contribution.*

ball¹ *n.* sphere, globe, spheroid *The centre-forward kicked the ball into the goal.*

ball² *n.* dance, social, party *We were invited to the ball given to raise money for charity.*

balloon *n.* ball, sphere, globe; bag, bubble *We used to tie messages to balloons and let the wind carry them away.*

balmy *adj.* mild, gentle, soothing, pleasant *I enjoy nothing more than a balmy day by the seaside.* ANT. stormy, tempestuous.

ban *vb.* forbid, prohibit, disallow, outlaw *Smoking is banned in the buses.* *n.* prohibition, taboo *There is a ban on staying out in the streets after nine o'clock.* ANT. *vb.* permit, allow.

band¹ *n.* group, company, society, association, body, crew, gang *The band of robbers met secretly in a hut in the forest.* *vb.* unite, group, join forces *We had to band together for our own protection.*

band² *n.* strip, belt *There was a narrow band of carvings around the base of the column.*

bandit *n.* outlaw, thief, robber, highwayman, hijacker, marauder, brigand *Bandits used to roam the countryside and rob coaches.*

bang *vb.,n.* boom, crash, shot, blast *The guns banged loudly in the distance and we knew the enemy was coming nearer. We heard a huge bang at the end of the street and found out later that a bomb had gone off.*

banish *vb.* exile, deport, expel; transport *In the eighteenth century, criminals were banished from the country.* ANT. receive, admit, welcome.

bank *n.* 1 savings bank; building society *The local bank holds the mortgage on our house.* 2 embankment, shore, ridge, mound *I swam to the edge of the lake and climbed out onto the bank.*

bar *n.* 1 barrier, obstacle, barricade, obstruction, hindrance, impediment *Peace should not be a bar to progress in science or business.* 2 counter; saloon, cocktail lounge, café *The businessmen met at the bar before going in for dinner.* *vb.* prevent, obstruct, hinder, impede, stop, deter, prohibit, block *All those who were not members of the club were barred from entering.* ANT. *n.* (1) encouragement, aid. *vb.* permit, allow; welcome, encourage.

barbarian *n.* savage, brute, boor, ruffian *The manager of the football stadium called the police because the boys were acting like barbarians.* *adj.* savage, rude, primitive, uncivilized, uncultured, cruel, barbaric, barbarous *A barbarian tribe never before seen was discovered in the Philippines.* ANT. *adj.* cultivated, civilized, tasteful.

barber *n.* hairdresser, hair stylist, coiffeur *Why do men go to barbers and women to 'hair stylists'?*

bare *adj.* 1 nude, naked, unclothed, uncovered, undressed *In many European countries, small children run about bare on the beaches.* 2 plain, unfurnished, empty, barren *The room was entirely bare.* 3 mere, scarce *Robinson Crusoe was marooned with just the bare necessities of life.* *vb.* reveal, disclose, expose, publicize *The newspaper reporter bared the details of the political scandal.* ANT. *adj.* (1) clothed, dressed. *vb.* hide, conceal, disguise.

barely *adv.* scarcely, hardly, just *I had barely got home when it started to rain.*

bargain *n.* deal, agreement, arrangement, contract *I'll make a bargain with you. I'll let you use my bicycle if you let me use your car.* *vb.* agree, contract, arrange *The two farmers bargained until a fair agreement was reached.* *vb. phr.* **bargain for** expect, anticipate, foresee *He got more than he bargained for when the bull suddenly turned nasty.*

barren *adj.* sterile, unproductive, unfruitful, bare, childless *What did you do when you found that your wife was barren?* ANT. fertile, fruitful.

barricade *n.* barrier, obstruction, fence, enclosure *The barricade prevented the horses from leaving the pen.* *vb.* shut in, obstruct, block, bar *The hunters barricaded themselves in the cabin for protection against the wolves.* ANT. *vb.* release, free, open.

barrier *n.* 1 bar, barricade, fence, wall, railing, obstacle *The barrier was opened to allow passengers through.* 2 obstruction, hindrance, impediment, restraint, obstacle; limit *Neither the mountains nor love of home was a barrier to the tribe's travelling great distances.* ANT. (2) encouragement, aid, assistance.

barrister *n.* lawyer, counsel, advocate; solicitor *My solicitor said that I would not be permitted to speak directly to the barrister representing me.*

barter *vb.* trade, exchange *We bartered pigs for lambs with our neighbours.*

base[1] *n.* bottom, support, stand, rest, foundation *The base of this column is carved from marble.* *vb.* found, establish *A careful*

scholar bases his theory on sound examination of the evidence.
ANT. *n.* top, peak, pinnacle.

base² *adj.* **1** low, immoral, bad, evil, depraved, wicked, mean, selfish *Anyone who would allow a kitten to starve is really base.* **2** cheap, tawdry, worthless, poor, debased, alloyed, (of coin) counterfeit *The clasp on your brooch didn't last long because it was made of base material.* ANT. (1) noble, exalted, virtuous. (2) refined, valuable.

bashful *adj.* shy, timid, sheepish, modest, coy, shamefaced, ashamed *You needn't feel bashful taking your clothes off for a medical examination.* ANT. self-assured; immodest, arrogant.

basic *adj.* main, chief, essential, fundamental *Kindness to others has always been one of my basic principles.* ANT. subordinate, subsidiary.

basis *n.* foundation, ground, reason, justification *The basis of our relationship is that we like the same things.*

batch *n.* bunch, collection, cluster, group, collection, handful *Take a batch of these files and sort them alphabetically.*

batter *vb.* beat, pound, hit, strike *The victim was found with his skull battered in.*

battle *n.* fight, combat; war, warfare; conflict, action, campaign *After the battle, each side looked after its wounded and buried its dead.* *vb.* fight, struggle against, strive against *Battling against great odds, the team finally won.*

bawl *vb.* cry, wail, caterwaul, scream, weep *I couldn't sleep because the neighbours' baby was bawling all night long.*

bay *n.* gulf, inlet, estuary, lagoon *We sailed into the bay just as the sun was setting.*

beach *n.* strand, sands, shore, seashore, coast *I love stretching out on a beach in the hot sunshine.*

bead *n.* **1** ball, sphere, globule *Her necklace was made of blue and red beads.* **2** drop, droplet *Because of the intense heat, there were beads of sweat on his face.*

beam *n.* **1** rafter, support, girder *The main beams of the roof are being eaten by termites.* **2** ray, pencil, gleam *The beam shone through the slit to light up the golden statue in the crypt.* *vb.* shine, gleam, glisten, glitter *When the moon beams on the water it looks like a silvery path.*

bear *vb.* **1** carry, support, hold up *The columns bear the weight of the roof.* **2** carry, transport, convey *Beware the Greeks bearing gifts!* **3** endure, stand, suffer, abide, tolerate *I cannot bear to hear a baby crying.* **4** give birth to, produce, beget *The mother bore six children.* *vb. phr.* **bear on** relate to, affect, be relevant to, be connected with *Whether you work hard at school bears very much on your exam results.* **bear out** substantiate, confirm, prove *My prediction was borne out by your losing the key on the first day.* **bear up** endure, carry on, keep up *I just don't see how Martha can bear up under the strain of caring for fifteen children.* **bear with** be patient with; tolerate *Please bear with me until I can straighten the problem out.*

bearing *n.* **1** posture, carriage; manner, behaviour, deportment, conduct *The girl's regal bearing made everyone notice her when she walked into the room.* **2** reference, relation, application, connection *What you think has no bearing on what we ought to do.* **3** direction, course, position *It took a few minutes with the chart to get our bearings.*

beast *n.* animal; brute, monster *During the divorce action it was revealed that her husband had behaved like a beast.*

beastly *adj.* **1** hateful, loathsome, detestable, mean, low, base, scurrilous, vile, despicable, cruel, offensive, nasty, obnoxious, unpleasant *He treated her in the most beastly way, so she divorced him.* **2** awful, nasty, uncomfortable, annoying, irritating *I have this beastly cold which I cannot get rid of.*

beat *vb.* **1** hit, strike, pound, batter, thrash *When we came into the garden, Jan's mother was beating the carpet.* **2** throb, pound, pulse, pulsate *I can feel my heart beating if I put my hand here.* **3** defeat, conquer, overcome *The home team beat the visitors 3–2.* *n.* stroke, blow; throb, pulse, pulsation *The beat of the jungle drums could be heard for miles.*

beautiful *adj.* pretty, lovely, handsome, attractive *Did you think that last year's Miss Universe was particularly beautiful?* ANT. unattractive, plain, ugly, hideous.

beauty *n.* loveliness, comeliness, attractiveness *Helen's beauty was legendary throughout the eastern Mediterranean.* ANT. plainness, ugliness, unsightliness.

because *conj.* since, as, for, for the reason that *Because you are a married man, I must refuse to see you again.*

become *vb.* **1** grow, change, come to be *When I told him what his friend had said, he became angry.* **2** suit, befit, be appropriate *or* attractive to *The green dress becomes you, but I don't care for the red one.*

becoming *adj.* attractive, pleasing, seemly, graceful *Grace was wearing a most becoming hat.*

bedlam *n.* pandemonium, chaos, commotion, furore, uproar, madhouse *The floor of the stock exchange became a bedlam as prices continued to fall.*

before *adv.* earlier, previously *The couple had been doctors in Africa many years before.* *prep.* in front of, ahead of *He knelt before the altar and prayed.* ANT. *adv.* later, afterwards. *prep.* behind.

beg *vb.* **1** ask, request, entreat, beseech, petition, solicit, implore *Kathy begged her mother to be allowed to go to the party.* **2** cadge, ask alms, ask charity, (*slang*) scrounge *He was so poor he had to beg in the streets for something to eat.*

beggar *n.* pauper, mendicant, supplicant; tramp, loafer *The beggars in the streets are the most embarrassing sight in a supposedly affluent society.*

begin *vb.* 1 start, commence; initiate; inaugurate *Don't begin until everyone is ready.* 2 originate, create, arise, come into being *The practice of working five days a week didn't begin until fairly recently.* ANT. stop, end, finish, terminate.

beginner *n.* amateur, nonprofessional, apprentice *We employ beginners and train them to become proficient in their work.* ANT. professional.

beginning *n.* 1 start, outset, commencement, emergence, initiation, inauguration *At the beginning of a new enterprise everyone works very hard.* 2 origin, source, rise, birth, creation *The beginning of modern scientific thought can be traced to the sixteenth century.* ANT. ending, finish, termination.

behalf *n.* part, support, interest, aid *I should like to say something on behalf of the Labour candidate.*

behave *vb.* act, conduct oneself, deport oneself *I thought that Jerry behaved quite well considering his age.* ANT. misbehave, rebel.

behaviour *n.* conduct, deportment, manners *Because of their behaviour, the children were made to do extra homework.* ANT. misbehaviour, misconduct, mischief, rebelliousness.

behind *prep.* at the back *or* rear of *Look out for that snake behind you!* ANT. in front of, before.

belief *n.* 1 view, opinion, conviction, creed, credo *His belief is that all men are equal.* 2 faith, trust, confidence, assurance *Nothing could shake his belief that his parents were the most wonderful people.*

believe *vb.* 1 accept, be convinced; hold, think, trust *He believed in God.* 2 think, suppose, assume, gather *I believe he's coming to dinner, but I'm not sure.*

belittle *vb.* diminish, demean, deprecate, depreciate, minimize, slight, discredit, humiliate *It was terribly cruel to belittle him in front of his friends.* ANT. build up, commend, flatter.

belong (to) *vb.* 1 be owned *or* possessed (by) *This book belongs to me.* 2 be a member of, be a part of *Which sports club do you belong to?*

belt *n.* band, stripe, tape, girdle, strap, strip *A belt of red ochre runs right round the middle of the column.*

bench *n.* 1 seat; bank *The benches in the hall are most uncomfortable.* 2 table, trestle, board *The carpenter worked away at his bench for hours making the fine carvings.*

bend *vb.* 1 curve, bow, deflect *You could never bend that steel bar with your bare hands.* 2 stoop, kneel, crouch, bow *Martin bent to look through the keyhole in the door.* 3 submit, yield, bow, stoop, agree *The foreman had to bend under the pressure from the board of directors.* 4 subdue, suppress, oppress, influence, cause to yield *The president was accustomed to bending all his people to suit his will.* ANT. (1) straighten.

beneficial *adj.* good, advantageous, helpful, useful, profitable, wholesome *Fresh air and sunshine are beneficial.* ANT. unwholesome, disadvantageous.

benefit *n.* good, profit, advantage; service, favour, help, support *Dick won't do anything unless it's for his own benefit.* *vb.* help, aid, support, profit, serve *Every time you help someone else you benefit yourself.* ANT. *n.* disadvantage.

benevolent *adj.* good, kind, well-wishing, kindly, kind-hearted, humane, well-disposed; generous, open-hearted, liberal, charitable *Benevolent members of the club donated the money to expand the library.* ANT. malevolent, mean, cruel, evil.

bent *adj.* 1 crooked, curved *The lock was so crude we could open it with a bent nail.* 2 determined, resolved, set, decided, firm *Although I tried to discourage him, Jim was bent on sailing across the ocean alone.* ANT. (1) straight.

bereavement *n.* loss; sense of loss, affliction; death *Poor George suffered two bereavements last year.*

beseech *vb.* beg, implore, ask, entreat *I beseech you to allow me to help.*

besides *adv.* furthermore, moreover, in addition, further *You can't go out to play because it's raining and, besides, you haven't finished your homework.* *prep.* in addition to, except for, other than *Besides me, there's no one else who cares about winning the game.*

besiege *vb.* blockade, lay siege to, surround *Ten thousand troops besieged the palace of the king.*

best *adj.* finest, highest, supreme, excellent *That is the best steak I have ever tasted.* ANT. worst.

bestow *vb.* give, confer, present, award *The Queen bestowed on him the Order of Merit.* ANT. withhold, withdraw.

bet *vb.* wager, lay *or* put (money), gamble *I have never bet on a horse race in my life.* *n.* wager, stake, ante, pledge *Madame DeTour placed a bet at roulette and won.*

betray *vb.* 1 deliver, be treacherous *or* disloyal *The traitor betrayed the location of the arsenal to the enemy.* 2 reveal, expose; display, show, exhibit *Although she seemed very angry, her smile betrayed her real feelings.* ANT. safeguard, protect, shelter.

better *adj.* 1 greater, superior *My school is better than yours.* 2 recovering, improving; well, healthy *'How are you today,' she asked her child. 'Better, Mummy.'* *vb.* improve, ameliorate; amend, polish up *I could better my tennis game if I practised more.* ANT. *adj.* (1) worse, inferior. (2) worse; ill. *vb.* worsen.

bewilder *vb.* confuse, puzzle, perplex, mystify, overwhelm *We were totally bewildered at the attention we received from the dignitaries.* ANT. enlighten, clarify.

bewitch *vb.* enchant, charm, captivate *Tanya so bewitched Gregory that he would do anything for her.*

bias *n.* prejudice, tendency, inclination *The executive has a bias in favour of employing only friends.* *vb.* influence, prejudice, bend, warp *The politician's opinion was biased because he had received gifts from the manufacturers.* ANT. *n.* impartiality, fairness.

bicker *vb.* argue, quarrel, wrangle, dispute *Stop this bickering about who is the better swimmer.*

bid *vb.* **1** command, order, direct *When the chairman bids you to stand, you are expected to immediately get up.* **2** greet, say, wish *I bid you good day, sir.* **3** offer, tender, propose *Mother bid only three pounds for the chair at the auction, but she got it.* *n.* offer, proposal *I made an unsuccessful bid of two pounds for the lamp.*

bide *vb.* **bide one's time** *vb. phr.* wait, remain, delay *After they refused to allow me in, I merely bided my time till the proper opportunity came along.*

big *adj.* **1** large, great, huge, immense, enormous, gigantic, tremendous *If it has thirty-seven rooms, I'd certainly agree that it's a big house.* **2** important, significant, prominent *The big event of the year was the Christmas party.* **3** generous, kind, outgoing, bighearted *It was very big of you to let us use your pool.* **ANT.** (1) small, little, tiny.

bill *n.* invoice, statement, charge, account *Please send me a bill for the work you have done.*

bind *vb.* **1** tie, fasten, band *Don't bind that bundle of clothes too tight or they'll tear.* **2** oblige, require, command, obligate *He was bound by the contract.* **ANT.** (1) loosen, free, untie.

birth *n.* coming, creation, appearance; beginning, start, foundation *I shall never forget having been in at the birth of this political party.* **ANT.** death, passing.

bit *n.* scrap, particle, fragment, speck, drop *May I have just a bit more sugar in my coffee?* *n. phr.* **bit by bit** gradually, slowly *Bit by bit, Jim saved enough money to buy a bicycle.*

bite *vb.* nip; gnaw, chew *They say that barking dogs don't bite, but let someone else prove it.* *n.* **1** nip, sting *A dog bite is more serious than a mosquito bite.* **2** *Informal:* morsel, mouthful; snack *May I have a bite of that hot dog?*

biting *adj.* **1** piercing, sharp, keen, stinging *The wind turned biting cold as we approached the seashore.* **2** penetrating, sarcastic, incisive *Her biting comments hurt him deeply.*

bitter *adj.* **1** acrid, harsh, biting *If you chew aspirin instead of swallowing it whole, it leaves a bitter taste in your mouth.* **2** distressing, distressful, painful, grievous *I had the bitter experience of studying hard but failing the examination.* **3** hostile, hated, severe, vicious *The citizens of the two countries were bitter enemies.* **ANT.** (1) sweet, bland.

black *adj.* **1** dark, sooty, inky, swarthy *The black man stood in the doorway.* **2** soiled, dirty, filthy, stained *When he finished repairing the car, he was black from head to toe.* **3** gloomy, dismal, sad, depressing, dark, sombre *It was a black day for the country when our party lost the election.* **ANT.** (1) white, light-skinned. (2) clean, pure, pristine. (3) bright, cheerful.

blame *vb.* reproach, condemn, criticize *The taxi driver was blamed for causing the accident.* *n.* responsibility, guilt, fault *Before you* *place the blame on me, you'd better find out the facts.* ANT. *n.* honour, credit.

blank *adj.* 1 empty, unmarked *The application was blank except for where Michael had filled in his name.* 2 uninterested, expressionless *A sea of blank faces greeted the teacher on the first day of school.* *n.* void, area, form, vacancy *Just fill in the blanks with the correct information, please.* ANT. *adj.* (1) filled. (2) animated, alert; excited.

blast *n.* explosion, detonation, eruption; noise, bang *The blast from the quarry was heard far away.* *vb.* detonate, explode, blow up *The explosion blasted the house sky-high.*

blaze *n.* flame, fire; holocaust, inferno *The firemen fought the blaze at the department store in the high street.* *vb.* burn, flare up, flame, shine *The fire was blazing in the hearth when we arrived for the Christmas party.* ANT. *vb.* dwindle, die.

bleach *vb.* whiten, blanch; pale *The blue jeans were bleached pale blue by the sun.* *n.* whitener *Don't use so much bleach in the wash.* ANT. *vb.* darken, blacken.

bleak *adj.* 1 bare, desolate, barren, windswept *The bleak landscape offered no shelter.* 2 depressing, cheerless, gloomy, dreary *The financial future of the company was bleak after the fire.* ANT. (2) hopeful, cheerful, promising.

bleed *vb.* lose *or* shed blood; issue, weep, ooze *The wound is still bleeding.*

blemish *n.* flaw, stain, tarnish, blotch, defect *It may take years to remove the blemish from his reputation.*

blend *vb.* mix, intermingle, mingle, combine *Before pouring the batter into the baking dish, you should blend all the ingredients thoroughly.* *n.* mixture, combination, compound *That pipe tobacco smells like a mild blend.* ANT. *vb.* separate, divide.

blight *n.* epidemic, disease, sickness, affliction *The blight killed off the entire crop.* *vb.* damage, ruin, harm, spoil, destroy *His career was blighted by his poor school record.*

blind *adj.* 1 sightless, unseeing, purblind *A blind person's hearing is often very acute.* 2 unaware, unknowing, unconscious, ignorant, thoughtless, unthinking *Irena was blind to the fact that no one really liked her.* *n.* screen, shade, curtain, cover *The sun is in my eyes; please pull down the blind.* ANT. *adj.* (1) sighted, seeing. (2) clearsighted, knowing, discerning, aware.

blink *vb.* 1 wink *She blinked when you shone the light in her eyes.* 2 flicker, twinkle *The stars are blinking in the black sky.*

bliss *n.* happiness, joy, gladness, ecstasy, rapture *It was sheer bliss to be with Carrie again.* ANT. misery, unhappiness, torment.

block *n.* obstacle, obstruction, impediment, hindrance, blockade *The police stopped every car at the road block, looking for the escaped men.* *vb.* stop, obstruct, impede, retard, hinder, blockade, check *The fallen trees blocked our passage to freedom from the wood.* ANT. *n.* aid, advantage. *vb.* aid, assist, forward, promote.

blood *n.* **1** gore, bloodshed, murder, slaughter *Cain had his brother's blood on his hands.* **2** lineage, heritage, ancestry *The Prince of Wales is of royal blood.*

bloody *adj.* bloodthirsty, cruel, inhuman, pitiless, ruthless, murderous, ferocious *Thousands lost their lives in one of the bloodiest battles of the century.* ANT. gentle, kind.

bloom *n.* flower, blossom *My new roses are growing with huge blooms.* *vb.* flourish, blossom, flower *Rose of Sharon blooms in September in this part of the country.* ANT. *vb.* wither, shrivel.

blossom *n.* flower, bloom *The cherry blossoms are beautiful in the spring.* *vb.* bloom, flower, flourish *The century plant is so called because it is said to blossom only once every hundred years.* ANT. *vb.* wither, shrink, dwindle, fade.

blot *n.* **1** spot, stain, inkstain, inkblot *I got that awful blot on my skirt when Ronnie spilled ink on me.* **2** blemish, taint, disgrace, dishonour *The blot on his record harmed his career.* *vb.* **1** spot, stain, spatter, soil *You've blotted my book with your leaky pen!* **2** dry, soak up, sponge up *If you blot the ink it won't smear when you turn the page.* *vb. phr.* **blot out** eliminate, destroy, obliterate, erase, rub out, cancel *I've blotted that terrible experience from my mind.*

blow¹ *n.* **1** thump, hit, slap, rap, cuff, box, knock, stroke *The boxer knocked his challenger out with a blow to the stomach.* **2** shock, tragedy, calamity *The news of the death of her turtle was a terrible blow to Joanne.*

blow² *vb.* **1** move, spread, drive *The leaves started to blow down the street in the breeze.* **2** whistle *The siren blew at noon each day.* *vb. phr.* **blow up** **1** explode, detonate *The spies blew up the bridge.* **2** enlarge, inflate *Blow up that balloon.*

blue *n.* azure, sapphire, turquoise *On a clear day, blue is the colour of the sky.* *adj.* sad, gloomy, depressed, unhappy, dejected, melancholy *I felt blue at the thought of leaving home.* ANT. *adj.* happy, cheerful, optimistic.

bluff¹ *adj.* **1** vertical, perpendicular, steep, precipitous, abrupt *The cliff was too bluff to climb.* **2** hearty, rough, frank, blunt, open *The manager's bluff approach sometimes put them off.* *n.* cliff, precipice *The edge of the bluff hangs out over the sea.* ANT. (1) shallow, gentle, sloping. (2) subtle, indirect.

bluff² *vb.* mislead, deceive, fool, pretend *The gambler bluffed the others into thinking he had a good hand.* *n.* pretence, lie, fraud, fake, deceit *Bill's tough manner is just a bluff—he's really soft inside.*

blunder *n.* mistake, error *Telling Kitty about the party when she hadn't been invited was a stupid blunder.* *vb.* stumble *I blundered into the lamp and knocked it over in the dark.*

blunt *adj.* **1** dull, unsharpened, rounded, worn *That blunt knife could hardly cut butter.* **2** rude, crude, direct, impolite, abrupt, short, curt, brusque, gruff *I don't invite Walter any more because his*

manner is too blunt. *vb.* dull *He blunted the axe on the rock.*
ANT. *adj.* (1) sharp, keen, pointed. (2) diplomatic, tactful.

blur *vb.* stain, sully, obscure, dim, dull; confuse *My spectacles were
blurred by the mist. The medication blurred Harriet's senses and she
was unable to drive.* *n.* smudge, smear, stain, spot *A blur of
smoke on the horizon marked the passing ship.* ANT. *vb.* clarify,
clear.

blush *vb.* redden, go red, colour; glow *Whenever she was told how
pretty she was, Alexandra blushed.*

board *n.* 1 plank, slat *He put a board over the hole so that people
wouldn't fall in.* 2 committee, council, body, group *Robert has
joined the board to help with the company's finances.*

boast *vb.* brag, crow, exaggerate *Nobody could stand being with Bill
because he was always boasting about how great he was.* *n.* brag-
ging, braggadocio *Despite his boast, Bill was unable to jump across
the stream.*

boat *n.* vessel, craft; ship *It is dangerous to take a boat out in this
stormy weather.*

body *n.* 1 corpse, cadaver; carcass *The body of the dead man was
taken away. The body of the wolf was buried in the snow.* 2 trunk,
torso *He had spots all over his body but none on his arms, legs, or
head.* 3 group, party, company, band *We walked out of the meeting in a body.*

boil *vb.* seethe, foam, bubble, simmer, stew *When the soup boils,
please turn off the gas.*

boisterous *adj.* noisy, lively, unruly; rude; stormy, turbulent *That
was certainly a boisterous party you had last night.* ANT. quiet,
calm, composed.

bold *adj.* 1 brave, unafraid, fearless, intrepid, courageous, daring,
valiant, heroic, gallant *The four bold men stormed the machine-gun
and captured it.* 2 rude, disrespectful, insolent, impudent, shameless *Richard was bold enough to answer back to the teacher.* ANT.
(1) afraid, cowardly, fearful, timid, timorous. (2) courteous, polite,
deferential.

bolt *n.* bar, rod *The bar on this lock is strong enough to hold the gate
shut.* *vb.* lock, secure, close, shut *People should bolt their doors
at night to stop burglars breaking in.*

bond *n.* 1 fastening, fastener, rope, tie, cord, band *The prisoner was
unable to release the bonds on his wrists.* 2 connection, tie, attachment, link *The bonds of friendship are very strong between Alice and
me.* 3 promise, promissory note, obligation, I.O.U. *My word is
my bond and everyone knows that I pay all my debts.*

bonus *n.* reward, premium, gift, bounty *The box of chocolates was a
bonus for the winner of the first prize.*

book *n.* volume, tome, publication, work; hardback, paperback;
novel, text *The library contains hundreds of thousands of books.*

boom¹ *vb.* 1 reverberate, thunder, roar *The huge guns boomed in the
distance.* 2 prosper, flourish *The late 1960s was a time of booming*

prosperity: business was booming. *n.* **1** blast, roar, thunder *I couldn't hear the music over the boom of the aeroplanes.* **2** prosperity, rush *Just before Christmas there is always a big boom in toy sales.* ANT. *n.* (2) recession; depression.

boom² *n.* spar, pole *The wind changed suddenly, causing the boom to swing around and hit me.*

boon *n.* blessing, benefit, help *The tax allowance on mortgage interest was a boon to homeowners.*

boost *n.* support, help; improvement, rise, increase *The visit from the Prime Minister was a real boost to morale. We were grateful for the boost in pay.* *vb.* promote, encourage, assist, increase, expand *The government's plans will boost exports in a big way.*

booth *n.* stall, stand; compartment, enclosure, cubicle *Our company had a large booth at the book fair.*

border *n.* **1** frontier, boundary, limit *We crossed the border between France and Italy.* **2** edge, margin *There was a border of blue flowers around the tablecloth.* *vb.* join, adjoin, edge, abut *Scotland is bordered by England.* ANT. *n.* (2) centre, middle.

bore *vb.* **1** weary, tire *We were all so bored by the film that we almost fell asleep.* **2** drill, hole, perforate *This machine bores into the steel plate in thirty-six places at the same time.* ANT. (1) interest, excite, arouse, captivate.

bosom *n.* **1** breast, chest *The nurse clutched the infant to her bosom.* **2** heart, feelings, mind, thoughts *His bosom swelled with pride when his son was awarded the top prize.*

boss *n.* manager, director, supervisor, employer, foreman *My boss had me on the carpet this morning for being late.* ANT. employee, worker.

botch *vb.* spoil, mess up, bungle, mishandle, mar *Whitney botched the job so badly that we had to do it over again.*

bother *vb.* irritate, trouble, worry, disturb, annoy, vex, pester, upset, inconvenience *It bothered me that I couldn't recall the name of the last prime minister.* *n.* trouble, inconvenience, upset, distress, anxiety *I never wanted to cause any bother—I only tried to help.* ANT. *n.* comfort, solace.

bottle *n.* jug, jar, flask; carafe *We took along bottles of fresh water in case we got thirsty.*

bottom *n.* **1** base, foot, depths *I heard the bucket strike the ground at the bottom of the dried-out well.* **2** underside *The mark on the bottom of the cup shows the maker's name.* **3** seat, buttocks, behind, rear *Billy's mother gave him a sharp slap on his bottom for breaking the window.* ANT. (1, 2) top, topside.

bough *n.* branch, arm, limb *The boughs of the tree are laden with fruit.*

bounce *vb.* rebound, recoil, spring (back) *The golf ball bounced along the ground and into a tree.*

bound¹ *vb.,n.* leap, jump, spring, bounce, skip *The dog bounded along next to the car. With one bound Barbara had crossed the stream.*

bound[2] *adj.* **1** tied, trussed; shackled, fettered *The prisoner was bound hand and foot.* **2** sure, certain, destined; required, compelled *Suzanne knew that her father was bound to say no when she asked him if she could go.* ANT. (1) unfettered, free.

bound[3] **(for)** *adj.* on the way to, destined for *The train is bound for Edinburgh.*

bound[4] *n.* (usually **bounds**) boundary, limit *Within the bounds of reason, there is no limit to how far you can push your imagination.*

boundary *n.* limit, bound, border, outline, margin, circumference, perimeter, edge, frontier *The fence marks the boundary between the properties.*

bounty *n.* **1** generosity, liberality; gift *The early settlers in America were grateful for the bounty from the earth.* **2** reward, award, bonus, prize, premium *The farmers offered a bounty of 30p for every dead mole.*

bouquet *n.* bunch, garland, spray, nosegay, wreath *We brought a bouquet of flowers to Aunt Margaret at the hospital.*

bourgeois *adj.* middle-class, common, conventional *Harold's bourgeois notions of dress require us to wear ties at all times.* ANT. aristocratic, upper-class.

bout *n.* match, round, fight, contest; conflict *The main bout of the evening was fought between Louis and Schmeling.*

bow *vb.* **1** stoop, bend *The porter was bowed down under the weight of the trunk.* **2** yield, submit *You ought to bow to the force of a stronger argument.* **3** curtsy, salaam, kowtow, kneel *Everyone bowed when the king came into the room.*

bowl *n.* dish, plate; basin, vessel; pot *There is nothing like a bowl of hot porridge on these cold mornings.*

box *n.* case, carton; coffer, trunk; bin; container, receptacle *When Giles arrived at Susan's house, he brought a box of chocolates for her mother.*

boy *n.* lad, youth, youngster; (*informal*) kid *Mr Housman has three boys to help with the harvest this year.* ANT. man; girl.

brace *n.* support, prop, stay, strut, bracket; crutch *This wall ought to have a steel brace to hold it in place.* *vb.* support, prop, steady *Brace yourself for some bad news.*

bracelet *n.* bangle, circlet, armband *Jennifer always wears the bracelet you gave her.*

brag *vb.* boast, gloat, swagger *It is bad manners to brag about yourself.* ANT. deprecate, depreciate.

braid *vb.* plait, wreath, weave, twine *The girls braided daisies into their hair.*

brain *n.* (usually **brains**) intelligence, sense, common sense, intellect, reason, understanding *Philip doesn't have the brains to come in out of the rain.* ANT. stupidity, dullness, imbecility.

brake *n.* restraint, fetter; curb, hindrance, discouragement *You must release the brake before you drive off.* *vb.* slow down, decelerate, retard, curb *The car braked as it came near to the corner.*

branch *n.* **1** limb, bough, shoot *The branches on this tree grow very close to the ground.* **2** offshoot, tributary *The two branches of the stream join here.* **3** division, part, subdivision, department *The restaurant opened a new branch on the main road.*

brand *n.* **1** kind, make, manufacture, trademark, label, trade name *What brand of shampoo do you use?* **2** stamp, mark, blaze *The stolen cattle bore the brand of our farm.* *vb.* mark, label; burn; stamp *He branded the sheep with a red dye.*

brandish *vb.* flourish, flaunt, swing, wave *The knight brandished his sword, preparing to attack.*

brave *adj.* courageous, gallant, fearless, daring, valiant, intrepid, unafraid, heroic, bold *The brave lad jumped into the river to save the dog.* ANT. timid, cowardly, fearful, craven.

bravery *n.* courage, daring, valour, fearlessness, heroism, boldness *It took a lot of bravery to stand up to the headmaster.* ANT. cowardice, timidity, fearfulness.

brawl *n.* fight, mêlée, fray, fracas, donnybrook, riot, disturbance; dispute, disagreement *The police were called when the brawl broke out at the club.*

brazen *adj.* bold, shameless, impudent, insolent, rude, immodest *Alan's teacher said she would not tolerate his brazen disregard of the rules.* ANT. modest, retiring, shy, self-effacing.

breach *n.* **1** break, rift, rupture, fracture, crack, opening, gap *The explosion tore a breach in the wall big enough for the tank to pass through.* **2** violation, breaking *Her failure to deliver the merchandise by Monday was a breach of our agreement.* ANT. (2) keeping, observation.

breadth *see* **width.**

break *vb.* **1** fracture, rupture, shatter, smash, wreck, crash, atomize, demolish *When Jack sat on the antique chair he broke it into a hundred pieces.* **2** violate, disobey *I have no respect for those who break the law.* **3** disintegrate, fall apart, collapse, splinter, smash, shatter *The old vase might break if you looked at it!* *n.* **1** crack, gap, opening, breach, rupture *The water poured through the break in the dike.* **2** suspension, stop, hesitation, interruption *We all took a ten-minute break and then went back to work.* *vb. phr.* **break down** fail, falter, stop *Our car broke down on the steep hill.* **break in** **1** educate, train, initiate, prepare, instruct *The foreman had to break in the new machinist.* **2** invade, trespass *The burglars broke in and stole goods worth hundreds of pounds.* **break off** interrupt, discontinue, stop, cease *Roger broke off when Marie entered the room and didn't continue until after she had left.* **break out** **1** start, initiate, begin, commence *A riot broke out among the strikers.* **2** escape, flee, depart, leave *Three prisoners broke out of the local prison last night.* **3** erupt *Her face broke out in a rash.* **break through** penetrate, invade *The platoon finally broke through the enemy lines.* **break up** **1** divide, separate, split *I see Ellie has broken up with her boyfriend again.* **2** disassemble, separate, divide, dismantle, take

apart *The boss insisted that the clique be broken up at once.* ANT.
vb. (1) mend, repair. (2) obey, keep.

breathe *vb.* inhale, exhale; gasp, sigh; pant; blow *The painting is so
fragile that you will destroy it if you breathe on it.*

breed *vb.* 1 bear, conceive, beget, father, mother; create, produce,
originate, generate *The farmer bred prize cattle from stock he had
imported.* 2 rear, raise, nurture, bring up; educate, train, teach
The Forsters' children are very well bred. *n.* kind, sort, variety,
species, strain *The dogs on the farm were of mixed breed.*

breeze *n.* wind, breath, air, flurry, zephyr *The austral breeze rippled
the surface of Fimkin's martini.*

bribe *vb.* tempt, entice, lure; influence, pervert, corrupt *The mayor
was accused of accepting a bribe, but it was never proved.*

bridle *n.* curb, check, restraint, control, halter *The leather bridle for
his favourite horse was studded with brass.* *vb.* curb, control,
check, restrain, govern *Walter would get along better with people if
he could learn to bridle his temper.* ANT. *vb.* loose, free, release.

brief *adj.* 1 short, temporary, fleeting *The life of some insects is so
brief that it lasts only a day.* 2 short, terse, concise, condensed,
compact *The brief reports did not leave time for any details.* *vb.*
advise, teach, instruct *The men were briefed before going into the
meeting.* ANT. *adj.* (1) long, extended, protracted. (2) extensive,
comprehensive, exhaustive.

bright *adj.* 1 shining, shiny, gleaming, brilliant, sparkling, shimmer-
ing, radiant *The seaman had bright brass buttons on his uniform.*
2 lively, cheerful, happy, lighthearted *Her bright personality makes
her a pleasure to be with.* 3 vivid, intense, brilliant *That bright
green dress becomes you very well.* 4 intelligent, quick-witted,
clever, keen *The bright children were mixed with the average ones to
stimulate them.* 5 promising, encouraging, favourable *Bob seems
to have a bright future in that new job.* ANT. (1) dull, dim, lustreless. (2) boring, dull, colourless. (4) stupid, slow, backward.

brilliant *adj.* 1 bright, splendid, radiant, shining, sparkling, glittering
Mrs Van Patten was wearing a brilliant diamond necklace. 2 talented, intelligent, gifted, ingenious *That fellow George is a brilliant
engineer.* ANT. (1) dull, lustreless. (2) mediocre, second-rate.

brim *n.* edge, lip, rim, margin, border *Be careful, as the brim of the
glass is chipped.* ANT. centre, middle.

bring *vb.* carry, take, fetch *Please bring that chair over here.* *vb.
phr.* **bring about** cause, accomplish, effect *The judge brought about
a compromise between the two parties.* **bring round** convince, persuade *If you argue enough, you can bring him round to your way of
thinking.* **bring to** or **round** revive, restore *It took twenty minutes to
bring Vickie round after she had been knocked unconscious.* **bring up**
1 rear, raise, nurture, educate, train, teach *Anita's parents were
away a great deal, so she was brought up by her aunt.* 2 introduce,
raise, propose *Why did he bring up the question of her honesty?*
ANT. *vb.* withdraw, remove.

brink *n.* edge, rim, verge, margin, limit *Luckily, the car stopped just at the brink of the cliff.*

brisk *adj.* 1 lively, active, animated, energetic, nimble, quick, agile, spry *Every morning Harry would take a brisk walk in the park.* 2 sharp, cool, stimulating, keen, invigorating *On these November mornings the air can be very brisk.* ANT. (1) slow, sluggish, lethargic. (2) heavy, still, oppressive.

brittle *adj.* frail, fragile, breakable, weak *These cookies are so brittle that they crumble when you pick them up.* ANT. flexible, elastic, supple.

broad *adj.* 1 wide; large, expansive, extended, roomy *The broad plain stretched out before them.* 2 general *In a broad sense, intolerance should be against the law.* 3 extensive, wide, full *He was appointed a judge because of his broad knowledge of the law.* ANT. (1) narrow, constricted. (2) detailed. (3) limited, negligible.

broadcast *vb.* spread, distribute, send, transmit, announce, relay *The BBC World Service broadcasts throughout the world.* *n.* programme, show *Did you hear yesterday's late-night news broadcast?*

broaden *vb.* extend, widen, expand, grow, increase *Those who continue their education broaden their horizons.* ANT. narrow.

broad-minded *adj.* tolerant, open-minded, unprejudiced, liberal *Peggy's parents are quite broad-minded about the boys she goes out with.* ANT. narrow-minded, prejudiced, bigoted, petty.

brokenhearted *adj.* sad, depressed, miserable, grief-stricken, inconsolable, disconsolate, forlorn, heartbroken *I was brokenhearted when my best friend moved away to another city.*

brood *n.* litter, young, offspring *The mother hen defended her brood of chicks from the kitten.* *vb.* ponder, think about, meditate on *or* about, consider, reflect on, deliberate on *The old man was brooding over the unfriendly things he had done in his youth.*

brook *n.* stream, rivulet, branch, run, rill, creek *The trout in that brook just seemed to want to be caught.*

brother *n.* 1 sibling *Any son of my parents is my brother.* 2 fellow man, kinsman; comrade *All men are brothers.* ANT. (1) sister.

brow *n.* forehead, front, face *The sweat stood out on his brow as he strained to lift the log.*

brown *adj.* copper, rust, bronze, chestnut, russet *The brown leaves of autumn lay on the ground.*

browse *vb.* glance, scan, skim, thumb through, peruse *The owner of the bookshop doesn't mind if people browse, as long as they buy something once in a while.*

bruise *vb.* injure, hurt, wound, damage *Alan was bruised on his arm when the mast fell against him.* *n.* abrasion, injury, wound, damage, harm *Beth suffered multiple bruises when she fell off her bicycle.*

brush *n.* 1 hairbrush; broom; whisk; paintbrush *I keep my brush alongside my comb.* 2 bush, bushes, scrub, thicket *We lost sight of the fox when he ran into the brush.* 3 encounter, meeting, affair, contact, skirmish *After he was released from prison, he never again had a brush with the law.*

brutal *adj.* cruel, mean, savage, pitiless, inhuman, barbaric, ferocious *The brutal attack on the bank clerk was inexcusable.* ANT. kind, kindhearted, gentle, mild.

brute *n.* beast, monster; savage, barbarian *We caught the brute and put him into a cage.* *adj.* physical; savage, wild *He picked up the two men using just brute strength and flung them away.*

bubble *n.* foam, froth, lather, effervescence *Soap makes the water full of bubbles.* *vb.* froth, foam, seethe, boil *The oil bubbled on the stove when we dropped in the potatoes for frying.*

bucket *n.* pail; container, can, canister, pot *Fetch a bucket of water from the well.*

buckle *n.* fastening, fastener, clasp *He wears a gold buckle on his belt.* *vb.* **1** fasten, clasp *Don't buckle your belt too tightly.* **2** bend, collapse, warp, yield, fail, give way *The bridge buckled under the weight of the huge lorry.*

budge *vb.* move, stir, shift *I haven't budged an inch since you left.*

buffet[1] *vb.* strike, beat, hit, slap *The winds buffeted the house for three days.* *n.* blow, hit *A quick buffet to the side of the head brought him to his senses.*

buffet[2] *n.* **1** sideboard, cabinet, counter *The food was set out on the buffet so that each person could help himself.* **2** meal, snack *Come round for a buffet tonight.*

build *vb.* construct, erect, put together, assemble *In their spare time the children built kennels and sold them to neighbours.* *vb. phr.* **build up** increase, strengthen, expand, develop *Over the years he built up the size of his record library considerably.* *n.* physique, form, figure *Kathy has the build of an athlete.* ANT. *vb.* demolish, pull down, raze.

building *n.* structure, edifice; residence, house, office building *My father's offices are in the new building on the high street.*

bulge *n.* swelling, lump, protrusion, protuberance, bump *The bulge at the side of the building looked dangerous.* *vb.* swell, protrude, extend *As he blew air into the balloon, it began to bulge.* ANT. *n.* depression, hollow.

bulk *n.* **1** size, volume, magnitude *The package wasn't heavy but its huge bulk made it difficult to carry.* **2** majority, most, main part *The bulk of my income comes from my salary.*

bulky *adj.* large, big, huge, clumsy, unwieldy, cumbersome, massive *How did you manage to carry such a bulky package up the stairs?* ANT. delicate, small, handy.

bully *n.* rowdy, ruffian, rascal, scamp *The village bully used to set upon the young lads.* *vb.* domineer, harass, intimidate *You could tell that he was a coward because he was always bullying the smaller children.*

bump *vb.* knock, bang, collide with, hit, strike *The first day he took out his new bicycle Alan bumped into a car.* *n.* knock, bang;

bun • 42

collision, blow *For trying to help the shopkeeper, Jim was given a bump on the head by the thief.*

bun *n.* roll, bread, scone, cake, pastry *We have hot buns with butter and jam for tea.*

bunch *n.* cluster, group, batch, bundle, collection *Take this bunch of flowers round to old Mrs Plunkett.*

bundle *n.* bunch; package, parcel, packet *We make up small bundles of kindling for use in the fireplace.*

bungle *vb.* mess up, spoil, ruin; fumble *Jonathan really bungled the painting of the fence, getting paint all over the pavement.*

burden *n.* load, weight; worry, trial; trouble *The donkey is a beast of burden. Concern about his father's health was too much of a burden for a child to manage.* *vb.* load, weigh down, overload, oppress *I don't want to burden you with my troubles.* ANT. *vb.* disburden.

bureau *n.* 1 desk *You'll find the keys in the top drawer of my bureau.* 2 office, agency *Let's go down to the travel bureau to see about our tickets.*

burglar *n.* thief, robber, housebreaker *The police think that all the thefts were committed by the same burglar.*

burial *n.* funeral, interment *The burial took place at the church cemetery on Monday.*

burn *vb.* 1 blaze, flame *The fire burned for three days in the forest.* 2 scorch, sear, char, set on fire, consume *The wooden carving was burned beyond recognition.* *n.* scorch, injury, singe, scald *There were some burns on her arms where the boiling water had accidentally been poured.*

burrow *n.* lair, den, hole, tunnel *The rabbit was back in its burrow before we could catch it.*

burst *vb.* explode, blow up, erupt *The electric light bulb burst into lots of pieces when I dropped it.* *n.* explosion; breach, rapture; outburst, outbreak *A sudden burst of firing broke the silence of the prison.* ANT. implode.

bury *vb.* 1 inter, entomb *The men were buried for two hours by the avalanche.* 2 hide, conceal, cover, secrete *The book I was looking for was buried under the pile of magazines.* ANT. (1) disinter, raise.

bus *n.* coach, minibus; tram *I am not sure that the bus runs after midnight.*

bush *n.* shrub, plant; shrubbery *There is a trick to trimming the bushes into the shapes of animals.*

business *n.* 1 trade, occupation, commerce *What business is your father in?* 2 company, firm, concern; partnership *After graduating from college, Victor went into his father's business.* 3 affair, concern *My personal life is none of your business.*

bustle *vb.* hurry, rush, hasten *I just saw Mr Carstairs bustling down the street to catch his bus.*

busy *adj.* active, occupied, engaged, employed, industrious, hardworking *I am sorry not to have phoned, but I have been very busy this week.* ANT. inactive, unemployed, indolent, lazy.

but *conj.* however; nevertheless, yet; on the other hand, though, still, although *We wanted to go to the cinema but it was too late. My sister went but I didn't.*

buy *vb.* purchase; procure, obtain, get *I am not sure that one can buy fresh tuna at our fish market.* ANT. sell.

by *prep.* near, at, close to, next to *There is a newsagent's shop over by the railway station.*

c

cab *n.* taxi, taxicab, minicab *We took a cab home from the party.*

cabin *n.* **1** compartment, berth, stateroom *Our cabin on the ship was on the lower deck.* **2** hut, shack *The hermit lived in a cabin in the woods.*

cabinet *n.* **1** council, committee, ministry *The prime minister depends on the members of his cabinet for advice.* **2** cupboard, wardrobe, chest *We bought a fine nineteenth-century cabinet at an auction.*

cable *n.* wire, rope, line *The cable is too weak to hold the boat at the mooring.*

cackle *vb.* cluck, quack; laugh, giggle, chortle, chuckle *When Old McDonald laughs, it sounds like a hen cackling.*

café *n.* snack-bar; cafeteria, restaurant *We stopped at a roadside café for tea.*

cagey *adj.* evasive, secretive, uncommunicative *It was very cagey of Wilmot to say nothing about the loaded gun.* ANT. frank, open, straightforward.

cajole *vb.* persuade, coax, flatter *Frank was trying to cajole Helen into going to dinner with him.*

cake *n.* pastry, roll, bun, patisserie, tart *Mrs Quimby makes the most delicious cakes.*

calamity *n.* disaster, bad luck, misfortune, distress, trouble, hardship, catastrophe *The drought proved to be a great calamity for everyone.* ANT. boon, blessing, godsend, windfall.

calculate *vb.* work out, reckon, compute, measure; add, multiply, divide *Can you calculate the time it will take to finish the job?*

calculating *adj.* scheming, crafty, cunning, shrewd *The count has a reputation for being calculating, so don't trust him.* ANT. ingenuous, simple, direct, guileless.

calculation *n.* reckoning, working out, computation *According to my calculations, we should be home by midnight.* ANT. guess, estimate.

call *vb.* **1** call out, cry out, exclaim, shout *I hear my name being called.* **2** name, designate, dub, label *Her name is Catherine but they call her Sophie.* **3** telephone, phone, ring, ring up *Please call me when you arrive at the hotel.* **4** collect, assemble, convene *The directors called a meeting.* **5** wake up, awaken, waken, wake, rouse, arouse *They called us at five o'clock to start on the hike.* *n.* **1** cry, shout, yell, exclamation *I heard the call of the hunters trying to find me in the forest.* **2** demand, need, occasion, claim *There isn't much call for fountain pens these days.* *vb. phr.* **call off** cancel, postpone *The match was called off at the last moment.* **call on** visit *I called on our new neighbours yesterday.*

callous *adj.* hardened, insensitive, unfeeling *I have never met anyone so callous as that prison warder.* ANT. tender; merciful.

calm *adj.* 1 quiet, peaceful, still, tranquil, mild, serene, smooth *The sea became calm towards sunset.* 2 composed, collected, unruffled, levelheaded, cool, unexcited; detached, aloof *Nell remained quite calm after I told her the bad news.* *n.* calmness, stillness, serenity, quiet; composure *The wind and rain stopped suddenly in the calm before the storm struck.* *vb.* pacify, soothe *When he learned that it had not been his son who had been in the accident, Bill calmed down.* ANT. *adj.* (1) tempestuous, stormy. (2) emotional, disturbed, excited. *n.* turmoil, upheaval, disturbance. *vb.* upset, excite, disturb.

camouflage *n.* disguise, covering; mask, blind, veil; deception *We used camouflage to conceal the tanks from the enemy.*

campaign *n.* operation, exercise, task; fight, crusade, offensive *We must carry the campaign forward if we are to win.*

cancel *vb.* 1 call off, rescind, set aside *I'm sorry but I have to cancel our appointment for dinner tonight.* 2 delete, cross out *or* off, erase *She cancelled his name and substituted hers on the list.*

candid *adj.* frank, open, straightforward, honest *If he were completely candid he would not hesitate telling you what he thinks.* ANT. devious, dishonest; cagey.

candidate *n.* nominee, aspirant, applicant *We selected the best person to be a candidate for this important office.*

capable *adj.* able, skilled, fit, skilful, accomplished, competent *John is a capable driver and you can feel safe.* ANT. inept, incompetent, unskilled.

capacity *n.* 1 volume, content *This tank has a capacity of 40 litres.* 2 ability, capability, aptitude, talent, faculty *If he would only study harder, John has the capacity to be a first-class student.* ANT. (2) incapacity, inability.

capital *n.* cash, money, assets, property, wealth, principal, resources *My father started his business with capital of £2000.* *adj.* major, chief, first, primary, leading, important, principal *St Peter's Church is of capital interest to visitors to Rome.* ANT. *adj.* trivial, unimportant, secondary.

capsize *vb.* turn over, tip up, overturn *After everyone was safely in the lifeboats, we watched as the ship capsized.*

captain *n.* 1 supervisor, commander, director, authority, leader *The teacher appointed Eugene to be the captain of the group.* 2 (of a ship) skipper, commander, commanding officer, master *The captain ordered the lifeboats to be lowered over the side.*

captivate *vb.* fascinate, charm, enchant, delight *Fred found Mary a totally captivating woman.*

captive *n.* prisoner, convict, hostage *The hostages remained as captives for five years.*

captivity *n.* imprisonment, confinement, detention, custody; slavery, bondage *Why were these innocent civilians kept in captivity?* ANT. freedom, liberty.

capture *vb.* seize, take prisoner, trap, grab, catch, arrest *We set the trap to capture rabbits, but not one fell into it.* *n.* seizure, catching; recovery *The escaped tiger avoided capture for three hours.* ANT. *vb.* release, free, liberate.

car *n.* automobile, vehicle, motorcar *I really must think about buying a new car.*

carcass *n.* body, corpse, remains, cadaver *The carcass of the gnu was surrounded by hyenas and vultures.*

cardinal *adj.* important, chief, principal, primary, prime, major, leading, essential *My cardinal reason for coming was to see you.* ANT. secondary, subordinate, auxiliary.

care *n.* **1** worry, concern, anxiety, trouble *Although his business was very bad, my father acted as though he didn't have a care in the world.* **2** carefulness, attention, regard, concern, consideration *Like many parents, Bob and Diane treated their first child with much more care than the later children.* **3** charge, custody, protection, keeping, supervision, guardianship *We left our dog in the care of the vet when we went away for a holiday.* *vb.* **1** mind; attend, consider *I don't care what you do with that eggshell.* **2** look after, keep; watch, guard, supervise *Who's going to care for me when I'm old?* ANT. *n.* **(2)** indifference, unconcern, apathy.

career *n.* profession, occupation, job, vocation *Herbert has made a career out of helping young people get established in business.*

careful *adj.* **1** cautious, watchful, wary, guarded, vigilant *You have to be careful of what you say when you're talking to the headmaster.* **2** thorough, concerned, painstaking, meticulous *I thought that Tim did a very careful job when he painted the railings.* ANT. **(1)** incautious, heedless. **(2)** careless, messy, sloppy.

careless *adj.* messy, sloppy, unthoughtful, unconcerned, negligent, reckless, thoughtless, uncaring *Although his writing was fine, Stuart was very careless about his spelling.* ANT. careful, cautious, prudent, painstaking.

caress *n.* embrace, pat, kiss *Under his mother's gentle caress, Billy was soothed enough to stop crying.* *vb.* pat, pet, stroke, fondle, cuddle *Dad took the photograph of Jennie while she caressed her kitten.*

cargo *n.* load, freight, baggage *These packing cases will go aboard the plane as cargo.*

carriage *n.* vehicle, coach; cart, wagon, chariot *The railway carriages are much more comfortable these days.*

carry *vb.* bear, transport, move, transfer; take, bring *The porter will help carry your luggage to the train.* *vb. phr.* **carry off** abduct, seize, kidnap, capture *When the bandits attacked a village, they would often carry off all the girls.* **carry on** **1** continue, go on, proceed *Please excuse the interruption: you may carry on with your* *conversation now.* **2** fuss, misbehave *Victor carried on so about being left behind that he was finally allowed to go.* **carry out** fulfil, complete, succeed, accomplish, win, effect *The plan sounds good, but will they be able to carry it out?*

cart *n.* barrow, wagon, carriage *The donkey was pulling a small cart.*

carton *n.* box, case, container; can, canister *Philbert arrived with a large carton of assorted biscuits.*

carve *vb.* cut, chisel, sculpt, hew, whittle, shape *These figures were all carved by hand.*

case¹ *n.* **1** instance, occurrence, example, happening; sample, illustration *The detectives were investigating a case of murder.* **2** action, suit, lawsuit, claim *The prosecution opened the case at the Old Bailey.*

case² *n.* container, crate, box, carton, chest; receptacle *When he opened the case of wine, it contained only eight bottles, not twelve.*

cash *n.* money, currency; banknotes, coins, change *Shall I pay in cash, or do you want to charge it to your credit card?*

cast *vb.* **1** throw, hurl, fling, toss, pitch, sling *To avoid being caught with the stolen papers, Ezra cast them into the deep well.* **2** direct, shed, impart *The lamp cast a strange yellow glow about the room.* **3** direct, turn *Whenever her name was mentioned, Elizabeth cast her eyes downward in embarrassment.* **4** mould, shape, form *I cast this bronze statue in my own shop.* *n.* players, actors, performers *There was a party for the entire cast after the first performance of the play.*

castle *n.* palace, mansion, château *Few people today can afford the upkeep on a castle.*

casual *adj.* **1** chance, accidental, unintentional, unexpected, offhand, unplanned, spontaneous *The whole trouble can be traced to their casual meeting in the garden.* **2** informal, sporty *At weekends we wear casual clothes unless we expect company or go out.* ANT. **(1)** planned, calculated, deliberate, premeditated. **(2)** formal, dressy.

catalogue *n.* list, roll, inventory, record, directory; file; index *I was just looking at the catalogue of the books in your next sale.*

catastrophe *n.* disaster, calamity, accident, misfortune, mishap *The loss of Egbert's job was a major catastrophe for his family.* ANT. boon, blessing, triumph.

catch *vb.* **1** seize, capture, take, grasp, grab, nab *Did they catch the thief who stole the car?* **2** trap, snare, entrap, ensnare *We caught two rabbits in the trap but let them go after a while.* **3** go down with, contract, succumb to *You'll catch a cold if you don't wear your hat.* *vb. phr.* **catch on** become popular, become fashionable *That new style of dress has really caught on these last few months.* **catch out** trap, trick, trip up *Jane tried to catch her brother out by asking him a trick question.* **catch up** reach, pass *Your brother has just left, so if you go now you'll soon catch him up.* *n.* **1** seizure; capture, arrest, apprehension *The fishermen made a great catch of fish.*

2 bolt, latch *The catch on the door is broken again.* ANT. *vb.*(1, 2) release, free, let go.

cause *n.* 1 reason, origin, creation, occasion, ground *The cause of the accident was a broken brake lever.* 2 aim, purpose, object *We managed to raise £20 for the cause of orphans.* *vb.* occasion, give rise to, bring about, originate, effect *According to the report, the breakdown caused the accident.*

caution *n.* 1 wariness, watchfulness, vigilance, heed, care *Exercise caution when you approach that dog—he may be unfriendly.* 2 warning, advice *She gave me a caution about the broken stair.* *vb.* warn, admonish, forewarn *The lifeguard cautioned us about the strong undercurrent.* ANT. *n.* (1) heedlessness, carelessness, incaution.

cautious *adj.* careful, watchful, wary; vigilant *Be cautious when handling those snakes—they're poisonous.* ANT. heedless, headstrong, indiscreet, foolish.

cave *n.* grotto, cavern, hole *Bears hibernate in a cave during the winter.* *vb. phr.* **cave in** collapse, fall in *Just as we were about to leave, the roof caved in and trapped us.*

cease *vb.* stop, end, put a stop *or* an end to, terminate *I wish that Elsie would cease her complaining.* ANT. begin, start.

celebrate *vb.* honour, observe, keep, commemorate *Do you celebrate birthdays in your family?* ANT. ignore, disregard.

celebrated *adj.* famous, renowned, famed, well-known, noted, illustrious, eminent; popular *One of Scotland's most celebrated writers will address us next week.* ANT. unheard of, unknown.

celebrity *n.* notable, dignitary; hero, heroine *He may be well known, but his wife is more of a celebrity than he is.*

cell *n.* room, cubicle, compartment, recess, den *The monks lived in small, bare cells.*

cellar *n.* basement, vault, crypt *We keep the wine in the cellar because it is cool there.*

censor *n.* examiner, inquisitor *They were afraid that the censors would ban the publication of the book.*

censure *n.* disapproval, criticism, reproach *The commission's vote for censure of the judge was unanimous.* *vb.* disapprove, criticize, condemn, reproach *After the dishonest things the mayor did, the town council had to censure him.* ANT. *n.* approval, praise. *vb.* praise, approve, applaud.

central *adj.* 1 middle, mid, focal, inner, halfway *The chief's hut was central in the arrangement of the village.* 2 principal, chief, dominant, basic, fundamental, necessary *The central issue for the workers was more pay; increased pensions were secondary.* ANT. (2) secondary, auxiliary, side, incidental.

centre *n.* 1 middle, midst, inside, midpoint *The centre of the earth is said to be a sphere of molten iron.* 2 focus, hub, heart, core *The monument is at the centre of the city.* *vb.* focus, direct, concentrate *The attention of the crowd centred on the clown in the red costume.* ANT. *n.* (1) edge, brim.

ceremony *n.* ritual, rite, service, formality *We all attended the ceremony at which Father was awarded his medal.*

certain *adj.* 1 confident, sure, positive, assured *After all he'd done for the town, his election as mayor was certain.* 2 definite, particular, special *It would not be wise for me to name certain people who were seen together at the party.* ANT. (1) doubtful, uncertain, questionable.

certainly *adv.* surely, absolutely, definitely, unquestionably, undoubtedly, doubtless *You certainly deserve everything you get.* ANT. doubtfully, dubiously, questionably.

certificate *n.* document, credential(s), declaration, affidavit *On the walls of my doctor's office are all the certificates he has been given.*

chain *n.* string, link; set, series *It is a curious chain of events that has brought me here.*

chair *n.* seat, bench, stool *You might have to stand on a chair to reach the platter.*

challenge *n.* dare, threat *The supermarket met the challenge of competition by reducing prices.* *vb.* dare, threaten *John challenged Peter to a duel.*

chamber *n.* room, salon; cell *The private audience with the king was held in a small chamber alongside the throne room.*

champion *n.* hero, winner, victor *The champion of the heavyweight boxers was Joe.* *vb.* defend, support *The housewives championed the cause of the poor in their area.*

chance *n.* 1 opportunity, possibility, prospect *I'll tell you what you want to know if you'll stop talking and give me a chance.* 2 luck, accident, fate *You ought to make absolutely certain that he's coming and leave nothing to chance.* *adj.* accidental, casual *A chance meeting at the club resulted in my getting the job.* ANT. *n.* (2) certainty, inevitability.

change *vb.* 1 exchange, substitute, replace *We changed our clothes before going out.* 2 vary; modify, alter *I wish you would change your mind and let us go swimming.* 3 exchange, trade *I have to change this five-pound note into coins to use in the telephone.* *n.* variation, modification, alteration *Ellie had a change of heart and came with us.* ANT. *vb.* endure, remain. *n.* endurance, steadfastness, immutability.

channel *n.* canal, duct, trough, way, runway, groove *The water runs through a narrow channel into this receptacle.*

chant *n.* song, singing, hymn, incantation *Certain kinds of chants have been used in church music for centuries.* *vb.* sing, recite, intone *The children started to chant, 'Kitty is a baby! Kitty is a baby!'*

chaos *n.* disorder, confusion, turmoil *You cannot imagine the chaos on the last day of the school semester.* ANT. tranquillity, order, organization, tidiness.

chaotic *adj.* disordered, confused, messy, disorganized *My files are completely chaotic and I need help getting them organized.* ANT. ordered, organized, neat, tidy, systematic.

character *n.* 1 qualities, features, characteristics *The judge is a man of outstanding character.* 2 person, role *The characters in the play were all very well acted.* 3 *Informal:* individual, eccentric *That fellow is quite a character.*

characteristic *adj.* typical, distinctive, distinguishing, special *Dictionaries often give examples of characteristic uses of words.* *n.* character, feature, quality, trait *A characteristic of the Pygmy people is their short stature.*

charge *vb.* 1 price at, sell for *They charge too much for a service at that garage.* 2 attack, assault, assail *The cavalry charged up the hill.* 3 accuse, indict, blame *Even though he had a perfect alibi, they charged Evans with robbery.* *n.* 1 accusation, blame, indictment, allegation *The charge against us was trespassing on private property.* 2 care, management, custody *The teacher left a student in charge of the class.* 3 price, cost *The charge for making a phone call increased again this year.* ANT. *vb.* (2) retreat, flee. (3) absolve, excuse, pardon.

charitable *adj.* kind, generous, liberal; considerate *Lady Binkley has always been most charitable when we raised money for the church.* ANT. mean, petty, stingy, narrow-minded.

charm *n.* 1 attractiveness, allure, enchantment; spell, magic witchery *When she used her charm on Rudolf, she could make him do anything she wanted.* 2 amulet, good-luck piece, talisman *The bearded pirate wore a strange charm on a chain around his neck.* *vb.* attract, enchant, lure, fascinate, captivate, bewitch *When you were in India, did you see any men charming snakes?*

chart *n.* plan, map; diagram *This chart shows the location of the treasure.*

chase *vb.* pursue, run after, follow, hunt *The farmer chased us out of the field.* *n.* pursuit, hunt *At first, I ran after the thief alone, but two other people later joined in the chase.*

chaste *adj.* virtuous, pure, innocent, decent; virginal *He had always thought of Melissa as a chaste young girl.* ANT. impure, worldly, sinful.

chasten *vb.* discipline, rebuke, reprove *Edward was severely chastened for disobeying his mother.*

chat *vb.* talk, converse *I chatted for a while with Mrs Philbey about where she was going for her holiday.* *n.* conversation, talk *During our chat, she told me she loved to go to the mountains.*

chatter *vb.* talk, chat; prattle, gossip, gabble *Mrs Gable paid no attention to the spider and just kept chattering on.*

cheap *adj.* 1 inexpensive, low-priced, low-cost *Fresh fruit is cheaper when it's in season.* 2 shoddy, inferior, poor *If you buy cheap clothes, you rarely get good value.* ANT. (1) costly, expensive, dear. (2) well-made.

cheat *n.* swindler, fraud, phoney, charlatan; crook, thief, confidence trickster, con man *The man who offered to sell Tower Bridge was nothing but a cheat.* *vb.* swindle, trick, defraud, deceive, victimize, dupe, hoax *The crook cheated me out of my life savings.*

check *vb.* 1 stop, halt, arrest, block *The tanks checked the advance of the enemy's soldiers.* 2 restrain, control, curb; hinder *This valve checks the flow of gas.* 3 review, investigate, test, examine, compare *Please check the inventory against the list.* *n.* control, curb; hindrance, barrier, bar, obstacle, restriction *When running a household you have to keep a check on the amount of money you spend. Bill doesn't seem able to keep a check on his temper.* ANT. *vb.* (1, 2) advance, continue, foster, promote.

check-up *n.* examination, medical *or* physical (examination) *My doctor gives me a check-up every year.*

cheek *n.* impudence, impertinence, nerve, gall, effrontery *He had the cheek to ask my mother her age.*

cheer *n.* 1 approval, applause, encouragement *A large cheer went up from the crowd as Bob won the race.* 2 glee, joy, mirth, gaiety, cheerfulness *Be of good cheer: happiness is just around the corner.* *vb.* 1 encourage, comfort *The coach's words cheered us, and we won.* 2 shout, yell, applaud *The crowd cheered for the new champion.* ANT. *n.* (1) discouragement, derision. *vb.* (1) discourage, sadden. (2) boo, hiss.

cheerful *adj.* cheery, happy, joyous, joyful, merry *Alexa has a cheerful disposition that puts people at ease.* ANT. sad, gloomy, morose, downhearted.

cherish *vb.* 1 treasure, hold dear, value, prize *She cherished the memories of her days at summer camp.* 2 nurse, comfort, nurture *I cherish the relationship I have with my brothers and sisters.* ANT. (1) scorn, undervalue, deprecate, disparage.

chest *n.* 1 breast, bosom *The little girl clasped the puppy to her chest.* 2 box, trunk, coffer, case, casket *The treasure chest contained rubies, pearls, diamonds and gold.* 3 (of drawers) dresser, cabinet, commode, chiffonier, bureau *My father's cufflinks were on the chest.*

chew *vb.* bite, munch, gnaw; nibble *The puppy chewed up my slipper.*

chic *adj.* stylish, up-to-date, fashionable, smart, (*informal*) trendy *Penelope Gastleigh's wardrobe is very chic.* ANT. old-fashioned, out-of-date.

chide *vb.* scold, criticize, admonish, reprimand, rebuke, reprove *Vincent's mother chides him for the slightest error.* ANT. praise, extol, commend.

chief *n.* leader, ruler, commander, boss, head *The chief of the robber band was masked.* *adj.* leading, principal, main; head *The chief reason for going to school is to learn something.* ANT. *adj.* secondary, incidental.

chiefly *adv.* mostly, mainly, principally, especially *We go to the seashore chiefly to cool off on hot summer days.*

child *n.* infant, youth, youngster, boy, girl *Treat her gently—she's only a child.* ANT. adult, grown-up.

childish *adj.* child-like, immature, babyish, infantile *You are too old for such childish behaviour.* ANT. adult, grown-up, mature, seasoned.

chill *n.* cold, coldness, coolness, cool *You will need a pullover in the chill of the evening.* ANT. warmth, heat.

chilly *adj.* cool, brisk, frosty *It is too chilly to go outside without a coat.* ANT. warm, heated, hot.

chip *n.* bit, fragment; flake, slice, wedge *Chips of wood were thrown up by the lathe.* *vb.* break, cut, hew, splinter, crumble *The paint is beginning to chip because of the weather.*

chirp *vb.,n.* twitter, peep, tweet, warble, cheep, chirrup *The birds were chirping happily in the trees. The chirps of the crickets and the birds woke me up.*

chivalrous *adj.* brave, noble; polite, courteous, gallant, gentlemanly *Wasn't it chivalrous of Tony to help that lady cross the street!!* ANT. rude, impolite, crude, uncivil.

chivalry *n.* nobility, knighthood; courtesy, gallantry *When someone is that considerate, you know that the age of chivalry cannot be dead.*

choice *n.* selection, option, pick *The saleslady offered us a choice of styles and colours.* *adj.* select, fine, rare, uncommon, valuable, precious *The mare in the pasture is a choice example of the best horsebreeding.*

choke *vb.* strangle, throttle; gag, gasp, suffocate *The pepper in that dish almost made me choke.*

choose *vb.* select, pick, decide between *or* on, settle on *or* for *There are thousands of records to choose from at the shop.*

chop *vb.* cut; hew, fell *These trees are the ones to be chopped down.*

chorus *n.* refrain, song, melody, tune *We rehearsed the chorus of the song several times.*

chronic *adj.* continuing, persistent, continuous, lingering, sustained, constant, lifelong, permanent, unending, eternal, everlasting *I wish I could get rid of this chronic cough.* ANT. fleeting, temporary; acute.

chuckle *vb.,n.* giggle, titter, laugh *The teacher chuckled over the story that Marjorie had written. Every few minutes, he gave a little chuckle.*

church *n.* 1 congregation; denomination, faith, tradition *The Church was learning to respond to the Word of God more.* 2 chapel, cathedral, abbey, sanctuary *Our church is full at Harvest, Christmas and Easter.*

circle *n.* 1 ring; loop, disc *The magician drew a circle in the sand.* 2 group, set, class, club *In her circle of friends, everyone now buys Elvis records.* *vb.* encircle, surround, round, enclose *The road circled our farm.*

circuit *n.* orbit, circle, revolution; course, tour, journey *This road makes a circuit of the entire city.*

circular *adj.* round, ring-like, disc-like *Most drinking glasses are* *circular. n.* advertisement, handbill, leaflet *We received a circular advertising the sale at the department store.* ANT. *adj.* straight.

circulate *vb.* distribute, send *or* pass round *Please circulate this memorandum for everyone to read.*

circumference *n.* periphery, border, edge, perimeter *A circle with a diameter of one foot has a circumference of a little more than three feet.*

circumstances *n.pl.* situation, conditions, facts, factors, grounds, background *Unless the circumstances change, I shall not be returning.*

cite *vb.* quote, mention, refer to *My comments were cited in the minister's speech on transport.*

citizen *n.* inhabitant, native, national, subject, denizen, dweller, resident *You are not allowed to vote unless you are a citizen.*

city *n.* town, capital, metropolis, conurbation *After several centuries, what started as a village became the big city you see today.*

civil *adj.* 1 municipal, public *Every citizen has his civil rights.* 2 polite, courteous, respectful, gracious, well-mannered *Roger has always been very civil to me.* ANT. (2) impolite, rude, crude.

civilization *n.* culture, society *Martin has written a book on the civilization of the Outer Hebrides.*

civilize *vb.* cultivate, refine, polish, tame, teach, instruct *Civilized people eat with a knife and fork.*

claim *vb.* 1 demand, require, request, ask for *After my grandfather died, my father claimed for himself all his property.* 2 assert, state, maintain, insist, declare *Donald claimed that he knew nothing about the theft of the statue.* *n.* 1 demand, request, requirement *The court ruled that the miner's claim was invalid.* 2 title, right, interest *I told you that Kitty has no claim to the brooch.*

clairvoyance *n.* premonition, precognition, foreknowledge; insight, discernment; intuition *It doesn't require clairvoyance to know that the traffic is bad at this corner.*

clamour *n.* din, noise, shouting, uproar *When the teacher announced another exam, there was such a clamour from the students that he cancelled it.* *vb.* demand, shout *The girls in the audience clamoured for the guitar player to come back on stage.* ANT. *n.* quiet, serenity, tranquillity.

clan *n.* family, set, group *He is a member of clan McLeod.*

clang *vb.,n.* jangle, jingle, ring *The metals clanged as the tins fell on the scrap heap. The clang of the alarm could be heard all over the building.*

clap *vb.* applaud, acclaim, praise, cheer *Everyone clapped at the end of the play.*

clarify *vb.* explain, clear, define *There are a few things in this story that I would ask you to clarify.* ANT. confuse, muddle, obscure.

clarity *n.* clearness, lucidity; precision; distinctiveness *Because of the clarity of the air, we could see the towers of the city from far off.*

clash *n.* 1 clang, crash, clank *The clash of armour could be heard far* *away as the knights fought.* **2** conflict, opposition, struggle, disagreement; collision *There was a clash between those in office and those who sought to replace them.* *vb.* **1** contrast, mismatch, jar *Your tie clashes with your shirt.* **2** conflict, disagree, interfere; collide *We always clash over our different points of view.* ANT. *n.* (2) harmony, agreement, accord. *vb.* (1) harmonize, blend. (2) agree, match, coincide.

clasp *vb.* grasp, embrace, hug, clutch, hold *Her father was so happy to find her safe and sound that he wept as he clasped her to him.* *n.* hook, catch, pin, fastening, brooch, buckle *These two parts of the dress are held together by a silver clasp.*

class *n.* **1** classification, rank, order, grade, division, subdivision, family, sort, kind, set, species, group *I don't know whether this animal belongs to the fish or reptile class.* **2** form, group, set, year *I'm in Miss Clarendon's class next year.* *vb.* classify, rank, grade *I wouldn't class you in the same category as your sister.*

classic *n.* masterpiece: Paradise Lost *is considered one of the greatest classics in the English language.* *adj.* model, definitive, standard; highest *California is the classic haven for tax exiles.*

classification *n.* **1** category, order, class *Into which classification should I put this book, science or philosophy?* **2** arrangement, grouping, ordering, organization *The librarian's classification of new books takes a great deal of time.*

classify *vb.* class, arrange, sort, order, organize, group, grade, index *The books are classified according to subject matter.*

clause *n.* paragraph, article, condition, limitation *There is a clause in this contract that needs revision.*

claw *n.* nail, talon, hook *The cat's claw caught in the curtain and tore it.* *vb.* scratch, tear; rip *The dog kept clawing at the door, trying to get in.*

clean *adj.* **1** clear, dustless, immaculate, unsoiled, unstained *My mother made me scrub the floor till it was clean.* **2** pure, untainted, uncontaminated, purified *Don't drink from a glass that isn't clean.* *vb.* **1** dust, mop, vacuum, scour, scrub, sweep, wipe, wash, rinse, cleanse *If you don't clean your room, you can't go out to play.* **2** purify, decontaminate; sterilize *All surgical instruments must be cleaned after every use.* ANT. *adj.* dirty, soiled, impure, contaminated. *vb.* soil, dirty, pollute.

cleanse *see* **clean.**

clear *adj.* **1** plain, understandable, distinct, lucid, obvious *I want to make the entire matter as clear as possible.* **2** uncloudy, unclouded, bright, light; sunny, fair *Water is a clear liquid. Saturday was such a clear day you could see the mountains in the distance.* **3** certain, sure, doubtless, obvious *Alan's innocence was clear.* **4** open, free, unobstructed, unblocked *The road was clear early in the morning.* *vb.* **1** empty *Please clear the room so that it can be painted.* **2** acquit, free, release, emancipate, let go *The statements the murderer made about his other crimes cleared two men who had been* *arrested for them.* **3** rid, free, remove *If they clear the channel of debris, we shall be able to sail the boat through it.* ANT. *adj.* (1) confused, muddled. (2) overcast, cloudy, dark. (3) dubious, questionable. (4) obstructed, blocked, blockaded. *vb.* (1) fill, clutter. (2) implicate, involve. (3) obstruct, block, blockade.

clearly *adv.* obviously, definitely, plainly, evidently, unmistakably, certainly, surely. *Cuthbert is clearly not the right person for the job.* ANT. dubiously, questionably.

cleave[1] *vb.* split, cut, sever, divide *The thunderstorm cleft the tree trunk in two.*

cleave[2] **(to)** *vb.* stick, cling, adhere *The Bible says a man cleaves to his wife when he marries her.*

clergy *n.* ministers, ministry, priesthood *Francis studied for the clergy at the local seminary.*

clergyman *n.* minister, parson, priest, vicar, pastor, preacher *Now that Francis is a clergyman, he gets a lot more respect.*

clerical *adj.* **1** priestly, ministerial, churchly, pastoral, ecclesiastical; sacred, holy *The bishop's other clerical duties did not prevent him from conducting services.* **2** stenographic, secretarial *After leaving school, Anne was lucky to get a clerical job in town.*

clerk *n.* office worker; office girl, office boy, junior, typist *Please hand in your application to the clerk at the reception desk.*

clever *adj.* **1** bright, intelligent, shrewd, quick, talented, expert, gifted, smart *A clever person could move ahead in that company.* **2** skilful, adroit, dexterous, handy *My brother is so clever with his hands that he finished a model aeroplane in two hours.* ANT. (1) stupid, slow, backward, dull. (2) clumsy, maladroit, inept.

client *n.* customer, patron *We treat all our clients with respect.*

cliff *n.* rock, hill, precipice *Philbert almost ran the car off the cliff.*

climb *vb.* go up, scale, ascend, mount *We start to climb the mountain at dawn.* ANT. go down, descend.

cling *vb.* stick, adhere, hold fast, cleave *Don't you hate the way your skirt clings on those crisp, dry days?*

clinic *n.* hospital, infirmary, sick bay *The injured were taken by ambulance to the clinic.*

clip[1] *vb.* cut, mow, crop, snip *They clipped my lawn too short.*

clip[2] *n.* fastener, paper clip, clasp *Please put a clip on those papers to keep them together.*

clique *n.* coterie, faction, group, party; splinter group *Anne joined that clique of girls who go out with the fellows on the football team.*

cloak *n.* cape, mantle, wrap, shawl *Count Dracula wrapped his black cloak round him and beckoned to her.* *vb.* conceal, hide, cover, mask *Her smile cloaked her real feelings about him.* ANT. *vb.* reveal, show, display.

clock *n.* timepiece; watch; chronometer *This clock operates on a battery and never needs winding.*

close[1] *vb.* **1** shut, fasten, bolt, lock *Be careful and make sure to close your doors at night.* **2** end, terminate, conclude *The speaker closed* *his remarks with a few compliments to the mayor.* ANT. (1) open, unlock. (2) begin, start.

close² *adj.* **1** near, nearby *If the supermarket were closer to the house, I wouldn't have to walk so far to shop.* **2** stuffy, unventilated, oppressive *With the windows closed and the heater on, it feels very close in this room.* **3** stingy, mean, mingy, tight *Scrooge was certainly a close man with his money.* ANT. (1) far, distant. (2) fresh, clear. (3) generous, open-handed, charitable.

cloth *n.* material, fabric, textile; tablecloth *It took two yards of cloth to make the skirt.*

clothe *vb.* dress, apparel, garb *How much does it cost today to clothe and feed a family of four?* ANT. undress, strip.

clothes *n.pl.* garments, clothing, dress; garb, attire, apparel, costume *We found only a pile of his clothes on the beach.*

cloud *n.* **1** haze, mist, fog *The clouds made it a gloomy day for our picnic.* **2** collection, mass *The stagecoach rattled into town in a cloud of dust.* *vb.* dim, obscure, shadow *The politician clouded the issue with his evasive answers.*

cloudy *adj.* **1** dim, obscure, vague, indefinite, blurred, unclear, confused *If your thinking is cloudy on a subject, you cannot write about it clearly.* **2** overcast, clouded, gloomy *It was a cloudy morning when we set sail for the island.* ANT. (1) clearheaded, lucid, clarified. (2) sunny, clear, brilliant, cloudless.

club *n.* **1** association, society, organization, circle, set *There was a long waiting list for membership in the club.* **2** cudgel, bat, stick *The thieves were carrying clubs with which they threatened their victims.*

clue *n.* hint, suggestion, trace, sign, indication *Didn't Jennie give you any clue where she hid the key?*

clumsy *adj.* awkward, ungraceful, unskilful, bungling, ungainly, inept *Will is too clumsy to build that model aeroplane by himself.* ANT. graceful, adroit, skilful, polished, dexterous.

cluster *n.* group, batch, bunch *A cluster of flowers grew near the rock.* *vb.* group, gather, assemble, pack, crowd *The students clustered around the notice board where the examination results had been put up.*

clutch *vb.* seize, grip, grasp, hold, grab *The old lady was clutching a bag that held all her possessions.*

coach *n.* **1** vehicle, bus; carriage *The coach for Brighton leaves at three o'clock.* **2** instructor, trainer, teacher; manager *Mr Smith is the coach for the winning team.* *vb.* instruct, train, drill, exercise *The trainer has a very difficult job trying to coach the members of the team during the season.*

coarse *adj.* rough; crude, rude *This file is too coarse for this gold ring. Harold sometimes uses very coarse language.* ANT. fine; refined, cultivated, genteel.

coast *n.* beach, seashore, shore, shoreline, seaboard *We like to spend our holidays on the South coast.* *vb.* glide, ride; drift *Pete came* *coasting down the hill on his sledge. Some people just coast through life letting nothing disturb them.*

coat *n.* jacket, raincoat, overcoat *Take off your coat and make yourself at home.*

coax *vb.* persuade, wheedle, cajole, urge *Can't we coax you to stay for dinner?* ANT. bully, force, coerce.

coil *vb.* wind, ring, twist, loop, roll *Please coil the string round this stick.* *n.* curl, ring, loop *I had to buy a whole coil of wire to do this job.*

coincide *vb.* correspond, agree, match, harmonize *These parts of the jigsaw coincide exactly. Our opinions coincide on how to treat naughty children.*

coincidence *n.* chance, accident *By coincidence, the father of one of my classmates was a classmate of my father's.* ANT. plan, scheme, plot, prearrangement.

cold *adj.* **1** cool, chilly, chill; frigid, freezing *Winter in Scotland can be very cold.* **2** unemotional, unfriendly, unfeeling, indifferent, heartless *Susan's attitude toward her classmates was so cold that she had no friends at all.* ANT. (1) hot, warm, temperate. (2) friendly, warm, compassionate, outgoing.

cold-blooded *adj.* cruel, unfeeling, pitiless, callous *I shall report him for the cold-blooded way he treats that animal.* ANT. feeling, sensitive.

collaborate *vb.* work together, cooperate *If we collaborate on this project, it will be completed in half the time.*

collapse *vb.* fall; fail, drop *The walls of the building collapsed during the fire.* *n.* failure, downfall, destruction *The kingdom was doomed to collapse when the dictator overthrew the government.*

colleague *n.* associate, co-worker; collaborator *I should like you to meet one of my colleagues from the office.*

collect *vb.* **1** gather, assemble, accumulate *I used to collect seashells as a hobby, but now I collect stamps.* **2** obtain, procure, secure, get, raise *The charity collected hundreds of pounds to help the handicapped.* ANT. (1) disperse, dispel, scatter.

collection *n.* accumulation, hoard, store, pile *When are you going to get rid of that collection of old newspapers?*

college *n.* polytechnic, university; institution, institute; school *We enrolled Desmond at college a few days after he was born.*

collide *vb.* crash, smash, strike, hit *When the atoms collide, enormous energy is released.*

collision *n.* crash, smash, smash-up *A collision on the motorway tied up traffic for hours.*

colloquial *adj.* popular, everyday, familiar, conversational, informal *Kurt writes in a colloquial style that is easy to read and understand.*

colossal *adj.* enormous, huge, immense, gigantic *The statue of Apollo that straddled the mouth of the harbour at Rhodes must have been truly colossal.* ANT. tiny, miniature, minuscule, microscopic.

colour *n.* hue, shade, tone, tinge, tint *I can't tell the colour of your* *eyes through those dark glasses.* *vb.* tint, paint, tinge; decorate *The walls should be coloured to match the carpet.*

column *n.* 1 pillar, post, support, prop *The columns at the front of that building look most impressive.* 2 article, feature; comment; review *Lionel writes the fishing column for the local paper each week.*

combat *vb.* fight, battle, oppose, contest, struggle *The economists seem to be unable to combat inflation effectively.* *n.* fight, battle, contest, conflict, war, struggle *The two knights were locked in mortal combat.* ANT. *vb.* surrender, yield, succumb.

combination *n.* 1 blending, mixing, compounding *The combination of flour and water makes a light paste.* 2 blend, mixture, compound, composite *Gunpowder is a combination of three simple ingredients.* ANT. (1) separation, division.

combine *vb.* blend, mix; unite, join, connect *Combine the ingredients in a large bowl. We ought to combine our forces for greater strength.* ANT. separate, divide.

come *vb.* 1 approach, advance, near *I want you to come here when I call you.* 2 arrive, reach *Dick came home late last night.* *vb. phr.* **come about** happen, occur, take place *The accident came about because you were driving recklessly.* **come across** find, stumble upon, discover; meet *Who should I come across in town today but Old Smithy!* **come into** inherit, receive, acquire, obtain *He came into a thousand pounds when his aunt died.* **come to** *or* **round** revive, recover, recuperate *After the blow on his head knocked him out, it took ten minutes for George to come round.* **come upon** discover, find *Betty came upon an old photograph album in the attic.* ANT. go, leave, depart.

comeback *n. Informal:* recovery, revival, return *After six years, it might be difficult to make a comeback as a comedian.*

comedian *n.* comedienne, humorist, comic, funnyman, wag, wit, gagman *Many comedians had their early training in the old variety theatres.*

comedown *n. Informal:* disappointment, blow; defeat, failure; reversal *Taking a job as a labourer after being a company director was quite a comedown for Harrigan.*

comedy *n.* farce, satire, revue; slapstick *The comedy playing at the Leicester is screamingly funny.*

comfort *vb.* soothe, relieve, console, ease, calm, cheer *Whenever Victoria was upset, her mother was always there to comfort her.* *n.* 1 solace, consolation *The comfort of knowing that you will stand by is all I need.* 2 relaxation, rest, satisfaction, luxury, ease *Because she had saved carefully, the old lady was able to live in comfort.* ANT. *vb.* upset, agitate, disturb, discompose. *n.* (1) uncertainty. (2) discomfort.

comfortable *adj.* 1 relaxed, easy, rested, contented, cheerful *The teacher's friendly manner made us all feel comfortable.* 2 restful, cosy, snug *This is a very comfortable armchair.* ANT. (1) uncomfortable, strained, tense, edgy.

comical *adj.* funny, ridiculous, humorous; absurd, ludicrous *We watched the comical antics of the pandas at the zoo.*

command *vb.* order, direct, demand, decree, rule *The major commanded his men to appear in his office.* *n.* order, demand, direction, rule, decree, charge, authority *By whose command was this ship sent into battle?* ANT. *vb.* obey.

commemorate *vb.* celebrate, remember, observe, honour *This tablet commemorates the contributions made by those who died in the service of their country.*

commence *vb.* begin, start, open *When do negotiations commence for the exchange of prisoners?* ANT. end, stop, terminate, finish.

commend *vb.* praise, recommend, applaud, laud *The teacher commended me for my penmanship.* ANT. blame, censure, criticize.

commendable *adj.* praiseworthy, deserving *Isn't it commendable how well the boys behaved throughout the recent ordeal?* ANT. deplorable, bad, lamentable.

commendation *n.* praise, approval, recommendation; applause; medal, honour *Father received a commendation for bravery in the war.* ANT. condemnation, criticism, censure.

comment *n.* remark, observation; explanation, commentary, review, report, criticism, judgement *Your comments on how the programme succeeded will be helpful in planning one for next year.* *vb.* remark, explain, observe *He commented that the carpet might be a little bright for this room.*

commerce *n.* business, trade, marketing *Commerce between the countries has increased over the years.*

commercial *adj.* financial, economic, business, trading *Why not consider the artistic as well as the commercial aspects?*

commiserate *vb.* sympathize, console, comfort, feel for *I really commiserate with you, for I lost a beloved pet myself.*

commission *n.* 1 committee, board *The price commission refused to allow any increases during the coming year.* 2 order, command, permission, permit *His commission as a second lieutenant came through today.* 3 fee, share, royalty; (*informal*) rake-off *The salesman was paid a very good commission on every car he sold.* *vb.* appoint, delegate, authorize, commit, entrust, deputize *I have been commissioned to bring you home.*

commit *vb.* 1 entrust, delegate, empower, authorize, commission *The association is committed to raising funds to help the blind.* 2 do, perform, carry out *The murder was committed by a person or persons unknown.*

commitment *n.* pledge, promise, duty, responsibility *He made a commitment to reduce taxes but has failed to honour it.*

committee *n.* board, commission, council *Ronald agreed to serve on the dance committee.*

commodity *n.* goods, merchandise, article, wares *We can achieve a favourable trade balance by exporting selected commodities.*

common *adj.* 1 joint, communal, mutual, shared *My neighbour and I have a common area of ground between our houses. Our common friend, Danny, invited us together.* 2 customary, usual, regular *This is a common variety of flower and not rare at all.* 3 ordinary, natural, conventional, plain, commonplace, stale, trite *The film had rather a common plot.* 4 coarse, vulgar, low *He was nothing but a common criminal.* ANT. (1) separate, different. (2) unusual, rare. (3) distinctive, outstanding, extraordinary. (4) refined, cultivated, genteel.

commonplace *adj.* ordinary, common, everyday, usual, undistinguished, frequent, run-of-the-mill *He paid £1000 for what looks like a commonplace garden ornament.* ANT. unusual, distinctive, original.

commotion *n.* disorder, disturbance, upheaval; fuss; noise, din *There was such a commotion next door that we had to call the police.*

communal *adj.* common, shared, joint *This is a communal park, intended for use by every resident of the estate.*

communicate *vb.* impart, convey, transmit, reveal, disclose, divulge; advertise, publicize, publish *How can he communicate his needs if he can't talk?* ANT. conceal, withhold, dissemble.

communication *n.* 1 transmission, announcement, disclosure, notification, declaration, publication *The minister used his press secretary for the communication of his ideas to the media.* 2 message, information, news, report, account, announcement, advice *The secret communications between the governments were sent in code.*

community *n.* 1 town, village, city, township *We moved to a small community in the country.* 2 public, people; society, nation *The community felt that Mr Timpson was doing a good job as mayor.*

compact¹ *adj.* compressed, packed, tight, thick *The snow was so compact that I was hardly able to force a shovel into it.* *n.* makeup case, vanity case *I lost my silver compact at the restaurant when I went to powder my nose.* ANT. *adj.* loose, unconfined, sprawling, unfettered.

compact² *n.* agreement, treaty, contract, pact, covenant *A trade compact was reached by the two countries.*

companion *n.* associate, comrade, mate, partner, colleague, friend *I shall have a chocolate ice cream and my companion, here, will have vanilla.*

company *n.* 1 business, firm, partnership, concern *After all those years of hard work, Len was made chairman of a big paper company.* 2 group, band, party, assembly, throng *I told the company that had gathered at the steps why I thought they should obey the rules.* 3 companionship, fellowship *I enjoy the company of my friends.* 4 guest(s), visitor(s) *Are you expecting company for dinner tonight?*

comparable *adj.* relative, alike, like *Where could you find a suitcase* *of comparable quality for the same price?* ANT. different, unalike, dissimilar.

compare *vb.* 1 match, liken; contrast *The teacher asked us to compare the invention of the telephone with any invention from before 1800.* 2 compete, rival, vie *Your beauty and hers cannot compare.*

comparison *n.* likening, judgement, contrasting *There is no comparison between the paintings of Veronese and Lichtenstein.*

compartment *n.* section, division, part *The wheat is stored in several compartments on the ship.*

compel *vb.* force, coerce, drive, impel *The robber compelled his victims to lie flat on the floor.* ANT. coax, wheedle, cajole.

compensate *vb.* 1 repay, remunerate, recompense, reimburse *The insurance company compensated my father for the loss of the money.* 2 balance, counterbalance, offset *No amount of saying you are sorry could compensate for the broken vase.*

compensation *n.* indemnity, reparation, damages; defrayal *Will the airline pay any compensation for the loss of your luggage?*

compete *vb.* contest, vie, rival, oppose *She wants to compete on an equal basis with the boys.*

competence *n.* ability, skill, capability. *I have never questioned her competence to govern.* ANT. incompetence, ineptitude

competent *adj.* capable, skilful, qualified, able, proficient *Cartwright is an extremely competent administrator.* ANT. incompetent, inept, awkward.

competition *n.* rivalry, contest, tournament, match *Who is sponsoring the chess competition this year?*

competitor *n.* contestant, rival, opponent *The list of competitors for the title will be published tomorrow.* ANT. friend, ally, colleague.

compile *vb.* put together, compose, collect, gather, arrange *I have compiled a list of people whom we must invite to the wedding.*

complacent *adj.* self-satisfied, smug, pleased *She felt very complacent till she found out that someone else had won first prize.*

complain *vb.* protest, grumble, moan, groan, fret *Patrick complains about the slightest little things.*

complement *vb.* complete, add to, supplement *To complement your dinner, we suggest a fine liqueur.* ANT. conflict, clash.

complementary *adj.* completing, integral; corresponding, reciprocal *The scarf in dark grey silk provides a complementary touch to the yellow jacket.*

complete *adj.* 1 whole, full, entire *The complete chemistry set costs a great deal.* 2 ended, over, finished, done, concluded *The manuscript would be complete if the author could write the last chapter.* *vb.* finish, end, conclude, terminate; close *I've completed all my homework for tomorrow.* ANT. *adj.* unfinished, incomplete, partial. *vb.* begin, start, commence.

completion *n.* conclusion, end, termination, finale, finish, close, wind-up, culmination *At the completion of the project, we packed and went home.*

complexion *n.* skin; appearance *Suzanne has a peaches-and-cream complexion. Your explanation of how the theft was accomplished puts a different complexion on the matter.*

complicated *adj.* complex, involved, intricate *That is one of the most complicated plots I have ever heard.* **ANT.** simple, uncomplicated, rudimentary.

compliment *n.* praise, honour, admiration, approval, commendation, appreciation *She took it as a compliment when I told her she was too young to go to college.* *vb.* praise, honour, approve, commend, flatter *I'd like to compliment you on your new dress, Diane.* **ANT.** *n.* insult, aspersion, affront. *vb.* insult, affront, disparage.

complimentary *adj.* **1** free (of charge), gratis, on the house *The manager sent complimentary after-dinner drinks to our table.* **2** favourable, approving *The reviewer had many complimentary things to say about Thea's performance.* **ANT.** (1) costly, expensive, dear. (2) insulting, derogatory, uncomplimentary.

comply (with) *vb.* obey, agree to, conform to, fulfil *Whoever joins the club must agree to comply with the rules.*

component *n.* part, element, constituent, ingredient *We had to send to Japan for the components needed to complete the repair on my video.*

compose *vb.* **1** create, write, make up *My sister composes popular songs in her spare time.* **2** constitute, make up, comprise *There are thousands of minerals that compose the crust of the earth.*

composed *adj.* relaxed, calm, cool, untroubled, peaceful, serene, tranquil, quiet *The accused sat in the witness box, composed and undisturbed.* **ANT.** agitated, nervous, anxious, overwrought, hysterical.

composer *see* **author.**

compound *n.* mixture, combination, aggregate *Water is a chemical compound made up of the elements hydrogen and oxygen.* *adj.* complicated, complex; combined, mixed *Bobby suffered a compound fracture of his arm when he fell off the horse.* **ANT.** *adj.* simple, uncomplicated.

comprehend *vb.* understand, grasp, perceive *Now I comprehend your reason for wanting cash instead of a cheque.*

comprehension *n.* understanding, perception, awareness, knowledge *The tourists' comprehension of the guide's commentary was far from perfect.*

comprehensive *adj.* inclusive, broad, wide, complete, full *The directors requested a comprehensive study of the market.* **ANT.** partial, fragmentary, incomplete, limited.

compress *vb.* squeeze, compact, press, crowd, pack *It was hard to compress all those activities into one week's holiday.* **ANT.** stretch, spread, expand.

comprise *vb.* constitute, consist of; contain, include *The collection comprises some of the best Chinese artefacts of the Ming period.*

compromise *n.* settlement; concession; (*informal*) give and take, bargaining *How can one honestly reach a compromise between quality and price?*

compulsive *adj.* driving, obsessive *He is so compulsive that he has become a workaholic.* ANT. easy-going, relaxed, lackadaisical, lazy.

compulsory *adj.* necessary, required, unavoidable, obligatory *A note from a doctor is compulsory to be excused from PT.* ANT. optional, voluntary; unrestricted, free.

compute *vb.* calculate, reckon, work out, figure *It took him only a second to compute the square root of 32,041.*

computer *n.* microprocessor; calculator; electronic brain, automaton, robot *People who couldn't spell the word are now using computers daily.*

comrade *n.* companion, friend, associate *I went on a walking tour of Scotland with two of my comrades.*

conceal *vb.* hide, cover, obscure, secrete *The customs officials caught George trying to conceal the cigars he had bought in the duty-free shop.* ANT. reveal, show, display, expose.

concede *vb.* admit, allow, acknowledge, yield *George readily conceded that he should not have tried to smuggle in the cigars.* ANT. deny, dispute.

conceit *n.* vanity, egotism, self-esteem *Cora's conceit about her looks is unbearable.* ANT. modesty, humility, humbleness, self-effacement.

conceited *adj.* vain, arrogant, proud, smug, self-important, egotistical *Cora is so conceited about her appearance that she spends all day in front of the mirror.* ANT. modest, humble, self-effacing.

conceive *vb.* 1 create, think (up), invent, imagine *The prisoners conceived a clever plan to escape.* 2 understand, perceive, grasp *It is difficult to conceive why they chose purple wallpaper with pink polka dots.*

concentrate *vb.* 1 focus, localize, condense *The rays of light should be concentrated on one point by this lens.* 2 ponder, meditate, think *Please don't interrupt while I'm concentrating on my homework.* ANT. (1) diffuse, scatter, disperse, dissipate.

concentration *n.* application, study, attention *This lesson requires a great deal of concentration.* ANT. distraction, confusion.

concept *n.* idea, notion, thought, theory *He has no concept of the importance of what we are trying to do.*

concern *vb.* 1 interest, relate to, affect, touch, involve *I don't see why what I had for breakfast should concern the Prime Minister of Uganda.* 2 worry, trouble, disturb *I'm concerned about my teenager's staying out after midnight.* *n.* 1 interest, consequence *International politics are of concern to everyone.* 2 anxiety, worry, care *My concern about the safety of children is not limited to that of my own.* 3 business, firm, company, partnership *Larry resigned from one company and started a concern of his own.* ANT. *vb.* (1) bore, tire. (2) soothe, calm. *n.* (1) indifference.

concerning *prep.* about, regarding, respecting *I should like to talk to you concerning your absence last week.*

concert *n.* recital, performance, entertainment *We used to attend the Promenade concerts every year.*

concerted *adj.* joint, united, combined *We must make a concerted effort to overcome inflation.* ANT. unorganized, individual, separate.

concession *n.* yielding, admission, granting *The owner made a concession to allow us to enter despite the hour.* ANT. demand, insistence.

concise *adj.* brief, succinct, condensed *Please try to keep your statement concise, as I haven't much time.* ANT. long-winded, prosaic, rambling.

conclude *vb.* 1 finish, end, terminate, complete *We concluded our dinner with a toast to the guest of honour.* 2 arrange, settle, determine, decide *The treaty was concluded when Japan agreed to stop whaling.* 3 presume, assume, gather, understand, deduce *I conclude from your comments that you are a socialist.* ANT. (1)begin, start, commence.

conclusion *n.* 1 end, finish, termination, close *The chairman's remarks came at the conclusion of the conference.* 2 decision, resolution, determination *Don't jump to conclusions about Eddie just because he wears his shoulder-length hair in curls.* ANT. (1) beginning, start, opening, commencement.

concrete *n.* cement *The airport runway is made of concrete.* *adj.* firm, definite, solid, specific, precise *I couldn't tell her any concrete reason for not wanting to go without insulting her, so I went.* ANT. (2) vague, undetermined, general.

condemn *vb.* 1 denounce, rebuke, blame *You mustn't condemn a person just because he cannot do what you can do.* 2 judge, doom, punish, convict, sentence *The court condemned the man to ten years in jail.* ANT. (1) praise, laud, extol, applaud. (2) pardon, absolve, excuse.

condense *vb.* reduce, abbreviate, shorten, abridge, concentrate, compress, digest, diminish *The local opera group staged a condensed version of Aida.* ANT. expand, enlarge, increase.

condescend *vb.* humble oneself, lower oneself, deign, stoop *She condescended to let me have her autograph.*

condition *n.* 1 state, position, situation *The doctor told me that I was in excellent physical condition.* 2 requirement, necessity, provision, stipulation *One of the conditions of employment in that restaurant is that you agree to give all tips to the management.* *vb.* train; accustom to *He was conditioned to perspire whenever they rang a bell.*

conditional *adj.* provisional, dependent (on), subject (to) *Approval for the rise in salary is conditional on continuing productivity.* ANT. absolute, certain.

conduct *n.* behaviour, manners, deportment, actions *Your conduct is* *not proper for an officer of the Navy!* *vb.* 1 behave, act *I thought that Philip conducted himself very well, considering his lack of experience.* 2 lead, guide, escort *Kathy got a job conducting tours of York Minster this summer.*

confer *vb.* 1 give, award, bestow, grant *In his sixtieth year, the university conferred on him their highest honour.* 2 discuss, consult, deliberate *Don't you think we ought to confer before announcing a hasty opinion by one person?* ANT. (1) withdraw, retrieve.

conference *n.* meeting, discussion, council; consultation *A conference on fishing rights in the North Sea is scheduled for next week.*

confess *vb.* admit, acknowledge, grant, concede *She confessed to a crime that she did not commit.*

confide *vb.* disclose, reveal, tell, divulge *She confided in me that she craves a lot of attention.*

confidence *n.* 1 trust, faith, reliance *My confidence in your abilities has always been justified by your accomplishments.* 2 self-assurance, self-reliance, self-confidence, courage *Many people would be more successful if they just had more confidence in themselves.* ANT. (1) distrust, mistrust, doubt. (2) shyness, modesty, diffidence.

confident *adj.* sure, certain, self-assured, self-reliant, self-confident, dauntless *I am quite confident about our success in the horse trials.* ANT. timid, uncertain, shy, self-effacing.

confidential *adj.* secret, private; off the record *What I am going to tell you now is confidential.* ANT. open, disclosed.

confine *vb.* limit, restrict, bound, keep *Please confine your talks to ten minutes and no longer.* ANT. release, free.

confirm *vb.* 1 assure, verify, corroborate, substantiate; strengthen *I confirmed everything that she had told me.* 2 validate, approve, ratify *The higher court confirmed the lower court's findings.* ANT. (1) deny, disclaim, disavow.

confirmed *adj.* habitual, inveterate, established; chronic, regular *Mr Pendergast is a confirmed habitué of the Crown and Garter pub.* ANT. infrequent, occasional.

confiscate *vb.* take, seize, appropriate *If you don't stop playing with that knife, the teacher will confiscate it.*

conflict *vb.* oppose, clash, contend *It seems obvious that your ideas about bringing up children conflict with mine.* *n.* 1 fight, battle, struggle, encounter, engagement *We must recognize the eternal conflict between right and wrong.* 2 controversy, disagreement, contest *I don't want to be caught in the middle of a conflict between political enemies.* ANT. *vb.* agree, harmonize, concur, coincide. *n.* (2) agreement, harmony, concurrence.

conform *vb.* 1 comply, submit, yield, obey *If you wish to remain a member of this club, you must conform to the rules.* 2 agree, correspond *The work you are now doing does not conform to our plan.* ANT. (1) rebel; disobey. (2) disagree, vary.

confront *vb.* face, oppose, defy; challenge, meet, brave *When the teacher confronted Tommy with the evidence, he confessed.*

confuse *vb.* **1** puzzle, perplex, bewilder, mystify, baffle, mislead *The directions for putting the bicycle together confused my father.* **2** mistake, mix up, jumble *My aunt is often confused with my mother, whom she resembles closely.* ANT. (1) enlighten, edify, illuminate, clarify. (2) differentiate, distinguish.

confusion *n.* **1** perplexity, bewilderment, uncertainty *At first, there was some confusion among the actors as to where they should stand on stage.* **2** disorder, mess, turmoil, upset *Your belongings are in such a state of confusion that I don't see how you can find anything.* ANT. (1) enlightenment, understanding, comprehension. (2) organization, tidiness.

congenial *adj.* agreeable, pleasant; friendly *I go to the club in the evening for the congenial company of my friends.* ANT. unfriendly, disagreeable.

congested *adj.* crowded, full, blocked; dense, thick *The traffic was so congested that it took me hours to drive across London.* ANT. empty.

congratulate *vb.* compliment, honour, acclaim, praise *Why don't you congratulate me on winning the scholarship?*

congregate *vb.* meet, convene, gather *After dinner, the teenagers like to congregate at the youth centre.* ANT. disperse, scatter, dissipate, dispel.

congress *n.* conference, meeting; legislature, parliament, assembly *We attended the ninth international congress of lexicographers.*

conjunction *n.* junction, link, combination, connection *The two parties acted in conjunction to solve the problem.* ANT. disconnection, diversion, separation.

conjurer *n.* magician, wizard, sorcerer *The children watched with rapt attention as the conjurer did his tricks.*

connect *vb.* **1** unite, join, link, combine *The front of our train was connected to the rear carriages of the train in the station.* **2** associate, relate *Somehow, I failed to connect her leaving so suddenly with the disappearance of the vase.* ANT. (1) separate, disconnect, disjoin. (2) dissociate.

connection *n.* **1** junction, union, link; bond, tie *There was a loose connection that prevented the radio from working.* **2** association, relationship, bond, tie *I no longer have any connection with that company.* ANT. (2) dissociation.

conquer *vb.* **1** succeed, win, gain, achieve *The army conquered the fort in two days.* **2** defeat, overcome, overpower, subdue *It may be years before medicine will be able to conquer cancer. The small force conquered the enemy in hard fighting.* ANT. (2) give in, surrender, yield.

conquest *n.* triumph, victory *We celebrated the conquest of the Saracens with a week of festivities.* ANT. failure, surrender.

conscientious *adj.* diligent, painstaking, scrupulous, exact *David is a very conscientious student.* ANT. irresponsible, careless, slovenly.

conscious *adj.* **1** aware *I suddenly became conscious of a slow scratch-*

ing sound at the window. 2 awake, alert *When Marilyn became conscious again after the blow on her head, she recognized her mother beside her.* 3 deliberate, intentional, purposeful *I don't like him, so I make a conscious effort to avoid him.* ANT. (1) unaware, insensitive. (2) asleep, comatose.

consecrate *vb.* hallow, sanctify; dedicate *We consecrate this monument to the memory of those who died for their country.*

consecutive *adj.* successive, continuous, serial, in order *When he said three consecutive days, he meant Monday, Tuesday and Wednesday of next week.* ANT. discontinuous.

consent *vb.* agree, permit, allow, let, assent *I consented to Laura's going to the theatre with a friend.* *n.* permission, agreement, assent *You have my consent to leave school early today.* ANT. *vb.* refuse, dissent. *n.* refusal, dissent.

consequence *n.* 1 result, outcome, effect, issue *Eugene was rude in class and, as a consequence, was reprimanded by the teacher.* 2 importance, significance, value *Jenny's father is a man of some consequence in this town.* ANT. (1) cause, impetus.

conservative *adj.* 1 reactionary, right-wing, conventional *The conservative sections of society resist change.* 2 moderate, cautious, careful *After the accident, Ted became a much more conservative driver.* ANT. (1) liberal, radical. (2) reckless, rash, adventurous, foolhardy.

conserve *vb.* preserve, keep, retain *Conserve your energy—you'll need it later.* ANT. squander, waste, use.

consider *vb.* 1 study, think about, deliberate, reflect on, contemplate *The committee agreed to consider Janet's request for an increase in salary.* 2 think of, regard, look upon, judge, estimate *Shirley had never considered Tom to be particularly good-looking.* ANT. (1) ignore, disregard, disdain.

considerable *adj.* 1 quite a lot, much, a great deal *There was a considerable amount of snow last winter. The complaints from the public were considerable.* 2 worthwhile, noteworthy, important, significant *Albert Einstein was a man of considerable accomplishments.*

considerate *adj.* kind, thoughtful, polite *Geoffrey was very considerate to allow me to stay the night.* ANT. inconsiderate, thoughtless, selfish.

consideration *n.* 1 thoughtfulness, kindness, kindliness, concern, courtesy, politeness, sympathy, empathy *It was Mark's consideration for other people that made him an outstanding social worker.* 2 attention, thought, reflection, study *I'll give that matter immediate consideration.* 3 payment, fee, pay, recompense, compensation *For a small consideration, the steward will serve your meals in your cabin.*

consign *vb.* entrust, hand over; deliver, convey *All the unsold copies of the newspaper were consigned to the dustbin.*

consist *vb.* comprise, be composed of; include, embrace, contain *Dinner consisted of a hamburger with baked beans on toast.*

consistent *adj.* **1** agreeing, compatible, harmonious *Consistent with your wishes, I have asked that the meeting take place tomorrow.* **2** regular, faithful *He might have been irresponsible about repaying debts to the bank, but he was always consistent about returning money to his friends.* ANT. (1) contrary, opposed, antagonistic. (2) inconsistent, erratic, eccentric.

consolation *n.* solace, comfort, sympathy *It is of little consolation to me that you were also refused admittance.* ANT. discouragement, discomfort, burden.

console *vb.* solace, comfort, sympathize with *Turnbull went over to console widow Jennie Jensen on the death of her husband.* ANT. disturb, upset.

consolidate *vb.* unite, combine; incorporate, solidify *We would operate more efficiently if our offices were consolidated in one place.*

conspicuous *adj.* noticeable, visible, clear, prominent, obvious, outstanding *You certainly were conspicuous with that green Mohawk hairdo.* ANT. inconspicuous, neutral.

conspiracy *n.* plot, scheme, intrigue *Investigators suspect that there might have been a conspiracy amongst the prison warders.*

conspire *vb.* plot, plan, scheme, intrigue *The head of security conspired to release the leader of the revolutionary faction.*

constant *adj.* **1** unchanging, fixed, stable, invariable, unchangeable *The constant sunshine in the desert made me long for clouds and rain.* **2** loyal, faithful, steadfast, true, staunch, devoted, steady, firm *My constant companion during those years was Arthur.* ANT. (1) irregular, off-and-on, periodic. (2) occasional, infrequent.

constitute *vb.* **1** make up, compose, form *People once thought that all matter was constituted of four elements—earth, air, fire and water.* **2** found, establish, create, organize *The courts are a duly constituted authority for dispensing justice.* **3** delegate, appoint, commission, authorize *My father was constituted ambassador to Ethiopia.*

constitution *n.* **1** code, law *The nation's Constitution has been put to some severe tests during the last decade.* **2** health, physique, vitality *With your constitution, you should be able to eat anything.*

constrain *vb.* force, compel; restrain; urge *I am constrained to advise you against such a course of action.*

construct *vb.* build, erect, raise *Within a few weeks, a camp for 50,000 soldiers was constructed in the desert.* ANT. destroy, demolish, raze.

construction *n.* building, erection, fabrication *The construction proceeded quickly because modular sections were used.*

constructive *adj.* helpful, useful, valuable *Any constructive suggestions will be welcome.* ANT. destructive, ruinous.

consult *vb.* discuss, confer, deliberate *We must consult with our advisers before giving you our reply.*

consume *vb.* **1** use, use up, exhaust, expend; eat, devour *The people in this country consume more sugar than those of any other country.* **2** destroy, devastate *The barn was quickly consumed by the flames.*

consumer *n.* buyer, user, purchaser *Consumers are much wiser and more demanding than they used to be.*

contact *n.* touching, meeting *You must avoid any contact with someone who has this dread affliction.*

contagious *adj.* infectious; catching, spreading *Enthusiasm for the new library was contagious.*

contain *vb.* hold, be composed of, include *I doubt that this silo could contain more than 5000 bushels of grain.*

container *n.* receptacle, holder; box, case, bin, tin, jar *Have you a container in which I can put the jam you want me to take home?*

contaminate *vb.* pollute, soil, dirty, corrupt, infect, poison *The blood tests were invalid because the test-tubes were contaminated.*

contemplate *vb.* **1** think about, consider, study, deliberate on, reflect upon *Desmond was contemplating the outcome of the trial.* **2** intend, plan *Do you contemplate correcting your behaviour?* **3** view, look at, regard, observe *Irene was contemplating her reflection in the mirror.*

contemplative *adj.* thoughtful, meditative, studious, pensive *We seem to have caught Carruthers in one of his few contemplative moments—unless he's asleep.* ANT. indifferent, inattentive, thoughtless.

contemporary *adj.* **1** contemporaneous, simultaneous, coexisting, coexistent *It is useful to compare the diary of Samuel Pepys with other contemporary writings.* **2** modern, up-to-date, fashionable *The room was decorated in contemporary style.* ANT. (1) antecedent; succeeding.

contempt *n.* scorn, disdain, malice. *I have nothing but contempt for anyone who would hurt a person's feelings like that.* ANT. admiration, approbation.

contemptible *adj.* low, base, mean, detestable, miserable *That contemptible wretch insulted my sister.* ANT. admirable, honourable.

contemptuous *adj.* scornful, disdainful, insolent, sneering *It may be Drumhall's inferiority complex that makes him so contemptuous of others' accomplishments.* ANT. respectful, polite; flattering; humble, modest, self-effacing.

contend *vb.* **1** combat, dispute, struggle, contest *We need to contend for higher moral standards these days.* **2** claim, assert, maintain, argue *The lawyer contended that his client was innocent.*

content *adj.* happy, satisfied, pleased, contented *I shall be content to get through this alive.* ANT. dissatisfied, restless, discontented.

contentious *adj.* quarrelsome, combative, disputatious, argumentative, hostile *Ferncliff has turned into a contentious, testy old curmudgeon.*

contest *n.* competition, match, tournament *Class 3b won the contest for the best road safety poster.* *vb.* dispute, oppose *The miner contested the right of anyone to trespass on his property.*

contestant *n.* competitor, opponent, rival; player *Contestants who qualify for the final round will be notified.*

contingency *n.* possibility, likelihood, circumstance, occasion *The home insurance policy covers every contingency except flood damage.*

contingent *adj.* (usually with **on**) dependent (on), depending (on), conditional (on), provisional (on) *The quarterly profits are contingent on the costs of fulfilling the government contract.*

continual *adj.* regular, consecutive, connected *The neighbours kept up their continual partying throughout the night.* ANT. irregular, intermittent, occasional.

continue *vb.* **1** persist, carry on *If you continue in your present manner, you will be punished for it.* **2** proceed, resume, recommence, renew *The trial continued after an hour out for lunch.* **3** endure, last, remain, stay *After he was discovered to be dishonest, the manager realized he couldn't continue in his job.* ANT. discontinue, stop, cease, interrupt.

continuous *adj.* uninterrupted, continuing, ceaseless, incessant, unceasing, constant, unending *The flow of water through this pipe is continuous.* ANT. irregular, intermittent, sporadic.

contract *n.* agreement, bargain, pact; treaty *The contract between the company and the union was signed yesterday.* *vb.* **1** agree *The firm contracted to supply paper to the printers.* **2** diminish, reduce, condense, shrink *The armadillo contracts into a little ball when it is threatened.* **3** get, acquire, go down with *I contracted a bad cold while out fishing.* ANT. *vb.* (2) expand, swell, enlarge.

contradict *vb.* deny; oppose, object to; defy, challenge *If your father says something, it is rude to contradict him.* ANT. agree.

contrary *adj.* **1** opposed, opposite, disagreeing, conflicting, opposing *If you say he should be released and I say he should be jailed, we obviously hold contrary opinions.* **2** disagreeable, hostile, perverse, stubborn, obstinate, headstrong *If you agree with me, then why are you being so contrary?* ANT. (1) similar, like, complementary. (2) obliging, agreeable, tractable.

contrast *n.* difference, distinction, disagreement *There is a marked contrast between what you are saying today and what you said yesterday.* *vb.* distinguish, differentiate; contradict, differ *One of our exam questions was to contrast the American Revolution with the Russian Revolution.* ANT. *n.* similarity, agreement, likeness.

contribute *vb.* donate, give, bestow, grant, provide, offer *I doubt that Peter has much to contribute to the discussion.* ANT. withhold, deny.

contribution *n.* donation, gift, grant, offering *Claire made a substantial contribution to the drive to rebuild the church spire.*

contrite *adj.* remorseful, sorry, repentant, regretful; penitent *Penny was very contrite over forgetting to return the book to the library.* ·

contrive *vb.* **1** invent, make, form, hatch *We must contrive a plan to get even with those children who stole our bicycles.* **2** manage, arrange; engineer *Despite visiting hours being over, I contrived to see my sister in hospital.*

control *vb.* **1** manage, direct, rule, dominate, command *My uncle*

correspond *vb.* 1 match, compare, agree, coincide, fit, suit *The two parts of this machine don't correspond.* 2 communicate, write *While I was away at school, I corresponded regularly with my brothers and sisters.* ANT. (1) diverge, differ, vary.

corridor *n.* hall, hallway, passage, passageway; foyer, lobby *Please wait for me in the corridor, near the lifts.*

corroborate *vb.* support, confirm, uphold *The witness corroborated my testimony in every detail.*

corrode *vb.* eat away, erode, wear away *These pipes are all corroded and must be replaced.*

corrupt *adj.* 1 dishonest, untrustworthy, crooked, treacherous, unscrupulous *Before my uncle became mayor and improved matters, this town had the most corrupt officials you could find.* 2 wicked, debased, low, evil, perverted *The minister preached against all of the corrupt practices among some of the people.* *vb.* bribe, pervert, deprave, debase *The gangsters used money, then threats, to try to corrupt the detectives.* ANT. *adj.*(1) honest, upright, scrupulous. (2) pure, sanctified. *vb.* purify, edify, sanctify.

cost *n.* 1 price, value, charge *What is the cost of that puppy in the window?* 2 sacrifice, loss, penalty, damage *Risking the cost of our friendship, I must tell you that you are very mean to your mother.*

costly *adj.* expensive, dear *How can you afford such costly clothes on your income?* ANT. inexpensive, low-cost, cheap.

costume *n.* clothing, dress, attire, clothes, garb, apparel *What kind of costume is that to wear to the office?*

cosy *adj.* warm, snug, comfortable; friendly *On stormy nights like this I enjoy being home before a cosy fire.* ANT. unpleasant, uncomfortable; cold.

couch *n.* sofa, settee *We sat on the couch together, holding hands.*

council *n.* committee, board, cabinet *The council will vote on the new plans tomorrow.*

counsel *n.* 1 advice, opinion, guidance *Your counsel in matters relating to marriage is meaningless, since you were never married.* 2 barrister, lawyer *If learned counsel will permit, I should like to cross-examine this witness.* *vb.* advise, guide *He counselled me to remain quiet in court.*

counsellor *n.* adviser, guide, helper; friend *I have asked Pinken & Shear to act as my financial counsellors.*

count *vb.* 1 enumerate, number, reckon, total, compute, tally *I counted thirteen buns in the bag from the bakery—a baker's dozen.* 2 amount to something, add up, figure *Your score on the last test won't count because you copied the answers from a neighbour.* *n.* sum, total, number *Take a count of the books on that shelf.*

countenance *n.* 1 face, visage, aspect, appearance *I like to see the smiling countenances of my students each morning.* 2 approval, support, encouragement, assistance *I cannot give countenance to such activity.* *vb.* approve, support, favour, encourage, assist *I*

refuse to countenance absence from school to watch a football game.
ANT. *vb.* prohibit, forbid.

counter *n.* 1 table, board, bench, ledge *In this cafeteria we have to queue at the counter to get served.* 2 disc, token; coin *You can buy counters for the slot machines over there.*

counteract *vb.* offset, thwart, counterbalance, neutralize, defeat *What can we do to counteract attacks of poison gas?*

counterfeit *adj.* 1 fake, fraudulent, spurious, false *I thought we had become millionaires when the money was found, but it turned out to be counterfeit.* 2 pretended, pretend, simulated, sham *Your counterfeit expression of love doesn't fool me.* *n.* forgery, imitation, fake *This document is a counterfeit.* *vb.* 1 forge, fake, falsify, imitate, copy *The police found the men counterfeiting bank notes in the basement.* 2 pretend, sham *At the funeral, those who were glad that George was gone counterfeited great sorrow.* ANT. *adj.* genuine, real, authentic.

country *n.* 1 nation, state *How many foreign countries have you travelled to?* 2 rural area, farmland, forest *We gave up our flat in the city and bought a house in the country.*

couple *n.* pair; team, brace *Hitch a couple of horses to the wagon.*

courage *n.* bravery, spirit, daring, fearlessness, valour, mettle, pluck *It took a lot of courage to defy Father's wishes.* ANT. cowardice, fear, fearfulness, weakness.

courageous *adj.* brave, fearless, dauntless, intrepid, plucky, daring, heroic, valorous *It was very courageous of the sergeant to rescue the men being held down by enemy fire.* ANT. cowardly, fearful, afraid, timid.

course *n.* 1 advance, progress, passage *In the course of life it often becomes necessary to suffer hardship for the sake of others.* 2 direction, way, bearing *When I saw St Paul's Cathedral I knew we were on the wrong course for Scotland.*

court *n.* 1 square, yard, courtyard, enclosure, quadrangle *The trees in the courts provide a good shade from the sun in summer.* 2 tribunal, assize, sessions *The witnesses went to court and gave evidence.* *vb.* woo, attract, pursue; make overtures; (*informal*) go out with *We courted for two years before we got married.*

courteous *adj.* polite, well-mannered, gracious, respectful *One doesn't expect the servants to bow and scrape, but they ought to be courteous.* ANT. rude, impolite, discourteous.

courtesy *n.* politeness, graciousness, respect *The watchword of Fawlty Towers Hotel is courtesy to everyone who walks—or is carried—through its doors.* ANT. rudeness, discourtesy.

cover *vb.* 1 coat, spread; protect *Please cover the furniture to keep the dust off.* 2 conceal, hide; mask *Miriam covered the scratch on the table with a lamp.* 3 include, embrace *This book covers every subject thoroughly.* *n.* 1 lid, top, stopper, covering *Evelyn couldn't get the cover off the box.* 2 shelter, protection, refuge *Dur-*

ing the thunderstorm, we sought cover under an overhanging rock.
ANT. *vb.* uncover, expose, reveal.

covetous *adj.* greedy, avaricious, grasping, acquisitive *Noel is pursuing you because he is covetous of your business connections.*

coward *n.* cad, weakling, poltroon, (*slang*) chicken *Fenwick is too much of a coward to stand up to the headmaster.* ANT. hero.

coy *adj.* bashful, shy, timid, modest *If you want another helping of food, don't be coy—just ask for it.* ANT. bold, brash, forward.

crack *vb.* 1 break, snap, split *Just as Walter was looking at himself in the mirror, it cracked.* 2 solve, decode, decipher, unravel *Have you cracked the code yet?* *n.* 1 snap *There was the crack of the rifle and the rabbit lay dead.* 2 break, flaw, split, fissure *Be careful not to drink from the side of the glass with the crack in it.*

cracker *n.* biscuit, wafer *They served only crackers and cheese at the party.*

craft *n.* 1 skill, ability, talent, expertness *Have you ever seen an expert cabinetmaker at his craft?* 2 handicraft, trade, occupation, profession *The harpooner has not plied his craft for many years.* 3 cunning, deceit, trickery, guile *Charles used every bit of his craft to get Jennie to marry him.*

craftsman *n.* artisan; specialist *It takes a true craftsman to do such finely detailed carving.*

crafty *adj.* cunning, clever, shrewd, sly *How very crafty of you to let your parents think we were only going for a walk.* ANT. guileless, gullible, open, naïve.

cramp *n.* pain, spasm, paralysis *He had cramp in his legs and found he couldn't get out of bed.* *vb.* restrict, confine; restrain, hamper, hinder *I feel cramped with six other people working in the same office.*

crank *n.* 1 starting handle; device, brace *The car won't start; I'll try using the crank.* 2 *Informal:* eccentric, (*slang*) weirdo, (*slang*) nutcase; fanatic *Only a crank would collect bits and pieces off old cars.*

cranky *adj. Informal:* eccentric, odd, strange, peculiar *Ferncliffe has gone a bit cranky in his old age.*

crash *vb.* shatter, smash, dash *It was a miracle that you weren't even scratched when the car crashed into the wall.* *n.* smash, smash-up *Twenty people were hurt in the crash.*

crass *adj.* stupid, gross; thick *It was crass of you to bring the teacher in on our secret.*

crate *n.* container, case, pack, box *A crate of oranges arrived for you this morning.*

crave *vb.* desire, yearn for, want, long for, hunger for *Gridley behaves that way because he craves affection.* ANT. renounce, relinquish.

crawl *vb.* creep, worm along *We managed to crawl through the tunnel to freedom.*

crazy *adj.* mad, insane, lunatic *You are crazy if you think I am going to dive off that cliff into the sea.* ANT. sane, rational, lucid.

creak *vb.*   squeak; grate *I can tell when someone is coming when I hear the garden gate creak.*

crease *n.*   fold, wrinkle, furrow; pleat *My shirts came back from the laundry full of creases.*

create *vb.*   1 originate, invent, beget *The composer created a new piece to honour his parents on their anniversary.*   2 make, form, construct, design *The early settlers in America created farms and homes out of the wilderness.*   ANT. destroy, abolish.

creation *n.*   1 beginning; invention; construction *The creation of the aeroplane was a marvellous feat.*   2 earth, universe, nature *As you look at creation, don't you sometimes think it wonderful?*

credible *adj.*   believable, conceivable; trustworthy *Henry did not give a very credible account of his whereabouts last night.*   ANT. incredible, unbelievable, inconceivable.

credit *n.*   1 honour, merit, recognition *Philip and Peter deserve a lot of credit for taking care of their aged mother.*   2 belief, trust, faith *How can anyone place any credit on what you say when they know how you lied in the past?*   3 repute, reputation, name, standing, rank *My credit is good enough to get a loan for a new car.*   *vb.* 1 believe, accept, trust *Even though I credit your explanation of the flat tyre, you shouldn't have been out so late.*   2 attribute *The museum experts credited the painting to my grandfather.*   ANT. *n.,vb.* discredit.

creditable *adj.*   praiseworthy, worthy *Maria turned in a very creditable performance as Lady Macbeth.*   ANT. unworthy, dishonourable, shameful.

credulous *adj.*   believing, trusting, gullible, naive, unsuspecting, unsuspicious *People are so credulous that you can sell them anything if you try hard enough.*

creed *n.*   belief, credo, doctrine, faith *No one should be discriminated against because of race, creed, or colour.*

creek *n.*   inlet, bay, cove, arm *We could sail up the creek only a mile because it was too shallow for our ship.*

creep *vb.*   crawl, worm along, sneak; slither *The shadowy figure crept through the shrubbery.*

crew *n.*   group, team, squad, company *How large a crew will you need to complete the work?*

crime *n.*   wrongdoing, misconduct, wrong, offence; violation, misdemeanour, felony *She was arrested for the crime of forgery.*

criminal *adj.*   illegal, unlawful, felonious *Maltreating a child is a criminal offence.*   *n.*   crook, lawbreaker, felon, convict, culprit, offender, delinquent *The escaped criminals were being sought by the police.*

cripple *vb.*   maim, disable, injure, hurt, damage *The fall from the second-storey window crippled him for life.*   *n.*   invalid, handicapped person, disabled person *Confined to a wheelchair after his accident, Jim remained a cripple for the rest of his life.*

crisis *n.* emergency, dilemma, trauma, climax *There was a crisis when it was found that £50,000 was missing.*

criterion *n.* standard, basis, principle, norm *If we went by your criteria of quality, nobody would ever publish another book.*

critic *n.* . 1 judge, reviewer, commentator *Who is the drama critic of that newspaper?* 2 faultfinder, censor, slanderer *I may make a mistake once in a while, but who appointed you as my critic?*

critical *adj.* 1 faultfinding, carping, condemning, reproachful, disapproving *Please stop nagging me: you have no reason to be so critical of everything I do or say.* 2 dangerous, risky, hazardous, perilous *His health was in a critical condition and the doctor ordered him to rest.* 3 crucial, important, decisive *The timing in putting a new product on the market can be critical.* ANT. (1) praising, flattering. (2) safe, sound. (3) unimportant, trivial.

criticism *n.* 1 censure, faultfinding, objection *Harsh criticism of my work resulted in its rejection by the publisher.* 2 review, commentary; evaluation, analysis *His criticism of Shakespeare's plays is masterly.*

criticize *vb.* judge, censure; scold, rebuke, chastise *Considering how you behave, you are scarcely the one to criticize others.*

crooked *adj.* 1 bent, twisted, curved, hooked, zigzag *A crooked path wove among the boulders to the pond.* 2 *Informal:* dishonest, criminal, corrupt *The directors were embarrassed when they discovered that the treasurer was crooked and had stolen money.* ANT. (1)straight. (2) honest, upright.

crop *n.* harvest, produce, yield *Because of lack of rainfall the crop will be poor this year.* *vb.* cut, lop, mow, clip *I think you look better with your hair cropped short.*

cross *vb.* 1 go across, traverse; intersect *Don't cross the street without looking first!* 2 mingle, mix, interbreed *If you cross a scottie with a poodle you get a 'scoodle'.* 3 thwart, frustrate, oppose *Once Reginald has his mind made up, it's not a good idea to cross him.* *adj.* irritable, annoyed, testy, ill-natured, bad-tempered, snappish; mean, angry *Our teacher was very cross with those children who hadn't done their homework.* ANT. *adj.* good-natured, cheerful.

crouch *vb.* stoop, duck *You have to crouch to get through the doorway.* ANT. stand.

crowd *n.* throng, swarm, host, flock, mob, pack *There was a crowd of people waiting in front of 10 Downing Street to see the prime minister.* *vb.* 1 throng, swarm, mob *We crowded onto the football field after the game.* 2 squeeze, cramp, pack; shove, push *We were crowded into the tiny cabin.*

crown *n.* 1 circlet, coronet, tiara *The princess wore a gold crown studded with precious stones.* 2 head, skull *Jack fell down and broke his crown.* *vb.* install, invest, endow *She was crowned queen in a ceremony that lasted for seven hours.*

. **crucial** *adj.* decisive, critical, significant, important *Defence of the coastline is crucial to our national security.*

crude *adj.* 1 rude, vulgar, coarse; unrefined, unpolished, graceless *Roy's manners are very crude.* 2 unfinished, raw, coarse *On the workbench stood a crude sculpture of a figure that I couldn't recognize until I was told it was of my sister.* ANT. (1) polite, cultured; refined. (2) finished, polished.

cruel *adj.* heartless, mean, merciless, pitiless, ruthless, brutal, inhuman *The prisoners were subjected to cruel torture.* ANT. kind-hearted, compassionate, merciful.

cruelty *n.* harshness, brutality, savagery *The cruelty of the advancing hordes of Mongols is legendary.* ANT. kindness, compassion.

cruise *vb.* travel, drift, coast; tour *The car cruised along at a steady speed.* *n.* tour, voyage, journey *My grandfather went on a world cruise when he retired.*

crumb *n.* bit, fragment, particle, scrap *I don't want to see a crumb of food left on your plate.*

crumble *vb.* break up, disintegrate, fall apart *After a few hundred years the building had crumbled to dust.*

crumple *vb.* collapse, crush; fold *The weight of the roof has caused the columns to crumple.*

crunch *vb.* bite, chew, munch; masticate *The noise at breakfast was deafening as everyone crunched his corn flakes.*

crush *vb.* break, smash, crash *The machine quickly crushed all of the stones into smaller sizes suitable for driveways and other uses.*

cry *vb.* 1 shout, yell, scream, roar, bellow *When I saw the rock falling I cried out as loudly as I could.* 2 weep, wail, sob, bawl *When the baby cries, either feed her, change her, or make sure nothing is hurting her.* ANT. (2) laugh.

cuddle *vb.* embrace, hug, kiss, caress *Randolph cuddled up with his teddy bear and was soon asleep.*

cue *n.* sign; hint, suggestion; reminder *If you want to learn to write well, take your cue from the many great authors.*

culminate *vb.* finish, end, conclude, reach a climax *The plan reaches its culmination in 1992, when we enter the Common Market.*

culprit *n.* offender; criminal *The police caught the culprit who has been harassing shoppers at the supermarket.*

cult *n.* 1 sect, group, faction, clique *My daughter's got caught up in a way-out cult and won't talk to me any more.* 2 fad, craze, fashion *This year's cult involves turtles and next year's may be insects from outer space.*

cultivate *vb.* 1 farm, till, plant, seed, harvest *Although he owns a huge area of farmland, Mr Snyder cultivates only half of it.* 2 educate, refine, teach, nurture *Our parents cultivated the habit of reading in all their children.*

cultural *adj.* educational, civilizing, instructive, elevating *Britain is known worldwide for cultural programming on TV.*

culture *n.* 1 civilization, society *Western and eastern cultures differ widely.* 2 refinement, breeding, cultivation, upbringing *From her* *bad manners and rude behaviour you could tell at once that she was totally lacking in culture.*

cumulative *adj.* increasing, intensifying, advancing, snowballing *Pollution of the river is the cumulative effect of the company's waste disposal programme.*

cunning *adj.* 1 clever, tricky, wily, foxy, crafty *Even at the age of three, Betsy was cunning enough to get what she wanted from anyone.* 2 skilful, clever, ingenious *That box was carved by a cunning hand from a solid piece of wood.* *n.* 1 wiliness, foxiness, shrewdness, cleverness, slyness, deceit *Another example of his cunning was the way he was able to persuade people to give him their money for his fake schemes.* 2 skill, ability *Her cunning was matched only by her beauty.* **ANT.** *adj.* (1) simple, naïve, gullible. *n.* (1) simplicity, openness.

curb *n.* check, restraint, control *The new tax law was an effective curb on expense accounts for executives.* *vb.* check, restrain, control *It required stern measures to curb wastage in the use of the country's resources.* **ANT.** *vb.* encourage, foster.

cure *n.* remedy, treatment, medicine *People used to think that sulphur and molasses were a cure for almost anything.* *vb.* heal, remedy *The salesman told us that snake oil would cure my broken leg.*

curious *adj.* 1 inquisitive, inquiring, interested; nosy, prying *If you weren't so curious about things that don't concern you, you wouldn't get into so much trouble.* 2 peculiar, odd, strange, unusual, queer *There was a curious animal with a red plume and a white tail and blue fur sitting on the fence.* **ANT.** (1) indifferent, uninterested.

curl *vb.* coil, twist, bend, loop, wind *Please curl the string around this stick.* *n.* curve, coil, spiral, lock, tress *My girlfriend has some lovely curls in her hair.*

current *adj.* present, up-to-date, modern *The current craze for horror films is bad for children.* *n.* stream, tide *The current carried the boat down the river and out into the sea.* **ANT.** *adj.* out-of-date, outmoded, old-fashioned.

curse *n.* 1 oath, ban *The witch's curse caused the children to shout and dance wildly.* 2 trouble, misfortune, evil *The rain, originally a blessing, turned into a curse after two weeks without stopping.* *vb.* swear, denounce, condemn *When the police finally caught the thief, he cursed them for finding him.* **ANT.** *n.* (1) benediction, blessing. (2) boon, advantage.

curtail *vb.* cut short, shorten, abridge, cut *We had to curtail the science programme because of lack of funds.*

curtain *n.* screen, shade, blind *The dark curtain will prevent any light from leaking out at night.*

curve *vb.,n.* bend, twist, arch *The road curves round to the left. The curves on that figure are most attractive.*

cushion *n.* bag; pillow, bolster, rest, support *There was a comfortable red cushion at each end of the couch.* *vb.* protect; lessen, suppress, absorb *This foam rubber is packed into the box to cushion the shock during shipping.*

custom *n.* habit, practice, convention *When you travel abroad you ought to participate in the customs of the countries you visit.*

customary *adj.* usual, common, habitual, regular *This is far better than the customary fare one gets on British Rail.* ANT. unusual, rare.

customer *n.* client, patron, buyer, consumer *Have you found a customer for that sculpture you had on display last week?*

cut *vb.* **1** gash, slash, prick, nick *I cut my finger on the point of the blade.* **2** sever, slice, carve, cleave, slit *That knife isn't sharp enough to cut the bread.* **3** mow, lop, chop, crop *The grass was cut once this week already.* **4** decrease, lower, lessen *The government may cut spending in order to reduce inflation.* *vb. phr.* **cut back** reduce, decrease *The budget for school supplies was cut back by twenty per cent.* **cut in** interrupt, interfere, butt in *When the teacher was talking, Phil cut in to ask if he could leave the room.* **cut off** stop, cease, end, terminate *The chairman cut off the debate after fifteen minutes.* **cut short** finish, stop, end *The performance was cut short by the power failure.* *n.* incision, slash, gash, slit *The nurse bandaged the cut on Janet's finger.*

cute *adj.* sweet, delightful, charming, appealing, attractive *You certainly were a cute baby, Martin.*

cycle *n.* **1** circle, series, revolution, period *Many poems have been written about the cycle of the four seasons.* **2** bicycle, bike; tandem; motor cycle *He rode his cycle to work.*

cynical *adj.* sarcastic, mocking, sneering, scornful, contemptuous *You can count on Robert to make some cynical comment about a pretty girl.*

d

dabble *vb.* play, trifle, fool *I don't really play the piano well—I merely dabble at it.*

daft *adj. Informal:* silly, foolish; simple, stupid *You are daft if you think I am going to go into the cage with that lion.* ANT. clever, bright, intelligent.

dagger *n.* sword, blade, knife *It was obvious that the dagger was the murder weapon.*

dainty *adj.* delicate, petite, pretty, beautiful, graceful, fine, elegant *Only Cinderella's dainty foot would fit into the glass slipper.* ANT. clumsy, oafish, lumpish.

dally (with) *vb.* play, toy, flirt *Furnival has the reputation of dallying with every girl he meets.*

dam *n.* barrier, dike, bank, wall *The beavers built a dam across our stream and flooded part of our land.* *vb.* obstruct, block, stop; restrict, check, slow *A huge tree fell down in the storm and dammed up the drain.*

damage *n.* impairment, injury, harm; destruction *The hurricane caused millions of pounds worth of damage on the island.* *vb.* impair, injure, harm, mar *The telephone lines were damaged in the storm. Gossiping about a person can damage his reputation.* ANT. *vb.* repair, rebuild, improve, fix.

damn *vb.* condemn; curse *Jack Ketch's descendants were damned forever to carry a birthmark in the shape of a gibbet.* ANT. bless.

damp *adj.* moist, soggy, dank; humid *When the weather is damp, I can't open this cupboard door because it sticks.* *n.* moisture, dampness, humidity, wetness *The damp in the walls causes a growth on them.* ANT. *adj.* dry, arid.

dampen *vb.* **1** moisten, wet *It is better to dampen clothes before ironing them.* **2** stifle, deaden; moderate *The noise of the traffic outside was dampened by the thick stone walls.*

dance *vb.,n.* step; polka, tango, waltz; (*slang*) boogie *Would you like to dance with me? The dance begins at eight tonight.*

danger *n.* peril, risk, hazard, uncertainty, threat *If you enter that cave you run the danger of being sealed in.* ANT. safety, security.

dangerous *adj.* perilous, hazardous, risky, uncertain, unsafe *Driving without a seat belt is very dangerous.* ANT. safe, secure.

dangle *vb.* hang; sway, droop *I like earrings that dangle.*

dare *vb.* **1** brave, risk *The acrobat dared to walk the tightrope over the river, a long way below.* **2** challenge *Rosemarie dared George to swim across the lake.*

daring *adj.* brave, fearless, intrepid, courageous, bold, valiant *Enter-*

ing the lion's cage carrying only a chair and whip is very daring. n. bravery, courage, valour *Vincent's reputation for daring began when he saved three children from a burning house.* ANT. adj. afraid, fearful. n. cowardice, timidity.

dark *adj.* 1 shadowy, unlit, murky, dim, dusky, shaded, sunless, black *The half of the earth facing away from the sun is always dark.* 2 dismal, sad, gloomy, unhappy *The period before the war was a dark time for many people.* ANT. (1) light, illuminated, bright. (2) cheerful, happy.

darken *vb.* 1 shade, blacken *My art teacher said that these areas of the drawing ought to be darkened for greater contrast.* 2 cloud over *The sky darkened suddenly and it began to rain.* ANT. brighten.

darkness *n.* dark, dusk, gloom; night *I could hardly seen anything in the darkness.* ANT. lightness, brightness; day.

darling *n.* beloved, dear, sweetheart, favourite *Anthony was the darling of all the teachers.* *adj.* dear, beloved *Robert's mother called him 'Darling baby' until he was twenty-five years old.*

darn *vb.* mend, repair; embroider *My girl friend offered to darn my socks for me.*

dart *n.* arrow, barb, missile *The dart hit the target but missed the bull's-eye.* *vb.* run, scurry, scamper, hasten, dash *From the top of the tall building, the people on the street below looked like ants darting to and fro.*

dash *vb.* 1 strike, smash, beat, break *In the darkness, we could hear the surf dashing on the rocks in front of the ship.* 2 run, scurry, scamper, rush, dart *In the rush hour, thousands of people dashed down the stairs into the underground station.* *n.* bit, sprinkling, scattering, pinch, hint *Add just a dash of pepper before serving.*

data *n.* information, facts, evidence; statistics *How did they gather this data about the memories of senile patients?*

date *n.* time, day, moment; year *On this date, ten years ago, I met my true love.*

daunt *vb.* frighten, discourage, intimidate *George is not easily daunted by threats.* ANT. encourage, inspirit.

dauntless *adj.* brave, fearless, undaunted, bold, intrepid, courageous, valiant *One could not imagine a more dauntless band of men than the 34th Brigade.* ANT. cowardly, timid, fearful.

dawdle *vb.* linger, idle, lag behind, dally *Come along, Samuel, and stop dawdling.* ANT. hurry.

dawn *n.* 1 sunrise, daybreak *The duel was arranged: it would be pistols at dawn in the park.* 2 beginning, origin, start *At the dawn of civilization, man already used a highly developed language.* ANT. (1) sunset, dusk, nightfall. (2) end, finish, conclusion.

daydream *vb.* muse, fantasize *You cannot get your work done if all you do is daydream.*

daze *vb.* stun, confuse, perplex, puzzle *The author was dazed by the publicity and fame his first novel had brought him. Roger was dazed by the blow he received on the head.* *n.* stupor, confusion, bewilderment *I just walked around in a daze after learning about winning the scholarship.*

dazzle *vb.* astonish, bewilder, surprise, stupefy, stun, impress *Ronald was dazzled by the beauty of the movie star.*

dead *adj.* 1 deceased, lifeless, defunct; gone, departed *Donald's great grandfather has been dead for twenty years. Janet forgot to water her violets for a week, and when she looked at them, they were dead.* 2 inert, motionless, still, inoperative, inactive *The engine went dead right in the middle of a traffic jam.* ANT. (1) alive, animate. (2) active, functioning.

deaden *vb.* numb, paralyse, anaesthetize *The dentist gave me an injection to deaden the tooth he was going to fill.*

deadlock *n.* stalemate, standstill, impasse *Labour and management had reached a deadlock in their negotiations.*

deadly *adj.* 1 fatal, lethal, mortal *He was going to take his own life by drinking the deadly poison but he came to his senses in time.* 2 deathly, ghastly, ghostly *Margaret's face turned deadly pale when she learned of the accident.*

deaf *adj.* 1 unhearing, stone-deaf *After the explosion, Tim was deaf in one ear for almost a week.* 2 unaware, stubborn, inattentive, oblivious *My father was deaf to my requests for more money.* ANT. (2) conscious, aware.

deal *vb.* 1 treat, cope, act, attend *Our former headmaster had methods for dealing with mischievous boys.* 2 trade, barter, do business, bargain *My company refuses to deal with anyone who isn't completely honest.* 3 give, distribute, apportion, deliver *I was dealt three aces and two kings.*

dear *qdj.* 1 loved, beloved, darling *His dear wife met his train every evening.* 2 expensive, costly, high-priced *That new hat was much too dear for someone on my salary.* ANT. (1) hateful. (2) cheap, inexpensive, reasonable.

dearth *see* **lack.**

death *n.* demise, decease, passing, extinction *It might have been a cooling of the earth that brought about the death of the dinosaurs.* ANT. life; birth.

debased *see* **corrupt.**

debate *vb.* argue, dispute, contend, discuss *We debated the merits of different types of wine until midnight.* *n.* discussion, dispute, argument, controversy *The debate in the House of Commons on the new education bill went on for a week.* ANT. *n.* agreement.

debt *n.* obligation, liability *Be careful not to allow your debts to exceed your assets.*

debut *n.* (first) appearance, introduction; presentation *Carr's daughter made her debut in society at the age of eighteen.*

decadent *adj.* corrupt, immoral, degenerate *One could not imagine a more decadent period of history.*

decay *vb.* 1 rot, spoil, decompose *If you don't keep fresh food under refrigeration, it will decay rapidly.* 2 deteriorate, decline, wither, perish, die *In the Dark Ages, western culture decayed so badly that there was little literature for several hundred years.* *n.* 1 decline, downfall, collapse *The decay of the Roman Empire was caused by internal corruption.* 2 rot, decomposition; mould, rottenness *The decay in her teeth was very bad because she ate so many sweets.* ANT. *vb.* grow, progress, flourish.

deceit *n.* deceitfulness, deception, fraud, dishonesty, guile *Mary's reputation for deceit comes from her having been a double agent.* ANT. honesty, uprightness; forthrightness, openness.

deceitful *adj.* insincere, false, dishonest, fraudulent, deceptive *It was deceitful to pretend to be friendly when you really despised him.* ANT. honest, sincere.

deceive *vb.* mislead, cheat, swindle, defraud, hoax, hoodwink, fool *We were deceived by Clement's calm appearance as he was really seething inside.*

decent *adj.* proper, becoming, respectable; fitting, appropriate *The decent thing to do would be to return the ring you stole.* ANT. indecent, improper, indecorous, unsuitable.

deception *n.* trickery, treachery, craftiness, deceit *Giles practised every deception imaginable to cheat his customers.* ANT. honesty, openness, frankness, probity.

deceptive *adj.* false, misleading, unreliable *A person's outward appearance can often be deceptive.* ANT. real, true, authentic.

decide *vb.* determine, settle, choose, resolve *You must decide for yourself what you want to do in life.* ANT. hesitate, waver.

decision *n.* conclusion, judgement, resolution, settlement *The decision of whether we stay or go is yours.*

deck *n.* platform, level, floor, storey *A stateroom on the deck above this is very costly.*

declaration *n.* announcement, pronouncement, statement, assertion, affirmation, notice *A representative made a declaration concerning the company's profits during the latest quarter.*

declare *vb.* say, state, proclaim, announce, pronounce, affirm, assert *Betty declared that she had never seen the man before.* ANT. deny, suppress.

decline *vb.* 1 refuse, deny, reject *He declined the nomination for the post of treasurer.* 2 lessen, deteriorate, weaken, fail, diminish *Profits continued to decline after the company stopped advertising.* *n.* 1 lessening, weakening, deterioration *After the accident, my brother's health went into a decline, but then he recovered completely.* 2 descent, slope, incline, hill *Sledges may be ridden down declines.* ANT. *vb.* (1) agree, accept. (2) improve, increase, grow. *n.* (1) improvement.

decompose *vb.* rot, decay, moulder; break up, disintegrate *The forest floor consisted of fallen trees that were decomposing.*

decorate *vb.* ornament, paint, colour, enhance, adorn *We are having the house decorated by professionals.* ANT. spoil, deface.

decoration *n.* 1 ornamentation, adornment, furnishing *The decora-

tions for our Christmas tree are stored in the attic. **2** medal, badge, citation, award *My father won seven decorations for bravery during the war.*

decrease *vb.* lessen, diminish, decline, dwindle *The number of complaints about the new cars decreased after the manufacturer recalled them for repairs.* *n.* lessening, reduction, decline *It will be a long time before we see any decrease in the cost of living.* ANT. *vb.* increase, expand. *n.* increase, expansion.

decree *n.* edict, order, declaration, proclamation *The new government issued a decree that petrol would be rationed.* *vb.* order, declare, announce, pronounce *The king decreed that all prisoners would have their sentences reduced.*

decrepit *adj.* **1** feeble, weak, weakened, enfeebled, infirm *The old man was so decrepit he could hardly walk.* **2** tumbledown, rickety, dilapidated, run-down *That decrepit barn is unsafe and ought to be torn down.* ANT. (1) strong, energetic.

decry *vb.* disapprove (of), criticize, disparage *The mayor decried the practice of parking in the high street.*

dedicate *vb.* **1** consecrate, sanctify, hallow *The grounds were dedicated as a cemetery for those who had died in the war.* **2** set apart or aside, apply, devote, assign *He dedicated all of his free time to helping the elderly.*

deduce *vb.* conclude, reason, infer *From the evidence, I deduce that you have just returned from Spain.*

deduct *vb.* subtract, take away *We shall have to deduct for the cost of the breakage during the party.* ANT. add, increase.

deed *n.* **1** act, action, achievement, feat *For his deed of heroism in rescuing the little girl, the boy received a medal.* **2** title, document, certificate *After we met the lawyers at the bank, we were given the deed to the house.*

deem *vb.* judge, determine, regard, consider, hold *We deem it unlikely that we shall ever return to Benidorm.*

deep *adj.* **1** low; bottomless, profound *They say that this pool is so deep that it has no bottom.* **2** serious, bad *That boy will find himself in deep trouble one of these days.* **3** learned, intellectual *I can see from your expression that you are thinking deep thoughts.* **4** absorbed, involved, engrossed *The two men were deep in conversation, and I didn't want to interrupt.* ANT. *adj.* (1) shallow. (3) light.

deface *vb.* spoil, mar, scratch, disfigure *Vandals defaced the Sheraton sideboard for no reason at all.* ANT. beautify, decorate.

defeat *vb.* **1** overcome, conquer, vanquish, overthrow, suppress *The small scouting patrol was completely defeated by the enemy's superior forces.* **2** thwart, foil, spoil, frustrate *The shower defeated our plans for a picnic.* *n.* conquest, overthrow *Loss of the fighter plane spelled defeat for us.* ANT. *vb.* (1) surrender, submit, yield.

defect *n.* flaw, weakness, imperfection, blemish *There was a defect in the new toaster, so we returned it and got our money back.* *vb.*

desert, abandon, leave, forsake *The men who defected from the army were all rounded up and punished.* ANT. *n.* perfection, flawlessness. *vb.* join, support.

defective *adj.* flawed, faulty, inoperable, inoperative, imperfect *I returned the defective radio to the shop and got a replacement.* ANT. perfect, flawless, faultless.

defence *n.* 1 protection, resistance *Until recently, man was unable to provide a natural defence against certain diseases.* 2 trench, bulwark, fortification, fort, barricade, rampart, fortress *The orange crates were no defence against the oncoming tanks.*

defend *vb.* 1 protect, guard, safeguard, shield *The main army went out into the battle and left only fifty men to defend the women and children in the fort.* 2 support, uphold, maintain *She tried to defend her son's behaviour, but everyone knew he had been wrong.* ANT. attack.

defer *vb.* delay, put off, postpone *I shall try to defer payment of my bill for another week or so.* ANT. hurry, speed, hasten, rush.

defiant *adj.* antagonistic, obstinate, rebellious, resistant, disobedient *The students were defiant when told that the sports programme would have to be curtailed.* ANT. submissive, yielding.

deficiency *n.* lack, scarcity, need, insufficiency *We take vitamin tablets to make up for any deficiency in our diet.* ANT. abundance, profusion.

deficit *n.* lack, shortage, deficiency; loss *Instead of a profit, we had a deficit in the second quarter.* ANT. excess; profit.

defile *vb.* corrupt, pollute, debase, adulterate *You have defiled the proud name of Grimsby and shall have to answer for it!!* ANT. purify, cleanse.

define *vb.* 1 explain, describe, interpret; name, designate *This dictionary defines words very thoroughly.* 2 set off, distinguish, mark off *I could see his outline defined against the curtain.*

definite *adj.* 1 certain, fixed, settled, determined *Our plans for Christmas are definite—we're having dinner at your house.* 2 clear, sharp, distinct, obvious, plain *There, in the stone, was the definite outline of a dinosaur's foot.* ANT. indefinite, undetermined.

definition *n.* meaning, sense, explanation, interpretation, description *Can anyone give me a good definition of 'dweeb'?*

deformed *adj.* misshapen, disfigured; twisted, warped, ugly *Most people are unaware that a beautiful soul is often concealed by a deformed body.*

defraud *vb.* cheat, swindle, trick *On their first visit to New York a couple of swindlers defrauded them of all their money.*

defy *vb.* challenge, oppose, dare, flout *You must not defy your parents' orders about staying out late.* ANT. yield, submit, surrender.

degree *n.* 1 measure, extent, standard, order *He reached a high degree of competence by sheer hard work.* 2 award, qualification *After three years at college she was awarded a BA degree.*

dejected *adj.* depressed, unhappy, disheartened, discouraged, downhearted, sad *Terry was quite dejected when our team failed to win the cup.* ANT. happy, cheerful, optimistic.

delay *vb.* 1 postpone, put off, hold up *The post was delayed for three days over the Christmas holidays.* 2 wait, hesitate, pause, hold back *When you hear the fire alarm, line up in the corridors and don't delay.* *n.* hold-up, pause, postponement *During the strike, there was a three-week delay in the delivery of fresh produce.* ANT. *vb.* hasten, forward, advance.

delegate *n.* representative; ambassador, emissary; envoy, deputy *Three universities sent delegates to the convention.* *vb.* appoint, nominate, deputize, commission, authorize *I was delegated to ask the teacher whether the class could·have a party.*

delete *vb.* cancel, erase, remove, cross out *You must delete any reference to East or West Germany and substitute just 'Germany'.* ANT. add, include.

deliberate *adj.* 1 intentional, considered, planned, calculated, premeditated *I believe that there was a deliberate effort to set fire to the house.* 2 careful, cautious, slow *The old man's deliberate walk was recognized by all who knew him.* *vb.* consider, reflect, ponder, weigh, judge *We deliberated for a long time before deciding what we would give to our teacher for a wedding present.* ANT. *adj.* (1) accidental, unintentional, unplanned.

delicate *adj.* 1 dainty, fine, fragile, frail *The delicate cobwebs sparkled in the morning dew.* 2 frail, weak, precarious *For a month after his operation my uncle was in delicate health, but he's fine now.* 3 sensitive, critical, precarious, perilous *The situation between Greece and Turkey has always been delicate.* ANT. (2) strong, healthy, robust.

delicious *adj.* tasty, appetizing, delectable, delightful *We used to buy the most delicious pastries at that shop.* ANT. unpleasant, horrible, unpalatable.

delight *n.* pleasure, joy, enjoyment *He is a loving father and takes great delight in his children.* *vb.* please, entertain, satisfy *Nothing delights me more than a good Christmas party.* ANT. *n.* revulsion, disgust, displeasure. *vb.* displease, revolt, disgust.

delightful *adj.* charming, pleasing, refreshing, pleasant, pleasurable *What a delightful way to start the day!!* ANT. disagreeable, unpleasant, nasty.

delinquent *n.* (young) offender, wrongdoer, criminal *It was a small group of delinquents that was vandalizing the cars.*

deliver *vb.* 1 distribute, give out; convey, hand over *The Post Office delivers millions of letters each day.* 2 address, present *Yesterday my father was to have delivered a speech to 400 people.* 3 liberate, set free, release, save, rescue *May God deliver us from evil.* ANT. (3) confine, imprison, enslave.

delivery *n.* 1 conveyance, handing over, transfer, distribution *The delivery of the goods took place at the station.* 2 manner, style, diction, articulation *It was clear that the minister was the right man to speak at the dinner: his delivery was faultless.*

deluge *n.* 1 downpour, cloudburst *It's rained nonstop all day—there's a deluge outside!* 2 flood, rush, overflow *There was a deluge of fan mail for the new rock star.* *vb.* flood; inundate, overwhelm *Last month the whole area was deluged by continuous rain storms.*

delusion *n.* fantasy, illusion, vision *Fred is having delusions of grandeur thinking he's Napoleon.*

demand *vb.* 1 ask for, claim, request *I demanded my rights.* 2 command, direct *The teacher demanded that the noisy pupils leave the room.* 3 require, need *This night job demands more than I expected.* *n.* 1 request, claim *Wage demands are increasing. Women's demands for voting rights equal to men's were a long time being met.* 2 obligation *This job puts too many demands on my free time.* 3 call, market *There is a great demand for felt-tip pens these days.* ANT. *vb.* (1) relinquish, waive, give up.

demolish *vb.* destroy, ruin, raze, devastate *The old shops were demolished to make way for a new shopping mall.* ANT. build, construct, erect.

demolition *n.* destruction, wrecking *No one was allowed in the area during the demolition of the tower block.* ANT. construction, erection.

demon *n.* devil, evil spirit, imp *That little demon is always getting into some mischief or other.* ANT. angel.

demonstrate *vb.* 1 prove, verify, establish *The prosecutor demonstrated the suspect's guilt beyond all shadow of doubt.* 2 explain, describe, illustrate *The simple screw demonstrates an application of the principle of the inclined plane.* 3 protest, march *The angry workers went to London to demonstrate about their low pay.*

demonstration *n.* 1 show, exhibition, exhibit, presentation, display *There was a demonstration at the planetarium that showed how the planets revolve around the sun.* 2 protest, march, rally *The trades union leaders called on their members to join the demonstration in the city centre.*

den *n.* lair, cave, cavern *It is best to avoid entering the lion's den if you can avoid it.*

denote *vb.* designate, indicate; stand for, mean *This signal denotes that the track is clear ahead up to the next signal.*

denounce *vb.* condemn, deplore; blame, accuse *The lieutenant was denounced by his men for his cruelty.*

dense *adj.* 1 thick, solid, impenetrable *A dense fog covered the moors.* 2 packed, crowded *On New Year's Eve a dense mass of people gathered in Trafalgar Square to see the new year in.* ANT. (2) sparse, scanty.

dent *n.* indentation, depression *That little knock, as you call it, caused a deep dent in my car door.*

deny *vb.* 1 contradict, disagree, dispute, repudiate *The suspect de-*

nied that he had taken the necklace from the case. **2** refuse, reject, disallow *You can't deny me the right to answer your charge.* ANT. (1) admit, concede, confess. (2) allow, permit.

depart *vb.* leave, go, set out *The ship departs at noon tomorrow.* ANT. arrive, come.

department *n.* section, branch, subdivision *In which department of the government does your mother work?*

departure *n.* going, leaving, setting out *As it was nearly midnight, I thought I had better take my departure.*

depend (on) *vb.* **1** rely, confide, trust *We are all depending on Samantha to win the swimming race.* **2** be dependent, hinge, rest *Whether we win or not will depend on the total score.*

dependable *adj.* reliable, trustworthy, steady, faithful *I found Evan Twinkell a dependable employee and would hire him again.*

depict *see* **describe.**

depleted *adj.* used up, consumed, exhausted, drained, empty *Our supply of rubbers is depleted, so stop making so many mistakes.*

deplorable *adj.* regrettable, grievous, lamentable *Isn't it deplorable how bad some of these new singers are?*

deposit *vb.* **1** put, place, put down, set down *The lorry deposited the goods at the quayside.* **2** save, bank; store *No matter how little money you have, you should get into the habit of depositing some in the bank regularly.* *n.* **1** sediment, lees, dregs *Port leaves a deposit at the bottom of the bottle.* **2** addition, entry *Please make this bank deposit for me when you go to town.* ANT. *vb.* (2) withdraw. *n.* (2) withdrawal.

depot *n.* store, warehouse, depository, wharf *The supplies will be kept at the depot till they are needed.*

deprave *see* **corrupt.**

depreciate *vb.* reduce, decline, decrease; decay, deteriorate *The longer you keep this fruit, the more it will depreciate.*

depress *vb.* **1** dispirit, dishearten, discourage; dampen *Paul was depressed for three days after losing the championship match.* **2** devalue, devaluate, cheapen *The pound was depressed yesterday on the international money market.* ANT. (1) cheer, exhilarate, exalt.

depression *n.* **1** cavity, dip, dent *All that remained of the flying saucer was a smoking depression in the ground where it had stood.* **2** despair, gloom, melancholy, sorrow, sadness, hopelessness *My mother went into a period of depression after my brother broke his arm.* **3** decline, recession, hard times *Some people thought that the business depression of the 1970s would be worse than that of the twenties.* ANT. (1) bank, elevation. (2) elation, happiness. (3) boom.

deprive *vb.* deny, strip; rob. *The claim is that he was deprived of his rights as a citizen.* ANT. supply, provide.

depth *n.* deepness, profundity *This is a well-written paper, but it has little depth.* ANT. height, tallness, loftiness; shallowness.

deputy *n.* assistant, lieutenant, aide, delegate *The director had no time to go so he sent his deputy.*

derelict *adj.* dilapidated, decrepit, neglected; deserted, abandoned, forsaken *These derelict buildings could be fixed up as shelters for the homeless.*

derive *vb.* receive, obtain, get, acquire *Mr Thomas derives his entire income from the sale of petrified prickly pears.*

derogatory *adj.* offensive, pejorative, disparaging, insulting *Manfred gets very upset if anyone makes derogatory remarks about his brother.* ANT. flattering, complimentary, appreciative.

descend *vb.* move lower, climb *or* go *or* move down *We descended the rock face with the aid of ropes.* ANT. ascend, climb (up).

descent *n.* fall, drop, decline *When the balloon deflated, our descent was very rapid.* ANT. ascent, rise.

describe *vb.* portray, characterize, picture, narrate, relate, recount *Please describe in detail exactly what you saw.*

description *n.* account, narration, report, record *The description of the fugitive is being broadcast on radio and television.*

desert[1] *n.* waste, wasteland, wilderness *It may sometime be necessary to irrigate the deserts to provide more farmland.* *adj.* wild, barren, uninhabited *Robinson Crusoe was cast ashore on a desert island.*

desert[2] *vb.* abandon, leave, forsake *When the cat deserted her kittens, our dog adopted them and took care of them.* ANT. join, accompany.

deserter *n.* fugitive, runaway, defector, renegade; traitor *The army deals very harshly indeed with deserters.* ANT. loyalist.

deserve *vb.* earn, merit, be worthy of, warrant *What has Penny done to deserve such a luxurious Christmas present?*

design *vb.* 1 plan, intend, scheme, plot *The trapdoor was designed to open if anyone tried to open the jewel case.* 2 create, originate *My sister designs clothes for a large manufacturer in Paris.* *n.* 1 pattern, plan, blueprint, sketch *These designs for the new monument were copied from old books.* 2 meaning, intention, purpose, end, aim *Veronica's design for the future did not include Harry as her husband.*

desirable *adj.* wanted, sought-after, wished-for; good, excellent *Honesty is a desirable characteristic to look for in anyone.* ANT. unwanted, hated; unattractive, repellent.

desire *vb.* 1 crave, long for, want, covet *What I desire most of all right now is a delicious nutty bar of chocolate.* 2 ask, request *If you call the servants, they will see that you have what you desire.* *n.* need, longing, want, craving, wish *The magician said he could satisfy every one of Harvey's desires.* ANT. *vb.* (1) loathe, abhor, detest.

desolate *adj.* 1 deserted, empty, lonely *During the winter, the beach was desolate.* 2 miserable, sad, unhappy, wretched *When you're away from me I am just desolate.* ANT. (1) crowded, populous, teeming. (2) cheerful, happy.

despair *n.* hopelessness, desperation, discouragement *When the hundredth experiment resulted in failure, the research staff were in deep despair.* *vb.* lose heart, lose hope *When I lost my watch while rowing on the lake, I despaired of ever seeing it again.* ANT. *n.* joy, hope, optimism.

desperate *adj.* despairing, hopeless, reckless *The escaped murderer was a desperate man who would stop at nothing to avoid capture.* ANT. calm, collected.

despicable *adj.* mean, base, low, contemptible, worthless *Beating that horse was a despicable thing to do.* ANT. admirable, honourable, worthy.

despise *vb.* scorn, dislike, disdain, condemn *They despise him for betraying his country.* ANT. admire, like, honour.

despite *prep.* notwithstanding, regardless of, in spite of, even with *Despite his poverty, Abraham Lincoln got a good education.*

despondent *adj.* dejected, discouraged, downcast, disheartened, sad *Charlotte was feeling despondent because business has been bad.* ANT. happy, joyful.

despot *n.* dictator, tyrant, autocrat, oppressor *The country was ruled for decades by a cruel despot.*

dessert *n.* sweet, pudding, (*informal*) afters *I am going to have ice cream for dessert.*

destiny *n.* fate, fortune, lot *I assume it was not my destiny to become a famous writer.*

destroy *vb.* 1 ruin, demolish; deface, spoil *These trees were destroyed by disease.* 2 kill, slay, end, extinguish *When I saw the train pulling out of the station, my holiday plans were destroyed.* ANT. (1) create, start, undertake.

destruction *n.* devastation, demolition, ruin, extinction *With the destruction of the old theatre we were left only with the memory of happy times spent there.* ANT. creation, beginning.

detach *vb.* separate, disengage, divide *The engine was detached from the rest of the train.* ANT. attach, connect.

detail *n.* feature, aspect; item, circumstance *Pomeroy has the responsibility to look after every little detail of the design.*

detain *vb.* delay, restrain, hold back, stop *The police detained a few people while they checked their credentials.* ANT. forward, hurry, rush.

detect *vb.* determine, discover, ascertain, learn, find out *I am trying to detect who it was that made the anonymous phone call.*

detective *n.* policeman, officer, investigator, private detective, sleuth, (*informal*) private eye *The detective found a clue to the murderer's identity.*

deter *vb.* prevent, discourage, dissuade *The newspapers tried to deter her from suing them for libel after that story.* ANT. encourage.

deteriorate *vb.* decay, degenerate, decline; impair; disintegrate *If you fail to maintain the roof, it will deteriorate over time.* ANT. improve.

determine *vb.* 1 decide, settle, resolve *It took only a few minutes to determine who had eaten the sweets—he had chocolate all over his chin.* 2 fix, establish, define *I wasn't able to determine exactly where my property ended and my neighbour's began.*

detest *vb.* despise, hate, loathe *If there is one thing I despise it is a hypocrite.* **ANT.** like, love, appreciate.

detriment *n.* harm, damage, injury, disadvantage *To his detriment, it must be said that he allowed the prisoners to be tortured.*

devastate *vb.* 1 lay waste, ravage; sack *The nuclear bomb devastated a large area of land.* 2 *Informal:* overwhelm, confound *The news of the death of her friend devastated her.*

develop *vb.* 1 grow, expand, enlarge, advance, mature *Anne has developed from a child into a beautiful, charming young lady.* 2 reveal, disclose, become known, unfold *The plot of the play developed only slowly.* **ANT.** (1) deteriorate, degenerate.

deviate *vb.* diverge, digress, wander, turn aside *Please try to stick to the subject and stop deviating.*

device *n.* machine, tool, utensil, instrument *What kind of device was used to pick this lock?*

devious *adj.* 1 underhand, insincere, dishonest; sly *The managing director was very devious in his approach to other firms.* 2 roundabout, indirect *Why did we have to drive the long way home along that devious route of yours?* **ANT.** (1) open, fair; honest. (2) direct.

devise *vb.* invent, create, originate, concoct *The boys devised a clever plan to escape from the cave.*

devote *vb.* apply, dedicate, give, commit *With eleven children, how could my mother devote a lot of time to any one of us?* **ANT.** relinquish, withdraw, withhold, ignore.

devour *vb.* gorge, gulp (down) *Chris was so hungry that he devoured three hamburgers in less than three minutes.*

devout *adj.* 1 religious, pious, devoted *He is a devout Christian and goes to church twice on Sunday.* 2 genuine, earnest, sincere, heartfelt *I am a devout believer in treating others the way I'd want them to treat me.* **ANT.** (1) irreligious. (2) indifferent, scornful.

diagram *n.* plan, outline; sketch; chart *Here is a diagram showing the layout of the bank.*

dictate *vb.* 1 speak, deliver, record *If he dictates too fast, I cannot take it down in shorthand.* 2 order, command, direct *The general dictated the conditions under which he would accept a surrender.*

dictator *n.* tyrant, despot *How can a people allow a dictator to get the upper hand?*

die *vb.* 1 decease, perish, expire, go, pass away *Because of the advances in medicine, people aren't dying until they are much older.* 2 decrease, diminish, fade, sink, decline, wither, wane, fail *The candle, like the roses in the vase, is dying.* **ANT.** (2) flourish, grow.

difference *n.* disagreement, inequality, contrast *There are big differences between the ways men and women view the same thing.* **ANT.** similarity, likeness, kinship, compatibility.

different *adj.* 1 unalike, unlike, differing, changed *You and your sister are as different as chalk and cheese.* 2 various, miscellaneous *There are five different flavours of ice cream to choose from.* ANT. (1) similar, alike, identical.

differentiate *vb.* distinguish, separate *The first thing he has to learn is to differentiate right and wrong.*

difficult *adj.* 1 hard, laborious, strenuous *Handling a horse-drawn plough is difficult.* 2 intricate, complicated, obscure *That college textbook is much too difficult for a child to understand.* ANT. (1) easy. (2) simple, uncomplicated.

difficulty *n.* 1 worry, hardship, trouble *Getting a good job after school can be a difficulty these days.* 2 predicament, fix, trouble *Barbie got herself into some difficulty at school last week.*

dig *vb.* excavate, burrow, scoop out *This is the third hole we have dug trying to find the treasure chest.*

digest *vb.* 1 eat, consume *After a huge meal, some snakes spend days digesting their food.* 2 study, consider, reflect on *Give me a few minutes to digest the teacher's remarks before replying.* 3 summarize, shorten, abridge *How can you digest the encyclopedia into such a small book?* *n.* summary, abridgement, abstract, synopsis, précis *Why should anyone want to read digests of great authors' books when the real pleasure comes from reading the originals?*

dignified *adj.* noble, serious, stately, solemn, elegant *A dignified gentleman came over to ask me what I wanted.*

dignify *vb.* exalt, ennoble, elevate, honour *I would scarcely dignify that disaster by calling it dinner.* ANT. humiliate, degrade, shame.

dignity *n.* distinction, stateliness, bearing *We must try to maintain a little more dignity in the classroom.*

dilapidated *adj.* old, shabby; decaying, tumbledown *The wall is so dilapidated that it might fall down any day.*

dilemma *n.* predicament, quandary *Not knowing which door conceals the lady and which the tiger can be a real dilemma.*

diligent *adj.* hardworking, persevering; careful, attentive *Ken has been very diligent to make certain that everyone is safe.* ANT. lazy.

dilute *vb.* water down, thin, weaken, mix *This flavouring is meant to be diluted with still or fizzy water.*

dim *adj.* unclear, faint, shadowy, vague *I could hardly make out the dim outline of the house in the fog.* *vb.* obscure, dull, darken *The houselights were dimmed as the curtain went up for the last act of the play.* ANT. *adj.* bright, brilliant. *vb.* brighten, illuminate.

dimension *n.* (usually **dimensions**) measure, size, extent *The dimensions of the room are 12 by 16 feet by 9 feet high.*

diminish *vb.* lessen, shrink, reduce, decline, wane *The horse has diminished in importance as a form of transportation since about 1915.* ANT. enlarge, increase, wax.

diminutive *adj.* little, small, tiny, minute *A diminutive man wearing a green suit stood defiantly in the path.* ANT. big, large, great, huge, gigantic.

din *see* **noise.**

dine *vb.* eat, feast, lunch, soup *We dine on steak tonight.*

dinghy *see* **boat.**

dip *vb.* plunge, immerse, submerge, wet *Dip the burning stick into the water to make sure it's out.* *n.* plunge, swim *I like to take a dip in the pool before breakfast.*

diplomat *see* **ambassador.**

diplomatic *adj.* polite, tactful, gracious, discreet *It would not be diplomatic to mention money at a time like this.* ANT. impolite, rude, thoughtless, ungracious, tactless.

direct *vb.* 1 command, manage, control, regulate *The new director directed the company through one of its most profitable periods.* 2 aim, sight, point, level *Completely frustrated, Betty directed her gaze skyward as if in appeal to a higher power.* 3 indicate, guide, conduct, show *Please direct me to the nearest police station.* *adj.* 1 straight, unswerving *When my son comes home after school, he makes a direct beeline for the kitchen to eat some biscuits.* 2 plain, straightforward, frank, sincere, earnest *Please stop wavering and give me a direct, honest answer to my question.* ANT. *adj.* (1) crooked, indirect, swerving. (2) dishonest, untruthful.

direction *n.* 1 way, route *After all I had told her, she drove off in the wrong direction.* 2 management, guidance, supervision *Under her direction, the school became one of the best in the country.*

directly *adv.* straight, immediately, at once *I shall be there directly.*

director *n.* manager, leader, executive; supervisor *We are having a meeting of the board of directors tomorrow.*

directory *n.* list, classification, record *The new directory has our company name misspelt.*

dirt *n.* soil, filth, pollution, filthiness *Don't come into the house with all that dirt on your wellies.* ANT. cleanness, cleanliness.

dirty *adj.* soiled, unclean, filthy, polluted *I wouldn't drink that dirty water if I were you.* *vb.* soil, foul, befoul, spot, pollute *The town's water was dirtied by the drains from the chemical-company plant.* ANT. *adj.* clean, pure, spotless. *vb.* clean, cleanse, purify.

disability *n.* incapacity, unfitness, injury *Father receives a small pension for the disability he has from the war.*

disable *vb.* cripple, incapacitate, weaken *The way she carries on, you'd think that a broken fingernail could disable you for life.*

disadvantage *n.* 1 inconvenience, drawback *The only disadvantage of my new job is that I have to get up at five o'clock.* 2 handicap, hindrance, obstacle *Her disadvantage is that she cannot type.* ANT. benefit, advantage, convenience.

disagree *vb.* argue, object, oppose *Terence wants to expand the car park, but the council disagrees.* ANT. agree.

disagreeable *adj.* quarrelsome, offensive, rude *My neighbour becomes very disagreeable if I throw my grass cuttings into his garden.* ANT. friendly, agreeable, pleasant.

disagreement *n.* conflict, controversy, quarrel, clash, opposition *I* *was unaware that there was any disagreement between the two of you.*

disappear *vb.* vanish, fade *The leprechaun disappeared into the forest.* ANT. appear, emerge.

disappoint *vb.* fail, dissatisfy; disconcert *Quentin was terribly disappointed that you didn't take him to the zoo.* ANT. satisfy, please, gratify.

disappointment *n.* defeat, dissatisfaction, failure, discouragement *We all have to learn to face disappointment at some time or other.* ANT. satisfaction, pleasure, gratification.

disapproval *n.* condemnation, censure; discontent, dissatisfaction *Nell found it very difficult to withstand her father's disapproval.* ANT. approval, praise.

disaster *n.* calamity, misfortune, accident, catastrophe *There was another rail disaster yesterday in which forty-three people died.*

disastrous *adj.* unfortunate, catastrophic, calamitous *The decision to focus all the company's resources on making paraffin lamps proved disastrous.*

disbelief *n.* incredulity; doubt, scepticism *Politicians' campaign rhetoric is usually greeted with disbelief by realistic voters.* ANT. credulity, certainty.

disc *n.* 1 record *Have you bought the number one disc yet?* 2 counter, token *We have to buy discs for the buses in this town.*

discard *vb.* throw away, get rid of, reject *Discard once and for all any idea of going to the cinema tonight.*

discern *vb.* see, distinguish, recognize, differentiate, perceive *I discerned a slight movement in the snowbank, dug down, and saved the dog.*

discharge *vb.* 1 let go, dismiss *When business got bad, three of us were discharged from our jobs.* 2 relieve, unload, unburden *Marie's responsibilities were not discharged until she finished washing the dishes.* 3 fire, shoot *The rabbit ran off into the woods when the gun discharged.* *n.* 1 explosion, firing, detonation *The sudden discharge of the gun made me jump.* 2 release, liberation; dismissal *My father's discharge from the Navy became final this week.* ANT. *vb.* (1) employ. *n.* (2) employment.

disciple *n.* follower, supporter; student, pupil *Plato was a disciple of Socrates.* ANT. teacher, leader, guide.

discipline *n.* 1 training, practice, exercise, drill *If you want to do well in sports, you must follow a strict discipline. Discipline in the armed services is not as severe as it once was.* 2 order, system, control *A neatly written paper shows good discipline.* *vb.* 1 train, control, drill, teach *Your puppy will make a better pet if you discipline him properly.* 2 punish, correct, chastise *In the old days, parents disciplined their children much more strictly than they do now.* ANT. *n.* (2) carelessness, negligence, sloppiness, messiness.

disclose *vb.* reveal, show, expose, uncover *It was disclosed that Ka-*

trina had borrowed the money without telling anyone. ANT. hide, disguise, mask, conceal.

disconcerted *adj.* agitated, uncomfortable, ill-at-ease, disturbed, upset *Tom was disconcerted to learn that he was wanted by the police.*

disconnect *vb.* separate, divide, unhook, detach, disengage *The engine was disconnected from the passenger carriages.* ANT. connect, engage, attach, bind.

discontinue *vb.* cease, end, stop; interrupt *Please discontinue my subscription to your magazine till further notice.* ANT. begin, start, launch, initiate.

discord *n.* conflict, disagreement *There is always discord between the far left, the centre and the far right factions in the party.* ANT. agreement, accord, concord.

discount *n.* rebate, deduction, allowance, concession, premium *If you buy a dozen, they'll give you a ten per cent discount.*

discourage *vb.* dishearten, depress, deject *Getting poor grades at school can be very discouraging.* ANT. encourage, inspire.

discourtesy *n.* disrespect, impoliteness, rudeness *Failing to address the headmaster as 'Sir' is a serious discourtesy.* ANT. courtesy, politeness.

discover *vb.* find; learn, find out, ascertain, determine *Was it Balboa who discovered the Pacific Ocean? I am trying to discover whom I should see about this notice I received in the post.* ANT. conceal, hide.

discreet *adj.* tactful, judicious, prudent, wise; cautious, careful *We can only hope that Harold will be discreet about the family secrets.* ANT. careless, incautious, tactless, indiscreet, imprudent.

discretion *n.* tact, prudence, wisdom, carefulness, thoughtfulness *Mary must exercise more discretion in selecting her friends.* ANT. carelessness, indiscretion, tactlessness, imprudence.

discriminate *vb.* distinguish, differentiate, tell apart *Anyone who wishes to be a gardener must learn to discriminate between weeds and flowers.*

discuss *vb.* talk about, deliberate, consider *Come round to my office and we'll discuss the possibility of a job.*

discussion *n.* talk, conversation; dialogue; conference *Tim readily joined in the discussion of where we should go for a holiday.*

disdain *vb.* scorn, reject *She disdains the way her sister dresses.* *n.* scorn, contempt, haughtiness *He treats everyone who has less money than he with disdain.* ANT. *vb.* admire, respect, esteem, prize. *n.* admiration, respect, honour.

disdainful *adj.* scornful, contemptuous, haughty, arrogant *You shouldn't be disdainful of those who are less well off than you.* ANT. admiring; humble.

disease *n.* illness, sickness, affliction, ailment, complaint, disorder, malady, infirmity *The Malay waste-away is almost as serious a disease as the Barcoo rot.*

disfigured *adj.* marred, scarred, damaged, deformed, defaced *This* *disfigured skin condition could come only from prolonged exposure to the sun.*

disgrace *n.* shame, dishonour, embarrassment *Tim had to live with the disgrace of having been caught cheating.* *vb.* shame, dishonour, embarrass, humiliate *The army deserter was told that he had disgraced his country.* ANT. *n.* honour, esteem. *vb.* honour, respect.

disguise *vb.* mask, hide, screen, conceal, camouflage *The detective disguised himself as a woman and waited in the street for the robber to attack.* *n.* mask, camouflage, cover *In her disguise as a flower girl, no one could recognize the society lady at the party.* ANT. *vb.* reveal, display, show.

disgust *vb.* nauseate, sicken; offend, revolt, repulse *The sight of an operation disgusts me.* *n.* distaste, nausea; aversion, revulsion *Looking at the dead horse filled him with disgust.* ANT. *n.* liking, admiration.

disgusting *adj.* revolting, repulsive, nauseating, repugnant *We thought that the horror show was too disgusting for Nancy to watch.* ANT. attractive, appealing.

dish *n.* 1 plate; bowl, container *Who's going to wash the dishes after dinner?* 2 food, meal; course *That dish certainly looks tasty!*

dishonest *adj.* corrupt, fraudulent, crooked *The company directors were accused of dishonest handling of the shareholders' money.* ANT. honest, straightforward, upright.

dishonour *n.* shame, disgrace, indignity, loss of face, defamation, obloquy *The students who had been caught cheating faced the dishonour of having their names posted.*

disintegrate *vb.* break down, shatter; divide, separate; decay *It is not long before metals disintegrate in this steamy, tropical climate.*

disinterested *adj.* impartial, neutral, unbiased, unprejudiced, open-minded *Nicky took a disinterested view of the dispute.*

dislike *vb.* disapprove of; hate, detest, loathe *Why must we associate with people I dislike?*

dismal *adj.* gloomy, sorrowful, depressing, melancholy, dreary, sombre *The dismal winter weather lasted through much of the spring this year.* ANT. cheerful, happy, charming, lighthearted.

dismay *vb.* scare, frighten, alarm: discourage, dishearten *We were dismayed to learn that the only roads to town were blocked by snow.* *n.* fear, terror, horror, dread *You can imagine the neighbours' dismay when the poisonous snake escaped.* ANT. *vb.* hearten, encourage.

dismiss *vb.* discharge, release, let go *As business declined, more and more people were dismissed from the plant.* ANT. engage, employ, hire.

disobey *vb.* break, violate, transgress; neglect, ignore, disregard *If you continue to disobey the traffic signals, you will have a serious accident.* ANT. keep, obey.

disorder *n.* confusion, turmoil, tumult, chaos *By the time the police* *arrived, what had started as disorder had become a riot.* ANT. order, neatness, organization.

dispatch *vb.* **1** send off *or* away *I dispatched the letter the very same day the request came.* **2** conclude, achieve, finish *I had only one more thing to do and dispatched that as quickly as I could.* *n.* **1** message, report, communication, communiqué *The dispatch from the front lines said that our troops were advancing.* **2** speed, promptness, quickness, swiftness *My next visitor is a bore, and I shall get rid of him with dispatch.* ANT. *n.* (2) slowness, reluctance, hesitancy.

dispense *vb.* distribute, apportion, give out *A shop assistant is dispensing coupons for free ice cream.*

disperse *vb.* scatter, spread (out), separate *The seeds are dispersed by the wind.* ANT. gather, collect, assemble.

display *vb.* **1** exhibit, show, demonstrate *There are strict rules about how flags should be displayed.* **2** reveal, uncover, show *Many people display their lack of knowledge as soon as they start talking.* *n.* showing, exhibit, exhibition, demonstration *I have never seen such a display of community spirit as during the parade.* ANT. *vb.* (2) disguise, hide, conceal, cover.

displeasure *n.* dissatisfaction, dislike, distaste, discontent, disapproval *I have already written to the maker to express my displeasure with the results of this anti-wrinkle cream.*

disposition *n.* nature, character, temperament, personality *Why do you spend so much time with someone who has such a disagreeable disposition?*

dispossess *vb.* evict, oust, dislodge, throw out, expel *Ulrika was dispossessed for nonpayment of rent.*

disprove *vb.* refute, invalidate, deny, controvert *The fact that he was being detained by the police in Cardiff disproves your contention that he was robbing a shop in Leeds.*

dispute *vb.* **1** argue, debate, quarrel, contest *How can you dispute my statement that my birthday is March 21st?* **2** oppose, deny, contradict *The committee disputed the wisdom of the report's recommendations and rejected them all.* *n.* argument, quarrel, debate, controversy *There was a dispute at the door about whether the tickets were valid or not.* ANT. *vb.* agree, concur. *n.* agreement, unanimity.

disqualify *vb.* debar, incapacitate, disable *Ian was disqualified from the competition for having stepped over the line.*

disregard *vb.* ignore, overlook, neglect *In taking on people, employers must learn to disregard race, colour, creed and sex and to consider only character and qualifications.* *n.* inattention, neglect, oversight *The policeman jumped into the icy waters with total disregard for his own safety.*

disrespectful *adj.* rude, impudent, impolite, impertinent; cheeky *Youngsters are terribly disrespectful of the elderly these days.* ANT. respectful, polite, courteous.

disrupt *vb.* interrupt, break; upset; intrude *The trial was disrupted by a disturbance in the rear of the courtroom.*

dissatisfaction *n.* disappointment, discouragement, discontent *Consumers must show their dissatisfaction with products if they expect the manufacturers to improve them.* ANT. satisfaction, enjoyment.

dissolve *vb.* 1 liquefy, melt, run *Salt dissolves in water.* 2 discontinue, terminate *Parliament was dissolved before the general election.* ANT. (1) harden, solidify.

distant *adj.* remote, far, afar, away, separated *A distant star may look larger than one that is nearer. Reptiles emerged from the sea at a distant point in time.* ANT. near, close.

distinct *adj.* 1 individual, separate, different *In nature each species is distinct from every other, even though some may seem alike.* 2 clear, definite, obvious, plain *I have a distinct recollection that you promised to take me to the ice rink.* ANT. (2) indistinct, vague, uncertain, obscure.

distinction *n.* 1 honour, renown, fame, repute, prominence, importance *It is a great distinction to be selected a winner of the Nobel prize.* 2 difference; characteristic *Until a child is taught what they mean, he is unable to make a distinction between right and wrong.*

distinguish *vb.* 1 separate, divide, differentiate, classify *It is hard for anyone but the specialist to distinguish one seashell from another.* 2 perceive, discern, recognize *Even at that great distance I was able to distinguish George in the crowd.* ANT. (1) blend, join, confuse.

distinguished *adj.* renowned, famous, honoured, eminent, illustrious, noted, important, celebrated *Maggie's father is a distinguished professor of music.* ANT. obscure, unknown, undistinguished.

distort *vb.* 1 deform, contort, twist, warp *His face had been distorted by old age.* 2 misrepresent, alter, misinterpret, pervert *Do news bulletins sometimes distort the truth?*

distract *vb.* 1 divert, occupy *I always found the radio too distracting when I was trying to do my homework.* 2 confuse, bewilder *Penny seemed distracted and unable to concentrate on what I was saying.* ANT. concentrate, focus.

distraction *n.* 1 amusement, entertainment, diversion *After studying for days for examinations, Jonathan felt he needed some distraction and went to the disco.* 2 confusion, turmoil, conflict *She felt a great distraction within herself at the enormity of the decision she had to take.*

distress *n.* 1 anguish, trouble, anxiety, worry, wretchedness; pain *Maggie caused her mother great distress whenever she stayed out late at night.* 2 danger, peril; disaster *The small boat was in distress because of the storm.* *vb.* worry, trouble, grieve, make wretched *Bill was distressed to learn that the headmaster had written to his father.* ANT. *n.* (1) happiness, tranquillity, peacefulness. *vb.* please, charm, satisfy.

distribute *vb.* share, deal, dispense, issue, mete out, allocate, apportion *We leave it to the charities to distribute the food that we contribute.* ANT. collect, gather, assemble.

district *n.* region, area, neighbourhood, section *Herman would prefer to go to school in his own district.*

distrust *vb.* suspect, doubt, mistrust *The bank manager distrusted the new cashier.* *n.* suspicion, doubt, mistrust *A good relationship between people must be founded on confidence, without distrust.* ANT. *vb.* trust. *n.* trust, confidence.

disturb *vb.* 1 annoy, bother, vex *Please don't disturb me when I am practising on the piano.* 2 worry, trouble *Even though the doctor said you were fine, the condition of your cold disturbs me.* ANT. calm, pacify.

disturbance *n.* 1 commotion, disorder, confusion *The marchers in the street caused quite a disturbance to the traffic.* 2 riot, brawl, fight *The police were called to control a disturbance between the political groups.* ANT. calm, serenity, tranquillity.

disuse *n.* neglect, decay, abandonment *Through disuse the old summerhouse has become dilapidated.* ANT. use, employment.

ditch *n.* channel, furrow, trench *He lost control of the car, which rolled off the road into a ditch.*

dive *vb.* plunge, dip, plummet, submerge *We watched the pelicans diving for their dinner.*

diverge *vb.* branch off, separate, fork *The two carriageways diverge when they reach the river.* ANT. join, converge, merge.

diverse *adj.* assorted, various, different *There are diverse ways of looking at the problem of educating children.* ANT. same, similar.

diversion *n.* 1 detour, redirection *There is a long diversion on the Oxford road because of road works.* 2 entertainment, amusement, sport, recreation *What do you do as a diversion if you live in such a small town?*

divert *vb.* turn aside *or* away, deflect *Galloway is not easily diverted from his goal.*

divide *vb.* 1 separate, split, part, detach, sever *Divide that apple into six pieces so we can share it.* 2 apportion, share, allot, allocate, distribute, deal *or* dole out *After the apple is cut up, we can divide it among the six of us.* 3 disunite, split up, estrange *Disagreements about women's rights divided the political party from the start.* ANT. (1) join, merge, combine. (2) gather, collect. (3) unite, unify.

divine *adj.* godly, heavenly, almighty, holy, transcendent *It was only through divine guidance that Grumbleigh arrived in the nick of time.* ANT. earthly, worldly.

division *n.* 1 separation, partition, sharing *In olden times, conquering soldiers were entitled to a division of the valuables in the cities and towns they captured.* 2 section, part, segment, portion *My father fought in the 3rd Division during the war.* ANT. (1) agreement, union.

divulge *vb.* reveal, release, disclose, expose; admit *Gerry divulged where he had hidden the treasure.* ANT. conceal, hide.

dizzy *adj.*   giddy, unsteady, lightheaded *I was still a bit dizzy from that blow on the head.*   ANT. clearheaded, rational, unconfused.

do *vb.*   1 perform, execute, enact, carry out, accomplish, effect *Success depends on everyone doing his job the best he can.*   2 finish, conclude, complete, achieve, attain *Don't just talk about it, do it!* *vb. phr.*   **do away with** kill, murder, execute *The pirates did away with all those who refused to join them.*   **do down** belittle, humiliate *Some elder brothers always do their younger brothers down.*   **do in** *Slang:* kill, murder *The thugs did the old lady in savagely.*   **do up** 1 wrap, enclose, tie *This is a beautiful gift—all done up with a red ribbon!*   2 redecorate, remodel *The Robinsons have done up their entire house.*

docile *adj.*   submissive; meek, mild, humble, tame *After a few weeks of training, the horse was as docile as a kitten.*

doctor *n.*   physician, general practitioner, surgeon; specialist *You had better see a doctor about that rash.*

doctrine *n.*   teaching, teachings; dogma, belief, principle *He accepts the doctrine that all men are created equal.*

document *n.*   form, certificate, record *The proper documents have been filed with our solicitors.*

dodge *vb.*   evade, elude, avoid; equivocate *One must not dodge one's responsibilities.*

dole *n.*   unemployment benefit *Don's father has been on the dole ever since he lost his job at the factory.*   *vb.*   deal, distribute, mete *The Red Cross doled out the food to the flood victims.*

domestic *adj.*   1 home-loving, homely *I am really very domestic and like nothing better than a good book and a comfortable chair by my own fireside.*   2 native, home-grown, homemade *If you buy domestic products, you stimulate the economy of your own country.*   ANT. (2) foreign, alien, outside.

domesticate *vb.*   tame, train, teach; housetrain *They say that it is almost impossible to domesticate wild beasts like tigers.*

dominant *adj.*   ruling, commanding, governing; prevailing, predominant *Among many animal groups the dominant male drives away the other males before the mating season.*

dominate *vb.*   control, rule, govern, influence, manage, subjugate, tyrannize *Some men are completely dominated by their wives.*

donation *n.*   gift, contribution, present, offering *Please make as large a donation as you can afford to the charity of your choice.*

doom *n.*   1 fate, destiny, fortune *The criminal had to wait till the judge passed sentence before learning his doom.*   2 death, ruin, destruction *The entire regiment rode to its doom as the flood waters closed in on them.*   *vb.*   destine, predestine, ordain, foreordain; decree; condemn *The entire project is doomed to failure if you take that attitude.*

door *n.*   entrance, opening, gateway; gate, portal *A huge man stood at the door, blocking my way.*

dot *n.* mark, spot, point, speck, particle *Inspection revealed several small dots of colour that identified the car as mine.*

double *adj.* twofold; dual, repeated, coupled *Give me a double portion of chips, please.* *vb.* multiply, duplicate *The inflation rate doubled last year.*

doubt *vb.* distrust, mistrust, question, suspect *The detective doubted that Professor Twinkle had been home all evening after he noticed the mud on his shoes.* *n.* **1** uncertainty, misgiving, scepticism, disbelief *I have my doubts about the truth of your story of being brought up by wolves.* **2** indecision, hesitancy *When we saw the fox running away with the chicken between its jaws, we no longer had a doubt about the identity of the culprit.* **ANT.** *vb.* trust, believe. *n.* belief, trust, confidence, reliance.

doubtful *adj.* dubious, uncertain, questionable, unsettled, undetermined, unsure *It is doubtful that we shall arrive on time, considering the weather.* **ANT.** certain, definite, sure, settled.

downcast *adj.* dejected, sad, depressed, downhearted, discouraged, unhappy, dispirited, despondent, crestfallen *David has been downcast because his parents would not allow him to keep a pet.* **ANT.** cheerful, happy, lighthearted, encouraged.

downfall *n.* ruin, fall, destruction *Every tyrant eventually meets his downfall.*

downgrade *vb.* lower, reduce, decrease, diminish; depreciate *After she lost yesterday's race, everyone downgraded Shirley's chances of winning tomorrow.* **ANT.** upgrade, improve, appreciate.

downhearted *adj.* sad, gloomy, depressed, downcast *Charles has been downhearted at the prospect of having to give up polo.* **ANT.** cheerful, happy, enthusiastic.

doze *vb.* nap *Father often dozes off while watching television.*

drab *adj.* dingy, dull, shabby; dreary *Why did you paint the kitchen such a drab colour?*

draft *n.* sketch, plan, drawing, outline *Here is the first draft of the changes we hope to make in the village square.*

drag *vb.* pull, draw, tow *The child entered, dragging a wagon behind her.*

drain *vb.* **1** draw off, empty, tap *The man drained his glass in one gulp. The conservationists fight the draining of swamps where birds, fishes, and other wildlife breed.* **2** exhaust, sap, waste; milk *Your annoying manner drains me of all patience.* *n.* tap, duct, channel, pipe *I pulled the stopper out of the sink and watched the water go down the drain.* **ANT.** *vb.* **(1)** fill, refill, replenish.

drama *n.* play, piece, show, production *The amateur group in Wendover staged the drama* Krapp's Last Tape *last evening.*

dramatist *n.* playwright *George Bernard Shaw was one of the most important dramatists of the century.*

drastic *adj.* severe, extreme; excessive, flagrant *They have made drastic changes to the traffic patterns around London.* **ANT.** moderate, cautious.

draw *vb.* **1** sketch, trace, depict, picture *The artist drew an excellent likeness of Anne in only a few minutes.* **2** drag, haul, tow, pull, tug *The oxen drew the heavy wagon up the muddy hill.* **3** attract *The parade drew a large crowd to the arena where the circus was to take place.* *vb. phr.* **draw back** withdraw, recoil, retreat *She drew back when she saw the box was full of snakes.* **draw on** employ, use, exploit *When you want to get something done properly, you must draw on all your resources.* **draw up** draft, prepare *Our lawyer drew up the documents for us to sign.* ANT. *vb.* (2) push, propel.

drawback *n.* disadvantage, hindrance, defect, shortcoming *The drawback to raising the price is that people may not be willing to pay so much for a newspaper.* ANT. advantage.

drawing *n.* sketch, picture, plan, rendering *Clumpett's drawings, which he used to throw away, today fetch prices in the thousands.*

dread *vb.* fear *I used to dread being in that teacher's class.* *n.* fear, terror, horror *Moriarty never overcame his dread of high places.* ANT. *n.* confidence, security.

dream *n.* **1** reverie, daydream *I had a dream about you yesterday.* **2** fantasy, hope, wish, fancy *His dreams of glory included landing on Mars and becoming a millionaire.* *vb.* imagine, fantasize, invent, fancy *She dreams of becoming a model.*

dreary *adj.* dismal, gloomy, cheerless, chilling, depressing *The weatherman predicted another dreary day for northern Scotland.* ANT. cheerful, hopeful, bright, encouraging.

dress *n.* **1** frock, skirt *I like that low-cut dress on you.* **2** costume, attire, garb, wardrobe, clothing, garments, clothes, apparel; habit; livery *Will Nancy's party require everyone to wear evening dress?* *vb.* **1** clothe, garb, don, wear, attire; robe *How are you going to dress for the masked ball?* **2** prepare, treat, attend *The doctor dressed my cuts and bruises and I was almost as good as new.* ANT. *vb.* (1) undress, disrobe, strip.

drift *vb.* float, sail, wander *The empty boat drifted about in the current until it finally came to rest on the beach.* *n.* tendency, intention, direction *In women's fashions there seems to be a drift toward repeating the styles of the 1930s and 1940s.*

drink *vb.* swallow, sip, gulp *You shouldn't drink a lot of cold water when overheated from exercise.* *n.* sip, gulp; beverage, potion, refreshment *There's nothing like a drink of tea when you're thirsty.*

drip *vb.* drop, dribble, trickle *The tap dripped all night, keeping me awake.*

drive *vb.* **1** control, direct, run, handle *Do you know how to drive a car?* **2** impel, propel, push, urge *I tried to reach the canoe but was driven back by the wind and the waves.* *n.* **1** ride, journey, trip, outing, tour, run *On Saturdays we go for a drive in the country.* **2** pressure, energy, urge, vigour, effort, force *Some people just have more drive than others.*

drivel *vb.* dribble; drip, slobber, drool *The dog drivelled at the* *mouth.* *n.* nonsense, twaddle, balderdash *What drivel some people speak!*

droop *vb.* sag, sink, settle *In the still air, the flag drooped.* ANT. straighten, rise.

drop *vb.* 1 drip, dribble, trickle *The rain ran down the roof and dropped into the barrel.* 2 fall, tumble *At the sound of the first shot, the soldiers dropped to the ground.* *n.* 1 droplet, gob, drip; trickle *There's a drop of rain right at the end of your nose.* 2 decrease, reduction, fall, slump, slip, decline *I haven't noticed a drop in the price of gum.*

drove *n.* herd, flock *Jimmy moved a drove of cattle into the south pasture.*

drowsy *adj.* sleepy, nodding *The children were drowsy after the long drive from the seashore.* ANT. alert, awake, energetic.

drug *n.* medicine, remedy *There's a drug for almost everything today; whether it cures or not is another matter.* *vb.* anaesthetize, stupefy, numb, benumb *The doctor drugged me so I wouldn't feel the pain when he set my broken arm.*

drum (up) *vb.* attract, summon, call; obtain, evoke *The men in the market stalls called out their wares, hoping to drum up some sales.*

drunk *n.* drunkard, drinker, alcoholic; dipsomaniac *Her first husband was a drunk who was unable to hold a job.*

dry *adj.* 1 arid, dehydrated, waterless, parched *If you don't believe that the desert is dry, you've never been there.* 2 dull, boring, tedious, tiresome *I found that course on lampshade making too dry to hold my interest.* *vb.* dehydrate, desiccate *Partly dried plums are called prunes.* ANT. *adj.* (1) wet, soaked, moist. (2) interesting, attractive, fascinating.

dubious *adj.* doubtful, questionable, suspect *As an honest dealer in antiques, I avoid handling anything of dubious origin.*

due *adj.* 1 owing, payable, owed, unpaid *My rent is due at the end of the month.* 2 expected, imminent *The ship was due yesterday.*

dull *adj.* 1 boring, tiring, tiresome, uninteresting *Instead of seeing a film on the history of piracy, we saw a dull one on how to grow turnips.* 2 blunt, dulled *That knife is so dull it couldn't cut a banana.* 3 slow, dumb, stupid, unimaginative *That fellow is the dullest one in our class.* 4 unfeeling, insensible, lifeless, dead *She's so dull that nothing interests her except eating and sleeping.* ANT. (1) fascinating, interesting, engaging. (2) sharp, keen. (3) bright, intelligent, quick. (4) alert, animated, spirited.

dumb *adj.* 1 dull, stupid, ignorant *Sadie is so dumb she failed every subject in school.* 2 speechless, mute *Some people who seem to be dumb are really only deaf.* ANT. (1) intelligent, bright, lucid, quick.

dump *n.* heap, pile *We put the old fridge on the dump.* *vb.* throw down, empty, unload *He dumped the heavy bags on the floor.*

dungeon *n.* prison, cell, jail, keep *The old man had been in the castle dungeon for thirty years.*

durable *adj.* lasting, firm, enduring *We thought that the synthetic paint might be more durable.* **ANT.** perishable, short-lived.

duration *n.* length, span, term, period *It was announced that food would be in short supply for the duration of the war.*

duress *n.* compulsion, coercion, constraint; force *Barbara only confessed to the crime under duress.*

dusk *n.* gloom, twilight *The street lights began to twinkle on at dusk.*

dutiful *adj.* faithful, obedient, docile *He used to come home for dinner, like any dutiful husband.* **ANT.** disobedient, headstrong, unruly.

duty *n.* 1 obligation, responsibility, conscience, faithfulness *It is every citizen's duty to report a crime when he sees one.* 2 function, responsibility, part, assignment *Every person in this naval unit is expected to perform his duty no matter what the cost may be.*

dwarf *n.* runt, midget *Only a dwarf could have crawled through that opening.* *vb.* stunt, reduce, minimize *I'm quite tall, but that football player dwarfed me easily.* *adj.* small, tiny, minuscule *A dwarf apple tree gives large apples.* **ANT.** *n.* giant.

dwell *vb.* reside, live, abide *I dreamt I dwelt in marble halls.*

dwindle *vb.* diminish, wane, lessen, decrease *As supplies of food began to dwindle, we became increasingly worried.* **ANT.** increase, wax, gain, grow.

dynamic *adj.* energetic, active, lively, vigorous, forceful *Ernest, a dynamic salesman, soon became sales manager.* **ANT.** listless, lazy.

e

eager *adj.* enthusiastic, keen, fervent *We were very eager to go to the model railway exhibition.* ANT. indifferent, uninterested, uninvolved.

earn *vb.* deserve, merit, win; realize, collect; clear, net *He made his money in the old-fashioned way—he earned it.*

earnest *adj.* sincere, serious, determined, eager *Alan is an earnest supporter of United.* ANT. insincere, frivolous, indifferent.

earth *n.* 1 world, globe *The earth is about 93 million miles from the sun.* 2 sod, turf, dirt, soil, ground *When planting tomatoes, make sure the earth is pressed firmly around the roots.*

earthly *adj.* worldly, everyday, mundane *When he made up his mind to study for the clergy, he denied himself earthly pleasures.* ANT. heavenly, divine.

earthy *adj.* 1 earthen, earthenware, earthlike *The earthy pots lay about the Indian campfire.* 2 coarse, unrefined, crude, vulgar *The audience was shocked by the comedian's earthy humour.* ANT. (2) refined, elegant, tasteful.

ease *n.* 1 naturalness, facility, skilfulness, cleverness *It is such a pleasure to watch the ease with which a master craftsman works.* 2 comfort, rest, relaxation, repose, contentment, contentedness *My father takes his ease on Sundays by watching football on TV.* *vb.* comfort, relieve, alleviate, soothe; lighten, lessen, reduce *That liniment certainly helped ease the pains in my legs. If you'll ease up on the brake, we can let the car roll ahead a little.* ANT. *n.* (1) difficulty, trouble, effort. *vb.* aggravate, worsen, heighten, intensify.

easy *adj.* 1 simple, effortless *Preparing a dictionary is not as easy as it may seem.* 2 comfortable, unhurried, leisurely *After a heavy Christmas dinner we used to take an easy walk on the common for half an hour.* ANT. difficult, awkward, strenuous.

easygoing *adj.* relaxed, carefree, calm, light *Will's easygoing manner makes people feel friendly.*

eat *vb.* 1 consume, chew, devour, swallow *Eat your spinach and you'll be as strong as Popeye.* 2 dine, lunch, breakfast; feast *We eat at about seven o'clock in the evening, after my father returns from work.*

eavesdrop *vb.* listen in, overhear, tap, (*slang*) bug *You only know about Cynthia's engagement because you were eavesdropping again.*

eccentric *adj.* odd, peculiar, strange *Mr Crotchet does some eccentric things, like dancing along the pavement, shouting at passers-by.*

economical *adj.* thrifty, sparing, careful, frugal *We find it more eco-*

nomical to buy the larger boxes of cereal. ANT. wasteful, lavish, unsparing.

ecstasy *n.* rapture, delight, pleasure *Listening to that concerto is pure ecstasy.* ANT. misery, unhappiness, agony.

ecstatic *adj.* delighted, overjoyed, elated, thrilled, happy *Susan was ecstatic when told the baby was a boy.* ANT. miserable, sad.

edge *n.* border, rim, brink, threshold, boundary, margin *The northern edge of the lake is where we swim. Don't cut yourself on the sharp edge of that piece of paper.* *vb.* 1 border, trim *She edged the neck and sleeves of the dress with lace.* 2 inch, move little by little, sidle *Roger edged over to Michele and grasped her hand.* ANT. *n.* middle, centre.

edgy *adj.* nervous, tense, irritable, touchy *Miles gets a little edgy when he hasn't had enough sleep.* ANT. tranquil, undisturbed, peaceful, bland.

edit *vb.* 1 revise, alter; compile, arrange *It requires several people to edit manuscripts before books or newspapers can be published.* 2 be in charge of, direct, publish *I know the man who edits the local newspaper.*

educate *vb.* teach, train, instruct *Carruthers has spent his entire life educating young children.*

education *n.* 1 instruction, training, schooling *There are many excellent schools and colleges where you can get a good education.* 2 culture, learning, knowledge *It is almost impossible to do the things you want to do without the proper education.*

eerie *adj.* weird, strange, fearful, spooky *The old deserted mansion had an eerie feeling about it.*

effect *n.* 1 result, outcome, consequence, end *Some scientists believe that global warming is the effect of burning petrol.* 2 significance, importance, meaning *Some kinds of punishment have almost no effect at all.* *vb.* accomplish, achieve; cause, make; bring about *Conservation of our natural resources has effected many changes in the development of large cities.* ANT. *n.* (1) cause.

effective *adj.* productive, efficient, practical *What is the most effective way of presenting our merchandise?* ANT. ineffective, wasteful, useless.

efficient *adj.* 1 effective, useful, serviceable *The lever is a very efficient machine.* 2 competent, apt, adept, able, capable, talented, skilled, clever *Phil has proved himself to be one of the most efficient workmen in the plant.* ANT. (1) useless, unworkable. (2) inefficient, ineffective, clumsy, awkward.

effort *n.* endeavour, attempt, try; struggle *It was a huge effort for such a small boy to jump over the barrier.*

eject *vb.* force out, expel, discharge, emit *The volcano began to eject lava and boulders a week ago.*

elaborate *adj.* ornate, ornamented, decorated, decorative; complicated, complex *The Victorian style of architecture is one of the most elaborate that was ever developed.* *vb.* decorate, embellish; develop, detail *The director of the department elaborated on his plan for reorganizing the division.* ANT. *adj.* simple, unadorned, stark.

elapse *vb.* pass (by), transpire *We ought to let a little time elapse before trying to phone her again.*

elastic *adj.* flexible; resilient, pliable *A typical elastic material is, of course, rubber.* ANT. rigid, inflexible, stiff.

elect *vb.* choose, select, vote for *The candidates all make a serious effort to get elected.*

elegant *adj.* fine, refined, cultivated; tasteful, choice *The Bell Inn is known as a place for elegant dining.* ANT. crude, unpolished, coarse, tasteless.

elementary *adj.* 1 basic, primary, fundamental *An elementary rule of competition is good sportsmanship.* 2 simple, uncomplicated *The explanation of how the prisoner escaped from the locked cell is elementary.* ANT. (2) complex, complicated, involved, sophisticated.

elevate *vb.* raise, lift *Attempts have been made to elevate the level of the public taste, but with little success.* ANT. lower, drop.

eligible *adj.* qualified, fit, worthy, suitable *Only UK residents are eligible to take advantage of the low rates we offer.* ANT. ineligible, unqualified.

eliminate *vb.* remove, get rid of, leave out, omit *I wish you would eliminate the words 'I can't' from your vocabulary.*

elope *vb.* run away, abscond *John and Eve are planning to elope because they want to avoid a big wedding.*

elude *vb.* evade, avoid, dodge *The fugitive has so far eluded capture.*

embargo *n.* restriction, restraint, prohibition *There is an embargo on the export of dried fruits.*

embarrass *vb.* shame, abash, confuse *I was embarrassed at not being able to answer such simple questions.*

emblem *n.* sign, token, symbol, badge, mark *The plaque on my car is an emblem of my membership in the club.*

embrace *vb.* 1 hug, clasp *When I found her in the crowd, I embraced my mother.* 2 include, contain, cover *The categories of animal, vegetable and mineral embrace most things on earth.* ANT. (2) exclude, bar.

emerge *vb.* come forth, appear; surface *We waited for the star to emerge from the stage door.* ANT. recede, retreat, disappear.

emergency *n.* crisis, predicament *Please do not call on me unless you have an emergency.*

eminent *adj.* distinguished, famous, celebrated, renowned, important, prominent *Georgette is one of our most eminent specialists in physical medicine.* ANT. unknown, undistinguished, ordinary, commonplace.

emit *vb.* see **eject.**

emotion *n.* feeling, sentiment *Cadwallader watched the aeroplane crash without showing any emotion.*

emotional *adj.* 1 passionate, ardent, stirring *That display was one of the most emotional scenes I've ever seen.* 2 hysterical, overwrought, zealous, enthusiastic, impetuous *I can't understand why my mother gets so emotional just because I keep breaking my arm playing football.* ANT. calm, tranquil, placid.

emphasis *n.* stress, accent *In the word 'emphasis' the emphasis is on the first syllable.*

emphasize *vb.* stress, affirm; highlight, underline *The ideas that he wants to emphasize are printed in red.*

emphatic *adj.* definite, positive, energetic, forceful, strong *Fred was most emphatic in his refusal to leave without Carrie.* ANT. quiet, lax, unforceful.

employ *vb.* 1 take on, engage, hire *The company employs people according to their skill.* 2 use, apply, utilize *He employed underhand tactics to achieve his own purposes.*

employee *n.* worker, labourer, wage-earner *The problem in that company is that there are almost as many bosses as there are employees.* ANT. employer, boss.

employer *n.* boss, proprietor, owner, management, manager, supervisor, superintendent *How many employers would give the entire staff a week's holiday at Christmas?* ANT. worker, employee.

employment *n.* work; job, position *Ewan has found employment with a computer company in Oxford.*

empty *adj.* bare, unoccupied, void, blank *Except for the gold coin, the box was empty. I sat staring at the empty sheet of paper, wondering what to write about.* *vb.* void, clear, unload, evacuate *Empty that bucket of water outside.* ANT. *adj.* full, filled. *vb.* fill.

enable *vb.* allow, sanction; empower, authorize *Only through the scholarship grant scheme was I enabled to attend college.*

enchant *vb.* charm, fascinate, delight, bewitch *Margo is the most enchanting woman I know.* ANT. bore, tire.

enclose *vb.* surround, encircle *The village square is enclosed by fencing during the construction work.*

encounter *vb.* meet, come across, face *We encountered our old neighbours while shopping at the supermarket.* *n.* meeting; appointment, rendezvous *Let me tell you about an encounter I once had with a king from the East.*

encourage *vb.* cheer up, hearten, help, strengthen, comfort *The teacher encourages all the students to do better.* ANT. discourage, depress.

encouragement *n.* support, reassurance, inspiration, stimulus; approval, help *The purpose of the programme is to offer encouragement to people to own their own houses.* ANT. discouragement, disapproval.

end *n.* 1 extremity, termination *After winding it for three hours, I finally came to the end of the string.* 2 limit, bound *Before Einstein, scientists used to think that space had no end.* 3 finish, conclusion, close *The symphony came to an end and we all applauded.* 4 aim, purpose, object, intent *What end have you in reading all those books?* *vb.* stop, finish, terminate, close, halt *I wish that* *nations could end all their arguing so we could have peace.* ANT. *n.* beginning, start, opening, launch. *vb.* begin, start, initiate.

endeavour *vb.* try, attempt, strive, struggle *If you promise to be good, I'll endeavour to forgive you.* *n.* try, attempt, exertion, effort, struggle *She has made a serious endeavour to memorize her part in the school play.*

endless *adj.* perpetual, repeated, continual, persistent *We have to put up with the neighbours' endless bickering.*

endorse *vb.* **1** confirm, approve, sanction, uphold *The chairman endorsed the comments of the speaker from the floor of the meeting.* **2** sign *He endorsed the cheque before it could be cashed.*

endow *vb.* give, bestow *Cynthia is endowed with beautiful hair.* ANT. divest.

endure *vb.* **1** last, continue, persist *The kinds of governments that limit the power of the people cannot endure for long.* **2** suffer, bear, undergo, experience *I don't think I could endure the pain and discomfort of another broken arm.* ANT. (1) cease, end, perish, die.

enemy *n.* foe, adversary, opponent, antagonist, rival *Even in a chess game one must regard the other player as one's enemy.* ANT. friend, colleague, cohort, ally.

energetic *adj.* vigorous, active, forceful, potent *Only the energetic pursuit of justice can ensure that we can all enjoy it.* ANT. lazy, indolent, sluggish, lax.

energy *n.* power, force, strength, vigour *Put as much energy into studying as you do into football and you would be the best in the school.* ANT. lethargy, feebleness.

engage *vb.* **1** employ, hire, take on *He was engaged as a departmental manager but soon rose to be a director.* **2** occupy, involve, absorb, engross *She was engaged in a new research project.* ANT. (1) dismiss, fire, discharge.

engaged *adj.* **1** betrothed, spoken for *Vera and Alan were engaged for only a few months before their marriage.* **2** occupied, busy *I can't connect you now, the line is engaged.*

engaging *adj.* beguiling, enchanting, charming, winning *Kathryn has a most engaging smile.* ANT. boring, ordinary.

enhance *vb.* heighten, intensify, improve, increase *Martha's figure is greatly enhanced by a princess-style dress.*

enjoy *vb.* have a good time; delight (in), like *Do you enjoy going to the theatre?*

enjoyment *n.* delight, pleasure, satisfaction *Some people derive enjoyment from making others happy.* ANT. displeasure, dissatisfaction.

enlarge *vb.* increase, amplify, extend, expand, magnify *An enlarged view of this section definitely shows a man in the window.* ANT. decrease, diminish, wane, shrink.

enlighten *vb.* inform, teach, educate *Please enlighten me as to what is expected of me.* ANT. confuse.

enlist *vb.* enrol, enter, sign up, register *We must enlist the help of two more people to push this car.* ANT. leave, abandon, quit.

enormity *n.* wickedness, heinousness, barbarity, savageness, atrociousness *The enormity of her crimes could not even be hinted at in the newspapers.*

enormous *adj.* huge, immense, gigantic, vast, colossal, stupendous *No one knows who carved those enormous stone heads on Easter Island.* ANT. small, diminutive, tiny, slight, infinitesimal.

enough *adj.* sufficient, adequate *Have you enough milk for tomorrow's breakfast?*

enquire *vb.* ask, question; investigate, examine *Someone came round while you were out enquiring if you lived here.*

enquiry *n.* examination, study, investigation *Tony has been asked by the police to help them in their enquiries.*

enrage *vb.* infuriate, anger, madden *Roger was enraged at being denied membership in the Clampett Society.* ANT. soothe, appease, calm.

enrol *vb.* enlist, register, sign up *I am going to enrol as a student in the new cooking school.* ANT. leave, quit, abandon.

ensue *vb.* follow, succeed; arise, result. ANT. precede.

ensure *vb.* guarantee, secure, assure *How can you ensure a return of at least twenty per cent on my investment?*

enter *vb.* come *or* go in, turn into, make one's way into *When poverty enters the door, love flies out of the window.* ANT. leave, depart.

enterprise *n.* **1** project, venture, undertaking *America is one of the few countries where an enterprise like yours could succeed.* **2** initiative, courage, boldness, drive, energy *Bob has the enterprise necessary to do well in anything he gets involved in.*

enterprising *adj.* resourceful, energetic *It was very enterprising of you to solicit business from all the neighbours.* ANT. indolent, lazy, unresourceful, sluggish.

entertain *vb.* amuse, divert; interest *Do you find clowns entertaining?* ANT. bore, tire.

entertainment *n.* amusement, enjoyment, pleasure, fun; sport, games, recreation *In Las Vegas there is continuous entertainment, twenty-four hours a day.*

enthusiasm *n.* eagerness, zeal, earnestness *My enthusiasm for sky diving diminished when I reached eighty.* ANT. indifference, unconcern.

enthusiast *n.* fan, fanatic, devotee; supporter *Are you an enthusiast of American football?*

enthusiastic *adj.* eager, zealous, earnest *Young is a very enthusiastic railway buff.* ANT. indifferent, aloof, unconcerned.

entice *vb.* attract, draw, lure, tempt *Is there nothing I can say to entice you to have another piece of chocolate cake?*

entire *adj.* whole, complete; intact, undivided *The entire question of moving to Australia has been put off for another year. The newspaper* *was still entire even after the magician apparently shredded it into bits.* ANT. partial, incomplete, separated, divided.

entitle *vb.* authorize, allow, empower *Knowing the Queen's first name scarcely entitles one to call her 'Lizzie'.*

entrance *n.* entry, door, access, gate, opening *The building has a very grand entrance.* ANT. exit.

entreat *vb.* beg, plead, implore *I entreat you to help these poor children by contributing now.*

entreaty *n.* appeal, plea, request, supplication *Her entreaties for help fell on deaf ears.*

envelop *vb.* surround, wrap, enclose, contain *Maddie ran into the house and her mother enveloped her in her arms.*

environment *n.* surroundings, habitat, conditions *Only in the past decade or so have people become seriously concerned about the environment.*

envisage *vb.* contemplate, expect, foresee *What do you envisage as the next step in the development of the town centre?*

envy *n.* jealousy, covetousness *Millie regarded her sister's new coat with envy.* *vb.* covet; grudge *You shouldn't envy your friends' property.*

epic *n.* saga, story, legend *The* Iliad *and the* Odyssey *are probably the best-known epics.*

epicure *n.* gourmet, epicurean, gourmand, gastronome, aesthete, connoisseur *Cuthbert is a true epicure, insisting on the proper wine with each dish.*

epidemic *n.* plague, scourge, pestilence *There seems to be an influenza epidemic every year.*

episode *n.* event, occurrence, incident *I cannot wait till the next episode of the soap opera I watch every afternoon.*

equal *adj.* 1 equivalent; same, identical *All men and women are supposed to be equal in the eyes of the law. Four is equal to two plus two.* 2 even, regular, uniform *Equal rights are provided for in the constitution.* *vb.* match *The wealthy man said that he would equal any contribution to the library fund.* *n.* match, counterpart; competitor, rival; double, twin *Herr Schmidt is my equal in our firm in Germany.* ANT. *adj.* (1) unequal, different. (2) uneven, irregular.

equip *vb.* furnish, provide, supply, fit out *If you are going camping, make certain that you are properly equipped.*

equipment *n.* material, materials, utensils, apparatus *Some of that mountain-climbing equipment can be very expensive.*

equivalent *adj.* equal, same; comparable; interchangeable *Turps and turps substitute have many equivalent uses.* *n.* counterpart, equal; match *The equivalent of a tape recorder for recording pictures is a video recorder.*

equivocate *vb.* prevaricate, hedge *Every time I ask Braithwaite when he will repay the money he borrowed, I get an equivocating reply.*

era *n.* period, time, age *The electronic era began with the invention of the transistor.*

eradicate *vb.* destroy, obliterate, stamp out *It was thought that smallpox had been eradicated once and for all.*

erase *vb.* remove, obliterate, expunge; cancel *It will take many years before Greyling will be able to erase the bad marks against her.* ANT. include, add.

erect *adj.* upright, vertical, straight *Sometimes I get a little dizzy when I stand erect after bending over.* *vb.* build, construct, raise; set up *The men erected the temporary building in less than two days.* ANT. *adj.* horizontal, flat. *vb.* demolish, knock down, flatten.

erode *vb.* wear down, grind down *The wind has eroded these rocks into weird shapes.*

errand *n.* job, task; mission *Simon viewed it as his errand to make certain that the standards of scholarship were maintained.*

erroneous *adj.* mistaken, wrong, inaccurate, incorrect, false, untrue *Most of the answers he gave were erroneous.* ANT. correct, right, accurate, true.

error *n.* mistake, oversight, inaccuracy, slip, blunder *There are a lot of spelling errors in this report.*

erupt *vb.* break out, start up, begin *Fighting has again erupted along the border.*

escalate *vb.* increase, go up *Wage demands continue to escalate despite the warnings of recession.*

escape *vb.* **1** run away, steal away, flee *Three prisoners have escaped from the county jail.* **2** avoid, elude, evade *Running away through the swamp, the men escaped their pursuers.* *n.* flight, departure; release *The criminal's escape was reported on the radio.*

escort *n.* guard, protection, convoy; guide *The murderer was brought to the jail by an armed escort.* *vb.* accompany, attend, usher; guard, protect *The shipment of gold was escorted by ten men with guns.*

especially *adv.* particularly, unusually, chiefly, specially *An especially heavy guard was placed round the embassy.*

essay *n.* composition, commentary, article; theme, thesis, dissertation *Hartfield's essay has been accepted for publication.*

essence *n.* root, character, principle, nature, basis *The essence of Reggie's problem is that he does not get along with the other students.*

essential *adj.* important, necessary, vital, critical, indispensable *In addition to knowing the subject he is teaching, it is essential that a teacher be kind and understanding.* *n.* necessity, requirement *Oxygen is an essential for all mammals.* ANT. *adj.* unimportant, dispensable, inessential, unnecessary.

establish *vb.* found, form, set up, begin *A new department was established to process the complaints received from customers.* ANT. discontinue.

estate *n.* property, land, grounds, holding *The estate has been passed down through the family for generations.*

esteem *vb.* prize, value, regard highly, revere, respect *The students as well as the teachers esteemed the headmaster of the school as a great educationalist.* *n.* respect, reverence, regard, honour, admiration *The captain was held in esteem by his crew.* ANT. *vb.* disdain, disregard, scorn. *n.* scorn, contempt.

estimate *vb.* value, gauge, evaluate, judge *The expert estimated that our paintings were worth almost one million pounds.* *n.* value, evaluation *The insurance company considered the estimate too high for repairing the old car.*

estimation *n.* opinion, judgement, point of view, viewpoint *In her estimation, the award should have been given to Carstairs.*

eternal *adj.* everlasting, endless, perpetual *Most religions have gods that are eternal.* ANT. brief, passing, temporary, transient.

etiquette *n.* decorum, (good) manners, social graces *It is bad etiquette to seat all the men together at a dinner table.*

evacuate *vb.* withdraw, abandon, leave, desert *As soon as the bombs began to fall, the town was evacuated.*

evade *vb.* elude, avoid, escape, dodge *Drumfey will do anything to evade his responsibilities.* ANT. meet, confront, face.

evaporate *vb.* vaporize; disappear, vanish *In the desert, the water evaporates quickly. Our picnic plans evaporated when the rain started.* ANT. appear; condense.

evasive *adj.* equivocating, deceitful, cagey *Grenville gave only evasive answers when asked the whereabouts of the money.* ANT. straightforward, open.

even *adj.* 1 level, smooth, flat *It was easier to walk where the ground was even.* 2 equal, balanced, square *If I give you the pound I owe you we'll be even.* 3 parallel *The police car drew up even with us.* *adv.* just, exactly *Even as I was watching, the sun disappeared and it started to rain.* ANT. (1) bumpy, irregular. (2) unequal, unbalanced, (3) divergent.

evening *n.* dusk, twilight, nightfall, sundown *Towards evening the stars came out.* ANT. dawn, sunrise.

event *n.* occurrence, incident, episode *This book deals with current events.*

eventual *adj.* ultimate, consequent *I never did learn the eventual outcome of that episode with the tiger.* ANT. current, present.

ever *adv.* 1 always, continuously, constantly *The sea, like the clouds in the sky, is ever changing.* 2 at all, at any time *Haven't you ever told a lie?* ANT. never.

evict *vb.* expel, dismiss, remove. oust *Lily was evicted for failing to pay the rent.*

evidence *n.* 1 proof, testimony. grounds *I know you think he took your umbrella, but have you any real evidence?* 2 indication, sign *The best evidence I have is that I saw him using it when it was raining.*

evident *adj.* clear, plain, obvious, apparent *It was evident that the* *child had nothing to do with the crime.* ANT. unclear, obscure, doubtful, uncertain.

evil *adj.* 1 sinful, immoral, wicked, bad *Some people think that any kind of entertainment on Sunday is evil.* 2 harmful, injurious *Drinking alcoholic beverages is an evil practice.* *n.* harm, woe; badness, wickedness, sin *Evil to him who does evil.* ANT. *adj.* (1) virtuous, moral, upright, good. (2) beneficial, advantageous, useful. *n.* goodness, virtue, uprightness.

evoke *vb.* call up, summon, arouse *Pictures of wounded animals and starving children always evoke pity and sympathy.*

evolve *vb.* develop, grow, emerge, result *The way society evolved in that country, there was neither need nor opportunity for education.*

exact *adj.* correct, accurate, precise; faultless *The exact time will be noon when you hear the signal.* ANT. inexact, inaccurate, faulty.

exactly *adv.* precisely, accurately; just *She is repeating exactly what I said last week.*

exaggerate *vb.* overstate, magnify *The need for reform of the educational system may be exaggerated.* ANT. minimize, understate, diminish.

examination *n.* 1 inspection, scrutiny, investigation *The jury was cautioned to rely only on a careful examination of the testimony and the evidence.* 2 test *I haven't yet revised for my geography examination.*

examine *vb.* inspect, investigate, scrutinize *Did you examine the murder weapon?*

example *n.* instance; sample, specimen, model; illustration *These are fine examples of sand paintings.*

exasperate *vb.* annoy, infuriate, bother, disturb *After trying unsuccessfully to set matters right for so long, I became exasperated and resigned.*

exceed *vb.* beat, surpass, outdo, excel *The fund drive this year has exceeded our most optimistic speculations.*

excel *vb.* outdo, surpass, exceed *The Grendel children excel at almost every sport.*

excellence *n.* superiority, distinction *Frank was given an award for excellence in seamanship.* ANT. inferiority, poorness, badness.

excellent *adj.* fine, superior, wonderful, marvellous *The Bluetts always serve an excellent claret with dinner.* ANT. poor, bad, terrible, substandard.

except *prep.* save, but, excepting, barring, excluding *Everyone wanted to go skiing except Donald.*

exceptional *adj.* unusual, different, strange, irregular, abnormal *A real house made out of gingerbread would be very exceptional indeed.* ANT. unexceptional, ordinary, commonplace.

excess *adj.* profuse, abundant, immoderate *The government checked up on all companies they thought might be making excess profits.* *n.* profusion, lavishness *An excess of wealth can lead people to forget God.* ANT. *adj.* sparse, inconsequential, meagre.

excessive *adj.* immoderate, inordinate, extreme, extravagant *Please avoid using excessive force when taking prisoners.* ANT. moderate, reasonable.

exchange *vb.* swap; transfer, trade, barter *I exchanged the damaged article for a new one.* *n.* 1 trade, interchange *In exchange for the three neckties, Suzie took a pair of warm gloves.* 2 market *Don't invest all your money in the stock exchange.*

excite *vb.* stir up, arouse, stimulate; move *Sandra is not easily excited but she thinks the new advertising is superb.* ANT. lull, bore.

excitement *n.* enthusiasm, stimulation, agitation *The public showed considerable excitement when the new model cars were unveiled.*

exciting *adj.* moving, interesting, stimulating; impressive *If you want to see a really exciting film, go see* Interspatial Slime. ANT. boring, dull.

exclaim *vb.* shout, cry, speak out; yell *The critics all exclaimed how much they liked the play's ending.*

exclamation *n.* outcry, shout, clamour *With an exclamation of disgust, he rose and stormed out of the room.*

exclude *vb.* keep out, shut out, bar *Kim says that she always feels excluded from your conversation.* ANT. include, embrace, involve.

exclusion *n.* bar, exception, rejection *The boys' rowdy behaviour led to their exclusion from the cinema.* ANT. inclusion.

exclusive *adj.* 1 limited, restricted, restrictive, selective *Do I have your exclusive permission to represent you?* 2 select, fashionable, choice *We can't afford to stay at an exclusive hotel, so we go to a boarding house.* ANT. (1) general, unrestricted. (2) ordinary, unfashionable, common.

excuse *vb.* forgive, pardon *Please excuse Phil for speaking rudely; he didn't mean it.* *n.* explanation, reason, plea, apology *The teacher accepted Sam's excuse for lateness.* ANT. *vb.* condemn, denounce; deplore.

execute *vb.* 1 carry out, do, complete, achieve *Every employee is expected to execute the orders given to him by his boss.* 2 kill, put to death, hang *Three men convicted for murder were executed last week.*

executive *adj.* administrative, managing *The executive powers of government are in Whitehall.* *n.* manager, administrator, official, supervisor *The aircraft shuttle service between the cities is intended primarily for business executives.*

exempt (from) *vb.* release, free, excuse *John was exempted from doing his exam because of his illness.* *adj.* free, excused, not liable, not subject to *Some people are exempt from paying tax.*

exercise *n.* 1 practice, drill, training; gymnastics *The old man said he did exercises every morning.* 2 use, application, employment *The exercise of a citizen's rights is a duty.* *vb.* train, drill, practise *The soldiers exercised on the parade ground.*

exertion *n.* effort, attempt, endeavour, strain *The exertion of carrying the bed upstairs made us all out of breath.*

exhaust *vb.* 1 wear out, tire, fatigue *I was exhausted from chopping wood for three hours.* 2 use (up), consume; spend *If man isn't careful he may exhaust many of the natural resources of the earth.* ANT. (1) refresh, renew. (2) replenish, replace.

exhaustive *adj.* thorough, comprehensive, inclusive, complete, thorough-going, extensive *We did exhaustive research into women's colour preferences.*

exhibit *vb.* 1 show, display, demonstrate *At the Trade Fair some manufacturers exhibited their future product designs.* 2 betray, reveal *With a sneer Sophie exhibited her scorn for modern art.* *n.* show, display, demonstration, exhibition *We saw an interesting exhibit of weaving at the country fair.* ANT. *vb.* conceal, hide, disguise.

exhibition *n.* display, presentation, show, demonstration, performance *The school put on a fascinating dance exhibition.*

exhilarating *adj.* invigorating, enlivening, inspiring *It was exhilarating to get out into the fresh air after that stuffy room.*

exile *vb.* banish, cast out, expel, deport *The government once exiled criminals to distant colonies.* *n.* banishment, deportation, expulsion *The exile of the king was forced by the revolutionaries.*

exorbitant *adj.* outrageous, excessive, unreasonable, preposterous *At times of shortage, prices for essentials rise to exorbitant levels.*

expand *vb.* enlarge, swell, inflate *The balloon expanded and began to rise.* ANT. shrink, shrivel, contract.

expanse *n.* area, stretch, extent, reach, span, sweep *We floated without power in the vast expanse of outer space.*

expect *vb.* anticipate, await, look forward to *We expected to get a lot of presents at Christmas.*

expedition *n.* journey, voyage, trip, excursion *The expedition into the Amazonian jungle has been gone for a month.*

expel *vb.* drive out *or* away, discharge; banish, deport, exile *Expel from your thoughts any consideration for the victims of the disaster.* ANT. invite; accept.

expend *vb.* use, consume, exhaust *One always expends far more energy than expected in the marathon runs.* ANT. conserve, reserve, ration.

expense *n.* cost, price, charge, payment *Spare no expense in making this the best swimming pool you have ever built.*

expensive *adj.* dear, costly, high-priced *We bought a smaller car because petrol was so expensive.* ANT. cheap, inexpensive, modest, low-priced.

experience *n.* 1 skill, wisdom, judgement; knowledge, contact; observation *I have had a little experience in dealing with naughty children.* 2 incident, event, adventure *His trip to the USA was an experience he'd never forget.* *vb.* feel, live through, undergo *No one can know what war is like until he has experienced it.* ANT. *n.* inexperience, naïvety.

experienced *adj.* skilled, accomplished, expert, practised, able, quali-

fied *My mother is an experienced teacher of foreign languages.*
ANT. inexperienced, untutored, naïve, unpractised.

experiment *n.* test, trial; research *Some people don't approve of doing experiments on animals.* *vb.* test, prove, try, examine *The scientists are going to experiment on human beings for the next space launch.*

expert *n.* authority, specialist *It takes years of training to become an expert in Chinese art.* *adj.* skilful, experienced, knowledgeable, skilled *The factory has three job openings for expert tool makers.* ANT. *adj.* unskilled, untrained, inexperienced.

expire *vb.* 1 terminate, end, cease *My subscription expires with the next issue of the magazine.* 2 die *The old man expired on the steps of the church.*

explain *vb.* 1 clarify, define, interpret *Scientists cannot explain precisely how the earth began.* 2 justify, account for *How do you explain what you were doing at the cinema when you were supposed to be at school?*

explanation *n.* 1 description, definition, interpretation *Please give me an explanation of how a dictionary is written.* 2 account, justification; reason; excuse *The teacher refused to accept Beth's explanation of why she was late.*

explicit *adj.* expressed, express, specific, specified, stated, plain *I left explicit instructions for the work to be done during my absence.* ANT. implicit, implied.

explode *vb.* blow up, burst, detonate, go off *The bomb was set to explode at noon.*

exploit *n.* feat, accomplishment, achievement *Among his many exploits Richard included sky-diving.* *vb.* use, take advantage of *You can be sure that Rupert will exploit everyone he can for his own ends.*

explore *vb.* investigate, examine *I want to explore the use of a cheaper fuel than petrol.*

explosion *n.* blast, burst, detonation, firing *The entire house was demolished in the explosion.*

export *vb.* sell or send abroad *If we export more than we import, then we have a favourable balance of trade.* ANT. import.

expose *vb.* reveal, bare, uncover, display, disclose *The newspaper reporters exposed the corruption in the city government.* ANT. conceal, hide, cover, mask.

express *vb.* state, declare *A civilized person learns to express himself clearly.* *adj.* 1 specific, precise, exact, special *I went to the market for the express purpose of buying celery and then forgot it.* 2 nonstop, quick, direct, rapid, fast *The express train doesn't stop at those small stations.* ANT. *adj.* (2) local, stopping.

expression *n.* 1 statement, declaration *The teacher asked for an expression of interest from all those who wanted to go to the museum.* 2 look; air *Michele had a horrified expression on her face when we showed her the snake.*

exquisite *adj.* 1 delicate, dainty, elegant, beautiful *Have you ever noticed the exquisite workmanship of the crown jewels?* 2 fine, excellent, superb, matchless, perfect *The exquisite furnishings of the palace were known throughout the world.*

extend *vb.* 1 stretch, stretch out *The forest extended as far as the eye could see.* 2 lengthen *The ladder can be extended by as much again.* 3 give, offer, grant; yield *We all extend to you our best wishes on your birthday.* ANT. (2) shorten, abbreviate, curtail.

extension *n.* stretching, expansion, enlargement, increase *We must have an extension of time to complete the tunnel.*

extensive *adj.* wide, broad, spacious, vast *The extensive timber in the Amazonian rainforest will soon be depleted.* ANT. confined, restricted, narrow.

extent *n.* degree, measure, amount, range *Do you know the extent of your father's holdings in Australian property?*

exterior *n.* outside, face, surface, covering *The exterior of our school is painted white.* *adj.* outside, outer, external *Exterior paints are made with materials that resist weathering.* ANT. *n.* interior, inside, lining. *adj.* inner, internal, interior.

external *adj.* exterior, outer, outside *The committee voted to hire an external agency to handle the advertising.* ANT. internal, interior, inner, inside.

extinct *adj.* dead, lost, gone, vanished *More and more animals and plants are in danger of becoming extinct every day.* ANT. alive, present, extant, flourishing.

extinguish *vb.* put out, quench, smother, choke *The foam extinguished the fire very quickly.*

extra *adj.* additional, supplementary, another; spare, reserve *Buy some extra crisps for the party.*

extract *vb.* draw out, withdraw, pull out, remove *The knight extracted the sword from the stone where it had been embedded.* *n.* essence, distillate *I bought a jar of yeast extract from the grocer's.* ANT. *vb.* insert, introduce, penetrate.

extraordinary *adj.* unusual, exceptional, rare, uncommon, remarkable *I heard the most extraordinary story yesterday.* ANT. ordinary, commonplace, usual.

extravagant *adj.* wasteful, lavish, excessive *If you hadn't been so extravagant you would have had plenty of money for your retirement.* ANT. frugal, economical, prudent, thrifty, provident.

extreme *adj.* 1 utmost, greatest *Tim's extreme nervousness made his hands shake.* 2 furthest, outermost, endmost, ultimate *In the picture at the extreme right you can see a mouse.* 3 excessive, immoderate *This morning I am suffering from an extreme pain in the neck.* *n.* end, limit, extremity *I can understand your being angry, but jumping up and down is going to extremes.* ANT. *adj.* (3) modest, moderate, reasonable.

f

fable *n.* 1 parable, tale, legend, myth, story *Aesop's* Fables *are among the most popular in the world.* 2 falsehood, fib, fiction, tale; lie *That story about his getting a medal for swimming was a complete fable.*

fabric *n.* cloth, material, textile *This is too lightweight a fabric for a winter coat.*

fabricate *vb.* make, manufacture, assemble, construct, form *Various parts of the house were fabricated in the plant, then transported here for assembly.* ANT. destroy, demolish, raze.

fabulous *adj.* fantastic, unbelievable, amazing, astonishing, astounding *The returning explorer told a fabulous tale about his discovery of a mountain of gold.* ANT. commonplace, ordinary.

face *n.* 1 look, expression; features, visage, countenance *Roger made a funny face when the teacher wasn't looking. She has a friendly face.* 2 front, façade *The face of the cliff was too steep for us to climb.* *vb.* meet, encounter, confront *I'll never be able to face Louis now that I know he tried to kiss my sister.* ANT. *vb.* avoid, evade, shun.

facetious *adj.* jocular, joking, flippant *Fenwick is never serious, always making a facetious remark.*

facility *n.* 1 ease, skill, skilfulness, ability *The instructor skis down that steep slope with such great facility.* 2 equipment, material *This laboratory is equipped with every modern research facility.* ANT. (1) difficulty, effort, labour.

fact *n.* truth, certainty, actuality, reality *It might be a fact that the earth is round, but I cannot see it.*

faction *n.* (splinter) group, clique, gang, party *There is a small faction that is opposed to free speech for all but their members.*

factor *n.* element; part, constituent; cause *The rate of interest is an important factor in inflation.*

factory *n.* (assembly) plant, workshop, shop *Blatty worked in a piano factory all his life.*

factual *adj.* real, actual; accurate *The reporter gave a factual account of the disaster.* ANT. invented, fabricated, incorrect.

faculty *n.* ability, capacity, talent *Spencer has the faculty of making everyone like him.*

fad *n.* craze, fashion, vogue *The company is hoping that fright wigs will become a fad and earn them a lot of money.* ANT. custom, convention.

fade *vb.* 1 pale, bleach, discolour *These curtains have faded from being in the bright sunlight.* 2 diminish, weaken, fail *My strength* *began to fade and I was afraid I couldn't hold on any longer.* ANT. (2) increase, grow.

fail *vb.* **1** fall short, miss, founder *The explorer failed in his attempt to find the source of the Nile.* **2** disappoint *Don't fail me now that I've invested so much in your success.* **3** fade, weaken; dwindle *Her strength failed when she reached the top.* ANT. (1) succeed.

failure *n.* **1** nonperformance, breakdown, collapse, loss, decline *The failure of the bank was brought about by poor investments.* **2** failing, lack of success *The team's failure to win was blamed on lack of training.* **3** deficiency, insufficiency *Tim was dismissed because of his failure as a supervisor.* ANT. success, achievement, accomplishment.

faint *adj.* **1** dim, faded, indistinct *The writing on the wall of the tomb was too faint to read.* **2** feeble, weak, halfhearted *We heard faint cries coming from inside the chest.* *vb.* collapse, swoon, lose consciousness *Ted's mother fainted when the hospital phoned about his accident.* ANT. *adj.* (1) clear, sharp, distinct. (2) strong, forceful, loud.

fainthearted *adj.* timid, shy, bashful; cowardly *Surgery ought not be watched by fainthearted people.* ANT. brave, courageous, stouthearted, fearless.

fair¹ *adj.* **1** just, impartial, unbiased, objective, unprejudiced; honest *The umpire made a fair decision when he said the batsman was out.* **2** ordinary, average, not bad *My marks for maths were fair.* **3** blond(e), light, white *She had fair hair but a swarthy skin.* **4** beautiful *Every knight yearned to save a fair damsel in distress.* **5** sunny, pleasant, bright, unclouded *The weather man predicted it would be fair for our picnic tomorrow.* ANT. (1) unfair, unjust, biased. (3) dark, black, swarthy. (5) stormy, cloudy, threatening.

fair² *n.* exhibit, exhibition, festival, bazaar, carnival *Are you coming to the fair with us?*

fairy *n.* pixie, sprite, elf, brownie *Don't you believe in fairies?*

faith *n.* **1** trust, reliance, belief *I have faith in everything you say.* **2** belief, religion, creed *The rights of every human being are equal regardless of their faith.* ANT. (1) mistrust, distrust, disbelief.

faithful *adj.* **1** loyal, devoted, trustworthy, trusty, true *My dog is the only faithful friend I have.* **2** credible, accurate, strict *The artist had painted a faithful copy of the picture.* ANT. (1) disloyal, faithless, treacherous. (2) inaccurate, erroneous, wrong.

fake *adj.* false, counterfeit, phoney *The counterfeiters were printing fake five-pound notes until they were arrested.* *n.* fraud, cheat; counterfeit, forgery, imitation *The man who promised to cure your cold is a fake. This diploma is a fake.* ANT. *adj.* genuine, real, authentic.

fall *vb.* **1** drop, descend; plunge, topple *After lightning had struck it in the storm, the tree began to fall.* **2** die *Two thousand brave soldiers fell in the last battle of the war.* **3** lower, decrease, diminish *The price of sugar has fallen during the last month.* *n.* drop, decline, collapse, spill *Prices haven't taken a fall like that for many years.* ANT. vb. (1) rise, soar, ascend. (3) rise, increase, climb. *n.* rise, ascent, increase.

false *adj.* 1 untrue, wrong, fanciful, inaccurate *I knew that your excuse was false, because I saw you do it.* 2 artificial, fake, unreal *False eyelashes don't suit you.* ANT. (1) true, accurate. (2) real, authentic, genuine.

falsehood *n.* fib, story, untruth, lie *That liar tells so many falsehoods that no one believes him when he tells the truth.* ANT. truth.

falsify *vb.* distort, warp, misquote, misrepresent *Our report has been falsified, leading to the arrest of the wrong man.*

falter *vb.* stumble, hesitate, tremble *Once your mind is made up, you should not falter.*

fame *n.* name, reputation, renown, honour, glory *The person who comes up with a cure for the common cold is assured everlasting fame.* ANT. anonymity.

famed *adj.* renowned, known; famous *My grandfather was famed far and wide as an excellent shot.* ANT. unknown, anonymous, obscure.

familiar *adj.* 1 known, common, frequent, well-known *That song sounds familiar—I think it's* 'Greensleeves'. 2 close, intimate *Jennie was a familiar friend at our house.* 3 well-acquainted, well-versed *I am quite familiar with the rules of the club.* ANT. (1) unfamiliar, unknown, foreign, alien. (2) rare, distant. 4 ignorant, unaware.

familiarity *n.* knowledge, understanding, awareness, comprehension *After working on the engine for so long, Don has some familiarity with its operation.* ANT. ignorance.

family *n.* relatives, tribe, relations *During their first years of marriage, the young couple was helped financially by John's family.*

famine *n.* want, hunger, starvation *The famine, owing to the crop failure, resulted in the deaths of thousands.* ANT. plenty.

famished *adj.* starving, hungry, ravenous *After all that work, I was so famished I could have eaten a horse.*

famous *adj.* well-known, renowned, celebrated, famed, eminent, illustrious *My father was one of the more famous residents of the town.* ANT. unknown, obscure, anonymous.

fan *n.* follower, enthusiast, aficionado, devotee *She was a fan of the Beatles for all those years.*

fanatic *n.* enthusiast, zealot, devotee; fiend; addict; (*informal*) crank *Mother is a fanatic when it comes to cleanliness.*

fancy *n.* imagination, fantasy; taste *My mother said that the pink tiles in the kitchen didn't suit her fancy.* *adj.* 1 ornate, ornamented, elaborate *The decorations on that dress are too fancy for my taste.* 2 special, deluxe *We received a basket of fancy fruit for Christmas.* *vb.* like, desire, wish *I just fancy an ice cream.* ANT. *adj.* plain, unadorned, simple, undecorated.

fantastic *adj.* unbelievable, incredible, unreal, unimaginable *You* *look fantastic in that new dress. They told us a fantastic story about a monster rising out of the loch.*

fantasy *n.* illusion, dream, daydream, mirage, delusion, vision *Despite leaving school at sixteen, Bindley never gave up his fantasy of winning a Nobel prize in medicine.*

far *adj.* distant, removed, remote *We have bought a house on the far side of the lake.* ANT. close, near.

fare *n.* charge, tariff, ticket; fee *I could not pay my fare, so I was put off the bus.*

fascinate *vb.* attract, charm, bewitch, enchant *We were fascinated by the wild animal exhibits at the natural history museum.* ANT. bore.

fashion *n.* 1 manner, way, method · *The teacher spoke to the children in a friendly fashion.* 2 style, mode, custom, vogue *Alexandra's mother dresses in the fashion of the 1930s.* *vb.* make, shape, mould, form *The potter fashioned the vase in a few minutes.*

fashionable *adj.* stylish, chic, modish, smart *Nicole's mother is always dressed in the most fashionable clothes.* ANT. unfashionable, dowdy.

fast *adj.* 1 quick, rapid, swift, speedy *A fast car could get me to the airport in an hour.* 2 secure, solid, staunch, firm *Before leaving the house, we made sure that the lock was fast on the door.* *adv.* 1 quickly, rapidly, swiftly, speedily *How did you get back here so fast?* 2 tightly, securely, firmly *The fishermen held fast to the overturned boat.* ANT. *adj.* (1) slow, crawling. (2) loose, insecure.

fasten *vb.* attach, fix, join, secure *You can't even fasten a button to a shirt!!* ANT. loosen, loose, free, release, unclasp.

fat *adj.* 1 fatty, oily, greasy *The doctor told me not to eat so many fat foods.* 2 obese, plump, stout, chubby *Betty used to be fat, but since she has started slimming, she has lost a lot of weight.* 3 thick, wide *The lawyer carried a fat briefcase into court.* ANT. (2) thin, lean, emaciated, slim, scrawny.

fatal *adj.* 1 deadly, lethal, mortal *The wound from the sword proved to be fatal, and the soldier died that night.* 2 disastrous; critical, decisive *Any mistake in timing during a rocket launching could be fatal for the entire project.*

fate *n.* fortune, luck, chance, destiny *It was fate that we should meet here, at the edge of this cliff.*

fatherly *adj.* paternal, paternalistic, protective, kind *My cousin gave me some fatherly advice before I left to live in Glasgow.*

fathom *vb.* penetrate, comprehend, understand *I find it difficult to fathom why Arthur is always so unpleasant to me.*

fatigue *n.* weariness, exhaustion, tiredness *Two days later, the child was found in the woods suffering from fatigue and exposure.*

fault *n.* 1 defect, imperfection, flaw, blemish, weakness *The mechanic could find no fault with the engine in my car.* 2 blame, responsibility *It's your own fault you have a cold if you won't wear your scarf.*

faultfinding *adj.* critical, carping, cavilling, censorious, *(informal)* nitpicking *Alan's faultfinding attitude is not winning him many friends at the club.*

faulty *adj.* defective, imperfect, damaged, broken, malfunctioning *The thieves had no trouble getting in, as the door lock was faulty.* ANT. perfect, flawless, whole.

favour *n.* good deed, good turn, service, kindness *He did Ken a favour by helping him to clean his car.* *vb.* support, want to *We favour going on a tour of Germany for our holiday.* ANT. vb. disapprove of.

favourable *adj.* hopeful, encouraging, promising, beneficial *The prospects for increasing the dividend look quite favourable.* ANT. unfavourable, discouraging.

favourite *n.* pet, darling *Jane is the teacher's favourite.* *adj.* favoured, preferred, liked *My favourite ice cream is chocolate.*

fear *n.* fright, dread, terror, alarm, dismay, anxiety *As the killer approached him with knife drawn, Ron felt his fear overcome him.* *vb.* · dread, be afraid of *This snake is completely harmless, and you have nothing to fear.*

fearful *adj.* afraid, frightened; apprehensive *It was not because of my safety—I was fearful for the sake of the children.*

fearless *adj.* brave, courageous, bold *Our fearless leader walked up to the pirate chief and demanded his surrender.* ANT. fearful, timid, cowardly.

feasible *adj.* practicable; possible, likely; probable *Considering the recent losses, wage increases do not seem feasible at the moment.*

feast *n.* banquet; dinner, barbecue *After the wedding ceremony, we were all treated to a feast at the bride's father's home.* *vb.* dine, banquet *We feasted on venison and roasted ox.*

feat *n.* achievement, act, deed *Leaping across the river on a motorcycle was a feat.*

feature *n.* quality, characteristic, trait *One of the features of life in a democratic country is political independence.* *vb.* star, promote *Last week the television programme featured my favourite pop star.*

fee *n.* pay, payment, remuneration *What sort of fee do you expect to pay your solicitor?*

feeble *adj.* weak, frail; ineffective, powerless *The old lady made a feeble attempt to fight off the robbers.* ANT. strong, powerful, potent.

feed *vb.* nourish, satisfy *My father had six mouths to feed and always worked very hard.* *n.* fodder, forage, food *The farmer stocked up on feed for his cattle for the winter.*

feel *vb.* **1** touch, stroke; grasp, grip *The blind lady felt the raised dots in her Braille hymnbook.* **2** experience, sense; perceive *I tried to feel pity for the doomed criminal.*

feeling *n.* **1** emotion, sentiment, sympathy *Finding her lost kitten gave Susan a feeling of joy.* **2** attitude, belief, thought, opinion *My mother had a feeling that I would do well in school.*

fellow *n.* man, chap, guy; boy *What sort of fellow did she think I was?*

female *adj.* feminine, womanly *Alistair insists that the female mind works differently.* ANT. male, masculine.

fence *n.* rail, barrier, paling *My neighbour has erected a high fence between our gardens to keep out my chickens.*

ferocious *adj.* fierce, savage, bloodthirsty, wild *I keep a ferocious Rottweiler for protection.* ANT. gentle, playful, calm, harmless.

fertile *adj.* productive, rich, fruitful *The entire story was a product of Anne's fertile imagination.* ANT. barren, sterile, unproductive.

festival *n.* celebration, carnival *Every year our town has a Christmas festival in the market square.*

festive *adj.* merry, gay, joyful, joyous *All his friends had a festive time at Miles's birthday party.* ANT. sad, mournful, morose, gloomy.

fetching *adj.* *Informal:* attractive, charming, pleasing *Kathy was wearing a fetching new hat.*

feud *n.* quarrel, argument, dispute, strife *The long feud between our families was finally settled peaceably.*

fever *n.* illness, disease, sickness *Tom has a fever and his mother won't let him come out to play.*

fiasco *n.* disaster, calamity, catastrophe *The theatre group's attempt to stage* King Lear *turned into a fiasco.*

fickle *adj.* changeable, capricious, inconstant *As Gillian is fickle, it makes no difference what she tells you, as she is bound to change her mind.* ANT. steady, constant.

fictitious *adj.* made-up, invented, fabricated, imaginary, false, make-believe, fictional *Did you believe that fictitious story about his being a war hero?*

fidget *vb.* squirm, wriggle *Stop fidgeting and answer the question!!*

field *n.* land, ground, plot, patch; meadow, pasture *We used to keep a cow in the field behind the house.*

fiendish *adj.* demonic, devilish, diabolic(al), satanic *Thewless came up with a fiendish plot for getting even with the headmaster.*

fierce *adj.* savage, ferocious, furious, violent, wild *The circus advertised the wild-animal act as having the fiercest lions and tigers in the world.* ANT. gentle, peaceful, harmless.

fight *n.* battle, war, conflict, combat *When the enemy gunboat fired a shot across our bows, we knew we had a fight on our hands.* *vb.* combat, battle, struggle *Brothers shouldn't fight each other.*

figure *n.* 1 pattern, design *The wallpaper has some pretty figures on it.* 2 form, outline; shape; mould; frame *We could see the figure of a man against the sky at the top of the hill.*

file¹ *n.* 1 line, row, rank, column *The soldiers stood in one long file.* 2 cabinet, index, portfolio, pigeonhole *He kept all his papers in a file.* *vb.* 1 classify, arrange, index *The secretary filed her boss's letters.*

file² *n.* steel, sharpener *He used the file to remove the loose ends.* *vb.* smooth, scrape, rub down *The craftsman filed the wood.*

fill *vb.* stuff, pack, plug; occupy *Cynthia's luggage alone filled the boot of the car.*

filter *vb.* screen, strain, sieve *If you filter the coffee there won't be any grounds.*

filth *n.* dirt, foulness, pollution, sewage *The town is responsible for dumping that filth into the river.*

filthy *adj.* dirty, foul; polluted, contaminated *These socks of yours are filthy because you never wash them. The lake where we swam as children is now filthy because of the factory wastes.* ANT. clean, pure, unspoiled.

final *adj.* last, ultimate, terminal, concluding *This will be the final call for dinner.* ANT. first, initial, beginning, starting.

finally *adv.* at last, in the end, at long last, ultimately, eventually *We were finally able to get the plumber to repair the pipe.*

find *vb.* discover, come across; observe *I found the car keys next to the telephone.*

fine *adj.* 1 excellent, superior, superb, choice, exquisite, perfect *After living in France, we developed a taste for fine foods and wines.* 2 thin, minute; powdered *The holes in the strainer are too fine to allow the tea leaves to pass through. The stone was ground down to a fine consistency.* ANT. (1) inferior, poor, squalid. (2) coarse, broad.

finicky *adj.* finical, fussy, fastidious, meticulous *Sarah is very finicky about her food and her clothes.*

finish *vb.* 1 end, terminate, close, conclude *Please finish whatever you are doing so that you can help me wash the dishes.* 2 consume, use up, complete *Finish your first course and then we'll see if you deserve ice cream for dessert.* *n.* 1 conclusion, end, close, termination *I've written a new finish for my play; do you want to read it?* 2 surface, gloss, polish *We had to have a new finish put on the table because you spilled paint on it.* ANT. *vb.* (1) begin, start, open. *n.* (1) opening, start, beginning.

firm *adj.* 1 rigid, stiff, solid; unchanging, inflexible, steadfast, unshakable *Quentin was firm in his conviction that his father was innocent of the theft. The house was on a firm foundation.* 2 compact, dense, hard *For a really sound sleep, I prefer a firm mattress.* *n.* company, business, concern; partnership *My uncle works for a firm that manufactures paint.* ANT. *adj.* (1) limp, drooping, soft, weak. (2) soft, squashy.

fit *adj.* 1 suited, suitable, appropriate, proper, fitting *It wasn't a fit night out for man or beast.* 2 ready, prepared, suited, fitted *We had all our equipment and were fit to go camping.* 3 healthy, strong; sound, well *The doctor said I could keep fit if I continued to get exercise.* *vb.* 1 hang, be comfortable for *That dress doesn't fit you at all.* 2 agree, suit, harmonize *They made the punishment fit the crime.* 3 equip, provide *We were fitted out for the safari by the biggest store in London.* *n.* 1 fitting, tailoring; measure *The* *shoes were a good fit.*   **2** spasm, convulsion, seizure, attack *Dinah was doubled up in a fit of laughing.*

fitting *adj.*   suitable, apt, proper, due *It is not fitting for a young person to be impolite to adults.*   ANT. unsuitable, inappropriate, improper.

fix *vb.*   **1** attach, rivet, fasten, pin, tie, secure, affix *The teacher fixed the sign to the notice board.*   **2** repair, mend *The man at the shop on the corner is good at fixing record players.*   **3** determine, establish, settle, arrange *We fixed a time for my next appointment.*   *n. Informal:*   predicament, dilemma *There he was, alone in the middle of London, with no money: in a real fix.*

flabbergast *vb.*   astound, amaze, confound *I was flabbergasted when they gave me the bill after dinner.*

flair *n.*   flamboyance, style, panache, élan, dash, drama *You might not like everything that Irena does, but you must admit that she does it with flair.*

flake *n.*   layer, chip; wafer, slice, shaving *After he finished scraping the cabinets, the flakes of paint were all over the floor.*

flame *n.*   fire, blaze *The flame from a match can be seen from miles away on a dark night.*

flap *vb.*   wave, flutter, fly *The flag flapped lazily in the light breeze.*

flare *n.*   flash, blaze, sparkle, glimmer *After the fuse was ignited, there was a brief flare before the firework fizzled out.*

flash *n.*   **1** flame, flare *The people's faces were lit up by the flash from the camera.*   **2** instant, wink, second, twinkling *In a flash, Santa Claus was back up the chimney.*   *vb.*   gleam, sparkle, twinkle, glitter *Maureen's eyes flashed with anger.*

flat *adj.*   **1** level, even, smooth *The land was as flat as a pancake as far as the eye could see.*   **2** dull, uninteresting, boring, lifeless *We all found the play a little flat.*   *adv.*   evenly, smoothly *That rug should lie flat on the floor. The poster was pasted down flat against the wall.*   ANT. *adj.* **(1)** uneven, rough, bumpy.   **(2)** interesting, stimulating.

flattery *n.*   praise, compliment(s) *Don't think that your flattery is going to make me like you any more.*

flaunt *vb.*   display, exhibit, parade, show off *Harold was rude to flaunt his new car before his poor relations.*   ANT. hide, conceal.

flavour *n.*   **1** taste, savour, tang *This pie has the flavour of lemon.*   **2** quality, characteristic, essence, character *That painting really gives you the flavour of the sea.*   *vb.*   season, spice *Vickie flavoured the salad with mayonnaise.*

flaw *n.*   imperfection, spot, fault, blemish, defect *All cars of that model were recalled because of a flaw in the braking system.*

flee *vb.*   run away, desert, escape *When we saw the watchdog coming for us, we fled.*

fleece *vb.*   purloin, steal, rob, filch; swindle, cheat, defraud *Sylvia was known to have fleeced eight elderly ladies out of their life's savings.*

fleet *adj.* swift, fast, rapid, quick, speedy *In ancient times, fleet runners were relied on to carry the news between cities.* ANT. slow, sluggish.

fleeting *adj.* temporary, brief, passing, swift *I caught only a fleeting glance at the sign as we hurtled past.* ANT. permanent, fixed, stable, lasting.

flexible *adj.* **1** elastic, supple, pliant, pliable *You'll need a flexible wire to reach into that clogged drain.* **2** yielding, easy, agreeable, adaptable *My plans for this evening are flexible, so I can meet you at any time.* ANT. inflexible, rigid, firm, unyielding, fixed.

flicker *n.* twinkle, glimmer, flash *I could just make out a flicker of light deep in the tunnel.*

flight *n.* **1** departure, leaving, take-off *The plane's flight was delayed by the fog.* **2** fleeing, running away, escape; retreat *The flight of the Israelites from Egypt is recorded in the Bible.*

flighty *adj.* frivolous, giddy, irresponsible, light-headed *Eustace is too flighty to be relied on for a responsible task.* ANT. stable, reliable, solid, responsible.

flimsy *adj.* weak, wobbly, frail, fragile *Don't put that heavy lamp on that flimsy table. A pain in the toe is a flimsy excuse for staying home from school.* ANT. strong, firm, stable.

fling *vb.* toss, throw, pitch *Walter flung the curtain aside and stepped into the room.* *n.* party, celebration, fun *Roberta has had her fling and can now get back to more serious things.*

flippant *adj.* frivolous, offhand; impudent, rude, impertinent *I only asked her the time and she gave me a flippant answer.* ANT. serious, sober, earnest.

flirt *vb.* make advances, toy with, ogle (at) *Does Marsha still flirt as she did when we were at school?*

flit *vb.* fly, skim, dart *The hummingbird flits from flower to flower drinking up the nectar.*

flock *n.* group, gathering; herd, flight, swarm, school *A huge flock of people attended the presentation ceremony.*

flog *vb.* beat, whip, thrash, strike *If a crew member was found guilty of a crime, he was flogged.*

flood *n.* deluge, overflow *After two weeks of rain, we knew that the river would rise over its banks and cause a flood.* *vb.* deluge, overflow, inundate *When the sink drain clogged up, the water flooded the kitchen floor.*

flop *vb.* **1** bend, fall, tumble, slump *Relaxed, her head flopped backwards.* **2** *Informal:* fail, founder *The whole scheme flopped when we couldn't raise any interest.* ANT. (2) succeed.

flourish *vb.* **1** grow, succeed, prosper *Because of his hard work, Dick's business flourished, and he was soon employing twenty people.* **2** wave, brandish *The Samurai flourished his great sword.* ANT. (1) decline, die.

flow *vb.* **1** stream, pour, run *The mill stream flowed right under the middle of the building.* **2** spurt, squirt, gush, spout *We couldn't* *stop the oil from flowing out of the broken pipe.* n. outpouring, discharge, stream *The doctor first tried to stop the flow of blood from the wound.*

fluctuate *vb.* waver, vary *The price of petrol fluctuated wildly during the crisis in the Middle East.*

fluent *adj.* eloquent, articulate, glib *Joanna is a fluent speaker of Spanish.*

fluid *n.* liquid; gas *Water is one of the most common fluids on earth.* *adj.* flowing, liquid, liquefied, running *You have to heat the butter or lard until it is fluid, for this recipe.*

flush *adj.* even, level, flat *The top of the counter ought to be flush with the top of the cabinet.*

fluster *vb.* agitate, flurry, make nervous or uneasy, rattle, upset *Anne was so flustered by the surprise party that she couldn't speak.*

fly *vb.* **1** soar, wing, hover, flit *At the sound of our footsteps, the scarlet bird flew away.* **2** flee, escape; rush, dart *The minute the door was left open unguarded, the prisoners flew out.*

foam *n.* lather, froth *The foam from the washing-up liquid overflowed the kitchen sink.*

focus *n.* centre, middle, nucleus, core *For years the church was the focus of social activity in the town.* *vb.* concentrate *Focus your attention on the problem at hand.*

foe *n.* enemy, adversary, antagonist, opponent *It is about time that they made peace with their political foes.* ANT. friend, ally.

fog *n.* **1** mist, cloud, haze *We couldn't see our way in the dense fog.* **2** confusion, daze, stupor *Millie is in such a fog that she hardly recognizes her friends.*

foil[1] *n.* **1** metal, sheet, leaf *The mirror had tin foil on the back of it.* **2** contrast, setting, background *The blue scarf serves as a good foil for the colours of the enamel brooch.*

foil[2] *vb.* frustrate, thwart, baffle, hamper *The police foiled the robbers' plans by turning up just as they were about to break into the bank.*

fold *vb.* bend, double, crease *After folding your paper in half, write your name at the top on the left.* *n.* lap, pleat, tuck, overlap *Put two folds into the napkin when you set the table.*

follow *vb.* **1** succeed, ensue *The mother duck swims along first, and the baby ducklings follow.* **2** obey, heed, observe *If you want to play any game at all, you must follow the rules.* **3** chase, pursue, track; trace *Bloodhounds can follow even the faintest scent.* ANT. (1) lead, precede.

follower *n.* pupil, disciple, adherent *The founder of the religion had many followers after a short time.* ANT. leader, director.

following *n.* supporters, disciples, public *For a young woman, she has quite a large following.*

folly *n.* silliness, stupidity, absurdity *Men were criticized for the folly of trying to build a flying machine.* ANT. wisdom; sensibleness.

fond *adj.* **1** attached, partial *I am very fond of chocolate ice cream.*

2 affectionate, loving, tender *Julie was aware of the fond looks being given her by Patrick.*

fondness *n.* liking, affection, partiality *I am developing a great fondness for you, Molly.* ANT. unfriendliness, hostility.

food *n.* sustenance, bread, nourishment, provisions, victuals *We had food for only three days.*

fool *n.* 1 clown, jester *The king always insisted on having the fool at his side.* 2 idiot, dunce, simpleton, blockhead, ninny, nincompoop, (*informal*) nitwit, oaf *If you think you can commit a crime without getting caught you are a fool.* *vb.* 1 jest, joke, play *I didn't mean anything cruel—I was just fooling.* 2 deceive, trick, hoax, hoodwink *The magician had us all fooled—we were sure the hat was empty, but he pulled two rabbits from it!*

foolish *adj.* silly, senseless, stupid, simple *Playing with matches is a foolish thing to do.* ANT. sensible, sound, reasonable, rational.

forbid *vb.* ban, prohibit. *They forbid parking at the entrance to the school.* ANT. allow, permit, let.

force *n.* strength, power, energy, might *The force of the wind is strong enough to knock down that building.* *vb.* 1 compel, oblige, coerce, make *I was forced to accept a purple car because it was the only one available.* 2 drive, impel, push *We forced our way through the crowd.*

foreboding *n.* suspicion, apprehension, misgiving *It was with a sense of foreboding that we entered the cave.*

forecast *vb.* predict, foresee; prophesy *He forecast that he would win the race—and he did.* *n.* prediction, prognosis *Let's hear the weather forecast to find out what the weather will be like tomorrow.*

forefather *n.* ancestor, forebear; predecessor *Our forefathers established this city.*

foregoing *adj.* previous, preceding, former; above *The foregoing material was supplied by researchers.* ANT. following, subsequent; below.

foreign *adj.* strange, unfamiliar, alien, different, exotic *Many of the customs were foreign to us.* ANT. familiar, ordinary, commonplace.

foreigner *n.* alien, stranger, outsider, newcomer *In those days, few foreigners came to visit our village.* ANT. native, resident.

foreman *n.* supervisor, superintendent, overseer, boss *I was told to get the approval of the foreman to leave early.*

foresight *n.* prudence, forethought, provision *George was praised for his foresight in preparing for the storm.*

forest *n.* wood, woods, woodland, grove, copse *The children entered the forest and found a tiny house made of gingerbread.*

for ever *adv.phr.* always, evermore, everlastingly *Nobody lives for ever.* ANT. temporarily, fleetingly.

forever *adv.* constantly, continuously, always *Margaret is forever bothering me to take her to the cinema.*

forfeit *vb.* lose, give up, abandon, relinquish *If you sign that paper you will forfeit your right to the estate.*

forget *vb.* 1 think no more of, not remember *We should both forgive and forget other people's wrongs.* 2 disregard, neglect, overlook, ignore *You can forget Old Scottie when you're picking the football team; he's not played for years now.* ANT. (1) remember, recall.

forgive *vb.* pardon, excuse *Father never forgave me for telling Mother where he had been.* ANT. censure, blame.

forgo *vb.* release, relinquish, renounce *She had to forgo any claim to the inheritance if she married Oscar.*

forlorn *adj.* miserable, desolate, wretched *The poor child looked so forlorn we took her inside.*

form *n.* 1 shape, figure, outline *The prince disappeared, then reappeared in the form of a frog.* 2 kind, sort, type, style *Vinyl is one of the many forms of plastic.* 3 blank, paper, document *Please fill in this form on both sides.* 4 mould, frame, pattern *My father made this form so that I could cast my own lead soldiers.* *vb.* 1 mould, fashion, make, model, construct *As we watched, the glassblower formed a goblet from a blob of molten glass.* 2 instruct, teach, develop, educate *Many people believe that parents have more influence in forming a child's mind than do teachers.* 3 take shape, grow, develop, appear *I have watched clouds form in the sky directly over that mountain.*

formal *adj.* 1 conventional, established *The formal way to do it is to send in an application.* 2 ceremonial, dignified, solemn, stately *There will be a formal marriage ceremony at the church, and you are expected to wear formal clothes.* ANT. informal, unceremonious.

former *adj.* previous, earlier, erstwhile, one-time *This car was not looked after properly by its former owner.* ANT. present, current; future.

formidable *adj.* imposing, alarming, terrifying, frightful, terrible, horrifying *Ed is a formidable chess player.*

formula *n.* 1 form, method, order, procedure *Is there a formula for a happy life? Yes, there is!* 2 equation, rule *The chemical formula for water is H_2O.*

forsake *vb.* desert, give up, abandon, forgo *We have forsaken the excitement of the city for a peaceful life in the country.*

fort *n.* fortress, castle, citadel *It was doubtful that the soldiers in the fort could withstand the siege much longer.*

forth *adv.* forward, onward, out *The knight rode forth to joust with the enemy.*

forthcoming *adj.* future, approaching, prospective, expected *The forthcoming issue of the magazine contains my latest story.*

forthright *adj.* direct, honest, candid, frank, outspoken *Please be forthright with me and stop hedging.* ANT. devious, tricky, roundabout.

forthwith *adv.* immediately, at once, without delay *The police surrounded the building and the fugitive came out forthwith.*

fortify *vb.* strengthen, bolster, buttress *We must fortify our position if we are to survive another attack.*

fortunate *adj.* lucky, blessed, charmed *How fortunate we are to have Angela as our cooking teacher!!* ANT. unfortunate, unlucky, cursed.

fortune *n.* **1** luck, chance, lot, fate *By good fortune, the gypsies were very kind to the lost boy.* **2** wealth, riches *Nellie will inherit a fortune when her grandfather dies.*

forward *adv.* onward, ahead *We marched forward till given the order to halt.* *adj.* **1** front, first, leading, foremost *The forward carriages sank into the marsh before they could stop.* **2** rude, bold, arrogant, fresh, impertinent, impudent *Manuel's forward attitude made him few friends.* ANT. *adv.* backward, rearward. *adj.* (1) rear, last. (2) reserved, shy, demure, retiring.

foster *vb.* promote, support, encourage, nourish, cherish *The purpose of the programme is to foster education among pensioners.*

foul *adj.* **1** dirty, filthy, unclean, impure, polluted *The people who live in that factory town are always breathing foul air.* **2** evil, wicked, vile, sinful *What a foul deed, stabbing someone in the back!* **3** stormy, bad, rainy *We sailed through some foul weather as we rounded Cape Horn.* ANT. (1) clean, pure, immaculate. (2) saintly, good. (3) clear, sunny, calm.

found *vb.* establish, organize *This company was founded in 1852.*

foundation *n.* basis, establishment, ground *Their guiding principles provided the foundations of liberty.*

fracas *n.* dispute, brawl, (*informal*) scrap *Everett caused a terrible fracas at the restaurant when they served him cold soup.*

fracture *n.* break, crack; rupture *There was a slight fracture in the dam, but it increased to a dangerous size overnight.* *vb.* break, crack; rupture *When I fell, my arm was fractured in two places.*

fragile *adj.* delicate, breakable, frail, weak *These champagne glasses are very fragile and must be packed carefully.* ANT. sturdy, hardy, stout, strong.

fragment *n.* bit, part, piece, scrap, remnant *The police had only a fragment of the box that had held the bomb.* ANT. whole.

fragrance *n.* smell, odour, aroma, perfume, scent *The fragrance of the orange blossoms filled the air.*

fragrant *adj.* sweet-smelling, aromatic, perfumed, scented *The florist's shop was fragrant with the scent of flowers.* ANT. noxious, smelly.

frail *adj.* weak, fragile, feeble, delicate *The old lady looks much frailer than she is.* ANT. strong, sturdy, hardy, powerful.

frame *n.* **1** skeleton, framework, support *The frame of this house is too weak to support a slate roof.* **2** border, case *The paintings in the museum have gold frames around them.* *vb.* **1** mount, enclose, border *I have sent the painting of my father out to be framed.* **2** plan, construct, compose, outline *Let us try to frame our activities for the next few months.*

framework *n.* structure, skeleton, frame *I doubt that such a flimsy framework can support my full weight.*

frank *adj.* candid, open, forthright, honest, unreserved, sincere, direct *If I were frank, I would tell you what I think of you.* ANT. devious, dishonest, tricky.

frantic *adj.* wild, frenzied, delirious, excited; hysterical, mad, crazy *The woman was frantic because her little boy had wandered off in the supermarket.* ANT. calm, tranquil, composed.

fraud *n.* deceit, trickery, treachery *The tax examiners suspected the company accountant of fraud.*

fraudulent *adj.* fake, deceitful, tricky, dishonest *The company had sent in fraudulent tax returns for five years.*

freak *n.* abnormality, oddity, curiosity *The carnival always had a collection of very weird freaks, like a headless woman.*

free *adj.* 1 independent, unrestrained, unrestricted, liberated *Britain is a free country, but that doesn't mean it costs nothing to live there.* 2 gratuitous, without charge *The shop was giving away one free bar of chocolate for every five you bought.* 3 loose, unfastened, unattached *We tied one end of the string to a tree and fixed the balloon to the free end.* *vb.* release, liberate, set free, emancipate *The hunter freed the animals caught in the traps. William Wilberforce wanted to free the slaves.* ANT. *vb.* enslave, entrap, snare.

freedom *n.* liberty, independence, release *People everywhere are struggling for freedom from want.* ANT. slavery, servitude, bondage.

freeze *vb.* 1 harden, solidify, ice up *or* over *The lake near us froze during the winter.* 2 cool, refrigerate, chill *My mother froze the meat by putting it in the freezer.*

freight *n.* cargo, load, shipment *The vessel has room for 10,000 tonnes of freight.*

frenzy *n.* excitement, agitation; craze *In a frenzy, the mob attacked innocent bystanders.*

frequent *adj.* common, customary, habitual *The wren was a frequent visitor to the birdtable in our garden.* *vb.* go to, visit often, attend *The teacher noticed that you have not been frequenting the library lately.* ANT. *adj.* infrequent, uncommon.

fresh *adj.* 1 new, crisp, raw; recent, current; late *These eggs are very fresh. The farmer had already planted a fresh crop of wheat.* 2 pure, sweet, drinkable, safe *The fresh water from the stream tasted delicious to the mountaineers.* 3 rested, healthy, energetic, vigorous *The cowboy exchanged his tired horse for a fresh one.* 4 different, original *We need some fresh ideas for the project.* 5 inexperienced, unskilled, untrained *Let's give that young fellow a chance even though he's fresh from college.* ANT. (1) stale, deteriorated; musty; old, out-of-date. (2) impure, polluted, foul. (3) exhausted, tired. (4) stale, unoriginal. (5) mature, experienced.

fret *vb.* worry, anguish, grieve; distress, torment *Don't fret about me—I feel fine.*

friction *n.* 1 rubbing, abrasion, wearing away *The friction of my bicycle wheel against the mudguard slowed my bike down.* 2 disagreement, tension, conflict, discord *I came down for breakfast and could tell there was some friction between my parents.*

friend *n.* companion, chum, mate *I invited a few friends to dinner last night.* ANT. enemy, opponent, foe.

friendly *adj.* kind, helpful, sympathetic, kindly *It was very friendly of you to ask if I needed help carrying my shopping.* ANT. unfriendly, antagonistic.

friendship *n.* comradeship, fellowship, camaraderie, fraternity *Our friendship is more important to me than taking that job in Flitwick.*

fright *n.* fear, terror, alarm, panic *I cannot tell you the fright I felt at seeing Henry, knowing he had died ten years ago.*

frighten *vb.* scare, terrify, panic *You are just trying to frighten the children by telling them ghost stories.*

frightful *adj.* awful, horrible, alarming, distressing *Jason had the most frightful scars where the dogs bit him.*

frigid *adj.* icy, freezing, cold, frosty, wintry, arctic, glacial *It's frigid in this room without the heat on.*

fringe *n.* border, edge; hem, edging, trimming *The farms are around the fringes of the city. The fringes on her skirt are torn.*

fritter (away) *vb.* waste, squander, misspend *Why do you fritter away your time watching soap operas on television?*

frivolous *adj.* silly, trivial, light, foolish *Father regarded learning as important and sports as frivolous.* ANT. serious, sensible.

frolic *vb.* frisk, cavort, play, gambol, romp *You should have seen the headmaster frolicking on the beach!!*

front *n.* **1** face, façade *The front of the house is painted green.* **2** beginning, start, head *Paul always tries to sneak in at the front of the line for ice cream.* *vb.* face, border, look out on *Our house fronts on the main street.* ANT. n. (**1, 2**) back, rear.

frontier *n.* boundary, border *The researchers in Cambridge are working at the frontier of scientific discovery.*

froth *n.* foam, lather, spray; scum *Use a slotted spoon to skim the froth from the top as the stew begins to cook.*

frown *vb.,n.* scowl, grimace, glare *The teacher frowned sternly at the children's misbehaviour, but did not say anything. Paul gave a frown as he didn't want to do what his mother asked.*

fruitful *adj.* fertile, productive, rich, abundant *I think that our meeting has provided me with many fruitful ideas.* ANT. barren, lean, unproductive, fruitless.

fruitless *adj.* sterile, unproductive, barren; vain, futile *The police conducted a fruitless search in the area for the lost dog.* ANT. fruitful, productive, fertile.

frustrate *vb.* defeat, discourage, prevent *I cannot understand why Allyson would want to frustrate our attempts at finding the thief.* ANT. satisfy.

fugitive *n.* runaway, deserter, refugee, escapee *The fugitives from the jail break were caught within a few hours.*

fulfil *vb.* complete, do, accomplish, realize, effect, carry out *Will Carrington be able to fulfil all the duties of his position?*

full *adj.* 1 filled, complete; replete *Don't talk with your mouth full. Since the heavy rains, the reservoir has been full.* 2 taken, occupied, in use *Get to the cinema early, because later on every seat will be full.* ANT. empty, vacant.

fumble *vb.* 1 grope, feel for *He fumbled for his keys in his pocket.* 2 bungle, botch, mishandle *He fumbled the speech because he was so nervous.*

fume *n.* smoke, vapour, steam, gas *The fumes from the back of the car were very strong.* *vb.* 1 smoke *The acid fumed as it ate through the steel.* 2 rage, rave, storm *The customer was fuming because the waiter spilled the soup on him.*

fun *n.* pleasure, amusement, entertainment, merriment, enjoyment, sport, gaiety *We always have fun when we go to the zoo with Uncle Merton.*

function *n.* 1 use; purpose; activity, operation *The function of a teacher is to teach; that of a student, to learn. The function of a watch is to keep accurate time.* 2 ceremony, affair, celebration, party, gathering *The ambassador attended the function at the embassy.* *vb.* operate, work, run *My new radio doesn't function properly.*

fund *n.* reserve, money, capital; supply *Please contribute to the fund for retired lexicographers.*

fundamental *adj.* basic, elementary, essential, principal, underlying, primary *The conservation of matter is a fundamental law of physics.* *n.* basics, elements, essentials, principle *Before learning the details, you must learn the fundamentals.*

funny *adj.* humorous, amusing, comic, comical, laughable *You can count on Murphy to be ready with a funny story.* ANT. serious, sad.

furious *adj.* enraged, angry, raging *Mother was furious when she found that the pie was gone.* ANT. calm, serene.

furnish *vb.* 1 supply, provide *My uncle Harry is in business to furnish companies with the very best staff.* 2 decorate, appoint, outfit *We furnished our living room with a new corner suite.*

further *adj.* more, additional *I doubt that we shall need any further help, thank you.*

furthermore *adv.* further, also, moreover *I don't want to go because I don't like ballet and, furthermore, I have a headache.*

fury *n.* 1 rage, anger, wrath, frenzy *Imagine my father's fury when he found the scratch on his new car!* 2 violence, ferocity, ferociousness, fierceness *After a short period of calm, the hurricane struck again in its full fury.* ANT. serenity, calmness.

fuse *vb.* join, combine, integrate, merge *It is fascinating to see how the artist has fused together the various materials for this collage.*

fuss *n.* bother, to-do, commotion *Why make so much fuss about some water on the kitchen floor?* *vb.* bother, annoy, pester, irritate *I'll get the work done faster if you stop fussing about it all the time.*

fussy *adj.* fastidious, over-particular, choosy, finicky, pedantic *The waiter said I was just being fussy when I refused to eat the steak that had fallen on the floor.* **ANT.** careless, casual.

futile *adj.* 1 useless, pointless, vain, idle, worthless *Trying to persuade Thomas to do his homework is futile during the cricket season.* 2 unimportant, minor, trivial *Don't waste your time on futile activities.* **ANT.** (1) worthwhile, valuable. (2) important, serious, weighty.

future *adj.* coming, to come, approaching, impending, imminent, destined *The future plans for my career have not yet been decided.* **ANT.** past, bygone, former.

fuzzy *adj.* blurred, blurry, indistinct, out-of-focus *How can you tell who that is in such a fuzzy photograph?* **ANT.** clear, lucid, well-defined.

g

gab *vb.* (*informal*) chatter, gossip, jabber, prattle, babble *Sam was just gabbing away, and I couldn't get a word in edgewise.*

gadget *n.* device, contraption, appliance *Ellis invented some sort of gadget for refilling ballpoint pens.*

gag¹ *vb.* stifle, choke, muffle, stop up *The prisoner was gagged to keep him quiet.*

gag² *n. Slang:* joke, story; hoax *John likes to crack lots of gags to make his friends laugh.*

gain *vb.* **1** obtain, get, acquire, win, earn *The home team gained a victory in the last few minutes of the game.* **2** improve, better, advance *The profits from the investments gained value over the years.* **3** increase in *The train gained speed as it travelled downhill.* *n.* **1** addition, increase *The gains by the winning party in the election totalled 30 seats.* **2** improvement *We have been making gains in our fight against poverty.* **ANT.** *vb.* lose. *n.* loss.

gallant *adj.* **1** brave, valiant, bold, courageous *Many gallant soldiers died in that battle.* **2** polite, chivalrous, courteous, noble *Our grandfather had a reputation among the ladies for being gallant.*

gallop *vb.,n.* leap, jump, spring *The horses galloped along the track. The sudden gallop of the pony frightened the little girl.*

gamble *vb.* **1** bet, wager, game *The countess gambled until she lost all of her money at the casino.* **2** trust, hope, expect *Don't gamble on it being fine tomorrow.* *n.* chance, risk *It's a gamble whether my talk with Lester will do any good.* **ANT.** *n.* certainty.

game *n.* **1** amusement, entertainment, play, sport, pastime *The games will start as soon as all of the children arrive.* **2** contest, competition *The game between the two teams was cancelled because of rain.*

gang *n.* band, troop, group, company, crew; horde *The ship was captured by a gang of pirates.*

gangster *n.* crook, criminal, gunman, hit man *There is a rumour that gangsters have taken over the local betting shop.*

gap *n.* space, interval; break *We must fill the gap between the floor and the wall.*

gape *vb.* stare, gaze; wonder, be amazed *When I arrived, the crowd was gaping at the constable standing on his head.*

garbled *adj.* distorted, twisted, mixed-up, confused *We couldn't make head or tail of his garbled story.* **ANT.** clear, straight.

garish *adj.* gaudy, showy; ostentatious; colourful *Mrs Cramwell insisted on having the sitting room painted in the most garish hues of red.* **ANT.** unobtrusive, unassuming, modest; dull, drab, dowdy.

garments *n.pl.* clothing, clothes, attire, garb, apparel *We took some old garments to Oxfam for the poor.*

gasp *vb.* puff, pant, wheeze *Harold finally reached the surface of the pond, gasping for breath.* *n.* breath; puff, pant *She gave a gasp as she saw the door handle turn.*

gather *vb.* 1 assemble, collect, accumulate, come *or* bring together *At Christmas, we gather our friends around us for a party. The relatives of the dead man gathered at the grave.* 2 understand, learn, assume *I gathered from what the teacher said that the exam would be next week.* ANT. (1) disperse, scatter, dispel.

gathering *n.* crowd, meeting, assembly, company, throng *There was a huge gathering in front of the county offices.*

gauge *vb.* estimate, judge; measure, check *The chairman gauged the atmosphere of the meeting and called on the members to vote.* *n.* 1 instrument, device *We measured the tyre pressures with a pressure gauge.* 2 standard, criterion, mark *Exams are a gauge of one's abilities.*

gay *adj.* 1 joyful, joyous, jovial, gleeful, merry, cheerful, happy *What a gay time we had at Cecile's house last night!* 2 bright, colourful, brilliant *The ballroom was decorated in gay colours for the dance.* ANT. sad, mournful, sombre, sorrowful.

gaze *vb.* stare, gape, goggle at, look *We gazed with wonder as the car slowly rose in the air by itself.*

gear *n.* 1 wheel, cog, lever *The driving mechanism on a car has a number of gears.* 2 equipment, material, supplies *The angler took his fishing gear with him.* 3 *Slang:* clothes, accessories *Young people's gear is by no means cheap.*

gem *n.* jewel, stone, ornament *The brooch is set with valuable gems.*

general *adj.* 1 indefinite, miscellaneous, inexact, vague *Our general plans mean that we will be leaving tomorrow, but we haven't worked out the details yet.* 2 common, usual, regular, customary *The general way to do it isn't good enough.* ANT. (1) definite, specific, exact, precise.

generate *vb.* create, produce, make *Does the atomic plant generate electricity economically?*

generous *adj.* 1 charitable, liberal, unselfish *Mr Storm made a generous contribution to the museum.* 2 noble, (*informal*) big, honourable *The committee has been very generous with its efforts to help the elderly.* ANT. (1) stingy, mean, selfish, tightfisted.

genial *adj.* easygoing, cheerful, warmhearted, cordial *Thomas and Regina are the most genial host and hostess I know.* ANT. unfriendly, cold.

genius *n.* 1 ability, talent, intellect, gift, aptitude *My brother has a genius for mathematics.* 2 prodigy, brain *My brother is a genius at mathematics.*

gentle *adj.* 1 mild, kindly, kind *Ken is so gentle he'd never say anything to hurt anyone's feelings.* 2 tame, cultivated, civilized

That tiger cub is as gentle as a lamb. ANT. (1) rough. (2) uncivilized.

genuine *adj.* 1 real, actual, true *If that were a genuine diamond, you'd be able to scratch glass with it.* 2 sincere, unaffected, definite *When I told you that I loved you, my feelings were completely genuine.* ANT. (1) fake, bogus, counterfeit, false. (2) insincere, pretended, sham.

germ *n.* microbe, bacterium, (*informal*) bug *He caught some germ while on holiday in Ibiza.*

get *vb.* 1 acquire, obtain, secure, procure, gain *Where did you get that funny hat?* 2 become, grow, develop *We all get old.* 3 fetch *Go and get your coat: we're leaving.* 4 carry, take *Get that bicycle out of the street!* 5 prepare, ready, make ready *You'll have to get your own breakfast.* 6 persuade, induce, urge *Sam can get anyone to do anything.* 7 come, approach, near *Get over here to my house as soon as you can.* 8 arrive at, reach, come to *When does the train get to London?* *vb. phr.* **get along** succeed, prosper *Will he be able to get along without his mother?* **get by** manage, survive *I'll get by all right on a few pounds a week.* **get in** enter; arrive *Get in the car at once! My train gets in at noon.* **get off** disembark, alight *The train stopped with a jerk and he got off.* **get over** 1 overcome, recover, survive *My father had malaria during the war and he's never got over it.* 2 appreciate, understand, believe *I can't get over seeing you again after all these years.* **get up** arise, rise *I get up at eight o'clock to go to school.*

ghastly *adj.* 1 *Informal:* horrifying, horrible, frightful, frightening, dreadful *Being in a war is a ghastly experience.* 2 pale, wan, white, deathly *When Clare put down the phone she looked ghastly.*

ghost *n.* 1 spectre, phantom, spirit, (*informal*) spook *Have you ever seen a ghost?* 2 trace, glimmer, vestige, hint, suggestion *Without a lot of practice, our team hasn't the ghost of a chance of winning the game.*

giant *n.* ogre, colossus, monster *The giant broke the telephone pole as if it were a matchstick.* *adj.* gigantic, huge, colossal, monstrous, enormous *I had a giant ice-cream cornet and now I can't eat my dinner.* ANT. *n.* dwarf, midget. *adj.* small, tiny, minuscule, infinitesimal.

gibberish *n.* nonsense, rubbish, claptrap, balderdash *They were speaking Swahili, but it sounded like gibberish to me.*

giddy *adj.* dizzy, unsteady, lightheaded *Sophie gets very giddy when she's in the room with Derek.*

gift *n.* 1 present, offering, donation *Although I like to receive gifts, I get much pleasure from giving them, too.* 2 talent, genius, ability, aptitude *Martin's gift for playing the oboe won him a scholarship.*

gigantic *adj.* huge, enormous, giant, large *I never realized how gigantic the moon rockets are till I saw one up close.* ANT. small, little, tiny, infinitesimal.

gingerly *adj.* cautious, timid, gentle *We made gingerly progress* *along the slope of the cliff.* *adv.* carefully, cautiously, gently *The bomb squad handled the mysterious package very gingerly.* ANT. *adv.* roughly.

girl *n.* lass; miss *Carrie was still a girl when the family moved from Linlithgow.* ANT. woman; boy.

gist *n.* substance, essence, point *I couldn't understand every word, but I got the gist of what she was saying.*

give *vb.* **1** provide, donate, supply, contribute, grant, present *I never realized how much your father has given to the town, both in time and money.* **2** yield, give in, give way *I felt the floor begin to give a little where we were standing.* **3** produce, develop, yield *This orchard won't give fruit for seven years.* **4** sacrifice, give up, donate *I have but one life to give for my country.* *vb. phr.* **give away** betray, reveal, divulge *Whenever Peter tells a lie, he gives himself away by stuttering.* **give in** yield, submit, surrender; admit *The weather was so beautiful that the teacher finally gave in and let the children go home early.* **give off** emit, discharge *The chemicals give off a smell like burning rubber.* **give out** **1** distribute, deal, dole *The man at the corner is giving out free sweets.* **2** weaken, tire *My arm gave out and I couldn't play tennis any more.* **3** publish, make known or public, publicize, advertise *The office refused to give out any information until the dead man's relatives had been informed of his death.* **give up** **1** stop, cease, discontinue, end *I've tried to give up smoking, but I can't.* **2** surrender, yield, submit, cede *The robbers gave up when surrounded by the police.* ANT. *vb.*(1) take.

glad *adj.* **1** pleased, happy, satisfied, delighted *I'm so glad that you're coming to my party!* **2** good, encouraging, pleasing *I heard the glad tidings: Marie is going to get married!* ANT. (1) unhappy, sad, morose. (2) gloomy, sombre, dismal.

glamour *n.* allure, charm, attraction *What can match the glamour of Hollywood in the 1930s?*

glance *vb.,n.* peek, glimpse, look *She glanced in my direction but I still tried to avoid her. I caught a glance of the car as it sped around the corner.*

glare *n.* dazzle, flash, brilliance *I couldn't make out who it was in the glare of the spotlight.* *vb.* scowl, stare, glower *The speaker would glare in the direction of anyone who caused a disturbance.*

glaze *vb.* coat, cover, gloss, shine, burnish *We like ham that has been glazed with honey.*

gleam *vb.,n.* beam, glow, glimmer; shine, sparkle *The moon gleaming on the water looked like a silver path to the horizon. The gleam of candlelight on silver and crystal will always remind me of my father's home.*

glee *n.* merriment, joy, cheer, mirth *All you have to do is mention ice cream for dessert and the children jump with glee.*

glib *adj.* easy, slick, smooth *One of those glib salesmen tried to sell me double glazing.*

glide *vb.* slide, slip, flow *We glided silently along the river in the canoe.*

glimpse *n.* sight, glance, impression *I caught a glimpse of the robber's face when his mask fell off.*

glisten *vb.* shine, glitter, shimmer, glimmer, sparkle *Mandy's eyes glistened with tears at the end of the sad story.*

glitter *vb.* sparkle, glisten, shimmer, glimmer, shine *The calm sea glittered in the sunlight.* *n.* light, sparkle, splendour, brilliance *The pop star stood on stage amidst the glitter of all the lights.*

global *adj.* worldwide, international, universal; round-the-world *The company I work for has global interests.*

globe *n.* sphere, orb, ball *The astronauts could see the earth hanging in space like a blue globe.*

gloom *n.* 1 darkness, shade, shadows, dimness *I heard footsteps but could see nothing in the gloom.* 2 sadness, melancholy *A feeling of gloom came over us when we thought about the hungry people.* ANT. (1) brightness. (2) cheerfulness, happiness.

gloomy *adj.* 1 sad, downcast, downhearted, glum, unhappy *The staff were gloomy because the prospect of redundancy hung over them.* 2 dark, dim, shadowy, dismal *The gloomy old house had not been lived in for years.* ANT. (1) happy, cheerful, merry, high-spirited. (2) sunny, bright.

glorify *vb.* 1 praise, worship, exalt *The congregation glorified God as the missionaries told them that many people had been converted.* 2 honour, acclaim, commend, extol, eulogize *The headmaster glorified the achievements of his senior pupils.*

glorious *adj.* 1 famous, renowned, noted, famed, distinguished, splendid, celebrated *It is our glorious tradition that attracts members to the club.* 2 *Informal:* delightful, admirable, wonderful *I've had a glorious day here in York.*

glory *n.* 1 honour, eminence, renown *His bravery in battle has won him much glory.* 2 splendour, magnificence, grandeur *Can we ever forget the glory that was Greece?*

glossary *n.* lexicon, dictionary *Any words you do not understand are explained in the glossary.*

glow *n.* 1 gleam, light *I saw the glow of the city against the sky as we approached.* 2 warmth, heat *The fire cast a warm glow on the children's faces.* *vb.* 1 gleam, glimmer, shine *The hot embers glowed in the fireplace after the flames died down.* 2 radiate, shine *The children's faces glowed with the expectation that Santa Claus would soon be there.*

glowing *adj.* favourable, complimentary, enthusiastic *The critics gave her new play glowing reviews.*

glue *n.* adhesive, paste, gum *A little glue ought to hold the handle on the cup.*

glum *adj.* sad, gloomy, unhappy, dismal, sullen, dejected *Susan is glum because her mother won't allow her to go to the cinema.*

glut *n.* surplus, excess, saturation *Because of over-production there is* *glut of teddy bears on the market.* ANT. insufficiency, deficiency, deficit.

gluttony *n.* hoggishness, piggishness, swinishness *Gluttony is one of the seven deadly sins.*

gnaw *vb.* eat, chew, erode *I found the book, but mice had gnawed it to pieces.*

go *vb.* 1 leave, depart, withdraw *All evening long, people kept coming and going in the large hall.* 2 proceed, move, travel, visit *Let's go to the cinema. My parents went to the United States for a holiday.* 3 become *Stop teasing me or I'll go crazy.* 4 operate, function, work, run *The car won't go unless you turn the key.* 5 pass, elapse *When you're busy, the day goes very quickly.* *vb. phr.* **go about** be busy, work, engage in *Mrs Smith went about her daily business quietly and efficiently.* **go by** pass, proceed *I go by your house every day.* **go off** explode, blow up *Don't let that firework go off in your hand!* **go on** 1 continue, persevere, persist *I just can't go on without you.* 2 happen, take place, occur *At our house there's a lot going on all of the time.* **go over** examine, scan, study *The actor went over his lines again before the rehearsal.* **go through** experience, undergo, endure *Please don't ask me any more questions: I've gone through enough for one day.* **go with** harmonize, match, suit, agree, complement *This grey hat will go with almost anything in my wardrobe.* **go without** fall short, want, need, require, sacrifice *When times are hard, we sometimes have to go without.* ANT. *vb.* (1) come.

goad *vb.* urge, spur, prod, incite, provoke *He blamed her for goading him into saying things he was sorry for.*

goal *n.* aim, object, target, end, purpose *It was his goal to become a doctor.*

go-between *n.* mediator, intermediary, middleman, agent *We should not try to deal with them directly but get someone to act as go-between.*

goings-on *n.pl.* events, happenings, occurrences *With such goings-on all night, I am surprised you got any sleep at all.*

good *adj.* 1 well-behaved, obedient; upright, moral, righteous *If you are a truly good person, other people won't always like you.* 2 qualified, suited, suitable, apt, proper, capable, fit *We have had a great many good applicants for the job.* 3 generous, kindly, kind, friendly, gracious, obliging *There's nothing more important than having good neighbours.* 4 pleasant, agreeable, pleasurable, satisfactory, fine *Did you have a good time at the party?* 5 healthy, sound, normal *You have good hearing to be able to hear a footstep at that distance!* 6 favourable, excellent, profitable *Business prospects are good for the future.* *n.* 1 benefit, welfare, advantage, profit *You'll do it now, if you understand it's for your own good.* 2 virtue, righteousness *Embrace the good and shun evil.* 3 kindness, beneficence *The good that men do is often buried with them when they die.* ANT. *adj.* (1) disobedient, naughty; bad, evil, corrupt. **(2)** unsuitable. **(3)** unkind, unfriendly. **(4)** unpleasant, (*informal*) lousy. **(5)** unhealthy, ill, sick. **(6)** unfavourable, hopeless, desperate. *n.* **(1)** disadvantage. **(2, 3)** evil, wickedness.

good-bye *interj.* cheerio, so long, see you soon, au revoir, adieu, farewell *I had to say good-bye to her at the railway station.* ANT. hello.

good-for-nothing *adj.* worthless, valueless, useless *I wish you'd get rid of that good-for-nothing teapot once and for all.* *n.* idler, malingerer, lazybones, sluggard, layabout *My brother-in-law is a good-for-nothing who hasn't worked for five years.*

good-hearted *adj.* kind, kind-hearted, considerate, thoughtful *It was very good-hearted of you to ask if we needed any help.* ANT. evil-hearted, nasty, cruel, mean.

good-looking *adj.* attractive, beautiful, pretty; handsome *Randolph was good-looking enough to be a movie star.* ANT. ugly; plain.

good-natured *adj.* kind, friendly, amiable, pleasant, cheerful, gracious *Daphne is looking for a husband who is good-natured, not necessarily rich.*

goodness *n.* honesty, virtue, good, integrity *He believed that there was some goodness even in the most evil person.* ANT. dishonesty, badness, evil, corruption, sin.

goods *n.pl.* **1** commodities, wares, merchandise; freight *The goods were brought out of the factory and put onto the lorry.* **2** property, possessions *I've got so many goods; what am I going to do when I move?*

gorge *n.* pass, defile, ravine *The outlaws lay in wait for the stagecoach at the edge of the gorge.* *vb.* stuff, cram, fill *Of course you can't eat your dinner after gorging yourself on sweets.*

gorgeous *adj.* splendid, magnificent, grand, dazzling *Dolly wears the most gorgeous clothes I have ever seen.* ANT. ugly, squalid.

gossip *n.* **1** prattle, hearsay, rumour *Don't believe what you hear about Henry—it's just gossip.* **2** scandalmonger, blabbermouth, meddler *That nosy Mrs Parker is just a loud-mouthed gossip.* *vb.* prattle, tattle, chatter, blab *I knew they must have been gossiping about me because they stopped talking the minute they saw me.*

govern *vb.* rule, control, guide, run; command *The laws governing the use of firearms are complex.*

government *n.* **1** rule, control, command, direction, authority, jurisdiction *The United Kingdom has a democratic form of government.* **2** Parliament, council *Both central and local government can levy taxes.*

gown *n.* dress, frock; robe *Nicole was dressed in a silver lamé ball gown.*

grab *vb.* seize, clutch, grasp *When they shouted 'Fire!!' I grabbed what I could and ran out of the house.*

grace *n.* **1** gracefulness, ease, elegance *I admire the grace with which you got rid of that awful person.* **2** charm, attractiveness, beauty *The princess is noted for her grace.*

graceful *adj.* elegant, artistic, becoming *Virginia certainly has a graceful way of declining an invitation. These models are trained to have a graceful walk.* ANT. awkward, clumsy, ungainly.

gracious *adj.* 1 kind, friendly; courteous, polite *It was very gracious of you to allow me to invite my friend for dinner.* 2 tender, merciful, compassionate *How gracious your wife is to take care of me when I'm ill.* ANT. (1) rude, impolite, discourteous, thoughtless.

grade *n.* 1 position, degree, class, category *There are several grades of blue.* 2 mark, evaluation, award *She got a poor grade in her maths test.* *vb.* arrange, class, categorize *She graded the eggs according to size.*

gradual *adj.* little by little, slow, moderate *The meteorologists have detected a gradual warming of the climate.* ANT. sudden, swift, abrupt.

graft *vb.* join, unite, splice *The hybrid is created by grafting this scion into the branch of the orange tree.*

grand *adj.* 1 elaborate, great, royal, stately *Kings and queens have always lived in a grand style.* 2 splendid, magnificent, sumptuous *A grand feast was arranged for the visitors.* ANT. poor, mediocre; plain.

grandiose *adj.* flamboyant, elaborate, rich, splendid *Arthur had such grandiose plans for a party if he was to win the lottery.*

grant *vb.* 1 give, bestow, confer, award *Charles was granted a leave of absence from the university.* 2 agree, allow, concede, accept *The detective reluctantly granted that I couldn't have been at the scene of the crime.* *n.* award, bequest, gift *My sister received a £1,000 grant for study abroad.* ANT. *vb.* (1) deny, withhold.

graphic *adj.* vivid, distinct, expressive; strong *I wish you would dispense with such a graphic description of your operation.*

grasp *vb.* 1 seize, hold, grab, clasp, grip, clutch *Howard grasped the gun by the barrel and wrenched it from the robber's hand.* 2 perceive, understand, comprehend *I don't quite grasp what you're trying to tell me.* *n.* 1 grip, clutches, clasp, hold *The coin fell from my grasp and slipped down between the bars of the grating.* 2 reach, understanding, capacity *That book is beyond the grasp of a seven-year-old.*

grasping *adj.* greedy, acquisitive, possessive, avaricious, selfish *Jones is a grasping old miser who made his fortune taking advantage of others.* ANT. generous.

grateful *adj.* appreciative, thankful *Don't think that I am not grateful for everything you have done for me, but I won't marry you.* ANT. ungrateful, thankless, grudging.

gratify *vb.* satisfy, please *I was gratified when I saw the results of the plastic surgery.* ANT. frustrate.

gratitude *n.* thankfulness, appreciation, indebtedness *Tell me how I can express my gratitude for everything you have done to help.* ANT. ingratitude, ungratefulness.

grave¹ *n.* tomb, vault, crypt *The mourners stood round the grave as the coffin was laid in it.*

grave² *adj.* 1 sober, thoughtful, solemn, serious *When I saw the doctor's grave expression I knew something was wrong.* 2 important, serious, weighty *Solving the problems of inflation and unemployment are very grave matters.* ANT. (1) happy, merry, frivolous, jolly. (2) trivial, unimportant.

gravity *n.* 1 gravitation, pressure, force *Objects fall to the ground because of gravity.* 2 seriousness, importance; concern *It wasn't until fourteen people had to go to hospital that we realized the gravity of the disease.* ANT. (2) triviality.

graze¹ *vb.* scrape, brush *The child grazed its knee on the side of the fence.*

graze² *vb.* feed, pasture, forage *The sheep were grazing on the grass.*

great *adj.* 1 large, big, huge, enormous, immense, gigantic *A great mountain loomed before us.* 2 noteworthy, significant, important, worthy, distinguished, remarkable *Shakespeare is undoubtedly a very great writer.* 3 chief, leading, main, principal *Sheldon has always been a great friend of mine.* ANT. (1) small, diminutive. (2) insignificant, trivial. (3) minor.

greed *n.* avarice, greediness, covetousness *The director's greed led him to steal money from the safe.* ANT. generosity, selflessness, unselfishness.

greedy *adj.* selfish, covetous, grasping, avaricious *The greedy old man ate all the food, leaving nothing for his children.* ANT. generous, giving, unselfish.

greet *vb.* meet, welcome, salute, address *The hotel manager stood at the door to greet guests.*

grid *n.* framework, network, system *The electricity is sent out over the wires by a huge grid system.*

grief *n.* sorrow, sadness, distress, suffering, anguish, woe, misery *You have caused your mother a lot of grief by staying out so late.* ANT. joy.

grieve *vb.* 1 lament, mourn, weep *Peggy grieved over the loss of her puppy for weeks.* 2 distress, sorrow, sadden, hurt *It grieves me to realize that all people are not honest.* ANT. (1) rejoice, celebrate.

grievous *adj.* dreadful, awful, gross, shameful, outrageous, regrettable, lamentable *Lending Bobby my car was a grievous error.*

grim *adj.* 1 stern, severe, harsh *The headmaster gave the students a grim warning about mugging old ladies.* 2 ghastly, sinister, frightful, horrible, grisly *The skull nailed to the tree was a grim reminder that we were far from being safe.*

grime *n.* dirt, filth; soil; soot *You can wash the grime off with some hot, soapy water.*

grin *vb.,n.* smile, beam *The little girl grinned with delight as she was given the huge teddy bear for her birthday. His broad grin showed that he knew the answer to the riddle.*

grind *vb.* 1 powder, pulverize, mill, crush *The corn was ground* *between the two stones.* **2** sharpen; smooth, even *Try to grind down the rough spots.*

grip *n.* hold, grasp, clutch, clasp *My grip on the branch was weakening and I was about to plummet to the rocks below.* *vb.* seize, grasp, hold, clutch *Grip the handle tightly and don't let go until I tell you to.*

groan *vb.* moan; sob *Did you have a bad dream? I heard you groaning in your sleep last night.* *n.* moan, sob, cry *The old man's groans could be heard throughout the whole hospital ward.*

groggy *adj.* stupefied, dazed, dizzy, stunned *I was groggy from lack of sleep, having driven all night.* **ANT.** alert.

groove *n.* slot, channel, scratch, furrow *The cabinet door slides in this groove.*

grope *vb.* feel for, touch; fumble *I was groping in the dark for the light switch when I was struck and knocked out.*

gross *adj.* **1** improper, rude, coarse, indecent, crude, vulgar *Her gross behaviour shocked her parents.* **2** flagrant, outrageous, extreme; grievous, shameful *The innocent man's conviction was a gross miscarriage of justice.* **ANT.** (1) refined, cultivated, polite.

ground *n.* **1** land, earth, soil *My great-grandfather built his house on a small plot of ground.* **2** grounds, basis, reasons, foundation, base *You have no ground for saying such things about me.* *vb.* train, educate, instruct *I was well grounded in history.*

groundless *adj.* unfounded, baseless *His charge that I hit him first is completely groundless.*

group *n.* gathering, collection, set, assembly, assemblage *A group of us went out for pizzas. There is an interesting group of exhibits at this end of the hall.* *vb.* gather, collect; sort, classify *Group all of the red flowers together.*

grovel *vb.* crawl, fawn, sneak *The boss likes to see people grovel before him when asking for a rise in salary.*

grow *vb.* **1** enlarge, increase, swell, expand *Watch that house grow.* **2** develop, flower *The rosebushes grow very well in this soil.* **3** cultivate, raise, produce, nurture *My father grows tomatoes every year.* **ANT.** (1) shrink, decrease.

growl *vb.,n.* rumble, snarl *The surly old man growled an excuse angrily. The dog gave out a steady growl as we came nearer.*

growth *n.* increase, development *The growth of the sunflower has been incredible!!*

grudge *n.* resentment, ill will, spite, bitterness *Harvey has a grudge against me because I took away his girlfriend.*

gruff *adj.* surly, rough, abrupt, blunt *Tom may be a bit gruff, but he is really very good-hearted.*

grumble *vb.* complain, protest, fuss *Stop grumbling and get on with your work!!*

guarantee *n.* warranty, commitment, promise, pledge *The manufacturer's guarantee says that they will replace any defective parts for* *nothing.* *vb.* warrant, promise, pledge, ensure *I can safely guarantee you'll be home before midnight.*

guard *vb.* protect, preserve, shield, defend *Two armed men were guarding the security van.* *n.* sentry, patrol, watchman, sentinel *There is a guard at every door during the king's visit.* ANT. *vb.* neglect, ignore, disregard.

guess *vb.* estimate, surmise, reckon *Guess what's for tea!* *n.* notion, opinion, hypothesis, theory *I'll give you three guesses how I got here last night.*

guest *n.* visitor, caller, company *Are you expecting guests for dinner?* ANT. host.

guide *vb.* 1 lead, direct, conduct, steer, pilot *I wish I had someone who could guide me through the forest.* 2 influence, affect *Let good judgement guide you throughout your life.* *n.* director, pilot, helmsman, leader *We were able to hire a Sherpa guide for the climb.* ANT. *vb.*(1) follow. *n.* follower.

guilt *n.* blame, fault; responsibility; remorse, self-reproach *He tried to place the guilt on me for something that he had done.*

guilty *adj.* responsible, culpable, blameworthy *The jury found her guilty of murder in the first degree.* ANT. innocent, blameless, guiltless.

gulf *n.* 1 chasm, abyss, ravine, canyon *The gulf that separated us from the lion was fortunately too wide for him to leap over.* 2 inlet, sound, bay *Have you ever been to the Gulf of Mexico?*

gullible *adj.* unsuspecting, trusting, trustful, unsuspicious, naive *Maurice is so gullible that he'll believe anything you tell him.* ANT. sophisticated, suspicious, sceptical.

gulp (down) *vb.* swallow, bolt down; eat, drink *Every morning he gulps down his breakfast and runs to school.*

gush *vb.* spout, spurt, flow, pour, stream *The water gushed out of the hosepipe the minute you turned it on.*

gutter *n.* drain, ditch, sewer *A passing car splashed water from the gutter all over my clothes.*

h

habit *n.* **1** addiction, compulsion, disposition *Reginald has a nasty habit of biting his nails.* **2** custom, practice *You ought to get into the habit of brushing your teeth after every meal.*

haggard *adj.* gaunt, drawn, worn *The survivors were haggard after their long ordeal in the lifeboat.* **ANT.** fresh, animated, bright, clear-eyed.

haggle *vb.* bargain, dicker *After haggling for an hour, the rug-dealer dropped his price by half.*

hail *vb.* greet, welcome, address *The tax refund was hailed by many as the solution to the crisis.*

hairdo *n.* coiffure, hairstyle, haircut *Jane's new upswept hairdo reminds me of the 1940s.*

hale *adj.* hearty, healthy, robust, vigorous *We are very happy to see you looking so hale and hearty.* **ANT.** feeble, weak.

halfhearted *adj.* indifferent, uncaring, cool, unenthusiastic *Will showed his indifference by his halfhearted attempt at being polite.* **ANT.** enthusiastic, eager, earnest.

halfwit *n.* dunce, idiot, dope, fool, simpleton *Anyone who spent hours trying to buy striped paint must be a real halfwit.*

hall *n.* passage, corridor, hallway; vestibule, lobby, foyer *Who is standing in the hall outside my door?*

hallow *vb.* set apart, consecrate, sanctify *These hallowed halls are where my family has lived for generations.*

halt *vb.* stop, cease, hold *The train halted in the station to let passengers get on and off.* *n.* stop, end *The government has called a halt to wasteful spending.* **ANT.** *vb.* start, begin. *n.* start, beginning.

hamper[1] *vb.* hinder, prevent, obstruct, thwart *I was hampered from swimming by my clothes and heavy shoes.*

hamper[2] *n.* basket; pannier, creel *We carried our sandwiches in a wicker hamper.*

hand *n.* **1** fingers, palm, fist *Stretch out your hand, please.* **2** helper, farmhand, assistant, labourer *We have three hired hands at the farm.* **3** aid, help, support *Can someone please give me a hand with this piano?* *n.phr.* **at hand** near, nearby, close *The boy's tenth birthday was at hand.* **by hand** manually *This desk was made entirely by hand.* **on hand** available, ready, convenient, in stock *We always keep spare parts for the engine on hand.* *vb.* give, pass, deliver *Please hand me that wrench.* *vb.phr.* **hand down** pass on, bequeath, give *That hunting rifle has been handed down from generation to generation in our family.* **hand in** deliver, submit, give in

We handed in our essays yesterday. **hand out** distribute, pass out *A man in the street was handing out these leaflets.*

handicap *n.* disadvantage, hindrance *A person's lack of education is a handicap in getting some jobs.* *vb.* hinder, thwart, hamper *The brace on the girl's teeth handicapped her speech.*

handicapped *adj.* disabled; crippled *There are special facilities for handicapped people at the supermarket.*

handle *n.* knob, crank, grasp *Take hold of the door handle and turn it.* *vb.* feel, touch *It is dangerous to handle certain chemicals.*

handsome *adj.* 1 good-looking, fine, comely *Don is as handsome as a film star.* 2 generous, large, big, liberal, ample *My employer gave me a handsome bonus at Christmas.* ANT. (1) ugly, unattractive. (2) mean, petty, stingy, niggardly.

handy *adj.* 1 ready, at hand, near, nearby, close *I always keep a notepad handy by the telephone.* 2 helpful, clever, useful *A can opener is a very handy gadget.* ANT. (2) inconvenient.

hang *vb.* 1 suspend, dangle, drape *The flag was hung from the railing of the balcony.* 2 execute, kill, lynch *The murderer was hanged the next morning.*

haphazard *adj.* random, chance, accidental *The selection of players is haphazard and totally unsystematic.* ANT. intended, designed, deliberate.

happen *vb.* occur, take place, come to pass *What do you think happened once they were alone?*

happiness *n.* joy, delight, joyfulness, elation, ecstasy *Children can bring so much happiness into a home.* ANT. sadness, gloom, melancholy.

happy *adj.* 1 pleased, contented; satisfied *I'm so happy to see you I could hug you! Jimmy was happy to be home again.* 2 lucky, fortunate *By a happy coincidence, the policeman came along just then and the thief ran off.* ANT. (1) sad, gloomy, sorrowful. (2) unlucky, inconvenient, unfortunate.

harass *vb.* 1 torment, bother, trouble *Mother was always harassing me to do my homework.*

harbour *n.* port, haven, anchorage *Rotterdam is one of the busiest harbours in the world.* *vb.* shelter, protect *The farmer and his wife harboured the runaway criminal for two weeks and then the police found him.*

hard *adj.* 1 firm, solid, rigid, unyielding, compact, dense *I could not dig the shovel into the hard ground. This stale bun is as hard as a rock.* 2 difficult, laborious, exhausting *Hard work never hurt anybody.* 3 difficult, complicated, puzzling, tough, intricate *We won't get any of the really hard problems to solve till we get to college.* 4 severe, stern, harsh, strict, demanding *Things will be hard for anyone who disobeys.* 5 shrewd, hardheaded, unsympathetic, cool, cold *Shirley really drives a hard bargain.* *adj. phr.* **hard up** *Informal:* poor, up against it, poverty-stricken; broke *When Jack became unemployed, his family were really hard up.* *adv.*

energetically, vigorously, forcefully, earnestly *My father has worked hard all his life.* ANT. *adj.* (1) soft, pliable, yielding. (2) easy, undemanding, comfortable. (3) simple, uncomplicated, direct. (4) lenient, easygoing.

harden *vb.* solidify, petrify *Once the concrete hardens the post will be secure.* ANT. soften, loosen.

hardly *adv.* scarcely, barely *I hardly know her. I was hardly home a minute when the doorbell rang.*

hardship *n.* difficulty, trouble, affliction *My aunt suffered terrible hardship after the death of my uncle.*

hardy *adj.* vigorous, sturdy, tough, strong *Are these plants hardy enough to survive an arctic winter?* ANT. weak, feeble, frail, fragile, decrepit.

harm *n.* 1 damage, hurt, injury *Your father wouldn't let any harm come to you.* 2 evil, wickedness, wrong *Although they don't want to admit it, gossips really want to do harm.* *vb.* hurt, damage, injure *Alan is so gentle, he wouldn't harm anyone.*

harmful *adj.* mischievous, hurtful, injurious *Some of the plants may be harmful to the cattle.* ANT. beneficial, advantageous.

harmless *adj.* innocent, painless *The colouring matter in food is supposed to be harmless.* ANT. harmful, injurious, dangerous.

harmonious *adj.* 1 melodious, tuneful *Those boys certainly make a harmonious trio.* 2 amicable, congenial *The two companies reached a harmonious settlement of the legal case before it came to court.* ANT. (1) discordant, dissonant. (2) quarrelsome, discordant, disagreeable.

harmony *n.* agreement, accord, unity *We get along in a spirit of harmony and friendship.* ANT. discordance, disagreement, conflict.

harness *n.* bridle, yoke, straps *The horse's harness was attached to the cart.* *vb.* yoke, control *For many years scientists have been developing means for harnessing tides for electric power.*

harrowing *adj.* tormenting, nerve-racking, distressing *The people who were held hostage have gone through a harrowing ordeal.*

harsh *adj.* 1 rough, severe, tough, unpleasant, unkind, stern, cruel *The police may have to take harsh measures to control hooliganism.* 2 rough, coarse, jarring *The harsh cry of the raven was heard in the woods.* ANT. (1) easy, soothing, gentle. (2) melodious, pleasing.

harvest *n.* crop, yield *The new fertilizers helped give the most successful harvest ever.* *vb.* gather, collect, pick, glean, reap *What is not sown cannot be harvested.*

haste *n.* 1 rush, hurry, rapidity, speed *Those who were not fighting the fire left the dangerous area with haste.* 2 scramble, hurry, flurry, rush, heedlessness *If you marry in haste, you may repent at leisure.* ANT. (1) sluggishness, sloth.

hasten *vb.* 1 hurry, rush, run, scurry, scamper, dash, sprint *Timothy hastened to be first in the line to receive the prize.* 2 quicken, urge, press, speed *Mother hastened us on to school in the mornings.* ANT. (1) dawdle, linger, tarry.

hasty *adj.* quick, rapid, swift *When the dog saw the puma, he beat a hasty retreat.* ANT. slow, dawdling.

hat *n.* cap, hood, bonnet, headgear, headpiece; helmet *In this weather you really ought to wear a hat.*

hatch *vb.* brood, breed, bring forth, incubate *The eggs finally hatched and the birds started cheeping at once.*

hate *vb.* detest, abhor, loathe, despise; dislike *I have never understood why Cinderella's stepmother and half-sisters hated her so.* *n.* hatred, loathing, abhorrence; dislike *Judges have a hate of injustice.* ANT. *vb.* like, love, admire. *n.* liking, love, esteem.

hateful *adj.* detestable, loathsome, offensive *Nobody gets along with Martin because he's such a hateful little boy.* ANT. lovable, likable, admirable.

hatred *n.* hate, loathing, aversion. *How do you explain Tessa's hatred of toasted cheese sandwiches?* ANT. liking, appreciation.

haughty *adj.* aloof, proud, prideful, arrogant *Carruthers is too haughty to have anything to do with the likes of you.* ANT. humble, simple, unaffected.

haul *vb.* drag, draw, pull, tow *It took three of us to haul the fallen tree off the road.*

have *vb.* 1 hold, possess, own *Dick has a pony that he got for his birthday.* 2 contain, include *The van has room for all our furniture.* 3 get, receive, obtain, take, gain, acquire *Have another biscuit with your tea.* 4 engage in, experience, undergo *My father had twenty years of army service.* 5 maintain, uphold, hold, believe, say, assert, testify *As the officer would have it, we drove into the river on purpose.* 6 bear, give birth to, bring forth, beget *Anne has just had twins.* *vb. phr.* **have to** must, be compelled to; need to *Do you have to go now?*

hazard *n.* peril, risk, danger *Driving too fast is a hazard not only to yourself but to other drivers.* *vb.* offer, tender, dare *I'd hazard a guess that you're fifteen years old.*

hazardous *adj.* perilous, dangerous, risky *Smoking may be hazardous to your health.* ANT. safe, secure.

hazy *adj.* 1 misty, murky, unclear *The day began hazy, but it later became very hot.* 2 vague, obscure *I don't understand what you mean: what you said is still rather hazy in my mind.* ANT. (1) clear. (2) definite.

head *n.* 1 skull *Robert was hit on the head and he fell down, unconscious.* 2 leader, commander, director, supervisor, chief *We went to talk to the head of the English department about our exams.* 3 source, start, beginning, origin *It took explorers many years to find the head of the Nile.* *vb.* lead, direct, command *Isaac will head this project and tell the workers what they must do.* *adj.* chief, leading, principal, main *The head buyer for the firm has been with them for forty years.*

headquarters *n.pl.* head office, base, centre *The headquarters of our company are situated in Newcastle-upon-Tyne.*

headstrong *adj.* stubborn, obstinate, wilful *Johnny is too headstrong to be easily persuaded to go.* ANT. amenable, easygoing.

headway *n.* progress, movement, advance *Are you making much headway with your plans for the new house?*

heal *vb.* cure, mend *This medicine will help the cut to heal.*

health *n.* wholeness, fitness, soundness, strength *I might not be rich, but I have my health, which counts for a lot.*

healthy *adj.* strong, robust, vigorous, sound *Two weeks after his operation, Adam was healthy enough to go camping.* ANT. unhealthy, ill, sick, unwholesome.

heap *n.* pile, stack, mound, collection, accumulation *There was a heap of rubbish at the side of the road.* *vb.* pile, stack, collect, accumulate *We kept heaping the sand in one place till there was a very high mound.*

hear *vb.* listen; detect, perceive *Hear what I have to say.*

heart *n.* 1 centre, core *The heart of the problem was that we didn't believe anything Jack said.* 2 sympathy, feeling, sentiment; tenderness; pity *Dave has so much heart he'd do anything for you.*

heartbroken *adj.* sad, miserable, wretched, crestfallen, downhearted, brokenhearted, dejected *Tony's script was turned down by the studio and he's heartbroken about it.*

heartless *adj.* cruel, mean, hardhearted, ruthless, pitiless *The heartless hunters killed the mother of the fawn.* ANT. kind, sympathetic.

heartrending *adj.* heartbreaking, depressing, agonizing *The refugees told many heartrending stories about the suffering of little children.*

heat *n.* 1 warmth, hotness, temperature *The heat from the fire singed the blanket.* 2 passion, excitement; ardour, zeal *They said that he struck her in the heat of the moment.* *vb.* warm, inflame, cook *It takes a long time to heat water on a wood-fired stove.* ANT. *n.* (1) coolness, cold, coldness, iciness, chilliness. *vb.* cool, freeze, chill.

heated *adj.* fiery, vehement, passionate, intense *The men engaged in a heated argument till finally one pulled out a gun.*

heathen *adj.* pagan, ungodly, unchristian, barbaric *The Incas took part in heathen rites involving human sacrifices.* ANT. godly.

heave *vb.* 1 hoist, boost, raise *With one final push they heaved up the box.* 2 haul, pull, tug *Three men heaving on the rope couldn't lift the safe.*

heaven *n.* paradise; the empyrean *When he awoke surrounded by such luxury, Aladdin though he was in heaven.* ANT. hell.

heavenly *adj.* 1 blissful, divine, saintly, angelic, holy, blessed *The minister had a heavenly expression on his face.* 2 celestial *Astronomers observe the motions of the heavenly bodies.* 3 (*Informal*) wonderful, marvellous, superb *That gâteau we had for tea was absolutely heavenly.*

heavy *adj.* 1 weighty, ponderous *That trunk is too heavy for you to lift by yourself.* 2 intense, concentrated, severe *There was a very heavy snowfall last week.* 3 burdensome, oppressive, harsh, depressing *The atmosphere was heavy when I walked into the court-*

room. **4** sad, oppressed, serious, grave, gloomy, mournful, melancholy, dismal *He told us the bad news with a heavy heart.* **5** boring, dull, tiresome *I found the play quite heavy going.* ANT. **(1)** light, buoyant, airy. **(2)** light, insignificant, minimal. **(4)** cheerful, happy.

hectic *adj.* active, rushed; excited *Someone always phones during the hectic minutes before I have to catch a plane.*

heed *vb.* obey, regard, observe *You'd better heed the advice your parents give you.* *n.* attention, mind *Don't pay heed to what Jean says, as she's only teasing you.* ANT. *vb.* ignore, disregard, overlook, disdain.

heedless *adj.* unmindful, deaf, blind, inattentive *Heedless of his own safety, Roger dived into the icy water to save the boy.*

height *n.* **1** altitude, elevation, tallness *What is the height of that block of flats?* **2** mountain, peak, prominence *We looked down on the valley from the height.* **3** extreme, climax, maximum *Crossing the street with your eyes closed is the height of stupidity.* ANT. depth.

heir *or* **heiress** *n.* inheritor, successor, descendant *When the old man died, he named you the heir to his fortune.*

hell *n.* perdition, inferno, underworld *He committed so many sins that he will spend eternity in hell.* ANT. heaven.

hello *interj.* hi!, how do you do, good morning, good afternoon, good evening *I said hello to everyone when I arrived.* ANT. good-bye, farewell, cheerio.

help *vb.* **1** aid, assist, support; back, encourage *Can someone please help me lift this piano? In these times we help all the needy people we can.* **2** avoid, prevent *I can't help hiccuping.* **3** serve *Please, help yourself to some more corned beef.* *n.* aid, assistance, support, relief *We need all the help we can get.*

helper *n.* assistant, aide; supporter *Each driver has a helper to load and unload the lorry.*

helpful *adj.* advantageous, profitable, valuable *Your advice has been most helpful.* ANT. useless, futile, worthless.

helpless *adj.* **1** dependent, feeble, weak, disabled *My brother has been helpless in a wheelchair since his operation.* **2** unresourceful, incompetent, inept, incapable *Sarah is completely helpless when faced with a machine that won't work.* ANT. **(1)** strong, independent. **(2)** competent, resourceful, enterprising.

hem *n.* edge, border, edging *Shorten the hem at the bottom of this skirt by two inches, please.*

herd *n.* flock, crowd, group, drove, pack *A herd of elephants stampeded towards us, and we had no place to hide.* *vb.* group, gather, crowd *The guide herded all of the tourists into the coach for the ride home.*

heritage *n.* inheritance, legacy, patrimony *The British take great pride in their heritage.*

hermit *n.* recluse, anchorite, eremite *He lives alone, like a hermit, not talking to anyone.*

hero *n.* champion, idol, star, paladin *Who are the teenagers' heroes this year? A medal was awarded to the hero of the battle.*

heroic *adj.* valiant, brave, dauntless, gallant, courageous, bold, fearless *The fireman made a heroic effort to save the family.* ANT. cowardly, fainthearted, timid.

heroism *n.* bravery, valour, gallantry, courage, boldness *The knight was given huge estates by the king for his heroism.* ANT. cowardice, timidity.

hesitate *vb.* 1 pause, wait, delay *He who hesitates is lost except when crossing the street.* 2 stutter, stammer *The actor hesitated for a moment or two at the beginning of his speech.* ANT. (1) proceed.

hidden *adj.* concealed, latent; obscure; invisible, unseen *The box of letters has lain hidden in the garret for all these years.* ANT. showing; revealed.

hide *vb.* conceal, cover, mask, screen, camouflage, cloak, shroud, veil *You can't hide your true feelings from me.* *n.* skin, pelt, leather, fur *The hides of buffaloes were once worth a lot of money.* ANT. *vb.* show, display, reveal.

hideous *adj.* ugly, frightful, frightening, shocking, horrible, horrifying, terrible, terrifying, monstrous, gross, grisly *Because of the hideous nature of his crime, the people wanted the man hanged.* ANT. beautiful, lovely.

high *adj.* 1 tall, lofty, towering . *That's a very high building.* 2 raised, shrill, high-pitched, strident, sharp *She speaks in a very high voice that gets on my nerves.* 3 important, prominent, powerful *A high official in the government gave me the news.* 4 dear, expensive *The jeweller asks high prices for gold these days.* ANT. (1) low, short. (2) deep. (3) lowly, unimportant, insignificant. (4) reasonable, inexpensive.

highlight *n.* outstanding feature, best part *The highlight of our holiday was a day at the zoo.* *vb.* emphasize, stress, feature *The politician highlighted low investment in industry in his speech.*

highly *adv.* very, extremely *The police say that her behaviour was highly irregular that evening.*

hike *n.* walk, trek, ramble *Let's take a hike through the Pennines.*

hill *n.* mound; headland, incline *We stood on the hill where we could see the surrounding countryside.*

hinder *vb.* interrupt, hamper, slow, delay, obstruct, interfere with, block, thwart, prevent, stop *Nothing could hinder the relentless advance of the avalanche.* ANT. advance, further, promote.

hindrance *n.* delay, interruption, obstruction, interference, barrier, obstacle *The committee's approval removed the last hindrance to the funding of the new civic centre.*

hinge *n.* pivot, link, joint, flap *The door has two hinges attaching it to the door frame.* *vb.* depend, rely, pivot *Success of the project hinges attaching it on getting enough people to support it.*

hint *n.* suggestion, tip, clue; whisper, taste, suspicion *If you don't get the answer in ten seconds, I'll give you a hint. There was just a hint of curry in the soup.* *vb.* suggest, mention *Are you hinting that Felix has been going out with my girlfriend?*

hire *vb.* 1 employ, engage, retain, enlist *The factory hired 200 people today.* 2 rent, lease, charter *We hired a car at the airport and drove it about on holiday.* *n.* rent, rental, lease, let, charter *The marina advertised boats for hire.* ANT. (1) dismiss, fire.

hiss *vb.* 1 boo, disapprove, shout down *The hecklers hissed loudly while the prime minister spoke to the crowd.* 2 spit, buzz, fizz, seethe *The snake hissed and frightened the little boy.*

historic *adj.* significant, important, famous *This will be a historic day in the development of the computer.*

history *n.* chronicle, record, account, narrative, tale, memoir, story *This book contains an entire history of the family, going back ten generations.*

hit *vb.* 1 strike, smite *The ball hit the wall and bounced off. Stop hitting children smaller than yourself.* 2 find, come upon, discover *The young couple hit upon a plan to elope, avoiding their parents' protection.* *n.* blow, stroke *She gave him a hit right in the face.*

hitch *vb.* tie, fasten, tether, harness *The cowboy hitched the horses to the wagon.* *n.* hindrance, interruption, interference *There's been a hitch in our plans and we can't go on the picnic.*

hoard *vb.* amass, save, store *During the shortage, some people hoarded sugar and coffee.* *n.* store, stock, cache *The police found a hoard of gold coins in a box in the chimney.* ANT. *vb.* spend, use, squander.

hoarse *adj.* rough, raucous, deep, husky, grating, harsh *After the test match, all of us were hoarse from cheering for our team.* ANT. clear.

hoax *n.* (practical) joke, trick, prank; deception *Telling the police that their teacher was a drug dealer was nothing more than a schoolboy hoax.*

hobble *vb.* limp, stumble, dodder, totter *Jack has been hobbling round with a sprained ankle all week.*

hobby *n.* pastime, diversion, leisure activity *My uncle collects seashells for a hobby.*

hoist *vb.* lift, raise, heave, elevate *It will take four men to hoist that ladder up to the roof.* *n.* crane, derrick; lift *The hoist was too weak to lift the piano.*

hold *vb.* 1 grasp, clasp, grip, clutch *The woman disappeared into the crowd, leaving me there holding the baby.* 2 have, keep, retain *I am holding onto the book and don't intend to lend it to anyone.* 3 contain *This bottle holds exactly one litre.* 4 possess, have *My uncle holds a history degree from Oxford.* 5 conduct, observe, engage in *The society is holding a meeting next month.* 6 think, believe, maintain, consider, judge *We hold these truths to be important: life, liberty, and the pursuit of happiness.* 7 remain, stick, adhere, cohere, cling *Will that tiny drop of glue hold the entire* *model together?* **8** exist, be valid, be true *Laws still hold even when people break them.* *n.* **1** grasp, grip *Get a good hold on the fishing rod.* **2** sway, influence, control *Geoff's new girlfriend has quite a hold on him.*

hole *n.* **1** opening, tear, rip, aperture *I'm so embarrassed! I had a hole in my sock when I took off my shoe.* **2** burrow, pit, cave, den, lair *The bear crawled into his hole to hibernate for the winter.*

holiday *n.* time off, leave, vacation, rest *After working flat out on painting the house, I need a holiday.*

hollow *adj.* **1** empty, unfilled *The wall made a hollow sound where it was tapped, so we knew it wasn't solid.* **2** empty, false, flimsy, meaningless *We lost so many men in the battle that ours was a hollow victory.* *n.* cavity, hole, depression, pit *The dog crawled into the hollow in the rock and went to sleep.* *vb.* excavate, dig, shovel *The pirates hollowed out a place in the hillside where they hid the treasure.* ANT. *adj.* (1) full, filled, solid.

holy *adj.* **1** blessed, sacred, hallowed, consecrated *We visited many holy places in our tour of Jerusalem.* **2** saintly, pious *Holy people take time to worship God every day.* ANT. (1) profane, unconsecrated, unsanctified.

homage *n.* respect, reverence, honour *I have found ways to do homage to my teachers, who helped me so much when I was young.*

home *n.* **1** family *Wherever my wife and children are is home to me.* **2** house, residence, abode, dwelling *Several thousand homes have been built in the area already.*

homeless *adj.* destitute, desolate; wandering, vagrant *The area is becoming crowded by homeless people who are sleeping rough.*

homesick *adj.* nostalgic; lonely *Of course I get homesick for the green hills near Wanganui.*

homework *n.* study, assignment, (*informal*) prep, work *I am not allowed to go out to play till I have finished my homework.*

honest *adj.* **1** truthful, trustworthy, moral, upright, honourable *The bank tries to employ honest people.* **2** open, candid, forthright, frank, straightforward *If you want my honest opinion, I think you treated her very badly.* ANT. (1) dishonest, fraudulent.

honesty *n.* **1** integrity, uprightness, trustworthiness, fairness, honour *Honesty is a virtue that we seek in all people.* **2** frankness, candour, sincerity *In all honesty, you did steal the money, didn't you?* ANT. (1) dishonesty, fraud.

honorary *adj.* complimentary, gratuitous *Aunt Constance was given an honorary degree by the university.*

honour *n.* **1** respect, esteem, distinction *It was an honour to be selected to head the social committee.* **2** principle, character, honesty, uprightness *Although Jane didn't have to return the money, she did so as a matter of honour.* *vb.* **1** respect, esteem *We honoured the memory of the past president with a special dinner.* **2** admire, revere *The returning football team were honoured by thousands of supporters.* **3** accept, acknowledge, clear *The bank refused to hon-*

our my cheque. ANT. *n.* (1) dishonour, disgrace, shame. *vb.* (1) dishonour, disgrace, shame.

honourable *adj.* 1 honest, noble, just, fair *The hero fought well and went to an honourable death.* 2 illustrious, famed, distinguished *The honourable chairman of the council received a special award.* ANT. (1) dishonourable, shameful, humiliating.

hoodwink *vb.* deceive, fool, dupe, (*informal*) bamboozle *Uncle Don was hoodwinked into giving the fortune-teller fifty pounds.*

hoot *vb.,n.* howl, bellow, yelp; screech, shriek *The workers hooted with laughter at jokes all afternoon and forgot their work. The owl's hoot could be heard a long way away in the stillness of the night.*

hop *vb.,n.* leap, jump *Why do you keep hopping about on one leg? Because with each hop I am giving the other leg a rest.*

hope *n.* 1 expectation, anticipation; desire *My parents have high hopes for me, which is why I am going to university.* 2 trust, faith, confidence *There may not be food on the table, but there's hope in our hearts.* *vb.* desire, aspire, expect *I hope Hugh will invite me to the dance.* ANT. *n.* (2) hopelessness, despair.

hopeful *adj.* confident, optimistic *I am hopeful that we can get this matter settled diplomatically, without resorting to war.* ANT. hopeless, despairing.

hopeless *adj.* 1 despairing, desperate, forlorn *With the score five-nil, the situation looks hopeless.* 2 incurable, fatal, disastrous *His condition is hopeless: I don't think your horse will live.* ANT. hopeful, promising.

horizontal *adj.* level, even, plane, flat, straight *The table is not horizontal, so everything keeps sliding off.* ANT. vertical, upright.

horrible *adj.* horrifying, horrendous, awful, terrible, horrid, dreadful, ghastly *I look horrible after a sleepless night.* ANT. wonderful, splendid.

horrid *adj.* shocking, horrifying, horrible, revolting, repulsive *A horrid little man was standing at the entrance to the carnival.*

horror *n.* 1 terror, dread, alarm *The horror of the murders shocked the nation.* 2 loathing, hatred, aversion *Phil had a great horror of seeing the animal in such pain.*

hospital *n.* clinic, infirmary, medical centre; rest home, nursing home *We must get him to the emergency room at the hospital.*

hospitality *n.* generosity, liberality, graciousness, warmth, welcome *Because of Harold's hospitality, we stayed with him after the fire in our house.*

host *n.* entertainer, master of ceremonies, compère *Chris is working as a host on one of the cruise ships to the Caribbean.*

hostage *n.* security, captive, prisoner *The bank robbers are holding two women as hostages till the police provide an escape car.*

hostile *adj.* unfriendly, antagonistic, warlike *The invasion was regarded as a hostile act of aggression by the United Nations.* ANT. friendly, hospitable.

hot *adj.* 1 burning, fiery, blazing; sizzling, roasting, frying, broiling, boiling, scorching, searing *It can get very hot in the middle of the desert at noon.* **2** spicy, sharp, biting *If you didn't put so much pepper on that curry, it wouldn't be so hot.* **3** violent, passionate, intense, ardent *The question of how to save fuel and energy is a hot issue today.* **ANT.** (1) cold, cool, chilly, freezing. (2) bland, tasteless.

hotel *n.* guest house, inn, motel, hostel *We shall have to stay at a hotel while the plumbing in our house is replaced.*

hotheaded *adj.* reckless, rash, unruly; touchy, testy, short-tempered, irritable *Jerry is too hotheaded to be given so much responsibility.* **ANT.** calm.

hound *n.* dog, beagle, greyhound *The local gentry took part in the fox hunt with hounds.* *vb.* pursue, harass, harry, pester *Pete was constantly hounded by the people to whom he owed money.*

house *n.* building, dwelling, residence *I have to be back at my house by noon.* *vb.* accommodate, shelter, lodge *The new hall of residence will house more than 500 students.*

hover *vb.* float, glide, fly *The hummingbird is able to hover like an insect while sipping nectar from a blossom.*

howl *vb.,n.* wail, yowl, cry; yell *Crowded in the lonely hut, we heard the wolf howling in the distance. With a howl, the dog leaped at the robber.*

hubbub *n.* noise, commotion, fuss, uproar, turmoil *What was all that hubbub at the pub last night when the police were called?*

huddle *vb.* crowd, throng, bunch, nestle *The children huddled together for warmth after the fire went out.*

hue *n.* colour, shade, tone, tint *The hues of the sunset are like those of a rainbow.*

hug *vb.,n.* embrace, clasp, press, grasp *Monica hugged the frightened puppy close to her. Laura's father came home and gave her a big hug and a kiss.*

huge *adj.* enormous, gigantic, immense, colossal, tremendous; large, big *There is a huge difference between what she says and what she means.* **ANT.** small, tiny, miniature.

hum *vb.,n.* buzz, drone, whirr, murmur *The sound of bees humming in the garden is a real delight. The constant hum of traffic in the town is something you can get used to.*

humane *adj.* kind, thoughtful, kindly, merciful, kindhearted, tender, gentle, softhearted *The charity is supported by people who want to ensure the humane treatment of animals.* **ANT.** cruel, mean, heartless.

humble *adj.* **1** lowly, unassuming, modest, unpretending, unpretentious *My father came from humble origins but is now the general director of a bank.* **2** polite, courteous, respectful *You should be more humble when talking to your elders.* *vb.* lower, reduce, degrade, downgrade, shame *Meeting the Prince of Wales face to face humbled me greatly.* **ANT.** *adj.* (1) vain, proud, haughty.

humid *adj.*   moist, damp, close, muggy, sticky *I didn't mind the heat, but it was so humid that you could hardly breathe.*

humiliate *vb.*   degrade, disgrace, shame, humble *Besides its being untrue, it was humiliating for Grace to be accused of taking the money.*

humorous *adj.*   funny, comical, comic, amusing *Uncle Philip seems to have an endless supply of humorous stories to amuse the ladies.* ANT. serious, unfunny, sober, sombre.

humour *n.*   1 amusement, joking, clowning, fun *I really like the style of humour of the Marx Brothers.*   2 mood, temper, disposition *If you want to ask Dorothy for a favour, you'd better wait till she's in a good humour.*

hump *n.*   bump, mound, protuberance, elevation *The dromedary has one hump, the Bactrian camel two humps.*

hunch *n.*   guess, feeling, intuition, notion *I had a hunch I would find you here.*

hungry *adj.*   famished, starved *Not having eaten for two days, of course I am hungry!!* ANT. full, sated, glutted.

hunt *vb.*   1 chase, track, pursue, stalk *Do you want to come to our country house and hunt game at the weekend?*   2 seek, probe; scour *She's been hunting for that book everywhere.*   *n.*   chase, pursuit; search *I went along on a fox hunt just for the ride.*

hurdle *n.*   1 fence, barricade, barrier *The athletes ran the race, leaping over the hurdles.*   2 difficulty, impediment, obstacle *There are many hurdles to overcome in life.*

hurl *vb.*   fling, throw, pitch, cast *The soldier picked up the grenade and hurled it back at the enemy.*

hurry *vb.*   1 rush, run, speed, race, hasten *Dinner is probably ready, so I'd better hurry home.*   2 rush, hasten, urge, accelerate *The police hurried the people along the street away from the fight.*   *n.* rush, haste, bustle *Stop pushing! What's the hurry?* ANT. *vb.* (1) linger, tarry, dawdle.

hurt *vb.*   1 damage, harm, injure *Did you hurt yourself when you fell down the stairs?*   2 wound, distress, afflict, pain *If you tell Liz that she can't go because she's too young, you'll hurt her feelings.*   *n.* injury, harm, pain *I feel the hurt of knowing I'll never see him again.*

hush *vb.,n.*   silence, quiet, still *Hush the children, will you; I'm trying to read! It is so peaceful in the hush of the evening.*

hustle *vb.*   hurry, hasten, race, run, speed *You will have to hustle if you want to catch the five o'clock train.*

hut *n.*   cottage, shed, lodge, shelter *The fisherman lived in a tiny hut by the sea.*

hypnotize *vb.*   mesmerize, entrance, charm, fascinate *Sonia is beautiful enough to hypnotize any man.*

hypocrisy *n.*   sham, hollowness, affectation, pretence *Don't you hate the hypocrisy of people who give to charity only to impress others?*

hypocrite *n.*   actor, pretender, deceiver, fraud *The politicians who* *always try to reduce taxes and increase benefits before an election are the worst hypocrites.*

hypothetical *adj.*   theoretical, speculative, conjectural   *To take a hypothetical case, suppose you were a knight in King Arthur's court.*

hysterical *adj.*   raving, frenzied, uncontrolled, delirious   *Thea was hysterical with grief over the death of her father.*

i

icy *adj.* freezing, frozen; cold *Be careful, as the roads are icy. You had better dress warmly against the icy weather.*

idea *n.* 1 thought, conception, concept *I've just had a great idea: let's go to the zoo this afternoon!* 2 notion, understanding *I haven't the slightest idea what you're talking about.* 3 opinion, plan, belief, view *The head of the company asked me what my ideas were for expansion.*

ideal *n.* 1 model, example, paragon, standard *My ideal kitchen appliance is one that does the dishes by itself.* 2 aim, objective, target, goal *The ideals of the United Nations are peace and friendship throughout the world.* *adj.* perfect, complete, fitting, supreme *This is an ideal spot for a picnic.*

identical *adj.* alike, indistinguishable, like; same *Angela bought the identical dress for ten pounds less.* ANT. unalike, different.

identify *vb.* name, describe, classify; recognize *Gerald was able to identify the woman who had stolen his car.*

identity *n.* individuality, character, uniqueness, personality *Have you any papers to establish your identity?*

ideology *n.* belief, doctrine, credo, principles *Our ideologies might differ, but I recognize that you have a right to yours.*

idiosyncrasy *n.* peculiarity, quirk, mannerism, eccentricity *His obsession with keeping a dozen cats is one of Paul's idiosyncrasies.*

idiot *n.* fool, nincompoop, dunce, moron *Only an idiot would try to hold his breath for five minutes.*

idiotic *adj.* stupid, senseless, foolish, inane, moronic, half-witted, simpleminded, dim-witted. ANT. intelligent, bright, brilliant, smart.

idle *adj.* 1 unemployed, inactive, unoccupied, unused *Five hundred men were made idle by the redundancies at the factory.* 2 lazy, sluggish *An idle mind finds nothing interesting in the world.* ANT. (1) active, busy, occupied, engaged.

idol *n.* 1 image, symbol, graven image, god, statue *The natives fell to their knees before an idol of their water god.* 2 favourite, pet, darling *The Monster was the name of the new rock group that was the idol of the teenagers.*

idolize *vb.* adore, worship, revere *Once idolized by millions, the star is now largely forgotten.* ANT. despise.

ignorant *adj.* 1 untrained, uneducated, illiterate, untaught *Some of the applicants were too ignorant to qualify for the job.* 2 unaware, unmindful, uninformed *Ignorant of the fact that she had just written* *him a letter, Bill tried to ring her up.* ANT. (1) educated, cultivated, cultured, schooled, learned. (2) aware, informed.

ignore *vb.* disregard, overlook, omit, neglect *Our appeal for help has again been ignored by the social services office.* ANT. notice.

ill *adj.* sick, unwell, unhealthy, diseased, ailing *It was the turkey with the chocolate sauce that made me ill.* ANT. well, healthy, fit.

illegal *adj.* unlawful, forbidden, illicit *It is illegal to bring certain goods into the country.* ANT. legal, lawful, legitimate.

illegible *adj.* unintelligible, unreadable, indecipherable *The kidnappers sent a ransom note, but it was illegible and we don't know what to do.* ANT. legible.

ill-mannered *adj.* rude, impolite, uncouth *Cuthbertson is the ill-mannered boor who insulted your wife.* ANT. polite, courteous.

illness *n.* sickness, infirmity, disease, ailment *The family has been advised that Curley's illness is terminal.*

illogical *adj.* irrational, absurd, preposterous *It is illogical to expect sympathy from someone you treated so badly.*

ill-treated *adj.* abused, harmed, maltreated, mistreated *There was a programme on TV last week about ill-treated children.*

illuminate *vb.* 1 light, light up, brighten, lighten *A strange green glow illuminated the sky.* 2 enlighten, explain, clarify, interpret *The difficult lecture was illuminated by many illustrations and examples.* ANT. (1) darken, shadow, becloud, obscure.

illusion *n.* delusion, hallucination, vision, fantasy, mirage *The film was so vivid that I had the illusion I was falling!!* ANT. reality, actuality.

illustrate *vb.* 1 illuminate, decorate, adorn, embellish *The book was illustrated with colour photographs.* 2 demonstrate, show *The salesman illustrated the use of the gadget by peeling potatoes with it.*

illustration *n.* 1 picture, photograph *This book contains hundreds of illustrations.* 2 example, explanation *Dictionaries often give illustrations of how words are used.*

illustrator *n.* artist, painter *The illustrators for this encyclopedia have been careful about every detail.*

image *n.* 1 likeness, representation, reflection *Betsy stared at her own image in the mirror.* 2 idea, picture, notion, conception *In my mind there is an image of what I would want to become when I grow up.*

imaginary *adj.* unreal, fanciful, whimsical *The unicorn might be an imaginary animal to you, but you've never seen one.* ANT. real, actual.

imagination *n.* imaginativeness, originality, inventiveness, ingenuity *It takes a lot of imagination to devise a plan for robbing the Bank of England.*

imagine *vb.* 1 conceive, picture, envisage, envision *Imagine yourself sitting in a restaurant eating your favourite food.* 2 suppose, believe, think *I couldn't imagine what had happened to you.*

imbecile *n.* (*Informal*) fool, idiot, bungler *Only an imbecile would* *believe that the magician had made the rabbit really vanish and reappear.*

imitate *vb.*   follow, copy, mimic, duplicate, reproduce *Try to imitate exactly my pronunciation of these French words.*

immaterial *adj.*   unimportant, trivial, inconsequential, insignificant *Anything you say after the trial is over will be immaterial.*

immature *adj.*   youthful, young; simple, naive *Gregory is too immature to take on the support of the entire family.* ANT. mature, wise, experienced.

immediate *adj.*   1 instant, instantaneous, present *My immediate reaction to your request for a loan is 'no'.*   2 near, next, close; prompt *Let's take care of the immediate problems now and leave the others till later.*   3 direct *The immediate result of the plan was to give housing to the elderly.* ANT. (1) long-range, distant. (2) future.

immediately *adv.*   at once, instantly, forthwith, directly, promptly *I told him to go and he went immediately.*

immense *adj.*   huge, enormous, vast, gigantic, great, large, big *It is impossible to grasp how immense the universe is.* ANT. small, tiny, minuscule.

immerse *vb.*   dip, plunge, submerge *Millie relaxes by immersing herself in a hot bath.*

imminent *adj.*   approaching, forthcoming, impending *With Christmas imminent, everyone is scurrying about shopping for gifts.*

immobile *adj.*   fixed, motionless, stationary *The thief remained totally immobile in the dark, and the police didn't see him.* ANT. mobile, moving.

immoderate *adj.*   excessive, extravagant, extreme *The recent increase in mortgage rates was criticized by the Chancellor as immoderate and inflationary.* ANT. moderate, reasonable.

immoral *adj.*   corrupt, wicked, dissolute *The immoral inspectors were accepting bribes to approve unsanitary restaurants.* ANT. good, upright.

immortal *adj.*   everlasting, eternal, timeless, undying, endless *Cultures may have real heroes, but their gods are always immortal.* ANT. mortal, perishable.

immune *adj.*   insusceptible, protected; exempt *After these injections will I be immune to yellow fever, Doctor?*

impact *n.*   1 contact, striking, collision *The bullet struck the wall with such impact that it went right through.*   2 impression, effect, result, consequence *The impact of the Reformation on Church history was very great.*

impair *vb.*   mar, damage, spoil, destroy *It was a leaking pipe that impaired the operation of the furnace.*

impartial *adj.*   unbiased, unprejudiced, fair *The referees are supposed to be impartial.* ANT. biased, prejudiced, unfair.

impatient *adj.*   restless, anxious *We were all impatient to be on our way.* ANT. patient, self-controlled.

impediment *n.* hindrance, obstruction, obstacle *They put every impediment in our way when we tried to investigate the crime.*

impend *vb.* loom, menace, threaten *The impending storm was correctly forecast by the Met Office.*

imperfection *n.* flaw, blemish, defect *The inspectors will not pass any product that has an imperfection.*

impersonal *adj.* detached, objective, disinterested *As I have nothing to gain or lose, I take an impersonal view of the problem.* ANT. personal.

impersonate *see* **mimic.**

impertinent *adj.* impudent, insolent, rude, disrespectful, saucy *The teacher will not tolerate impertinent behaviour.* ANT. polite, courteous, respectful.

impetuous *adj.* rash, hasty, impulsive *Ken was much too impetuous to have bought his wife a car he cannot afford.* ANT. careful, cautious, thoughtful, prudent.

implant *see* **instil.**

implement *n.* tool, utensil, instrument, device *The die-cutter uses precision implements in his trade.* *vb.* complete, fulfil, achieve, realize *The government implemented their election promises and lowered income tax.*

implicate *vb.* incriminate, involve *Why did John implicate Jacquelyn in the plot to steal the Manet painting?*

implicit *adj.* **1** implied, indirect *The meaning of what he was trying to say was implicit rather than immediately obvious.* **2** unquestioning, absolute, certain *Young children have an implicit trust in their parents.* ANT. explicit, plain.

implore *vb.* beg, beseech, entreat *The children implored their father to allow them to go to the fun park.*

imply *vb.* hint, suggest, indicate, mention *Are you implying that it was I who told the police where he was hiding?* ANT. state, declare.

impolite *adj.* rude, unpleasant, discourteous, insolent, impertinent, uncivil *The shop assistant at Stacey's was very impolite when I asked for a refund.* ANT. polite, courteous, respectful.

import *vb.* bring in, ship in; buy abroad *Britain must import most of the wood used in building and furniture manufacture.* ANT. export.

important *adj.* **1** significant; essential, primary, principal *Filling in a form is an important part of applying for a job.* **2** famous, distinguished, notable *We have had some very important people visiting us.* ANT. (1) unimportant, trivial, trifling, secondary. (2) inconsequential, anonymous.

impose *vb.* require, levy, demand *The government has imposed high taxes on luxuries.*

impossible *adj.* inconceivable, unimaginable, unworkable, preposterous *Many of the things we take for granted today were thought impossible a hundred years ago.* ANT. possible; probable, likely.

impostor *n.* pretender, charlatan, cheat, dissembler *He was an im-*

postor, posing as a man from the gas company just to see what might be worth stealing in your house.

impotent *adj.* weak, powerless, inept *When we ran out of ammunition we were impotent to stop the advance.* ANT. powerful, strong.

impoverish *vb.* make poor, ruin, bankrupt *Many people were impoverished by the huge increases in mortgage interest rates.*

impractical *adj.* unworkable, unrealistic, unreal *Tom's plan for rebuilding the old car proved impractical.* ANT. practical, workable, plausible, viable, feasible.

impregnate *vb.* soak, saturate, fill up, permeate, pervade, infuse *The sponge must be impregnated with the polish before applying it.*

impress *vb.* 1 influence, affect; awe *All of the parents were impressed by their children's achievements in the art class.* 2 imprint, emboss, indent, mark, print *The Roman general impressed his seal on the document.*

impression *n.* 1 effect, mark, influence *The prime minister's speech made a deep impression on me.* 2 mark, dent, indentation, depression *The thief's shoe made an impression in the flower bed outside the window.* 3 opinion, belief, guess, theory *I have the impression that you'd rather not go.*

impressive *adj.* striking, awe-inspiring, stirring, moving; grand, magnificent *The banker lived in that impressive mansion up on the hill.* ANT. boring, tedious.

improbable *adj.* doubtful, unlikely *It is improbable that Carter's wife will let him go fishing.* ANT. likely, probable.

impromptu *adj.* off-the-cuff, spur-of-the-moment, unprepared, casual, offhand, extemporaneous *For an impromptu speech, the foreman's talk was effectively phrased.*

improper *adj.* 1 unsuitable, unfit, inappropriate *The manager told us that blue jeans and sweatshirts were improper attire for the restaurant.* 2 indecent, naughty, unbecoming *My father used to punish any of us whom he heard using improper language.* ANT. proper, fitting, appropriate.

improve *vb.* better, amend, repair, ameliorate. *We are trying to improve our relations with the countries in that part of the world.* ANT. worsen, impair.

improvement *n.* change, development, growth; addition; modernization; amelioration *The improvement of the dockside area will bring much new business to the city.* ANT. deterioration, worsening.

improvise *vb.* ad-lib, extemporize; invent, devise *We had no tools at all and had to improvise in order to repair the engine.*

impudent *adj.* impertinent, fresh, insolent, insulting, rude *That impudent waiter told me that this is not his table.* ANT. courteous, polite, respectful.

impulse *n.* 1 whim, hunch, fancy, caprice, urge *Fanny got an impulse to place a bet on a horse called 'Bottoms Up'.* 2 force, surge, pulse *The impulse of the waves keeps the pump going automatically.*

impulsive *adj.* hasty, rash; spontaneous, automatic *Barry is an im-*

pulsive shopper, preferring to buy what he finds in the shop rather than making a list. ANT. careful, cautious, prudent.

impure *adj.* adulterated, contaminated, mixed, tainted; unclean *The cattle were being affected by the impure water in the area.* ANT. pure, spotless, clean.

inaccessible *adj.* far, remote, (*informal*) ungetatable *The upper windows are inaccessible without a ladder.* ANT. near, close.

inaccurate *adj.* incorrect, wrong, mistaken, faulty *Why bother reading a columnist whose predictions are usually inaccurate?* ANT. accurate, correct, right.

inactive *adj.* motionless, still, inert, idle *During cold periods, reptiles remain generally inactive.*

inadequate *adj.* insufficient; weak, feeble; unsatisfactory *Your bid for the painting was inadequate and a man from Birmingham bought it.* ANT. adequate, sufficient, satisfactory.

inanimate *adj.* lifeless, mineral, inorganic. *In their religion, they believe that inanimate objects have spirits.* ANT. animate, lively.

inappropriate *adj.* unsuitable, improper, unfit; untimely *After some inappropriate remarks about my clothing, the bank manager agreed to give us the loan.* ANT. appropriate, suitable.

incapable *see* **incompetent.**

incense *vb.* enrage, infuriate, anger *Terry's father was incensed to learn that he had taken the car without his permission.*

incentive *n.* inducement, stimulus, impulse, encouragement, influence *When business is bad, some shops offer incentives to draw in customers.* ANT. discouragement, disincentive.

incessant *adj.* unending, eternal, continuous, perpetual, constant, relentless *The woodpecker kept up the incessant hammering, preventing me from sleeping.* ANT. intermittent, irregular, spasmodic, sporadic.

incident *n.* event, occurrence, happening *The police reported that there was another incident at the golf club last night.*

incidental *adj.* secondary, unimportant, trivial *How you feel about orphans is incidental compared with what you can do to help them.* ANT. fundamental, basic.

incidentally *adv.* by the way *Incidentally, how do you expect to pay for this party?*

incite *vb.* provoke, stir up, arouse *Charles was arrested and charged with inciting people to riot.*

inclination *n.* 1 tendency, predisposition, preference, prejudice *My inclination is to do nothing for a week and see what happens.* 2 slope, slant, incline, lean *The inclination of the Leaning Tower of Pisa continues to increase every year.* ANT. (1) disinclination, reluctance. (2) uprightness, straightness.

incline *vb.* 1 lean, slope, tilt, slant *The hill inclines steeply near the top.* 2 tend, be disposed *I incline to think you're right.*

include *vb.* embrace, encompass, involve *The package tour includes a trip in a glass-bottomed boat.* ANT. exclude, omit.

incoherent *adj.* disordered, unclear, inarticulate *The witness gave an incoherent report of how the accident had taken place.*

income *n.* salary, earnings, wages, pay; revenue, receipts, return *At five per cent, your income from savings would be only five pounds on a hundred.* ANT. expenditure.

incomparable *adj.* matchless, peerless, unequalled *The orchestra played Handel's incomparable Water Music.*

incompatible *adj.* conflicting, inconsistent, contrary, contradictory *As the two plans are incompatible, one will have to be discarded.*

incompetent *adj.* unfit, incapable, unqualified; clumsy, awkward *Why must employers be forced to hire incompetent help?* ANT. competent, able, skilled.

incomplete *adj.* unfinished, imperfect *After five years, the Greystones' house is still incomplete.* ANT. complete, finished.

incomprehensible *adj.* undecipherable, unintelligible *The message was written in an incomprehensible script.*

inconceivable *adj.* unimaginable, unbelievable, impossible *It is inconceivable that Tim could have passed the exam without cheating.* ANT. believable, possible.

inconsiderate *adj.* unthoughtful, unthinking, thoughtless, unmindful, careless *It was inconsiderate of you to leave the tools you borrowed out in the rain.*

inconsistent *adj.* contradictory, self-contradictory, illogical *It is inconsistent to swear that you love your country and then spy for Spivonia.* ANT. consistent, logical, coherent.

inconspicuous *adj.* unnoticed, retiring, unostentatious *That inconspicuous old lady down the street won the Nobel prize for physics last year.* ANT. prominent, conspicuous, obvious.

inconvenient *adj.* inappropriate, awkward, troublesome, untimely *The telephone always seems to ring at an inconvenient time.* ANT. convenient, handy.

incorrect *adj.* wrong, inaccurate, mistaken, erroneous *32 is an incorrect total for the numbers 12, 15, and 4.* ANT. correct, accurate, proper, suitable.

increase *vb.* swell, enlarge, extend, grow, prolong, lengthen, broaden *My boss increased my salary this year.* *n.* enlargement, growth, expansion *There has been a huge increase in the price of cheese during the past year.* ANT. *vb.* decrease, shrink, lessen, diminish. *n.* decrease, lessening, shrinkage.

incredible *adj.* unbelievable, improbable, inconceivable *Your excuse that you are late because an elephant stepped on you is absolutely incredible.* ANT. credible, plausible, believable.

incriminate *vb.* involve, accuse, blame, implicate *There is enough evidence to incriminate them in the murder.*

indebted *adj.* appreciative, grateful, thankful *I am deeply indebted to you for your help.*

indecent *adj.* immoral, offensive, shocking, shameful *The students* *have been severely reprimanded for their indecent behaviour.* ANT. decent, upright.

indecision *n.* hesitancy, irresolution, uncertainty *Owing to Dana's indecision, we missed buying the table at auction.*

indeed *adv.* really, in fact, truthfully, surely, honestly *This cabinet proves that David is indeed a fine craftsman.*

indefinite *adj.* uncertain, unsure, vague, unsettled, confused; confusing *The time of the train's arrival is indefinite, so we shall just have to wait.* ANT. definite, decided, unequivocal.

indemnity *n.* compensation, reimbursement, restitution *The indemnity received for the broken vase was much less than its value.*

independence *n.* liberty, freedom; sovereignty, autonomy *People fight and die for their independence.* ANT. dependence, reliance.

independent *adj.* **1** free, autonomous, self-ruling, self-determining *Many African countries, once under British rule, have become independent.* **2** unconventional, uninhibited, self-confident *Karen is an independent girl for her age.* ANT. (1) dependent, subject.

indicate *vb.* **1** signify, symbolize, mean *Yellow lines near the kerb indicate that you cannot park there.* **2** point out, show, designate *The policeman indicated that the best route to the park would be straight ahead.*

indifferent *adj.* unconcerned, uncaring, cool, insensitive, nonchalant *My supervisor was indifferent about my taking a holiday in July or August.* ANT. concerned, caring, earnest.

indignant *adj.* angry, irritated, aroused, exasperated, irate *I was indignant at being told to remain when my classmates were let go.* ANT. serene, calm, content.

indiscreet *adj.* tactless, rash, imprudent *It was quite indiscreet of you to tell Barbara's husband about our lunching together.* ANT. tactful, cautious.

indispensable *adj.* necessary, essential, required *A thorough knowledge of the subject is indispensable if you want to teach it.* ANT. dispensable, unnecessary.

indisposed *adj.* ill, sick, unwell *Mandy cannot talk on the telephone because she is indisposed.* ANT. well, healthy.

indistinct *adj.* vague, blurred, blurry, hazy *The faces in this photograph are too indistinct to identify the people.* ANT. distinct, clear.

individual *adj.* single, separate, apart, different, distinct; special *Each member of the team has his own individual number.* *n.* person, human, being *Each individual will be given his own reading list for the summer.*

indoctrinate *vb.* teach, influence, inculcate, brainwash *It is your responsibility to indoctrinate new students regarding the rules.*

indolent *adj.* lazy, idle, slow, sluggish, inactive *Caperthwaite is much too indolent to be with the company for long.* ANT. vigorous, active, dynamic.

induce *vb.* persuade, influence, convince *We induced Cassie to go to the cinema with us.* ANT. dissuade, discourage.

inducement *n.* lure, enticement, incentive, stimulus *What sort of inducement did they offer you to have double glazing installed?* ANT. discouragement.

indulge *vb.* yield to, gratify, satisfy *Why does Theodora indulge Harry's every whim?*

industrious *adj.* hard-working, busy, diligent, persistent *Being most industrious, I was able to complete the work quickly.* ANT. lazy, indolent.

inefficient *adj.* wasteful, extravagant; incompetent, incapable *The old calculators were much too inefficient for our purposes.* ANT. efficient; effective.

inept *adj.* 1 awkward, clumsy *He is too inept with his hands to become a good watchmaker.* 2 inappropriate, unseemly, improper, unfitting *When Mrs Keane told you she had just lost her husband, it was inept of you to say 'How careless of you'.*

inert *adj.* motionless, unmoving, fixed, static, immobile, lifeless, inanimate *The frog's inert little body lay before me, ready for dissection in biology class.* ANT. moving, quivering, active, lively.

inevitable *adj.* unavoidable, inescapable, sure, certain *Once the fugitive ran into the cul-de-sac, his capture was inevitable.*

inexpensive *adj.* low-priced, modest, economical; cheap *Every time I buy an inexpensive pair of tights they tear in no time.* ANT. expensive, costly, dear.

inexperienced *adj.* untrained, green; uninformed, naive *We pay inexperienced labourers less than our experienced staff.* ANT. skilled, experienced, seasoned, trained.

infamous *adj.* 1 scandalous, shocking, shameful, disgraceful *Her infamous conduct was known to many in the town.* 2 notorious, wicked, evil, bad *Everyone knows about the infamous Spanish Inquisition.*

infantile *adj.* childish, immature, babyish, naive *How could grown men have behaved in such an infantile way?* ANT. grown-up, mature, adult.

infatuated *adj.* fascinated, inflamed, charmed *The moment Arthur met Nellie he was infatuated with her.*

infect *vb.* contaminate, taint, pollute *Be careful to avoid infecting the utensils with dirty hands.*

infectious *adj.* catching, communicable, contagious, transferable *Eustace has a highly infectious disease and must remain in quarantine.*

inferior *adj.* lower, second-rate; mediocre *Alan was sold an inferior diamond for Margaret's engagement ring.* ANT. superior, higher.

infinite *adj.* vast, boundless, innumerable, endless, unlimited, limitless *There are not an infinite number of ways to solve this problem.* ANT. finite, limited.

inflame *vb.* excite, arouse, incite, fire *The speaker was trying to inflame the crowd so they would riot.* ANT. calm, soothe.

inflammation *n.* irritation, soreness, redness; infection *The inflammation is from scratching a mosquito bite.*

inflate *vb.* swell, expand, blow up, distend *Gradually, the huge balloon was inflated with hot air and began to rise.* ANT. deflate, collapse.

inflexible *adj.* rigid, unbending, firm, unyielding, immovable, steadfast *The teacher was inflexible in his requirement that the papers had to be handed in by Tuesday.* ANT. flexible, pliant, yielding, giving, elastic.

inflict *vb.* **1** give, deliver, deal *The gang that attacked us inflicted serious injuries to those who resisted.* **2** impose, levy, apply *The government inflicts heavy taxes on rich people.*

influence *n.* effect, sway, weight, control *The politician had great influence throughout the city.* *vb.* affect, control, sway, impress *The scientist insists on keeping an open mind and will be influenced only by actual facts.*

inform *vb.* notify, advise, tell, relate *Please inform the absent members about what happened at the meeting.*

informal *adj.* relaxed, friendly, easygoing *We just had some friends over for an informal evening at home.* ANT. official, formal, conventional.

information *n.* facts, data, knowledge; intelligence *The information in these reference books is checked and verified.*

informative *adj.* enlightening, instructive, educational *We had a most informative talk with your cousin about the murder weapon.*

informer *n.* betrayer, traitor, tattler, (*slang*) rat *Ellis was the informer who told the club's secrets to his mother.*

infrequent *adj.* occasional, scarce, sparse *Our visits to Grannie's house became more and more infrequent.* ANT. frequent, regular.

infuriate *vb.* anger, annoy, enrage *Father was infuriated when he learnt that Roger had taken the car.*

ingenious *adj.* clever, skilful, imaginative, inventive *Peter has come up with an ingenious solution to the problem.*

ingenuous *adj.* naive, simple, innocent, unsophisticated *The idea of losing weight by starving yourself is ingenuous to say the least.*

ingredient *n.* element, component, constituent *Don't leave out the baking powder, a most important ingredient.*

inhabit *vb.* occupy; live, dwell, *or* reside in *Poor families now inhabit the B and B's in town.*

inhabitant *n.* resident, citizen; native *The inhabitants of certain parts of the city pay very high rents.*

inheritance *n.* heritage, legacy, patrimony *Bennie thought his uncle was rich, but the entire inheritance was only a hundred pounds.*

inhibit *vb.* curb, repress, control, restrain *The presence of the police was the only thing that inhibited the robbery that night.*

inhuman *adj.* barbaric, savage, brutal, bestial *An international commission was investigating the inhuman treatment of prisoners.*

initial *adj.* first, basic, primary, elementary *When I heard the news,* *my initial reaction was to tell everyone I knew.* ANT. last, final, terminal.

initiate *vb.* start, begin, commence, open *The ceremonies were initiated by the welcoming speeches of the council.* ANT. stop, finish, terminate.

initiative *n.* enterprise; enthusiasm; energy, vigour *Bill raked the leaves in the garden on his own initiative!!*

inject *vb.* inoculate, vaccinate *The doctor injected me with some antibacterial drug which reduced the swelling.*

injure *vb.* harm, hurt, wound, damage *How many people were injured in that car crash?*

injury *n.* harm, damage, hurt, impairment *The driver sustained an injury to his toe.*

inmate *n.* prisoner, convict, internee; patient *We met when we were fellow inmates at the hospital.*

inn *n.* public house, tavern; hotel *Some of the country inns serve excellent food.*

innocent *adj.* 1 not guilty, blameless, faultless, virtuous *The defendant was found to be innocent and was set free.* 2 unknowing, naive, unsophisticated *Innocent young people are not allowed to see that kind of film.* ANT. (1) guilty, blameworthy. (2) sophisticated, wise, worldly.

innumerable *adj.* numberless, countless, immeasurable *Innumerable people attended the political rally.*

inquisitive *adj.* prying, curious, intrusive, (*slang*) nosy *Why are you so inquisitive about where I buy my bread?* ANT. uninterested, incurious.

insane *adj.* 1 mad, crazy, deranged, lunatic, demented, mentally unsound *The murderer was declared legally insane.* 2 foolish, stupid, idiotic *You're insane to dive off that tower into a small tank of water.* ANT. (1) sane, coherent, rational.

insecure *adj.* shaky, nervous, uneasy, uncertain *I feel insecure about investing all my money in hula hoops at this time.*

insensitive *adj.* callous, hard, tough, unfeeling *The officials' insensitive attitude towards the elderly is unforgivable.*

insert *vb.* introduce, put in *Insert the key in the lock and turn it to the right.*

inside *n.* interior, lining; heart, centre *How could the inside of such an ugly building be so beautiful?*

insignificant *adj.* unimportant, irrelevant, trifling *Price increases always seem major, while the decreases are always insignificant.* ANT. important, significant.

insincere *adj.* deceitful, dishonest, false *By the way he said 'I love you', Sylvia knew that Michael was insincere.*

insipid *adj.* boring, uninteresting, tasteless *I cannot understand how Mrs Hastings can be so proud of such an insipid collection of antiques.* ANT. lively.

insist *vb.* demand, require, command *The solicitors insisted on seeing the financial director.*

insolent *adj.* impertinent, rude, disrespectful, insulting *That boy has to learn not to be insolent to his elders.* ANT. polite, courteous, respectful.

inspect *vb.* examine, investigate, study *All our products are carefully inspected before being offered for sale.*

inspiration *n.* impulse, stimulus, spur, motivation, incentive; thought, idea *Edward's inspiration led to the development of a new kind of apple.*

inspire *vb.* stimulate, encourage, invigorate; animate, quicken *A truly gifted teacher can always inspire some of his students.*

instability *n.* unsteadiness, imbalance *The basic instability in the structural steel caused the building to quiver in a wind.* ANT. stability, balance.

install *vb.* establish, set up, put in *The men came to install the new boiler today.*

instance *n.* case, example, occasion, illustration *Last night's robbery is another instance of the rise in crime in that neighbourhood.*

instant *n.* moment, flash, twinkling *She called and he was beside her in an instant.*

instantly *adv.* at once, immediately, right away, directly, instantaneously *When the sergeant gives an order, he expects it to be obeyed instantly.*

instil *vb.* implant, infuse, imbue; introduce *The teachers are trying to instil in their students a respect for knowledge.*

instinct *n.* feeling, intuition *They used to think that pigeons found their way home by instinct.*

institute *vb.* establish, organize, found, launch, begin, initiate *We had to institute a new set of regulations when they hired women.*

institution *n.* organization, establishment, association; college, hospital *They say that marriage is a marvellous institution, but who wants to live in an institution?*

instruct *vb.* **1** teach, educate, train, tutor, school, drill *The gym teacher instructed us in the art of self-defence.* **2** order, command, direct *We were instructed to be very quiet during the ceremony.*

instruction *n.* **1** teaching, training, education, guidance *Miles plays the violin beautifully, but he's never had any instruction.* **2** direction, order, command *The instruction was to proceed to the end of the street and turn right.*

instrument *n.* tool, implement, device, equipment *The surgeon's instruments are already in the autoclave.*

insufficient *adj.* inadequate, unsatisfactory; poor, meagre *Who can live on the insufficient funds provided by the state?*

insult *vb.* offend, outrage, humiliate *I won't insult you by telling you what I think of that cake you baked.* *n.* offence, affront, outrage, scorn *Even though you love your dog, telling me that I look like him is an insult.* ANT. *vb.* flatter, praise. *n.* flattery, praise.

integrity *n.* **1** soundness, wholeness, solidity, stability *You cannot remove a brick from that wall without threatening the integrity of the entire structure.* **2** honesty, uprightness, honour, principle, virtue *We need more people of integrity in government.*

intellect *n.* **1** judgement, understanding *The men who planned the raid were of low intellect.* **2** intelligence, mind, mentality, brains *There can be no doubt that Albert Einstein was a man with enormous intellect.*

intellectual *adj.* intelligent, learned *I don't think you will find this comic too intellectual.* *n.* academic, scholar *The intellectuals are all in favour of higher government grants to the arts.*

intelligence *n.* ability, skill, aptitude; understanding *Herman is a student of high intelligence who gets good marks.*

intelligent *adj.* bright, clever, quick, astute, alert *The more intelligent students learn all the time, not only when they are studying.* ANT. stupid, slow, unintelligent, dumb.

intelligible *adj.* comprehensible; clear, plain *We relied on the analysts to make the economic statistics intelligible.*

intend *vb.* mean; expect; plan, propose *What do you intend to do about your dog when you go away on holiday?*

intense *adj.* **1** deep, profound, concentrated, serious, earnest *Felicity was wrapped up in her own intense thoughts.* **2** concentrated, great, heightened, intensified, exceptional *The intense heat from the burning building scorched the trees nearby.*

intensify *vb.* raise, magnify, reinforce, sharpen *The more companies that bid on the project the greater the intensity of the competition.*

intent *n.* aim, purpose, intention *The man had been arrested for attacking the pedestrian with intent to kill him.* *adj.* concentrated, set; steadfast *Philip was intent on becoming a doctor, and after years of study, his ambitions were fulfilled.*

intention *n.* plan, intent, purpose, expectation, design, aim *Is it your intention to marry the baker's daughter?*

intentional *adj.* purposeful, deliberate, planned, intended *What makes you think that his stepping on your toe was intentional?* ANT. accidental, chance.

intentionally *adv.* purposefully, on purpose, deliberately; maliciously *Mrs Murphy would never intentionally insult anyone.* ANT. accidentally.

intercept *vb.* stop, seize, ambush; deflect, (*informal*) head off *The customs agents intercepted a huge shipment of drugs yesterday.*

interest *n.* **1** concern, care, attention *The scientist examined the fossil with interest.* **2** profit, advantage, benefit, gain *It's in your own interest to do well at school.* **3** right, share, ownership, claim *Yes, I do have a small interest in that publishing company.* **4** addition, increase *Nowadays the interest you have to pay if you borrow money is about ten per cent.* *vb.* **1** attract, engage, absorb *What you say about your uncle's jewel collection interests me.* ANT. *n.* (1) disinterest, apathy. *vb.* bore, weary.

interested *adj.* 1 absorbed, engrossed; stimulated, excited, inspired *Are you interested in model railways?* 2 concerned, involved, affected *You cannot be impartial: since you own a share in the property, you are an interested party.* ANT. (1) bored. (2) disinterested, indifferent.

interesting *adj.* attractive, fascinating, absorbing, engrossing *That was one of the most interesting books I have ever read.* ANT. uninteresting, boring, tedious, wearisome.

interfere *vb.* meddle, butt in, intervene *If only people would not interfere and allow us to get on with our work!!*

interference *n.* 1 meddling, prying, intrusion *Your interference in matters that don't concern you has gone far enough.* 2 obstruction, obstacle, barrier *Every time I have tried to settle the question the others have created some interference.*

interior *n.* inside, centre *The interior of the house was painted yellow.* *adj.* inside, central, inner, internal *The interior sections of the island were mostly swamplands.* ANT. *n.* exterior, outside. *adj.* external, outer, outside.

interminable *adj.* endless, never-ending, unending, long, tedious *We had to listen to another one of Castro's interminable speeches.*

intermittent *adj.* occasional, periodic, spasmodic, discontinuous, continual *I picked up the phone and heard an intermittent buzzing sound.*

internal *adj.* 1 inner, interior, inside; private, intimate *They received internal injuries in the car crash.* 2 domestic, native *Diplomatic relations are an international, not an internal matter.* ANT. external, outer, surface.

international *adj.* global, worldwide, multinational, universal *An international commission has been appointed to investigate the drug problem.* ANT. national, domestic, internal.

interpret *vb.* 1 explain, define; make sense of; understand *The way Lorenzo interpreted your remark, he thinks you don't like him.* 2 translate, paraphrase *Because the ambassador understood not one word of Russian, he hired Ivan to interpret what was being said.*

interpretation *n.* explanation; account, rendition, reading *I should like to hear your interpretation of the substance of that meeting.*

interpreter *n.* translator, linguist *All the summit leaders brought their own interpreters.*

interrogate *vb.* cross-examine, question, ask *The police interrogated him for hours before releasing him.*

interrupt *vb.* 1 intrude, break in, interfere, cut in (on) *Please don't interrupt me when I'm talking. If you always interrupt, how can you know what others think?* 2 discontinue, stop, hinder, obstruct *The trees on this side of the house interrupt the view of the seashore.*

interval *n.* gap, pause, intermission *There should be a two-second interval between the strikings of the clock.*

intervene *vb.* come between, interfere, interrupt, intrude *Two years have intervened since we last met.*

intimate *adj.* **1** close, familiar, personal *Shellie is one of my most intimate friends.* **2** private, personal, confidential, secret *We have always shared the most intimate details of our lives with each other.* **3** thorough, complete, detailed *I have an intimate understanding of the way in which a car engine works.* *vb.* hint, suggest, imply *Charlie intimated that if I were to offer to lend him my car, he would accept.*

intimidate *vb.* scare, frighten; threaten *If you think you will intimidate me by waving that pistol about ... you are absolutely right!!*

intolerable *adj.* unbearable, insufferable; painful *The weather has become intolerable.* ANT. tolerable, bearable.

intolerant *adj.* prejudiced, biased, bigoted *You cannot expect fair treatment for yourself if you are intolerant of the rights of others.* ANT. tolerant, broadminded, fair.

intrepid *adj.* bold, fearless, daring, courageous *An army expert has won the George Cross for his intrepid actions in defusing a bomb.* ANT. cowardly.

intricate *adj.* complex, involved, convoluted, tangled; puzzling, tricky *The relationships of the people in that family are extremely intricate.* ANT. clear, easy.

intrigue *vb.* attract, charm, interest, captivate *The dark-haired girl at the table in the corner intrigues me.* *n.* plot, scheme, conspiracy *The cafés of Casablanca were famous as the scenes of many international intrigues.*

introduce *vb.* **1** present; acquaint *We were introduced to each other at Flora's house in Putney.* **2** submit, propose, present, offer *The government has introduced a bill to change the education system in this country.*

introduction *n.* **1** presentation, acquaintance, contact *The meeting began with the introduction of three new members.* **2** preface, foreword, preliminaries; prelude *The introduction in this book is very short: just two pages.*

intrude *vb.* interfere, infringe, interrupt *I do not mean to intrude on your conversation, but could you tell me where the loo is?*

intruder *n.* prowler, thief, trespasser, robber *The defendant swore that it was the bushy-haired intruder who slew his wife.*

intuition *n.* instinct, sixth sense, clairvoyance, insight *Intuition tells me that I have made a very fortunate decision today.*

invade *vb.* attack, penetrate, occupy, overrun; encroach upon *The shore defences prevent anyone from invading that part of the coast.*

invalid[1] *n.* patient, sufferer, convalescent *We visited the invalids in hospital.*

invalid[2] *adj.* inoperative, null and void; abolished *The return half of a day-return ticket is invalid on the day after you bought it.* ANT. valid, operative; permitted.

invasion *n.* intrusion, attack, encroachment *The invasion of Europe by the Allies began on 6 June 1944, D-Day.*

invent *vb.* **1** originate, create, devise *Thomas Edison invented the* *electric light bulb.* **2** make up, concoct, contrive *I think Andrew invented the story about being in the army, as he's only nine years old!*

invest *vb.* lay out, put money in, speculate *At the moment, I am investing in real estate.*

investigate *vb.* examine, inspect, explore, study *We have been investigating everyone who knew the victim and would like to talk now to you.*

investigation *n.* examination, exploration, enquiry, study, research, search *Having completed their investigation, the auditors left.*

invigorating *adj.* stimulating, vitalizing, bracing, fortifying *An invigorating cold shower is good for you in the morning.*

invisible *adj.* imperceptible; unseen, hidden, concealed, inconspicuous *When Charlotte sees Allen, all other men become invisible.* ANT. obvious, visible, clear.

invite *vb.* **1** ask, request the company of *After we got to know them a little, we invited our neighbours for dinner.* **2** request, encourage, urge *Applications are invited for the teaching post at the school.*

inviting *adj.* alluring, luring, appealing, tempting, attractive, encouraging *The girl gave me an inviting smile, so I asked her to dance.* ANT. uninviting, unattractive.

involuntary *adj.* automatic, reflex, uncontrolled; unintentional *Grimsby has either developed an involuntary twitch in his eye or he is winking at my wife.* ANT. voluntary, willed, wilful.

involve *vb.* **1** include, contain, embrace *If your plans for having dinner involve me, please remember I don't like cauliflower.* **2** complicate, confuse, entangle: *'This is one of the most involved cases I have ever tried,' said the judge.*

irony *n.* satire, absurdity; ridicule, mockery *It is a pity that you cannot see the irony in your wife's going off with Kermit.*

irrational *adj.* **1** illogical, absurd, unreasonable *The girl's irrational behaviour baffled the doctor for months.* **2** senseless, stupid, incoherent *Man sometimes behaves as an irrational being.*

irregular *adj.* **1** uneven, unequal, crooked *The irregular surface of this wall must accumulate a lot of dust.* **2** disorderly, random, unsettled, disorganized *The hours kept by the staff are irregular, and you can never be sure when someone is in the office.* ANT. (1) regular, even.

irrelevant *adj.* unapt, unrelated, unconnected, extraneous *What you think about my business acumen is totally irrelevant.*

irresistible *adj.* compelling, alluring, overwhelming *You must admit that Janice looks quite irresistible in that black gown.*

irresponsible *adj.* untrustworthy, unreliable *Philip is too irresponsible to be entrusted with the job of security guard.*

irreverent *adj.* disrespectful, impolite; sacrilegious, profane, blasphemous *Evan has written another of his irreverent Christmas poems in which he twits everyone, including the Queen.*

irritable *adj.* sensitive, touchy, testy, peevish, short-tempered *Irena* *is so irritable that every little thing annoys her.* ANT. cheerful, happy.

irritate *vb.* **1** annoy, vex, pester, bother *I find your constant whining about going swimming very irritating.* **2** redden, chafe, inflame *Stop scratching your eye or you'll irritate it.* ANT. (1) soothe, pacify, calm.

isolate *vb.* separate, disconnect, segregate, detach *Anyone who has been exposed to this disease ought to be isolated.*

isolation *n.* separation, detachment; loneliness, solitude, seclusion, confinement *Crusoe began to feel the effects of his isolation.*

issue *n.* **1** number, copy, edition *Have you seen Wednesday's issue of the newspaper?* **2** problem, question, concern; matter, subject *The television programme dealt with current events and with issues of importance to all of us.* *vb.* **1** appear, emerge, come out, come forth *The smoke issued from the chimney in great black clouds.* **2** publish, distribute, put out, send out, circulate, release *A quarterly magazine is issued four times a year.*

itemize *vb.* list, record, detail, register *When doing the inventory, you must itemize every book in stock.*

j

jail *n.* prison *After spending twenty years in jail, the man was afraid to face the responsibilities of freedom.* *vb.* imprison, confine, detain, lock up *She was jailed for shoplifting.*

jailer *n.* keeper, guard, warden *The prisoners tied up the jailer and escaped.*

jam *vb.* pack, crowd, force, ram, push, squeeze, wedge *I don't see how they can jam eight tomatoes into that tiny can.* *n.* preserve, conserve *Do you like jam in sandwiches?*

jar¹ *n.* pot, jug, bottle, pitcher; container *I bought a jar of honey from the supermarket.*

jar² *n.* jolt, shock *The fall gave her system quite a jar.* *vb.* clash, disagree, grate *The colours in your living room jar.*

jealous *adj.* envious; covetous *You are jealous of anyone who has more than you.*

jealousy *n.* envy; covetousness *David never looked at another woman because he feared his wife's jealousy.*

jeer *vb.,n.* laugh, scoff, taunt *The boys jeered as the headmaster went by. A huge jeer rose from the crowd as the prisoners came out of the courtroom.*

jerk *vb.* twitch, quiver, shake *When you jerked the tablecloth, you spilled the milk.* *n.* twitch, spasm, shake, quiver *With a quick jerk, the horse threw the boy to the ground.*

jet *n.* 1 spurt, squirt *When I turned on the tap, a jet of water hit me in the face.* 2 aeroplane, jumbo jet *The jet took off from Heathrow bound for the United States.*

jewel *n.* gem, gemstone, precious *or* semi-precious stone *The crown was made of gold and set with diamonds and other jewels.*

job *n.* 1 work, employment, trade, profession, position, calling, career, business *With so many people unemployed, my father was lucky to have a job.* 2 task, chore, duty *Mother told me she had some jobs she wanted done around the house after school.*

jog *vb.* 1 push, shake, jar *Sandra jogged her boyfriend when he fell asleep.* 2 run, trot *Many people now go jogging to keep fit.*

join *vb.* unite, connect, couple, assemble, link, fit, attach *The pieces of the puzzle joined together to form the picture of a sunset.* ANT. split, separate, divide, sunder.

joint *n.* connection, link, coupling, union, junction *I could see where the glue was oozing out of the joint between the parts.* *adj.* common, mutual, combined, connected *If we make a joint effort, we can do it more quickly.* ANT. *adj.* separate, divided.

joke *n.* jest, prank, game, caper, antic; anecdote *Tying a tin to a* *dog's tail isn't a funny joke.*   *vb.*   jest, banter, laugh *You go to your office by helicopter every day? You must be joking!*

jolly *adj.*   joyful, spirited, happy, cheerful, glad.   ANT. sad, sombre, gloomy, melancholy.

jolt *vb.,n.*   jar, bump, bounce, shake, shock *The electric wire touched my finger and jolted me. Everett got quite a jolt when he sat on that drawing pin.*

journal *n.*   1 diary, account, record *Some people keep a journal every day of everything that happens to them.*   2 periodical, magazine, newspaper *The reading room contains many journals.*

journalist *n.*   reporter, correspondent, columnist *Only journalists were given press passes to allow them to interview the Prime Minister.*

journey *n.*   trip, voyage, excursion, tour *Our journey to Istanbul took three days on the train.*   *vb.*   travel *The student journeyed for two weeks to visit his old professor.*

jovial *adj.*   jolly, convivial, hearty *We enjoy visiting Desmond because he is such a jovial host.*

joy *n.*   delight, pleasure, happiness, gladness, satisfaction *It is gratifying to see the joy in the children's faces at Christmas.*   ANT. unhappiness, misery, sadness, gloom.

judge *n.*   1 justice, magistrate *The judge pronounced judgement on the men and sentenced them to eighteen months' imprisonment.*   2 arbiter, referee, umpire, arbitrator *How can you be a judge of the matter when you don't know all of the facts?*   *vb.*   1 sentence, condemn, convict *Mr Justice Smith judged the prisoners in the dock.*   2 decide, determine, consider, reckon *He judged the festivities worthy of his support.*

judgement *n.*   1 decision, verdict, estimation, opinion *In our judgement, the horse should not have been disqualified.*   2 understanding, wisdom, discretion, sense, common sense, intelligence *I think you showed good judgement when you reported that suspicious man to the police.*

jug *n.*   jar, bottle, flagon, flask, pitcher *You will find a jug of milk in the fridge.*

jump *vb.,n.*   leap, spring, bound, vault, skip, hop *Don't try jumping over that puddle or you'll fall into it. He's going to attempt a jump over the river next year while riding a horse.*

jumpy *adj.*   nervous, apprehensive, touchy, sensitive, excitable *Sally has been so jumpy lately that I asked the doctor to give her something to calm her down.*   ANT. calm, tranquil, unruffled.

junction *n.*   1 intersection, crossroads *The accident happened at the junction, as the two cars collided.*   2 connection, joint, weld, seam *The rust started at the junction where the two sides of the box come together.*

jungle *n.*   bush, forest, thicket, undergrowth *As we stepped into the darkness of the jungle, I expected to see Tarzan any minute.*

junk *n.*   rubbish, waste, salvage, scraps *After the crash, the car was worth ten pounds as junk.*

just *adj.* **1** fair, impartial *I think that the umpire's decision was just—the man was out.* **2** rightful, lawful, legal; proper; deserved *Since we had paid for the land, we had just title to it.* ANT. (1) biased, unfair, partial.

justice *n.* fairness, equity, impartiality, fair-mindedness *It is the responsibility of the judge to see that justice is done.*

justify *vb.* **1** vindicate, clear, acquit, excuse *I don't see how you can justify murder except in self-defence.* **2** defend, explain, excuse *Tom tried to justify his actions by claiming that he had been very tired.*

juvenile *adj.* childish, puerile, babyish, infantile *If you keep up this juvenile behaviour you'll be treated as a child.* *n.* youngster, teenager, youth *The juveniles were charged with speeding on their skateboards.* ANT. *adj.* mature, adult. *n.* adult, grown-up.

k

keen *adj.* **1** enthusiastic, eager, interested *I don't know if Ward is so keen to publish the book any more.* **2** sharp, acute *This hunting knife has such a keen edge I can split a hair with it.* **3** quick, shrewd, bright, clever, intelligent *John has a keen wit.* ANT. (1) apathetic, reluctant. (2) blunted. (3) dull, stupid, slow, obtuse.

keep *vb.* **1** retain, hold, withhold, preserve, maintain *When you borrow books from the library, you're supposed to return them, not keep them.* **2** continue, persist in *I wish you wouldn't keep saying the same thing over and over again.* **3** save, store, hold *You can't keep eggs for a month outside the refrigerator without their becoming rotten.* *vb. phr.* **keep back** delay, hinder, hold, check *I couldn't keep back a sneeze.* **keep on** continue, persist in *If you keep on shouting you'll get hoarse.* **keep up** maintain, sustain, support *The firm kept up its rate of progress for three years and then went bankrupt.* *n.* **1** living; room and board, maintenance, subsistence *The farmhand worked just for his keep during hard times.* **2** tower, dungeon *The knight rescued the damsel from the keep of the king's castle.*

keeper *n.* jailer, warden, custodian, guard *The lion attacked his keeper at the zoo.*

kernel *n.* core, heart, nucleus *The kernel is the only edible part of the nut. The kernel of the problem lies in getting the message to the public.*

key *n.* **1** latchkey; master key; skeleton key *He opened the front door with his key.* **2** clue; answer, solution *The key to the puzzle is to spell the words backwards.*

kidnap *vb.* abduct, capture, seize, carry away, make off with, hold for ransom *The men kidnapped the child and demanded five thousand pounds in ransom.*

kill *vb.* **1** slay, execute, assassinate, murder *The tiger killed two people and then ran into the jungle.* **2** destroy, cancel, abolish *Your attitude could kill any feeling of love I might have towards you.*

kind¹ *n.* sort, class, type, variety *What kind of bird is that?*

kind² *adj.* friendly, gentle, kindly, mild, kindhearted, goodhearted, warm, tender, affectionate *He was very kind to his elderly neighbours.* ANT. cruel, brutal, mean, hardhearted.

kindle *vb.* **1** ignite, fire, light *You'll need some paper to kindle a fire.* **2** excite, arouse, inflame, provoke *The new girl in the class knew how to kindle a spark of dislike into a flame of hatred.*

kingdom *n.* monarchy, realm, domain, empire *At one time the kingdom of Spain was one of the most powerful in the world.*

kiosk *n.* booth, stall, stand *Let's stop at the newsagent's kiosk and buy a magazine to read on the train.*

kiss *vb.* 1 embrace *The friends kissed as they met again.* 2 touch, brush, graze *The billiard balls kissed lightly.*

kit *n.* set, collection; outfit, equipment *Randolph got a tool kit for Christmas.*

knack *n.* talent, skill, ability, aptitude *Even when he was a child, Kenneth had a knack for repairing watches.*

knife *n.* blade, cutter; penknife *The artisan uses a special kind of knife for carving wood.*

knob *n.* 1 handle, doorknob *You have to turn the knob if you want to open the door.* 2 bump, projection, protuberance *There's a knob on my head where the ball hit me.*

knock *vb.,n.* rap, thump, whack, thwack, tap *Please knock on my door at seven tomorrow morning. I have a headache from that knock I got yesterday.*

knot *n.* 1 tie, splice, hitch *The bowline is a secure knot that is easy to tie and to untie.* 2 twist, tangle, snarl *I couldn't untie the knot in my bootlaces.*

know *vb.* 1 recognize *I don't think I know you—have we met?* 2 understand, comprehend, see *Do you know what I'm talking about?* 3 distinguish, discriminate *I wouldn't know him from Adam.*

knowledge *n.* 1 facts, information, learning, data *Sidney's knowledge of physics is rather limited.* 2 understanding, wisdom, judgment *Man's knowledge of himself has increased enormously in the past century.*

l

label *n.* marker, mark, sticker, tag, stamp *The label on this vase says it was made in Denmark.* *vb.* mark, stamp *All medicines should be labelled to show their ingredients.*

laborious *adj.* difficult, tiring, burdensome, hard *Shovelling coal is laborious work.* ANT. easy, simple, restful, relaxing.

labour *n.* 1 work, toil, drudgery *Clearing out your attic would provide labour for five men for a week.* 2 workingmen, workers, working class *Management and labour reached an agreement last night, and the bus drivers returned to work today.* *vb.* work, toil, strive *My father laboured for many years for others before he could buy his own farm.*

lack *n.* shortage, need, dearth, want, scarcity *Driving over the speed limit shows a lack of good judgement. The lack of vitamins and protein in their diet made many of the people very weak and ill.* *vb.* want, need, require *We are lacking three people to make up the football team.* ANT. *n.* abundance, quantity, plenty, profusion.

lad *n.* boy, youth, fellow, chap, stripling *Ted is a fine lad, but he may be too young to become team captain.*

lag *vb.* fall behind, dawdle, linger, loiter, tarry, straggle *Deliveries are lagging two weeks behind orders.* *n.* slack, slowdown, tardiness *The lag in sales is due to economic difficulties.*

lame *adj.* 1 crippled, disabled, limping; deformed *The horse is too lame to run in the Grand National.* 2 poor, unsatisfactory, weak, inadequate, faulty *Having to wash your hair is a pretty lame excuse for not arriving at work on time.* ANT. 2 convincing, believable, plausible.

lament *vb.* mourn, weep, bemoan, grieve; regret *The widows of the men killed in the explosion lamented their loss.* *n.* mourning, lamentation, moan, wail, moaning, wailing, weeping *The widow's lament was great for many days after the accident.*

lamentable *adj.* deplorable, unfortunate, shocking *The conditions in which the family was living were lamentable.*

lamp *n.* light, light bulb, lantern *Shine the lamp over here so I can see the book titles.*

land *n.* ground, earth *The hovercraft moved off the land into the sea.* *vb.* come down, touch down, arrive *The aeroplane landed at Gatwick airport.*

lane *n.* passage, alley, way, alleyway *The lane behind the houses is overgrown with rose bushes.*

language *n.* 1 tongue, speech *My uncle speaks three foreign lan-*

guages. **2** dialect; jargon; patois *The technical language of mathematics is hard to understand.*

lapse *vb.* stop, end, cease; decline, deteriorate, weaken *When interest in films lapsed, many cinemas went out of business.*

large *adj.* big, great, massive, huge, vast, enormous, immense *A particularly large and ferocious elephant blocked the path.* ANT. small, little, tiny, diminutive.

largely *adv.* mainly, chiefly, mostly, principally *The spring floods were caused largely by the melting winter snows.*

lash *n.* whip, thong, cane, rod, knout *The thief received five lashes in the public square.* *vb.* whip, strike, scourge, beat *The prisoner was lashed as a punishment.*

lass *n.* girl, maiden, damsel *When I first met Susan, she was a lovely lass of sixteen.*

last *adj.* final, latest, ultimate, extreme, concluding *The last time I saw her, she was wearing a green hat and coat.* *vb.* continue, remain, endure *This pair of blue jeans has lasted for three years.* ANT. *adj.* first, initial, starting, beginning.

late *adj.* overdue, behind time; slow *The train to Aylesbury is late again.* ANT. early.

lather *n.* foam, suds, froth *This shampoo creates a lot of thick lather.*

latitude *n.* freedom, scope, range, extent *If you give me only ten pounds to buy a pair of shoes, I don't have much latitude of choice.*

laugh *vb.,n.* chuckle, giggle, snicker, guffaw *I wasn't laughing at you because you're not funny. Margaret gave a little embarrassed laugh when asked why she was late.*

laughable *adj.* amusing, funny, humorous, comical, ridiculous *It was laughable to watch Evans trying to saddle the Shetland pony.*

launch *vb.* **1** fire, drive, propel *The rocket was launched to the moon at dawn.* **2** initiate, originate, start, begin *The firm launched its sales offensive in October.* ANT. (2) stop, finish, terminate.

lavish *adj.* generous, profuse, abundant, liberal *The apartment was decorated with the most lavish furnishings.* ANT. meagre, scanty; sparing; mean.

law *n.* rule, statute, order, decree, ruling *The new law covers employee contributions to pension schemes.*

lawful *adj.* legal, legitimate *The constable was not sure whether parking at that spot was lawful or not.* ANT. illegal.

lawless *adj.* uncontrolled, uncivilized, wild, untamed, savage, violent *The early days of the West in America are depicted in fiction as lawless.* ANT. law-abiding, obedient, tame.

lawlessness *n.* anarchy, chaos, mob rule, mobocracy *In the period following the end of the war, lawlessness prevailed in many parts of the country.* ANT. order.

lawyer *n.* solicitor, barrister, counsel, advocate *If you want to take the matter to court, you will have to engage a lawyer.*

lax *adj.* lenient, slack, remiss *The teachers have been lax about enforcing discipline lately.* ANT. strict.

lay¹ *vb.* **1** put, place, set, deposit *Please lay the book on the table.*
2 attribute, reckon *The blame was laid fair and square on Peter.*
3 wager, bet, risk, hazard, stake *I'll lay you five to one that my horse wins.*

lay² *adj.* **1** unordained, laic, laical *John's uncle is a lay member of the church, not a minister.* **2** amateur, nonprofessional *Since I wasn't a scientist, I could give only a lay opinion about the effects of the atomic power plant.*

lay³ *see* lie².

layer *n.* coat, coating, stratum, bed *Before pouring the concrete, you must put down a layer of sharp sand.*

layout *n.* arrangement, plan, design *There is a new road layout at the Hen & Chickens roundabout.*

lazy *adj.* idle, indolent, inactive, sluggish, slothful *If you weren't so lazy, you would have finished your work by now.* ANT. ambitious, active, forceful.

lead *vb.* **1** guide, conduct, direct, steer *The blind man's dog led him carefully across the street.* **2** command, direct *We need a strong man to lead us through the coming difficulties.* ANT. follow.

leader *n.* director, chief, commander, head, manager, ruler *The small green woman stepped out of the saucer and asked to be taken to our leader.* ANT. follower, disciple.

league *n.* alliance, union, combination *One faction has formed a league in an attempt to unseat the incumbent.*

leak *vb.* drip, flow *Tighten the joint and the pipe will stop leaking.*

lean¹ *vb.* **1** slant, tilt, slope *The Tower of Pisa leans over a little more each year.* **2** rely, depend, trust *When you go in to take the examination, you won't be able to lean on your teacher's help.*

lean² *adj.* slender, slim, thin, lanky, skinny *The tall, lean cowboy sauntered into the saloon.* ANT. *adj.* fat, heavy, obese.

leap *vb.,n.* jump, vault, spring, bound *Jennie leapt up to kiss me when I entered the room. With a leap, the tiger was attacking the elephant.*

learn *vb.* master, acquire, gain; determine, find out, discover; memorize *How did you learn so many foreign languages? I learnt that Maria was not coming to my party. I learnt the poem by heart.*

learned *adj.* scholarly, wise, educated, knowledgeable, well-informed *Three learned men served as advisors to the university.* ANT. ignorant, uneducated, unlettered, illiterate.

learning *n.* knowledge, scholarship, education *Hulbert has great respect for men of learning.*

lease *vb.* let, hire, rent, charter *I should like to lease a sailing boat for a week's holiday.*

least *adj.* **1** smallest, tiniest, minutest *Mother gave me the least amount of rice she could: one grain!* **2** slightest; trivial *Don gets annoyed at the least little thing.* ANT. (1) most.

leave *vb.* **1** depart, go, quit; desert, abandon *Evelyn left two days ago. The man in the witness box admitted to leaving his wife and two* *children.* **2** bequeath, will *Oscar's grandmother left him some money when she died.* **n.** **1** permission, allowance, liberty, freedom, consent *Do I have your leave to speak to the minister?* **2** vacation, holiday *Andy will be on leave from the Navy all next month.* ANT. *vb.* (1) arrive, come.

lecture *n.* speech, talk, address, lesson *Last night we attended an illustrated lecture on bird watching.* *vb.* speak *or* talk (to), address, teach, instruct *The professor lectured the students about the plays of Shakespeare.*

leftovers *n.pl.* remains, scraps, remainder, residue *We have to eat leftovers for dinner again.*

legacy *n.* inheritance, bequest *Aunt Millicent's legacy was only one acre of land ... but it happens to be in the middle of Mayfair.*

legal *adj.* lawful, legitimate; honest *It is not legal here for shops to sell bottled spirits on Sunday.* ANT. illegal.

legend *n.* story, tale, myth, folk tale, fable *According to legend, those who kiss the Blarney Stone acquire the gift of the gab.*

legendary *adj.* **1** mythical, fictitious, fanciful, imaginary *Nobody is exactly sure whether King Arthur was real or legendary.* **2** famous, celebrated, notorious *The wealth of the Rhodes family is legendary in these parts.*

legible *adj.* decipherable, readable, plain *I admire anyone with legible handwriting.* ANT. illegible, unclear.

legitimate *adj.* legal, lawful, right, proper, correct, valid *My aunt is the legitimate heiress of the king of Transylvania.* ANT. illegitimate.

leisure *n.* relaxation, ease, recreation, rest *Because of my work schedule, I have little time for leisure.*

leisurely *adj.* unhurried, casual, relaxed, comfortable *Let's take a leisurely stroll around the square.* ANT. hectic, hurried, pressed, forced, rushed.

lend *vb.* loan, entrust, advance *Could you lend me ten pounds till next week?* ANT. borrow.

length *n.* extent, measure; reach, longness *The length of time needed to complete the mission depends on what we encounter. Do you know the length of the Forth Bridge?*

lengthen *vb.* extend, stretch, reach, prolong, grow, increase *As spring approaches, the hours of daylight lengthen in England.* ANT. shorten, contract, shrink.

lenient *adj.* tolerant, indulgent, pardoning; soft, gentle *Many believe that the courts have been too lenient with criminals.* ANT. severe, strict, austere.

lessen *vb.* reduce, diminish, decrease, shrink, dwindle, decline *We are doing what we can to lessen the threat of war.* ANT. increase, swell, expand, multiply.

lesson *n.* **1** exercise, drill, assignment, homework *I hope that all the students have completed the lesson for today.* **2** instruction; example, model *Your catching a cold ought to be a lesson to you to wear your coat.*

let *vb.* **1** permit, allow, grant *Please let me go to the disco.* **2** lease, rent *There's a flat to let in our block.*

lethal *see* **fatal.**

letter *n.* note, message, communication, epistle *The poet's collected letters will be published next year.*

level *adj.* **1** even, smooth, flat, uniform *The new board you put into the floor isn't level with the others.* **2** horizontal, plane, flat *On a level road, this car runs very smoothly.* **3** equivalent, equal *My boat drew up level with the leader's and then we started to pull ahead.* *vb.* **1** even, equalize; smooth *I have to level the ground before planting the seeds.* **2** demolish, destroy, raze, flatten *The entire centre of the city was levelled by the bomb.*

levelheaded *adj.* sensible, reasonable, collected, calm, cool *You can rely on Chris to remain levelheaded in a crisis.*

levy *n.* tax, charge, fee, duty *The levy on imports was raised to reduce the trade deficit.*

lewd *adj.* obscene, immoral, indecent *The bookshop owner was arrested for selling lewd materials.*

liable *adj.* subject, accountable, answerable, responsible *Parents are liable for damage done by their children.*

liar *n.* falsifier, prevaricator, deceiver, fibber, cheat *Once someone is known to be a liar, we tend to disbelieve anything he says.*

liberal *adj.* **1** generous, openhanded, unselfish, kind *Arnold has always been a very liberal tipper in this restaurant.* **2** tolerant, unprejudiced, unbigoted, openminded *I have always taken a liberal attitude towards women's rights.* ANT. (1) stingy, mean, niggardly, tightfisted, selfish.

liberate *vb.* free, release, loose, deliver *The invading army liberated prisoners of war in each city they conquered.* ANT. imprison, confine, jail.

liberty *n.* freedom, independence *Liberty means the freedom to do as one pleases within the law.* ANT. bondage, servitude, slavery.

licence *n.* permit, authorization *You may not drive without a licence.*

license *vb.* permit, allow, sanction, authorize *The new restaurant is not yet licensed to sell spirits.*

lid *n.* cover, top, cap *Make sure that the lid is screwed on tight.*

lie¹ *n.* falsehood, prevarication, fib, untruth, fiction, perjury *It's a lie to say that I stole that cherry pie—my twin brother did it.* *vb.* fib, prevaricate, misinform *Don't lie to me! I know you have no twin brother.*

lie² *vb.* **1** recline, repose *I lay in bed till noon today.* **2** be situated *or* located *The valley lies between the two mountains.* *n.* position, situation, location, site *I've just started this job, so give me a chance to see the lie of the land.*

life *n.* **1** being, animation, existence, vitality *There's still a breath of life in the injured man.* **2** biography *I've just finished reading a life of Churchill.* **3** vigour, vitality, energy, spirit, sparkle *Irene is always the life of the party.*

lifeless *adj.* dead; inanimate; heavy, dull, slow *The critics found the new play to be completely lifeless.*

lift *vb.* raise, elevate *That box is too heavy for you to lift by yourself.*

light¹ *n.* **1** illumination, radiance, brilliance, brightness *There's not enough light here to read by.* **2** lamp, fixture, chandelier, candle, bulb *Please turn off the lights when leaving the room.* *vb.* **1** illuminate, brighten *That one candle isn't enough to light this room.* **2** ignite, fire, burn, kindle *I lit a fire in the sitting room.* *adj.* **1** bright, clear, luminous, lit, illuminated *This is a pleasant light room to be in.* **2** pale, whitish, bleached *Your light yellow dress looks very good on you.* **ANT.** *n.* (1) dark. *vb.* (1) darken. (2) extinguish. *adj.* dark.

light² *adj.* **1** unsubstantial, airy, buoyant, dainty *If all the books are removed this bookcase is very light.* **2** giddy, frivolous *Sometimes I think you're a bit light in the head.* **3** trivial, shallow, slight *I enjoy a little light reading before going to sleep.* **ANT.** (3) serious, heavy, weighty.

lightheaded *adj.* **1** silly, frivolous *Why do you always get so lightheaded when you're playing games at a party?* **2** giddy, dizzy *The effects of the anaesthetic made me feel lightheaded.* **ANT.** (1) sober, rational. (2) clearheaded.

lighthearted *adj.* gay, carefree, cheerful, merry, happy, glad *Priscilla's lighthearted manner gave no hint of her serious problems.* **ANT.** sad, melancholy, sombre, serious.

like *vb.* admire, esteem, fancy, care for, cherish, adore, love *Do you like me as much as I like you? I like scones for tea.* *adj.* alike, similar; resembling *The two brothers were very like each other.* **ANT.** *vb.* dislike, hate. *adj.* dissimilar, different.

likely *adj.* probable, liable, possible, reasonable *It seems likely that I shall be able to attend the meeting.*

likeness *n.* **1** resemblance, similarity *Yes, there is a likeness between you and Napoleon.* **2** image, representation, picture, portrait *The king's likeness appears on all postage stamps, coins and bank notes.*

likewise *adv.* similarly; besides, also *Watch me peel this apple and then do likewise.*

liking *n.* affection, partiality, fondness *If the managing director takes a liking to someone, that person will go far.* **ANT.** dislike, antipathy.

limit *n.* **1** boundary, bound, extent, frontier, end *The limits of our property are marked by those huge trees.* **2** restraint, check, restriction *There is no limit to your rudeness!* *vb.* check, hinder, restrain, restrict, confine *You ought to limit the amount of sugar you eat.*

limp¹ *adj.* flabby, soft, supple, flexible *After being left out in the rain, the pages of the book were all soggy and limp.* **ANT.** stiff, rigid, hard.

limp² *vb.* hobble, falter, stagger *The pirate came limping into the* *cabin on his pegleg.* *n.* hobble, lameness *This limp comes from my sprained ankle.*

line *n.* 1 row, array, file, sequence, series *There was a line of medicine bottles on the shelf.* 2 mark, stroke; outline *After drawing a line at the top of your paper, write your name on it.* 3 seam, crease, wrinkle *The palmist told my fortune from the lines on my hand.* 4 division, limit, boundary *I draw the line when it comes to five packets of crisps in one day.* 5 wire, cable; pipe; track *When digging along the railway line, the men had to be careful to avoid cutting the telephone, power and gas lines.* *vb. phr.* **line up** align, file, array *I want all the children who are going to the zoo to line up outside at once.*

linger *vb.* loiter, stay, remain, tarry, dawdle *Please do not linger near the doors as you leave the theatre.*

link *n.* tie, bond, connection, connector, loop, coupling *I cannot see any link between your wanting to see a film and Bob's washing his car.* *vb.* connect, tie, couple *The chains were linked to each other.*

lip *n.* brim, edge, rim *Catch that drop clinging to the lip of the cream pitcher.*

liquid *see* **fluid.**

list *n.* series, roll, record, register *Is Bob's name on the list of candidates?* *vb.* record, register, post, file *At the bottom of the application form, please list all personal references.*

listen *vb.* hear, attend *I warned them, but they wouldn't listen to me.*

literal *adj.* word for word, verbatim, exact, faithful, precise *This is a literal translation from the original.*

literate *adj.* educated, informed; intelligent *Every literate person knows who Shakespeare was.* ANT. illiterate, unread, unlettered, ignorant.

literature *n.* writings; poetry, plays, novels, essays *Victor is taking a course in German literature.*

litter *n.* rubbish, waste, refuse *Please don't throw litter on the streets.* *vb.* strew, scatter, disorder *The park was littered with sweet wrappers after the children had left.*

little *adj.* 1 small, tiny, wee, minute *This little book has more information in it than many large ones.* 2 brief, short *There's only a little time left before my plane leaves.* *adv.* slightly *Aren't you even a little hungry?* ANT. *adj.* (1) large, big, huge. (2) long, extended.

live¹ *vb.* 1 abide, reside, dwell *I am going to live in India when I grow up.* 2 exist, be; survive *No animal, including man, can live without any water at all.*

live² *adj.* 1 alive; surviving *My grandmother used to go visiting carrying a live white mouse on a gold chain.* 2 unrecorded *Shall we go to town to see a live show tonight?* 3 controversial; important *The television programme dealt with live issues.* ANT. (1) dead. (2) recorded.

lively *adj.* 1 active, live, vigorous; spry, nimble, quick *Jack's grand-mother is pretty lively for a woman of ninety-two.* 2 animated, spirited *That certainly was a lively party last night.* ANT. slow, dull, sluggish.

livid *adj.* angry, furious, enraged *When told that his daughter had eloped, Alan was livid with rage.*

living *n.* livelihood; support *What does your son-in-law do to make a living?*

load *n.* burden, weight; cargo, shipment, delivery *That's quite a load you're carrying. I've ordered another load of coal for the winter.* *vb.* weight, burden; lade *We loaded the luggage into the boot of the car.*

loaf *vb.* loiter, lounge, idle *After spending the summer loafing about, it is about time you got down to work.*

loan *n.* advance; credit *I asked the bank to approve a loan of £1000 for my new car.* *vb.* lend, entrust, advance *The library loans books freely.*

loathe *see* **hate.**

lobby *n.* vestibule, foyer, entrance hall, anteroom *Please meet me in the lobby in ten minutes.* *vb.* influence, induce, persuade *The pressure group tried to lobby the MPs.*

locate *vb.* 1 find, discover, unearth *I haven't been able to locate a copy of the book you asked for.* 2 situate, site, place *I've been planning to locate the new factory near the motorway junction.*

location *n.* site, situation, spot, place *The top of that hill would be a fine location for our new home.*

lock[1] *n.* tress, braid, plait *Betty's golden locks flowed down to her shoulders.*

lock[2] *n.* latch, hasp, bolt, padlock *I have nothing that anyone would want, so I don't have a lock on the door.* *vb.* latch, padlock, bolt, fasten *Lock the door carefully after I leave and don't let anyone in.*

lodge *n.* cottage, cabin, hut; chalet *The prince had a hunting lodge in the mountains.* *vb.* 1 stay, reside, abide, board, room, dwell *I've been lodging with my aunt while looking for a job.* 2 settle, fix, put *Trying to get the pencil out of the rifle barrel, my finger became lodged in the hole.*

lofty *adj.* 1 tall, high, towering *A lofty tower block can be seen as you approach the city.* 2 exalted, elevated *His lofty ideas of himself annoyed everyone.* 3 proud, scornful, haughty *She's much too lofty to have anything to do with us.* ANT. (1) low. (3) humble.

logical *adj.* reasonable, rational, sensible *It is not logical to assume that because we know the same people we know each other.* ANT. irrational, crazy.

loiter *see* **linger.**

lone *adj.* sole, alone, solitary; apart *A lone rider was seen in the distance.*

lonely *adj.* solitary, friendless; rejected *I feel very lonely when you are gone for more than a day.*

long[1] *adj.*   extensive, lengthy, extended *You have kept me waiting for a long time.*   **ANT.** short, brief, limited.

long[2] **(for)** *vb.*   crave, desire, wish *I long for a tall glass of iced tea.*

longstanding *adj.*   enduring, longlasting, established, persistent *The longstanding feud between the families still raged after a century.*

long-suffering *adj.*   tolerant, patient, forbearing *Why should a long-suffering parent have to put up with such ungrateful children?*

long-winded *adj.*   wordy, verbose; dull, boring *The speech was so long-winded that I fell asleep in the middle.*   **ANT.** terse, curt.

look *vb.*   **1** gaze, glance, survey, watch, regard, see, study *Look at the girl in the window.*   **2** appear, seem *It looks as if we won't be able to go on our picnic now that it's raining.*   **3** seek, search for *Please look for your keys yourself.*   *n.*   **1** glance, peek, peep, glimpse *I've only had one look at the page, but I've memorized it.*   **2** gaze, stare; contemplation, study, examination *The fixed look she gave me made me nervous.*   **3** appearance, expression *You should have seen the look on her face when I told her!*

loom *vb.*   threaten, menace, impend *Storm clouds loomed on the horizon.*

loop *n.*   circle, coil, ring *The railway line formed a loop round the city centre.*

loose *adj.*   **1** unfastened, untied, free, undone *There's a lion loose from the circus!*   **2** wobbly, insecure, unscrewed, movable *The arm of the chair is loose.*   **3** baggy, draped, slack *Now that I've lost all that weight, my trousers are too loose on me.*   *vb.*   loosen; release, set free *Whenever anyone came too close to the property, they would loose the guard dogs.*   **ANT.** *adj.* **(1)** fastened, tied, secure.   **(2)** firm, secure, steady.   **(3)** tight, confining.

loosen *vb.*   loose, untie, undo, unchain, unfasten *The man was choking, so I loosened his collar.*   **ANT.** tighten, tie, secure.

loot *n.*   plunder, booty *The bank robbers escaped with the loot.*   *vb.* rob, steal, plunder, rifle, sack *It was the manager of the bank who had looted the customers' accounts.*

lord *n.*   nobleman, peer; master, ruler, governor *The lord of the castle signalled for the festivities to begin.*

lose *vb.*   mislay, misplace *How could you have lost your shoe in the underground?*   **ANT.** find, discover, locate.

loss *n.*   **1** damage, injury, hurt *The insurance was barely enough to cover our losses in the fire.*   **2** want, bereavement, need; misfortune, trouble; death *The loss of Ben's mother was a loss to us all.*

lost *adj.*   **1** missing, mislaid, misplaced, gone, absent *The ring, which I thought was lost, turned up in John's pocket.*   **2** wasted, spent, misspent, squandered *The money lost in gambling every year amounts to millions of pounds.*   **ANT.** **(1)** found.

lotion *n.*   balm, salve, cream, liniment *Use hand lotion after doing the washing-up and your skin will stay smooth.*

loud *adj.*   noisy, ear-splitting, thunderous, blaring *Loud noises were coming from the next house.*   **ANT.** soft, quiet, murmuring.

lounge *vb.* loaf, idle, laze *Stop lounging about the house and go out and get yourself a job!* *n.* living room, sitting room *Let's go into the lounge and wait for Hattie there, where it's more comfortable.*

love *n.* adoration, warmth, devotion, tenderness, liking, friendliness, affection *How can you compare a person's love for his family with his love of ice cream?* *vb.* worship, adore, treasure, cherish, like *Darling, when I say I love you, I mean I want to be with you for ever.* ANT. *n.* hate, loathing. *vb.* hate, detest, loathe.

lovely *adj.* attractive, fair, charming, comely, pretty, beautiful, handsome *The bride looked lovely in her wedding gown.* ANT. ugly, hideous.

low *adj.* 1 low-lying, stooped, crouched *Sarah jumped over the low wall.* 2 cheap, inexpensive *The greengrocer was asking low prices for the vegetables at the end of the day.*

lower *vb.* 1 reduce, decrease, lessen, diminish *If you don't eat a balanced diet you lower your resistance to disease.* 2 soften, quiet, turn down *Please lower the volume of your stereo.* 3 degrade, disgrace, humble *I wouldn't lower myself to talk to someone who's such a bigot.* 4 sink; drop; *Martin lowered himself carefully into the hot bath. Lower the leaf of the table gently.* ANT. (1, 2, 4) increase, raise.

loyal *adj.* faithful, true, devoted, dependable; patriotic *Have you any reason to think that Cadwallader might not be loyal to the Crown?* ANT. disloyal, treacherous, traitorous.

loyalty *n.* faithfulness, devotion, fidelity; allegiance, patriotism *Only if you have any doubts do you have any reason to test a person's loyalty.* ANT. disloyalty, treachery, treason.

luck *n.* fortune, chance, fluke *Winning the lottery is simply a matter of luck.* ANT. misfortune.

lucky *adj.* fortunate, favourable, blessed *I have been very lucky at cards.* ANT. unlucky, unfortunate.

ludicrous *adj.* laughable, absurd, ridiculous, preposterous *Why does Elizabeth insist on wearing such ludicrous clothes to the office?*

luggage *n.* baggage, suitcases, bags, trunks *The customs inspectors will examine the contents of your luggage.*

lukewarm *adj.* tepid, unenthusiastic, spiritless, wishy-washy *Danny's suggestion that we play poker received a lukewarm reception.*

lull *vb.* calm, soothe, quiet *We were lulled to sleep by the sound of the waves beating on the shore.* *n.* calm, hush, quiet, stillness, silence; pause *I took advantage of a lull in the activities to steal away unnoticed.*

luminous *adj.* light, glowing, bright, luminescent, fluorescent *Millions of luminous particles danced in the wake of the boat at night.*

lump *n.* 1 bump, protuberance *I still have the lump on my head where she hit me.* 2 cube; piece, block *I have two lumps of sugar in my tea.*

lunatic *n.* madman, maniac, psychotic *There is no way of predicting what a lunatic might do.*

lure *n.* attraction, temptation, bait *The salesman used the promise of a free information service as a lure to sell the encyclopaedia.* *vb.* entice, attract, tempt, draw *The spider attempted to lure the fly to land on its web.*

lurid *adj.* shocking, sensational *The tabloids are always full of lurid stories about famous people.*

luscious *adj.* juicy, delicious, delectable *Those apples look positively luscious.*

lust *n.* desire, drive, passion, craving, appetite *The dance that Salome did for King Herod was to arouse his lust.* *vb.* desire, long for, crave for *As he was lusting after money, the poor man found himself committing murder.*

lustre *n.* 1 sheen, gloss, glitter; brightness, brilliance, radiance *The lustre of the pearls showed up best in candlelight.* 2 fame, glory, repute, honour, distinction *Although the lustre of his accomplishments had won him praise, he was then awarded the Nobel prize.*

luxuriant *adj.* lush, dense, rich, rank *The luxuriant growth of the jungle hid the ancient ruins completely.*

luxurious *adj.* lavish, rich, splendid, deluxe *The luxurious furnishings took my breath away.* ANT. sparse, Spartan, simple, crude.

lyrics *n.pl.* words, text, libretto, book *I know the lyrics of all the published songs written by Sandy Wilson.*

m

macabre *adj.* gruesome, horrible, horrifying, ghastly, grim: On Hallowe'en, the children wanted to hear macabre tales of the supernatural.

machine *n.* device, contrivance, engine, motor, mechanism *This machine prints four colours on both sides of the sheet simultaneously.*

mad *adj.* 1 insane, crazy, mentally ill, deranged *The composer finally went mad and had to be confined in a hospital.* 2 angry, furious, enraged, irate, raging *I'm very mad at Nora for not telling me about Ted's surprise party.* ANT. (1) sane, rational, lucid. (2) happy, cheerful, content.

madden *vb.* enrage, infuriate, anger, vex, annoy *Waving that red flag in front of his face will madden the bull even more.* ANT. mollify, calm, please.

magazine *n.* 1 periodical, journal, review, publication *Do you subscribe to any nature magazines?* 2 arsenal, armoury *An enemy shell hit the magazine and blew it sky-high.*

magic *n.* sorcery, wizardry, sleight-of-hand, witchcraft *The way that rabbit appeared in the silk top hat was magic.* *adj.* magical *This is a magic wand that turns into a snake unless I'm holding it.*

magical *adj.* magic, marvellous, miraculous; mystical *A magical change took place as, before my eyes, the pretty little green frog turned into an ugly princess.*

magician *n.* conjuror, sorcerer, wizard *The best entertainment for a children's party is a magician.*

magnanimous *adj.* generous, unselfish, kind, benevolent *It was very magnanimous of Lady Blackley to donate so much to the fund.*

magnificence *n.* splendour, grandeur, luxury *The magnificence of the Taj Mahal is truly awesome.*

magnificent *adj.* 1 splendid, luxurious, rich, lavish, grand *The throne room of the palace is the most magnificent I've ever seen.* 2 marvellous, wonderful, extraordinary, impressive *From our bathroom windows we have a magnificent view of the mountains.* ANT. plain, simple.

magnify *vb.* enlarge, increase *Use this lens to magnify the image still further.* ANT. diminish, reduce.

magnitude *n.* 1 extent, dimension, size, measure *Nobody had any idea of the magnitude of the disaster because all telephones and other communications had been cut off.* 2 importance, consequence, significance *The results of the research were of some magnitude for all mankind.*

maid *n.* 1 maidservant, housemaid, chambermaid, servant *We left

the hotel room early so the maid could clean up and make the beds.
2 maiden, girl, young woman, lass *The shepherd was singing a song to a pretty maid who had brought his lunch.*

maim *vb.* disable, cripple, injure, mutilate, disfigure *The accident left many people maimed for life.*

main *adj.* chief, principal, foremost *The main reason she comes here is for the free dinners.* ANT. secondary, accessory.

maintain *vb.* 1 keep, continue, keep up, preserve, support *Despite opposition, Johnson maintained his leadership of the political party.* 2 preserve, keep, keep up, renew *If the town maintained the park in good condition, the people would be able to use it.* 3 assert, state, hold, declare; claim, contend *The man whom the police are questioning maintains that he was nowhere near the scene of the crime.* ANT. (1) discontinue.

maintenance *n.* 1 upkeep, preservation *This is a delicate machine, and maintenance and repairs are costly.* 2 support, living, subsistence, bread, livelihood *On the salary you are paying me I don't even have enough money for maintenance.*

majestic *adj.* 1 royal, kingly, princely, regal, noble, grand, stately *The star of the play made a majestic entrance and everyone applauded.* 2 splendid, magnificent *The decorations in the grand ballroom of the hotel are truly majestic.* ANT. (1) lowly, base. (2) squalid.

majesty *n.* dignity, nobility, grandeur *The majesty of the ceremony was not lost on the children, who were very impressed.*

major *adj.* greater, larger; important, chief *Is there a major difference in our points of view on the issue?* ANT. minor, inconsequential.

majority *n.* greater part, preponderance, mass, bulk *A survey reveals that the majority of voters would like a change.* ANT. minority.

make *vb.* 1 fabricate, manufacture, produce, form, build, construct, create *By using assembly lines, it became possible to make a car in an hour.* 2 become, develop into *I think that Barbie would make an excellent prefect.* 3 cause, render; occasion *Eating chocolate all afternoon made him feel sick.* 4 do, effect, execute, perform, accomplish *Alan made a bow and the curtain came down at the end of the play.* 5 compel, cause, force *Patrick's mother makes him wear the velvet suit with the lace collar whenever they go visiting.* 6 earn, gain, obtain, acquire, get *My guess is that, as a director of the company, Abernathy makes about £25,000 a year.* 7 reach, arrive at *I don't see how we can make Edinburgh if you drive so slowly all the time.* 8 appoint, elect, select, assign *Ernie's father was made head of the town committee on preservation of trees.* 9 amount to, add up to, equal, total *6 and 3 makes 9.* *vb. phr.* **make believe** pretend, fantasize, imagine *Let's all make believe that we're sailing across the ocean in a big ship.* **make do** get by, manage, survive *'I expect we'll make do somehow', Mother used to say, and we always did.* **make for** head towards, aim for *We're making for the Lake*

District on our holiday. **make good** repay, compensate, reimburse *The company had to make good the loss of my wallet.* **make it** succeed, triumph *After working hard for twenty years, Kelly has finally made it to the top of his profession.* **make out** discern, perceive, understand, recognize *Hubert mumbles so, I can hardly make out what he's saying.* **make up** 1 create, invent, fabricate *The students made up a story about life as a lorry driver and then put it on as a play.* 2 compose, form, join, constitute *Do we have enough people to make up a football team?*

male *adj.* masculine, manly, virile *Before they allowed in women reporters, team locker rooms were a male stronghold.* ANT. female, feminine, womanly.

malice *n.* spite, resentment, viciousness, grudge, bitterness *I stepped on your toe by accident, not out of malice.* ANT. love, kindness.

maltreat *vb.* hurt, abuse, injure, mistreat *I had no idea that so many children were maltreated by their parents.*

mammoth *adj.* huge, colossal, enormous, immense, gigantic *They are opening a mammoth supermarket in the shopping precinct nearby.* ANT. small, tiny, minuscule.

man *n.* 1 mankind, humanity; human beings *Man has lived on earth for thousands of years.* 2 gentleman, chap, fellow *The men came in the room and the ladies left.* 3 manliness, courage, bravery *The man in him was quickened as he contemplated the task before him.*

manage *vb.* 1 direct, guide, lead, supervise, superintend, control, conduct, administer, rule *My uncle manages an aircraft factory.* 2 succeed, contrive; arrange, bring about *I managed to cling to a small tree that saved me from falling off the cliff.* ANT. (1) mismanage, bungle.

manageable *adj.* controllable; docile, tractable, willing; obedient *An animal born in captivity is more manageable than one born in the wild.* ANT. unmanageable; wild, recalcitrant.

management *n.* 1 control, supervision, direction, regulation, administration, care *The management of the company was in the hands of the owner's son.* 2 directors, authorities *The management consulted with the union officials before declaring the redundancies.*

manager *n.* supervisor, superintendent, overseer, executive, director, boss *Frances is the first woman to be appointed manager of the plant.*

mandate *n.* commission, authority, support; command *We have a mandate from the people to give the news impartially and fully.*

mandatory *adj.* required, compulsory, obligatory *A good education is mandatory for anyone who wants to get anywhere in the world.*

mangle *vb.* mutilate, destroy, disfigure, tear *My teddy bear was mangled out of recognition in the washing machine.*

mania *n.* craze, obsession, passion *The mania for the Beatles began in the 1960s.*

maniac *see* **lunatic**.

manifest *adj.* evident, obvious, apparent *It was manifest from the* *tracks that the elephant had passed this way.*   ANT. hidden, concealed.

manipulate *vb.*   1 handle *It requires dexterity to manipulate the controls of a huge passenger aeroplane.*   2 manage, use, exploit *Grimsby manipulates people to get them to do what he wants.*

manly *adj.*   masculine, manful, strong, brave, courageous *They call boxing the manly art of self-defence.*

manner *n.*   way, method, style, fashion, custom *I do not like the rude manner in which you address your teacher.*

mannerism *n.*   habit, quirk, peculiarity, eccentricity *Rudolph's thumbing his nose is merely one of his mannerisms.*

manoeuvre *n.*   plan, action, strategy, tactics *In war, political and military manoeuvres are both important.*   *vb.*   plot, scheme, contrive *Three men manoeuvred for the leadership, when they heard that the present director was retiring.*

manual *n.*   handbook, guidebook, instruction book *I looked in my car manual to see how to change the oil.*   *adj.*   1 physical *Ian sometimes did a manual job in his holidays.*   2 human *Manual cataloguing of books takes a long time; doing it by computer would be much quicker.*   ANT. *adj.* (1) mental.   (2) automatic, computer-operated.

manufacture *vb.*   make, assemble, fabricate, construct *The company manufactures toys in the factory down the road.*   *n.*   making, assembly, fabrication, construction, production *The Black Country is an important centre for the manufacture of locks and drains.*

many *adj.*   numerous, abundant, plentiful *There are many varieties of fish in the sea.*   ANT. few.

map *n.,vb.*   chart, graph, plan *This map of England doesn't show the county boundaries. The survey team was mapping the area using photographs taken from an aeroplane.*

mar *vb.*   spoil, impair, harm *I don't want anything to mar our friendship.*

march *n.*   walk, parade, advance; procession *The march, which covered a distance of twenty-five miles, tired the soldiers out.*   *vb.* move, proceed, walk, parade *The protesters marched to Trafalgar Square and held a rally.*

margin *n.*   edge, rim, border *The margin on the napkins matches that on the tablecloth.*

marginal *adj.*   borderline, nonessential, unnecessary, noncritical *Being able to read and write seems to be a marginal requirement these days to enter university.*   ANT. principal, main.

marine *adj.*   maritime, oceanic, nautical *My brother is studying marine biology.*

mark *n.*   1 impression, effect, trace, imprint, stamp, brand *The teachers at the school have left their mark on their students.*   2 sign, symbol, emblem, badge *The king made his mark on the treaty by using his signet ring.*   3 target, goal *The first three arrows were wide of the mark, but the last hit the bull's-eye.*   *vb.*   1 stamp, brand,

imprint, identify *The bookplate marks this book as one of mine.*
2 distinguish, characterize *Her face was marked by anger.* **3** note,
heed, notice, pay attention to, attend, register *Mark what I say
about these chemicals or you may get hurt.* *vb. phr.* **mark down**
reduce, cut *The prices of cars have been marked down ten per cent.*
mark off separate, segregate, designate *These spaces in the car park
have been marked off for executives' cars.* **mark up** increase, raise
These cameras were marked up for only a small profit over cost.

market *n.* marketplace, stall, bazaar; supermarket, shop, store *We
have to go to the market to do our week's shopping tomorrow.* *vb.*
sell, merchandise *This company has been marketing cosmetics for
almost fifty years.*

marriage *n.* **1** wedding, nuptials *There aren't many people old
enough to remember the marriage of the king.* **2** matrimony, wed-
lock; union *Marriage is a solemn condition, but it can be rewarding
for the right couple.* **3** alliance, association, confederation *The
marriage of the company making toothpaste with the one making
toothbrushes worked out very successfully.* ANT. divorce, separation.

marry *vb.* wed; betroth *Bill and Penny are to be married tomorrow.*

marsh *n.* swamp, bog, fen, morass, quagmire *In the spring, the
marsh is teeming with young birds and other wildlife.*

marshal *vb.* arrange, order, organize, rank *The military forces have
been marshalled in readiness for the big battle.*

marvel *n.* wonder, miracle, phenomenon *The electric light was one
of the marvels of the late nineteenth century.* *vb.* wonder, stare,
gape *The children marvelled at how an elephant could dance so
gracefully.*

marvellous *adj.* wonderful, miraculous, wondrous, extraordinary,
amazing, astonishing, astounding *I have never seen anything so
marvellous as the eruption of a volcano.* ANT. commonplace, ordinary, usual.

masculine *adj.* male *Boxing is pretty much a masculine sport.* ANT.
feminine, female, unmasculine.

mask *n.* protection, protector; disguise, camouflage *You must wear a
mask when operating this machinery. The beautiful ladies all wore
masks to the ball.* *vb.* conceal, hide, disguise, veil, screen *I find
it difficult to mask my contempt for someone who would strike a
person when he's down.*

mass *n.* **1** pile, heap, quantity, aggregation *A huge mass of building
materials was being accumulated near the foundation.* **2** size, bulk,
magnitude, extent *The mass of the sun is many times greater than
that of the earth.* *vb.* gather, amass, accumulate, collect, marshal,
assemble *The armies were massed on the battlefield.*

massacre *n.* slaughter, genocide, killing, butchery, extermination
The massacre of the missionaries horrified the rest of the population.
vb. slay, murder, kill, butcher, exterminate *The Nazis were guilty
of massacring millions of innocent people.*

massage *vb.* rub, knead, caress; stimulate *Your leg will feel better after I have massaged it.*

massive *adj.* 1 huge, immense, gigantic, tremendous *Behind the town was a massive pile of rocks from the last avalanche.* 2 large, bulky, weighty, ponderous *A massive rock was balanced on the edge of the cliff, about to topple into the valley below.* ANT. (1) small, little, tiny. (2) light, weightless.

mast *n.* spar, pole; post *Run the flag up the mast upside down to show that the boat is in trouble.*

master *n.* 1 expert, maestro, genius *From what the museum curator could see, this artist was a master with a brush.* 2 ruler, leader, chief, commander, captain, boss, director, supervisor, superintendent *In ancient Greece and Rome, slaves assumed the names of their masters.* *vb.* 1 learn, understand, grasp *Jane eventually mastered the German language.* 2 conquer, overcome, subdue, overpower *The inexperienced chessplayer was easily mastered by the professional.* *adj.* 1 major, chief, principal *The man was a master bridge player.* 2 expert, skilful, skilled *My cousin Peter has a licence as a master mariner.*

masterful *adj.* domineering, commanding, dictatorial, bossy *My sister wants to marry someone who is masterful.*

masterly *adj.* skilful, expert, superb, adroit *The captain handles the team in a masterly manner.* ANT. clumsy, maladroit, awkward.

mastermind *n.* genius, expert *Robin is a mathematical mastermind who can solve these problems in seconds.* *vb.* manage, direct, supervise; organize *The woman who masterminded the bank robbery escaped and now lives in Brazil.*

masterpiece *n.* masterwork, perfection, model, classic *Da Vinci's paintings are all masterpieces.*

match *n.* 1 equal, equivalent, peer *Stan is very good at tennis, but he's finally met his match in Paul.* 2 competition, contest, sport *The wrestling match has been postponed.* *vb.* 1 even, equal, balance, equate *I'm afraid that with your experience of the game you won't match the champion.* 2 agree, resemble, harmonize *I'm sorry to tell you that your green polka-dot tie doesn't match that pink and purple shirt.*

matchless *adj.* unequalled, unrivalled, peerless, incomparable *The acrobat turned in a matchless performance on the parallel bars.* ANT. unimpressive, ordinary.

mate *n.* associate, companion, comrade *The man said he'd get two of his mates to help him move the piano.* *vb.* breed *What would happen if you mated a goat with a bluebottle? You'd get a butterfly!*

material *n.* 1 substance, matter, stuff; fabric *We were unable to identify the material of which the flying saucer was made.* 2 cloth, fabric, textile *The shop sells material by the metre.* *adj.* physical, real, touchable, palpable, tangible *You cannot discuss the spiritual world in terms of material objects.* ANT. *adj.* immaterial, intangible, spiritual.

maternal *adj.* motherly; loving, caring, sympathetic; protective *Matilda's feeling towards the young men is strictly maternal.*

matter *n.* 1 substance, material *The matter of which the universe is composed is almost infinite in its variety.* 2 subject, affair, business, interest *We have a matter to discuss before you can go.* 3 trouble, difficulty *What's the matter? You look pale.* *vb.* count, signify, mean *Does it matter whether you paint the table before or after the bookcase?*

mature *adj.* 1 ripe, aged, ready, seasoned *When these tomatoes are mature, each will weigh a lot.* 2 adult, full-grown, matured, grown *The play my parents saw last night is suitable only for mature audiences.* *vb.* age, ripen, develop *This tree hasn't matured enough to be transplanted.* ANT. *adj.* (1) young, youthful. (2) immature, innocent, naive.

maximize *vb.* increase, develop, enlarge, extend *The party is trying to maximize its influence in Parliament.* ANT. minimize, reduce.

maximum *n.* height, climax, greatest number *We are trying to do the maximum for every one of our constituents.* ANT. minimum.

maybe *adv.* perhaps, possibly *If it is warm tomorrow, maybe I'll go to the seashore.* ANT. definitely, certainly.

maze *n.* network, labyrinth, tangle *Hugh seems unable to extricate himself from the maze of paperwork on his desk.*

meadow *n.* pasture, field, plain *We went into the meadow to pick wildflowers.*

meagre *adj.* scanty, sparse, frugal, mean *The profits from the business have been pretty meagre this year.* ANT. plentiful, bountiful, ample, abundant.

meal *n.* snack, refreshment; breakfast, dinner, lunch *When Chugg was given a cold meal at Dartmoor, he sent it back to be reheated.*

mean¹ *vb.* 1 intend, plan, expect, propose *What do you mean to do when you arrive in Manchester?* 2 indicate, denote, signify, say, express, suggest *You ought to know that I say what I mean, and I mean what I say.*

mean² *adj.* 1 unkind, cruel, nasty, rude *I think it was very mean of you to tell Sarah that her dress is ugly.* 2 stingy, miserly, tight, selfish *Scrooge was so mean that he didn't even give his employees a day off at Christmas.* ANT. (1) gentle, thoughtful, kind. (2) generous, openhanded.

mean³ *n.* average, centre, middle *Each family has a mean number of 2.4 children.*

meander *vb.* wind, twist, turn; wander *The river meanders through the valley below.*

meaning *n.* sense, signification, denotation; significance, import, gist *The meaning of the speech is clearly that we must pay higher taxes if we are to beat inflation.*

meaningless *adj.* senseless, nonsensical, preposterous, unreasonable *I cannot understand this article—it reads like a meaningless jumble of words.*

means *n.pl.* 1 wealth, riches, money *The bank manager is a man of means and should contribute more than just a pound to charity.* 2 support, agency, resources *What means can we use to persuade him to give more?*

measure *n.* 1 extent, size, weight, volume, bulk, dimension; depth, breadth, height, length *It is difficult to comprehend the measure of the universe because the earth is so small by comparison.* 2 rule, test, standard, trial *By that measure, all the students in the class have done rather well.* *vb.* rule, weigh, count, estimate, gauge *How do astronomers measure the distance from the earth to the nearest star? Not in the same way you measure flour for baking a cake or cloth for making a coat.*

measureless *adj.* limitless, immeasurable, boundless, immense, vast, infinite *From the surface of the moon we could look out into the measureless blackness of space.* ANT. measurable, ascertainable.

mechanic *n.* machinist, operator *Only skilled mechanics are allowed to operate this machine.*

mechanical *adj.* automatic, machinelike *After a while at this job, everything becomes mechanical.*

mechanism *n.* machine, machinery, device, tool, contrivance *Where is the mechanism that controls the windscreen wipers?*

mechanize *vb.* equip, industrialize, automate *The only way to reduce labour costs is to mechanize the factory.*

medal *n.* award, decoration, medallion, badge, reward *The highest peacetime medal in Britain is the George Cross.*

meddle *vb.* interfere, pry, intrude, snoop *Stop meddling in other people's business!!*

meddlesome *adj.* meddling, troublesome, interfering, obstructive *Mrs Walton is a meddlesome old woman.*

mediate *vb.* intervene, intercede, reconcile *We need a fair-minded person to mediate our dispute with the union.*

medical *adj.* pathological, healing, remedial, pharmaceutical *The medical treatment restored him to health in no time.*

medicine *n.* drug, remedy, medication, potion, prescription, cure *This medicine won't cure your cold, but it will make you feel better.*

mediocre *adj.* average, ordinary, fair, dull *I liked the music, but I found the dancing mediocre.* ANT. excellent.

meditate *vb.* think, ponder, reflect, contemplate *I should like time to meditate on what you have proposed.*

medium *n.* 1 average; mean *There must be some medium between your being either very good or very naughty.* 2 means, mechanism, factor; agency, instrument *The telephone is the medium by which we can communicate with people across a distance.* *adj.* average; middling *The medium-priced suits are on this rack.*

medley *n.* mixture, variety, conglomeration *The orchestra played a medley of Cole Porter tunes.*

meek *adj.* humble, patient, submissive *Cooley is much too meek to ask for help.*

meet *vb.* 1 encounter, come across *I don't think that we have met before.* 2 converge, connect, join, unite *This road meets the motorway at the new intersection.* 3 settle, satisfy, fulfil, answer, discharge *I don't know if Hugo has the money to meet his obligations.* 4 convene, gather, assemble, congregate *The committee is supposed to meet next week.* *n.* contest, meeting, competition, match *The athletes' meet took place on the cinder track.* ANT. *vb.* (1) miss. (2) diverge, split. (4) scatter.

melancholy *n.* sadness, gloom, depression *Since she moved from the country to the city, Janet seems so full of melancholy.* *adj.* sad, gloomy, depressed, downcast, downhearted, unhappy *The cry of the owl sounds so melancholy—like the howl of the wolf.* ANT. *adj.* happy, joyful, jubilant.

mellow *adj.* 1 ripe, mature, full-flavoured *This pear is so mellow I can eat it with a spoon.* 2 smooth, sweet, melodious *The mellow sounds of the orchestra filled the room where we were dining.* *vb.* ripen, mature, develop, soften *This whisky has mellowed with age.* ANT. *adj.* (1) immature, unripened.

melodious *adj.* tuneful, harmonious, sweet, dulcet; pleasant *For a beginner, Tessa certainly has a melodious voice.* ANT. jarring, grating, discordant, tuneless, unmelodious.

melody *n.* tune, air, music, song *I think I recognize that melody.*

melt *vb.* 1 liquefy, dissolve *The ice in my ginger ale has melted.* 2 fade out, blend, dwindle, vanish, disappear *As we approached their village, the natives seemed to melt away into the jungle.* 3 soften, relax *The giant's heart melted when he saw the children, and he let them play in his garden.* ANT. (1) harden, freeze, solidify.

member *n.* partner, sharer, participator *Are you a member of this committee?*

memorable *adj.* historic, unforgettable, important, significant *My discharge from the hospital was a memorable day for all the family.* ANT. forgettable, passing, transitory.

memorial *n.* commemoration, remembrance; pillar, column; inscription *The townspeople subscribed to erect a memorial to those who died in the war.*

memorize *vb.* learn, remember, record *Try to memorize the code number and not write it down anywhere.* ANT. forget.

memory *n.* 1 recollection, recall, remembrance, retrospection *As she got older, her memory grew worse.* 2 mental image, thought, representation *After more than ten years, my memory of the conversation is not very accurate.*

menace *n.* threat, warning, intimidation *That driver is a menace to everyone else on the road.* *vb.* threaten, intimidate, warn *As I stepped nearer to the gate, a huge dog leapt out and menaced me.*

mend *vb.* 1 repair, patch, restore, fix *There's a man down the street who mends broken china.* 2 improve, recover, recuperate, heal *Greg's broken arm mended very quickly.* ANT. (1) ruin, destroy, spoil. (2) worsen, deteriorate.

menial *adj.* lowly, common, servile *Geoffrey was finally able to get a menial job sweeping out offices.*

mental *adj.* intellectual, reasoning, thinking. ANT. physical.

mention *vb.* refer to, introduce, touch on *Please don't mention the subject of your leaving to Mother.* *n.* reference, remark *I do seem to remember that the speaker made some brief mention of the other candidates.*

merchandise *n.* wares, stock, goods, commodities *The shopkeeper said that he doesn't keep that kind of merchandise and would have to order it.* *vb.* sell, promote *The sales manager suggested merchandising the posters through bookshops.*

merchant *n.* storekeeper, shopkeeper, retailer, trader, dealer; businessman *Mr Harris is a well-thought-of wine merchant in London.*

merciful *adj.* kind, compassionate, lenient, forgiving, tenderhearted, kindhearted, sympathetic *We begged the king to be merciful when punishing people for slight offences.* ANT. unjust, unforgiving, harsh, mean.

merciless *adj.* cruel, ruthless, pitiless, savage, hard, hardhearted, unfeeling *The spy was subjected to merciless torture to find out the truth.* ANT. merciful, benevolent, kindhearted.

mercy *n.* 1 compassion, sympathy, pity, consideration, leniency, kindness, tenderness *The prisoners begged for mercy, and the chief allowed them to be released.* 2 disposal, discretion, disposition *The poor fly was caught in the web and was now at the mercy of the spider.* ANT. (1) cruelty, ruthlessness, pitilessness.

mere *adj.* bare, scant. *I was a mere lad when I shipped aboard a Liverpool liner as cabin boy.* ANT. considerable, substantial

merely *adv.* barely, hardly, only, simply *When I offered to carry your packages, I was merely trying to be helpful, not to steal them.*

merge *vb.* join, unite; blend, fuse *If the companies merge, their combined strength could be significant.*

merger *n.* amalgamation, combination, incorporation *I look forward to a merger between our two companies.*

merit *n.* worth, value, quality, worthiness *I think that there is a great deal of merit in wanting to conserve energy.* *vb.* deserve, earn, qualify for, be worthy of *Joe merited that commendation for bravery for saving the girl from drowning.*

merry *adj.* cheerful, cheery, joyful, happy, jolly, jovial *We certainly had a merry time at the office party!!* ANT. sad, doleful, gloomy.

mesh *n.* network, net, web, screen *Some debris has clogged the mesh, preventing the water from flowing through.*

mess *n.* 1 untidiness, confusion, disorder, muddle, jumble *I've never seen a mess like the one in Sophie's room—everything's strewn about.* 2 difficulty, trouble, predicament *Pete has got himself into a mess with the history teacher again: something about late homework.* *vb.* confuse, muddle, dirty *It takes an hour to straighten up and clean a room that you mess up in a minute.*

message *n.* 1 communication, note, letter; memorandum, memo

The courier carried the message for three weeks through the jungle.
2 information, news, word, advice *I have a message for you from your mother: Don't forget to brush your teeth.*

messenger *n.* courier, bearer, runner, agent *Although he ran all the way, the messenger did not arrive till after David had left.*

messy *adj.* dirty, disorderly, disordered, confused, confusing; untidy, sloppy, slovenly *The teacher refused to accept any homework that was too messy.* ANT. neat, orderly, tidy.

mete (out) *vb.* administer, distribute, allot *The charity saw to it that the food was meted out fairly.*

meter *n.* device, recorder, gauge; measure, scale *The gas company sends someone round to read the meter periodically.*

method *n.* way, technique, manner, approach, means *Using your method, it would take four people five days to complete the work.*

methodical *adj.* systematic, orderly, businesslike *Curtis may not be very fast, but his methodical procedures are very accurate and well organized.* ANT. irregular, disconnected, confused.

meticulous *adj.* precise, accurate, exact, painstaking, scrupulous *Sergeant MacLowe is a meticulous stickler for the rules.*

middle *n.* centre, midpoint, median *You are not allowed to walk down the middle of a motorway.* *adj.* centre, central, halfway, intermediate *Bill lives in the house at this end, John in the one at the other end, and Betty lives in the middle one.* ANT. beginning, end.

middleman *n.* agent, broker, dealer, representative, distributor *Our prices are lower because you don't have to pay a middleman—you buy directly from the manufacturer*

midst *n.* middle, centre, thick, heart *In the midst of the forest is a bare circular track, which they call a fairy ring.*

might *n.* power, strength, force, vigour *It would take the might of a giant to lift that stone from the door of the cave.* ANT. weakness, frailty, vulnerability.

mighty *adj.* strong, powerful, muscular *The blacksmith was a mighty man who could bend a steel bar with his bare hands.* ANT. weak, frail.

migrate *vb.* move, resettle; immigrate, emigrate *Where shall we put all the people who migrated from the continent after the war?* ANT. remain, stay, settle.

mild *adj.* 1 calm, gentle, temperate, pleasant *After a bitter cold winter, we experienced a mild spring.* 2 amiable, kind, compassionate, peaceful, calm *Tom is known to have a mild disposition.* 3 bland, soothing *This is a sharp, not a mild, cheese.* ANT. (1) stormy, turbulent. (2) violent, excitable, hot-tempered.

militant *adj.* aggressive, belligerent, offensive, pugnacious *The present government is trying to suppress the militant tendencies of the opposition.*

military *adj.* armed, martial; operational, strategical *We suffered a military setback, but our diplomatic advances more than made up for it.*

mimic *vb.* impersonate, copy, imitate, ape *Have you seen Stuart mimicking the headmaster?* *n.* impersonator, comedian, mime *I love seeing mimics imitating famous people!*

mind *n.* 1 intellect, brain, intelligence, reason, understanding, sense *Albert Einstein had the mind of a genius.* 2 inclination, intention *I have a mind to dismiss the entire class early for being so good.* *vb.* 1 object (to), care (about), dislike *Do you mind moving your car a little, so I can drive mine out?* 2 care for, look after, watch, tend *Stefanie minds three children after school.* 3 pay attention, obey, heed, attend *Mind what your father says to you now!*

mindful *adj.* aware, open-eyed, alert, watchful *Mindful of all the dangers, Basil still wanted to become a commando.* ANT. heedless, uncaring.

mine *n.* 1 pit, shaft, excavation; lode, vein *The mine was rich in coal and could be worked for twenty-five years.* 2 source *Jim was a mine of information about football.* *vb.* dig, excavate, drill, quarry *My grandfather mined in South Africa.*

mingle *vb.* combine, mix, blend *After sifting the flour, mingle it with the other ingredients.* ANT. separate, sort.

miniature *adj.* tiny, small, midget, little, minute *I dreamed that a mouse was driving across my bed in a miniature car.* ANT. large, giant.

minimize *vb.* diminish, decrease, lessen, reduce *The best you can do with investments these days is to minimize your losses.* ANT. maximize, enlarge.

minimum *n.* least, lowest *Try to pay the minimum when you buy at auction.* ANT. maximum.

minister *n.* clergyman, pastor, parson, preacher, vicar, curate, chaplain, deacon, cleric, reverend *The minister's sermon was about kindness to people being more important than kindness to animals.*

minor *adj.* smaller, lesser, secondary, petty, unimportant *The department stores no longer consider shoplifting a minor offence.* *n.* boy, girl, child, youth, adolescent *No minors were allowed to attend the film.* ANT. *adj.* major. *n.* adult, grown-up.

mint *vb.* coin, punch, stamp, strike *The government has stopped minting pure silver coins.*

minute¹ *n.* jiffy, moment, instant, second *When my wife says 'Wait a minute', I sometimes have to wait an hour.*

minute² *adj.* tiny, wee, microscopic, minuscule *I've never understood how the fly's minute wings could carry it so quickly.* ANT. large, huge, immense.

miracle *n.* marvel, wonder, phenomenon *Every religion has a god who works miracles.*

miraculous *adj.* marvellous, wonderful, incredible, phenomenal, extraordinary; *Jeanne has made a miraculous recovery after her accident.* ANT. ordinary, commonplace, everyday.

mirror *n.* looking-glass, glass; reflector *I don't always like what I see* *when I look in the mirror.* vb. reflect *The image of the building is mirrored in the pond.*

mirth n. glee, joy, gaiety, joyousness, jollity, joyfulness, merriment, laughter *Some regard New Year's Day as a time for reflection and not for mirth and frivolity.* ANT. gloom, sadness, seriousness.

miscarry vb. fail, go wrong *or* awry *Our plans for a surprise party for Fingal miscarried when his wife told him about it.* ANT. succeed.

miscellaneous adj. diverse, different, mixed, varied *This filing cabinet seems to contain a lot of miscellaneous files.*

mischief n. 1 playfulness, roguishness, rascality *That redheaded boy is full of mischief—putting a drawing pin on teacher's chair.* 2 trouble, harm, damage, injury *The vandals who broke into the school last night did a lot of mischief.*

mischievous adj. roguish, playful, naughty. *Peter isn't really a bad child, he's just mischievous.* ANT. good, well-behaved

miser n. niggard, skinflint, tightwad, Scrooge; hoarder *That miser never spent anything on anyone but himself.* ANT. philanthropist, benefactor.

miserable adj. 1 unhappy, uncomfortable, wretched, heart-broken *Ted was miserable when he wasn't chosen for the team.* 2 poor, penniless, needy, poverty-stricken *The miserable people in other countries have no one to turn to for help but us.* 3 mean, contemptible, hateful, low, wretched, bad *What rotten miserable person has been teasing these animals?* ANT. (1) happy, joyful, content. (2) wealthy, well-off, prosperous. (3) noble, honourable. (4) lucky, fortunate.

miserly adj. stingy, tightfisted, pennypinching, cheap, mean; selfish *Mrs Cutter was so miserly that she used paraffin lamps instead of electric lights.* ANT. generous, openhanded, extravagant.

misery n. 1 unhappiness, suffering, anguish, woe, agony, distress *During the famine I saw almost more misery than I could stand in one lifetime.* 2 grief, sorrow *We all tried to console the widow in her misery.* ANT. (1) delight, joy.

misfortune n. bad luck; calamity; disappointment, nuisance *Finnegan always felt that it was a misfortune to have been born in the twentieth century.* ANT. good fortune, good luck.

misgiving n. doubt, hesitation, suspicion, mistrust, uncertainty *Father's misgivings about letting me use the car were confirmed when I had an accident.*

mishap n. accident, misadventure *I understand that the mishap with your computer was easily remedied.*

misjudge vb. prejudge, misconstrue, misinterpret *I must have misjudged your talent at chess.*

mislay vb. lose, misplace *Have you mislaid the car keys again?* ANT. find, discover.

mislead vb. deceive, delude, take in; trick *Do not be misled by what the double-glazing salesman tells you.*

mismatched *adj.* unsuitable, unfit, unsuited, incompatible *Herbert and the princess as a couple are totally mismatched.*

misprint *n.* error, mistake; literal *The misprint in the headline of the play review made it read 'Goon Show' instead of 'Good Show'.*

miss *vb.* 1 need, want, desire, yearn for *His wife missed him very much when he was away from home.* 2 drop, fumble, bumble *Sonia missed the ball completely, even when we threw it gently.* *n.* slip, failure, error, blunder, fumble *A miss is as good as a mile.*

missile *n.* projectile, shot, weapon *The guided missiles that were stockpiled in Europe have largely been dismantled.*

mission *n.* task, duty, work, undertaking *Thurfoot feels that it is his mission in life to help others.*

mist *n.* fog, cloud, haze, steam *The mist was so thick we couldn't drive another foot.*

mistake *n.* error, slip, fault *Lester, this homework is full of mistakes and you must do it again.* *vb.* misunderstand, misjudge, confuse; misinterpret *I mistook the reflection of the searchlight on the clouds for a flying saucer.*

mistaken *adj.* wrong, incorrect, confused, misinformed, inaccurate *Alan is mistaken about having had an appointment with me for today.* ANT. correct, right, accurate.

misunderstand *vb.* misinterpret, misjudge, confuse, jumble, mistake *Philippa misunderstood my intention when I sent her flowers for her birthday.* ANT. comprehend, perceive.

misunderstanding *n.* disagreement, clash, conflict, dispute *The little misunderstanding between Vincent and his girlfriend was settled when she shot him.*

mix *vb.* combine, blend, mingle *When you mix the chemicals together be careful that they do not explode.* *n.* combination, blend, mixture *The people on that island are an unusual mix of natives and immigrants. Use a cake mix when preparing this cake.* ANT. *vb.* separate, divide.

mixture *n.* 1 mix, confusion, jumble, medley, hotchpotch *Your jacket and your trousers are a curious mixture of styles.* 2 blend, combination *I made up this mixture so that we could dip bread in it for French toast.*

moan *vb.,n.* groan, wail, lament, cry *When I went to see what it was, it turned out to be the wind moaning in the chimney. I thought I heard someone in the next room give a loud moan.*

mob *n.* swarm, crowd, rabble, throng *There was a mob of people gathered near the ice-cream vendor.* *vb.* swarm, crowd, throng; riot *The rock star was mobbed when he left the theatre by people wanting his autograph.*

mobile *adj.* movable; free; portable *The great thing about this barbecue is that it is mobile enough to move wherever you want it.* ANT. immobile, stationary, fixed.

mock *vb.* scorn, deride, ridicule, tease, jeer *When the singer came out on stage, the audience mocked him, and he wept.* *adj.* imitation, fake; fraudulent, sham *Mock turtle soup doesn't taste like the real thing.* ANT. *vb.* praise, honour, applaud. *adj.* real, genuine, authentic.

mockery *n.* 1 ridicule, scorn, derision *Bernard's painting was held up to the mockery of the other students.* 2 travesty, sham, pretext, pretence *You have made a mockery of a very serious matter by ridiculing it.* ANT. praise, admiration.

mode *n.* manner, method, style, technique, practice, way, fashion *This mode of working while lying flat on my back is new to me.*

model *n.* 1 example, pattern, ideal *I tried to make a vase, using the one over there as a model.* 2 copy, representation, imitation, facsimile *This aeroplane is an actual·working model of the real thing.* 3 version, style, design *This car is a late model.* 4 mannequin, sitter *I'd very much like to have you sit as a model for my next painting.* *vb.* 1 form, shape, mould, fashion, pattern, design *Dick has modelled a figure out of clay. Sandra tries to model herself on her teacher.* 2 sit, pose *Cordelia models for that high-fashion boutique in town.*

moderate¹ *adj.* 1 reasonable, average, medium, fair *The doctor said that a moderate amount of coffee would do me no harm.* 2 conservative, middle-of-the-road, cautious *The minister's plans for economic recovery were moderate, not extreme.* ANT. (1) immoderate, excessive.

moderate² *vb.* 1 arbitrate, referee, judge, umpire *The head of the department moderated the debate between the two teams.* 2 weaken, pacify, lessen, calm, sober, temper *As the sun sank towards the horizon, the scorching heat of the day was moderated by a cool breeze.* ANT. (2) intensify, increase.

modern *adj.* present-day, up-to-date, recent, novel, new, fresh, modish, stylish *A modern house is much easier to keep clean than an older one.* ANT. old-fashioned, antique, out-of-date, outmoded.

modernize *vb.* refurbish, rebuild, improve, renovate, renew *It cost the Johnstons quite a lot to modernize their kitchen.*

modest *adj.* 1 humble, unassuming; meek *Geoffrey was very modest regarding his achievements.* 2 decorous, chaste *Harriet was wearing a modest black dress buttoned up to the neck.* ANT. (1) vain, proud, arrogant. (2) ostentatious, pretentious, showy, gaudy.

modesty *n.* humility, simplicity, decency, propriety *Modesty prohibits my describing what went on in the headmaster's study.* ANT. vanity, conceit, pride.

modify *vb.* 1 change, alter, vary, adjust *If you expect to remain as a student in this school, Patrick, you'll have to modify your behaviour.* 2 moderate, temper *Since she was elected, I think that the record will show that the MP has modified her views on education.*

moist *adj.* damp, humid; muggy, clammy, wet *The sponge must be kept moist throughout the procedure.* ANT. dry, arid, parched.

moisten *vb.* dampen; wet; humidify *You must moisten the earth round the base of the plant every week.* ANT. dry.

moisture *n.* dampness, wetness; condensation; mist *The moisture from my hot bath condensed and froze on the window.* ANT. dryness, aridity.

molest *vb.* annoy, disturb, pester; attack, assault *Several women have complained about being molested while walking through the park.*

moment *n.* 1 instant, (*informal*) jiffy, flash, twinkling *The receptionist asked me to sit down and wait a moment.* 2 importance, significance, import, gravity, seriousness, consequence *It is of no great moment to me whether you go tomorrow or tonight.*

momentary *adj.* brief, temporary, short-lived, fleeting, ephemeral *I caught only a momentary glimpse of the Queen as she rode by.*

momentous *adj.* important, serious, consequential, far-reaching *Only an event of momentous proportions could prevent my being on time to meet you.* ANT. unimportant, trivial, trifling.

monarch *n.* king, queen, ruler, emperor, empress, sovereign *When the monarch entered the room, we all bowed our heads in respect.*

money *n.* 1 coin, cash, currency, notes *Can you lend me some money to go to the cinema?* 2 funds, capital *I doubt that the company has the money it needs for expansion.*

monitor *n.* supervisor; director, adviser *Felicity will be the dining room monitor for today and will try to keep the children under control.* *vb.* watch, observe, control, supervise *We were able to monitor the actions of the robot from the control booth.*

monopoly *n.* 1 control, domination *Some nationalized industries have a monopoly in the supply of their services.* 2 cartel, ring *The firm had a monopoly on spare parts for cars.*

monotonous *adj.* boring, dull, tedious, humdrum, tiring, tiresome, wearisome *Watching a record turning on a record player is terribly monotonous. The politicians gave one monotonous speech after another.* ANT. interesting, fascinating, riveting.

monster *n.* beast, brute, fiend, villain, wretch, demon *This little monster pulls the wings off butterflies.*

monstrous *adj.* horrible, revolting, shocking, repulsive, hideous, dreadful, terrible; outrageous *The guards were known for their monstrous torturing of prisoners.*

monument *n.* column, pillar, obelisk, stone; statue *They have erected a monument to commemorate the battle.*

monumental *adj.* 1 huge, enormous, immense, colossal, gigantic *At the top of the mountain stands a monumental cross.* 2 significant, important *The invention of the wheel allowed man to make monumental progress.* ANT. (1) miniature, tiny. (2) insignificant, trivial.

mood *n.* temper, humour, disposition, frame of mind *Ferncliff seems to be in a happy mood today.*

moody *adj.* temperamental, changeable; short-tempered, irritable, peevish, fretful, spiteful *Maria has been very moody lately—I wonder if anything is wrong.* ANT. calm, even-tempered, good-natured.

mop (up) *vb.* wipe, wash, clean *Whoever made this mess must mop it up at once.*

mope *vb.* grieve, lose heart, despair, sulk *Why not go out for some fresh air instead of moping about the house all weekend?* ANT. cheer up.

moral *adj.* upright, honest, ethical, just, good, honourable *The moral people—those who never seem to do anything wrong—those are the ones to keep an eye on.* ANT. immoral, dishonest, sinful, corrupt.

morale *n.* spirit, confidence, assurance *The salesmen need an inspirational talk to improve their morale.*

morbid *adj.* unhealthy, unwholesome; pessimistic; morose *Louis is known for his lugubrious manner and his morbid sense of humour.*

more *adj.* additional, extra, further *More money can be budgeted only with the consent of the treasurer.* ANT. fewer.

moreover *adv.* also, further, furthermore, in addition, besides *Lenore won first prize in diving, moreover she won a medal in the relay race.*

moron *see* **idiot.**

morsel *n.* bite, titbit, bit, piece *The beggar shared a few morsels of bread with the dog.*

mortal *adj.* **1** perishable; temporary; human *Since all men are mortal, we must all die sometime.* **2** lethal, deadly, fatal *The knight received a mortal wound from the sword and lay dying.* ANT. **(1)** immortal, imperishable. **(2)** superficial.

most *adj.* nearly all, a majority of *Most people would do exactly what you did.*

mostly *adv.* generally, chiefly, mainly, for the most part, largely, principally *Sometimes our dog goes out for walks with us, but mostly he just lies around.*

motherly *see* **maternal.**

motion *n.* movement, change, action *Because of the breeze, the branches of the trees are constantly in motion.* *vb.* gesture, signal, indicate *I was about to say something, but Vincent motioned to me to be quiet.* ANT. *n.* stillness, immobility.

motivate *vb.* stimulate, move, cause, prompt *What motivates Dennis to behave that way?*

motive *n.* reason, purpose, idea, cause, ground *What was Edward's motive in telling people that I hate ice cream?*

motor *n.* engine, machine *We were able to repair the motor that drives the lawn-mower.*

motto *n.* slogan, maxim, byword, catchword; proverb, saying *The mattress manufacturer's motto is 'We stand behind every product we sell'.*

mould *n.* **1** cast, cavity, form, pattern *Joyce makes her jellies in a pretty mould.* **2** decay, mildew *Mould developed on the damp walls.* *vb.* shape, form, fashion *Sandra moulds the clay into delicate figures.*

mound *n.* hill, hillock, pile, heap *The picnickers left behind a mound of rubbish that we had to clean up.*

mount *vb.* 1 ascend, climb, go up *The cowboy mounted his horse and rode away. Frank had to mount a ladder to reach the light bulb.* 2 rise, increase, ascend *As the costs of raw materials mounted, the manufacturers passed them on to the consumer in higher prices.* 3 prepare, make ready, set up *The enemy was going to mount an attack at dawn.* *n.* 1 horse, steed, charger *The comical knight rode an old nag as his mount.* 2 mountain; hill *Mount Everest is the highest peak in the world.* 3 backing, setting; margin *The drawing on white card was set off well against the black mount.* ANT. *vb.* (1, 2) descend.

mountain *n.* peak; height, ridge, range *The Andes are the most impressive mountains I have seen.*

mourn *vb.* lament, grieve, sorrow, bemoan *David is mourning the loss of his pet mongoose.* ANT. rejoice, celebrate.

mournful *adj.* sad, sorrowful, unhappy *At night we could hear the mournful cry of the wolf.* ANT. cheerful, joyful, happy.

mouth *n.* entrance, opening, aperture *We huddled inside the mouth of the cave.*

move *vb.* 1 advance, proceed, progress, go on; stir, budge, travel, shift; retreat *As soon as anyone moved, the dogs would begin to growl.* 2 push, propel, shift *Please move your chair closer to the table.* 3 affect, touch, influence *I was deeply moved by the play.* *n.* movement, motion, action *Hilary made a move as if to leave.*

movement *n.* 1 move, motion, action, activity *I noticed a slight movement of the door and knew someone was behind it.* 2 effort, action, crusade *There was a movement among the students to help the vagrants of the town.*

muddle *n.* confusion, trouble *I seem to be in such a muddle today, I can't get anything straight!* *vb.* confuse, mix up, jumble up *The clerk in the NHS office muddled up our files and they almost sent me to hospital for surgery.*

muddy *adj.* soggy, miry, marshy *You had better wear your wellies as it's very muddy outside.*

muffle *vb.* deaden, soften, quieten, mute, stifle *Stuff cotton wool in your ears to muffle the noise of the explosion.* ANT. amplify, louden.

multiply *vb.* 1 increase; double, triple, treble *The number of readers of the new magazine multiplied in the beginning.* 2 reproduce, propagate *Rabbits multiply very rapidly.* ANT. decrease, lessen.

multitude *n.* throng, crowd, mass, swarm, mob *The pope spoke to the multitude assembled in the square below his balcony.*

mumble *see* murmur.

munch *vb.* chew, crunch *The silence was broken by the noise of Ferdinand munching on brazil nuts.*

murder *n.* killing, death, slaying, slaughter; manslaughter *The suspect was accused of the murder of three people whose bodies had been* *found in his cellar.* *vb.* kill, destroy, massacre; slaughter, slay, assassinate *It was found that the killer had murdered the people out of revenge.*

murderer *n.* killer, slayer, assassin; gangster *Convicted murderers were hanged in the old days.*

murky *adj.* dim, dark, gloomy; dirty *The murky atmosphere prevented our seeing more than a few feet ahead.*

murmur *n.* mutter, mumble, grumble, complaint; whimper *A murmur of protest was heard from the audience when the new rules were announced.* *vb.* mutter, mumble, grumble; whimper *The trees murmured under the onslaught of the icy winds.*

musical *adj.* tuneful, harmonious, melodious *Hazel has a truly melodious voice.*

musician *n.* artist, player, performer; composer *On weekend evenings, there were musicians to entertain visitors to the restaurant.*

musty *adj.* old, dusty, fusty, mouldy *When the old trunk was finally pried open a musty odour of old papers wafted up to us.*

mute *adj.* dumb, voiceless, silent *Despite threats, the prisoner remained mute during the questioning by police.*

mutilate *vb.* maim, weaken, damage, injure *On his first day at work, Morris mutilated his hand in a machine.*

mutinous *adj.* rebellious, revolutionary, unruly *After five weeks in the tropical heat, the crew was beginning to become mutinous.* ANT. obedient, dutiful, compliant.

mutiny *n.* rebellion, revolt, uprising *All of the men who took part in the mutiny were sent home in chains.* *vb.* rebel, revolt, rise up *The crew of the* Bounty *mutinied against Captain Bligh and set him and a few men adrift in a boat.*

mutter *see* **murmur.**

mutual *adj.* **1** reciprocal, alternate *If you give our employees a discount in your shop, we'll give yours a mutual discount in ours.* **2** common, shared *Albert is our mutual friend.*

mysterious *adj.* secret; puzzling, strange *There have been a few mysterious sightings of Lord Lucan in various parts of the world.* ANT. open, direct, obvious.

mystery *n.* **1** puzzle, riddle, enigma *The mystery developed as a second man suddenly disappeared.* **2** strangeness, inscrutability *There is a strange mystery surrounding the woman who lives in the castle, and we may never know the solution.*

mystify *vb.* confuse, bewilder, puzzle, perplex *I am totally mystified by this letter from my brother because I have no brother.*

myth *n.* **1** legend, tradition, fable *The ancient Greek and Roman myths still have a profound effect on our literature and language.* **2** lie, fib, prevarication, fiction *That whole story she told about being an heiress is just a myth.*

n

nag *vb.* annoy, pester, irritate, torment, vex *Warren's mother is always nagging him about cleaning up his room.* *n.* faultfinder, carper; pest, nuisance *Phil's wife is an awful nag.*

naïve *adj.* innocent, credulous, simple, ingenuous *Peter is naïve enough to believe anything you tell him.* ANT. experienced.

naked *adj.* **1** unclothed, undressed, bare, uncovered, nude *At night, when it was hot, we used to go swimming naked.* **2** simple, stark, plain, obvious, unadorned, undisguised *Jack finally told me that he had done the deed, and that's the naked truth.* ANT. (1) covered, clothed, garbed. (2) suppressed, concealed.

namby-pamby *adj.* insipid, wishy-washy, weak, colourless *It turned out that Percy had not been too namby-pamby to become a commando.*

name *n.* **1** title, appellation, designation *My name is George; what's yours?* **2** reputation; character *Rick has made a name for himself as an author of historical novels.* *vb.* **1** call, title, term, christen, baptize *We named our first child Nancy.* **2** designate, signify, mention *By the time he was two, Dan could name all the days of the week and the months.* **3** elect, nominate, appoint *We named Betty chairwoman of our committee.*

nap *n.* rest, snooze, forty winks, siesta, doze *Van likes to take a short nap before dinner.*

narrate *vb.* tell, relate, describe, recount, report *As we gathered round the fire, the old man narrated a tale from long ago.*

narrative *n.* story, tale, account, history, description *In the old days, before many people could read, history was passed on by poets and storytellers in the form of narratives.*

narrow *adj.* **1** slender, thin, tapering, tight *The passageway at the end of the cave was too narrow for me to squeeze through.* **2** close, precarious, perilous, dangerous *The driver leapt clear of the wreck just as it burst into flames—a narrow escape!* ANT. (1) wide, broad.

narrow-minded *adj.* limited, illiberal *How will you ever learn anything if you are too narrow-minded to listen to others?* ANT. broad-minded, liberal.

nasty *adj.* **1** disagreeable, unpleasant, foul *We sometimes get a spell of very nasty weather in February.* **2** dirty, filthy, foul, disgusting, loathsome, polluted, offensive *There was a very nasty pool of sewage where the factory dumped its wastes.* **3** dirty, filthy, obscene, indecent, improper *How dare you use such nasty language in the classroom!* **4** ill-natured, mean, spiteful *Manuel has a very nasty* *temper.* ANT. (1) pleasant, fair, seasonable. (2) clean, pure. (3) proper, decent. (4) pleasant, even-tempered.

nation *n.* country, state, realm, kingdom, republic *Forty nations agreed to sign the peace treaty.*

nationality *n.* citizenship; allegiance *His parents were of Italian nationality, but he now has British citizenship.*

native *adj.* 1 natural, innate, inborn, inbred, hereditary *English is my native language.* 2 local, original *Kangaroos are native to Australia.* *n.* national, citizen, inhabitant, resident *I don't come from around here at all—I'm a native of the Channel Isles.* ANT. *adj.* (2) foreign, alien. *n.* stranger, foreigner, outsider.

natural *adj.* 1 inbred, inborn, innate, inherited, hereditary; original, basic, fundamental *It's natural for a frightened animal to attack when cornered.* 2 normal, customary, typical, usual; characteristic *Instead of trying to act in a particular way, just do what is natural for you.* ANT. unnatural, alien, contrary.

naturally *adv.* 1 normally, usually, typically, ordinarily, customarily *Naturally I expect everyone to respect his parents.* 2 freely, readily, simply, openly, sincerely *Please try to behave naturally when you go for the interview: don't put on an act.* ANT. (2) artificially.

nature *n.* 1 world, universe; creation *It's against the laws of nature to expect things to fall upward.* 2 character, quality, essence *What is the true nature of water that makes it expand when cooled and contract when warmed?* 3 sort, kind, variety, character *I don't understand the nature of your question.* 4 manner, disposition, personality, character *I didn't think it was in Mr Robinson's nature to get upset over small matters.*

naughty *adj.* 1 disobedient, unruly, unmanageable, insubordinate, mischievous *Don't be naughty: just do as you are told and behave yourself.* 2 titillating, indecent, improper, rude *The boys told naughty stories in the locker room after the game.* ANT. (1) good, well-behaved, obedient.

nausea *n.* sickness, vomiting, queasiness *A feeling of nausea comes over me when I look down from such a great height.*

nauseate *vb.* disgust, repel, sicken *The stench from the rotting flesh nauseated us.*

nautical *adj.* marine, maritime, naval; sea-going *The chandlery over there sells nautical gear for yachtsmen.*

navigate *vb.* direct, guide, steer, pilot *It is no mean feat to navigate a vessel halfway round the world.*

near *adj.* close, nearby, neighbouring, adjoining *Take a chair near the fire if you're cold.* ANT. far, distant, remote.

nearly *adv.* almost, practically *I forgot it was supposed to be a surprise party and nearly told Bernard.*

neat *adj.* clean, orderly, tidy, trim; dapper, natty, smart, elegant *I want this room to be neat when I return or no pudding for a week!! Vincent has always been a very neat dresser.* ANT. messy, sloppy, unkempt, disorganized.

necessary *adj.* needed, required, important, essential *These days, a car is necessary if you are going to live in the country.* ANT. unnecessary, dispensable, unneeded.

necessity *n.* requirement, essential, prerequisite . *So many of the things we used to think of as luxuries have become necessities.*

need *n.* 1 want, lack, necessity *I feel the need of a holiday after working so hard for two years.* 2 requirement, necessity *The need for energy is increasing all of the time in the industrialized nations.* 3 poverty, pennilessness, want *Every Christmas we make a contribution to families that are in need.* *vb.* want, lack, require, miss *The poor children needed shoes and clothing and food after the flood had destroyed their home.*

needle *vb.* prod, goad, provoke, tease *Don't let George needle you about the way you look after the house.*

needless *adj.* unnecessary, unessential, nonessential, superfluous *By not phoning to say you would be late, you caused your mother needless hours of worry.*

needy *adj.* poor, poverty-stricken, penniless, destitute *They are taking up a collection for needy children.* ANT. wealthy, well-to-do, affluent, well-off.

neglect *vb.* 1 disregard, overlook, ignore *The judge ruled that the man had to take better care of the family he had neglected.* 2 omit, skip, miss *The speaker neglected mentioning all those who had helped elect him.* *n.* disregard, negligence, inattention *The soldier was reprimanded by his commanding officer for neglect of duty. The house was suffering from neglect and needed painting and some repairs.* ANT. *vb.* (1) care, attend. *n.* attention, concern, regard.

negligent *adj.* careless, inattentive, neglectful *It was negligent of you to leave your skateboard about where anyone could trip over it.*

negligible *adj.* trivial, trifling, unimportant, insignificant *There is only a negligible difference between these two editions of Hamlet.*

negotiate *vb.* arrange, settle, transact *We negotiated with the bank to pay only a small fee for the transfer of the funds.*

neighbourhood *n.* area, vicinity, section, district, locality *The value of the property in this neighbourhood has increased steadily.*

nerve *n.* 1 courage, boldness, bravery, spirit *It takes some nerve to move to a new district where you don't know anyone.* 2 *Informal:* effrontery, impudence, rudeness, impertinence *You have a lot of nerve walking into my home without knocking or ringing!* ANT. (1) cowardice, weakness, frailty.

nervous *adj.* 1 restless, excited, agitated *The threatening phone calls made everyone in the town nervous.* 2 timid, shy, fearful *Mona was very nervous about her interview.* ANT. (1) calm, tranquil, placid. (2) bold, courageous, confident.

nestle *vb.* settle, shelter, huddle, snuggle, cuddle *The dogs nestled together for warmth.*

nettle *vb.* needle, irk, irritate, pester, vex *Janice was becoming nettled by Byron's incessant questions.*

network *n.* system, organization, complex, structure *A network of agencies throughout the world represents our interests.*

neutral *adj.* 1 uninvolved, inactive, nonpartisan *I am going to remain neutral in the argument between Cecile and Roger.* 2 dull, drab *The car was a neutral colour.* ANT. (1) prejudiced, biased.

new *adj.* 1 novel, fresh, unique, original, unusual *Ken announced that he'd discovered a new way to cook chicken.* 2 recent, modern, current, latest *The new fashions aren't really very becoming to shorter people.* ANT. (1) old, ancient, usual. (2) outmoded.

newcomer *n.* new boy, beginner, novice *As he is only a newcomer, allow him some time to learn the routine.*

news *n.* information, knowledge, data, report *Is there any news about the hostages being held on that airliner?*

next *adj.* 1 adjacent, beside, close, touching *The house was next to the church.* 2 following, succeeding, subsequent *Who will be the next ruler of the country?* ANT. (1) distant. (2) preceding, previous.

nibble *vb.* peck, nip, bite *There won't be any left for dinner if you keep nibbling away at the pie.*

nice *adj.* 1 pleasant, agreeable, pleasing *Maria certainly has a nice disposition.* 2 kind, thoughtful, friendly, cordial *Be nice to your sister.* 3 accurate, precise, exact; subtle *People should learn to make a nice distinction between the meanings of words.* ANT. (1) unpleasant, disagreeable, nasty. (2) thoughtless, unkind. (3) careless, inexact.

nickname *n.* sobriquet, byname, cognomen, moniker, handle *My real name is Launcelot but my nickname is 'Animal'.*

nil *n.* nothing, nought *or* naught, zero *As they scored no points, the score was seven to nil.*

nimble *adj.* agile, spry, lively, quick *You'll have to be pretty nimble to catch that cat of ours.* ANT. clumsy, awkward.

nincompoop *n.* fool, idiot, simpleton, ninny, nitwit, dunce *Why have they made that nincompoop head of the school?*

nitty-gritty *n.* meat, substance, essentials, nub, crux, essence, pith *Let's stop talking about the trivialities and get down to the nitty-gritty.*

nitwit *see* **nincompoop.**

noble *adj.* 1 honourable, honest, upright, virtuous, dignified *It is more noble to give than to receive.* 2 aristocratic, titled, high-born, well-born, blue-blooded *The man who will marry the princess comes from a noble family.* ANT. (1) ignoble, base, dishonest. (2) low-born.

nod *vb.* say 'Yes', approve, agree, consent *When I asked him if he would like some coffee, he nodded.*

noise *n.* tumult, uproar, clamour, din, racket, outcry *The noise from the neighbours is unbelievable.* ANT. quiet, silence, peace.

noisy *adj.* loud, tumultuous, booming *It can be very noisy living near the railway line.* ANT. quiet, silent, peaceful.

nominal *adj.* theoretical, titular, ostensible *Richard is nominal head of the company, but Gladys really runs things.*

nominate *vb.* name, select, choose, propose *Whom do you think they will nominate for the first ballot?*

nonbeliever *n.* infidel, heathen, pagan; atheist, sceptic *Some religions urge their followers to destroy all nonbelievers.*

nonchalant *adj.* uninvolved, unconcerned, uncaring, indifferent; easygoing *I cannot see how she can be so nonchalant about a missing child!!*

nonconformist *n.* rebel, dissenter, radical *Gregory has always been somewhat nonconformist in his views, going his own way.*

nondescript *adj.* indescribable, unclassifiable, indefinite *Bonita thinks herself a fashion plate, but I find her clothing nondescript.*

nonessential *adj.* unnecessary, needless *During the war everyone did without nonessential items, like nylons and chocolates.*

nonsense *n.* trash, rubbish, balderdash, twaddle *Don't believe the nonsense people tell you about me.*

nonsensical *adj.* ridiculous, absurd, silly, stupid, senseless *The notion that you can make better time taking the shore road is nonsensical.*

nonstop *adj.* endless, incessant, unceasing, constant, continuous: Fred couldn't put up with Bessie's nonstop nagging so he slipped a sleeping potion into her tea.

norm *n.* standard, model, measure; average *This summer temperatures have generally been higher than the norm.*

normal *adj.* regular, usual, customary, typical, common; standard, routine *When the watchman made his round he saw nothing that wasn't normal.* **ANT.** odd, irregular, peculiar.

normally *adv.* usually, customarily, regularly, frequently *Normally, I stop by to visit my aunt when I am in Birmingham*

nosy *adj.* prying, inquisitive, curious, snooping *Our neighbours are always nosy to find out who our guests are.*

notable *adj.* noteworthy, remarkable, noted, unusual, uncommon, conspicuous, distinctive, distinguished *The union and management negotiators made notable progress in their discussions.* *n.* celebrity, personality, star *Notables of the stage, film and television attended the gala dinner.* **ANT.** *adj.* ordinary, usual, commonplace.

notation *n.* representation, system; signs, symbols *The system of musical notation, while uniform, is subject to interpretation.*

note *n.* 1 message, memorandum, memo, record *The secretary took notes of what the members of the council said.* 2 notice, heed *I have taken note of what you said and will act as you suggest.* 3 eminence, importance, distinction, repute, reputation *Many people of note came to the farewell party.* *vb.* 1 notice, attend, observe, heed, regard *The witness testified that he had noted that the back door of the house was open.* 2 write down, record, register *I noted in my diary all of the interesting things that happened to me and my friends.*

noted *adj.* famous, well-known, celebrated, distinguished, famed, notable *A noted artists was selected to paint the president's portrait.* ANT. unknown, anonymous.

notice *n.* 1 sign, poster, announcement, advertisement; note *In addition to the notices we posted on the board, we also placed one in the newspaper.* 2 observation, attention, heed, note *Please take notice of the No Smoking signs in the trains.* 3 warning, advice, admonition *The mechanic gave the garage manager one week's notice of his intention to leave.* *vb.* observe, note, heed, regard, pay attention to *Notice how carefully the painter works on these miniatures.* ANT. *vb.* ignore, disregard, overlook.

noticeable *adj.* observable, apparent, perceptible; obvious, conspicuous *Did Frances really believe that she would be less noticeable in such a tight dress?*

notify *vb.* inform, advise, tell *We were notified that the power would be shut off if we didn't pay the bill at once.*

notion *n.* idea, fancy, impression, concept, conception *My notion of what you ought to do is less important than yours.*

notorious *adj.* infamous, ill-famed; disreputable *You get what you deserve if you play cards with such a notorious cheat.*

nought *or* **naught** *see* **nil.**

nourish *vb.* sustain, support, feed, supply *Children ought to have at least one nourishing meal a day.*

nourishment *n.* sustenance, support, food, nutriment *Evidently, hydroponic farming provides plants with the nourishment they need.*

novel *n.* book, story, tale; fiction *Have you read any good novels lately?* *adj.* new, original; unusual, different, odd, strange *He's so old-fashioned that he thinks the waltz is a novel dance.*

novelty *n.* newness, originality; freshness, recentness *Myrtle tired of Jacques as soon as the novelty of going out with a Frenchman wore off.*

novice *n.* beginner, learner, tyro; amateur *Be a little more tolerant of Bruce, as he's only a novice.*

nude *see* **naked.**

nuisance *n.* irritation, annoyance, bother, trouble *After fifty years I found it a nuisance to get up to go to work every morning.*

nullify *vb.* annul, cancel, abrogate, abolish *When the council saw how angry the shopowners became, they nullified the new parking bans.*

numb *adj.* dead, deadened, paralysed *I was sitting in the waiting room for so long that when the doctor gave me a shot of penicillin my bottom was too numb to feel anything.*

number *n.* 1 total, sum, collection, quantity, amount *A large number of people visit the museum every year.* 2 numeral, digit, figure *Pick a number from one to ten but don't tell me what it is.* *vb.* count, total, add, work out, calculate; estimate *Number the desks in this classroom.*

numerous *adj.* many, copious; numberless *Numerous people have already seen this film.* ANT. few, scanty.

nurse *n.* attendant, orderly; sister, matron *Nurse, will you see to this patient, please?* *vb.* take care of, tend, care for, attend *When you were sick, wasn't it your mother who nursed you back to health?*

nurture *vb.* nourish, feed; support *In their early stages, all new programmes need a bit of nurturing.*

nutrition *n.* food, nutriment, nourishment, sustenance *The school dietitian might be an expert on nutrition, but she has a terrible sense of taste.*

O

oaf *n.* clod, boor, yokel, hillbilly, bogtrotter *That oaf Olaf has the table manners of a retarded cannibal.*

oath *n.* **1** pledge, promise, vow *I have sworn an oath never to reveal the secret.* **2** curse, profanity, swearword *When the hammer struck his finger the carpenter uttered an oath that I shall not repeat.*

obedience *n.* submission, docility *We sent our dog to a school where he was given obedience training.* ANT. disobedience, rebelliousness.

obedient *adj.* docile, yielding, respectful, obliging *Till he was ten, Clark was very obedient and did what he was told.*

obese *adj.* fat, overweight, plump, corpulent *For some reason, Rollo didn't mind being called obese, but he insisted he wasn't fat.* ANT. slender, slim, thin, lanky.

obey *vb.* comply with, follow, conform to *If you want to remain here, you must obey the rules.* ANT. disobey; break.

object *vb.* protest, disapprove of, complain *My mother objected when I said I wanted to climb the mountain alone.* *n.* **1** objective, goal, target, aim *Our object in staging the rally was to demonstrate against the use of nuclear weapons.* **2** thing, article *The object on the table was a golden statue.* ANT. *vb.* approve, agree, assent.

objection *n.* protest, disapproval, doubt *Have you any objection to my leaving work early today?* ANT. agreement, assent, concurrence.

objective *n.* aim, goal, purpose *Our objective was to reach the border before dawn.* *adj.* fair, just, impartial, unbiased *Since you are not involved and won't profit either way, perhaps you can give us an objective opinion.* ANT. *adj.* subjective, biased.

objectivity *n.* impartiality, disinterest, indifference, neutrality *Because of his objectivity, I would accept Solomon's judgement.*

obligation *n.* **1** requirement, responsibility, duty *Anyone who is elected to an office should be prepared to assume its obligations.* **2** contract, agreement *The company has taken on the obligation to supply clean towels to the school.*

oblige *vb.* require, force, compel, bind *In those days, every young man was obliged to serve in the armed forces for two years.* ANT. free.

obliging *adj.* agreeable, accommodating, kind *It was very obliging of you to allow us to stay the night.*

oblique *adj.* slanting, sloping, inclined *This oblique line ruins the composition of the painting.* ANT. vertical, perpendicular.

obliterate *vb.* destroy; erase, wipe out, delete *The harsh environment has obliterated all signs of a previous civilization.*

oblivion *n.* forgetfulness, unmindfulness; blankness, emptiness *At the end of each day in that dungeon I sought only the oblivion of sleep.*

oblivious *adj.* forgetful, unaware, unconscious *John is so wrapped up in himself that he is oblivious to the concerns of others.*

obnoxious *adj.* unpleasant, annoying, disagreeable *How can he stand living with that obnoxious woman?*

obscene *adj.* offensive, outrageous; dirty, filthy *They have cut the obscene passages from the film to show it on television.*

obscure *adj.* 1 hidden, dim, unclear, indistinct *The sign was too obscure for me to read what it said.* 2 unknown, inconspicuous *The best play of the year was written by an obscure playwright.* *vb.* screen, veil, hide, conceal, cover *The car was completely obscured by the bushes.* ANT. *adj.* (1) clear, lucid, illumined. (2)famous, noted, distinguished. (3) bright.

observance *n.* honouring, keeping; celebration *The banks are closed during the observance of national holidays.*

observant *adj.* watchful, alert, keen, vigilant, attentive *How observant of you to notice the registration number of the getaway car!!* ANT. unobservant, inattentive.

observation *n.* 1 watching, attention *Our observation of the cave was rewarded when we saw the men emerge.* 2 comment, remark, opinion *Wendy made the observation that she considered the book very boring.*

observe *vb.* 1 see, notice, look at, regard, watch *Observe the way the amoeba surrounds its food, then absorbs it with its body.* 2 honour, keep, celebrate *I observe the Queen's birthday by putting a flag outside my window.* 3 obey, follow, abide by *Please observe the speed limit.* ANT. (1, 2) ignore, disregard.

obsession *n.* fixation, infatuation, craze, mania, delusion *Collecting matchbook covers is an obsession of Lucinda's.*

obsolete *adj.* old-fashioned, outdated, outmoded, antiquated *'Olde' is an obsolete spelling for 'old'.* ANT. new, modern, up-to-date, current, fashionable.

obstacle *n.* block, stop, barrier, interference, obstruction *The foreman continually put obstacles in the way of my advancement.* ANT. aid, support.

obstinate *adj.* stubborn, opinionated, wilful, pigheaded, inflexible *Even when he knows he is wrong, Felix is too obstinate to admit it.* ANT. pliable, pliant, yielding.

obstruct *vb.* block, stop; hinder, interfere with *A police car was obstructing the road. Withholding evidence is obstructing justice.* ANT. help, further.

obstruction *n.* obstacle, block, blockage, interference, barrier *Owing to the obstruction, we had to drive home the long way round.*

obtain *vb.* 1 get, acquire, gain, procure, secure, attain *It is sometimes difficult to obtain foodstuffs in country areas.* 2 pertain, be valid, concern *Which laws obtain in this area?*

obtrusive *adj.* protruding, jutting; noticeable, prominent *Fern would be less obtrusive if she spoke more quietly.*

obvious *adj.* clear, unquestionable, transparent, plain, unmistakable *It was obvious what Jim's thoughts were as he gazed at the toys in the window.* ANT. subtle, hidden, unobtrusive.

obviously *adv.* clearly, plainly, certainly, surely, evidently *Obviously, everyone must be somewhere.*

occasion *n.* **1** time, occurrence, happening *The family gave Dad a gold watch on the occasion of his fiftieth birthday.* **2** opportunity, chance, excuse *Should the occasion arise, I would love to go the United States for a holiday.*

occasional *adj.* irregular, random, sporadic *Henry's occasional absences were forgiven by his employer.* ANT. regular, constant.

occasionally *adv.* now and then, infrequently, seldom, irregularly *I occasionally visit the village where I was born.* ANT. often, regularly.

occupant *n.* resident, tenant, inhabitant *The former occupant of this flat left it in a shambles.*

occupation *n.* **1** trade, profession, business, job, employment *For many years, my uncle's occupation was as an architect.* **2** seizure, capture *When the soldiers defending the castle surrendered, the enemy's occupation of the mountain was complete.*

occupy *vb.* **1** take up, use, fill, hold *The parents occupied the back part of the theatre at the school play.* **2** obtain, seize, capture *The invading army soon occupied the city and its suburbs.* **3** engage, employ, busy, absorb *Worries about the coming exams occupied Nellie's mind.*

occur *vb.* happen, take place, befall *What has occurred since yesterday to make you change your mind?*

occurrence *n.* event, happening; incident *Our family picnic is an annual occurrence.*

ocean *n.* sea, deep, main, Davy Jones's locker *Many brave sailors have perished in the ocean.*

odd *adj.* strange, unusual, peculiar, queer, weird, extraordinary *How very odd that your children have the same names as mine!!* ANT. ordinary, regular, unexceptional; straightforward.

odious *adj.* hateful, detestable, despicable *Informing on one's friends is the most odious act imaginable.*

odour *n.* smell, aroma, scent, fragrance, bouquet, perfume *Once the bottle was opened, the odour permeated the room.*

offence *n.* **1** sin, wrong, transgression, trespass, crime, wrongdoing, misdemeanour *The policeman said that the offence I had committed was driving through a red traffic light.* **2** resentment, indignation, anger *Bill took offence when we suggested he was too cowardly to ask Lucy for a dance.*

offend *vb.* **1** irritate, annoy, vex, anger, provoke, displease *Marie was offended at Paul's suggestion that she should get rid of her new* *hat.* **2** outrage, insult *The sight of the concentration camp offended all of us.* ANT. (1) please, flatter, delight.

offender *n.* culprit, criminal, lawbreaker, transgressor *The police had little patience with habitual offenders.*

offensive *adj.* **1** unpleasant, disagreeable, revolting, nauseous, sickening, nauseating, disgusting *Certainly, most people find the smell of rotten eggs offensive.* **2** aggressive, attacking *Our football team then made a number of offensive manoeuvres that gained some ground.* *n.* attack, assault, aggression *Our team took the offensive and we won.* ANT. *adj.* (1) pleasing, pleasant, agreeable, attractive. (2) defensive, defending.

offer *vb.* **1** present, tender, proffer, submit *The plan that Bill offered was to be voted on the next day.* **2** volunteer *Manuel offered to help with the collection at the school.* *n.* suggestion, proposal; presentation *We have received three offers to buy the car.* ANT. *vb.* refuse, deny. *n.* refusal, denial.

offhand *adj.* casual, informal, impromptu, unprepared *My offhand guess is that there are 2,137 beans in the jar.* ANT. planned, considered, calculated.

office *n.* **1** suite, offices, office building *I will be working late at the office tonight.* **2** position, post, situation; occupation *Which office do you hold in Parliament?*

official *n.* office-holder, functionary, bureaucrat, civil servant *When enquiring about my grant, I talked with an official in the education department.* *adj.* **1** formal, conventional *I think we'd better order the paper through the official channels.* **2** administrative; authorized, authoritative *The official records of births, deaths and marriages are kept in that building.*

officious *adj.* overbearing, aggressive, forward *Eleanor resents her parents' officious meddling in her personal affairs.*

offset *vb.* balance, counterbalance, set off, compensate for *The losses in one division were offset by the profits in another.*

offshoot *n.* branch, by-product, derivative *The sales office in Amsterdam is an offshoot of the main office in London.*

offspring *n.* children, descendants, issue, progeny *The male offspring in our family have always attended that school.*

off-the-record *adj.* unofficial, restricted, confidential *After the speech, the Prime Minister made a few off-the-record remarks that are best forgotten.*

often *adv.* frequently, regularly, usually *We often come here to watch the sunset.* ANT. rarely, seldom, hardly.

ogre *n.* monster, beast *She thinks her father is an ogre because he won't let her go to the cinema tonight.*

OK *adj.* *Informal:* correct, fine, all right *If it is OK with you, I'll go now.* *vb.* approve, allow, authorize *Did the doctor OK this drug?* *n.* approval, permission *Your OK must be on every order before it is sent out.*

old *adj.* **1** aged, elderly *My parents aren't very old.* **2** used, worn, dilapidated, faded, broken-down *There was an old hut in the woods where the boys would meet secretly.* 3 former, ancient, old-fashioned, antique *My aunt collects old cigar boxes.* ANT. (1) young, youthful. (2) fresh, brand-new.

old-fashioned *adj.* old, antiquated, outmoded, passé *Bertha was wearing one of her old-fashioned picture hats.* ANT. new, up-to-date, fashionable, current, modern.

omen *n.* portent, sign, indication, warning *Gerald regarded the death of the canary as an omen of evil days to come.*

ominous *adj.* threatening, menacing, foreboding, inauspicious *Ominous storm clouds began to gather on the horizon.*

omit *vb.* 1 leave out, exclude, bar *It was decided to omit from consideration all those with less than a B-average mark.* 2 ignore, neglect, overlook *By mistake your name was omitted from the list of members.* ANT. include.

one-sided *adj.* partial, biased, prejudiced, unfair *The book presents a one-sided view of the crisis in the Middle East.* ANT. impartial, just.

onlooker *n.* spectator, observer, witness, bystander *Though merely an onlooker, Nina was accused of complicity in the robbery.*

only *adj.* single, lone, solitary *When you have no brothers or sisters you are called an only child.* *adv.* merely, just, but, not more than *It took me only one hour to walk to work during the railway strike.*

onset *n.* beginning, opening, start, commencement *The onset of winter was marked by an advance of frigid air from Siberia.* ANT. end, conclusion, finale.

onwards *adv.* forwards, ahead *She walked onwards into the forest, without looking back.* ANT. backwards.

ooze *vb.* seep, exude, drip, emit, leak, flow *The oil oozed from the ground.* *n.* slime, mire, mud *Many fossils have been found in the bottom of the ooze at the bottom of the sea.*

open *adj.* 1 unclosed, uncovered, accessible *The door was open all night—anyone could have walked in. The jar of jam was left open and became mouldy.* 2 free, easy, candid; sincere, honest *Donald was very open about his plans for the next week.* 3 unoccupied, vacant, unfilled *The job advertised last week is still open.* *vb.* 1 start, begin, commence *The chairman opened the meeting with a short speech of welcome.* 2 expand, spread, extend *When Roger opened his fist, I saw the stain on his fingers, proving that he was the culprit.* ANT. *adj.* (1) closed, shut, sealed. (2) private, secretive. (3) filled, taken. *vb.* (1) finish, end, stop. (2) close, clench.

open-handed *adj.* generous, kind, charitable *People tend to be a bit more open-handed at Christmastime.* ANT. tight-fisted, stingy, mean.

open-hearted *adj.* honest, frank, candid *It isn't often that a politician is so open-hearted with his constituents.* ANT. devious, insincere.

opening *n.* 1 gap, hole *The dog escaped from our yard through an opening in the fence.* 2 beginning, start, commencement *At the* *opening of the ceremony, a huge limousine arrived.* **3** vacancy, opportunity, chance *We have an opening for a skilled typist.*

open-minded *adj.* fair, tolerant, liberal, just *The judge was open-minded enough to listen to both arguments before ruling.* ANT. bigoted, intolerant, prejudiced.

operate *vb.* **1** run, work, use, manage *Do you known how to operate a printing press?* **2** run, work, function, perform *After it had been repaired, the machine operated normally again.*

operation *n.* **1** performance, function, action *The operation of this motor is poor and irregular.* **2** administration, direction, supervision, handling *A new executive was brought in to take charge of the operation of the project.* **3** surgery *The operation on my toe will be tomorrow.*

operator *n.* operative, machinist, engineer, driver *The crane operator was skilled enough to pluck the kitten from the tree.*

opinion *n.* belief, view, sentiment, idea, viewpoint *In my opinion, the food in that restaurant is excellent and the service is execrable.*

opponent *n.* rival, competitor, contestant, antagonist *My opponent in the chess finals is a Life Master.* ANT. ally, colleague, teammate.

opportunity *n.* chance, time, occasion *Murphy had the opportunity to telephone to say he would be late.*

oppose *vb.* resist, battle, combat, withstand, thwart *As the club opposed the admission of women, Edgar resigned.* ANT. support, agree to.

opposite *adj.* **1** contrary, reverse, different *Ken turned the car round and drove off in the opposite direction.* **2** facing *I walked in and took my place on the opposite side of the room.* ANT. (1) same, like, similar.

opposition *n.* antagonism, resistance, defiance; disapproval *Did the new budget meet with much opposition?* ANT. support, help, cooperation.

oppress *vb.* burden, afflict, torment; depress, worry *The people were sorely oppressed under the dictatorship. Don't you sometimes feel your responsibilities oppressing?*

oppression *n.* tyranny, injustice, cruelty, persecution *The oppression of minorities in Cantharia was what made me move to France.* ANT. freedom, liberty.

oppressive *adj.* burdensome, difficult, hard; stifling *Unable to tolerate the government's oppressive practices, the people revolted. The atmosphere in the room became oppressive with the windows shut.*

opt (for) *vb.* choose, prefer, select *Offered a choice, I would opt for the roast turkey.*

optimism *n.* hopefulness, confidence, cheerfulness *Monica's parents expressed optimism that she would be admitted to study medicine.* ANT. pessimism, doubtfulness, cynicism.

option *n.* choice, preference, selection *Before I decide, may I know what the options are?*

optional *adj.* voluntary, elective, discretional *Formal attire is op-*

tional at the awards dinner. ANT. compulsory, obligatory, necessary.

oral *adj.* spoken, uttered, verbal, said, vocal, voiced *Were the complaints from customers oral or written?* ANT. written, printed.

oration *n.* speech, address, sermon, lecture *A long oration was delivered at the dedication of the memorial.*

orbit *n.* course, path, circuit, lap, revolution *The planets move in elliptical orbits round the sun.* *vb.* circle, revolve *The moon orbits round the earth, which orbits round the sun.*

ordeal *n.* trial, calamity, difficulty, misfortune, tribulation *Quentin has undergone the ordeals of trench warfare.*

order *n.* 1 command, direction, instruction, rule *The sergeant received the order to move the company into the front-line area.* 2 requisition, purchase order; contract *The shop acknowledged receiving our order for two boxes of stationery.* 3 goods, merchandise, shipment *Two weeks afterwards, our order arrived.* 4 arrangement, classification, system, sequence *The words in this book are in alphabetical order.* *vb.* 1 command, direct, instruct *The police were ordered to investigate a report of thefts from the supermarket.* 2 buy, obtain, request *That is not the stationery we ordered.* 3 arrange, classify, organize *The teacher thought the material in my essay had been well ordered.*

orderly *adj.* 1 neat, well-organized, regulated *In contrast to Mary's room, which is a mess, Anita's is very orderly.* 2 disciplined, well-organized, well-behaved *I want everyone to line up and to go into the corridor in orderly fashion during the fire drill.* ANT. (1) messy, sloppy, undisciplined. (2) disorganized, haphazard.

ordinarily *adv.* usually, commonly, generally, normally *Ordinarily, I would require you to type the letter again.*

ordinary *adj.* 1 usual, common, customary, regular, normal *Just do everything in the ordinary way and try to pretend nobody is watching you.* 2 average, mediocre, everyday, undistinguished *Although Annette wears fancy clothes for her job in the hotel, she dresses in ordinary clothes during the day.* ANT. (2) extraordinary, unusual, special.

organization *n.* 1 formulation, plan, classification *The experts disagreed on the organization of the information for the files.* 2 group, association, society, institute, league, guild *The members of the teachers' organization agreed to meet the education officials.*

organize *vb.* 1 arrange, compose, coordinate, shape, regulate, order, classify *The office manager asked Ronnie to organize the files.* 2 establish, found, form, constitute *Ten of us decided to organize a swimming and tennis club.*

organized *adj.* orderly, planned, neat, arranged *Norma likes to have all her papers organized so she can find things easily.*

orient *vb.* adjust, align, position *The building is oriented so that the sun shines in the windows during the winter.*

origin *n.* beginning, source, root, birthplace, rise, start *Scientists* *have been unable to pinpoint the exact origin of man.* ANT. end, termination.

original *adj.* **1** first, primary, beginning *The original people in this town were Anglo-Saxons.* **2** unique, new, fresh, novel, creative *The invention of the steam engine, by James Watt, was an original idea.* ANT. (1) secondary. (2) outmoded, old-fashioned.

originate *vb.* **1** arise, begin, start *The idea of coining money originated many centuries ago.* **2** invent, create, begin *I wonder who originated the idea of the Channel Tunnel.*

originator *n.* inventor, creator; discoverer *The originator of the wheel never visited the western hemisphere.* ANT. imitator, follower.

ornament *n.* decoration, adornment, ornamentation, embellishment *A curious gold ornament hung from the man's left ear.* *vb.* decorate, adorn, embellish *The cakes are ornamented with multicoloured icing.*

ornamental *adj.* decorative, ornate, embellishing, adorning *The gratings over the windows are for security and are not purely ornamental.*

orthodox *adj.* conforming, conservative, conventional, standard *Claude insists that we celebrate the holidays in the orthodox manner.* ANT. unorthodox, unconventional.

oscillate *vb.* waver, sway, swing; vibrate *He watched the pendulum of the clock oscillating back and forth, back and forth.*

ostensible *adj.* seeming, apparent, superficial *The ostensible reason for the attack was to regain lost territory, but the real reason was to recover the oil fields.*

ostentatious *adj.* showy, pretentious, flamboyant, pompous *I cannot imagine why Sophie feels she has to make an ostentatious show of herself.*

oust *vb.* eject, expel, deprive, dislodge *The president was ousted by a military junta.*

outbreak *n.* eruption, outburst *The outbreak of hostilities was traced to a minor border incident.*

outcome *n.* result, end, consequence, upshot *As I had to leave before the game was over, I didn't know the outcome.*

outdo *vb.* surpass, excel, beat *Nancy outdoes all her competitors in gymnastics.*

outfit *n.* **1** gear, clothing, get-up, garb *Stephanie arrived at the dance wearing a new outfit of gold lamé.* **2** kit, equipment *My father was given a whole new fishing outfit for his birthday by the family.*

outgoing *adj.* **1** departing, leaving *The outgoing officers were honoured at a ceremonial dinner.* **2** open, easy, friendly, congenial, cordial, amiable *Arthur is quite outgoing and would make a good salesman.* ANT. (1) incoming. (2) unfriendly, cold.

outgrowth *n.* development, result, effect, product *Many modern laws are an outgrowth of ancient Roman laws.*

outlandish *adj.* strange, weird, odd, peculiar, curious, exotic, unconventional *Waders, a wing collar, tam o'shanter and a net shirt make for pretty outlandish dinner attire.* ANT. ordinary, common.

outlaw *n.* criminal, bandit; fugitive *The outlaws were cornered and captured after a cross-country pursuit.* *vb.* prohibit, ban *The sale of all handguns should be outlawed.*

outline *n.* 1 edge, border, side *If you see it against the sky, you will be able to make out the outline of the jagged cliff in the distance. Draw an outline of the map of the British Isles.* 2 plan, sketch, framework *Nick handed in an outline of the essay he was going to write.* *vb.* draft, sketch, plan, draw *The playwright outlined the plot of his new musical.*

outlook *n.* 1 view, viewpoint *Because Tessie comes from a family that has money, her outlook on saving is different from mine.* 2 future, prospect, chance, opportunity *The outlook for people with qualifications is better than for those without when they leave school.*

outmoded *adj.* old-fashioned, dated, passé, unfashionable *Doublet and hose are outmoded dress, especially for swimming, Frobisher.* ANT. modern, up-to-date.

output *n.* production; productivity, yield *The average farm today has double the output of the same farm a hundred years ago.*

outrage *n.* affront, offence, insult *In wartime, soldiers commit outrages on the people whose land they capture.* *vb.* shock, injure, offend *I was outraged when I learned that Jim had borrowed the car after I had told him not to.*

outrageous *adj.* shocking, offensive, disgraceful, shameful, gross, contemptible *To say that I was with her last night is an outrageous lie!!* ANT. reasonable, sensible, prudent.

outset *n.* beginning, start, commencement *At the outset, I declared my innocence of any wrongdoing.* ANT. end, climax.

outside *n.* 1 exterior, surface, covering *The outside of the tin box was brightly coloured.* 2 limit, bounds *I would guess that, at the outside, 300 students live in that hall of residence.* *adj.* external, exterior, outer *The outside walls of my house need painting.*

outsider *n.* stranger, alien, foreigner; nonmember *We never let outsiders attend meetings of our secret club.*

outsmart *vb.* outwit, outmanoeuvre *Be consoled that you've been outsmarted by one of the best-known swindlers in the business.*

outspoken *adj.* bold, candid, blunt, frank *I prefer that you be outspoken rather than conceal your feelings.*

outstanding *adj.* 1 excellent, distinguished; notable, well-known, famous, prominent, conspicuous, leading *Alan's mother was one of the most outstanding violinists of her time.* 2 unpaid, overdue, due, owing *I keep all of the paid bills in this drawer and all of the outstanding ones in the other.* ANT. (1) ordinary, average.

outward *adj.* external, exterior, outside *She gave no outward sign that she heard or understood what I was saying.* ANT. inward.

outwit *vb.* confuse, bewilder, trick, baffle *The fox outwitted the hounds, which soon lost the scent.*

overall *adj.* general, complete, comprehensive, inclusive *The overall pattern of his behaviour has improved markedly.*

overbearing *adj.* domineering; proud, arrogant *Try not to be so overbearing and give the children a chance to think for themselves.*

overcast *adj.* cloudy, clouded, dark *They say that you can get just as good a tan on an overcast day.* ANT. clear, sunny.

overcome *vb.* 1 conquer, defeat, beat, subdue *The heavy-weight boxer easily overcame any challenger.* 2 overpower, weaken, overwhelm *The firemen were nearly overcome by the smoke.* ANT. (1) submit, yield.

overcrowded *adj.* congested, full, crowded *The trains are always so overcrowded on holiday weekends.*

overdue *adj.* late, delayed, due *Weren't you worried when Sally's plane was two hours overdue?*

overflow *vb.* run over, flood, spill over *In another second, the bath would have overflowed.*

overhaul *vb.* revamp, rebuild, recondition *I have just had my car's engine overhauled and it runs like a clock.*

overhear *vb.* eavesdrop, catch, listen in to, hear *She says she didn't mean to listen, but she overheard them plotting your murder.*

overlook *vb.* ignore, disregard, neglect, miss *The judge said he would overlook the past if we swore to behave.* ANT. notice.

overpower *vb.* overwhelm, vanquish, overcome, conquer, subdue, defeat, beat *The man easily overpowered the young lad, who was no match for him.* ANT. surrender.

overrule *vb.* disallow, override, nullify, cancel *The higher court overruled the finding of the lower court and released the defendant.*

oversight *n.* 1 error, overlooking, omission, blunder, neglect, fault *Through an oversight, the report cards weren't sent out on time.* 2 supervision *The elders exercise oversight in our church.*

overtake *vb.* catch, reach; pass *Our horse overtook all the other horses and won the race.*

overthrow *vb.* overpower, defeat, conquer; upset, overturn *The army succeeded in overthrowing the government so quickly that no one was hurt.* *n.* defeat, collapse, fall *The overthrow of the king was being plotted by spies in another country.*

overture *n.* 1 prelude, introduction *The overture to the opera was played very well.* 2 (often **overtures**) approach, suggestion, advance *I think we must begin making overtures to take over that company.*

overwhelm *vb.* defeat, overcome, crush, overpower *The tiny force protecting the village was quickly overwhelmed by the advancing army.*

own *vb.* possess, have, hold *Everything he owned was lost in the fire.*

p

pace *n.* **1** step *Take three paces to the right, then one to the left, and dig there for the buried treasure.* **2** speed, rate; velocity *Anne was typing only three letters an hour and was asked to increase her pace.* *vb.* walk, stride *John paced the room as he waited for news impatiently.*

pacific *adj.* peaceful, calm, peaceable, tranquil, quiet; gentle *Jan has a pacific nature and is seldom upset.* **ANT.** turbulent, excited.

pacify *vb.* calm, quiet, tranquillize, smooth, lull *Although Ben was about to lose his temper, we succeeded in pacifying him.* **ANT.** upset, excite, disturb.

pack *vb.* **1** prepare *Pack your suitcase right away—we're off for a holiday this afternoon.* **2** cram, ram, crowd, stuff, compress *Those sardines are packed in the can almost as tightly as people on a train during the rush hour.* *n.* **1** bundle, package, parcel, load *Each hiker carried a pack on his back.* **2** crowd, herd, gang, mob, group *The pack of wolves had attacked the sheep during the night.*

package *n.* bundle, parcel, pack, packet, load *The package was weighed at the post office.* *vb.* crate, box, bottle *The perfume comes packaged in a leakproof container.*

packet *n.* package, bundle; parcel *The postman delivered a small packet of letters this morning.*

pact *n.* agreement, contract, compact, arrangement, deal, settlement, treaty, bargain *There is a trade pact between the two countries.*

pad *n.* **1** cushion, wadding; stuffing, filling, padding *If you keep this pad under your sprained knee it will make you more comfortable.* **2** block; bundle *The detective made notes on a small pad of paper.* *vb.* cushion *This fragile vase should be carefully padded for shipping.*

paddle *n.* oar, scull, sweep *The first thing you did wrong was to lose the canoe paddle overboard.*

pagan *see* **heathen.**

page *n.* sheet, side; leaf *This book has sixty pages.*

pageant *n.* spectacle, exhibition, show, display, extravaganza *Marguerite will be the star of our annual pageant this year.*

pain *n.* **1** distress, suffering, misery, ache, pang, torment, agony *Harold kept on running in spite of the pain of his sprained ankle.* **2** anguish, misery *Betty's decision to live away from home caused her parents much pain.* **ANT.** (1) comfort, ease. (2) delight, joy.

painful *adj.* agonizing, aching, inflamed, sore, throbbing *I have a very painful headache.* **ANT.** soothing.

painstaking *adj.* careful, exacting, scrupulous *The miniature is fashioned with painstaking attention to detail.* ANT. careless, slipshod.

paint *vb.* portray, draw, sketch, depict *The reporter painted a picture of utter desolation after the battle.*

pair *n.* couple; brace, team *A pair of horses drew the carriage.* *vb.* match, mate, couple, join *The teacher paired us off and we marched out of the room two abreast.*

pale *adj.* 1 white, ashen, colourless, pallid *Before it becomes warm enough to go sunbathing and get a tan, everyone looks pale.* 2 dim, faint *The bedroom is being painted pale blue.* ANT. (1) ruddy, flushed. (2) dark, bright.

paltry *adj.* meagre, petty, trivial, trifling, insignificant *Considering all your wealth, we expected a contribution of more than a paltry hundred pounds.*

pamper *vb.* coddle, spoil, cosset, overindulge *Parents tend to pamper their first child, then sometimes ignore those that follow.*

pamphlet *n.* brochure, booklet, leaflet *We mailed a pamphlet to ten thousand customers to warn them about the fault in the toaster.*

pander (to) *vb.* please, gratify; provide, minister to *Harold panders to Janet constantly, indulging her every whim.*

panel *n.* 1 section, board, inset *Robert fixed some new panels on the wall.* 2 group, team; committee, commission *The panel on the television quiz programme consisted of two men and two women.*

pang *n.* pain, hurt, throbbing *I got a sudden pang in my calf from all that exercise.*

panic *n.* alarm, fear, dread, fright, terror *When they saw and smelled the fire, the horses' panic was so great they stampeded.* *vb.* terrify, frighten, alarm *The civilians were panicked by the scream of the bombs dropping nearby.* ANT. *vb.*calm, soothe, tranquillize.

pant *vb.* puff, gasp, throb; wheeze *Jack came panting up the hill.*

pantry *n.* storeroom, larder, cupboard, scullery *The stores are kept in the pantry, not the kitchen.*

paper *n.* 1 newspaper, journal *Have you read the paper today?* 2 document, record, certificate *When you apply for a job, you should bring all the necessary papers with you.* 3 article, report, essay *Only invited scholars read their papers at the international meeting.*

parade *n.* march, procession, review; pageant *Today is the annual church parade.* *vb.* march, walk, strut *The pretty girls were parading along the beach.*

paradise *n.* 1 heaven *Many people believe that if they're good, they'll end up in paradise when they die.* 2 utopia *We spent our holiday on what was promised in the travel brochure would be a tropical paradise.*

paradox *n.* puzzle, contradiction, mystery, enigma *How it could be pouring with rain while the sun shone was a paradox of the tropics.*

parallel *adj.* similar, corresponding, like, resembling *Our thinking has been parallel on the subject of liberty for many years.* *n.* 1 equal, match, counterpart *As a scientist, George has no parallel in* *this country.* 2 similarity, likeness, resemblance, correspondence *It isn't accurate to draw a parallel between twentieth-century rulers and those of the sixteenth century.* vb. resemble, correspond to, match, equal *My experience parallels yours when it comes to service in the army.* ANT. *adj.*divergent.

paralyse vb. deaden, benumb, numb; transfix *When the rat saw the snake, it was paralysed with fear.*

paramount adj. pre-eminent, supreme, greatest *It is of paramount importance that we meet as soon as possible.*

parcel n. package, bundle, packet *A strange-looking man delivered this parcel for you today.*

parch vb. dry up, dehydrate, brown. *The earth is all parched from the drought.*

pardon n. forgiveness; amnesty, acquittal, exoneration *The general refused to give pardons to the criminals convicted of major crimes.* vb. excuse, forgive, acquit, exonerate *On his birthday the king pardoned all his political opponents still in jail.* ANT. *vb.* condemn, sentence.

pare vb. 1 peel, skin *I know how to pare an apple so that the skin comes off in one long curly piece.* 2 diminish, reduce, cut, trim, crop, shave *The finance committee is meeting to see if the budget can be pared down a bit.*

park n. green, square, land *I sometimes go for a walk in the park near my home.* vb. leave, put, place *Where can I park my car?*

parody n. satire; imitation, mimicry, travesty, take-off *Sherman was famous for his hilarious parody of the headmaster.*

parsimonious adj. mean, selfish, stingy. ANT. generous.

part n. 1 portion, piece, section, fraction, fragment *Since I helped to pay for it, part of that apple pie should go to me.* 2 share, allotment, participation, interest *If everyone does his part, we shall be finished much sooner.* 3 role, character *Philip played the part of Macbeth.* vb. 1 divide, split, break up, disconnect *The curtains parted to reveal a striking stage set. We had to part at the barrier because only passengers were allowed beyond it.* 2 depart, go, leave, quit *It is late and we must part now.* ANT. *n.*(1) whole, entirety.

partial adj. 1 incomplete, unfinished, undone *I made a partial payment towards the cost of the car.* 2 prejudiced, biased, one-sided, unfair, unjust *The umpires and referees in sports should not be partial to one team or the other.* ANT. (1) entire, complete, comprehensive.

participant n. shareholder, partner, associate, colleague *I don't want to be a participant in a scheme to sell beach toys in the Kalahari Desert.*

participate vb. share, partake, join; engage in, be involved *The school expects all students to participate in the sports programme.*

particle n. bit, spot, grain, speck, shred, scrap *A particle of grit flew into my eye. There isn't a particle of truth in his story.*

particular adj. 1 special, specific, distinct *This particular house is* *where I once lived.* **2** careful, finicky, discriminating *Suzanne is very particular about the people she associates with.* **3** notable, exceptional, remarkable, unusual *This is a matter of particular importance for the future.* *n.* detail, point, item, feature *The report on the condition of the playground was correct in every particular.* ANT. *adj.* (2) careless, undiscriminating.

particularly *adv.* especially, specially, specifically, explicitly *The mysterious stranger seemed particularly interested in the doorknob of No. 4, St Mary's Row.*

partisan *n.* follower, disciple, supporter, backer *After the government was overthrown, its partisans continued to fight.* *adj.* partial, biased, prejudiced *Rupert presented a very partisan view of the conference when he got back.*

partition *n.* **1** division, separation, distribution *The Allies agreed to the partition of Germany after the war.* **2** divider, screen, separator, barrier, wall *A new partition was installed dividing the office in half.* *vb.* divide, separate, apportion *We ought to partition a section of the cellar for a workshop.* ANT. *n.*(1) joining, unification.

partly *adv.* partially, somewhat, comparatively *You are only partly right about who stole the tarts from the Queen of Hearts.*

partner *n.* associate, colleague, participant *My partner in this new venture is an expert engineer.*

partnership *n.* cooperation, alliance, union *The partnership between the two men lasted all their lives.*

party *n.* **1** gathering, social; fun *Are you coming to our party on Saturday?* **2** group; company, crowd *A party of tourists saw the sights of London.* **3** block, faction, body, organization *You don't have to join a political party to vote in an election.*

pass *vb.* **1** go, move, proceed, continue *Have you seen a ginger kitten pass this way?* **2** disregard, bypass, ignore *The manager passed over George when it was time to consider promotions.* **3** circulate, spend *The counterfeiter succeeded in passing some false ten-pound notes around.* **4** go by *or* away, end, terminate, cease, expire *The day of the horse and cart has passed.* **5** enact, establish, approve *Parliament has passed the new tax bill.* **6** exceed, surpass *The club passed its target in raising funds.* **7** spend, while away, fill *I passed the time waiting for the train in reading a book.* **8** elapse, flow, roll; advance, proceed *Time passes slowly when you are waiting for someone.* *n.* **1** gorge, ravine, gap *The army reached the mountain pass before dawn and launched an attack immediately.* **2** permit, admission, permission *You will need an official pass to visit the arms factory.* **3** toss, throw, hurl *Namath threw a forward pass that was caught by the fly-half.* ANT. *vb.*(2) consider, notice, note.

passable *adj.* acceptable, satisfactory, adequate, tolerable, fair *Jordan's work is passable, but not outstanding.* ANT. exceptional, extraordinary, superior.

passage *n.* **1** paragraph, section, text *The speaker read a passage from* Moby Dick *and then discussed its meaning.* **2** passing, transition, movement. *The passage of time seems to slow when you are waiting for someone.* **3** passageway, corridor, hall *The passage is so narrow that it is difficult for two people to pass.* **4** journey, voyage, trip, crossing, tour *When he was just a boy, my grandfather worked his passage from England to America as a cabin boy.*

passé *adj.* old-fashioned, dated, old hat, outmoded, out-of-date *I am sorry to break the news to you, Edgar, but gaiters are a bit passé.*

passenger *n.* commuter, traveller; tourist *How many passengers do the international airlines carry in one twenty-four-hour period?*

passion *n.* **1** emotion, feeling, zeal, rapture, excitement *The passion Victoria had for the women's lib movement sometimes made her say things she didn't mean.* **2** love, desire, affection, liking, fondness, enthusiasm *My mother has a strong passion for all of her nine children.* **ANT.** indifference, apathy, coolness.

passionate *adj.* emotional, excited, impulsive, zealous, enthusiastic, earnest, sincere *We elected Curtland because of his passionate devotion to environmental issues.*

passive *adj.* inactive, inert, lifeless; submissive *Thinking she might play a passive role on the committee, Sarah was in for a big surprise.*

past *adj.* **1** gone, over, finished, done, done with *The days of regular travel by steam trains are past.* **2** former, preceding, prior *The past president of the Cricket Club was at the dinner.* **3** recent, preceding *In the past few days nobody has seen Joan at school.* *n.* **1** antiquity, old times, the (good) old days, days of yore, yesterday *It always seem as though everything was better in the past.* **2** experiences, former life, secret life *She may be old now, but that author had quite an exciting past.* **ANT.** *adj.*(1) ahead. (2) present; future. *n.* (1) present; future.

paste *n.* adhesive, glue *Let's make some paste to stick the pieces of paper together.* *vb.* stick, glue, fix *The teacher pasted some paintings on to the boards.*

pastime *n.* amusement, recreation, entertainment; hobby *Roger has taken up model railways as a pastime.*

pastor *n.* minister, clergyman, priest *As the pastor of this flock, he must warn you against the evils of drink.*

pastry *n.* cake, tart, delicacy; patisserie *Irena served beautiful French pastries at teatime.*

pasture *n.* land, grass, field, meadow *The pasture is big enough for a hundred cows.*

pat *vb.,n.* tap, stroke; beat, hit *She patted the cake mixture firmly into the tin. She gave him a friendly light pat on the head.*

patch *vb.,n.* mend, repair *Do you think that the tailor can patch my torn trousers? My jacket has a patch over each elbow.*

patent *n.* protection, copyright, control, permit *Dick's got a patent on a new kind of fuel.* *vb.* license, limit, copyright *Some of the strangest devices you have ever seen have been patented.*

path *n.* walk, way, trail, track, footpath, lane, pathway *The path to our front door was icy, and I slipped and fell.*

pathetic *adj.* **1** pitiable, pitiful, moving, touching *The half-drowned kitten looked so pathetic that we had to take it home and care for it.* **2** *Slang:* worthless, awful, contemptible *Her first attempts at learning to drive were pretty pathetic.*

patience *n.* **1** calmness, composure, passiveness, serenity, courage *Our teacher's patience came to an end when Evelyn started to giggle again.* **2** endurance, perseverance, persistence *It takes a great deal of patience to stand in a queue for four hours to buy a ticket for a concert.* ANT. (1)impatience, restlessness, impetuosity.

patient *adj.* **1** persistent, untiring, persevering *If you'll be patient, the dentist will be with you in a few more moments.* **2** resigned, submissive *As Tom grew older, he became more patient with other people's faults.* **3** calm, serene, quiet, unexcited, unexcitable, self-controlled, unruffled, unshaken *The old pony was very patient when children wanted to ride him. After years of patient research, the scientists finally perfected the medicine.* *n.* invalid; case, inmate *Danny was a patient in the hospital for a week after he broke his leg.*

patrol *vb.* guard, watch; inspect *Three security guards are employed to patrols the factory at night.* *n.* guard, protector, watchman *The patrols walk regularly round the office block, making sure everything is all right.*

patron *n.* **1** customer, client, purchaser, buyer *The first patrons arrive at the restaurant at six-thirty for breakfast.* **2** supporter, benefactor, backer, philanthropist *The patrons of the arts centre have contributed thousands of pounds to its funds.*

patronize *vb.* **1** buy at, support *We always patronize our local shops.* **2** condescend, stoop, talk down to *The department head didn't like the new clerk because she spoke to him in a patronizing way.*

patter *n.* **1** tapping, patting, rattle *The patter of rain on the window became louder.* **2** chatter, jabber, prattle *The salesman's glib patter about the encyclopaedia helped him sell several sets.*

pattern *n.* **1** model, guide, example, original *Penny was building a model car, using a Rolls Royce as a pattern.* **2** design, decoration, figure *The dress has a beautiful pattern but I don't like the way it fits.* *vb.* model, copy, follow, imitate *The style of the building was patterned after Georgian designs.*

pause *n.* hesitation, rest, wait, interruption, delay, break, intermission, recess *After a short pause, the speaker went on to discuss the habits of lions in the wild.* *vb.* hesitate, rest, wait, interrupt, break, delay, recess *You ought to pause to think before replying to that question.* ANT. *n.* continuity, perpetuity. *vb.* continue, perpetuate.

pave *vb.* lay, cover, flag, metal *A special crew was able to pave the road overnight.*

pawn *n.* tool, cat's-paw, puppet, (*slang*) stooge *Carstairs has no authority, he's merely a pawn of the management.*

pay *vb.* **1** settle, remit, discharge *I have very few bills to pay this month.* **2** compensate, recompense, reward, return *Phil's new job* *pays him much better than his last one.* *n.* payment, salary, wage, wages, fee, income *How much is your pay per month?*

payable *adj.* due, owing, owed; unpaid *The invoice becomes payable on the tenth of the month.*

payment *n.* sum, recompense, remittance *Will they be able to make the monthly payment on their new car?*

peace *n.* 1 quiet, serenity, calm, peacefulness, tranquillity *Every time I spend a day in a big city, I yearn for the peace of the countryside.* 2 pact, treaty, truce, accord, armistice *A peace agreement was signed in Geneva this week.* ANT. agitation, upheaval, disturbance.

peaceable *adj.* peaceful, gentle, mild, calm, friendly, amiable, pacific *The peaceable reign of King Pflugmeister lasted for thirty years.* ANT. hostile, warlike, aggressive.

peaceful *adj.* peaceable, quiet, calm, serene, tranquil *The presence of the police ensured that the demonstration was peaceful.* ANT. disrupted, agitated, riotous.

peak *n.* 1 top, summit, point, crest *We could see the peaks of the Lake District mountains from the railway.* 2 top, maximum, pinnacle *Prices on the stock market reached their peak of the year today.* ANT. (2) base, bottom.

peal *vb.* sound, ring, chime, resound *The bells of St Mary's pealed out to celebrate the New Year.*

peculiar *adj.* 1 unusual, odd, strange, unfamiliar, uncommon, queer, outlandish, curious *The camel is a very peculiar animal.* 2 characteristic, special, unique, exclusive *A love of eucalyptus leaves is peculiar to the koala, which looks like a teddy bear.* ANT. (1) ordinary, regular, unspecial.

peculiarity *n.* characteristic, distinctiveness, individualness *Martin's one peculiarity is that he constantly hums to himself.*

pedantic *adj.* academic, overprecise, fussy *Our foreman is very pedantic when it comes to following the safety regulations.*

peddle *vb.* hawk, vend, sell *Did you know that wealthy Mr Costa used to peddle vegetables door to door?*

pedestrian *n.* walker, stroller *Pedestrians should watch how they cross the road.* *adj.* ordinary, common, everyday, dull, commonplace *The comedian told some very pedestrian jokes that weren't funny at all.* ANT. *adj.* unusual, fascinating, extraordinary, special.

pedigree *n.* family, descent, ancestry, parentage, line, lineage *This dog's pedigree has been traced back to the winner of the first Crufts Show.*

pedlar *n.* salesman, hawker, seller, barrow boy *A century ago, most goods were sold to the public by pedlars.*

peel *n.* skin, rind, peeling *I slipped on a banana peel and everyone laughed when I fell down.* *vb.* skin, strip, pare *My uncle can peel an orange so that the skin comes off in one piece.*

peep¹ *vb.,n.* cheep, chirp, squeak *The baby chicks peeped constantly*

*when they were awake. I don't want to hear a peep out of you after
you get into bed.*

peep² *vb.,n.*   peer, glimpse, look   *Close your eyes and count to
twenty—and no peeping! We got a peep at what they were doing
without their seeing us.*

peer¹ *n.*   1 equal, parallel, match, rival   *As a high-jumper, Kim has no
peer.*   2 nobleman, lord   *The peers of the British realm are listed in
this book.*

peer² *vb.*   scrutinize, examine   *The old lady peered at me closely, trying
to see if I was someone she knew.*

peg *n.*   holder; dowel, pin, tack, fastener   *The table is held together
entirely by wooden pegs.*

pelt *vb.*   1 throw, hurl   *The natives pelted stones at the visitors.*
2 hurry, speed, dash   *We pelted along the road trying to catch the
robbers.*   3 rain, pour   *It was pelting down outside.*

pen¹ *n.*   fountain pen, ball-point pen, biro   *Can you lend me a pen so I
can write down your name?*

pen² *n.*   enclosure, cage, coop, sty   *Domestic animals like chickens and
pigs are often kept in pens.*

penalize *vb.*   punish, condemn; dock   *Should a tennis player be penal-
ized for arguing with the referee and using foul language?*

penalty *n.*   punishment; forfeit; fine   *Death by hanging is no longer
the penalty for murder in England.*

penetrate *vb.*   1 pierce, enter, bore, hole   *The bullet penetrated the
wall, just missing my head.*   2 permeate, spread, seep   *The smoke
from the fire penetrated all the rooms, and we had to have everything
cleaned.*

penetrating *adj.*   shrewd, astute, intelligent, perceptive; sharp, acute
*Alan can usually be relied on to make a penetrating observation in
class.*

peninsula *n.*   point, neck, spit, headland   *At high tide, much of the
peninsula is under water.*

penniless *adj.*   poor, poverty-stricken, needy, destitute   *Penniless and
unable to get work, Harold applied to the council for help.*   ANT.
rich, wealthy, well-off, prosperous.

people *n.*   1 human beings, humans, persons   *Many people have
moved from the country to the cities.*   2 race, nation, tribe, clan,
family   *A primitive people was found recently, living in the Philippine
Islands.*   *vb.*   populate   *Australia was originally peopled by the
Aborigines, long before the white man came.*

perceive *vb.*   1 see, discern, notice, observe, distinguish, make out   *It
is very difficult to perceive the differences between the monarch and
the viceroy butterflies.*   2 understand, comprehend, grasp   *I cannot
perceive the purpose in your trying to swim across the river.*

perception *n.*   understanding, apprehension, comprehension   *Mary
has a completely different perception of what took place in the bank
holdup.*

perceptive *adj.* discerning, sharp, acute, observant *It was very perceptive of you to notice that the letter was missing.*

perfect *adj.* 1 faultless, excellent, flawless, pure, ideal *The acrobat's style was perfect.* 2 complete, finished, whole *The robbers' plan was perfect: they had thought of everything.* 3 complete, utter, total *He might have told you he was my brother, but he was a perfect stranger to me.* 4 exact, precise, sharp, correct *The two pieces of ancient sculpture turned out to be a perfect match.* *vb.* complete, achieve, finish, accomplish *No one has yet been able to perfect a perpetual-motion machine.* ANT. *adj.*(1) imperfect, flawed, second-rate.

perfectionist *n.* pedant, precisionist, precisian, stickler, purist *Hortense is too much a perfectionist to allow a shirt to be sold with a button missing.*

perform. *vb.* 1 do, carry out, accomplish, achieve, complete *With a little coaxing, Harry would perform the trick of walking on his hands.* 2 present, act out, give, produce *The children performed the play on an outdoor platform in the park.*

performance *n.* presentation, offering, exhibition, appearance *There will be two performances of the play on Wednesdays.*

performer *n.* actor, actress, entertainer *The performers worked in the theatre because they loved it, not for the money.*

perfume *n.* 1 scent, essence; toilet water, cologne *Every Mother's Day I give my mother a bottle of perfume.* 2 odour, scent, fragrance, smell, aroma *The perfume of the orange blossoms filled the night air.*

perhaps *adv.* maybe, possibly, conceivably *If David can take a holiday this summer, perhaps he'll join us at the seaside.* ANT. definitely, absolutely.

peril *n.* danger, hazard, risk *You go into that lion's den at the peril of your life.* ANT. security, safety.

perilous *adj.* dangerous, risky, hazardous, unsafe *The trail through the mountains is steep and perilous.* ANT. safe, secure.

perimeter *n.* edge, boundary, border, outline *Guards are posted around the perimeter of the property.*

period *n.* 1 time, interval, term; era, age, epoch *My uncle spent a brief period in the navy. The fifteenth to seventeenth centuries were a period of exploration and migration.* 2 course, cycle; timing *The period of the day is marked by the revolution of the earth on its axis.*

periodical *n.* magazine, review, journal: VERBATIM *is the most popular quarterly periodical on language.*

perish *vb.* die, expire; pass away, depart *Thousands perished in the eruption of Mt Vesuvius.*

perishable *adj.* biodegradable, decayable, decomposable *Perishable foods must be kept in the refrigerator.*

perk up *vb.phr.* liven up, revive, cheer up *Irwin always perks up when the grandchildren come to visit.*

permanent *adj.* 1 enduring, lasting, stable, continuing, long-lived, persisting, persistent; perpetual, everlasting *Stainless steel is a more permanent material than aluminium for building.* 2 unchanging, unaltered, unchanged, constant, unvarying, invariable *Because of the accident, Tim has a permanent scar on his arm.* ANT. passing, temporary, fluctuating.

permeate *vb.* pervade, penetrate, fill, saturate *The water permeated the cracks and flooded the cave.*

permission *n.* consent, leave; freedom, liberty *You have my permission to leave. He has permission to come and go as he pleases.*

permit *vb.* allow, let, tolerate, suffer *No one is permitted to talk during class.* *n.* permission, authorization *Only councillors have permits to park in that area.* ANT. *vb.* forbid, prohibit, disallow.

perpendicular *adj.* vertical; upright, standing *The flagpole seems to be leaning a little from the perpendicular. I was so dizzy I was unable to remain perpendicular.* ANT. horizontal.

perpetual *adj.* unceasing, continuing, continuous, continual, everlasting, permanent, constant, eternal, ceaseless, undying *Marvin pledged his perpetual love to Catherine.* ANT. intermittent, inconstant, fluctuating.

perplex *vb.* confuse, puzzle, mystify, bewilder *Dana was completely perplexed by the algebra problem.*

persecute *vb.* oppress, torment, ill-treat, maltreat, victimize, abuse *Minorities have always been persecuted in that country.*

persevere *vb.* endure, persist, last, continue *If you work hard and persevere, you will go far in any field.* ANT. lapse, desist, discontinue, stop.

persist *vb.* persevere, continue, remain, endure *The police are persisting in their effort to find the criminal.* ANT. stop, desist.

person *n.* human, human being, individual, someone, somebody; personage *Three unknown persons broke in and stole my typewriter.*

personal *adj.* 1 private, secret *Linda revealed many personal things about herself that I wouldn't repeat to anyone.* 2 individual, special, particular *My personal opinion is that each one of us ought to do what he does best.* ANT. (1) public, general.

personality *n.* character, nature, make-up, disposition *Alexa's easygoing personality makes her a welcome addition to any group.*

personify *vb.* represent, symbolize; embody *The company chooses a different woman to personify the Homemaker of the Year.*

personnel *n.* people, staff, workers *It is increasingly difficult to hire skilled personnel.*

perspective *n.* aspect, viewpoint, outlook *I am afraid that Rosalinda's perspective on her husband's infidelity is a bit warped.*

persuade *vb.* 1 influence, induce, convince *Peter persuaded me to try to get a job for the summer holidays.* 2 urge, coax, prompt *You don't have to persuade Anne to eat everything on her plate.* ANT. (1) dissuade, discourage.

persuasive *adj.* convincing, influential, winning, alluring, compelling

Arguments against the death penalty become persuasive when you consider unjust convictions. ANT. unconvincing, dubious.

pertinent *adj.* relevant, appropriate, suitable *Those comments are not pertinent to the subject being discussed.*

perturbed *adj.* upset, flustered, disturbed, agitated *Don't be perturbed—I just came in to brush my teeth.*

pervade *vb.* permeate, spread, fill *The odour of jasmine pervaded the room.*

perverse *adj.* wayward, contrary *Elbert is in a perverse mood today and is saying No to every request.*

perverted *adj.* abnormal, unnatural, distorted *Putting a fly in your soup is another example of Ferncliffe's perverted sense of humour.*

pest *n.* 1 nuisance, irritation, irritant, annoyance, (*informal*) tease, bother *Why must you be such a pest about my keeping my room neat?* 2 disease, germ, virus, bug, insect *The pests damaged the crops.*

pester *vb.* annoy, irritate, vex, nag, trouble, harass, torment, tease, bother, worry *If you don't stop pestering the dog, you'll get bitten.*

pestilence *n.* epidemic, plague, disease *A pestilence wiped out half the population of the village.*

pet *n.* favourite, darling *Eunice is the teacher's pet.* *vb.* fondle, caress *Phoebe had great fun petting the new kittens.*

petition *n.* request, application, appeal, solicitation, entreaty *Most of the residents signed the petition to save trees along the streets.* *vb.* request, apply, appeal, entreat *The students got together to petition the teachers to give them less homework.*

petrify *vb.* stun, daze, dumbfound *When the beast advanced towards him, Osbert was petrified.*

petty *adj.* 1 unimportant, trivial, insignificant, paltry, trifling *My mother always seems to tell me off about very petty things.* 2 stingy, mean, miserly *Some people are very generous with themselves but very petty when it comes to others.* ANT. (1) important, vital, significant. (2) generous, bighearted.

phantom *n.* spectre, ghost, apparition *The old man swore that he had seen a phantom who haunted the ghost town.* *adj.* unreal; imaginary *He insisted that the ghost was a phantom cowboy who had been killed in a gunfight.*

phase *n.* 1 stage, period, state *The Neanderthal was thought to be an early phase in the development of modern man.* 2 aspect, side, view, condition *Each phase of the project should be handled by the person who knows most about it.*

phenomenal *adj.* extraordinary, remarkable; stupendous; unusual *Genevieve made a phenomenal recovery from her illness.* ANT. ordinary.

phobia *n.* fear, dread, neurosis *Many people have a phobia about being in small, enclosed places.*

phenomenon *n.* 1 happening, occurrence, fact, incident *The fish that climbs trees in Borneo is a very strange phenomenon.* 2 marvel, wonder *Anyone who can balance himself on only one toe is truly a phenomenon.*

phone *see* telephone.

photograph *n.* photo, picture, snapshot; print; slide *The neighbours asked us over to look at photographs of their grandchildren.*

physical *adj.* 1 bodily, corporeal, corporal *I have a complete physical examination once a year.* 2 real, material. natural *Man cannot fly—it's a physical impossibility.* **ANT.** (1) mental, spiritual.

pick *vb.* 1 choose, select *I was picked to represent our school in the debating contest.* 2 gather, harvest, reap, collect, pluck *Every autumn our family goes to an orchard where you can pick all the apples you want.* 3 steal, rob *My pocket was picked while I was in the bus.* *n.* choice, selection; best *When Josie's dog had puppies, we were allowed the pick of the litter.*

picture *n.* 1 painting, drawing, photograph, illustration *I love the pictures in my family album.* 2 image, likeness, representation *Jean is the picture of health.* 3 description, account *Try to give us a picture of the events of last Saturday.* *vb.* 1 describe, represent *In his story, the writer pictured a world where there was no evil.* 2 imagine, conceive of *Can you picture yourself winning the Miss World contest?*

picturesque *adj.* striking, scenic; attractive, pleasing *The cottage by the lake makes a very picturesque scene.*

piece *n.* quantity, unit, section, portion, part *How big a quantity of cake did he eat to get so sick?*

piecemeal *adv.* partially, gradually, bit by bit *We finally dragged the story out of George piecemeal.* **ANT.** entire, whole, complete.

pierce *vb.* 1 stab, perforate, puncture *Once you pierce the skin of the sausage with a fork, all the juices and fat run out.* 2 affect, rouse, touch, move, excite, thrill *Cory's sad story about the death of her cat pierced our hearts.*

pigheaded *adj.* stubborn, obstinate, inflexible *Clara is being pigheaded in her refusal to taste my stew.*

pile *n.* heap, collection, accumulation *There's a pile of dirty clothes in the corner of your room and I want it taken away.* *vb.* heap (up), accumulate, amass, assemble *Please ask the men to pile that firewood near the shed.*

pilfer *vb.* steal, take, (*slang*) nick, pinch *Customers have pilfered almost as much merchandise from our shop as they have bought.*

pilgrim *n.* traveller, wanderer *We met many pilgrims on their way to the Holy Land.*

pilgrimage *n.* tour, journey, trip, expedition *I make an annual pilgrimage to Shipston-on-Stour to visit my aunts.*

pill *n.* tablet, medicine, dose, capsule *Cuthbert forgot to take his pill, so of course he feels worse.*

pillar *n.* column, shaft, support, prop *The roof of the temple was supported by twenty-four marble pillars.*

pillow *n.* cushion, pad, bolster *Sleeping without a pillow can some-times help a bad back.*

pilot *n.* aviator; steersman, helmsman *My uncle was a fighter pilot in the Air Force. That's nothing: my father is a pilot on a transatlantic 747.* *vb.* steer, guide *A man who knows the harbour waters was brought aboard to pilot the ocean liner up to the pier.*

pin *n.* 1 fastening, fastener, clip, peg *A wooden pin was used to hold the door shut.* 2 brooch, tiepin *Sandy's mother wore a diamond pin to the opera last night.* *vb.* fasten, fix *Hugh pinned the notice onto the board.*

pinch *vb.,n.* nip, squeeze *Why do grown-ups all like to pinch children's cheeks? The pinch of these tight new shoes is more than I can stand.*

pinnacle *n.* peak, summit, climax, crest, zenith *It was in the late nineteenth century that the dynasty reached its pinnacle of power.*

pioneer *n.* 1 settler, explorer, discoverer *The spread westward of American civilization was due chiefly to the early adventurous pio-neers.* 2 leader, initiator *Ivor was a pioneer in the field of digital computers.*

pious *adj.* devout, religious, reverent *A pious woman, Maria could often be found at prayer.* ANT. impious, irreligious, profane.

pipe *n.* tube; channel, duct, conduit *This pipe was clogged with debris, preventing the water from running through.*

piquant *adj.* pungent, tart, spicy, hot *The sauce is a bit too piquant for my taste.*

pirate *n.* buccaneer, corsair, privateer, plunderer *Some books make pirates seem romantic, when in fact they were killers and thieves.* *vb.* steal, rob, plagiarize *The novel sold very well over here, and soon it was pirated for publication in Taiwan.*

pistol *n.* gun, firearm, revolver, automatic *The smoking pistol was still in her hand when I entered the room.*

pit *n.* hole, cavity, hollow, well, excavation *A camouflaged pit for catching large animals is called a deadfall.*

pitch *vb.* 1 set up, establish *We pitched camp near the river.* 2 throw, toss, fling, hurl *It was John's turn to pitch the ball.* 3 plunge, rock *The huge ship was pitching like a matchbox in the typhoon.* *n.* slant, angle, incline, grade *In countries where it snows a lot, the roofs of the houses have a very steep pitch.*

pitcher *n.* jug, container, ewer *This pitcher of milk is empty.*

pitfall *n.* trap, deadfall, snare *One encounters many pitfalls in a career in the theatre.*

pithy *adj.* terse, succinct, concise, pregnant *You can always count on Sidonie to make a pithy comment about men.*

pitiful *adj.* pitiable, pathetic, distressing, heart-rending *The croco-dile, completely trussed up, gave a pitiful cry.*

pitiless *adj.* unpitying, merciless, unmerciful, ruthless, mean, cruel, hard-hearted, stony-hearted *The pitiless overseers beat the slaves cruelly.* ANT. kind, kindly, gentle.

pity *n.* sympathy, compassion, charity, mercy, tenderheartedness, softheartedness *I feel so much pity for the animals in zoos that I want to set them free.* *vb.* feel for, sympathize (with), commiserate (with) *Pity the poor children elsewhere in the world, many of whom have nothing to eat.* ANT. *n.* cruelty, pitilessness, vindictivensss.

pivot *n.* lever, fulcrum, hinge, axis *The door turns on this iron pivot.*

pivotal *adj.* central, focal, crucial, critical, essential *Pensions are a pivotal issue in the strike.* ANT. unimportant, peripheral, side, trivial.

placard *n.* card, notice, poster *The animal rights people went round tearing down the bullfight placards.*

place *n.* 1 space, plot, region, location, area, spot *There's a place I know where the sun always shines and the swimming is marvellous.* 2 residence, home, house, dwelling *I love your new place, Anna! Too bad you can't afford to furnish it!* *vb.* 1 put, set, arrange, locate *Place your hands on top of the table, palms up.* 2 engage, appoint *We have placed three new people in the accounts department this month.* 3 identify, recognize, connect *I know that face, but I just can't place it.*

placid *adj.* calm, peaceful, quiet *Inez has such a placid disposition it is difficult to imagine her in a rage.*

plagiarize *vb.* copy, appropriate, forge *The entire second chapter was plagiarized from your book on whales.*

plague *n.* 1 pestilence, Black Death, epidemic *The plague in Europe in the Middle Ages killed about one quarter of the population.* 2 trouble, vexation, nuisance, irritation *A plague of locusts destroyed almost the entire crop.* *vb.* trouble, vex, annoy, irritate, pester *Financial troubles always plagued this family.*

plain *adj.* 1 simple, undecorated, unembellished, ordinary, unadorned *Sophie was wearing a plain black dress with a shocking-pink collar and cuffs.* 2 unattractive *Peter married a plain girl.* 3 clear, understandable, unmistakable, obvious *I made it quite plain that Sue would not go out with anyone who drank or smoked.* 4 candid, blunt, outspoken, frank, open, honest, sincere *If you don't mind some plain speaking, I'd like to know why you arrived home so late.* *n.* plateau, prairie, steppe, savanna, tundra *The central plains of the United States are extensive farming areas.* ANT. *adj.*(1) fancy, elaborate, ornamented. (2) pretty, beautiful, attractive. (3) disguised, hidden, unclear.

plan *n.* 1 plot, procedure, scheme, design, method *Donald outlined his plan for selling the textbooks to schools and colleges.* 2 drawing, rendering, map, chart, diagram *When I checked the plan of the building I found the hidden passageways.* *vb.* plot, scheme, design, arrange, contrive *The engineers planned to build the plant near the river. If it's sunny on Saturday, we plan to go on a picnic in the park.*

plane *n.* 1 level *If you are going to be rude, then the plane of this* *conversation is too low for me.* **2** aeroplane, aircraft *Tony just got off the plane from London.*

plank *n.* board, timber, wood *A deal table is made from plain planks of wood fastened to a supporting frame.*

plant *n.* **1** shrub, bush, bulb, flower *Your garden plants look lovely.* **2** factory, works, installation; machinery *The printers opened a new plant on the industrial estate.* *vb.* sow, seed *Sue planted some seeds in her garden.*

plaster *n.* **1** mortar, binding; cement *We put some plaster on the walls and then wallpapered them.* **2** bandage, dressing, lint *I think we'd better put a plaster on that cut.*

plastic *adj.* **1** pliant, supple, mouldable, pliable, flexible *Clay is a plastic substance that can be shaped into many forms.* **2** synthetic, artificial *Plastic surfaces are less attractive than natural ones but are easier to keep clean.*

plate *n.* dish *Michael got the plates out of the cupboard for dinner.* *vb.* coat, layer, cover *The metal was plated with gold.*

platform *n.* **1** stage, pulpit *The primitive theatre was nothing more than a raised platform on which the actors stood.* **2** policies, principles *The politicians met to work out the party platform for the coming elections.*

plausible *adj.* reasonable, likely, probable, believable, credible *Did you think Hargreaves' story about the mermaid was plausible?.*

play *n.* **1** show, drama, performance *Each year at Christmas our class put on a play for the rest of the school.* **2** amusement, sport, entertainment, recreation, game, pastime *There is a time for work and a time for play, and play comes after work.* *vb.* **1** act, perform, present, represent, impersonate *Richard played the part of the grandfather in our melodrama.* **2** have a good time; sport, frisk, romp, caper, frolic *After school was over, we all went out to play on the beach.* **3** compete, participate, contend *My brother taught me how to play chess.* **4** perform on *Can you play the piano?* *vb. phr.* **play ball** *Informal:* collaborate, cooperate *If we can get the teacher to play ball, maybe we'll have less homework.* **play down** minimize, belittle, make light of *If I were you, I would play down my experience as a pickpocket.* **play up** **1** *Informal:* annoy, irritate, antagonize *Why do you children always play up when we have visitors?* **2** highlight, emphasize, stress *You ought to play up your good points, like your ability to draw.*

player *n.* sportsman, participant, team member; contestant, competitor *Just who are the players in this game you have organized?*

playful *adj.* frolicsome, frisky, sportive *The cat didn't mean to scratch you, she was just being playful.*

plaything *n.* toy, game, gadget, trinket *Put away your playthings when you finish with them.*

playwright *n.* dramatist, dramaturge, scenarist, scriptwriter *The best playwrights of the century can be counted on the fingers of one hand.*

plea *n.* **1** appeal, request, entreaty *Ted's plea for fair treatment by his* *teammates was sincere.*   2 excuse, apology, answer, reply *My only plea for having given George a box on the ears was that he hit me first.*   3 defence, pleading, case *The lawyer entered a plea of not guilty for his client.*

plead *vb.*   1 beg, entreat, appeal *Sonia pleaded with her captors to let her go.*   2 answer, declare, present *The man pleaded guilty to driving on the wrong side of the road.*

pleasant *adj.*   1 enjoyable, nice, agreeable, pleasurable, satisfying, satisfactory, adequate, acceptable *We had a pleasant visit at my cousin's, but it could have been much more fun.*   2 affable, agreeable, charming, mild, amiable, friendly, personable, courteous *Fred's a pleasant enough fellow, but he's not my best friend.*   ANT. horrid, disagreeable; sour, nasty.

please *vb.*   1 gratify, satisfy *It pleases me to think of my parents getting a good rest from work.*   2 desire, choose, wish *You may do as you please about going to the concert.*   ANT. (1) displease, annoy, vex.

pleased *adj.*   happy, satisfied; delighted *I am very pleased to see you again, Meadle.*

pleasing *adj.*   pleasant, agreeable, charming, delightful, engaging *A pleasing melody wafted over to us across the pond.*   ANT. irritating, annoying.

pleasure *n.*   1 delight, satisfaction, enjoyment, gladness, happiness, joy, well-being, gratification *Stefan gets a great deal of pleasure out of spending a day with his grandchildren.*   2 luxury, indulgence *His pleasures are his greatest weakness.*   ANT. (1) pain, discomfort, torment.

pledge *n.*   promise, agreement, commitment, oath *Ronnie gave his pledge to abide by the rules of the club if he became a member.*   *vb.* promise, agree; swear, vow *Timothy has pledged to help at home after school.*

plentiful *adj.*   abundant, bountiful, fruitful, copious *The farmers thanked God for a plentiful harvest.*   ANT. scarce, rare, scanty.

plenty *n.*   abundance, fullness, fruitfulness, bounty, plentifulness *Many people went to America, believing it be the land of plenty.*   ANT. need, want, scarcity.

pliable *adj.*   flexible, mouldable, adaptable, plastic *If you soak the wood in water for a few hours, it becomes pliable enough to bend.*

plight *n.*   difficulty, predicament, dilemma, situation, state, condition *Consider the plight of the orphan, with no family.*

plod *vb.*   tread, walk, trudge; stump *The remains of the troop plodded wearily back to the base after the battle.*

plot *n.*   1 plan, scheme, design, intrigue, conspiracy *Some think that the oil shortage is the result of an international plot.*   2 story, theme, outline, thread *The acting in the play was good, but the plot lacked something.*   *vb.* plan, scheme, design, contrive, conspire *The prisoners spent six months plotting their escape.*

pluck *vb.*   snatch, pull, jerk, yank *You have to pluck the feathers out of* *a chicken before cooking it, not after.* *n.* courage, bravery, nerve, boldness, determination, spirit *It takes pluck to admit when you've done something wrong.*

plucky *adj.* brave, courageous, undaunted, bold, spirited *Harvey is the plucky fellow who dived in to save me.*

plug *n.* stopper, cork, bung *She pulled out the plug and let all the water out of the bath.* *vb.* stop (up), block, obstruct *The rust inside the pipes plugged up the whole system.*

plump *adj.* chubby, fat, stout, portly *Esmeralda is much more plump than she was when we were classmates.* ANT. slim, thin, skinny.

plunder *vb.* rob, pillage, sack, ravage, strip, raid, loot *The conquering armies plundered the city till nothing of value remained.* *n.* **1** booty, loot, spoils *The soldiers needed many wagons to carry off their plunder.* **2** pillage, robbery, sacking, sack *The plunder of Troy lasted two months.*

plunge *vb.* **1** submerge, dip, immerse *I plunged my burnt finger into the cool water.* **2** dive, jump, rush *Davey plunged into the river to try to save the drowning girl.* *n.* leap, dive, jump *We all took a plunge into the swimming pool before dinner.*

pocketbook *n.* purse, handbag, bag; wallet, portfolio *I think I left my pocketbook lying on the desk.*

poem *n.* verse, lyric, sonnet, ballad *'Evangeline' is one of the longest poems in the English language.*

poetry *n.* verse; metre; rhyme *My brother-in-law writes poetry that doesn't rhyme.*

poignant *adj.* distressing, intense, severe, strong, keen *Seeing you again brought back many poignant memories, Simon.*

point *n.* **1** locality, position, location, spot *Don has reached a point in his life where he doesn't want to waste time any more.* **2** aim, object, intent, purpose, idea *The point of my story is to show that you cannot afford to be dishonest.* **3** meaning, import, drift *You don't get the point of the joke, do you?* **4** headland, cape, ness, promontory *We stood out on the point, near the lighthouse, watching the boats sail past.* *vb.* **1** indicate, show, designate *The boy pointed to the place in the wall where the man had disappeared.* **2** direct, guide, head, lead, steer; aim *I pointed the canoe homeward to arrive before sunset. Don't ever point a gun at anyone!*

point-blank *adv.* directly, bluntly, explicitly, plainly *She told me point-blank that she never wanted to see me again.* ANT. indirectly, vaguely.

pointless *adj.* purposeless, vain *The argument about what I should have done last week was totally pointless.*

poise *n.* **1** self-control, control, assurance, composure, dignity; carriage *Although she's only fourteen, Suzanne has the poise of a twenty-one-year-old.* **2** balance, steadiness, equilibrium *That acrobat on the high wire has unbelievable strength and poise.*

vb. balance; hesitate *The diver poised on the edge of the high platform before diving into the pool.* ANT. *n.*(1) coarseness, ineptitude. (2) awkwardness, instability, uncertainty.

poison *n.* venom, virus, toxin, bane *Children should never be allowed to touch or use poison of any kind. The spitting cobra can project its poison a very long way.* *vb.* infect, contaminate, pollute *Exhaust fumes from cars poison the atmosphere in large cities.*

poisonous *adj.* toxic, deadly, lethal; dangerous, harmful *Poisonous chemicals are constantly polluting the water and air.*

poke *vb.,n.* stab, thrust, jab, punch *Don't poke that broom handle into the hornets' nest. When I teased Peter he gave me a poke in the ribs.*

policy *n.* tactic, strategy, procedure, approach, system, rule *The government's policy is to retire people at the age of fifty-five.*

polish *vb.* 1 shine, brighten *When you've finished making the beds, you can polish the silver.* 2 refine, finish *The president polished his speech while on his way to the meeting.* *n.* 1 gloss, shine, sheen, lustre, brightness *The furniture has such a high polish that you can see yourself in it.* 2 refinement, finish, elegance *The lady has excellent taste and polish.* ANT. *vb.*(1) dull, tarnish.

polite *adj.* courteous, thoughtful, considerate, cordial, respectful, mannerly, considerate *You must be more polite to your elders.* ANT. impolite, rude, discourteous, uncivil.

pollute *vb.* contaminate, dirty, befoul, taint *The fumes from the refinery are polluting the atmosphere.* ANT. clean, purify.

pomp *n.* magnificence, splendour, brilliance *The coronation was attended by unbelievably glorious pomp.*

pompous *adj.* vain, arrogant, stuffy, pretentious, self-important *Cheedle has behaved like a pompous fool since his knighthood.*

ponder *vb.* weigh, consider, study, reflect, deliberate, think, contemplate *Have you ever pondered whether the country is the best place to bring up children?*

ponderous *adj.* heavy, weighty *Count on Postlethwaite to bore everyone with his ponderous discussion of party politics.*

poor *adj.* 1 impoverished, poverty-stricken, needy, destitute, penniless, hard up *There are many more poor people in India than in all the western countries combined.* 2 bad, substandard, faulty, inferior, worthless *The machinery made in this factory is of such poor quality that no one wants it.* 3 unfortunate, unlucky, doomed, luckless, unhappy, miserable, pitiful, pitiable *After the man's wife went away, the poor fellow just didn't know what to do.* ANT. (1) rich, wealthy, prosperous. (2) good, excellent. (3) lucky, fortunate.

poppycock *n.* nonsense, twaddle, piffle, rubbish *Surely you don't believe that poppycock about Greg's sailing round the world single-handed!!*

popular *adj.* 1 well-liked, well-thought-of, approved, accepted, favourite, celebrated, admired, famous *Jane was one of the most pop-*

ular girls in our class at school. 2 common, general, familiar, ordinary, current, prevailing *The popular view of the scholar is of someone out of touch with the world, buried in books.* ANT. (1) unpopular, disliked.

populous *adj.* thronged, crowded, teeming, dense *Tokyo is one of the most populous cities in the world.*

port *n.* harbour, haven, refuge, dock *We finally reached port after forty days at sea.*

portable *adj.* movable, transportable; handy *Putting a handle on this TV doesn't make it portable—it's much too heavy to lift.*

porter *n.* 1 carrier *The porter took my suitcases off the train.* 2 gatekeeper, doorman; caretaker *The porter at the door told me where to go.*

portion *n.* 1 share, part, quota, section, segment *Only a small portion of money from the sale of a book goes to the author.* 2 serving, helping *Tom ate three portions of apple pie with ice cream after that big dinner.* *vb.* apportion, allot, distribute, deal out *The profits from the sale were portioned out to us.*

portly *adj.* corpulent, stout, fat, heavy, obese *Gilbert has to buy his clothes in a shop where they fit portly men.* ANT. slim, thin, slender.

portrait *n.* picture, likeness, representation; painting *A portrait of Queen Mary shows her with her grandchildren.*

portray *vb.* represent, depict, picture *The painting portrayed a man riding a horse. Penny portrays an old lady in the school play.*

pose *vb.* 1 model, sit *When Janet was a student, she made money posing for fashion commercials.* 2 pretend, feign, act *Donald posed as an expert on computers, but he'd never even seen one.* 3 assert, state, set forth *Getting an elephant for a pet poses the problem of how to feed it.* *n.* posture, position, attitude *The pose you took before would make a better photograph.*

position *n.* 1 location, place, locality, site *The position of that building causes it to block out sunlight during the summer.* 2 condition, situation, state, status *The position of all the students was the same: all had taken the one-year course and all now had to face the exam.* 3 job, post, employment, situation, office, occupation *Raquel has just got a very good position in the printing company.* 4 posture, pose, deportment, bearing *For how long can you maintain that position of standing on one leg?* 5 belief, view, attitude, opinion *My position is that the teachers ought to be paid as much as the government can afford.* *vb.* put, place, situate, locate *The painting must be carefully positioned in the frame for the best effect.*

positive *adj.* 1 clear, definite, sure, certain, direct, unmistakable *We gave the tourists positive directions on how to get there, but they still got lost.* 2 sure, certain, definite, obstinate *Betty was positive that Jim had said to meet him at eight o'clock.* 3 practical, real; beneficial *I want to see some positive effects before I approve another test of this plane.* ANT. (1,2) unsure, dubious, mixed-up, confused. (3) negative, adverse.

positively *adv.* definitely, certainly, absolutely, unquestionably, surely *The witness testified that Wayne was positively the last man she saw leave the theatre on Saturday.*

possess *vb.* 1 have, own, hold *Everything Tim possesses can fit into his one small knapsack.* 2 occupy, control, dominate, hold *Whatever possessed you to act in such a way? Dave was possessed by a fit of laughter.*

possession *n.* 1 ownership, occupancy, custody *When are we taking possession of the house?* 2 property *That fountain pen is one of my prized possessions.*

possible *adj.* conceivable, imaginable; practical, practicable, feasible. ANT. impossible, unthinkable, inconceivable; impractical.

possibly *adv.* maybe, perhaps, conceivably *Can there possibly be anything more perfect than a sphere?*

post *n.* 1 shaft, column, pole, pillar *We built a bird house and put it on top of a tall post in the garden.* 2 job, position, office *Donna's father was appointed to an important post in the embassy.* 3 position, station, location *The sentry left his post to investigate the eerie noises.* 4 fort, camp, base *The soldiers from the nearby post came into town on Sundays to go to church.* *vb.* 1 send *The letter I posted in London yesterday was delivered in Leeds today.* 2 assign, station, position *There were two guards posted at the gate.*

postpone *vb.* delay, defer, put off *The game was postponed because of rain.*

poster *n.* advertisement, bill, placard *The kiosks are plastered with posters advertising the new play at Drury Lane.*

posture *n.* carriage, stance, deportment *You get pains in your lower back because of your poor posture.*

pot *n.* saucepan, pan, vessel *That pot won't be big enough to hold all this spaghetti.*

potent *adj.* powerful, strong, mighty; influential, convincing, effective *Lady Belling has long been a potent force in the art world.* ANT. impotent, weak, powerless, feeble.

potential *adj.* 1 possible; likely *Ken is a potential member of the swimming team.* 2 latent, hidden, dormant *The potential energy of the hydrogen atom is unbelievably great.* *n.* potentiality, capacity, ability *Renee has great potential as a soprano.*

pottery *n.* ceramics, china, earthenware *Childers has given up woodcarving and turned to making pottery.*

pouch *n.* sack, bag; container *The hunters returned from the duck shoot with their pouches full of game.*

pound *vb.* beat, bang, strike, hit *The police came at midnight and pounded my door with their truncheons.*

pour *vb.* flow, run, discharge *Watch the water pour through the tunnel after a storm.*

poverty *n.* 1 need, want, destitution, distress, pennilessness *Many of Dickens's characters lived in the worst of poverty in nineteenth-century England.* 2 scarcity, lack, scantiness, scarceness *Comic books* *may be fun to read sometimes, but they suffer from a poverty of expression.* ANT. (1) wealth, richness, comfort. (2) abundance, fruitfulness.

power *n.* **1** ability, capability *It isn't within my power to grant you permission to stay away from school.* **2** force, energy, strength, might, vigour *It takes a lot of power to hit a six in cricket.* **3** authority, command, control, rule, sovereignty *When our party comes into power, they will sponsor laws dealing with tax reform.*

powerful *adj.* **1** strong, mighty, potent *The blacksmith was a powerful man who could lift an anvil with one hand.* **2** influential, effective, convincing *The police force is a powerful arm of law enforcement.* ANT. (1) weak, powerless. (2) ineffectual.

practical *adj.* possible, workable, doable, achievable, attainable *The practical way to get something done is not always the cheapest.* ANT. impractical, visionary.

practice *n.* **1** habit, custom, usage, tradition *Breaking a bottle over the bow of a ship at its launching is a well-established practice.* **2** operation, action, performance *Your theory sounds fine, but how can it be reduced to actual practice?* **3** exercise, drill, repetition *Practice makes perfect.*

practise *vb.* **1** exercise, drill, repeat *If you practise, they may let you play the piano in the school orchestra.* **2** observe, follow, pursue *You should practise what you preach.* **3** do, exercise, work at; function *My uncle practises medicine in Bombay.*

practised *adj.* skilled, adept, expert, able *Castillo is a practised violinist.* ANT. inept, unskilled.

pragmatic *adj.* practical, realistic, workable, functional *Henry's approach is pragmatic—he wants to get the job done in the best way.*

praise *vb.* commend, laud, applaud, admire, celebrate *Fran's dog was very pleased when she praised him for doing a trick correctly.* *n.* commendation, compliment, approval *Praise from one's friends is often more valued than praise from one's parents.* ANT. *vb.* disapprove, condemn, criticize. *n.* criticism, condemnation, disapproval.

prank *n.* trick, joke, caper *Andrew's prank of putting glue on the teacher's chair did not go unpunished.*

pray *vb.* ask, beseech, beg, entreat, urge, importune *I pray you to forgive me—I didn't know what I was doing.*

prayer *n.* request, appeal, entreaty *The arrival of the rescue ship was the answer to their prayers.*

preach *vb.* teach, address, urge, encourage; lecture, moralize *Persuading bankers that they should lend money is preaching to the converted.*

precarious *adj.* perilous, dangerous; uncertain, doubtful *With sales decreasing, the business is in a precarious state.* ANT. safe.

precaution *n.* safeguard, measure, step *Please take every precaution to ensure your safe return.*

precede *vb.* go before, go first *The sheik let his wife precede him* *everywhere only because he feared land mines.* ANT. go after, follow, succeed.

precedence *n.* priority, preference *The wishes of the community must take precedence over the desires of the individual.*

precedent *n.* example, criterion, model *Entertaining visitors with a thousand dancers set a very expensive precedent.*

precept *n.* rule, principle, maxim *His precept has always been the Code of Hammurabi—an eye for an eye and a tooth for a tooth.*

precious *adj.* **1** valuable, costly, priceless, expensive, dear *She kept her most precious jewels in the bank.* **2** beloved, dear, cherished, favourite *The memory of the ball is so precious to Miranda that she'll never forget it.*

precipice *n.* cliff, crag *In another second, we would have plunged over the precipice to the rocks below.*

precipitate *adj.* sudden, swift, hasty, speedy *Wasn't your decision to move to Ouagadougou a bit precipitate?* ANT. considered, gradual.

precipitous *adj.* steep, abrupt, sharp *On one side of the trail was a precipitous drop of a mile to the valley below.*

précis *n.* summary, abstract, abridgement, outline *I don't have time for the full story, so just give me a précis.*

precise *adj.* **1** definite, exact, well-defined *The pirates gave me a precise description of where I could find the buried treasure.* **2** rigid, stiff, inflexible, careful, severe *Only precise adherence to the rules is tolerated in this school.*

precisely *adv.* exactly, specifically *Just let me know precisely what you want me to do.*

precision *n.* exactness, accuracy, correctness *The stunt pilots maintain the formation with extraordinary precision.*

predicament *n.* quandary, dilemma, difficulty *My predicament was that I did not have enough money for both ice cream and pizza.*

predict *vb.* foretell, forecast, prognosticate, prophesy *Who can predict the future?*

prediction *n.* forecast, prophecy *Her prediction is that we will be married within a year.*

predominant *adj.* prevalent, dominant, prevailing *These peoples have been predominant in influence in Turkestan for thousands of years.* ANT. secondary, accessory.

predominate *vb.* prevail, rule *When it comes to a vote, those who want a holiday by the sea always seem to predominate.*

pre-eminent *adj.* distinguished, outstanding; incomparable *Allison's father is a pre-eminent physicist.* ANT. inferior, secondary.

preface *n.* introduction, foreword, prelude, preamble, prologue *To find out what an author has in mind, it's a good idea to read the prefaces of books.* *vb.* precede, introduce, begin *The speaker prefaced his remarks with some jokes that established a relaxed atmosphere.*

prefer *vb.* favour, select, elect, fancy *Given a choice between chocolate ice cream and coffee, I prefer coffee.*

preference *n.* choice, selection, option, decision, pick *Sally's preference is for a husband who will look after her tenderly.*

prejudice *n.* favouritism, bias, partiality, unfairness *He has a strong prejudice against people who make up their minds without weighing both sides of the question.* *vb.* influence, convince, bias, warp *If everyone claims to be prejudiced in favour of peace, why are there wars?*

preliminary *adj.* preparatory, introductory *Before you start recording the talk I'd like to make some preliminary remarks.* *n.* **preliminaries** introduction, preface, prelude *Now that the preliminaries are over, let's get down to business.*

premature *adj.* untimely, early, unexpected *Owing to their premature return home, they surprised a burglar.* ANT. prompt.

preoccupied *adj.* distracted, absorbed, engrossed; busy *Leave Monty alone for now—can't you see he's preoccupied?* ANT. alert, aware, conscious.

preparation *n.* arrangement, plan; measure, provision *Did you make adequate preparation for your guests' arrival?*

prepare *vb.* get ready, arrange, plan *How do you expect to prepare for tomorrow's exam if you go out tonight?*

preposterous *adj.* absurd, ridiculous; fantastic, impossible *It is preposterous to suggest that cholesterol is good for you.*

prerogative *n.* privilege, right *As it is the dealer's right to choose the game, Arthur has the prerogative to play pontoon if he wishes.*

prescribe *vb.* direct, designate, order, recommend *The doctor prescribed some new medication which might have bad side effects.*

presence *n.* **1** attendance *Samuel's presence at the meeting will be important to its success.* **2** nearness, vicinity, closeness *Please don't use such language in my presence.* **3** bearing, personality, appearance *The king of Madagascar was a man of tremendous presence.* ANT. (1) absence.

present¹ *adj.* **1** existing, current; being *The present membership of the club is 25.* **2** here, attending; near, nearby *If you hear your name called, please answer 'Present'.*

present² *vb.* **1** give, donate, grant *The retiring employee was presented with a gold watch.* **2** introduce, acquaint *May I present my cousin, Andrew?* **3** show, display, exhibit, offer, furnish *Please present your tickets to the person at the door of the theatre.* *n.* gift, donation, gratuity, tip, largess *Toby received more presents for his birthday than anyone I know.*

presently *adv.* soon, shortly, anon; right away, directly, immediately *The doctor will see you presently.*

preserve *vb.* **1** keep, save, maintain *Preserve your energy for the next race.* **2** can, conserve, cure, salt, pickle *All of the vegetables we don't eat fresh we preserve and eat during the winter.* ANT. (1) squander, waste, use.

preside *vb.* officiate, direct *Helen was asked to preside over the conference on terrorism.*

press *vb.* 1 push *Press the button and the lift will come.* 2 squeeze, compress *After the grapes have been pressed, the skins and pulp are used to make brandy.* 3 embrace, hug, clasp *Suzie pressed the shivering kitten to her bosom.* 4 iron, smooth *Do you think you can press this skirt for me?* 5 urge, insist on *If I press you, would you be able to buy something for me when you go to town?* 6 push, crush, crowd *So many people pressed into the underground train that I could hardly breathe.* *n.* journalists, reporters, newspapermen, the fourth estate, the second oldest profession *The trades union leader gave a full briefing to the press after leaving the meeting.*

pressure *n.* stress, constraint; force *They put pressure on me to quit. There is a lot of pressure building up in the tank and it might burst.*

prestige *n.* reputation, importance, influence, distinction: renown, fame *Your parents enjoy great prestige in this community.*

presume *vb.* suppose, assume, believe; take for granted *I merely presumed that you were leaving when you put on your coat.*

presumption *n.* 1 supposition, assumption, guess *Your presumption that I am going out just because you see me wearing a hat happens to be false.* 2 impudence, insolence *What presumption he displayed in calling the teacher by his first name!* ANT. (2) humility; shyness; modesty.

presumptuous *adj.* impertinent, bold, impudent, fresh, rude, arrogant, forward *It was presumptuous of you to comment on Sir Ronald's shabby appearance.*

pretence *n.* 1 deceit, falsification, fabrication *Tom made a pretence of trying to appear innocent.* 2 lie, falsehood, deception *Your story about going to the library was nothing but pretence.*

pretend *vb.* 1 imagine, make believe *Let's pretend that you are a knight and I a damsel in distress.* 2 deceive; falsify, fake, simulate, feign *Don't try to pretend to us that you didn't know you were absent from school yesterday.*

pretentious *adj.* ostentatious, showy, affected; showing off *Hiring a man to precede him everywhere, blowing a trumpet, seems quite pretentious.* ANT. humble, simple.

pretext *n.* appearance, guise; pretence, guise *Under what pretext can you get into the office at night?*

pretty *adj.* attractive, fair; lovely, beautiful *Too bad about Wilhelmina—she used to be so pretty.* ANT. plain; ugly.

prevail *vb.* 1 predominate *A belief in the supernatural still prevails in many parts of the world.* 2 succeed, win, triumph *Even though the forces of evil may seem to have the upper hand, in the end good will prevail.* ANT. (2) lose, yield.

prevailing *adj.* current, common, habitual, general, universal *The prevailing opinion is that I ought to accept the appointment.*

prevalent *adj.* common, prevailing, widespread, extensive *Raising ducks for market was a prevalent activity around Aylesbury.* ANT. rare, infrequent.

prevent *vb.* block, stop, thwart, interrupt, obstruct, retard, hinder, slow, deter, inhibit *Firemen prevented me from entering the burning building.* ANT. help; allow.

previous *adj.* prior, earlier, former *Her previous husband ran off to Tierra del Fuego with the children.* ANT. later, following, subsequent.

prey *n.* victim *The rabbit was easy prey for the lion.* *vb.* victimize; seize, raid *There was a band of thugs in the hills that preyed on the villages for food.*

price *n.* cost, charge, expense, value *The price of food in Britain has risen a lot in the past months.* *vb.* mark: value, rate *We shall have to price all these goods before putting them out for sale.*

priceless *adj.* **1** invaluable, inestimable *The gold jewels were priceless.* **2** *Informal:* extraordinary, remarkable, memorable, marvellous *That joke you told us was priceless—now tell it to the others!*

prick *vb.* stab, pierce *The needle pricked him slightly as it went through his skin.* *n.* stab, cut, mark *The prick of the nettles stung her.*

pride *n.* **1** conceit, vanity, arrogance, self-importance, egotism, pretension *John is so swelled up with pride over his new job that he won't listen to anything I say to him.* **2** self-respect *Stephanie's pride in her family's position is great but she doesn't boast about it all the time.* **3** enjoyment, fulfilment, satisfaction *Dick takes so much pride in his vegetable garden each summer.* ANT. (1) humility, humbleness.

prim *adj.* formal, strait-laced, priggish, puritanical, prudish *Gordon was so prim that he wouldn't allow anyone to say 'Gosh!!' in his presence.*

primarily *adv.* chiefly, mainly, essentially, firstly, originally *Isn't this book intended primarily for younger people?* ANT. secondarily.

primary *adj.* **1** chief, main, principal *My primary purpose in being here is to help you learn.* **2** first, earliest, prime, original *Our primary consideration should be the safety of the participants in the race.* ANT. (1,2) secondary.

prime *adj.* **1** primary; first; chief *The prime aim in education is to teach understanding rather than just knowledge.* **2** best, top-grade, superior, excellent *I wish I could eat a prime sirloin steak, medium-rare, right this minute.* *vb.* prepare, make ready *The speaker was well primed on how he should address his audience.*

primitive *adj.* **1** prehistoric, primeval *In primitive societies, the men went out to hunt and the women stayed at home.* **2** uncivilized, uncultured, unsophisticated, simple, rough, rude, brutish *Why is it that so many children today have such primitive table manners?* ANT. (2) cultured, sophisticated, cultivated.

principal *adj.* chief, main, leading, prime, first, essential, primary *The principal problem lies in selecting the right people to do the job.* *n.* chief, head, leader *The authorities appointed a new principal to the college.* ANT. *adj.* secondary, accessory.

principle *n.* **1** rule, standard *The cafeteria operates on the principle of* *first come, first served.*   2 truth, law, postulate, proposition *Democratic government was founded on the principle that all men have equal rights.*   3 honesty, uprightness, virtue, goodness *My father was a man of very high principles.*

print *vb.*   1 issue, publish; reissue, reprint *We printed 2000 copies of the book.*   2 develop; enlarge *I had the pictures printed on glossy paper.*   *n.*   1 mark, fingerprint, sign *The detectives found three identifiable prints on the door leading to the bedroom.*   2 type, printing *Make sure you read the small print at the end of the contract before signing it.*   3 copy, lithograph, picture, photograph, etching, engraving *The public library has a fine collection of prints by famous artists.*

prior *adj.*   earlier, sooner, preceding *I have a prior engagement and cannot come to your party.*   ANT. subsequent, later.

prise *vb.*   lift, raise, lever; open *You will never guess what they found in the old chest when they prised up the lid.*

prison *n.*   jail *Fifteen years in prison can have a sobering effect on even the hardest criminal.*

private *adj.*   1 personal, individual; special, particular *What I have in my bank account is my own private business.*   2 secret, confidential, hidden *The representative made his views known in a private communication to the reporter.*   ANT. (1) public, general.

privilege *n.*   freedom, liberty; permission, right, advantage *Why does Manuel enjoy the privilege of being able to come in late for work?*

prize *n.*   reward, award, premium, bounty, bonus *The company gives a yearly prize for the best suggestion made by an employee.*   *vb.* value, esteem; estimate, rate *Don's judgement is highly prized by the directors of the company.*   ANT. *vb.* undervalue, disregard.

probable *adj.*   likely; feasible; presumable *It is probable that Ken will be nominated for the Nobel prize this year.*

probe *vb.*   examine, investigate, inquire, scrutinize, explore *The committee was set up to probe gifts to political parties.*   *n.*   examination, investigation, inquiry, scrutiny, exploration *The probe of the MPs' bank accounts revealed nothing of an illegal nature.*

problem *n.*   1 difficulty, predicament, dilemma *A problem has arisen in connection with my tax refund, causing a month's delay.*   2 question; puzzle, riddle *I couldn't do the last problem in the maths exam.*

procedure *n.*   operation, process, method, system *Please tell me the procedure to follow to apply for a tax refund.*

proceed *vb.*   1 move ahead *or* on, go on, progress, continue *Let us now proceed to the next house and interview the people there.*   2 result, issue, spring, emanate *The next step in the operation will proceed from the last one.*   ANT. (1) withdraw, retreat.

proceedings *n.pl.*   record, account, minutes, annal, document *The proceedings of the conference will be published in three months.*

proceeds *n.pl.*   income, reward, intake, profit, return, yield *The proceeds from our investments paid for this new car.*

process *n.*   course; procedure, method, system, operation *In the pro-*

cess of saving the puppy, I lost my glasses. The scientist developed a new process for refining iron ore. vb. treat, prepare *George's grandfather is the man who invented the technique for processing wood into paper.*

procession *n.* parade, train, cavalcade *An entire procession of people filed through the doctor's waiting room ahead of me.*

proclaim *vb.* announce, advertise, declare *The week beginning 3 November has been proclaimed as International Lexicography Week.*

proclamation *n.* announcement, declaration; promulgation *The proclamation states that no one will be allowed on the streets after nine p.m.*

procure *vb.* get, obtain, win, secure, gain, acquire *I need to procure a late-model computer for use at home.*

prod *vb.* nudge, goad, push, jab *The cattle moved along briskly when prodded by an electrical rod.*

prodigious *adj.* vast, huge, immense, extensive *The crop was so successful that they were able to sell a prodigious amount of wheat abroad.*

prodigy *n.* marvel, wonder; freak, curiosity *Francis was a musical child prodigy, composing a song at the age of five.*

produce *vb.* **1** bear, bring forth, yield, supply, give *A ewe rarely produces twin lambs.* **2** create, make, originate, generate, occasion, bring about, give rise to, cause *Hydro-electricity produces electricity from the power of the flow of water.* **3** show, exhibit, present, display, demonstrate *The judge said that we had to produce proof of damages in order to have a valid case.* *n.* product, production, fruits, crops, harvest *We buy all the produce for the restaurant directly from the farmers to ensure freshness.*

product *n.* **1** result, outcome, output, produce *The product of all that hard work is an essay I'm very pleased with.* **2** goods, stock, commodity, merchandise *Some shops once refused to sell any products manufactured in your country.*

productive *adj.* fertile, fruitful, rich; creative *Carruthers has a productive imagination constantly yielding new ideas for projects.* ANT. wasteful, useless.

profess *vb.* declare, state, avow *Both of them professed their innocence, but I don't believe them.*

profession *n.* occupation, calling, vocation, employment *Medicine, law and education are professions, while carpentry, plumbing and so forth are trades.* ANT. hobby, pastime.

professional *n.* expert, specialist *Mark is a real professional at painting model aircraft.* *adj.* **1** trained, expert, qualified *Patrick is a professional lexicographer.* **2** paid *Some sports are open to both amateur and professional competitors.* ANT. amateur.

proficient *adj.* skilled, skilful; able, capable *I would never be afraid with Susan, as she is a proficient pilot.* ANT. unskilled, inexperienced.

profit *n.* **1** gain, return, earnings *If I buy something for £10, sell it for*

£20 and have expenses of £5, my profit is £5. 2 advantage, benefit, gain, improvement *I can't see any profit in continuing this dispute.* *vb.* benefit, improve, better *It doesn't profit you to say bad things about others.* ANT. *n.* (1) loss, debit. *vb.* lose.

profitable *adj.* beneficial, favourable, productive, useful, lucrative, gainful *To be profitable, a business must buy cheap and sell dear.*

profound *adj.* 1 deep, solemn, serious *There is a profound difference between effort and success.* 2 wise, knowing, knowledgeable, intelligent, learned *The speech was so profound that no one understood it.* ANT. (1,2) shallow, superficial.

profuse *adj.* abundant, plentiful, bountiful *The praise from our coach was profuse whenever we won a game.* ANT. meagre, scanty, inconsiderable.

programme *n.* record, plan, schedule, calendar, list, agenda; events *And now for a fully packed programme of entertainment.*

progress *n.* advance, advancement, movement, improvement, development *The doctor was pleased to see that I was making considerable progress towards recovery.* *vb.* advance, improve, proceed, develop *If Frank continues to progress in his studies, he may come first in the class.* ANT. *n.* regression. *vb.* regress, backslide.

prohibit *vb.* 1 forbid, disallow, ban *The fire laws prohibit smoking in some lifts.* 2 prevent, obstruct, stop, hinder *A sprained ankle prohibited Jane from walking any faster.* ANT. (1) allow, permit. (2) help, encourage.

prohibition *n.* ban, prevention, restriction, embargo *A prohibition has been placed on the shipment of arms to that country.* ANT. permission, authorization.

project *n.* 1 plan, proposal, outline, scheme, design *Your project for the new shopping centre must be approved by the district council.* 2 activity, task *The children are going to construct a model Indian village as a class project.* *vb.* 1 propose, plan *How much time do you project will be required to clear the land for the building?* 2 cast, throw *The image from the film was projected onto the screen.* 3 extend, protrude, bulge *The corner of the table projects too far to allow the door to be closed.*

prolific *adj.* fruitful, fertile, productive *The university has always been a prolific source of engineers.*

prolong *vb.* lengthen, extend, increase *With practice, we were able to prolong the time we could spend under water.*

prominent *adj.* 1 well-known, famous, noted, notable, noteworthy, important, eminent, distinguished, leading, celebrated *A prominent scientist had been invited to give the address on speech day.* 2 noticeable, obvious, conspicuous *The error in the statistics was too prominent to be ignored.* ANT. insignificant, unimportant.

promiscuous *adj.* immoral, loose, licentious, dissolute *Cora has been unlucky in selecting men friends who turn out to be promiscuous.*

promise *n.* assurance, pledge, oath, vow, word *The manager gave his promise that our new dishwasher would be repaired.* *vb.* pledge, vow, assure, swear *You promised that we could go to the cinema if we finished all our homework.*

promote *vb.* 1 advance, further, support, help, aid, assist *To promote the sale of the vacuum cleaners, the store offered a week's free trial.* 2 move up, advance *Vickie was so proud when her father was promoted to foreman of the whole factory.* ANT. (1) hinder, retard. (2) demote.

prompt *adj.* timely, punctual *The fireman's prompt action saved the lives of three old people. Please try to be more prompt at the dinner table.* *vb.* 1 urge, arouse, incite *Your reminder prompted me to phone to ask if you could come to dinner.* 2 hint, suggest, propose, mention *I don't need you to prompt me about buying flowers for my mother's birthday.* ANT. *adj.* late; slow.

pronounce *vb.* 1 utter, proclaim, announce *The minister said, 'I now pronounce you man and wife.'* 2 articulate, utter, enunciate *When he was about nine, Eugene had difficulty pronouncing the letter 'L'.*

pronounced *adj.* definite, clear, noticeable *There is a pronounced difference between parsnips and turnips.* ANT. indistinguishable, minor, unnoticeable.

proof *n.* 1 evidence, demonstration, testimony, confirmation *The man accused of the crime offered proof that he was far away when it was committed.* 2 test, trial *The proof of the pudding is in the eating.* *adj.* protected, impenetrable, impervious *This thick plastic is proof against bullets.*

proper *adj.* 1 suitable, correct, fitting, just *I think that making children who write on walls clean them is a proper punishment.* 2 polite, well-mannered, decent *When she's with grown-ups, Natalie is always very proper.* ANT. (2) rude, impolite, discourteous.

property *n.* 1 belongings, possessions, effects *Please remove all personal property from your lockers at the end of the school term.* 2 house; land, real estate, tract *My uncle has just bought a large property in Aylesbury.*

prophecy *n.* prediction, augury; forecast *Your prophecy that we would lose the cup this year proved false.*

prophesy *vb.* predict, foretell; divine, augur *The seer prophesied that the sky would become red, then green.*

prophet *n.* oracle, fortune teller, forecaster, seer, clairvoyant, soothsayer *If you predicted sunshine and it rained, I'd say you were a poor prophet.*

proportion *n.* 1 relation; comparison, balance *You must be careful to mix the ingredients in the correct proportion or you won't get an edible cake.* 2 part, section, share, piece *What proportion of the interest in the company do you think the investors have?* *vb.* adjust, balance, arrange *The club members proportioned the work among themselves.*

proposal *n.* 1 offer, suggestion; scheme, plan *The company accepted our proposal, and we'll soon have the contract to build the ship.*

2 proposition, engagement *My proposal of marriage was accepted immediately.*

propose *vb.* **1** present, offer, tender, recommend, suggest *The union proposed a settlement that would give each employee a 20% rise.* **2** plan, intend, expect, mean *How do you propose to climb up the face of a sheer cliff?* **3** offer marriage, *(informal)* pop the question; ask for the hand of *The young man proposed to his girlfriend rather nervously, thinking she might say no.*

prosecute *vb.* accuse, charge with, sue, bring an action against *As quickly as the government prosecuted criminals, the lawyers would get them released.*

prospect *n.* **1** expectation, hope *Your job prospects won't be very good if you don't complete your education.* **2** view, outlook, panorama *The prospect from the hotel window was marvellous.* **3** buyer, candidate *Dan's father will be entertaining two business prospects at dinner tonight.* *vb.* search, explore, dig *My forefathers went prospecting for gold, but they didn't find any.*

prospective *adj.* proposed, planned, hoped-for. *My prospective employer said they have plans for opening a Paris office.*

prosper *vb.* succeed, thrive, rise, flourish *Roger's career has prospered since he moved to Birmingham.* **ANT.** decline, sink, fail.

prosperous *adj.* wealthy, well-off, rich, thriving, flourishing, well-to-do *Any change in the tax laws seems to ensure that the accountants become prosperous.* **ANT.** poor, impoverished; failing; unfortunate.

protect *vb.* defend, shield, guard *If you want to live in that neighbourhood, I suggest you get a dog to protect you.*

protection *n.* **1** guard, security, shield, safety *The shed provided protection against the rain.* **2** security, assurance *Many people have life insurance to provide protection in case one partner dies.*

protest *n.* objection, complaint; opposition, disagreement *Our protest against the way children were treated had no effect on our parents.* *vb.* object, complain *If you didn't protest about the conditions here, no one would do anything to improve them.* **ANT.** *n.* approval, agreement. *vb.* approve, agree.

protocol *n.* etiquette, convention, procedure *I am unsure of the protocol when a head of state visits.*

protrude *vb.* stick out, project, jut out *The frame began to protrude through the fabric.*

proud *adj.* **1** arrogant, haughty, self-important, snooty; conceited, vain *The people next door are too proud to have anything to do with us.* **2** self-respecting *We are justly proud of our country's fine heritage.* **3** dignified, high-minded, honourable *It was a proud moment for my parents when I was given the prize.* **ANT.** humble, modest.

prove *vb.* **1** show, demonstrate, confirm, verify, affirm *Can you prove that the ring is pure gold?* **2** test, examine, try *Prove the answer by substituting the value of x in the equation.*

proverb *n.*   saying, adage, maxim, byword *Despite inflation, 'A penny saved is a penny earned' is a valid proverb.*

proverbial *adj.*   well-known, common, general *Scrooge's stinginess is proverbial.*

provide *vb.*   supply, furnish, equip, give, bestow *The army provides a uniform when you join, at no charge.*

province *n.*   area, territory, region, district *In which province did you receive your foreign service training?*

provision *n.*   arrangement, condition *Provision was made in case he failed to keep his side of the bargain.*

provisional *adj.*   temporary, transient, passing; tentative, conditional *Provisional arrangements will be made to shelter victims of the disaster.*

provisions *n. pl.*   store, supplies, stock *We had enough provisions to last us for only one week.*

provoke *vb.*   **1** bother, vex, irritate, annoy, irk, anger, enrage *Don't provoke me any more or I won't let you go to the game on Saturday.* **2** cause, occasion, bring about *The articles in the newspaper provoked many readers to write in.*

prowl *vb.*   slink, sneak, lurk *The police caught a man prowling around behind our house last night.*

prudence *n.*   **1** carefulness, care, caution, tact; discretion, circumspection *Junior employees have to exercise prudence when they notice the faults of their superiors.* **2** wisdom, judgement, foresight, common sense *Don showed prudence in not asking the teacher a lot of silly questions.* ANT. rashness, recklessness, foolishness.

prudent *adj.*   **1** wise, discreet, careful, sensible *Be more prudent in what you say to others lest you hurt their feelings.* **2** provident, reasonable, safe *Ask Donald if you want advice about prudent investments.* ANT. rash, reckless, foolish, foolhardy.

pry *vb.*   peep, peer, meddle *Why is Meg always prying into everybody's personal affairs?*

pseudonym *n.*   assumed name, alias; pen-name, *nom de plume:* *'Elia' was a pseudonym of Charles Lamb.*

public *n.*   society, community, people *The public has a right to know about the workings of government.* *adj.* common; community, municipal, civil *This is a public park and I have every right to be in it.* ANT. *adj.* private.

publish *vb.*   **1** issue, distribute, bring out *During his career, Alfred published many worthwhile works of literature.* **2** announce, declare, proclaim, disclose, reveal, publicize *The prime minister's honours list was published recently.*

pull *vb.*   drag, draw *Jack pulled the sledge back up the slope.* *vb. phr.* **pull apart** separate, divide *The referee couldn't pull the wrestlers apart.* **pull away** leave, depart *Just as I arrived, I saw the train pulling away.* **pull down** wreck, destroy, raze *The company is going to pull down the old factory.* **pull off** **1** remove *I pulled off my burning clothes and dived into the water.* **2** achieve, succeed *The*

task seemed impossible but she pulled it off very skilfully in the end.
pull out leave, depart *The coach pulls out at midnight.* **pull through** survive, recover *James has had a serious illness, but the doctor said he'll pull through all right.* **pull up** stop *I pulled up at the traffic light, waiting for it to change to green.* *n.* **1** wrench, jerk; haul, tow *I gave a hard pull and the handle came off.* **2** *Informal:* influence, weight *David's father has a lot of pull in this town.*

pulse *n.* beat, throb, vibration *I could feel the pulse of the deer's heart was still strong.*

pump *vb.* **1** lift, raise, drive *The natives pumped the water up.* **2** blow *Your bicycle tyres need pumping up.*

punch *vb., n.* blow, knock, hit *He punched me on the nose. The punch the boy got dazed him for a few seconds.*

punctual *adj.* prompt, timely, on time *Be punctual when arriving for work tomorrow.* ANT. early; late.

punish *vb.* discipline, chasten, reprove, scold, castigate *The worst feeling is being punished for something you didn't do.* ANT. reward; praise.

pupil *n.* student, learner *There are only three pupils in my Latin class.*

purchase *vb.* buy, obtain, get, acquire, procure *We drove into the village once a week to purchase groceries and other supplies.* *n.* acquisition *Ernest made two purchases in the hardware store.*

pure *adj.* **1** unmixed, genuine, simple, undiluted *This sweater is made of pure wool.* **2** spotless, untainted, clean, uncontaminated, unpolluted *The spring gave out abundant pure water.* **3** innocent, good, chaste, virtuous *The priest led a completely pure existence.* ANT. (1) adulterated, mixed. (2) dirty, foul, tainted. (3) immoral, licentious.

purely *adv.* completely, entirely, totally *Fred's comment was made purely in fun, so don't be insulted.*

purge *vb.* cleanse, eliminate, eradicate *The people could not purge themselves from their sins.* *n.* elimination, removal; purification. *Many were forced to resign in the purge on the radicals in the political party.*

purify *vb.* cleanse, refine, purge *In this vat the mixture is purified by passing it through fine screens.*

purpose *n.* **1** intention, intent, object, end, aim, objective, goal *My purpose in life is to help people learn as much as possible about the English language.* **2** use, application *What is the purpose of this device?* *n.phr.* **on purpose** intentionally, deliberately *You stepped on my toe on purpose!*

pursue *vb.* follow, chase, hound, track *The police pursued the fugitives for three days without catching them.*

pursuit *n.* chase, hunt *The pursuit of wild game is frowned on by some.*

push *vb.* **1** force, shove, thrust *Kim pushed a pencil through the hole* *in the wall.* **2** press, shove *The crowd pushed me right back onto the train I had just left.*

put *vb.* **1** place, set *Please put the tray on the table.* **2** attach, establish, assign *Don't put too much emphasis on how much money your friends have.* **3** express, state, say *It wasn't so much what George said as how he put it that was so clever.* *vb. phr.* **put across** communicate *The preacher put his message across very well.* **put aside** save, keep *My mother always put a little money aside for a rainy day.* **put away** **1** save, set aside, store *I had a little bit put away for your birthday.* **2** lock up *That crazy old man ought to be put away.* **put down** defeat, repress *The new commander had the rebellions in the provinces put down.* **put off** **1** delay, postpone *Don't put off till tomorrow what you can do today.* **2** disconcert *Stanley was put off by the rude way the hotel manager spoke to him.* **put on** **1** don; wear, dress, attire *Please don't put on your purple shirt with the green trousers.* **2** pretend, fake, feign *Don't put on airs with me, young man.* **3** stage, produce, present *The Royal Shakespeare Company is putting on* Macbeth. **put out** **1** extinguish, douse *Put out that match!* **2** inconvenience *I hope it won't put you out if I stay for tea.* **3** extend, offer *Sam put out his hand and I shook it warmly.* **put through** effect, achieve, do *The plan was put through with little delay.* **put up** erect, build, construct *They put up a statue to the statesman in front of the Town Hall.* **put up with** endure, stand, tolerate, suffer *I can't understand how you can put up with Deirdre's constant complaining.*

putrid *adj.* rotten, decayed, decomposed, mouldy *If you keep food too long—even in the fridge—it becomes putrid.*

puzzle *n.* confusion, question, riddle, problem *It's a puzzle to me how your cousin, who is so lazy, can keep his job.* *vb.* confuse, perplex, bewilder, mystify *I was puzzled by your comment, but now I understand what you meant.*

puzzling *adj.* baffling, enigmatic, perplexing *Married to and divorced from each other three times, Anne and Richard have a puzzling relationship.*

q

quack *n.* fake, faker, charlatan, fraud, impostor *Any doctor who prescribes surgery for a black-and-blue mark must be a quack.*

quaint *adj.* **1** strange, unusual, odd, curious, uncommon *Tourists often commented on the quaint customs of village life.* **2** old-fashioned, antiquated *My aunt still makes quilts using those quaint old stitches.* ANT. (1) common, ordinary.

quake *vb.* tremble, shake, quiver, shudder *The leaves of the aspen tree quake in the slightest breeze.* *n.* earthquake, tremor *A mild quake yesterday rattled doors and windows in the Ben Nevis area.*

qualifications *n.,pl.* accomplishments, attainments; experience, knowledge; abilities, skill *What are Franklin's qualifications to be a computer programmer?*

qualify *vb.* **1** suit, fit *The interviewer told Rosette that she wasn't qualified for the job.* **2** limit, restrict; restrain, moderate; change *Instead of making a general statement, you ought to qualify your remarks.*

quality *n.* **1** attribute, property, characteristic, character, trait, feature *A good doctor has the quality of sympathy in his basic nature.* **2** excellence, worth, value; grade, rank, status, condition *The quality of some television programmes leaves much to be desired.*

quandary *n.* dilemma, predicament *I was in a quandary as to what to get Ashley for her birthday.*

quantity *n.* amount, extent, mass, bulk, measure, number *Whoever comes closest to estimating the number of beans in the jar wins the bicycle.*

quarrel *n.* argument, dispute, disagreement, difference, tiff, fight *The quarrel between my brother and me arose because he wanted me to stay at home while he went to the bowling alley.* *vb.* argue, dispute, disagree, differ, squabble, bicker, fight *Our children seldom quarrel about anything.* ANT. *vb.* agree.

quarrelsome *adj.* edgy, irritable, disagreeable; cross *Because of his tendency to be quarrelsome, Stewart gets into many arguments.* ANT. even-tempered, genial.

quash *vb.* crush, suppress, subdue, put down *With insufficient evidence against his client, the barrister petitioned for the indictment to be quashed.*

queer *adj.* odd, peculiar, unusual, extraordinary, uncommon *I thought it queer when they notified me about winning the pools, as I had placed no bet.* ANT. ordinary, conventional, usual.

quell *vb.* subdue, suppress; allay *The calm voice of the president succeeding in quelling the uprising.*

quench *vb.* satisfy, slake *Sweet fizzy drinks do not really quench my thirst.*

query *n.* question, enquiry *If you have a query about your homework, please ask your teacher.* *vb.* question; doubt *When Andrew failed the exam, he queried the result with his teacher.*

quest *n.* search, journey, hunt *The quest for the Holy Grail was the subject of many medieval romances.*

question *n.* 1 query, enquiry *Timmy, if you have a question, please raise your hand.* 2 doubt, uncertainty *There has been some question about whether John could visit us.* *vb.* 1 query, ask; interrogate, interview *The police questioned the man closely.* 2 doubt; suspect *How dare you question my honesty?* **ANT.** *n.* (1) answer, solution. *vb.* (1) answer, reply, respond.

questionable *adj.* doubtful, dubious; debatable *We all thought that the referee's decision was questionable.*

queue *n.* line, file; train, retinue *British people seem to like standing in queues.* *vb.* line (up), file *I met my wife while queueing at a bus stop.*

quibble *vb.* argue, (*informal*) split hairs, take issue *Stop quibbling about the pence and worry about where you'll get the pounds.*

quick *adj.* 1 fast, rapid, swift, speedy *Walter plays a lot of tennis and is very quick on his feet.* 2 impatient, hasty *He must learn to control his quick temper.* 3 prompt, ready, immediate *The quick answer to your question is 'No', but I should explain that more fully.* **ANT.** (1) slow, sluggish.

quicken *vb.* hurry, hasten, accelerate *As I heard my train approaching the station, I quickened my pace.*

quick-witted *adj.* shrewd, astute, alert, acute, clever *It was quick-witted of Martin to catch the vase before it fell and broke.*

quiet *adj.* 1 silent, still, soundless, noiseless *Please be quiet in the library.* 2 tranquil, peaceful, calm, restful *The patient was finally quiet after a restless night.* *n.* silence, stillness, peace, peacefulness, calm, calmness *You could have heard a pin drop in the quiet of the meeting.* **ANT.** *adj.* (1) noisy, loud, boisterous. (2) perturbed, anxious.

quieten (down) *vb.* 1 still, hush, silence *You'd better quieten down or the neighbours will complain.* 2 calm, pacify, subdue *Though Dad was very angry to begin with, we managed to quieten him down when we explained how the accident had happened.*

quirk *n.* peculiarity, characteristic; mannerism, idiosyncrasy, foible *I cannot explain Fordyce's constant humming except to say it is one of his quirks.*

quit *vb.* 1 stop, cease, discontinue *Quit teasing Anne about having red hair.* 2 resign, leave *After twenty-five years without promotion Bill quitted his job.*

quite *adv.* 1 rather, somewhat *I was quite annoyed when the train was ten minutes late.* 2 completely, entirely, wholly *If you have quite finished talking, I should like to say something.*

quiver *vb.* shake, quake, tremble, shudder, shiver, vibrate *I feel the house quiver every time a lorry drives by.*

quiz *vb.* question, interrogate, cross-examine *The police quizzed him for hours about his whereabouts on Tuesday.*

quota *n.* portion, share, allotment, apportionment *Umbracho has already had more than his quota of brandy.*

quotation *n.* extract, citation; passage, sentence; saying *Hearn has nothing original to say—he can only spout quotations.*

quote *vb.* cite, recite; mention, refer to *Let me quote a passage from the Bible to illustrate my point.*

r

rabble *n.* mob, throng, crowd, horde *The royal family stood on the balcony and regarded the teeming rabble below.*

rabid *adj.* frantic, frenzied, raving, raging, violent *Some of the rock group's more rabid fans tore at their clothing.*

race[1] *n.* 1 contest, competition, match *When Mel entered the race, he had no idea he would win.* 2 stream, course *The race under the mill was strong enough to turn the paddle-wheel.* *vb.* 1 run, compete, contend *Phil wasn't allowed to race on Saturday because of his sore ankle.* 2 hurry, run, speed, dash, hasten *We raced to finish our homework before the deadline.* ANT. *vb.* (2) dawdle, linger, dwell.

race[2] *n.* family, kind, strain, breed, people, nation, tribe, stock *The Mongolian race developed in Asia.*

racist *adj.* bigoted, prejudiced, intolerant *Someone always makes a racist remark at these meetings and upsets a few people.* *n.* bigot *Boggley is one of the most prejudiced racists I know.*

rack *n.* framework, frame, bracket *The fish are hung out on racks to dry in the sun.*

racket *n.* noise, hubbub, disturbance, fuss, uproar, din, tumult *My neighbour's chickens make a terrible racket every morning.*

racy *adj.* lively, spirited, vigorous, fresh; sharp *Count on Dudley to come up with a racy bit of gossip every night.* ANT. dull, deadly.

radiant *adj.* bright, shining, beaming, brilliant *Angela looked absolutely radiant in her new ball gown.* ANT. dim, dark.

radiate *vb.* emit, spread, shed, diffuse *The sun radiates light and warmth.*

radical *adj.* 1 basic, fundamental, essential *We shall have to make radical changes in our plans if we can't use the hall.* 2 extreme, progressive, revolutionary, militant *The radical element in the organization has been warned about the disturbances.* *n.* progressive, militant, extremist, revolutionary *The radicals confronted the political leaders with their views.*

rag *n.* cloth; shred, scrap, piece *Use a soft rag to polish the silver.*

rage *n.* 1 anger, fury, wrath *The director's rage at the news that he had been left out of the screen credits was huge.* 2 fad, fashion, craze, vogue, mania *Except for a few fanatics, the skateboarding rage has passed.* *vb.* 1 fume, rant, rave, storm *When he found that the dog had eaten his dinner, Albert raged about the house for an hour.* 2 storm, overflow; burn *The storm raged all about us. The fire raged out of control for three hours.*

ragged *adj.* torn, tattered, shredded, worn *Please don't wear that ragged pullover when you go to church.*

raid *n.* 1 attack, assault, invasion *The commandos planned a raid on the submarine base.* 2 arrest; seizure *Aunt Martha was caught in the police raid on the gambling casino.* *vb.* attack, assault, invade, maraud *The ammunition dump was raided last night.*

rail *n.* fence, railing, bar *If they raise the rail any higher the horse won't be able to clear it.*

rain *n.* drizzle, sprinkle; shower; storm, deluge *I hope the rain keeps off.* *vb.* pour (down); drizzle *It's raining again today.*

raise *vb.* 1 lift, elevate, hoist *Please raise your hand if you wish to speak in class.* 2 rear, bring up; cultivate *My mother raised twelve children. Mr Green raises corn on his farm.* 3 rouse, awaken, excite *Our hopes were raised when we spied a sail.* 4 increase; enlarge *Your salary will be raised by ten per cent next week.* **ANT.** (1) lower. (4) decrease, lessen, reduce.

rakish *adj.* smart, saucy, dashing, daring *Derek tilted his hat at a rakish angle and addressed the girl in the bus queue.*

rally *vb.* 1 reassemble, attack *The soldiers rallied for the major assault on the town.* 2 summon, call up *A leader should try to rally other people's support.* *n.* gathering, meeting *The motoring enthusiasts assembled for their weekly rally.*

ramble *vb.* amble, stroll, saunter, wander, walk *We rambled through the meadow looking for wild flowers to pick.* *n.* stroll, walk *Let's take a ramble along the beach.*

rampant *adj.* unrestrained, unchecked; raging, violent *We had to deal with a rampant epidemic of the flu last month.*

rancid *adj.* rotten, bad, mouldy, rank, off *This butter cannot be eaten—it's rancid.*

random *adj.* chance, haphazard, unplanned, unscheduled, irregular, casual *Frank picked a random number and won £250 in a lottery.* **ANT.** particular, specific, special.

range *n.* extent, expanse, area, limit *Sue was interested in a very narrow range of subjects.* *vb.* 1 vary, change *The weather in our area ranges from bad to awful.* 2 wander, travel, roam, rove, stray *The prince ranged far and wide, through many lands, seeking adventure.*

rank *n.* grade, level, order, class, standing, degree *Morris achieved a high rank among the officers in the company.* *vb.* arrange, order, sort, classify *Eugene ranks at the top of his group.* *adj.* 1 wild, dense, lush, vigorous, luxuriant, abundant *The vegetation was so rank we could barely make our way through it.* 2 smelly, putrid, offensive, foul, rotten *A rank odour emanated from the sewer.*

ransack *vb.* 1 examine, search *We ransacked the attic looking for the lost medals.* 2 plunder, loot, take away *The enemy soldiers ransacked the town they had captured.*

ransom *n.* deliverance, release; compensation, redemption *The kidnappers were demanding a ransom of £10,000.*

rant *vb.* rage, rave, fume, harangue *Pettigrew stood ranting in the street as the traffic warden wrote out his ticket.*

rap *n.* knock, blow, thump *Every time he played a wrong note, the piano teacher gave him a rap on the knuckles.* *vb.* knock, thump, whack *When you get there, rap at the door three times and ask for Joe.*

rape *vb.* assault, ravish, take by force *I heard that a woman was almost raped in the neighbourhood last night.*

rapid *adj.* quick, swift, speedy, fast *The United Nations was planning for a rapid deployment of its peace-keeping force.* ANT. slow, sluggish, halting.

rapture *n.* joy, bliss, ecstasy, delight *Cassie experienced great rapture whenever she saw an Elvis Presley film.*

rare *adj.* 1 unusual, uncommon, scarce, infrequent *Good diamonds are expensive because they are rare.* 2 superlative, excellent, fine, choice, matchless *The museum has a collection of rare paintings by sixteenth-century artists.* 3 underdone, undercooked, red *I enjoy eating a rare steak.* ANT. (1) common, ordinary, usual, everyday. (3) well-done.

rascal *n.* 1 villain, scoundrel, rogue, trickster, swindler, scamp *The rascal told me one story and you another about how much money he needed.* 2 imp, mischief-maker *That little rascal ate all the biscuits.*

rash[1] *adj.* thoughtless, hasty, impetuous, foolhardy, reckless *If you think before you act, you can avoid doing many rash things.* ANT. considered, thoughtful, prudent.

rash[2] *n.* eruption, eczema, dermatitis *You know you have measles when you see a red rash on your chest.*

rate *n.* 1 pace, speed, velocity *Alex worked at a fast rate and finished everything in one day.* 2 price, charge *Phoning after six o'clock means you pay the cheap rate.* 3 proportion, ratio *The rate of inflation is increasing.* *vb.* 1 price, value *The dresses in this shop are rated too much over their cost.* 2 consider, regard; evaluate *Jeanette is rated as one of the top students in the school.*

ration *n.* allowance, portion *During the war, everyone was entitled to his ration of meat, butter, sugar and other foods.* *vb.* apportion, parcel out, distribute *The food was rationed out carefully among the marooned sailors.*

rational *adj.* 1 sensible, reasonable *The only rational way for us to find a new leader is to elect one.* 2 sane, clearheaded, normal *People who really believe that the moon is made of green cheese are not rational.* ANT. (2) irrational, insane, crazy.

rationalize *vb.* justify, defend, explain away, make excuses *How do the generals rationalize losing the battle in which they outnumbered the enemy two to one?*

rattle *vb.* shake, clatter *The collectors rattled their tins, wanting the passers-by to put some money in.* *n.* clatter, clack, click, shaking

The rattle of the wooden wheels on the cobbles could be heard down the street.

raucous *adj.* harsh, rough, gruff, loud *I could hear their raucous laughter in the next house.*

ravage *vb.* damage, devastate, wreck *During the 1940s, the country was ravaged by war.*

rave *vb.* 1 rant, rage, storm *The king raved on about how his generals were plotting against him.* 2 *Informal:* praise, laud *Mrs Johnston was raving about the new hairdresser in town.*

raw *adj.* 1 uncooked, undone *I love to eat raw carrots.* 2 unprocessed, untreated, rough, unrefined *The factory takes raw materials and converts them into finished products.* 3 immature, untrained, new *The raw recruits were ragged mercilessly.* **ANT.** (1) cooked. (2) processed, refined, finished. (3) experienced.

ray *n.* beam *He watched as a ray of sunshine crept across the floor.*

reach *vb.* 1 arrive at, get to, come to *We didn't reach home till after dark.* 2 stretch, extend *I could just reach up to the top of the door.* *n.* extent, distance, range, scope *The criminals fled to Brazil, beyond the reach of the law.*

react *vb.* respond, reply, answer *When the children were rude, Mother reacted by denying us sweets.*

reaction *n.* response, result, reply, answer *Clive's reaction to high food prices was to buy a farm and raise his own vegetables.*

readable *adj.* 1 legible, decipherable, clear *My handwriting was once illegible, but now it's readable.* 2 interesting, exciting; enjoyable, pleasant, well-written *The book I'm studying at the moment is very readable.*

readily *adv.* promptly, quickly; easily; willingly *The company responded readily to my letter of complaint.*

ready *adj.* 1 prepared, done; arranged, completed *The roast joint will be ready in an hour.* 2 quick, prompt, skilful *Whenever anyone said anything, the comedian was able to provide a ready wisecrack.*

real *adj.* true, actual, genuine, authentic *He used so many pseudonyms that his real name was in doubt.* **ANT.** false, counterfeit, sham, bogus.

realistic *adj.* practical, pragmatic *You may believe in miracles, but I prefer to take a more realistic approach to solving the problem.*

reality *n.* truth, actuality, fact *Whatever you might think, the reality is that if we don't get water soon, we'll die.*

realize *vb.* 1 understand, be aware of, appreciate, recognize *Do you fully realize whom you are speaking to?* 2 effect, complete, achieve, work out *Plans are easy to think up but harder to realize.* 3 sell for, make *The sale of paintings realized £25.*

really *adv.* actually, truly, honestly *Do you really believe that man can travel faster than the speed of light?*

realm *n.* 1 kingdom, domain *The queen's realm extended from one sea to the other.* 2 area, domain, sphere, province, department *In the realm of surgery, Dr Franklin has no equal.*

reap *vb.* harvest, cut, gather, mow, pick *This year we reaped a profitable harvest in rapeseed.* ANT. sow, plant, seed.

rear[1] *n.* back; bottom, rump, posterior *At the rear of the house stood an old car. Hugo was struck in the rear with the paddle.* *adj.* back *The rear window of the car was misted up.* ANT. *n.* front.

rear[2] *vb.* **1** raise, bring up *The little girl had been reared in a convent.* **2** lift, raise, elevate; rise *The horse reared on its hind legs.* **3** put up, build, construct, erect *The shed could be reared by two men in one afternoon.*

reason *n.* **1** purpose, motive, cause, object, objective, aim *What was your reason for phoning me at midnight?* **2** explanation; excuse *I have already given you two good reasons why you should study hard.* **3** judgement, understanding, intelligence, common sense *The decision is a matter of reason, not of opinion.* **4** sanity *The poor fellow painting the grass green seems to have lost his reason.* *vb.* **1** argue, justify *You cannot reason with an angry man.* **2** conclude, suppose, assume, gather, infer *I reasoned that the team that came first won the race.*

reasonable *adj.* **1** sensible, rational, logical *As a reasonable person, you must know that no family can survive on that amount a week.* **2** moderate, bearable *I think that £500 is a very reasonable price for that car, considering its condition.* ANT. (1) irrational, mad, crazy, insane. (2) outrageous.

reassure *vb.* comfort, console, encourage *The manager reassured me that the bank was solvent and my money was safe.*

rebel *n.* revolutionary, mutineer, traitor *The rebels attacked the president's palace last night.* *vb.* revolt, defy, overthrow *The peasants rebelled when told that there wouldn't be enough to eat.*

rebellious *adj.* defiant, insubordinate, refractory *When Brent was in his teens, he became a rebellious youth, like his friends.*

rebuff *vb.* snub, reject, spurn, slight *They rebuffed all my offers of help.* *n.* snub, rejection, repulse *The rebuff of my plans came as a great surprise as I had thought they would have been accepted.*

rebuke *vb.* upbraid, chide, reproach, scold *The teacher rebuked Peter for talking during an examination.* *n.* reprimand, reproach, scolding *After the first rebuke from their parents, the children never again went near the cliff.* ANT. praise.

recall *vb.* **1** remember, recollect *I recall having met you at last year's party.* **2** call in, withdraw *The company recalled all cars of the model that had faulty brakes.* *n.* memory, recollection, remembrance *Vincent has total recall and can remember everything that ever happened.*

recant *vb.* withdraw, retract, take back *When many of their products failed, the company recanted on their guarantee of free repair.*

receive *vb.* **1** accept, get, acquire, come by, obtain *I received my copy of the magazine today.* **2** entertain; greet, welcome *The ambassador is receiving guests in the front hall.* ANT. (1) give, offer.

recent *adj.* late, up-to-date, new, novel *A recent newspaper article described the situation in Nigeria.* ANT. old, out-of-date, dated.

reception *n.* party, gathering *The wedding reception took place in a hotel near the church.*

recess *n.* 1 hollow, niche, dent, opening, cranny, nook *The golden idol was concealed in a narrow recess in the cave.* 2 vacation; respite, rest, pause, break *Parliament is now having a recess.*

recipe *n.* formula, directions, instructions *If you don't follow the recipe to the letter, the dough will not rise.*

reciprocal *adj.* mutual, (*informal*) tit-for-tat; interchangeable, exchangeable *Our reciprocal arrangement calls for her to do the cleaning while I do the laundry.*

recite *vb.* repeat; report, list *Can you recite the names of all the monarchs of England in chronological order?*

reckless *adj.* thoughtless, careless, rash, wild *Ned's uncle was arrested for reckless driving.*

reckon *vb.* 1 calculate, compute; estimate, guess *Counting the rows of seats, I reckoned that there were fifty-four people in the room.* 2 consider, regard *I reckon your sister is very clever.* 3 think, suppose, believe *It'll be fine tomorrow, I reckon.*

recognize *vb.* 1 recollect, recall, know *I recognized the bank clerk as the man I had seen in the supermarket.* 2 acknowledge, admit *I recognize your authority to order me about, but I don't like it.*

recoil *vb.* draw back, withdraw, shrink, wince, flinch *The instant she saw the snake she recoiled.*

recollect *vb.* remember, recall *I cannot recollect the last time we met.*

recommend *vb.* 1 commend, praise, approve *I recommended Brad for the job.* 2 advise, counsel, suggest *The board has recommended that a new school be built on the hill.* ANT. (1) disapprove, veto.

recompense *vb.* reward, repay, compensate *The insurance company has already recompensed us for the theft of the bicycle.*

reconcile *vb.* 1 unite, bring together, mediate *The couple were reconciled after the misunderstanding.* 2 adjust, settle *Leon and Debbie have reconciled their differences and are friends again.*

recondition *vb.* overhaul, rebuild, restore *We could not afford a new dishwasher, so we bought one that had been reconditioned.*

reconsider *vb.* think again, re-evaluate, go back on *I do wish you would reconsider your decision to leave home.*

record *vb.* write, enter, register *The clerk recorded every transaction in the ledger.* *n.* 1 disc, recording *I bought a lot of new records yesterday.* 2 document, register; archive, annal *The records of births and deaths were destroyed in the fire.* 3 best place, top, first; highest attainment *Mark broke the record for the long jump.* *adj.* unbeaten, top, best *He completed the circuit in a new record time.*

recount *vb.* tell, narrate, describe; report *We gathered round the fire while Hafton recounted his adventures in Mogadishu.*

recoup *vb.* recover, regain, retrieve; repay *Ferncliffe kept on playing and finally recouped all his losses at baccarat.*

recover *vb.* 1 regain, retrieve, redeem, salvage, recapture *I recovered my balance after I tripped.* 2 improve, better; heal, mend, convalesce *The economic situation is bound to recover by the end of the year. Father has recovered completely from his illness.*

recreation *n.* amusement, entertainment, leisure, diversion, enjoyment, fun *What does your family do for recreation during the summer?*

recruit *n.* beginner, trainee; novice *Some of the new recruits have to be trained in order to be of any use to the army.*

rectify *vb.* put right, correct, improve, remedy *We know we made a mistake, and we have done our best to rectify it.*

recuperate *vb.* recover, convalesce, improve, rally *Throgmorton insists it took six weeks for him to recuperate from a sprained thumb.*

redress *n.* compensation, reparation, amends *She sought redress for her injuries.* *vb.* compensate for; correct; put right *Jake wanted to redress the distress caused to him by his opponents.*

reduce *vb.* 1 lessen, diminish, decrease *I wish they would reduce the price on that dress I saw in the window.* 2 impoverish, lower, degrade *Since Al's father lost his job, the family has been in reduced circumstances.* ANT. (1) increase, enlarge, swell. (2) promote, improve.

refer *vb.* 1 direct; recommend, commend *At the town hall I was referred to the office which deals with education grants.* 2 concern, regard, deal with, relate *The word 'energy' refers to any kind of power.* 3 mention, suggest, touch on, hint at *What do you suppose the doctor was referring to my when he suggested I lose some weight?*

referee *n.* umpire, arbitrator; arbiter, judge *The boxing referee took a very long time counting up to ten.* *vb.* umpire, arbitrate, judge *On Saturdays, my father enjoys refereeing soccer games.*

reference *n.* 1 direction; allusion, mention *Your mother made reference to my dirty shirt, so I'd better change for dinner.* 2 regard, concern, relation, respect *'With reference to your letter of 16 March, we would like to point out—' was how the letter began.*

refine *vb.* 1 improve, clarify *My summer job certainly refined my ideas on how restaurants are run.* 2 clean, purify *In this process we refine the gold till it is almost 100 per cent pure.*

refined *adj.* cultivated, polite, courteous, well-bred, civilized *The school turns out refined young ladies who will be at home in society.* ANT. rude, coarse, brutish.

reflect *vb.* 1 mirror; reproduce *The strange face was reflected in the window of the shop.* 2 think, ponder, consider, deliberate, contemplate *If you reflect on your experience a little, you'll realize that you are responsible for your own actions.*

reflection *n.* 1 image, appearance, likeness *I could see my reflection in the highly polished table top.* 2 deliberation, consideration, study, meditation *After some reflection, Len decided that he'd better go to the library after all.*

reflex *adj.* involuntary, automatic, unthinking, mechanical; spontaneous *My flinching was a reflex action when he threatened me with the cricket bat.*

reform *n.* change, correction, improvement *The new candidates campaigned on the promise to bring about reforms in government.* *vb.* change, improve, better, correct *The criminal promised to reform, so he was released on parole.*

refrain[1] *vb.* stop, cease, desist, abstain *The notice in the bus said 'Passengers are requested to refrain from talking to the driver while the vehicle is in motion'.*

refrain[2] *n.* chorus; melody, theme *You sing the refrain at the end of every verse of this song.*

refresh *vb.* renew, exhilarate, invigorate *I was completely refreshed after a cold shower.* ANT. tire, exhaust.

refreshment *n.* snack; food, drink *You must be tired—can I get you some refreshment?*

refuge *n.* safety, shelter, protection *We sought refuge from the storm in a cave.*

refugee *n.* exile, fugitive, castaway; evacuee; runaway *The refugees from the battle began to stream across the border.*

refund *n.* rebate, repayment, reimbursement *When I returned the chipped cup to the shop, they gave me a refund.* *vb.* reimburse, pay back, repay, make good, recompense *The garage refunded the customer £10 for their poor service.*

refuse[1] *vb.* turn down, deny, decline *The teacher refused us permission to leave school early.* ANT. accept, allow.

refuse[2] *n.* waste, rubbish *The refuse is collected on Mondays.*

regard *vb.* 1 look at *or* upon, consider, estimate *Philip always regarded his brother as a better tennis player.* 2 attend, respect, honour, value *I regard very highly your ability to get along well with so many people.* *n.* 1 reference, relation, concern *With regard to your summer cottage, would you rent it to us this year?* 2 respect, concern, estimation, esteem *I hold the English professor in very high regard.* 3 concern, thought, care *Toby has no regard at all for his mother's feelings.*

regardless *adj.* despite, notwithstanding, aside (from); besides *They expect you to do your duty regardless of your feelings about right and wrong.*

regime *n.* government, management, direction, administration *Under the new regime, foreign visitors must register at the police station.*

regimented *adj.* orderly, ordered, rigid, controlled, disciplined *Crapton enjoys the regimented life of a soldier.* ANT. free, loose, unstructured.

region *n.* area, place, locale, territory *Colour the coal-mining regions of Europe orange.*

regional *adj.* provincial, local, district *Is the increase in crime national or regional?*

register *n.* 1 record; catalogue *All transactions were entered in the register daily.* 2 list, book, record, roll *Every hotel guest must sign* *the register.* *vb.* enrol, record; enter, list, catalogue *Please register for your classes before the beginning of the academic year.*

regret *vb.* lament, bemoan, feel sorry about, be sorry for *I sincerely regret having hurt your feelings, but I didn't do it on purpose.* *n.* sorrow, concern, qualm, scruple, misgiving *My regret at having to leave before the end of the summer was heartfelt.*

regrettable *adj.* lamentable, deplorable, unfortunate *It is regrettable that Sophronisba lost the caber-tossing competition.*

regular *adj.* 1 usual, customary, habitual, normal *My regular routine gets me to the office at about eight-thirty in the morning.* 2 steady, uniform, even, systematic, orderly *I could hear his regular breathing from the room next door.* ANT. (1) irregular, odd, unusual.

regulate *vb.* 1 govern, control, direct, manage, legislate *The government doesn't regulate prices in a free economy like ours.* 2 adjust, set *Please regulate the heat in this room so that we don't freeze and boil alternately.*

regulation *n.* law, rule, statute *If you do not obey the parking regulations, you will get a ticket.*

rehabilitate *vb.* restore, re-establish, improve *The landlord has plans to rehabilitate the block of flats.*

rehearse *vb.* practise, repeat; train *I have to rehearse for the school play and cannot go out tonight.*

reign *n.* rule, dominion, sovereignty; power *How long was the reign of Henry VIII?* *vb.* rule, govern *Queen Elizabeth II is the reigning monarch of the United Kingdom.*

reimburse *see* **refund.**

reinforce *vb.* strengthen, support, back, assist *What you say about repeat offenders simply reinforces my argument.*

reject *vb.* 1 refuse, deny; renounce *I don't know why my application was rejected, unless I misspelled something.* 2 discard, expel, throw out *or* away *The inspector rejected the radio as faulty.* ANT. accept.

rejoice *vb.* delight; celebrate, enjoy *We rejoiced at the news that our team had won.*

relapse *vb.* retrogress, backslide, degenerate *After an energetic start, Gloria relapsed into a lethargy.* ANT. improve.

relate *vb.* 1 tell, report, narrate, recount, describe *I shall relate to you everything that took place at the haunted house.* 2 connect, associate, compare *How do the angles of a triangle relate to one another?*

relation *n.* 1 connection, association, relationship, similarity *The relation between cause and effect is sometimes difficult to understand.* 2 relative, kinsman *I spent last week visiting some relations in Bromley.*

relative *n.* relation, family, kinsman *The orphan had no living relatives.* *adj.* corresponding, comparative, analogous *The lecturer talked on the relative merits of different energy sources.*

relax *vb.* 1 loosen, slacken, let go *The shark relaxed its hold on the raft, allowing it to drift away.* 2 repose, recline, unwind, rest

When my father comes home from work, he likes to relax for a while, reading the newspaper. ANT. (1) tighten, increase, intensify.

relaxation *n.* ease, comfort, rest *Many people recommend the relaxation one can achieve from sleeping on a waterbed.*

release *vb.* 1 let go, relinquish, set loose, free, liberate, set free *Stefanie released me from the promise I made not to tell anyone. I found a knife and cut through the ropes, releasing the prisoner.* 2 let out, publish, proclaim, announce *The company finally released the story about the president's award.* *n.* 1 freedom, liberation *After his release from prison, the ex-convict was able to find a decent job through the help of some friends.* 2 record; film *The pop group's latest release soon became popular.*

relent *vb.* yield, give, bend, relax *I hope that Father will relent and allow Pavlova to go to the dance.*

relentless *adj.* pitiless, unmerciful, implacable, severe, harsh; inflexible *The relentless Mongol hordes drove all before them.*

relevant *adj.* pertinent, connected, appropriate, suitable, apt *Is what you have to say relevant to the subject at hand?*

reliable *adj.* trustworthy, dependable *I need a reliable car that won't break down.* ANT. unreliable, erratic; eccentric.

relic *n.* trace, vestige; token, remnant *The huge stone heads on Easter Island are probably relics of an ancient religion.*

relief *n.* 1 ease, comfort *The new medicine brought me some relief from the leg pains.* 2 aid, assistance, support, help *The relief plans for the sick have not yet been approved.*

relieve *vb.* 1 ease, comfort, soothe, lessen *That massage relieved the tension I felt.* 2 spell, replace *The new watchman relieved Bill at midnight so that he could go home early.*

religion *n.* faith, belief; creed, persuasion *The Muslim religion has flourished mainly in the Middle East and Africa.*

religious *adj.* 1 pious, devout, devoted, reverent, holy, faithful, godly *Porter's family is very religious and goes to church every Sunday.* 2 strict, rigid, exacting, conscientious *Religious observance of the rules will keep you out of trouble.* ANT. (1) irreligious, impious. (2) lax, slack, indifferent.

relinquish *vb.* give up, abandon, surrender, yield, renounce *Will Arnold relinquish control of the company when he is sixty-five?*

relish *n.* 1 satisfaction, enjoyment, delight, appreciation, gusto *Nicole ate the vegetables with such relish—yet I thought she didn't like them.* 2 condiment *I like relish on my food.* *vb.* enjoy, like, appreciate *Vincent relishes the idea of baking his own bread.* ANT. *n.* (1) distaste, disgust.

reluctant *adj.* unwilling, hesitant, disinclined, loath *June was reluctant to go to the party because she didn't know anybody.* ANT. ready, eager.

rely *vb.* depend, trust, count *You can rely on Alexa to get the job done.*

remain *vb.* stay, continue, linger *If you will remain for a few minutes, I'd like to talk with you.* ANT. depart, leave, go.

remainder *n.* residue, rest, remains *After the best part is used for furniture, the remainder of the wood is processed for other uses.*

remark *vb.* say, mention, comment, state, note, observe *Imogen remarked that she liked Sophie's new dress.* *n.* comment, statement, observation *Your remark about Teddy's nose was really very unkind.*

remarkable *adj.* unusual, special, extraordinary, exceptional, noteworthy, uncommon. ANT. average, ordinary, commonplace.

remedy *n.* cure, medicine, relief, medication *In the old days, people thought that snake oil was a good remedy for almost any ailment.* *vb.* cure, correct, improve *The town tried to remedy its financial problems by increasing the rates.*

remember *vb.* **1** recall, recollect *I never can remember my cousin's telephone number.* **2** memorize, retain, know by heart, keep *or* bear in mind *I remember every word of a poem I learned when I was ten years old.* ANT. forget.

remembrance *n.* **1** recollection, recall, memory *My remembrance of the incident is nothing like yours.* **2** keepsake, souvenir, memento *I keep the remembrances of my visit to Canada in a small brass box.*

remind *vb.* **1** bring back *Strawberries remind me of the summer.* **2** prompt, jog, prod; advise *I must remind my father to sign that letter.*

reminiscences *n.pl.* recollections, memories; account, story, anecdote *Cartwright's reminiscences of his service in India are about to be published.*

remiss *adj.* negligent, careless, inattentive *I was remiss in forgetting Aunt Agatha's birthday.*

remit *vb.* **1** pay; send, forward *Please remit £2 with your order.* **2** pardon, forgive, excuse, overlook *The judge remitted the convict's sentence, and he was released.*

remittance *n.* payment, disbursement *Your remittance has been received, and the books will be shipped at once.*

remnant *n.* remainder, remains, residue, rest *The remnants of fabric left after making the clothes were used for patchwork quilts.*

remodel *vb.* reshape, remake, rebuild, renovate, redecorate; change, modify *Do you like the way our kitchen has been remodelled?*

remorse *n.* regret, grief, contrition *Don't you feel any remorse over the way you treated your sister?*

remote *adj.* **1** distant, far off *or* away *Stanley went to a remote village in order to complete his book.* **2** slight, unlikely, inconsiderable *You don't have even a remote chance of winning the lottery.* ANT. (1) near, nearby, close.

remove *vb.* **1** doff, take off *Please remove your hat when you enter a building.* **2** transfer, dislodge, displace, take away, eliminate *The rotten stump was removed from the garden, leaving a big hole.*

removed *adj.* aloof, standoffish, distant, remote, cool *Percy is too* *removed from the everyday running of the business to think much of the employees.* ANT. involved.

remuneration *n.*   payment, compensation, wages, salary, pay, recompense *Arturo complains that remuneration for acrobats is very meagre.*

render *vb.*   1 make, cause to be *or* become *Thirty families were rendered homeless by the flood.*   2 do, perform *Norbert rendered us a great service by fetching the groceries from the market.*   3 present, submit, offer, give, deliver *I rendered an account of the conference to my superiors.*

rendition *n.*   version, interpretation, performance *The chamber music society's rendition of the Bach piece was excellent.*

renew *vb.*   refresh, revive; invigorate *I need a holiday during the winter to renew my energies.*

renounce *vb.*   1 give up, abandon, leave, abdicate, forsake, forgo *The hermit renounced all worldly goods and went to live in a cave.*   2 disown, reject, deny *When my aunt married a man her father didn't like, he renounced her.*

renovate *vb.*   renew, restore, reconstruct *The Carstairs renovated their house at considerable expense.*

renown *n.*   fame, repute, reputation, glory, distinction, prestige *Tom's mother and father are both poets of some renown.*   ANT. anonymity, obscurity.

rent *n.*   rental, payment *How much rent do they pay for the shop?*   *vb.*   lease, let, hire *We don't rent our house, we own it.*

repair *vb.*   mend, patch, restore, renew, adjust *The painting was repaired so that you couldn't see the damage at all.*   *n.*   1 patch *I can see where the repair was made on your jacket.*   2 reconstruction, rehabilitation, rebuilding *This old house is in need of repair.*

repartee *n.*   banter, badinage *Oscar was renowned for his quick wit and repartee.*

repay *vb.*   pay back, reimburse, recompense; refund *I cannot repay you for all the favours you have done for me.*

repeal *vb.*   cancel, abolish, end *The higher court repealed the action of the lower court.*   *n.*   cancellation, abolition, end *The repeal of the act made some people happy and some unhappy.*

repeat *vb.*   1 reiterate, restate *I've already told you three times, and I shall not repeat it again.*   2 redo, remake, reproduce *Don't repeat your performance of last week—it was awful.*   *n.*   repetition, remake *Many of the television programmes during the summer are repeats.*

repel *vb.*   1 repulse, check, rebuff *The small force at the fort repelled the attacks all day long.*   2 refuse, reject, decline, discourage *Frances repelled all friendly advances when she first came to town.*   3 revolt, offend, nauseate *The smell of the marigold repels insects.*   ANT. (1, 3) attract, lure.

repent *vb.*   regret, atone for, do penance for *It is not too late to repent for your sins.*

replace *vb.* 1 supersede, take over, substitute, supplant *Computers are replacing people in some jobs.* 2 put back, return, restore *Please replace the books where you found them.*

replica *n.* copy, reproduction, model, duplicate *The thieves stole a sculpture and replaced it with a replica.*

reply *n.* answer, response, rejoinder *The reply to your request is still 'No'.* *vb.* answer, respond, rejoin *'Are you feeling better now?' 'Yes,' I replied.*

report *n.* account, description, statement, record; outline *Harold wrote a report of the meeting.* *vb.* account, describe, inform *News teams try to report the news impartially.*

reporter *n.* journalist, newswoman, newsman, newspaperwoman, newspaperman *Reporters interviewed the prime minister after the cabinet meeting.*

repose *n.* sleep, rest, slumber *Please do nothing to disturb madam's repose.*

represent *vb.* 1 speak for, act for *An MP represents his constituency in Parliament.* 2 render, describe, interpret *The picture represents a wintry scene.*

representative *n.* agent, delegate; substitute, surrogate *We have a representative in Katmandu to process orders for skateboards.*

repress *vb.* control, restrain, suppress *For decades the people there have been repressed by a dictatorship.*

reprimand *vb.* rebuke, criticize, admonish, censure *Please avoid reprimanding the children in public.*

reproach *n.* condemnation, blame, censure *The manageress again reproached me for arriving late at work.*

repudiate *vb.* disown, reject, deny, disavow *After the war, many repudiated their Nazi beliefs.*

repulsive *adj.* repellent, offensive, horrid, repugnant, disgusting, distasteful *The film contained a number of repulsive scenes that made me feel ill.*

reputable *adj.* upstanding, honest, straightforward, trustworthy, reliable *Are you suggesting that Lord Lucan is not reputable?*

reputation *n.* 1 repute, name, standing *Your reputation as an expert on fossils is excellent. If you are unfriendly, you may get a bad reputation.* 2 fame, renown, distinction, prominence, prestige *The doctor's reputation for success in treating arthritis has spread far and wide.*

request *n.* petition, question, appeal, entreaty *Your request for a leave of absence has been approved.* *vb.* ask, appeal, petition, entreat, beseech *We requested 500 towels for the gym, and they sent us 500 trowels!*

require *vb.* 1 need, want *You will require petrol to run that car.* 2 demand, oblige; command, order *Students are required to bring their textbooks to the lessons.*

requirement *n.* 1 need, demand, necessity *What requirements should you provide for when you go camping?* 2 condition, prerequisite, provision *There is no requirement that an applicant have experience for the job.*

rescue *vb.* save, set free, liberate, release, ransom, deliver *The firemen rescued eight children from the burning building. The knight rescued the beautiful princess from the castle dungeon.* *n.* liberation, release, ransom, deliverance, recovery *The mountain climbers survived the rescue.* ANT. *vb.* abandon.

research *n.* study, scrutiny, investigation *Research has shown that women live longer than men.* *vb.* study, scrutinize, investigate, examine *Scientists are constantly researching the cause of major diseases.*

resemblance *n.* similarity, likeness. *Any resemblance to real persons, living or dead, is purely coincidental.*

resemble *vb.* take after, look like *David resembles his father in that they both have blond hair and blue eyes.*

resentment *n.* bitterness, displeasure, indignation *The workers' resentment is a result of the bad treatment they have suffered.*

reserve *vb.* save, keep, hold, maintain *Please reserve a table for two at André's for dinner. I wish you would reserve judgement till you have heard the whole story.* ANT. squander, waste.

reside *vb.* **1** abide, dwell, live, stay *Where are you residing now?* **2** lie, abide *Early scientists believed that the key to a person's health and personality resided in the fluids of the body.*

residence *n.* **1** home, abode, dwelling *The residence down the road was sold last week to a young couple.* **2** stay, sojourn *Because of my residence abroad, I don't have to pay any taxes here.*

resident *n.* inhabitant, native; householder; citizen *Are you a resident here or merely an occasional visitor?*

residue *n.* remainder, remains, rest, balance *The reddish residue left after burning the mercury is mercuric oxide.*

resign *vb.* give up, abdicate, leave, abandon *Since he resigned, Gregory has done nothing but play golf.*

resist *vb.* stand firm, withstand, endure; oppose *It was difficult to resist the attractions of the big city.* ANT. yield, give in, give way, surrender.

resolute *adj.* resolved, firm, determined, set, decided *Rebecca remained resolute in her determination to complete her education.* ANT. wavering, irresolute, vacillating.

resolution *n.* **1** resolve, determination *I thought that Jane had shown remarkable resolution in the performance of her work.* **2** statement, decision, recommendation, verdict, judgement *The committee has approved the resolution that we allow women to join the club.*

resolve *vb.* **1** determine, settle, conclude, decide, confirm *The students finally resolved to plan a picnic for the following Saturday.* **2** solve; explain *Politicians have been unable to resolve the energy problem.* *n.* intention, purpose, resolution, determination *Our firm resolve to return encouraged the downcast amongst the group.*

resort *n.* **1** holiday spot, rest-place *We often go on holiday to the* *resorts on the East coast.* **2** relief, recourse, refuge *Leaping across the chasm was the fugitive's only resort to avoid his pursuers.* *vb.* turn to, apply to, go to, use, employ *Food was so scarce that the shipwrecked crew resorted to eating leaves and berries.*

resource *n.* reserve, store, supply, source *What resources are available at the library for a student of philosophy?*

resourceful *adj.* inventive, ingenious, creative *These men are resourceful enough to survive in the desert for several days.*

respect *n.* **1** admiration, regard, honour, esteem, approval *I have the greatest respect for your abilities.* **2** particular, regard, detail, point, feature *In many respects, I find John the most suitable person for the job.* **3** reference, connection *With respect to your wanting to go on the outing, you have our permission.* **4** concern, consideration *You should have more respect for your elders.* *vb.* honour, esteem, revere *I respect your opinion, even though I disagree with you.* ANT. *n.* (4) disrespect, disregard.

respectable *adj.* **1** acceptable, proper, decent, respected *The manager of the bank ought to be a respectable citizen.* **2** fair, passable, presentable *I think that coming in second is a very respectable showing in a national contest.* ANT. (1) disreputable.

respectful *adj.* polite, courteous, well-bred, well-behaved, well-mannered *The children were brought up to be respectful to their elders.* ANT. rude, impertinent, flippant.

respite *n.* reprieve, interval, rest, pause *How can you keep going on such a work schedule with no respite?*

respond *vb.* reply, answer, react *I am not sure how to respond to these constant appeals for charitable contributions.*

response *n.* reply, answer, reaction *When you ask so unpleasantly you can scarcely expect a friendly response.*

responsibility *n.* **1** obligation, duty, trust *The responsibilities of a married man with six children are considerable.* **2** accountability, liability *His sense of responsibility prevented him from giving in.*

responsible *adj.* **1** accountable, answerable *Who is responsible for writing this on the blackboard?* **2** chargeable, culpable *The man responsible for the accident has been identified.* **3** able, reliable, capable, trustworthy, upstanding, honest *Do you consider yourself a responsible member of the community?*

rest¹ *n.* **1** repose, relaxation, inactivity, quiet, ease *The doctor told my mother that she needed a rest after all that hard work this winter.* **2** immobility, standstill *The wheel came to a rest on the number seventeen, and I had won £25.* *vb.* **1** relax, lounge *I have a cousin who does everything backwards: he works for two weeks, then rests for the other fifty.* **2** lie, lean, depend, hang *Our decision on when to leave for home rests on the weather.*

rest² *n.* remainder, residue, surplus, excess *After I have eaten everything I want, the rest goes to my dog.*

restful *adj.* quiet, peaceful, calm, tranquil *I welcome a restful week-*

end in the country after the turmoil of the city. ANT. disturbed, upsetting, tumultuous, agitated.

restless *adj.* nervous, fidgety, unquiet, restive *After a few days of doing nothing, Samuel becomes very restless.* ANT. calm, tranquil, peaceful.

restore *vb.* **1** return, replace *Please restore that book to the shelf where you found it.* **2** renew, repair, renovate, mend *The antique clock has been restored to its original condition.* **3** reinstate, re-establish, reinstall *After his military service, Len was restored to his old job at the press.*

restrain *vb.* control, check, hold, curb *Agatha, unable to restrain her enthusiasm, leapt up cheering.*

restraint *n.* control, self-control, reserve, constraint *It is best to exercise some restraint in dealing with children of that age.*

restrict *vb.* limit, confine, restrain *Please try to restrict your remarks to the subject at hand.*

result *n.* effect, outcome, consequence *As a result of your misbehaviour, the entire class will have to remain after school.* *vb.* arise, happen, follow, issue *The return of the watch resulted from the advertisement in the paper.* ANT. *n.* cause.

resume *vb.* continue, restart, recommence *After the interruption, the speaker calmly resumed his talk.*

retain *vb.* **1** hold, keep *Retain the ticket stub when you enter the theatre.* **2** remember, recall *Can you retain facts easily?* **3** hire, employ, engage *We retained a lawyer to look after our interests.* ANT. (1) free, release.

retaliate *vb.* take revenge, repay, return, avenge *It is difficult to know how the enemy will retaliate once they are trapped.*

retard *vb.* delay, hold back, slow, hinder, check, obstruct *This special material can retard flames for two hours.* ANT. advance, speed.

retarded *adj.* backward, slow, behindhand; slow-witted, dull, stupid *The children they used to call 'retarded' they now term 'special'.* ANT. advanced, quick.

reticent *adj.* reserved, quiet, silent, taciturn, close-mouthed *Adolf is somewhat reticent about describing what he did during the war.*

retire *vb.* **1** leave, part, withdraw, retreat *The knights retired from the battlefield in order to regroup their forces.* **2** resign, leave *In our company, anyone who reaches the age of seventy must retire.* ANT. (1) advance, attack.

retiring *adj.* shy, withdrawn, modest, reserved *Minerva has a retiring personality and refuses to run for any office.* ANT. bold, impudent, forceful.

retort *vb.* reply, respond, snap back, answer, rejoin *'You know what you can do with your cricket bat!' Tom retorted angrily.* *n.* reply, response, answer, rejoinder *Tom's retort to the abusive taunts was a rude word.*

retract *vb.* withdraw, go back on, take back *The boys said they were sorry and retracted the bad things they had said.*

retreat *vb.* retire, leave, withdraw, depart *Soundly defeated, the regiment retreated to the safety of the fort.* *n.* **1** departure, retirement, withdrawal *In the face of the huge numbers of the enemy, the battalion's retreat was expected.* **2** rest; privacy, solitude, seclusion *The church youth group went on a retreat for the weekend.* **3** shelter, refuge; sanctuary *Our local authority has a retreat to help drug addicts.* ANT. *vb.* advance.

return *vb.* **1** go back, come back *I returned home at midnight.* **2** bring *or* take back *When will you return the lawnmower you borrowed last summer?*

reveal *vb.* disclose, communicate, tell, divulge, publish, announce, publicize, broadcast *Rick and Norma revealed that they had been secretly married for a year.* ANT. conceal, hide.

revenge *n.* vengeance, reprisal, repayment, retaliation *Steve will get his revenge for Don's taking his bike by letting the air out of the tyres.* *vb.* avenge, repay, retaliate *We'll revenge the insults to our team by beating them in the championship.*

revenue *n.* income, take, profit, receipts, proceeds, return *Revenue from Christmas sales was lower than last year.*

reverberate *vb.* resound, echo, reflect, rebound *The sound of distant thunder reverberated through the house.*

revere *vb.* venerate, respect, admire *Mr Ashburton was widely revered for his many charitable acts.* ANT. despise.

reverence *n.* respect, homage, veneration *Peggy regards people who are financially successful with undue reverence.*

reverent *adj.* respectful, deferential; solemn, worshipful *One should enter a place of worship with a properly reverent attitude.* ANT. disrespectful, impious.

reverse *adj.* opposite, contrary *Why are the handlebars of your bicycle in reverse position?* *n.* **1** opposite, contrary *Bill said he would disapprove the action, but he did the reverse.* **2** back, rear *The reverse of a tapestry looks untidy, but the front is regular.* **3** defeat, setback, misfortune, catastrophe *The army suffered one reverse after another when fighting the enemy.* *vb.* **1** invert, transpose, turn *The middle letters of the sign were reversed, so it read 'LAIDES', which means 'ugly women' in French.* **2** repeal, revoke, overthrow *The higher court reversed the lower court's ruling.*

review *vb.* **1** re-examine; study *I reviewed the plans for the new theatre and made a few changes.* **2** criticize, survey, inspect *The new novel was reviewed in last Sunday's newspaper.* *n.* **1** examination, study *The review of the college's courses is going on now.* **2** criticism, critique, judgement, opinion *The film at the local cinema received a very bad review in the press.*

revise *vb.* alter, change, improve, amend, correct, update *The revised edition of the dictionary contains many new words. Please revise this paper to correct the errors I have marked.*

revive *vb.* **1** renew, refresh, reanimate, rejuvenate, reawaken *The* *new book revived people's interest in the Civil War.* **2** recover, recuperate, pick up *I revived after that fifteen-minute nap before dinner.*

revoke *vb.* repeal, rescind, withdraw *They refused to revoke the regulation against smoking on short commercial flights.*

revolt *vb.* **1** rebel, mutiny, rise up *The peasants revolted in England in the fourteenth century.* **2** disgust, nauseate, repel, sicken *The sight of the injured at the train wreck revolted me so much that I was unable to help.* *n.* **1** revolution, rebellion, mutiny, uprising *The revolt of the masses in Russia took place in 1917.* **2** disgust, revulsion, aversion, loathing *What a feeling of revolt the sight of a dead animal gives me!*

revolution *n.* **1** revolt, rebellion, uprising, overthrow, mutiny *The French Revolution followed soon after that in America.* **2** turn, cycle, rotation, spin, orbit *The earth makes one revolution about the sun each year, and one revolution on its axis each twenty-four hours.*

revolve *vb.* turn, rotate, spin, cycle, circle *The earth revolves on its axis once in twenty-four hours.*

revolver *n.* pistol, gun *Did all cowboys really carry revolvers in the Old West in America?*

revulsion *n.* loathing, disgust, repugnance *Arthur regarded working in a butcher shop with revulsion.*

reward *n.* prize, award, recompense, pay *As a reward for saving the dog from the river, Dirk received a medal from the society.* *vb.* compensate, pay *If you are good to people, you may be rewarded by their being good to you.*

rhyme *n.* **1** verse, poem, poetry *Putting the lesson in rhymes made it easier to learn.* **2** similarity in sound *Children are fascinated by stories told in rhyme, whether by Mother Goose or Dr Seuss.*

rhythm *n.* beat, accent; metre *The song is written in waltz rhythm.*

rich *adj.* **1** wealthy, well-off, well-to-do, affluent *The big house on the hill is owned by the richest man in town.* **2** abundant, bountiful, plentiful, fruitful, fertile *The farmers will have a rich harvest this year.* ANT. (1) impoverished, poor. (2) scarce, unproductive, scanty.

rid *vb.* clear, free, shed, eliminate *It was the Pied Piper who rid the town of Hamelin of its rats.* *adj.* clear, free, delivered *I'm happy to be rid of that awful cold I had last week.*

riddle *n.* problem, puzzle, question, mystery *How he escaped from the locked room is a riddle to me.*

ride *vb.* **1** journey, tour, motor, drive *We rode through the jungle on the back of an elephant.* **2** drive, manage, guide, control *Don't ride your bicycle on the wrong side of the road.*

ridicule *vb.* mock, deride, taunt, tease *Don't ever ridicule anyone because he's different—he may be much better, too.* *n.* mockery, derision, burlesque, satire *The writers held the politicians up to ridicule until they resigned.* ANT. respect, praise.

ridiculous *adj.* nonsensical, farcical, absurd, laughable, ludicrous, comic, preposterous *Charley looked ridiculous wearing his aunt's dress.* ANT. sensible, sound.

right *adj.* 1 correct, factual, accurate, true *The calculation is right, but you have the wrong answer.* 2 good, just, honest, upright, lawful, moral *I know that you want to do what is right.* 3 proper, suitable, apt, correct *Phoebe knows which is the right fork to use for her salad.* *n.* 1 justice, virtue, morality, goodness *Right shall prevail and evil will be conquered.* 2 title, claim, privilege *You have the right to think whatever you like.* *adv.* 1 properly, correctly, legally, honourably, fairly *I believe that the reporter didn't get the story right.* 2 directly, straight, straightway *I went right home after school.* ANT. *adj.* (1) wrong, incorrect, fallacious. (2) bad, dishonest. (3) unsuitable, inappropriate. *n.* (1) evil, wrong.

righteous *adj.* good, honest, virtuous, moral, just, fair, upright, honourable *A righteous observance of the law is a requisite of good citizenship.*

rigid *adj.* 1 stiff, unbending, unyielding, inflexible *The leather belt was so rigid that I had to oil it in order to bend it.* 2 severe, strict, stern, inflexible, harsh *Why must the headmaster be so rigid about the rules?*

rigorous *adj.* 1 severe, harsh, strict *Some people think the country needs a return to rigorous discipline.* 2 scrupulous, meticulous, exact, precise *His dissertation was written with a rigorous attention to detail.*

rim *n.* edge, lip, border, brim *Be careful!—The rim of that glass is chipped.* •

rind *n.* skin, shell, crust, peel *Before eating the cheese, you must cut off the rind.*

ring[1] *n.* band, circlet, loop, circle *The ring of mushrooms in the forest meant that fairies and elves had been dancing there. Why don't you wear your diamond ring tonight?* *vb.* circle, surround, encircle *Armed police ringed the scene of the crime.*

ring[2] *vb.* 1 peal, resound, sound, tinkle, jingle *The doorbell just rang.* 2 summon; announce, proclaim *Please ring for service by pressing this button twice.* *n.* tinkle, jangle, peal, jingle *To this day I can recall the ring of the old school bell.*

rinse *vb.* clean, wash *Rinse well to make sure you get out all the soap.*

riot *n.* disorder, disturbance, tumult, uproar, confusion *When the police prevented the people from buying food, there was a riot in which 200 people were injured.* *vb.* rebel, revolt *The prisoners rioted because there wasn't enough food and clean clothing.*

rip *vb.,n.* cut, tear, slit, slash *The sword ripped through the drapery like a hot knife through butter. Nancy was embarrassed because there was a big rip in her dress.*

ripe *adj.* ready, mature, developed, grown, aged *Till it is flecked with brown, this banana is not ripe enough to eat.* ANT. immature, ungrown.

ripen *vb.* mature, age, develop, mellow *Put these green apples on the window sill till they ripen.*

ripple *vb.* ruffle, wave, roll, swell, flutter *A light breeze rippled the surface of the pond.* *n.* wave; undulation *Tim threw a pebble in the lake and watched the ripples spread from the centre.*

rise *vb.* 1 arise, get up; awake *We rose at dawn to watch the animals drink at the watering place.* 2 ascend, mount, arise, climb *The string broke and Dottie's balloon rose up into the summer sky.* 3 prosper, flourish, advance, thrive, succeed, progress *After marrying the boss's daughter, Bill rose rapidly in the company.* *n.* 1 increase, addition, enlargement *A rise in wages is soon followed by a rise in the cost of living.* 2 ascent, climb *The rocket's rise from the launching pad was noisy but swift.*

risk *n.* peril, danger, hazard, chance *I don't think that the glory of having climbed the mountain is worth the risk of getting killed trying.* *vb.* chance, hazard, endanger; gamble *Would you risk your life running into a burning house to rescue a dog?*

risky *adj.* dangerous, chancy, perilous, hazardous, unsafe *Investing your life savings in a medieval theme park seems risky.* ANT. safe, secure.

ritual *n.* ceremony, custom, formality, convention *Every religion has more or less ritual associated with its worship of God.*

rival *n.* competitor, contestant, antagonist, opponent *My rival in the boxing match is a lot heavier than I.* *vb.* compete, contest, oppose *Your beauty rivals that of the rose.* *adj.* competing, opposing, opposed *A rival suitor won the hand of the fair maiden.*

river *n.* stream, brook, creek, tributary *This river has some of the biggest salmon I have ever seen.*

road *n.* way, street, avenue, drive; motorway; by-pass, ring road, orbital (motorway) *The important thing is how the car performs out on the road.*

roam *vb.* wander, ramble, rove, range *With an hour before the film started, we roamed through the shopping precinct.*

roar *vb.,n.* bellow, cry, shout, yell, brawl *When the tiger became caught in the net, it roared until the jungle seemed to shake. The roar of the crowd at the football stadium could be heard throughout the surrounding area.*

rob *vb.* steal, pilfer, rifle; sack, pillage, plunder *The manager suspected Sue of robbing the till. I returned home to find that thieves had robbed me of most of my clothes.*

robber *n.* thief, bandit, pilferer, swindler, criminal *The police caught the robber as he was leaving the scene of the crime.*

robbery *n.* theft, burglary, larceny *The robbery was committed while we were away for the weekend.*

robust *adj.* strong, firm, hardy, vigorous *We pick robust young people and train them for the elite attack corps.*

rock[1] *n.* stone, boulder; pebble *The children collected stones off the beach and took them home.*

rock² *vb.* sway, reel, totter *The dinghy rocked to and fro in the heavy waves.*

rod *n.* pole, bar, wand, staff, stick, baton *Stop waving that rod about or you'll poke someone in the eye with it!*

rogue *n.* rascal, scoundrel, cad, villain; criminal, outlaw *Alphonse is quite a rogue among the ladies.*

role *n.* 1 part, character *Theodora was selected for the leading role in the play.* 2 function, task *What role do temperature and dampness play in catching cold?*

roll *vb.* 1 turn, revolve, spin, rotate, whirl *A huge rock came rolling down the hill.* 2 wind, tie, wrap *Please roll up that cord so we can use it again.* 3 flatten, press, level, smooth *The baker rolled out the dough before cutting it to make biscuits.* *n.* 1 bun; bread *After eating two buttered rolls, I was no longer hungry.* 2 list, register, roster *Please read the roll so we can tell if everyone is here.*

romance *n.* 1 love affair, affair, enchantment *The entire court knew that the queen was carrying on a romance with the butler.* 2 novel, story, tale *Romances were always very popular reading.*

romantic *adj.* 1 sentimental; idealized; fanciful *Penny dreamt that she would meet a romantic lover one day.* 2 visionary; impractical; idealistic, extravagant, exaggerated, fantastic, wild *Your plans are always so romantic but they never quite come off.* ANT. realistic, down-to-earth.

romp *vb.* run, play, frolic, caper *The children are out romping in the meadow with the dogs.*

roof *n.* cover, shelter, top *There are some unfortunates who haven't even a roof over their heads.*

room *n.* 1 chamber; accommodation *We have an extra room if you'd like to stay a few days.* 2 space *There was room for one more person in the lift.*

roomy *adj.* spacious, commodious, capacious *This wardrobe ought to be roomy enough for your clothes.*

roost *vb.* perch, lodge, settle *All the pigeons came home to roost except one.*

root *n.* cause, origin, basis, reason, source *It is not money but the love of money that is the root of evil.*

rooted *adj.* stationary, fixed, firm, steadfast, fast, immovable *I stood rooted to the spot as Scorpio advanced, pistol at the ready.*

rosy *adj.* 1 pink, reddish *At dawn, the sky became rosy just before the sun came up.* 2 fresh, healthy, ruddy *After a week at the seashore, we all returned home in rosy condition.* 3 cheerful, happy, bright, promising, optimistic *Everything is beginning to look rosy again.*

rot *vb.* spoil, decompose, decay, mould, putrefy *The fruit will begin to rot on the trees if it isn't picked soon.* *n.* decay, mould *There was some rot in one of the planks of the boat, and we had to replace it.*

rotate *vb.* 1 turn, revolve, spin, orbit *The tray rotates in the centre of the table and everyone can help himself to pickles and relishes.* 2 alternate, take turns *Instead of your dealing the cards all evening, why don't we rotate?*

rotten *adj.* 1 mouldy, decayed, spoiled, decomposed, putrid, tainted *Food kept without refrigeration soon becomes rotten.* 2 corrupt, immoral, dishonest, deceitful *The government of some cities in the world has become rotten through bribery and greed.* ANT. (1) fresh.

rough *adj.* 1 uneven, unpolished, irregular, bumpy *The rough surface of the furniture would have to be sandpapered before painting.* 2 coarse, impolite, unpolished, rude, crude, unrefined *The farmer's rough manner made no difference to us because he was so kind.* 3 stormy, wild, violent, disorderly, turbulent *The sea was beginning to get very rough, and we knew a storm was brewing.* 4 uncomfortable, inconvenient *Life in earlier times was very rough.* 5 unfinished, hasty, crude, vague *I saw a rough draft of the article before it was rewritten.* ANT. (1) smooth, sleek. (2) suave, sophisticated. (3) calm.

roughly *adv.* about, approximately, nearly *There were roughly thirty people at our party. They left at roughly three a.m.*

round *adj.* 1 circular, curved, spherical *That serving platter isn't round, it's oval.* 2 arched, bowed, rounded *The top of the tree is round now that it has been trimmed.* 3 approximate, rough *In round figures, I'd say fifty people came.* *adv.* circularly, around *The merry-go-round went round and round.* *prep.* enclosing, encircling, circling *The costume called for her to wear a heavy steel collar round her neck.* *n.* routine, series, succession, cycle, course *The doctor makes his rounds in the hospital every day, visiting each patient in turn.*

roundabout *adj.* indirect, devious *Why don't you come right out and say what you mean instead of talking in a roundabout way?* *n.* junction, intersection *Take the third exit at the roundabout.* ANT. *adj.* direct, straightforward.

rouse *vb.* 1 awaken, waken, wake up *I was roused at four o'clock in the morning to stand watch on the ship.* 2 stir up, excite, stimulate *The band played a rousing march.*

rout *vb.* scatter, defeat, conquer, overcome *The enemy was completely routed by the attack from all sides.* *n.* flight, defeat, retreat *When reinforcements arrived from the fort, the attackers were put to rout.*

route *n.* track, way, course, road, path *Which is the best route to Banbury?*

routine *n.* way, method, system, habit *I generally follow the same routine every day, rising at seven and retiring by eleven.* *adj.* customary, usual *I'm going to the dentist for a routine check-up.* ANT. *adj.* uncommon, rare, unusual.

rover *n.* adventurer, traveller, voyager, wanderer *Swann was a rover till he finally settled down with Amanda at Bristol.*

row[1] *n.* series, rank, file, array, order *The commanding officer marched past a long row of soldiers who stood at attention.*

row² *n.* quarrel, squabble, disturbance *Whenever my sister threatened to move out of the house, there would be a big family row.*

royal *adj.* regal, majestic, noble, sovereign, ruling, imperial; kingly, queenly, princely *The presence of a royal personage ensured the success of the event.*

rub *vb.* scour, scrape; shine, polish *Rub the table surface with sandpaper till it's smooth.* *vb. phr.* **rub out** erase, delete, eradicate *The teacher rubbed out the writing on the board.*

rubbish *n.* **1** waste, litter, debris, trash *Please take the rubbish out when you leave.* **2** nonsense, drivel, balderdash *If she thought before speaking, maybe Mabel wouldn't talk such rubbish.*

rude *adj.* impolite, crude, unmannerly, uncivil, coarse, impudent, impertinent *Abernathy has such rude manners that we never invite him to our house.* **ANT.** polite, courteous, polished, cultivated.

rudiments *n.pl.* basis, fundamentals; beginnings *Penny learnt the rudiments of painting at the academy.*

ruffle *vb.* disturb, disarrange, disorder, rumple *The pages of the book were ruffled by so many children having read it.* *n.* frill, trimming *There was an old-fashioned dress in the museum with white lace ruffles at the collar and cuffs.*

rug *n.* mat, carpet, floor-covering *A silk prayer rug was recently sold at auction for a huge sum.*

ruin *vb.* **1** spoil, destroy, demolish, wreck *Barbie's hairdo was ruined in the rain.* **2** bankrupt, impoverish *My grandfather was ruined when the company in which he had invested went bust.* *n.* **1** rubble, wreck *The grass grew among the few walls of the ruin that still stood.* **2** destruction, devastation, decay, disintegration, dilapidation *The ruin of the beautiful ancient Greek temples has deprived us of much architectural knowledge.*

rule *n.* **1** order, ruling, law, regulation, guide *If you want to get along with a minimum of trouble, follow the rules.* **2** control, government, dominion, domination *The islands off the coast don't come under the rule of the king.* *vb.* **1** govern, control, manage, lead, conduct, direct *The king ruled the country with an iron hand.* **2** decree, decide, judge *The judge ruled that the defendant was guilty.*

ruler *n.* **1** leader, governor, commander, chief *The countries' rulers met for a summit conference.* **2** rule, tape measure, measure *Put the ruler along this edge of the cabinet and tell me how long it is.*

ruling *n.* decision, decree, judgement *MacEnline disputed the referee's ruling that the ball was on the line.*

rumble *vb.* thunder, resound *The echoes of the cannonshots rumbled across the valley.*

rummage *vb.* search, hunt, ransack *The cats rummage through the dustbins to find scraps to eat.*

rumour *n.* gossip, hearsay, news *What truth is there to the rumour that you are shortlisted for the Nobel prize?*

rumpus *n.* uproar, commotion, tumult *Ferncliffe threatened to cause a terrible rumpus if he was dismissed as manager.*

run *vb.* 1 speed, hurry, hasten, race *The man just snatched my purse and ran.* 2 operate, function, work, go *My car hasn't run properly since the accident.* 3 go, come, pass; ferry *The train runs only once a day. The boat runs between here and the island all the time.* 4 stretch, lie, extend, reach *This railway line runs from here right down the valley.* 5 flow, stream, pour *The tears came running down Anne's cheeks.* 6 compete, contest, oppose *Who will run for election next year?* *n.* 1 sprint, dash, rush *After a ten-minute run, I finally caught the train.* 2 series, sequence; spell, period *I've had a run of bad luck at cards lately.* *vb. phr.* **run away** escape, elope, flee *The children ran away after breaking a window.* **run down** hunt, seize, catch *The police dogs ran down the escaped convicts in a nearby swamp.* **run into** 1 crash, collide *The two cyclists ran into each other head on.* 2 meet, encounter *Guess whom I ran into at the cinema last night.* **run out** use up, exhaust, consume; squander *I ran out of petrol on the motorway.* **run up** incur *I ran up a large phone bill last quarter.*

run-down *adj.* 1 dilapidated, ramshackle, tumbledown *How could they have let the house get into such a run-down state!* 2 unhealthy, weakened, debilitated *After his illness Robert was in a terribly run-down condition.*

run-of-the-mill *adj.* ordinary, common, commonplace, everyday, average *The painting was merely a run-of-the-mill watercolour, with nothing unusual to recommend it.*

rupture *n.* break, burst *The water began to seep through a rupture in the dam.*

rural *adj.* country, rustic, countrified, pastoral, farm, agricultural *Electricity had only just reached the rural, outlying areas in the 1930s.* ANT. urban, citified.

rush *vb.* run, hasten, speed, hurry, dash *I rushed to the phone but it stopped ringing just as I got there.* *n.* haste, hurry *Dick came into the house in a rush—he'd forgotten his keys.* ANT. *vb.* linger, tarry.

rustle *vb.,n.* stir, whisper, swish; scratch, crackle *The leaves rustled in the wind. There was a great rustle of papers at the meeting.*

rut *n.* 1 groove, furrow, hollow, trench *The ruts in the road are getting worse as they are not being repaired.* 2 routine, habit *My life is in such a rut at the moment; how can I change?*

ruthless *adj.* pitiless, merciless, hardhearted *No one could approve of such ruthless treatment of the workers.*

S

sabotage *n.* treason, treachery, subversion *During the war, any suspicious act of damage was looked upon as possible sabotage.* *vb.* subvert, impair, damage, disable *I suspect Jonathan of trying to sabotage our efforts to escape from prison.*

sack *n.* bag, sac, pouch *We carried the coal home in an old potato sack.*

sacred *adj.* holy, hallowed, divine, consecrated *Sacred places ought to be treated with respect.* **ANT.** blasphemous, profane, sacrilegious.

sacrifice *n.* offering; atonement, propitiation *In olden days, animals were offered as a sacrifice to God.* *vb.* surrender, give up, forgo *We all have to sacrifice some things in life.*

sad *adj.* 1 unhappy, downhearted, sorrowful, depressed, dejected, melancholy, glum, downcast, gloomy, cheerless *Mimi's kitten is lost—that's why she looks so sad.* 2 saddening, discouraging, dismal, tragic *I was just sitting down to dinner when they phoned with the sad news about Grandpa.* **ANT.** happy, joyous.

sadden *vb.* dishearten, cast down, deject, depress *All the children were saddened to learn of the death of the zoo elephant.*

safe *adj.* 1 protected, secure *I ran down the street and didn't feel safe till I'd locked the house door behind me.* 2 reliable, trustworthy, dependable *Do you think that putting money in your firm might be a safe investment?* *n.* vault, strongbox, deposit box *We don't keep important papers around the house but in the safe at the bank.* **ANT.** adj. (1) dangerous.

safeguard *n.* protection, guard, shield, defence *This new lock should prove an excellent safeguard against thieves.*

safety *n.* security, protection; impregnability *The young animals returned to the safety of the burrow after foraging for food.*

sag *vb.* droop, fail, weaken; hang down *Pennants, ribbons and other decorations sagged in the pouring rain.*

sage *adj.* wise, sagacious, judicious, rational, logical *The old man gave me some sage advice about my career.* *n.* wise man, savant, scholar, expert *The ancients always consulted a sage before making any important decision.* **ANT.** adj. foolish, stupid, naive.

sail *n.* sheet, fabric, cloth *The sails were hoisted on the ship.* *vb.* travel, navigate, voyage, cruise *We sailed across the Channel.*

sake *n.* 1 reason, purpose, motive *The lieutenant said he would carry the flag for the sake of the regiment.* 2 benefit, welfare, advantage *I'll give some money for the sake of the elderly.*

salary *n.* wage, pay, compensation, payment *The increase in my salary barely covered the rise in inflation.*

sale *n.* 1 business, trade, commerce *Sales were bad last year.* 2 transaction, deal; trading; auction *The sale of the goods went well.* 3 clearance, reduction, auction *The sales after Christmas bring in a lot of money.*

saloon *n.* bar, lounge *We relaxed in the saloon with our beers.*

salute *vb.* greet, welcome, receive *When Lord Flimsy went to his club, his friends all saluted him with much respect.* *n.* greeting, welcome, celebration *Great was the salute at the return of the celebrity to his home town.*

salvation *n.* 1 rescue, liberation, deliverance; release *Grasping that root as I fell off the cliff proved to be my salvation.* 2 forgiveness, redemption; justification *Christ died on the cross and rose again for our salvation.*

same *adj.* identical, equivalent, corresponding *How embarrassing to be wearing the same party dress as Monica!*

sample *n.* example, specimen, token *The company was giving away free samples of soap and cologne.* *vb.* test, taste; examine, inspect *Would you care to sample some of this ham that I have just baked?*

sanctify *vb.* consecrate, purify; set apart *Tourists are not allowed to enter the sanctified part of the church.*

sanction *n.* 1 permission, authority, authorization, support, approval *I give you my sanction to put on a musical festival at Christmas.* 2 ban, embargo, penalty, punishment *Some nations declared sanctions against the countries that supported their enemies.* *vb.* approve, authorize, allow, permit, support *Does your mother sanction that kind of behaviour in public?*

sane *adj.* rational, sound, normal, balanced, reasonable *It is difficult to believe that anyone who behaves like that could be sane.* ANT. insane, mad, irrational, crazy.

sanguinary *adj.* bloody, bloodstained, gory, sanguineous *It turned out to be a very sanguinary battle indeed.*

sanguine *adj.* optimistic, confident *Pancho was quite sanguine about the outcome of the tennis match.*

sanitary *adj.* clean, disinfected, antiseptic, hygienic, purified *The lavatories in the motorway filling stations are kept quite sanitary.* ANT. dirty, unclean, filthy, fouled.

sap *vb.* exhaust, weaken, drain *You cannot be a good teacher if, as you claim, the children sap your patience.*

sarcasm *n.* mockery, irony, satire, derision, scoffing *Do I detect a touch of sarcasm in your voice when you acknowledge me as the greatest living pianist?*

satanic *adj.* devilish, diabolical, diabolic, demonic, demoniacal, fiendish *Miss Pebbles watched with satanic delight as the skiers sailed off the edge of the cliff into space.*

satire *n.* ridicule, irony, mockery, parody *The author has written a barbed satire on the weaknesses of Parliament.*

satisfaction *n.* 1 pleasure, contentment, gratification, enjoyment *My father got considerable satisfaction from my having been picked for* *the football team.*   **2** payment, repayment, amends *The refugees demanded satisfaction from the Germans after the war, and many of them got it in the form of pensions.*

satisfactory *adj.*   sufficient, all right, adequate *I found the dinner at the Prebendary restaurant quite satisfactory.*   ANT. unsatisfactory, poor.

satisfy *vb.*   **1** fulfil, meet *Will you be able to satisfy the camp's requirements for a swimming instructor?*   **2** cheer, comfort, please *Jane's mother wasn't satisfied till she heard that the children had arrived safely.*

saturate *vb.*   soak, drench, steep *Saturate the sponge with the cleaning liquid, squeeze some out, then rub the spot gently.*

saucy *adj.*   pert, insolent, impudent, bold, impertinent *The Bottle and Glass has quite a saucy barmaid at weekends.*

saunter *vb.*   amble, wander, stroll, walk *After dinner people saunter along the boulevard for a breath of fresh air.*

savage *adj.*   **1** wild, uncivilized, uncultivated, rough, rugged, crude, natural *The savage wilderness had never seen man's footprints.* **2** cruel, heartless, fierce, ferocious *The man was the victim of a savage attack on his way home that evening.*   *n.*   aborigine, cannibal, native, barbarian *The painted savages had begun their dance at the fire.*   ANT. adj. (1) tame, cultivated.

save *vb.*   **1** rescue, free, liberate; preserve, salvage *The fireman saved three people from the burning building.*   **2** preserve, keep, reserve; hoard *I managed to save £2 a week from the money I earned mowing lawns.*

savour *n.*   scent, taste, flavour, relish, tang *After being cooped up in the office, I like going home for the savour of the sweet country air.*

say *vb.*   speak, utter, remark, state, declare *I am not sure that Mother heard what you said.*

scale *n.*   measure, gradation, range; ratio, proportion *The people who do hard physical work are seldom paid on the same scale as office workers.*   *vb.*   climb, mount *The two men scaled the prison wall and ran away.*

scamp *n.*   scallywag, rogue, rascal *That's Raffles, the handsome scamp who took my jewels in Monte Carlo.*

scan *vb.*   **1** glance at *or* over *I only scanned the material and I don't remember what it says.*   **2** examine, study *After scanning the data carefully, the analyst was ready with his report.*

scandal *n.*   disgrace, disrepute, shame, dishonour *The scandal forced two members to resign.*

scanty *adj.*   sparse, scarce, meagre, inadequate, insufficient *Caught between unemployment and inflation, the family could afford only scanty sustenance.*   ANT. plentiful, abundant.

scarce *adj.*   rare, sparse, scanty, insufficient *The farther into the desert we went, the scarcer the water became.*   ANT. common.

scarcely *adv.*   hardly, barely *Scarcely had I got into the bathtub when the telephone rang.*

scarcity *n.* shortage, want, need, dearth, insufficiency, lack *There is a scarcity of good cabinet-makers available today.*

scare *vb.* frighten, shock, startle *You scared me when you jumped like that!*

scatter *vb.* spread, sprinkle, disperse *The seeds must be scattered within the furrows.* ANT. gather, collect, assemble.

scene *n.* view, display, exhibition, spectacle *A storybook scene lay before us as we looked down from the mountaintop.*

scent *n.* 1 odour, smell, fragrance, aroma, perfume *The scent of roses filled the morning air.* 2 trail, spoor, track *A bloodhound's sense of smell is so strong that he can follow a week-old scent.*

sceptical *adj.* cynical, suspicious, doubting *When first approached about the deal, I was justifiably sceptical.*

schedule *n.* timetable, programme, plan, calendar *We've a very tight schedule today and shall be busy.* *vb.* plan, programme; timetable *My English class is scheduled for ten o'clock every morning.*

scheme *n.* 1 plan, plot, design, programme *I have worked out a scheme that will allow me to have a library study period before my history class.* 2 plot, intrigue, conspiracy *The secret service discovered a scheme to assassinate the cabinet minister.* *vb.* plan, plot, intrigue, contrive *They're scheming how to get rid of him.*

schism *n.* division, split, faction *There appears to be a widening schism on unionism within the ranks of the party.*

scholar *n.* schoolboy, schoolgirl; student; academic, lecturer, professor *As a scholar in the humanities, Professor Dodd has written several books that have been well received.*

scintillate *vb.* shine, sparkle, twinkle *The stars scintillated in the black, cloudless sky above.*

scoff *vb.* mock, belittle, deride, ridicule *They scoff at scars who never felt a wound. The children scoffed when I said I had found a Tyrannosaurus Rex in the school basement.*

scold *vb.* reprove, berate, reprimand, criticize, censure, blame *Father scolded me for coming home late for dinner.*

scope *n.* range, reach, extent *The broad scope of the survey was intended to include all adults.*

scorch *vb.* char, burn, singe *The laundry scorched my shirt, ruining it.*

score *n.* 1 record, tally, reckoning *According to the score, the home team is winning. The coach asked me to keep score.* 2 mark, total *Dick received the highest score in the class.* 3 grievance, complaint, case *I have a score to settle with Dorothy because of what she has been telling people about me.* *vb.* record, tabulate, count *Brenda scored the highest of all the students in the maths test.*

scorn *n.* contempt *Betty turned up her nose to show her scorn for anyone who cheated in an exam.* *vb.* 1 despise, hate *All our friends scorned people who were dishonest.* 2 refuse, ignore, spurn, reject *I scorned his offer to behave because I knew he'd do the same thing again.*

scornful *adj.* contemptuous, disdainful *You would be less scornful of success if you had ever enjoyed any.*

scoundrel *n.* rogue, cad, villain, knave *That disreputable scoundrel is still breaking women's hearts at seventy-five years of age.*

scour *vb.* scrub, clean, wash *Company is coming, so you'd better scour that ring off the bathtub.*

scourge *n.* **1** affliction, plague *Lack of adequate food is the scourge of many countries.* **2** whip, lash *The slave-driver lay about him with a leather scourge.* *vb.* punish, chastise, afflict; torment *In the old days, criminals were scourged in public by beating with a cat-o'-nine-tails.*

scowl *vb.,n.* glare, frown, glower *The teacher scowled at anyone who gave a wrong answer. The old man looked unpleasant because of the scowl on his face.*

scramble *vb.* **1** mix, blend, combine *I had scrambled eggs for breakfast.* **2** hasten, scurry; clamber, climb *When the announcement came to abandon ship, the passengers scrambled into the lifeboats.*

scrap *n.* **1** piece, part, fragment, crumb *Please pick up every scrap of paper you can find.* **2** waste *Vincent's uncle is a dealer in metal scrap.* *vb.* discard, abandon *I should have scrapped that car months ago—it's not safe to drive any more.*

scrape *vb.* scour, rub; rasp, scratch *Every spring we scrape the paint off the bottom of the boat and apply a fresh coat.*

scratch *vb.,n.* scar, scrape *I scratched my finger with that saw, so I'll put some iodine on it. My mother was angry when she saw the scratch on the table.* *n. phr.* **from scratch** *Informal:* from the beginning, from the outset *You're better starting off from scratch when rewriting your idea.*

scrawl *vb.* scribble, scratch *Some vandal has scrawled his name on the newly painted wall.*

scrawny *adj.* skinny, bony, gaunt, spindly, thin *Are you trying to tell me that this scrawny little kid trounced the town bully?*

scream *vb.,n.* shriek, cry, yell, screech *We heard a woman scream so we called the police. When she saw that someone had walked on her flowerbed, my aunt let out a scream.*

screech *vb.,n.* scream, shriek, yell, cry *The owl screeched in the darkness, and we huddled together. When Anne saw us get off the plane, she gave a screech of joy and ran towards us.*

screen *n.* cover, protection, separation, partition *An ornate screen divided the room in two.* *vb.* shield, conceal, hide; separate, partition *The bookcase screened the other side of the room from my view.*

scrimp *vb.* economize, save, conserve *She scrimped to send her son to university, so it is only fair for him now to take care of her.*

script *n.* **1** handwriting, hand, penmanship, writing *The old man wrote his letters in a beautiful ornate script.* **2** copy, manuscript, lines, text *Maureen didn't know her part because, she said, she'd lost her script on the bus.*

scrub *vb.* scour, wash, cleanse, clean *You must scrub hard to get off all the dirt.*

scruple *n.* doubt, hesitation, qualm, compunction *Hervey has no scruples at all when it comes to making money.*

scrupulous *adj.* painstaking, exacting, careful, fastidious, careful *Only the most scrupulous scholarship could produce a history of such accuracy.* ANT. careless.

scrutinize *vb.* examine, study *The detectives scrutinized every inch of the area looking for clues.*

scurrilous *adj.* outrageous, abusive, insulting *The opposition party launched a scurrilous attack on the Prime Minister.*

scurry *vb.* scramble, hustle, hurry, hasten, scamper *The rabbit scurried round the hedge and into its burrow.*

scuttle *vb.* sink, ditch, swamp *The crew scuttled the ship to prevent its falling into enemy hands.*

sea *n.* ocean, waters, waves *Thousands crossed the sea to escape slavery under the tyrant.*

seal *n.* symbol, signet, insigne, mark, emblem, stamp, crest *I at once recognized the seal of the Brennenzollich family.* *vb.* approve, endorse, sign, stamp *Now that we have an agreement, let's seal it with a kiss.*

search *vb.* explore, examine, investigate, scrutinize, inspect *We searched everywhere but couldn't find a trace of the stolen coins.* *n.* exploration, examination, investigation; quest, hunt *The search for the kidnapped heir goes on.*

seasoned *adj.* experienced, skilled, veteran *Desmond, a seasoned sailor, has served with the navy for thirty years.*

seat *n.* **1** chair, stool, bench *Please find a seat and sit down.* **2** situation, location, centre, place *London is the seat of government in this country.*

secede *vb.* withdraw, resign, quit *If they persist in wanting war, we shall secede from the party.*

secluded *adj.* separate, isolated, sheltered, hidden, secret, private *We used to meet in a secluded place to avoid neighbours' prying eyes.*

secondary *adj.* subordinate, subsidiary, auxiliary *The needs of the individual are seen as secondary to those of the state.* ANT. primary.

secret *adj.* hidden, concealed, unknown *My brother and I used to talk together in a secret language.* *n.* confidence; mystery *If you can keep a secret, I'll tell you where Ma has hidden the chocolate.* ANT. adj. open, public.

sect *n.* denomination; group, faction *To which Protestant sect does your family belong?*

section *n.* part, segment, division, subdivision *I had a few orange sections for breakfast. Blanche lives in a dangerous section of town.*

secure *adj.* **1** firm, tight, fast, fastened, stable, fixed *'The lifeboats are all secure, Captain,' reported the seaman.* **2** safe, protected, defended *We felt secure, huddled in the warm room round the fire.* **3** assured, self-assured, confident, resolute *I envy Barbie when she* *applies for a job—she always seems so secure.* *vb.* **1** fasten, fix, tighten *Please secure the door when you go out.* **2** obtain, procure, acquire *The officer ordered the seamen to secure a supply of diesel fuel for the launch.* **3** protect, defend, guard *The fort will be secured from attack when the cavalry arrives.* ANT. adj. (1) loose, free. (2) endangered.

security *n.* **1** safety, protection, shelter *The attic offered security to the weary escapees.* **2** guarantee, surety, pledge, promise *I have savings in the bank as a security against hardship.*

sedate *adj.* **1** calm, unruffled, serene, calm, composed, controlled *The judge was a sedate, matronly woman.* **2** proper, dignified, prim *Charles is far too sedate to do such a dance in public.* *vb.* drug, tranquillize, narcotize *To calm him down, the doctor sedated Paul, who soon fell asleep.*

sediment *n.* dregs, lees, grounds, residue *I dislike drinking coffee that has sediment at the bottom of the cup.*

seduce *vb.* lead astray, allure, entice, tempt, lure *Vampira used many means to seduce men to do her bidding.*

see *vb.* **1** observe, perceive, look at, regard, examine, study, view, eye, notice *I can see a small red barn or boathouse across the river, but it's too far to see if anyone is near it.* **2** understand, comprehend, recognize, appreciate *Yes, I see what you mean about Louis.* **3** learn, determine, find out, ascertain *Please see who's at the door.* **4** experience, undergo, go through *I've seen a lot of suffering these last few years.* **5** escort, attend, accompany *I'll see you to your limousine, madam.* **6** think, deliberate, ponder *I'll see about that matter at another time.*

seedy *adj.* run-down, shabby, squalid, mean *Beppo was staying in a seedy hotel in another part of the city.*

seek *vb.* search for, look for *The police are seeking someone to help them in their enquiries.*

seem *vb.* appear, look *That child seems to be lost. Does it seem to you that winters are getting colder?*

seep *vb.* ooze, leak, percolate *The rainwater seeps into the ground, then into the aquifers.*

segment *n.* section, division, part, portion *Julian belongs to the conservative segment of the organization.*

segregate *vb.* separate, exclude; ostracize *The goats must be segregated from the sheep.* ANT. combine, include.

seize *vb.* **1** grab, grasp, clutch *The thief tried to seize the woman's handbag, but she held it tight and he ran off.* **2** capture, take *After a siege of forty days, the attackers finally seized the castle.* ANT. (1) release, loosen.

seldom *adv.* rarely, not often, infrequently, scarcely *These days, we rarely go out to dinner.*

select *vb.* choose, pick, prefer *In a supermarket you select the food you want by yourself.* *adj.* special, chosen, choice, preferred, selected, picked, elite *The select troops became the king's personal bodyguard.*

self-control *n.* restraint, discipline *To stop smoking you must exercise considerable self-control.*

self-important *adj.* egocentric, conceited, egotistical, proud *That self-important little man is always making speeches about his so-called accomplishments.*

selfish *adj.* self-centred, greedy, mean, miserly *Hurlbut is selfish and wants everything for himself.*

self-righteous *adj.* egoistical, sanctimonious, holier-than-thou *That self-righteous bank manager tried to justify foreclosing on our mortgage!*

self-satisfied *adj.* smug, complacent *Shirley looks so self-satisfied now that she has finally caught a husband.*

sell *vb.* trade, barter, market, retail, merchandise *She sells seashells by the seashore; the seashells that she sells are seashore shells.*

send *vb.* post, dispatch, transmit, forward, convey, ship *The goods were supposed to have been sent last week.*

senior *adj.* older, elder; superior *The senior members of the club sit on the various committees and hold office.* ANT. junior, minor.

sensation *n.* **1** sense, feeling, sensibility, perception, sensitiveness *The dentist gave me an injection, and I had no sensation in my lower lip.* **2** excitement, thrill, stimulation *The new rock group was an overnight sensation.*

sensational *adj.* thrilling, startling, exciting, marvellous, superb, spectacular *This book should be a sensational bestseller.*

sense *n.* **1** sensation, feeling, perception *The doctor asked me if I had any sense in my left leg.* **2** understanding, reasoning, intellect, judgement, wit, common sense, brains *I don't know what's the matter with Sadie, but she hasn't the sense she was born with!* **3** awareness, consciousness *Have you no sense of honour or of loyalty?* *vb.* perceive, feel, discern, appreciate *I sensed someone near me, even though I had heard nothing and couldn't see in the darkness.*

sensible *adj.* reasonable, rational; thoughtful, judicious; responsible *I am pleased that Donald is sensible enough to want to complete his education.* ANT. foolish.

sensitive *adj.* **1** sore, tender, delicate *The end of my finger is still sensitive where I burned it yesterday.* **2** touchy, tense, nervous *Donald is still very sensitive about his exam results last year.* **3** perceptive, keen, receptive *Bob has very sensitive hearing.*

sensual *adj.* **1** erotic, sexual, lustful, carnal *These books cater to the reader's sensual nature.* **2** lascivious, lewd, indecent *Flemburgh's sensual appetites have got him into trouble lately.*

sentiment *n.* **1** feeling, attitude, opinion *Roger never let his sentiments be known about the loss of his aunt.* **2** tenderness, emotion *The film was so full of sentiment that even the adults cried.*

separate *vb.* **1** divide, disconnect, split, break up *We finally separated the two fighting dogs.* **2** isolate, segregate *The boys and the* *girls are separated in our school.* *adj.* **1** apart, divided, detached *We were able to keep the dogs and the cats separate.* **2** distinct, different *Please sort the nuts and the bolts into separate containers.* **3** independent *Victor's mother and father have decided to lead separate lives.*

sequel *n.* consequence, result, development *Tonight's episode is a sequel to the programme shown last week.*

sequence *n.* order, succession, series, arrangement *There is something wrong with the alphabetical sequence.*

serene *adj.* peaceful, quiet, calm, tranquil *The lake was serene again after the storm had passed.* . ANT. agitated, turbulent, stormy.

series *n.* order, sequence, succession *Owing to the fog, there has been a series of rear-end collisions on the motorway.*

serious *adj.* **1** grave, earnest, sober, solemn *I think you ought to have more fun and try to be less serious.* **2** important, critical *Disobeying the school rules is a serious matter.* ANT. (1) frivolous, jocular, light.

sermon *n.* address, talk; lecture, discourse.

servant *n.* domestic, attendant; butler, valet, manservant, footman; maidservant, maid *Many of the stately homes can no longer function because of a lack of servants.*

serve *vb.* **1** attend, wait on *The waitress came over to our table and asked, 'May I serve you?'* **2** assist, help, aid *The solider re-enlisted in order to serve his country.*

service *n.* **1** help, aid, assistance *How can I be of service to you?* **2** worship, ceremony, ordinance *We went to the church service on Sunday morning.*

servile *adj.* menial, beggarly, submissive, obsequious, fawning *How can you tolerate having that servile toady about all the time?*

session *n.* meeting, sitting, gathering *The matter will be voted on at the next session of the executive committee.*

set *vb.* **1** put, place, position *You can set the armchair in the corner over there, please.* **2** assign, appoint, fix, settle, establish, determine *If you will set a time when we are to meet, I shall be there.* **3** harden, solidify, thicken, congeal, gel *The cement will set overnight.* **4** rate, price, value *The discount at the sale was set at twenty per cent.* *vb. phr.* **set apart** separate, divide *The children who refused to behave were set apart from the others.* **set aside** save, reserve *The man in the shop has set aside a transistor radio for me till I have the money to pay for it.* **set back** slow, retard, hinder, delay *Our original schedule was set back six weeks by a fire at the factory.* **set down** write, record *Each student should set down his own ideas before starting to write.* **set forth** begin, start *The explorers set forth on their journey from Plymouth.* **set free** liberate, release, free *We took the fawn into the forest and set it free.* **set off** **1** detonate, touch off, explode *The children are not allowed to set off the fireworks by themselves.* **2** embark, start out *I like to set off on a car trip early in the morning.* **3** contrast, offset *The red necktie sets off* *the pale pink shirt very well.* **set on** attack *The stagecoach was set on by robbers as soon as it left town.* **set out** begin, start, commence *There were ten people at the inn who had set out from London that morning.* **set up** establish, found *The children set up a business to sell lemonade during the hot summer.* *n.* 1 collection, assortment; kit *The stamp collector has a complete set of first-day covers. Do you have a chemistry set?* 2 group, company, clique, circle *I don't like the set that Margie is going with these days.* *adj.* settled, firm, unchanging *Agnes's father is very set in his ways, isn't he?*

setback *n.* hindrance, disappointment, adversity, defeat *Despite some setbacks, Craddock finally obtained his doctoral degree.*

settle *vb.* 1 agree upon, establish, decide *I think we ought to be able to settle who is going to clean the stairs.* 2 pay, satisfy *The insurance company settled the claim in two weeks.* 3 locate, lodge, reside, abide *My ancestors settled in Sydney, Australia.* 4 sink, subside *The ground under the new house settled, creating cracks in the walls.*

sever *vb.* cut off, separate *The mob impaled the severed head on a pike outside the prison.* ANT. join, connect, attach.

several *adj.* a few, some, a couple, a handful *Several new members were elected last evening.*

severe *adj.* 1 cruel, strict, harsh, rigid, firm, unyielding *The headmaster of our school is a severe disciplinarian.* 2 difficult, harsh, unpleasant *An especially severe winter has made our fuel bill much higher.* 3 violent, dangerous *The severe storm knocked down power lines all over the area.* ANT. (1) lenient, easygoing. (2) mild.

sew *vb.* stitch, seam, embroider; mend *Mrs Cranshaw just sits in her chair and sews.*

shabby *adj.* ragged, worn, threadbare *Uncle Ben still wears the same shabby old raincoat wherever he goes.*

shack *n.* hut, hovel, shed, shanty *For years we lived together in a tiny shack in the forest.*

shade *n.* 1 shadow, darkness, gloom, dusk *In the shade, I was unable to see who it was.* 2 tint, colour, hue *That shade of blue goes with your eyes very well.* *vb.* 1 darken, blacken *If you shade that part of the drawing, it will look more natural.* 2 screen, conceal, cover, block *I shaded the sun from my eyes with my hand.*

shadowy *adj.* shady, dark, gloomy, dim; indistinct, indefinite, vague *A person was huddled in a shadowy corner. A shadowy figure loomed up before me in the mist.*

shady *adj.* 1 shaded, sunless *Let's walk on the shady side, out of the hot sun.* 2 doubtful, questionable, shifty, devious *Gabriela doesn't like my spending so much time with those shady characters at the library.*

shaft *n.* 1 pole, rod, bar *The natives held the shafts of the spears ready to hurl them onto the strangers.* 2 ray, beam, streak *A shaft of light came in through the gap in the curtains.*

shaggy *adj.* woolly, hairy, uncombed, unkempt *Tom's story was that he had been given a shaggy dog for Christmas.*

shake *vb.* 1 quiver, tremble, quake, shiver, shudder *The tiny kitten was shaking with cold on our doorstep, so we took it inside.* 2 grasp, clasp, take *I shook John's hand as I was introduced to him.*

shaky *adj.* uncertain, (*informal*) iffy, questionable, faltering, unsteady *The deal might go through, but it looks very shaky.*

shallow *adj.* slight, superficial, inconsiderable *Bertie's relationship with Nancy is a very shallow one.* ANT. deep, profound.

sham *n.* fake, fiction, pretence *The company's guarantee turned out to be a complete sham.*

shame *n.* 1 embarrassment, humiliation *A feeling of shame came over me when I realized that Suzie had overheard me talking about her sister.* 2 disgrace, dishonour *The soldier's court martial brought shame to the entire platoon.* *vb.* 1 humiliate, humble, abash, mortify *Tony was shamed into admitting that he had taken all the sweets out of the jar.* 2 disgrace, dishonour, humble *Should a teacher be shamed by a student who misbehaves?* ANT. n. (2) pride, honour.

shameful *adj.* disgraceful, humiliating, dishonourable, scandalous *I think it shameful the way Aunt Agatha gossips about her friends.*

shameless *adj.* unashamed, unembarrassed; bold, brazen, insolent, impudent *They still talk about that shameless dance Griselda did on the table at the pub.*

shape *n.* 1 form, figure, outline; appearance *That swimming pool is in the shape of a letter 'C'.* 2 mould, frame, form, pattern, cast *The clay hardened into the shape of the container where it was kept.* *vb.* form, fashion, model; mould, cast *Try to shape this block of wood to look like an apple.*

shapeless *adj.* vague, undefined, indistinct, amorphous *A cloudy, shapeless apparition appeared before me.*

shapely *adj.* well-formed, curvy, well-built, well-proportioned, alluring, attractive *Dennis has been seeing Tanya, that shapely model from Paris.*

share *n.* portion, part, ration, allotment; helping *You have already eaten your share of the pie.* *vb.* 1 participate, partake *Everyone who does his work can share in the rewards.* 2 divide, distribute, apportion *I think you ought to share the chocolates among you equally.*

sharp *adj.* keen, acute, cutting, fine *The guide's hunting knife was sharp enough to shave with.* ANT. blunt, dull.

sharpen *vb.* hone, whet *The wood was so tough that we had to sharpen the axe every few minutes.*

shatter *vb.* 1 smash, break, burst, split; destroy *The ball went through Mrs Maloney's window and shattered it.* 2 upset, shock *The news that Andy had failed his exam shattered him.*

shave *vb.* cut, trim, clip *Arriving at 4.59 for the 5.01 to Paddington is shaving it pretty close.*

shawl *n.* scarf, stole *The beggarwoman drew her shawl close round her shoulders against the night chill.*

shed *n.* hut, lean-to, shelter, outbuilding *Father used to let travellers stay overnight in the shed where we kept farm tools.*

sheer *adj.* 1 utter, simple, absolute *Your story about the frog turning into a prince is sheer nonsense.* 2 steep, abrupt *We were faced with a sheer rocky cliff that no one could climb.* 3 fine, transparent, thin, clear *The model was wearing sheer stockings.*

sheet *n.* 1 covering, cloth; bed-linen *I'll change the sheets on the bed today.* 2 layer, leaf; film, coating *Put a sheet of paper over the top of the jar before sealing it. There's a sheet of ice on the roads tonight, so be careful.*

shelf *n.* ledge, plank, rack *I was too short to reach the topmost shelf without a ladder.*

shell *n.* crust, case, husk; covering, layer, outside *Remove the shell before eating the nut.*

shelter *n.* protection, haven, sanctuary *We sought shelter from the storm by crouching in a cave.* *vb.* protect, shield, harbour, guard *The farmer sheltered many fugitives who escaped from the gang.*

shield *n.* guard, defence, protection, shelter *We had to plant a row of trees alongside the house as a shield from the winds.* *vb.* guard, defend, protect, shelter *The man raised his arms to shield himself from the attack.*

shift *vb.* move, change, transfer *The foreman shifted three men from the factory to the warehouse. The wind, which had been from the south, shifted to the north.* *n.* 1 move, change, transfer *My shift to another job in the company meant I would earn more money.* 2 turn, spell, period *I work the day shift but I used to work nights.*

shiftless *adj.* lazy, idle, indolent, slothful *Mario Farniente is so shiftless that he spends his holidays in a hospital intensive care unit.*

shifty *adj.* tricky, slippery, crafty, clever, shrewd, cunning, sly *That shifty beggar sneaked out of the restaurant without paying.*

shimmer *vb.* shine, glimmer, glisten, gleam *The moonlight shimmered on the lake as we paddled along in our canoe.*

shine *vb.* 1 gleam, beam, glisten, glimmer, shimmer, glow, radiate *The sun shone every day of our holiday.* 2 polish, brush *I shined my riding boots in preparation for the horse show competition.* *n.* gloss, lustre, radiance, polish *My face was reflected in the shine of the chrome on the car.*

shiny *adj.* glossy, polished, bright, glistening *Your furniture would be shiny, too, if you'd only wax it.* **ANT.** dull, dingy.

shipshape *adj.* neat, clean, orderly, Bristol fashion *The sailors were ordered to make everything aboard shipshape.* **ANT.** messy, sloppy.

shirk *vb.* evade, avoid, dodge *Any employee who shirks his duty will be dismissed.*

shiver *vb.* quake, tremble, quiver, shudder, shake *We stood on the corner, shivering in the cold, waiting for the school bus.* *n.* shudder, tremble *A shiver ran down my spine when I thought of the way the kitten had been killed.*

shock *n.* **1** blow, clash, collision, impact *The shock of the huge lorry striking the wall broke all the windows in the house.* **2** disturbance, upset, agitation *The shock at the news of her son's death was too much for the mother to bear.* *vb.* **1** surprise, stagger, astound, stun, startle, bewilder *The parents were shocked when they saw the film.* **2** horrify, outrage, offend, revolt, appal *The world was shocked to discover what had been going on in the Nazi concentration camps.*

shoe *n.* footwear, boot, sandal *People were too poor to buy shoes and had to wrap rags round their feet.*

shoot *vb.* fire, explode, burst, discharge *You know that you are forbidden to shoot a firearm in this area!*

shop *n.* store, supermarket; department store; kiosk *All the shops will be having sales after Christmas.*

shore *n.* beach, coast, seaside, seacoast *As the boat neared the shore, he jumped out and waded to meet me.*

short *adj.* **1** brief, concise, abbreviated, condensed, curtailed, terse, abridged *The film is short—it lasts only twenty minutes.* **2** slight, little, undersized *The string is too short to go around the package even once.* ANT. long, lengthy.

shortage *n.* shortfall, deficiency, deficit *We shall have to make up the shortage in the accounts from our own pockets.* ANT. surplus

shortcoming *n.* weakness, frailty, failing, foible *I must admit that dishonesty would be a serious shortcoming in a bank clerk.* ANT. strength, asset, advantage.

shorten *vb.* **1** cut, curtail, abbreviate, abridge *The article is good, but it has to be shortened to fit into the space in our magazine.* **2** take in, lessen, reduce *The dressmaker had to shorten my sister's skirt a little.* ANT. lengthen.

short-handed *adj.* understaffed *With so many people away on holiday, we are short-handed at the moment.*

shortly *adv.* soon, anon, presently, directly *The manager said he would attend to us shortly.*

shortsighted *adj.* **1** myopic *The optician said that I was shortsighted and needed glasses.* **2** thoughtless, unthinking, unimaginative *It was quite shortsighted of you not to have foreseen what mother would do when she saw the ink on the carpet.* ANT. (1) far-sighted, presbyopic. (2) imaginative, thoughtful.

shot *n.* blast, burst, discharge *Did you hear a shot?*

shout *vb.,n.* yell, roar, cry, bellow *I shouted to my sister that she'd better hurry up. Jimmy gave a shout when I stepped on his toe.*

shove *vb.,n.* push, jostle *Can you help me shove this heavy bookcase? If you give the cart a good shove, it will roll down the hill.*

shovel *n.* spade, scoop, scuttle *Rick picked up the shovel and stoked the furnace.*

show *vb.* **1** display, present, exhibit *I have already shown you all the* *books I have on gardening.* 2 indicate, note, point *Show me the way to go home.* 3 explain, reveal, tell *I wish you would show me how to do that trick with the disappearing mouse.* 4 prove, demonstrate *If you expect me to believe your story about the purple banana, you'll have to show me.* 5 guide, usher, lead *The man in the green uniform will show you to your seats.* vb. phr. **show in** conduct, lead, direct *Please show Mr Gilbert in.* **show off** brag, boast *Every time the teacher looks at him, Oscar shows off.* **show up** 1 arrive, appear, turn up, surface *Ten o'clock is no time to show up for school!* 2 expose, belittle, discredit *The experienced pianist did not like being shown up by his own pupil.* n. 1 presentation, exhibit, exhibition, display *Mother and I went to a flower show yesterday.* 2 drama, play, musical *Where shall we meet after the show?*

shred *n.* fragment, piece, bit, tatter *After the fight, Jack's shirt was in shreds.* vb. cut, strip, tear *I like shredded carrots in my salad.*

shrewd *adj.* 1 cunning, sly, crafty, tricky *Putting a drawing pin on the teacher's chair was not a very shrewd move, Moriarty.* 2 clever, ingenious, intelligent, astute *My father is a very shrewd investor, and many businessmen seek his advice.*

shriek *vb.,n.* scream, screech, yell, howl *Mother shrieked when she saw the mouse run along the floor. We were very frightened when we heard a piercing shriek at midnight.*

shrill *adj.* sharp, piercing; high-pitched *The train whistle is shrill enough to damage your hearing.*

shrink *vb.* 1 contract, diminish, dwindle, shrivel *If you wash that shirt in hot water, it will shrink.* 2 recoil, withdraw, flinch, retreat *Dick shrinks from any responsibility you try to give him.* ANT. (1) swell.

shudder *vb.,n.* shiver, tremble, shake, quiver *I shuddered at the thought of going out into the bitter cold. The dog gave a violent shudder, making the rain from his coat fly everywhere.*

shuffle *vb.* 1 scuffle, plod, crawl, falter *The old man shuffled along the street.* 2 mix, jumble, disorder *It's your turn to shuffle the cards.*

shun *vb.* avoid, evade, elude *Frances has no idea why her friends are shunning her.*

shut *vb.* close; lock, seal *Please shut the door after you.* vb. phr. **shut up** *Informal:* be quiet, hush, still *Oh, do shut up, I'm getting so tired of hearing your voice.* ANT. vb. open.

shy *adj.* timid, bashful *Liz is no longer the retiring, shy child who seemed afraid of her own shadow.* ANT. bold, self-confident; brazen.

sick *adj.* ill, unwell, ailing, unhealthy, infirm *This insurance policy pays for surgery but not for every time you just get sick.* ANT. healthy, well.

side *n.* 1 face, surface *A cube has six sides.* 2 opponent, foe, rival *Which side are you for, the one in the green shirts or the one in white?* adj. secondary, indirect; unimportant *The main issue is the kind* *of television programmes we want; for the moment the cost of the programmes is a side issue.* *vb.* join, support, associate *Maggie sided with her husband in the argument.*

siege *n.* blockade, barrage *The siege successfully cut off all movement of food and water, in and out of the fortress.*

sieve *n.* strainer, colander, screen, riddle *Pass the mixture through a sieve to get out the bones, which you can save for soup.*

sift *vb.* 1 sieve, separate, sort, filter *Jean sifted the flour to remove the coarser grains.* 2 evaluate, examine, scrutinize *The detectives sifted the evidence before them.*

sigh *vb.* breathe, cry, gasp, groan, moan *Private Frobisher sighed when he learnt that he would have to stand a double watch again.*

sight *n.* 1 vision, eyesight *Bill's sight requires him to wear glasses.* 2 view, spectacle, scene, display *The trained porpoises leaping through the air together are quite a sight.* 3 *Informal:* eyesore *My mother told me that my room was a sight and that I must clean it up at once.*

sign *n.* 1 symbol, token, indication, suggestion, hint *Those black clouds on the horizon are the sign of a coming storm.* 2 signal, clue *The dog gave no sign that it would bite.* *vb.* authorize, approve, confirm *Please sign the contract on the dotted line.*

signal *n.* sign, beacon, flag *If we send them a signal, they might be able to avoid the trap.*

significance *n.* importance, consequence, weight, moment *The significance of my father's advice didn't sink in till years later.*

significant *adj.* important, meaningful, vital, crucial, critical *Do you really think it significant that the date of your birth is a prime number?* ANT. unimportant, insignificant, trivial, meaningless.

signify *vb.* 1 indicate, show, signal, communicate *The policeman signified his permission to cross the street by beckoning with his arm.* 2 mean *What do you suppose those strange hand movements signify?*

silence *n.* 1 quiet, stillness, noiselessness, soundlessness, hush *After the noise and bustle of the city, I really enjoy the silence and serenity of the country.* 2 muteness, speechlessness *Silence is golden, but speech is silver.* ANT. (1) noisiness, clamour, racket.

silent *adj.* 1 quiet, noiseless, soundless, still, hushed *I dived down into the lake, into its silent depths.* 2 mute, speechless, uncommunicative *My father was silent on the subject of where we were going for our holiday.* ANT. (1) noisy, clamorous. (2) talkative, communicative.

silly *adj.* senseless, foolish, stupid, ridiculous *Stop that silly giggling and get serious for a minute!!* ANT. serious, sober.

similar *adj.* like, resembling, alike *The shirts are similar, but not identical.* ANT. different, dissimilar.

similarity *n.* likeness, resemblance *I cannot see any similarity between your reckless behaviour and Randolph's act of bravery.* ANT. dissimilarity, difference.

simmer *vb.* boil, stew, bubble *This soup should simmer for ten min-*

utes. *vb.phr.* **simmer down** *Informal:* calm down, quieten down *Alfred got very angry for a while but he then simmered down.*

simple *adj.* **1** uncomplicated *Addition and subtraction are parts of simple arithmetic.* **2** clear, understandable, plain *I cannot give you a simple explanation of why plants are green.* **3** easy *That was a simple history exam.* **4** unadorned, plain, unimaginative *Sue liked to wear simple dresses.* ANT. (1) complicated, complex. (2) puzzling, abstruse. (3) difficult, demanding. (4) ornate, grand.

simulate *vb.* pretend, feign, imitate *It takes an expert to tell the difference between natural and simulated pearls.*

simultaneous *adj.* concurrent, coincident, contemporaneous *The sound and flash of the explosion were simultaneous.*

sin *n.* trespass, transgression, wickedness *The seven deadly sins are pride, anger, covetousness, lust, gluttony, envy and sloth.* *vb.* trespass, transgress *Jonah sinned by disobeying God.*

sincere *adj.* **1** honest, open, candid, faithful, trusty, trustworthy *Don is a sincere friend.* **2** genuine, real, true *Mabel shed sincere tears for her lost puppy.* ANT. dishonest, hypocritical, deceptive.

sincerity *n.* honesty, guilelessness; openness, frankness *I believed her because she spoke with such sincerity.* ANT. guile, deceit, insincerity.

sing *vb.* chant, croon *That was a song my mother used to sing to me.*

singe *vb.* burn, scorch *The explosion singed my hair and eyebrows.*

single *adj.* **1** one, lone, sole, solitary *A single man stood on the beach, looking out towards the horizon.* **2** celibate, unmarried, unattached *The party at the club next week will be for single people only.* **3** individual *I reserved a single room at the hotel.* ANT. (2) married, attached. (3) double.

singular *adj.* **1** remarkable, unusual, extraordinary, rare, uncommon, exceptional *Climbing Mount Everest is certainly a singular feat.* **2** strange, odd, peculiar, queer, eccentric, curious *These birds exhibit a singular mating dance.* ANT. common, ordinary, everyday.

sinister *adj.* ominous, unfavourable, adverse *Do you see nothing sinister about your friend, Doctor Fu Manchu?*

sink *vb.* descend, fall, drop *After letting go of the lifebelt, he sank like a stone beneath the waves.* ANT. rise, ascend.

sip *vb.* taste, drink *You should sip the hot lemonade slowly.* *n.* taste, swallow, drink *May I have a sip of your sherry?*

siren *n.* alarm, horn, signal, tocsin; warning *As soon as we heard the sirens, we would hurry down to the bomb shelters.*

sit *vb.* rest, squat, crouch, perch *Please do not sit on the floor.* *vb.phr.* **sit on** *Informal:* repress, suppress *The government sat on the committee's report and did not make its findings public.* ANT. *vb.* stand; recline.

site *n.* location, place, position *We selected a flat, grassy site to pitch our tent.*

situation *n.* **1** location, site, position *The situation of the house gives it magnificent views in three directions.* **2** condition, state, circumstances *In the present situation, it may not be easy to find a job after school.*

size *n.* dimension, measurement; extent, scope; largeness *What did you say was the size of the sailing boat you used to race in?*

skeleton *n.* bone(s); frame, framework *These form merely the skeleton of our plan, which we must flesh out with details.*

sketch *n.* drawing, picture *Here is a rough sketch of my home.* *vb.* draw, outline, represent *In the art class, the students were asked to sketch a model of a monkey.*

sketchy *adj.* vague, indefinite, indistinct, incomplete, rough *The police could get only a sketchy description of the attacker.*

skid *vb.* slide, slip, glide *The car skidded all over the road on the black ice.*

skilful *adj.* skilled, accomplished, expert, adept, proficient *Bentley is a skilful manager of the production line at the plant.* ANT. inept, clumsy, awkward.

skill *n.* ability, talent, aptitude *Vladimir plays the piano with great skill.*

skim *vb.* scan, loók through, (*informal*) flick through, browse *Although he barely skimmed through it, my teacher said that my essay was excellent.*

skimpy *adj.* meagre, scanty, thin (on the ground); cheap, stingy *The contributions to the fund have been quite skimpy this year.* ANT. lavish, generous.

skin *n.* covering, outside, peel, shell, rind *This lemon has a thick skin.* *vb.* peel, pare; flay *Skin these grapes for me, would you? The cruel pirate gave the man twenty lashes, almost skinning him alive.*

skinny *adj.* thin, scrawny, lean, gaunt, raw-boned *When Evan wears his tight jeans you can see how skinny he really is.* ANT. heavy, hefty, fat.

skip *vb.* jump, leap, spring, gambol, hop *Told she had won a new car in the draw, Hortense was skipping about the office all day.*

slack *adj.* **1** loose, lax, limp *Let the skipping rope hang slack, so that it touches the ground in the middle.* **2** lazy *Tim is very slack about getting his work done.* **3** slow, inactive, sluggish *Summer is the slack period in our business.* ANT. (1) taut, stiff, rigid. (3) active, busy.

slam *vb.* bang, push, close, fasten *Please do not slam the door when you leave.*

slander *n.* defamation, calumny, gossip, lies *The newspaper's reports about his meetings with Mrs Barfsky were pure slander.*

slang *n.* vulgarism; argot, cant; dialect, jargon *'Bog' is slang for 'lavatory'.*

slant *vb.* lean, incline, slope, tilt *Many roofs slant downwards.* *n.* **1** incline, slope, pitch *We came to a steep slant in the road and the car would go no further.* **2** angle, approach, view *I got a new slant on you when I heard you give that talk at the meeting.*

slap *vb.,n.* smack, blow, pat *I slapped him on the cheek for being naughty. He gave his friend a gentle slap on the back.*

slash *vb.* 1 slit, cut, gash *The recipe says to slash the roast in several places with a sharp knife and to insert garlic in the slits.* 2 reduce, lower, cut *Prices on clothing were slashed after Christmas.* *n.* slit, cut, gash *There were three slashes in my car tyre.*

slaughter *vb.* kill, butcher, massacre, slay *The cattle were slaughtered to produce food.* *n.* killing, butchery, butchering, massacre *We must do something to prevent the continued slaughter of wildlife.*

slave *n.* serf, vassal, captive *It was formerly common practice to make slaves of the people conquered in war.* ANT. master.

slay *vb.* kill, assassinate, murder *She was paid a huge sum in gold to slay the minister.*

sleep *vb.,n.* rest, repose, slumber, nap, snooze, doze *If you sleep too little, you're tired the next day. I had only five hours' sleep last night.*

sleepy *adj.* drowsy, tired, somnolent, fatigued *I am too sleepy to drive home.* ANT. alert, awake; energetic.

slender *adj.* slim, trim, slight, thin *One way to keep slender is to avoid overeating and to exercise.* ANT. heavy, fat, overweight.

slide *vb.* slip, glide, skid, skim *We had great fun sliding down snowy hills on an old board.*

slight *adj.* 1 small, sparse, scanty, spare *It takes only a very slight amount of insecticide to kill a fly.* 2 insignificant, unimportant, trivial *Irena has a terrible temper and gets angry at the slightest thing.* *vb.* ignore, disregard, snub, scorn *I felt slighted because I wasn't invited to the dance.* ANT. *adj.* (1) large, enormous, huge. (2) major, significant. *vb.* flatter, compliment.

slim *adj.* 1 slender, thin, slight; lank *Sophie is quite slim now that she has lost weight.* 2 small, poor, scanty, slight, weak; unimportant, insignificant *Ben stands a very slim chance of winning against Boris at chess.* ANT. (1) fat. (2) excellent.

slime *n.* mire, ooze, mud, filth *Wash the slime off your boots before setting foot in this house!*

sling *n.* bandage, dressing *Pete had his injured arm supported in a sling.* *vb.* hurl, throw, send *He slings the boomerang into the air and it returns to him.*

slip *vb.* 1 slide, glide; shift *I was about to slip off the edge of the cliff when a strong hand caught me and hauled me to safety.* 2 err, blunder *I slipped when I gave away your secret.* *n.* error, mistake, blunder *Your telling my father about where we went yesterday was an unfortunate slip.*

slipshod *adj.* careless, sloppy *The gardener has done a slipshod job of trimming this hedge.* ANT. careful.

slit *vb.* cut, slash *With one stroke, I slit open the fish.* *n.* cut, slash, slot, tear *The slit in the evening dress started at the hem and went up above the knee.*

slogan *n.* motto, cry, catchword *'Dieu et mon droit' is the slogan on the royal arms of Great Britain.*

slope *vb.,n.* incline, slant *The lawn behind my house slopes down to the river. The trees on that slope are all bent by the wind.*

slouch *vb.* droop, lounge, languish *Sit up straight and stop slouching!!*

slovenly *adj.* 1 unkempt, bedraggled, sloppy, messy *His dress was so slovenly that one would never know he's a prince.* 2 slipshod, careless, slapdash, sloppy *Katinka did a slovenly job of polishing the silver.* ANT. (1) neat. (2) meticulous.

slow *adj.* 1 unhurried, gradual, leisurely *The slow pace of life in the country is more to my liking than the hectic activity of the city.* 2 late, delayed, behindhand *My watch is five minutes slow.* 3 dull, boring, tedious *The play was very slow—I fell asleep.* *vb.* retard, hinder, obstruct, slacken *We slowed down when we came to the bend.* ANT. *adj.* (1) fast, quick. (2) fast, ahead.

sluggish *adj.* slow, lethargic, phlegmatic *When she is paid for completing a job, Mary works very fast, but she is sluggish if paid by the hour.* ANT. energetic, vivacious.

slumber *n., vb.* sleep, rest, repose *Nothing can disturb Della's slumber. Despite the noise of the bombs, Father slumbered on.*

slump *n.* decline, descent, drop, fall; depression *Business has hit a slump, I'm afraid.* *vb.* sink, decline, descend *George slumped in his chair when Bob told him he couldn't go to the match with him.* ANT. *n.* boom.

slur *vb.* 1 blur, garble, swallow *Jane is in the habit of slurring her vowels.* 2 discredit, smear, (*slang*) knock *Do you know what Tony's been saying to slur your reputation?*

sly *adj.* cunning, crafty, secretive, wily, foxy *That was a sly trick of Henry's to listen in on my phone conversation.*

smack¹ *vb.* smell, savour *The handkerchief smacked faintly of the lavender scent Olive uses.*

smack² *n.* slap, pat, spank *Shut up, or I'll give you a smack on the face.* *vb.* hit, strike, slap *Is it always good to smack a naughty child?*

small *adj.* 1 little, tiny, miniature *The watch was so small I could hardly see the face.* 2 unimportant, insignificant, minor, trivial *Whether you go to the theatre or not is a small matter to me.* ANT. (1) large, big, enormous.

smart *adj.* 1 modish, stylish; neat, tidy *Alec looks very smart in his new suit, doesn't he?* 2 clever, intelligent, bright *Donald was smart enough to get through all his exams.* *vb.* sting, hurt, burn *That witch hazel smarts when you put it on an open cut.* ANT. (1) untidy, unfashionable, dowdy. (2) stupid, slow, dumb.

smash *vb.* break, crash, crush, demolish *The car was badly smashed in the accident.* *n.* crash, shattering *I heard the smash of a pane of glass and thought it was a burglar.*

smear *vb.* 1 rub, spread, wipe *Your hands are smeared with grease from working on the car engine.* 2 slander, libel, defame *The tabloids smeared the minister in a report on his assumed treachery.*

smell *vb.* scent, sniff, detect *I can smell turkey roasting, and it's making me hungry.* *n.* **1** scent, odour, aroma, bouquet *The smell of orange blossoms filled the air.* **2** odour, stench, stink *I can't stand the smell of dead fish.*

smile *vb.,n.* grin, beam, smirk *Bill smiled when I handed him his birthday present. I can see the smile on your face when I start talking about ice creams.* ANT. scowl, frown.

smooth *adj.* even, level, flat, unwrinkled *There was no wind, and the lake was as smooth as glass. After he shaves, my father's cheek is so smooth!* *vb.* level, even, flatten, iron *Doris smoothed down the sheets on the bed before putting on the blankets.* ANT. *adj.* rough, uneven. *vb.* roughen.

smother *vb.* stifle, asphyxiate, suffocate *We were almost smothered by the smoke from the fire.*

smug *adj.* self-satisfied, complacent *Earnshaw seems very smug about winning today's chess match.* ANT. modest, shy.

snare *n.* trap, net *We set snares for the fox that was eating our chickens.* *vb.* trap, catch, capture *Dave built a large cage in which he hoped to snare a rabbit.*

snarl *vb.* **1** growl, gnarl *Our dog always snarls at the postman.* **2** tangle, ensnarl *The anchor rope is all snarled in the anchor.* ANT. (2) free, untangle, loose(n).

snatch *vb.* seize, grab, grasp *Dorothy just snatched the apple out of my hand and made away with it.*

sneak *vb.* slink, skulk, steal *Roger sneaked in when no one was looking and stole a pie.* *n.* informer, (*slang*) rat, turncoat; coward *Hugh was a sneak when he went and told teacher what I'd done.*

sneer *vb.* scorn, scoff, mock, jeer, taunt *Don't sneer at my swimming records unless you can do better.* *n.* jeer; disdain *With a sneer, Victor dismissed my attempt at drawing a plan for our new house.*

snip *vb.* cut, clip, nip *Someone has snipped the buds off all our rose bushes.*

snivelling *adj.* weepy, whining, whimpering, sniffling, blubbering *Stop that snivelling and pull yourself together!!*

snore *vb.* snort, wheeze, pant *John and Melissa cannot sleep in the same room because they keep each other awake when they snore.*

snub *vb.* slight, insult; rebuke *Mary was upset when her friends snubbed her at the party just because she was wearing a shabby dress.* *n.* slight, insult, humiliation *We all felt the snub when we weren't invited to dinner at the country club.* ANT. *vb.* accept. *n.* acceptance.

snug *adj.* **1** cosy, sheltered, comfortable *The children remained snug in bed while the storm raged outside.* **2** close-fitting, trim, tight *Don't you think that those trousers are a little snug round the hips?*

soak *vb.* drench, wet, steep, saturate *Soak that shirt overnight to remove the stain.*

soar *vb.* fly, glide, tower *High above, the hawk soared, motionless, in ever-narrowing circles.*

sob *vb.* lament, cry, weep *The boy was sobbing because the big boys had taken his ball.*

sober *adj.* 1 clearheaded, moderate *Whenever my grandfather has to drive a car, he doesn't drink and stays sober.* 2 serious, solemn, grave *The funeral service for the comedian was the only sober occasion he had ever been associated with.* ANT. (1) drunk, inebriated. (2) frivolous.

so-called *adj.* supposed, alleged *They enjoy visiting Blackpool, amusing themselves along the so-called Golden Mile.*

sociable *adj.* social, friendly, affable *The people I spoke with at the party seemed very sociable and outgoing.* ANT. antisocial, unfriendly.

social *adj.* 1 group, human, common *The country has many social problems in the area of community health.* 2 friendly, genial, sociable *All our neighbours are quite social and we spend a lot of time together.*

society *n.* 1 community, civilization, nation *Society's problems, like having enough food for everyone, cannot be solved easily or quickly.* 2 club, organization, association, circle, group *My mother is a member of two professional medical societies.* 3 association, companionship, company *I enjoy the society of people everywhere in the world.*

soft *adj.* 1 flexible, pliable, pliant; elastic *This clay is soft enough now for you to mould a figure out of it.* 2 smooth, velvety, satiny *My kitten's fur is so soft!* 3 quiet, low, gentle *The girl was singing in a soft voice.* ANT. (1) hard, rigid. (2) rough, abrasive. (3) harsh, raucous, shrill.

soften *vb.* moderate, mellow, weaken *George softened a bit in his attitudes as he grew older.*

soil *n.* earth, loam, dirt *You'll need more soil to plant that flower in such a large pot.* *vb.* dirty, stain, spot *Badly soiled clothes should be allowed to soak for a while before washing.*

sole *adj.* single, only, exclusive *The sole reason I came was to chat with you.*

solemn *adj.* 1 serious, sober, grave *The partners make solemn promises in the marriage ceremony.* 2 formal, dignified, important *The coronation of the monarch is a most solemn occasion.* ANT. (1) lighthearted, frivolous; merry.

solicit *vb.* request, seek, pray, beg, beseech *The candidates made many speeches to solicit votes from the constituency.*

solid *adj.* 1 firm, compact, hard, dense *The ball was made out of solid rubber.* 2 three-dimensional *A solid steel rod holds the door closed.* 3 unmixed, plain *Should I wear the solid green shirt or the check?* 4 reliable, trustworthy; sensible *I know that James is a solid type of person.* ANT. (1) hollow. (2) flat, thin, two-dimensional. (4) unreliable, untrustworthy; dishonest.

solitary *adj.* isolated, lonely, deserted; sole, only, single *A solitary tree remained standing after the hurricane.*

solution *n.* answer, explanation *The solution to the crossword puzzle will be published tomorrow.*

solve *vb.* answer, unravel, explain *When they identified the fingerprints, the detectives thought they had solved the case.*

sombre *adj.* 1 serious, sober, grave, gloomy, dismal *The sun hasn't shone for so many days that I am in a very sombre mood.* 2 dismal, mournful, sad, melancholy *The funeral was a sombre event.* ANT. (1) happy, cheerful.

sometimes *adv.* occasionally, now and then, at times *Sometimes, on a hot day, I enjoy an ice lolly.* ANT. always, invariably.

soon *adv.* shortly, in a little while, before long *The bus will come along soon, I hope.*

soothe *vb.* calm, pacify, comfort, quiet *Do you find that loud rock music soothing?* ANT. disquiet, upset, unnerve.

sordid *adj.* foul, dirty, filthy, unclean *The poor live in the most sordid surroundings.*

sore *adj.* aching, painful, hurting, tender, sensitive *My finger is still sore where I caught it in the door yesterday.* *n.* cut, bruise, burn, wound, injury *I have a sore on my knee where I scraped it playing games.*

sorrow *n.* sadness, grief, misery, anguish, depression *Sorrow hung over the country like a pall after the assassination of the president.* *vb.* mourn, grieve, lament *We tried to console the sorrowing family.*

sorrowful *adj.* sad, unhappy, melancholy, depressed *The cancellation of the school play was a sorrowful moment for all of us.*

sorry *adj.* 1 apologetic; remorseful, repentant *I'm sorry if I hurt your feelings, for I didn't mean to.* 2 pitiful, wretched, poor, paltry; shabby *She is in a sorry state having lost her husband.*

sort *n.* kind, variety, type *What sort of a dog did you get for your birthday?* *vb.* separate, classify, arrange, order *Please sort these words into alphabetical order.*

so-so *adj.* mediocre, middling, fair, *comme ci, comme ça,* OK, all right *After a very rough Channel crossing, we felt only so-so.*

sound[1] *n.* noise; din, racket *The silence was so great that we could hear the sound of a pin drop.* *vb.* echo, resound *The fire alarm sounded throughout the building.*

sound[2] *adj.* 1 secure, safe, uninjured, unharmed, whole, healthy *We returned home during the storm, safe and sound.* 2 trustworthy, reliable; sensible *I think we can rely on Philip's judgement to be sound.*

sour *adj.* 1 acid, tart *Those lemon sweets are so sour they make my mouth pucker up.* 2 bad-tempered, unpleasant, cross *That old man certainly has a sour disposition—he doesn't like anyone or anything.* ANT. (1) sweet. (2) good-natured, sunny, benevolent.

source *n.* origin, beginning *The source of this stream is a spring high in the mountains.*

souvenir *n.* memento, keepsake *I have a tiny silver Eiffel Tower as a souvenir of my trip to Paris.*

sovereign *n.* ruler, lord; monarch, king, queen, emperor, empress *Queen Elizabeth II is the sovereign of Great Britain.* *adj.* supreme, chief, principal *Freedom of speech is a sovereign right of our people.*

sow *vb.* scatter, plant, propagate *Carver is sowing the seeds of dissension among his classmates.*

space *n.* **1** area, location, room *Please put the desk into the open space against that wall.* **2** cosmos, galaxy, outer space *The Americans launched a further rocket into space.*

spacious *adj.* roomy, large *The corridor was spacious enough to drive a coach and four through it.* ANT. cramped, small, narrow, confined.

span *n.* extent, spread *This history book covers a span of four centuries.* *vb.* extend, reach, cross *The bridge spans the river about a kilometre north of here.*

spare *vb.* **1** save, set aside *or* apart, reserve *The police detective was able to spare just fifteen minutes to talk with our class.* **2** save; forgive; show mercy to *Because the robber was a great musician, the king spared his life.* *adj.* extra, additional, unoccupied *I think we can find a spare tennis racquet that you can borrow for today.*

sparing *adj.* frugal, thrifty, economical, parsimonious *While father was ill, we had to be very sparing in what we spent for food.* ANT. lavish, generous.

spark *n.* flash, glint; glitter, sparkle *Though they hadn't met for years, I saw a spark of recognition when they saw one another.*

sparkle *vb.* **1** shine, glisten, glitter, twinkle *The sea sparkled in the bright sunlight.* **2** bubble, effervesce *I like sparkling water with my dinner.* *n.* **1** shine, glitter, twinkle *The sparkle of the glasses caught my eye.* **2** spirit, liveliness, brilliance *Valerie's personality lent sparkle to the party.*

sparse *adj.* scanty, few, rare, scattered *The sparse vegetation was inadequate to support the cattle.* ANT. dense.

spasm *n.* convulsion, fit, attack, seizure *When the spasms increased in frequency, we phoned the doctor.*

speak *vb.* say, talk, utter; address *It is wrong to speak evil of people, especially behind their backs.*

special *adj.* **1** exceptional, unusual, extraordinary, distinguished, different *We have reserved this jewellery for our special customers only.* **2** particular, distinct, certain *I have made special plans to spend this weekend in the country.* ANT. (1) average, ordinary.

specialist *n.* expert, authority *You ought to have specialist examine your horse's fetlock.*

specific *adj.* definite, particular, distinct, precise *Is there a specific reason why I must wear red socks to your party?* ANT. general, nonspecific, vague.

specification *n.* description, designation, condition *If you provide the specifications for the gear, our plant can make it.*

specify *vb.* designate, name, define *The teacher specified which children would have extra work to do.*

specimen *n.* sample, example, model, type, pattern *The doctor took a blood specimen to test for various diseases.*

speck *n.* bit, spot; mite *I don't want to see a speck of food left on your plate!!*

spectacle *n.* show, scene, exhibition, display *Matilda certainly made a spectacle of herself at last night's dance.*

spectator *n.* watcher, viewer, observer, onlooker *At the golf tournament, a ball hit one of the spectators.* ANT. participant, player, contestant.

spectre *n.* ghost, phantom, apparition *Out of the gloom appeared a spectre of immense proportions, chilling me to the bone.*

speculate *vb.* guess, consider, surmise, view, suppose, theorize *You cannot speculate about the date of the document—it appears at the very beginning.*

speech *n.* **1** talk, address, oration, lecture, sermon *The MP gave a speech on the steps of the town hall.* **2** utterance, articulation, diction, accent, pronunciation, enunciation *From your speech I can tell that you come from Scotland.*

speed *n.* **1** rapidity, swiftness, haste *I could see that the girl hadn't eaten for a long time by the speed with which she gulped her food.* **2** velocity *The speed of the train decreased as it came into the station.*

spell *n.* **1** formula, incantation, enchantment *The witch cast a spell on the poor little girl.* **2** period, time, term, stretch *We had several spells of cold weather last winter.*

spellbound *adj.* entranced, fascinated, hypnotized, mesmerized, rapt *Richard could keep an audience spellbound for hours.*

spend *vb.* **1** pay, expend, lay out *I spent much too much money on that tie.* **2** use up, consume *I wish you wouldn't spend so much time watching television.* ANT. (1) save, hoard.

spendthrift *n.* wastrel, squanderer, profligate *Jean-Paul will soon be poor if he continues being such a spendthrift.*

sphere *n.* **1** ball, orb, globe *In nature, many objects have the form of a sphere.* **2** area, field, environment, domain *In my sphere of work, one must study for many years to become an expert.*

spice *n.* seasoning, condiment, flavouring, herb *This dish is too bland and needs a lot of spice.*

spicy *adj.* off-colour, risqué, indecent, suggestive, indelicate *Please don't let Harold tell any of his spicy stories in my aunt's presence.*

spike *n.* pin, nail, prong, point *The tent rope was tied to a spike driven into the ground.*

spill *vb.* scatter, drop; let go *I have spilt the sugar all over the floor.*

spin *vb.* **1** turn, revolve, whirl, rotate, twirl *When we were children, we used to spin our tops and try to do tricks with them.* **2** narrate, tell, relate *At night the old men would get together at the club to spin tales of long ago.*

spine *n.* backbone, spinal column *The term 'vertebrate' refers to animals that have spines.*

spineless *adj.* weak, feeble, limp; cowardly *That spineless poltroon deserted his men and left them to die.* ANT. strong, brave, courageous.

spirit *n.* 1 mood, attitude, outlook, feeling *Jim has been in very low spirits since his older brother went away to college.* 2 vitality, liveliness, energy *It takes a lot of spirit for an invalid like Betsy to remain cheerful.* 3 angel, fairy, devil, elf, sprite, goblin, demon *In the old days, many people blamed evil spirits for their own mistakes.* 4 ghost, phantom, spectre *That house—the deserted one—is inhabited by spirits.* 5 meaning, intention, intent *There is often a difference between the letter of the law and the spirit of the law.* 6 will; soul *After your body dies, the spirit still exists.*

spirited *adj.* animated, excited, active, lively, energetic, vigorous. ANT. lazy,indolent, sleepy.

spiritual *adj.* 1 immaterial, intangible; otherworldly *Spiritual beings are active in the world, although you cannot see them.* 2 religious, holy, consecrated *Gerald is very spiritual: he follows God's will in every way.* ANT. (1) material, physical, tangible.

spite *n.* malice, contempt, resentment *Margaret punctured your bicycle tyres purely out of spite.* ANT. goodwill, affection.

splash *vb.* spatter; dash, break *Don't you love to watch the sea splashing on the rocks at the bottom of the cliff?*

splendid *adj.* 1 magnificent, brilliant, gorgeous, sumptuous, elegant, luxurious *The king ordered the craftsmen to create splendid furnishings for the palace.* 2 excellent, superb, superior *That's a splendid painting of the Grand Canal in Venice.*

splendour *n.* magnificence, grandeur, display, brilliance *The splendour of the civilization of ancient Greece will never again be seen.*

splinter *n.* sliver, chip, piece, fragment *Be careful with that board or you'll get a splinter in your finger.* *vb.* split, shiver *The glass splintered into a thousand pieces when it dropped on the floor.*

split *vb.* divide, break, separate *Let's split the chocolate bar among the three of us. If you hammer a wedge into the crack in that log, it will split easily.* *n.* crack, opening *The split in the wood was repaired by the carpenter.*

splutter *vb.* stutter, stammer *In reply to the policeman's question, Gerald could hardly splutter out that he had been at the cinema.*

spoil *vb.* 1 damage, ruin, destroy *I left my painting out in the rain and it's completely spoiled.* 2 rot, go bad *If you leave milk out of the refrigerator too long it will spoil.*

spoken *adj.* oral, articulated, said, pronounced, uttered, vocal *The tapes contain a record of the spoken testimony, but the documents are at the library.*

spokesman *n.*   representative, agent *David has been elected to act as the spokesman for all of us.*

sponge *vb.*   mop, wipe, swab *Get some rags to sponge up this mess.*

sponsor *n.*   patron, supporter, promoter *Calisco Toys have agreed to be sponsors of our Christmas pageant.*

spontaneous *adj.*   natural, voluntary, unconscious, unplanned, spur-of-the-moment *Lending me your skates was a spontaneous act of friendship that I shall not forget.* ANT. studied, cautious.

sport *n.*   1 game, play, recreation *I play football for sport.*   2 mockery, jest, joke ridicule *You are making sport of me when you say I'm the greatest singer you've ever heard.*

sporting *adj.*   fair, considerate, sportsmanlike *Big-game hunters were not known for giving their quarry a sporting chance.*

spot *n.*   1 mark, blemish, blot, stain, flaw, speck *I wouldn't go near Peter—he has spots all over his face.*   2 place, location, site *We have built our new home in a beautiful spot right near the lake.*   *vb.* 1 mark, stain, blot, spatter *You've splashed tomato juice everywhere and have spotted the clean tablecloth.*   2 locate, find *I spotted you in the school photograph even though it was taken years ago.*

spotless *adj.*   immaculate, clean, unsullied *Garmont came out of ten years in the army with a spotless record.* ANT. dirty, impure.

spotty *adj.*   uneven, erratic, inconsistent, irregular *Eric's performance on the parallel bars has been spotty, and he'll have to perfect it if he is to qualify.* ANT. even, regular, reliable, steady.

spout *vb.*   squirt, spurt *The lava could be seen spouting out of the volcano from far away.*   *n.* nozzle, tube *The water comes out of the green spout and the milk out of the white one.*

sprawl *vb.*   lounge, relax, slouch, spread, loll, sit, rest *It is amusing to see our three cats sprawled out on the rug before the fire.*

spray *n.*   spatter; splash *There was a fine spray of cologne from the top of the bottle.*   *vb.* sprinkle, spatter, splash *I sprayed the roses with a fluid that would keep off the bugs.*

spread *vb.*   1 distribute; disperse *The icing must be spread evenly over the top of the cake before serving.*   2 open, unfurl, unroll, unfold *I helped to spread the sails on the lawn so they could dry in the sun.*   3 scatter *The news about the fire spread throughout the town.*   *n.* 1 extent, range; diffusion *The spread of nuclear weapons is terrifying.*   2 jam, jelly, preserve, conserve *I like to put a spread on hot toast after it has been buttered.*

sprightly *adj.*   spry, lively, vivacious, nimble *That sprightly old lady of ninety-two goes out dancing?*

spring *vb.*   1 leap, bound, jump *I sprang to my feet when the teacher entered the room.*   2 start, begin, arise, originate *Dave's eagerness to help with the cooking springs from his wish to be closer to the food.*   *n.* 1 leap, jump, bound *With one spring the cat was out of the door and scurrying down the hall.*   2 source; origin *This stream is fed by a spring in the mountains.*

sprinkle *vb.*   scatter, spread, strew *Sprinkle the pancake lightly with* *powdered sugar.* *n.* scattering, rain; drizzle *We were getting wet in the sprinkle that came from the garden hose.*

sprint *vb.* dash, rush, race *When the police siren was heard, the thief ran out the door and sprinted down the street.*

sprout *vb.* grow, develop *Restaurants serving nouvelle cuisine seem to be sprouting up everywhere.*

spry *adj.* lively, nimble, quick, alert, agile, energetic *Robert is quite spry for a man of eighty-seven.* ANT. inactive, lethargic.

spur *n.* goad; stimulus *The will to win is a spur to athletes to do their very best in competitive sports.* *vb.* goad, stimulate, urge *Thoughts of a warm fire spurred us on as we trudged home through the snow.*

spurious *adj.* unreal, fake, counterfeit *It was my job to sort the spurious coins from the real ones.* ANT. real, genuine.

spy *n.* informer, secret agent, agent *The spies were shot as soon as they were caught, even without a trial.* *vb.* watch, observe, pry *'Stop spying on me,' John told his younger brother.*

squabble *vb.* quarrel, argue, bicker, wrangle, row *How can you waste time by squabbling over whose hair is longer?* *n.* quarrel, row, argument, dispute *For forty years she has been having squabbles with her neighbour about which one of them owns that tree.*

squalid *adj.* filthy, dirty; foul *It is terrible that some people have to continue to live in such squalid surroundings.*

squander *vb.* waste, throw away, lavish, fritter away *Arthur squandered the fortune his father left him and is virtually poverty-stricken.*

squat *vb.* crouch, stoop *The young children squatted on the floor.* *adj.* thickset, stubby, dumpy; compact *Some modern squat chairs are not very comfortable.*

squeak *vb.,n.* cry, creak, squeal *The hinges of the door squeaked and I knew someone was approaching. The squeak of the mouse frightened us all.*

squeeze *vb.* pinch, clasp, press *Why did you have to squeeze my arm so hard?*

stab *vb.* pierce, gore, stick, spear; knife, bayonet *In the scuffle with the robbers, one man was stabbed in the leg.*

stable *adj.* steady, firm, robust, sturdy, steadfast, solid *The platform is not very stable and might give way at any moment.* ANT. unstable, shaky.

stack *n.* pile, mound, heap, mass *There's a big stack of firewood if you want to make a fire.* *vb.* pile, heap, accumulate *Please try to stack those stones more neatly next time.*

staff *n.* 1 stick, pole, club *Little John always carried his staff with him and used it as a weapon.* 2 employees, personnel, help, crew *The company has a skilled staff of thirty-five people at the main office.*

stage *n.* 1 theatre *When I was younger, I wanted to go on the stage, but I couldn't act well enough, so now I'm a star on television.* 2 phase, step, period *The project has reached a stage where we need* *more people right away.* *vb.* produce, direct; present, put on *Our school staged the musical comedy* The Boy Friend *this year.*

stagger *vb.* 1 sway, totter, reel, falter *Here comes Freddie, staggering down the street as if he'd been hit on the head.* 2 vary, alternate *If you could stagger your working days and your days off, you could get some rest.*

stagnant *adj.* still, dead; foul, filthy *The only water available was from a stagnant pool in the road.*

stain *n.* 1 spot, blemish, blot, mark *There's a big stain on your collar—it looks like blood.* 2 disgrace, smirch, blot *It will take many weeks of very good behaviour, Roberto, to clear up that stain on your record.* *vb.* 1 spot, blot, mark *You've stained the tablecloth with ketchup!* 2 tint, dye, colour *The cabinet-maker stained the wood a very dark mahogany.*

stair(s) *n.* stairway, flight of stairs, staircase, steps *The coat cupboard is under the stairs.*

stake *n.* 1 post, stick, pole, pale, picket, rod *The hunters tied the goat to a stake in the clearing to act as bait for the tiger.* 2 wager, bet *The stakes are too high for me to play poker with those men.* 3 interest, concern *I bought a stake in a silver mine but I lost everything.*

stale *adj.* 1 old, spoiled, dry; inedible *We break up any stale bread we have and feed it to the birds.* 2 uninteresting, flat, dull, trite *We had to sit through dinner listening politely and laughing whenever Bill told another of his stale jokes.* **ANT. (1)** fresh, new.

stalk¹ *vb.* follow, dog, pursue, shadow, track, hunt *Have you ever stalked a tiger in the jungles of India?*

stalk² *n.* stem, shaft *The stalks of the plants are now growing rapidly.*

stall *vb.* stop; hesitate, postpone, delay *My car keeps stalling in the middle of traffic.* *n.* stand, booth, kiosk *Sheila manned the cake stall at the fair.*

stammer *vb.* stutter; falter, hem and haw *Stop stammering and tell me where you've hidden the key!*

stamp *vb.* 1 trample, crush *Our guests stamped all over our newly seeded lawn and ruined it completely.* 2 brand, mark, imprint *Ellie stamped her name all over my shirt and I can't wash it out.* *n.* die, block, seal *My father gave me a rubber stamp with my name and address on it.*

stand *vb.* 1 rise, arise, stand up *Please stand when the band plays the national anthem.* 2 remain, stay *My original instructions still stand.* 3 tolerate, endure, abide, bear *I can't stand listening to rock 'n' roll all day long.* *vb.phr.* **stand down** resign *When are you going to stand down so I can take over?* **stand for** represent *This symbol stands for good quality.* **stand out** be prominent *The high buildings stood out in the landscape.* *n.* 1 position, attitude, opinion *His stand on the issue is that anyone who goes on strike ought to be fired.* 2 table, platform *The vase was knocked off that wooden stand in the corner.* **ANT.** *vb.* **(1)** lie, recline, repose.

standard *n.* 1 measure, gauge, example, model, criterion *Some peo-*

ple think that the standard for judging right and wrong depends on each situation. **2** banner, pennant, flag, emblem, symbol *In the ancient Roman army, the man who carried the legion's standard was very important.* *adj.* basic, typical, approved, official, regular *Light bulbs are manufactured in a few standard sizes to fit sockets.* **ANT.** *adj.* unusual, irregular, special.

standing *n.* position, rank, status, station *Because of his standing in the community, no one suspected Sir Leonard of being a drug dealer.*

standpoint *n.* viewpoint, position, attitude *Perhaps, from the standpoint of the animals in the zoo, it is the people who are being kept out.*

staple *adj.* principal, main, chief, necessary, essential *Bread is a staple food in most diets.*

stare *vb.* gaze, watch; gape *The crowd just stared as the two gigantic wrestlers battled it out in the ring.*

stark *adj.* **1** absolute, utter, complete, sheer *The stark truth is that your son did chop down the cherry tree, Mrs Washington.* **2** harsh, severe, rough, grim *The stark countryside was uninviting during the winter.*

start *vb.* **1** begin, commence, initiate *I wish you hadn't started Grandpa off on his storytelling—now he'll never stop.* **2** jump, jerk; twitch *Oh! You made me start! I didn't know anyone was here.* *n.* **1** beginning, commencement, outset, onset *At the start of a race no one knows who will win.* **2** shock, surprise *You gave me quite a start, peering in the window wearing that spooky mask!* **3** lead, head start, advantage *I have a start on the rest of the class because I've already read this book.*

startle *vb.* surprise; shock, alarm *The sudden banging on the door at midnight startled me.*

starve *vb.* *Informal:* be hungry, be famished: *I'm starving—is it time for lunch yet?*

state *n.* **1** nation, country *What were once colonies in Africa have mostly all now become independent states.* **2** condition, status; situation *The doctor told us that the state of the family's health is excellent.* *vb.* declare, say, assert, express; tell *For the second time in one hour, Mornie stated why she had come to see the show.*

stately *adj.* grand, dignified, imposing, elegant, impressive, majestic, magnificent *Mrs Thistlebotham is a stately dowager who resides in that large home overlooking the river.* **ANT.** mean, base, squalid.

statement *n.* **1** announcement, declaration, assertion *The minister issued a statement to the press after his trip abroad.* **2** account, record *The bank send me a statement regularly.*

station *n.* depot, post; stopping place *The police station is open twenty-four hours a day. I got on the bus at the bus station.* *vb.* place, position, put, locate *The colonel stationed eight men to stand guard duty last night.*

stationary *adj.* still, motionless, fixed *The main pier is stationary,* *but there are several floating docks alongside it.* ANT. mobile, movable.

statistics *n.pl.* data, figures, tables *The statistics will show how many people are in favour of and how many are against the new regulations.*

statue *n.* figure, bust, sculpture *Statues of Stalin have been torn down all over the Soviet Union.*

status *n.* rank, position, standing *What is the status of my request for a transfer? Because of John's status in the town, the police are reluctant to arrest him.*

statute *n.* law, rule, ruling, ordinance *There is a statute calling for a severe fine if your dog fouls the footway.*

staunch *adj.* firm, steadfast, loyal *We have always been staunch supporters of the local football club.*

stay *vb.* 1 remain, rest, tarry, linger *Please stay where you are for a moment.* 2 remain, continue *Do you stay happy all the time?* 3 delay, check, hinder, halt, hold *The judge stayed the execution of the convicted murderer because new evidence had been discovered.* *n.* 1 stop, hindrance, halt, delay *On Christmas Eve, a stay of execution saved six men who were to die the following week.* 2 brace, support; rope, line *When the stay snapped, the mast broke in two and we radioed for help.* ANT. *vb.* (1) go, leave, depart.

steady *adj.* 1 even, regular, stable, unremitting *A steady rain fell throughout the day.* 2 firm, steadfast, reliable *We need a steady hand at the helm if this boat is to sail across the Atlantic.* 3 firm, solid, stable *That wobbly little table isn't steady enough for the typewriter.*

steal *vb.* 1 take, pilfer, rob, shoplift, embezzle *Binks stole a dog biscuit and ran out into the yard to eat it.* 2 sneak, prowl *Dressed in black from head to toe, the thief silently stole down the hall towards the strongroom.*

stealthy *adj.* secret, sly, furtive *One robber gave a stealthy sign to his accomplice, who promptly subdued the guard.* ANT. open, direct, obvious.

steep *adj.* sheer, perpendicular, abrupt, sudden *The climbers are now moving up the steep face of the cliff.* ANT. gradual.

steer *vb.* guide, direct; navigate; drive *The pilot was steering the aeroplane right into the side of a mountain.*

stem *n.* trunk; stalk *The stems of the plants were so thick I couldn't cut them.* *vb.* 1 arise, originate *Some of the problems in schools stem from a shortage of money.* 2 stop, check, hinder, halt *We must do something to stem the tide of crime in the area.*

stench *n.* stink, fetor; smell *The stench from that sewer is overpowering.*

step *n.* 1 pace, stride *All those who want to go on the outing should take one step forward.* 2 action, move, measure *It was essential that we take steps to make certain the bank was locked up.* 3 stage *What's the next step in the process?* *vb.* walk, move, come, go

Please step this way if you want to watch the sea lions being fed.
vb.phr. **step up** *Informal:* increase, accelerate *You must step up your rate of work.*

sterile *adj.* infertile, impotent, barren *These hybrids are sterile and cannot produce offspring.* ANT. fertile.

stern *adj.* strict, severe, harsh, hard, rigid, unyielding *Our teacher is very stern with students who have not done their homework.* ANT. lenient, forgiving.

stew *n.* goulash, ragout *Mother made lamb stew for dinner.* *vb.* simmer, seethe, boil *You have to stew this kind of meat for three hours before you can chew it. You may think that Donald is not upset, but he's stewing about something.*

stick *n.* twig, stalk, branch, staff, rod, pole *I poked a wooden stick through a hole in the fence and something grabbed the other end of it.* *vb.* **1** stab, pierce, puncture, spear, gore *Get a needle—Gary has a splinter stuck in his finger.* **2** catch, adhere, hold, cling *Chewing gum was stuck to the bottom of my shoe.* **3** remain, abide, stay, persist; be faithful *No matter what you say, I'll stick by you.*

stickler *n.* perfectionist, nitpicker *The colonel is a stickler for regulations, so you'd better be on time.*

sticky *adj.* ticklish, tricky, awkward, delicate *Things got a bit sticky when Froggie and his girlfriend ran into his wife at the hotel.*

stiff *adj.* **1** rigid, unbendable, inflexible, firm, solid, hard *My mittens were frozen stiff, and I couldn't get them off.* **2** severe, harsh, strong *Ten years is a very stiff sentence.* **3** difficult, arduous *We had a very stiff exam at school today.* ANT. (1) limp, lax. (2) lenient. (3) easy, simple.

stiffen *vb.* thicken, harden *Do not remove the brace for the stanchion till the concrete has stiffened.*

stifle *vb.* smother, suffocate, strangle, choke, throttle *The children stifled their laughter when the teacher's hairpiece fell off.*

stigma *n.* mark, stain, blot, blemish *Arrest for drunken driving can put a permanent stigma on your licence.*

still *adj.* **1** motionless, stationary *Please be still while I try to bandage your finger.* **2** tranquil, peaceful, calm, serene *The room was so still you could hear a pin drop.* *conj.* but, nevertheless, however; besides *I realize that you have a job; still, you ought to continue your studies.* *vb.* **1** silence, quiet, hush *The crowd had to be stilled so that we could hear the speaker.* **2** calm, soothe, pacify *My fears for Ruth's safety weren't stilled until I learned that she'd arrived home.* *n.* stillness, quiet, calm, hush *Only a dog's barking broke the still of the night.* ANT. *adj.* (1) mobile. (2) noisy. *n.* noise.

stilted *adj.* forced, laboured, heavy, awkward *Penelope seems very stilted and not at all relaxed when she meets new people.*

stimulate *vb.* arouse, activate, excite, urge, animate; invigorate *Jan finds an ice-cold shower quite stimulating in the morning.*

sting *vb.* tingle, prick; burn, smart *My face still stings where Minerva slapped me for saying something rude.*

stingy *adj.* miserly, mean, tightfisted, penny-pinching, mingy, selfish *Ebenezer was so stingy that he gave his employees only Christmas Day as a holiday.* ANT. generous, openhanded, giving.

stink *vb.* smell, reek *After that bout with the skunk, our dog came home stinking to high heaven.* *n.* smell, stench, reek, odour *The stink of the mouldy food filled the kitchen.*

stint *n.* job, work, task, assignment *Kenneth completes his stint at the charity shop every Saturday morning.*

stir *vb.* **1** mix, beat, agitate *Adele puts five spoons of sugar into her coffee and then doesn't stir it.* **2** arouse, rouse, stimulate; move *The leader's patriotic speech really stirred his listeners.*

stitch *see* **sew**.

stock *n.* supply, store *The shop bought an ample stock of decorations for sale before Christmas.* *vb.* store, supply, keep, carry *The salesman told me that they didn't stock every size of shoe in that style.*

stone *n.* pebble, cobble; rock, boulder *The wall is made of stones set into concrete.*

stony *adj.* cold, unsentimental, insensitive *The giant's stony heart melted and he let the children play in his garden.*

stoop *vb.* bend, lean, bow, crouch *The man stooped to pick up the coins that had fallen from his pocket.*

stop *vb.* **1** cease, conclude, end, finish *I wish you'd stop calling me Bill: my name happens to be George.* **2** halt, stay, pause *When I heard footsteps behind me I started running and didn't stop till I was safe at home.* **3** intercept, obstruct, hold *Stop that man! He stole my purse!* *n.* **1** halt, end *You must put a stop to copying your homework from others.* **2** stay, delay, halt *The train makes a stop at Watford to let off passengers.*

stopgap *n.* substitute, makeshift, expedient *Tom borrowed a wheel from my car as a stopgap when two of his tyres went flat.*

store *n.* **1** shop, market *If you go to the store, please buy some eggs.* **2** supply, reserve, stock, deposit *There is a large store of food in the company's warehouse.* *vb.* keep, preserve, stock, save *My aunt stores tins in her larder for years.*

storey *n.* level, floor *Sheri lives on the tenth storey in one of those high-rise blocks of flats.*

storm *n.* tempest; gale, thunderstorm *In the middle of the storm, all of the lights went out when the house was struck by lightning.* *vb.* **1** rage, rant *Father went storming about the house because he couldn't find his slippers.* **2** attack, besiege, assault *The army stormed the enemy camp by night.*

story *n.* **1** tale, narrative, anecdote *Grandpa used to tell us funny stories at bedtime.* **2** lie, fabrication, fib *You have to learn not to tell such stories or no one will believe you when you tell the truth.*

stout *adj.* **1** fat, obese, overweight, plump, heavy, portly *If you make* *fun of someone who is stout, you might hurt his feelings.* **2** strong, sturdy *They tied up the prisoners with some stout twine and then called the police.* ANT. (1) slim, thin, skinny, lean. (2) flimsy.

straight *adj.* **1** direct, uncurving *Motorways have many straight sections.* **2** honest, upright, honourable, moral *Alan is one of the straightest people I know.* **3** orderly, tidy *Please try to keep your room straight.* *adv.* directly *You must come straight home from school today for your piano lesson.* ANT. *adj.* (1) crooked, twisted.

straightforward *adj.* direct, forthright, candid, open, aboveboard, frank *Be straightforward with me and say exactly what you think.* ANT. devious.

strain *vb.* **1** stretch, tighten *We strained the rope trying to pull the car out of the ditch.* **2** injure, harm, sprain *Bend at the knees to lift something heavy or you'll strain your back.* **3** filter, screen, sift *Strain the tea before serving it.*

strainer *n.* sieve, colander, filter *To remove any small bones, put the soup through a strainer.*

strait *n.* **1** channel, passage *Do you know where the Strait of Magellan is? I don't.* **2** (usually **straits**) difficulty, trouble, distress, crisis *The family has been in dire straits since Peter's father lost his job.*

stranded *adj.* abandoned, helpless *Selkirk was left stranded on a desert island for organizing the mutiny.*

strange *adj.* **1** odd, peculiar, unusual, curious, extraordinary, queer, bizarre *A small man, wearing strange silvery clothes, stepped out of the spaceship.* **2** foreign, unfamiliar, exotic *A strange odour lingered in the room after our mysterious visitor left.* ANT. (1) common, ordinary. (2) familiar, everyday.

stranger *n.* foreigner, alien, outsider *The people in this village seem to be wary of strangers.* ANT. friend, acquaintance.

strangle *vb.* throttle, choke, suffocate *Her attacker tried to strangle her but she broke his hold and screamed for help.*

strap *n.* belt, strip, band, thong *The catch on my suitcase broke, so I bound it with a leather strap.*

stratagem *n.* ruse, subterfuge, trick, wile *What stratagem will they use next to lure me into telling them the secret?*

strategy *n.* management; technique, approach, tactics *We must use the proper strategy to persuade the teacher to let us out early.*

stray *vb.* wander, rove, roam *The horse broke its tether and strayed off into the woods.* *adj.* lost, strayed *The dog was trained to find and return stray sheep to the farm.*

stream *n.* **1** brook, run, creek, rivulet, river *In the winter, the stream near our house froze over.* **2** flow, rush, torrent *A stream of abuse from the audience greeted the discredited leader when he rose to speak.* *vb.* flow, rush, pour, gush *Tears streamed down the girl's face.*

street *n.* road, way; avenue, boulevard *The street on which we live is lined with trees.*

strength *n.* **1** power, vigour, might *Sally's father showed off his* *strength by crushing a brick with his bare hands.* 2 durability, soundness *For its weight aluminium has remarkable strength.* ANT. (1) weakness, frailty.

strengthen *vb.* reinforce, fortify *While you recuperate, you must exercise to strengthen your muscles.*

strenuous *adj.* energetic, forceful, vigorous, active, determined *We made a strenuous effort to move the tree that was blocking the road.*

stress *vb.* emphasize, accent, accentuate *The minister said that he couldn't stress the importance of honesty enough.* *n.* 1 emphasis, accent, weight, importance *In my day, great stress was laid on a classical and literary education.* 2 pressure, strain *The stress on the cable was too great and it gave way.*

stretch *vb.* 1 extend, elongate, lengthen *The rope cannot be stretched to go around the package twice.* 2 expand, spread, extend *I can't wear that sweater because it's stretched out of shape.* *n.* extent, range *I had a long stretch in Germany—I was there for twenty years.* ANT. *vb.* contract, shrink.

strict *adj.* stern, unbending, inflexible, stiff, harsh *There are strict laws against parking in the main square.* ANT. lenient, easygoing.

stride *n.* walk, step, pace, gait *The major took large strides along the road.* *vb.* march, trudge; walk *We strode over the fields at a steady pace.*

strife *n.* conflict, disagreement, discord, difference, quarrel, unrest *Because of the current strife in the Middle East, travellers are forbidden to go there.* ANT. peace, tranquillity, concord.

strike *vb.* 1 hit, beat *The detective knocked the man down by striking him on the jaw with his fist.* 2 attack, assault *The commandos strike at dawn.* 3 impress, affect, overwhelm *I was struck by the similarity between the two books.* *n.* walkout, sit-down *The entire staff went out on strike for longer hours and less pay.*

stringent *adj.* rigorous, harsh, severe, uncompromising *The regulations have become more stringent since the new manager was hired.*

strip *vb.* 1 undress, disrobe *The doctor's nurse told me to strip for the examination.* 2 uncover, peel, remove *That test was as easy as stripping the skin from a banana.* *n.* band, piece, ribbon *I cut a strip of cloth to use as a bandage.*

strive *vb.* try, attempt, endeavour *I was striving to throw a rope to the man caught in the quicksand.*

stroke *n.* 1 blow, knock, tap, rap *The huge man knocked down the tree with one stroke of his axe.* 2 achievement, accomplishment, feat *Starting a restaurant in the country was a stroke of genius.* *vb.* touch, smooth, rub; caress, pet *The vet stroked the dog to calm it.*

stroll *vb.,n.* walk, amble, ramble, saunter *The robber casually strolled into the bank. We went for a stroll along the river before dinner.*

strong *adj.* 1 powerful, mighty; brawny, muscular *The man in the circus is strong enough to pick up an elephant.* 2 solid, resistant, unbreakable *The glass in the windscreen is almost strong enough to* *resist the blow of a hammer.* **3** sharp, spicy, hot; aromatic *The flavour of this dish is strong enough—don't add any more pepper.* ANT. (1) feeble,weak. (2) fragile. (3) bland, tasteless.

structure *n.* framework, construction, arrangement *The building's structure is supposed to withstand an earthquake.*

struggle *vb.* fight, strive, oppose *The two men struggled for possession of the gun.* *n.* **1** fight, encounter, clash, battle, conflict *At the end of the struggle thousands lay wounded on the battlefield.* **2** effort, exertion *It's a struggle getting up on time every day.*

stubborn *adj.* obstinate, unyielding, inflexible, rigid, unbending *Don't be so stubborn about learning new ways of doing things.* ANT. yielding, complaisant.

student *n.* pupil; scholar; learner *When it comes to understanding human nature, I am still a student.*

studio *n.* workshop, workroom, atelier *The artist's studio was on the top storey with a north-facing window.*

study *n.* attention, examination, research *The committee decided that much study must be given to the question of where the new airport was to be built.* *vb.* examine, investigate; consider, weigh *We ought to study the problem before giving a reply.*

stuff *n.* **1** substance, material *What kind of stuff do they make plastic out of?* **2** cloth, fabric, textile *The king's throne room was hung with gold-embroidered stuffs.* *vb.* ram, fill, pack, cram *I stuffed rags in the cracks to keep out the cold.*

stuffy *adj.* **1** close, sticky, unventilated, oppressive *The air is very stuffy in this room—can you open a window?* **2** dull, staid, stodgy, conservative *The old lecturer gave a very stuffy talk on the days of the Empire.*

stumble *vb.* trip; lurch, flounder *I stumbled on the stairs and almost fell.*

stun *vb.* **1** knock out *I was temporarily stunned when the ball struck me on the head.* **2** astonish, surprise, shock, amaze, astound *Ike was stunned when they told him that he'd won the gold medal.*

stunning *adj.* dazzling, brilliant, astonishing, astounding, ravishing, exquisite *I never knew that Alan's wife was such a stunning beauty.*

stunt *vb.* dwarf, check, hinder, restrict *Didn't your mother tell you that smoking would stunt your growth?*

stupefy *vb.* **1** deaden, stun, numb *Peter was stupefied when he got the news of his sister's death.* **2** amaze, astound, confuse *Rose was stupefied on hearing she had got a distinction in the exam.*

stupendous *adj.* amazing, astounding, marvellous *They staged a stupendous production of* Aida *to celebrate the opening of the Suez Canal.*

stupid *adj.* dull, half-witted, silly, idiotic, simple-minded, witless *Crossing the road without waiting for the green light is pretty stupid.* ANT. intelligent, smart, bright, quick.

stupor *n.* daze *I walked about in a stupor after that blow on the head.*

sturdy *adj.* firm, strong, well-built *Although the flagpole bent in the wind, it was too sturdy to break.* ANT. frail, flimsy.

stutter *vb.* stammer, stumble, falter *Cranshaw began to stutter whenever he talked with a girl he didn't know.*

style *n.* 1 kind, sort, type *What style of shoe were you looking for?* 2 elegance, chic, smartness *Greta's mother has a great deal of style, no matter what she does or wears.*

suave *adj.* sophisticated, smooth, urbane *Nigel is a suave man-about-town who knows all the right people.*

subconscious *adj.* inner, inmost, mental, hidden *I have a subconscious fear of being caught in a lift.*

subdue *vb.* 1 defeat, conquer, beat, overcome *The people, without any defence, were quickly subdued by the advancing army.* 2 lower, reduce, soften, tone down *The mourners talked in subdued voices at the funeral.*

subject *n.* 1 topic, theme *On what subject should I write the essay for the English class?* 2 subordinate, dependant *The people were considered subjects of the queen.* *adj.* 1 depending, dependent *Subject to your approval, we'd like to plan a picnic for the class.* 2 subordinate, inferior *The subject peoples of the world have come a long way towards independence.* *vb.* 1 dominate, influence, control, tame, subdue, suppress *Because of you, we were caught and subjected to punishment.* 2 expose *Why must I be subjected to constant abuse just because I have red hair?*

sublime *adj.* noble, exalted, lofty *When did people first exhibit the sublime notion of the freedom of the individual?*

submerge *vb.* dip, sink, subside, submerse *The strange craft submerged beneath the waves and was never seen again.* ANT. rise, surface.

submit *vb.* 1 yield, surrender *The few soldiers remaining finally submitted when the fort was bombed.* 2 offer, tender *Our class submitted a plan to the headmaster for cleaning up the grounds.* ANT. (1) resist, fight.

subordinate *adj.* inferior, lower *Ken was finally able to get a job subordinate to the head of department.* *n.* worker, assistant, inferior *Beth is a subordinate of Mrs White's in the company.* *vb.* lower, demean, reduce *You ought to learn to subordinate your desires to those of the entire group.* ANT. superior.

subscribe *vb.* 1 pay, contribute *I want to subscribe to the fund for the environment.* 2 support, approve *Great men subscribe to different theories about the origin of the universe.*

subsequent *adj.* following, later, succeeding *A subsequent ruling denied planning permission for a restaurant at that site.* ANT. previous, preceding.

subside *vb.* sink, lower; diminish *Enthusiasm for punk rock appears to have subsided.* ANT. erupt, arise.

subsidy *n.* grant, support, aid *We shall need a subsidy if we are to continue our research.*

substance *n.* 1 material, matter, stuff *This dress is made out of some strange synthetic substance.* 2 essence *Tom presented the substance of his argument but no one agreed with him.*

substantial *adj.* 1 considerable, large, sizable *The professor received a substantial fee for writing the introduction to the book.* 2 real, actual, tangible *The police have substantial reason to believe that the fire was not accidental.* 3 wealthy, influential *My uncle is a substantial member of this community, I'll have you know.* ANT. (1) trivial, unimportant, insignificant.

substantiate *vb.* establish, prove, confirm *My wife will substantiate my alibi that I was home in bed at the time of the murder.*

substitute *n.* replacement, relief, stand-in *I'm not good enough to be a regular player, but I'm a substitute.* *vb.* replace, exchange, displace *Rick was sent in to substitute for Bill when Bill broke his leg.*

subtle *adj.* indirect; suggestive; implied *There are subtle differences between Jainism and Buddhism.* ANT. obvious, overt.

subtract *vb.* reduce, diminish, deduct, lessen *Subtract all the unnecessary verbiage and what do politicians really have to say?* ANT. add.

subvert *vb.* overthrow; upset; corrupt *These fifth-columnists are trying to subvert the government.*

succeed *vb.* 1 thrive, prosper, flourish *Fred has succeeded very well in business.* 2 follow; ensue; replace *We were having such a wonderful time that the succeeding days meant nothing. Mr Kensington succeeded Mr Kew as chairman of the garden committee.* ANT. (1) fail, (*slang*) flop. (2) precede.

success *n.* 1 prosperity, fortune; luck *The headmaster of the school wished each student every success in the future.* 2 achievement, attainment, accomplishment *Your success at work is evident. Well done!* ANT. (1) misfortune. (2) failure.

successful *adj.* lucky, fortunate, prosperous, triumphant, victorious, favourable *Our business trip was very successful.*

succession *n.* series, course, sequence *Let me describe the succession of events after you left.*

successive *adj.* consecutive, sequential, serial *The earthquake was followed by successive minor tremors.*

successor *n.* follower, heir *The retiring chairman is leaving all his office furniture behind for his successor.* ANT. predecessor.

succinct *adj.* concise, brief, terse *Can you give me a succinct summary of what happened?*

succumb *vb.* give way, yield, submit, surrender *Once the discipline was removed, Curtis succumbed to all the weaknesses that pleasure could afford.*

suck *vb.* absorb, take in, swallow; engulf *The tornado sucked up everything in its path.*

sudden *adj.* unexpected, swift, abrupt, unforeseen *The sudden blizzard hit without warning and left us stranded.*

suffer *vb.* 1 undergo, experience, endure, go through *You must have* *suffered terribly from those burns.* **2** allow, let, permit *Why should I suffer these people to come to me with their complaints?*

sufficient *adj.* enough, adequate *We have sufficient water to last us for two days.*

suffocate *vb.* choke, stifle, strangle *The room was so hot and smoky that I almost suffocated.*

suggest *vb.* **1** offer, propose, recommend, hint *I suggested that they might try putting out the fire with sand, since water was unavailable in the desert.* **2** evoke, hint, imply *The colours in the picture suggested a note of optimism.*

suggestion *n.* **1** plan, proposal, idea *The teacher liked my suggestion that everyone in the class start his own project.* **2** hint, trace, touch *There was a faint suggestion of garlic in the soup.*

suit *n.* costume, outfit *I'm going to buy a new suit today.* *vb.* agree with, befit, fit *The arrangements suit us nicely, thank you.*

suitable *adj.* fitting, apt, becoming, proper *Have you been able to find suitable accommodation for the royal couple?* ANT. inappropriate.

sulk *vb.* mope *Is there anything you can say to make Charles stop sulking?*

sullen *adj.* **1** silent, moody, bitter, sulky *Try to say something to cheer up Bob this morning—he seems so sullen.* **2** dismal, sad, gloomy, sombre *These sullen winter days are very depressing.* ANT. (1) cheerful, cheery, jovial.

sultry *adj.* hot, oppressive, close, stifling *It is too hot and sultry for my taste in the tropics during the summer.*

sum *n.* amount *There is no need for you to keep on giving such small sums of money to me.* *vb.phr.* **sum up** summarize, review *The lecturer summed up his main points in conclusion.*

summary *n.* outline, digest, synopsis, abstract, précis *Please let me have a summary of the book in just 250 words.* *adj.* brief, concise, short, compact, condensed *A summary report of what happened at the meeting should be on my desk now.*

summit *n.* top, peak, crown *We were unable to catch sight of the harbour till we were at the summit of the hill.*

summon *vb.* call, request, send for, invite *We were summoned to the head teacher's office the following morning.* ANT. dismiss.

sumptuous *adj.* lavish, extravagant; splendid, magnificent *I cannot recall having stayed in such sumptuous surroundings before.*

sundry *adj.* various, several, diverse, miscellaneous *We found sundry items of interest in the old trunk.*

sunny *adj.* cheerful, happy, cheery, joyful *Kathleen has such a sunny disposition that one cannot help liking her.*

superb *adj.* wonderful, splendid, marvellous, extraordinary, superior, excellent, magnificent, fine *The turtle soup at this restaurant is superb.*

supercilious *adj.* disdainful, haughty, contemptuous, snobbish *So-*

nia's attitude is supercilious because she evidently cares little for anything.

superficial *adj.* shallow, trivial, slight, inconsiderable *Most of the criticism of the new play was quite superficial.* ANT. deep, profound.

superfluous *adj.* unnecessary, redundant, excessive *Any comment you might offer for improvement would be superfluous.*

superintendent *n.* supervisor, manager, director, overseer, administrator *If my uncle hadn't been superintendent of the plant, I wouldn't have got the job.*

superior *adj.* better, greater, finer *One can easily see that this painting is of superior workmanship.* · *n.* boss, employer, supervisor *Each worker must have his time sheet signed by his superior.* ANT. inferior.

supernatural *adj.* invisible, unknown, hidden, mysterious, occult *Dabbling in supernatural affairs can be very dangerous.*

supersede *vb.* replace, succeed, supplant *Can you remember when the present rules superseded those in place for decades?*

supervise *vb.* oversee, direct, manage *If the children had been properly supervised, the accident would not have occurred.*

supervisor *n.* foreman, forewoman, manager, manageress, boss, director *Buford fell in love with his supervisor because he liked the way she ordered him about.*

supple *adj.* flexible, lithe, limber, pliable *Only if you exercise will you develop a supple body like mine.*

supplement *n.* addition; complement; extension *The railway authorities issue supplements with details of changes to the main timetable.* *vb.* add, extend, complement *Tim supplements his pocket money by working in a shop after school.*

supply *vb.* provide, furnish, stock *The dealer who supplies our grocer with vegetables raised his prices again.* *n.* store, stock, inventory, quantity *Our supply of pencils is running low, so please order some more.*

support *vb.* **1** bear, hold up, sustain, prop *That flimsy chair cannot support the weight of an adult.* **2** maintain, sustain, finance *How can Oscar support his family on so little money?* **3** back, assist, aid, promote *I shall support your desire to travel to the States with financial help.* **4** strengthen, corroborate, verify, substantiate *The confession of the thief was supported by the evidence of his fingerprints at the scene.* *n.* **1** brace, prop, stay *I hope that these supports will hold in a storm.* **2** help, aid, assistance *We need all the support we can get in the fight against disease.*

suppose *vb.* **1** assume, presume *Suppose you are walking down a lonely street in the middle of the night: would you be scared?* **2** believe, think; judge *I suppose you're right about not trusting Philip to get here on time.*

suppress *vb.* subdue, overpower, crush; repress *The government saw to it that activities of small liberal groups were suppressed.*

supreme *adj.* best, highest, greatest *His supreme achievement was to have chewed an oyster instead of swallowing it whole.*

surcharge *n.* excess, supplement, extra *There is no surcharge for gift wrapping purchases at this shop.*

sure *adj.* **1** certain, positive, confident, convinced *Are you sure that Mary said to meet her here?* **2** reliable, steady, trustworthy, unfailing *A sure way to make someone angry with you is to punch him on the nose.* **3** firm, stable, solid, safe *My footing on the icy steps was far from sure, and I soon slipped and fell.*

surface *n.* exterior, outside, covering, cover *The surface of the sun has a temperature of millions of degrees.*

surge *vb.* swell, heave, grow *The tidal wave surged up the river, destroying everything in its path.* **ANT.** ebb, wane, diminish.

surly *adj.* unfriendly, antagonistic, hostile *The lorry driver became quite surly when I asked him to let me by.*

surmise *vb.* think, judge, suppose, assume, believe, presume, suspect *I surmise, from seeing your red face and from your jumping up and down, that you are excited about something.* *n.* guess, thought *It was your surmise that the sun would rise within an hour.*

surmount *vb.* overcome, conquer; scale, climb *If we can surmount these obstacles, we can get on with the task at hand.*

surpass *vb.* exceed, pass, outdo, excel *This play surpasses everything that Arriba has ever written.*

surplus *n.* excess, remainder *There will be a surplus of wheat in this year's harvest.* *adj.* extra *All surplus money will be added to the picnic fund.*

surprise *vb.* **1** amaze, astound, astonish, startle *I was surprised to see Georgina wearing a green dress—she looks so much better in blue.* **2** catch, startle *The teacher surprised three students hiding in the cubicle.* *n.* amazement, shock *The enemy took us by surprise and we surrendered.*

surrender *vb.* yield, submit, give up *Thousands of soldiers surrendered and we counted the battle won.* **ANT.** resist.

surround *vb.* encircle, circle, girdle *The entire building was surrounded by police, so we gave up.*

surreptitious *adj.* sneaking, underhand(ed), sly, furtive, sneaky *With a surreptitious movement of his hand he signalled the dog to attack.* **ANT.** open, aboveboard, straightforward, open-handed.

survey *vb.* examine, scan, view, inspect *Before moving into the territory, we surveyed it carefully.* *n.* **1** examination, inspection *A survey of the area yielded no information.* **2** poll *In a recent survey, more people said they preferred butter to margarine.*

survive *vb.* remain, persist, live, continue *I cannot see how anyone could survive for that long in the desert.* **ANT.** fail, die, succumb.

suspect *vb.* **1** doubt, mistrust, distrust, disbelieve *The police suspect the three men who were seen loitering near the bank.* **2** suppose, presume, assume *I suspect that Bob may be late because his car won't start.* *n.* defendant *The suspect was seen leaving the scene* *of the crime.* *adj.* suspicious, suspected, questionable, doubtful *Spending large amounts of money after a robbery makes certain people suspect.* ANT. *vb.* (1) know, believe, trust.

suspend *vb.* 1 hang; dangle *The flag was suspended from the rafters in the gymnasium.* 2 postpone, defer, withhold, delay, interrupt *We suspended payments on the television when it stopped working.*

suspense *n.* uncertainty, insecurity, anxiety, excitement *I can't stand the suspense waiting to see if my horse won.*

suspicion *n.* doubt, mistrust, misgiving, scepticism *Martha greeted with suspicion the telegram advising her she had won the pools.*

suspicious *adj.* 1 distrustful, suspecting, doubting, doubtful, dubious, suspect, questioning, sceptical *I was suspicious of Anne when she said she had memorized the entire telephone directory.* 2 questionable, suspect, irregular, unusual *There was a suspicious-looking person lurking near the back door.*

sustain *vb.* 1 support, bear, carry, uphold *That flimsy pole cannot sustain the weight of the entire roof.* 2 support, maintain, keep *Our hopes were sustained by the sounds of digging from the other side of the cave.* 3 undergo, endure, suffer; bear *The injuries sustained in the accident were all minor, and everyone was sent home.* 4 support, ratify, approve *The findings of the lower court were sustained by the higher court.*

swallow *vb.* eat, gulp, gorge *Jack was in a hurry and swallowed his dinner quickly.* *n.* gulp, mouthful *Take a swallow of water to help you to stop coughing.*

swamp *n.* bog, quagmire, fen, marsh, morass *Keep away from the swamp if you want to avoid a dangerous area.* *vb.* deluge, overcome, flood *After Sadie's singing debut, she was swamped with requests to sing.*

swap *vb.* exchange, barter, trade *We swapped our old Ford—and a little money, of course—for a new Jaguar.*

swarm *n.* horde, throng, mass, host *A swarm of insects hovered over the picnic table.* *vb.* throng, crowd *The fans swarmed around the football players after the game.*

sway *vb.* 1 wave, bend, swing *The palm trees swayed gently in the tropical breeze.* 2 influence, persuade, impress *The judge refused to be swayed by appeals to sympathy.*

swear *vb.* 1 vow, declare, state, assert, vouch, vouchsafe *The prisoner swore that he had never seen that man before in his life.* 2 curse, blaspheme *We don't allow students to swear in this school.*

sweat *vb.* perspire *Physical labour under that hot sun makes you sweat.* *n.* perspiration *The sweat ran down from my forehead into my eyes, stinging them.*

sweep *vb.* brush, clean, clear *When you get a chance, please sweep out the garage.*

sweeping *adj.* general, comprehensive, broad, all-embracing, all-inclusive *Geraldine is always making such sweeping generalizations about people.*

sweet *adj.* **1** sugary, honeyed *That chocolate is too sweet for me.*
2 pleasant, melodious, tuneful, musical, harmonious, mellow *Nicole has a very sweet singing voice.* **3** charming, agreeable, pleasant, attractive *Our parrot has a sweet disposition and would never bite anyone.* **ANT.** (1) sour, bitter. (2) discordant, harsh. (3) irritable, nasty, irascible.

swell *vb.* grow, increase, enlarge, expand *As they continued to pump hot air into it, the balloon swelled and slowly rose off the ground.* **ANT.** shrink, diminish.

swerve *vb.* turn, swing, veer *Driving home, I had to swerve to avoid hitting a deer in the road.*

swift *adj.* fast, quick, rapid, speedy: 'I am a swift runner,' said Tom slowly. **ANT.** slow, sluggish, laggardly.

swim *vb.* bathe, dip; paddle, wade; dive; float, drift *I prefer to swim in the warm, clear waters of the Caribbean.*

swindle *vb.* cheat, defraud, trick, deceive, (*informal*) con *I was once swindled out of £100.* *n.* fraud, deception, trickery *The company's guarantee is nothing more than a swindle to sell you the car.*

swing *vb.* sway, rock, wave *There was Tarzan, swinging on a vine, while Cheetah jabbered away on the ground below.*

swirl *vb.* roll, whirl, spin, reel, flow *When she dances, her skirt swirls about her, this way and that.*

switch *vb.* change, shift, turn *Some voters switched their vote from Labour to the Conservatives.*

swoon *vb.,n.* faint *Women swooned at the news of Valentino's death.*

swoop *vb.* dive, plummet, pounce *The eagle swoops down on the water and snatches a salmon from beneath the surface.*

symbol *n.* sign, token, figure, representation; design, logo *The universal symbol for peace is a white dove.*

sympathetic *adj.* compassionate, considerate, tender, kind *We should all be more sympathetic to the feelings of others.* **ANT.** unsympathetic, intolerant, indifferent.

sympathize *vb.* feel for, commiserate, weep for, comfort *I sympathize with anyone who has a son or daughter in the armed services.*

sympathy *n.* feeling, sentiment, compassion, understanding *Don't you feel any sympathy for that poor woman whose husband was killed?*

symptom *n.* sign, indication, mark *Red spots on your tongue are not a symptom of dandruff.*

synopsis *n.* summary, digest, outline, précis *Can you let me have a brief synopsis of your plan without all the details?*

synthetic *adj.* manmade, manufactured; artificial *This chair is covered in a synthetic material that simulates leather.* **ANT.** natural, real.

system *n.* procedure, arrangement, plan, order, scheme *We need a new system for controlling exhaust emissions from cars.*

systematic *adj.* organized, orderly, regular, methodical *One common systematic way of arranging information is in alphabetical order.* ANT. random, irregular.

t

taboo *adj.* prohibited, banned, forbidden *In some societies it is taboo for a woman to utter her husband's name.*

tacit *adj.* unspoken, silent, implicit, assumed, inherent, implied *We have a tacit agreement not to encroach on one another's territory.* ANT. outspoken, express.

tackle *n.* gear, equipment, rigging, apparatus *What kind of tackle would be used to raise a car from a dock onto a ship?* *vb.* **1** seize, grab, down, catch, throw *The player was tackled near the centre of the field.* **2** undertake, try *If they pay him enough, Jack will tackle any assignment they give him.*

tact *n.* judgement, sense, diplomacy, prudence *Have you the tact needed to get it across to Frobisher that he has bad breath?*

tactful *adj.* diplomatic, considerate, sensitive, skilful *If you were more tactful about pointing out her mistakes, Barbara might not burst into tears so often.* ANT. tactless, unfeeling.

tactics *n.pl.* strategy, plan, approach *Which tactics should be used to end the war quickly?*

tag *n.* label, sticker, ticket, tab *According to the tag, this dress is two sizes too small for you.*

taint *vb.* contaminate, spoil, pollute, corrupt *Your reputation has been tainted by that little affair in Tampico last year.*

take *vb.* **1** grasp, hold, catch, seize *They took the puppy from us because we couldn't keep it in the passenger section.* **2** win, capture, seize, acquire *After a two-hour battle, the pirates took the treasure ship. You take first prize.* **3** pick, choose, select; prefer *Take any number from one to ten; double it; then add the original number.* **4** guide, conduct, lead, escort, bring *Who is going to take the children to school today?* **5** remove, steal, shoplift, rob *Somebody took my left shoe.* **6** record, note, write, register *Have you hired a secretary who can take your letters in shorthand?* **7** require, need, demand *But it doesn't take two hours to wash your hair!* **8** charm, attract, engage, bewitch *I must admit that I am very much taken with Fiona.* **9** purchase, buy, pay for *I'll take one dozen of the red ones and two dozen of the blue.* *vb.phr.* **take after** resemble *You certainly take after your mother, Sophie.* **take away** deduct, subtract *Take 6 away from 11 and you're left with 5.* **take back** **1** reclaim, recover, regain *The French took back all the conquered land after the war.* **2** retract, recall, deny *You had better take back those things you said!* **take down** lower, remove *The teachers made us take down the poster from the wall.* **take for** mistake, misunderstand *Sorry, I took you for your twin brother.* **take in** **1** include, embrace

, *When you say 'mammal', that doesn't take in birds and snakes.*
2 deceive, dupe, fool *You certainly were taken in by that fellow who sold you a comb without teeth.*   **3** welcome, shelter, receive, accept *My mother won't let me take in every stray dog or cat.*   **4** shorten, reduce, lessen *The tailor took in all my clothes when I lost a lot of weight.*   **5** understand, comprehend *Marcia took in everything I said but didn't even smile.* **take it** **1** assume, understand, accept *I take it that you don't like eating raw eggs.*   **2** endure, survive *I guess that Merrill just can't take it.* **take off** **1** remove *You'll have to take off all your clothes if you expect to have a bath.*   **2** deduct, subtract, take away *The owner offered to take off another ten per cent if I paid promptly.*   **3** leave, depart, go *The plane takes off at three o'clock.*   **4** *Informal:* satirize, lampoon *In his new act, Gerald takes off some politicians perfectly.* **take on** **1** employ, hire, engage *We took on twenty-three more people at the plant last month.*   **2** undertake, assume *I think that with his job after school and on weekends, Peter has taken on more than he can handle.*   **3** assume, acquire *After not having seen another person for so long, Jim took on a lean, mean look.* **take out** **1** extract, remove *The dentist said he had to take out my last baby tooth.*   **2** entertain, escort, go out with *Are you old enough to take out girls?* **take over** seize, capture *A gang from the other side of town took over our clubhouse.* **take to** enjoy, like, favour *My new watchdog takes to strangers in the friendliest way.* **take up** **1** start, begin, commence *Don't you think that it's a little late to take up hang-gliding at the age of eighty-three?* **2** occupy, consume *All of my days are taken up with going to school or working afterwards.*

taking *adj.* captivating, charming, attractive, winning *When I said that Ida has taking ways, I did not mean she would be arrested for shoplifting.*

tale *n.* story, anecdote *Father tells the same old tales, year after year, when we get together for Christmas dinner.*

talent *n.* skill, ability, gift, aptitude *Has Dick lost his great talent for playing the kazoo?*

talk *vb.* **1** speak; communicate *Betty says she doesn't want to talk to you.*   **2** confer, discuss, consult *I think you ought to talk it over with someone before making a decision.* *n.* **1** conversation, chat, discussion *We had our talk before dinner.*   **2** lecture, address, speech *At the meeting I gave a short talk on butterflies.*

talkative *adj.* garrulous, loquacious, voluble, glib *The men she meets are either overly talkative or they open their mouths only to eat.* ANT. silent, mute.

tall *adj.* high, big, lofty, towering *As the availability of land diminishes, we tend to build tall buildings on what is left.* ANT. short, low.

tame *adj.* **1** domesticated, docile, mild, broken *Civilization began when man learned how to make animals tame.*   **2** dull, uninteresting, unexciting, flat, empty, boring *Life must be pretty tame for you* *now that the summer holidays are over.* vb. domesticate, break *It takes a lot of patience to tame a wild animal.* ANT. *adj.* (1) wild.

tamper vb. mess around, meddle, tinker *I should appreciate it if you would not tamper with the front door lock.*

tang n. savour, flavour, zest *That rice certainly has a spicy tang to it!*

tangible adj. material, physical, concrete *I wish I had something tangible to give you for Christmas.* ANT. spiritual, insubstantial, intangible.

tangle vb. knot, twist, confuse, snarl *You've tangled the kite string in the branches of the tree.* n. 1 knot, muddle *The string was in a complete tangle in the tin.* 2 confusion *Everything is in such a tangle in this office: we must clear things up sometime.*

tank n. container, cistern; basin, tub *After the petrol shortage Cyril acquired a huge storage tank which he filled in preparation for the next shortage.*

tap vb. rap, pat, strike, hit *If you tap the ball gently, it will roll into the hole and you'll win.* n. rap, pat, blow *A slight tap on the door or window and the dog will start barking.*

tape n. strip, ribbon *Please let me have a piece of tape from that roll.* vb. 1 bind, tie, fasten; bandage *I taped the sign on to the board.* 2 record *Brad taped the entire show and now can play it back any time he wants to hear it.*

taper n. candle *We lit a taper and the room sprang into light.* vb. decrease, narrow, lessen *A cone has a circular base and its side tapers to a point.*

tardy adj. late, overdue, unpunctual *This is the third time this week that Richard has been tardy getting to school.* ANT. prompt, punctual, timely.

target n. goal, objective, object, aim *Our target is to raise £250 to add to the fund for our team uniforms.*

tariff n. tax, levy, duty, rate *The tariff of ten per cent must be paid on all imported goods.*

tarnish vb. stain, soil, dirty *The scandal might have tarnished your reputation, but you will survive.*

tarry vb. linger, dawdle, loiter, dally *Jane and I tarried a bit after the others left so we could talk to George.*

tart adj. 1 acid, sour *Lemons are very tart.* 2 sharp, biting, cutting *Victoria's tart comment about my hat was not at all welcome.* ANT. (1) sweet, sugary.

task n. job, duty, chore, undertaking *Ben has some tasks to finish before he is free to go to the cinema.*

taste vb. 1 sip, try, savour, sample *Have you tasted Mrs O'Neill's apple pie?* 2 experience, undergo *Only someone who has never tasted war could want to go into battle.* n. 1 flavour, savour *I don't like the taste of orange juice in my milk.* 2 appreciation, discernment, discrimination, judgement *That book is in very bad taste.*

tasteful *adj.* chic, stylish, elegant, refined *Alma was wearing a tasteful black dress and a string of pearls for the prince's reception.*

tasteless *adj.* 1 insipid, flavourless, unpalatable *This tasteless dish cannot be boeuf bourgignon.* 2 unrefined, rude, boorish, uncultivated *When Mrs Bramble said she was sick, it was tasteless of you to remark 'You're telling me!'*

tattle *vb.* reveal, blab, inform on *Philip tattled to Mother about the missing chocolates, and I was punished.*

taunt *vb.* tease, annoy, bother, pester; mock, jeer, ridicule, make fun of *Why must you continue to taunt him just because he wears shorts?*

taut *adj.* tight, tense, stretched *Don't let that rope sag—pull it taut.*

tawdry *adj.* cheap, gaudy, showy, flashy *I haven't seen such a tawdry display since I visited a musical hall.*

tax *n.* tariff, levy, duty, rate *Will the government increase taxes in the budget?* *vb.* 1 assess *A government should not tax its citizens without giving them a voice in running the country.* 2 strain, burden, encumber, load, overload *The work taxed her so much she fell ill.*

taxi *n.* taxicab, cab *'Please call me a taxi.' 'All right: You're a taxi!'*

teach *vb.* instruct, train, educate, inform, tutor *It is his responsibility to teach students how to write clearly and well.*

teacher *n.* instructor; tutor; lecturer, professor; pedagogue *Teachers are hard to find, and good teachers are impossible to find.*

team *n.* 1 group, organization, club *It looks as if our team might win the cup.* 2 crew, gang *Put a team of six men on doing the job and it will be done much faster.*

teamwork *n.* cooperation, collaboration, partnership *The game requires cooperation, coordination and teamwork.*

tear[1] *vb.* rip, split, rend, divide *My father is so strong that he can tear a telephone book in half.* *n.* rip, split, rent *There's a tear in my coat that I have to sew up.*

tear[2] *n.* drop, teardrop *A tear ran down Penny's cheek when she peeled the onion.* *vb.* water *The pollution in the air makes my eyes tear.*

tease *vb.* irritate, annoy, pester, bother, vex, harass, hector *If you keep on teasing that dog, he'll bite you.*

technical *adj.* technological, industrial, mechanical; specialized *Repairing a computer is a technical skill which I lack.*

technique *n.* method, system, approach, routine, procedure *Scientists have developed new techniques for the treatment of certain diseases.*

tedious *adj.* tiring, tiresome, dull, boring, wearisome *Walking an hour each way to and from school every day can become tedious.* ANT. interesting, engaging, exciting.

tedium *n.* boredom, monotony, dullness *I cannot survive the tedium of another episode of that soap opera, 'Brighton University'.*

teem *vb.* swarm, abound, bristle *I joined the teeming masses of people on their way to work every morning.*

teeter *vb.* wobble, totter, sway, waver *The company is in a precarious condition, teetering on the brink of bankruptcy.*

telephone *n.* phone, (*informal*) horn, blower; receiver *When you get there, pick up the telephone and call home.* *vb.* phone, ring (up), dial *It distracts me when you telephone me at work.*

tell *vb.* **1** relate, narrate *Please tell us a bedtime story.* **2** inform, advise, explain *Can't you tell me where you live?* **3** reveal, disclose, divulge, declare *Doesn't Philip ever tell the truth?* **4** determine, discern, discover *I can't tell whether the car is blue or green in this dim light.* **5** command, order, bid *You tell Harvey that he'd better get to work on time or he won't have a job.* *vb.phr.* **tell off** scold, reprimand, rebuke *Why does Peter have to keep telling his children off? Because they're always naughty.*

telling *adj.* convincing, persuasive, forceful, effective *The threat of punishment is not a telling argument against crime.*

temper *n.* **1** mood, disposition, temperament; humour *Ellie seems to be in a bad temper this morning.* **2** self-control, patience *Edward loses his temper over very unimportant things.* *vb.* **1** moderate, soothe, soften, pacify *If you want to get along with people, you must learn to temper your outbursts.* **2** toughen, anneal *The first swords of tempered steel were made in Toledo, Spain.*

temperament *n.* disposition, nature, temper *The doorman at my club is of a very sour temperament.*

temperamental *adj.* moody, irritable, touchy, sensitive *You don't have to be temperamental to be a prima donna, but it seems to help.* ANT. calm, serene, unruffled.

temperate *adj.* moderate, controlled, restrained, cool, calm *Try to be less excitable and view the problem in a more temperate manner.*

tempest *n.* storm; tumult, commotion, turmoil *As the tempest raged outside, we were snug before the fire.*

tempo *n.* pace, beat, rhythm, cadence, measure *The tempo of the music quickened when they played Latin American tunes.*

temporary *adj.* passing, short-lived, short, fleeting, momentary *There was a temporary delay while a crew de-iced the wings of the aeroplane.* ANT. permanent, everlasting, fixed.

tempt *vb.* lure, allure, entice, seduce, attract, invite *I am tempted to go to the dance if Carol will be there.*

tenable *adj.* defensible, reasonable, possible *How can your contention be tenable that high interest rates cause inflation?*

tenacious *adj.* determined, persistent, unchanging, unyielding *When Gruber refused to release his tenacious hold as club treasurer, we began to suspect something.*

tend *vb.* **1** incline; lead, point *Students tend to be more intelligent people.* **2** guard, look after, care for, take care of *Who was left at home to tend Grandma?*

tendency *n.* inclination, trend, leaning, disposition *Even when he was a lad, Ted showed a tendency towards the outdoor life.*

tender[1] *adj.* **1** delicate, soft; fragile *That's the most tender steak I've* *ever eaten.* **2** loving, gentle, affectionate, sympathetic *I received a very tender note from a friend when I became ill.* **3** sensitive, sore, painful *My arm is still tender where I banged it last week.* ANT. (1) tough, chewy. (2) unfeeling, cruel.

tender² *vb.* offer, proffer, present, propose *The company tendered a bid of £50,000 to complete the road works.* *n.* offer, proposal *A tender of £55,000 has already been rejected.*

tenderhearted *adj.* sympathetic, compassionate, softhearted, kind, merciful *It was tenderhearted of Melissa to care for those stray dogs.* ANT. hardhearted, cruel.

tense *adj.* **1** stretched, strained, tight *My arm was tense from carrying so many books.* **2** excited, nervous, (*slang*) uptight, (*informal*) worked up *Bill was tense from lack of sleep.* ANT. (1) loose, relaxed, lax. (2) calm, composed, unruffled.

tentative *adj.* provisional, experimental, trial *Our company made a tentative proposal for the work but were rebuffed.*

term *n.* **1** word, expression, phrase, name *The technical term for salt is sodium chloride.* **2** period, interval *What is the term of your agreement?*

terminal *adj.* fatal, deadly, mortal *When the doctor told me I had a terminal disease, I decided to go out and enjoy myself for once.*

terminate *vb.* end, stop, cease, close, finish, conclude *The school year terminates with a series of examinations.* ANT. begin, commence, start.

terrible *adj.* horrible, awful, horrifying, dreadful, terrifying *Terrible damage has been done by the earthquake.*

terrify *vb.* frighten, scare, terrorize, petrify *I have seen the terrifying results of an atomic explosion.*

territory *n.* area, region, province; section *Each salesman has an assigned territory to cover over a three-month period.*

terror *n.* horror, dread, fear, fright, panic, alarm *Until the mad killer was caught, we all lived in terror.*

test *n.* trial, examination, exam, quiz *We are going to have a French test tomorrow.* *vb.* question, examine; review, inspect *Are we going to be tested on what was taught today?*

testify *vb.* warrant, declare, affirm, attest, state, witness *Patrick testified that he had been held up at knifepoint by the defendant.*

text *n.* book, textbook, manual *We shall be using a new physics text this year.*

textile *see* **cloth.**

texture *n.* surface, pattern, feel, fibre *Silk and satin have a similar smooth texture.*

thankful *adj.* grateful, obliged, appreciative *Gary was thankful to be home again after such a dangerous mission.*

thaw *vb.* melt, liquefy, dissolve *To thaw out this food place it in the microwave.* ANT. freeze, solidify.

theft *n.* robbery, thievery, stealing, larceny, burglary; pillage, plunder *The theft yielded the robbers a mere £5.*

theme *n.* 1 subject, topic, thesis, argument, point *The main theme that ran through the speech was that we must be good to each other.* 2 melody, tune, leitmotif *The theme in that symphony is easy to recognize.*

theoretical *adj.* unproved, tentative; ideal, hypothetical *My suggestion that we advertise on television is purely theoretical.*

theory *n.* explanation, opinion, hypothesis, guess, assumption *I can find no one to agree with my theory that the earth really is flat.*

therefore *adv.* consequently, thus, hence, so then, accordingly *As I am breathing, I must therefore still be alive.*

thick *adj.* 1 dense, solid *The crowd was so thick that I was unable to get through.* 2 heavy, compact, syrupy, viscous *The oil was quite thick and coated everything with a black goo.* **ANT.** (1) thin, slim. (2) watery.

thief *n.* robber, burglar, criminal *They think that the thief who stole your necklace might have been a woman.*

thin *adj.* 1 narrow, slim, lean, slender; sparse, meagre, scanty *Carolyn looks thin after losing weight. That's a pretty thin excuse for being late—you couldn't find a sock?* 2 watery, weak, light *The soup is so thin here that they seem to make it by boiling a pot of water with only one noodle in it for flavour.*

thing *n.* object, article; device, gadget, instrument *The man wore a strange thing on his head.*

think *vb.* 1 consider, contemplate, reflect, meditate *I have been thinking about going on holiday, but I cannot decide where.* 2 judge, deem *Don't you think that Mr Carson is an excellent teacher?* 3 suppose, assume, believe *I think that you'll want to go to the football match when you find out who's playing.*

thirst *n.* desire, appetite, craving, longing *The students in my history class exhibit an unusual thirst for knowledge.*

thorn *n.* barb, nettle, spine, prickle, bramble *Be careful that you are not pricked by these sharp thorns.*

thorough *adj.* complete, careful *The men have done a thorough job of cleaning out the cellar.* **ANT.** careless, haphazard, slapdash.

thoroughfare *n.* street, avenue, road, highroad, highway, avenue, boulevard *The main thoroughfare in this city is called High Street.* **ANT.** byway.

thought *n.* 1 meditation, deliberation, contemplation, reasoning, cogitation *I didn't want to disturb Irene because she was deep in thought.* 2 idea, belief *It was Patrick's thought that taking a holiday in Greece might help him get a good rest.*

thoughtful *adj.* 1 kind, considerate, attentive, courteous, friendly *Gerry is so thoughtful—he always brings wine when invited to dinner.* 2 absorbed, pensive, reflective *When he heard about how difficult it was for uneducated people to get a job, Tom became very thoughtful.* **ANT.** (1) thoughtless.

thoughtless *adj.* inconsiderate, careless; imprudent, negligent *It was *thoughtless of you not to visit your parents at Christmastime.* ANT. thoughtful, careful, kind.

thrash *vb.* beat, whip, flog, punish; defeat *If we did anything wrong, Father thrashed us soundly.*

threat *n.* warning; menace, intimidation *Though she said she would tell my mother, that turned out to be an idle threat.*

threaten *vb.* 1 warn, menace, caution, forewarn, intimidate *The bully threatened Percy with a beating if he didn't give him the ball.* 2 loom, advance, near, impend *The black clouds threatened from the west.*

threshold *n.* 1 sill, door, entrance, gate *It used to be customary for a husband to carry his bride over the threshold of their new home.* 2 edge, verge; beginning, start *I was on the threshold of telling the secret when they stopped torturing me.*

thrift *n.* economy, saving; care, caution, prudence *If you practise reasonable thrift, you should have enough money soon for a new hi-fi.*

thrifty *adj.* frugal, sparing, parsimonious, economical, saving *My grandmother was so thrifty that she saved every bit of string.* ANT. spendthrift, prodigal.

thrill *n.* excitement, stimulation, tingle *We all got a great thrill out of watching our team win the gold medal for swimming.* *vb.* excite, stimulate, rouse, arouse *The star said that she was thrilled to receive the award.*

thrive *vb.* prosper, succeed, grow, flourish *The family business thrived after we moved to Milton Keynes.* ANT. languish, expire, die.

throng *n.* crowd, multitude, swarm, mass, horde *A throng of people crowded round the plane to welcome the visitor from Yakutsk.* *vb.* crowd, swarm, teem *Spurred on by favourable reviews, people thronged to the theatre to see the play.*

throttle *vb.* strangle, choke, stifle *When I broke in, he had her by the throat and was throttling her.*

through *adj.* done, finished; complete, over *Are you through using my razor? The school year will be through in another few days.*

throughout *prep.* 1 everywhere, all through, all over *We searched throughout the house but couldn't find the cat.* 2 during *Throughout the last three days you have been nagging me constantly. Why?*

throw *vb.* toss, hurl, pitch, cast, fling, send *Throw the ball to me and I'll run with it.* *n.* thrust, shove, toss, pitch *That was a great throw from the boundary.*

thrust *vb.* push, shove; force *You don't have to thrust the thing right into my face just because I didn't see it at first.* *n.* push, shove, drive *With a single powerful thrust, the native's spear had killed the wild boar.*

thud *n.* plonk, plump, plop, bump *The box landed with a thud on the carpet.*

thump *vb.,n.* whack, rap, wallop, beat *I thumped her for being so horrid to me. She gave him a thump on the back in return.*

thwart *vb.* frustrate, obstruct, stop *They thwarted any attempt we made to repay them for their kindness.*

ticket *n.* permit, pass; note, slip; voucher, certificate *If you present this ticket to the guard, he will let you through.*

tickle *vb.* 1 rub, stroke, touch, titillate *Tickling young children is fun.* 2 excite, delight, amuse, stimulate *He was quite tickled to think he would shortly be in Africa.*

ticklish *adj.* delicate, sensitive, difficult *Because of the politics in the region, arriving at an agreement will be ticklish.*

tidings *n.pl.* news, information, word, report *The messenger brought tidings of a great battle having been won at Marathon.*

tidy *adj.* organized, neat, orderly *Why do teenagers have so much trouble keeping their rooms tidy?*

tie *vb.* 1 bind, secure, fasten *June is a little early to be wrapping up Christmas presents, isn't it?* 2 join, connect, knot, link, fasten *The captive was tied to a stake and the natives danced about him, singing. If you tie these two pieces together, then the cord will be long enough to go round.* *n.* 1 link, bond, connection; constraint *Harry has few ties: he has no family and his parents are both dead.* 2 cravat, bow tie, necktie *You must wear a tie and jacket to eat in the dining room of the hotel.*

tight *adj.* 1 firm, taut, secure, strong, fast, fixed *This knot was tied so tight that no one could open it.* 2 sealed, airtight, watertight, locked, fastened *I can't open this jar because the cover was screwed on too tight.* 3 *Informal:* tipsy, high, drunk, intoxicated, inebriated *Mother got a little tight from drinking champagne at her anniversary party.* 4 stingy, miserly, niggardly *Old Jack is too tight to donate any money to charity.* ANT. (1) loose, slack. (3) sober.

tilt *vb.* slope, incline, slant, lean, tip *You tilted the table when you leaned on it, spilling my milk and biscuits on to the floor.* *n.* slope, angle, incline *The plank was put at a tilt to help the workmen push their wheelbarrows up and down.*

time *n.* 1 period, interval, span, space, term *The time between spring and autumn is called summer. Don't spend so much time talking on the phone, Mabel.* 2 rhythm, tempo, beat, measure *The orchestra then played Beethoven's Eighth Symphony in fast time.* *vb.* regulate, gauge, adjust, measure *The engineers are trying to time the number of pulses per second.*

timely *adj.* opportune, convenient; favourable, auspicious *Are you certain it is timely to approach Father for permission to borrow his car?*

timetable *n.* calendar, schedule *What sort of timetable do you envisage for marketing the new soap powder?*

timid *adj.* shy, bashful, retiring, coy, fainthearted, diffident, fearful *Clement was far too timid to ask Anne-Marie to dance.* ANT. bold, forward, self-confident.

tinge *vb.,n.* tint, colour, dye, stain *We tinged our T-shirts a pale shade of blue. There's a slight tinge of pink in the sky at sunset.*

tingle *vb.* prickle, itch, sting; thrill *The mild shock from the battery made my fingers tingle.*

tinkle *n.* ring, jingle, chime *I enjoyed listening to the tinkle of the temple bells.*

tint *vb.,n.* tinge, colour, dye, stain *Some older people with white hair tint it a bluish shade. These walls need a warm tint in order to set off the colour of the carpet.*

tiny *adj.* small, wee, little, miniature *As I rubbed the box, a tiny figure leapt out of it and offered to grant me three wishes.* ANT. large, huge, enormous.

tip[1] *n.* end, point, peak, top *You can see the tip of the tower just over those buildings.*

tip[2] *vb.* tilt, upset, knock over *The canoe tipped, and we both fell into the cold water.*

tip[3] *n.* **1** gratuity, gift, reward *My father gave the waiter a good tip because the service had been so good.* **2** hint, clue, inkling, suggestion *The man in the green suit just gave me a tip on which horse would win the race.*

tire *vb.* weary, weaken, fatigue, exhaust *Since my illness, I find that I tire easily. All that exercise tired me out.* ANT. exhilarate, invigorate, refresh.

tired *adj.* exhausted, weary, run-down, fatigued, sleepy *I got so tired walking around in the museum that I had to sit down.*

tireless *adj.* energetic, active, strenuous, enthusiastic *Letitia has been a tireless advocate for women's rights.*

tiresome *adj.* boring, dull, tedious, monotonous *Standing watch is so tiresome that I often fall asleep standing up.*

title *n.* **1** name, heading, designation *What is the title of that book?* **2** ownership, deed, right, claim *The title to that property is held jointly by my mother and father.* *vb.* name, designate, entitle, call *I have titled my latest book* The Birth of an Iceberg.

toil *vb.* work, slave, sweat *Think about all those people toiling in the fields to harvest the food that you take for granted.* *n.* work, labour, drudgery, effort, exertion *After ten hours of toil, I just want to eat and go to sleep.* ANT. *vb.* relax, loll.

token *n.* sign, mark, sample *Ben gave Betty a bracelet as a token of his affection.*

tolerant *adj.* considerate, patient, liberal, impartial *Our teacher is not at all tolerant of misbehaviour in class.* ANT. intolerant, biased, bigoted, prejudiced.

tolerate *vb.* permit, allow, authorize, stand, condone *Smoking is not tolerated anywhere on school property.*

tomb *n.* grave, vault, sepulchre *We visited Napoleon's tomb in Paris.*

tone *n.* **1** sound, noise *The tone of the clarinet is soft and mellow.* **2** manner, mood, expression *Sheldon's voice reflected the angry tone of the argument.*

tonic *n.* stimulant, refresher, pick-me-up; preparation *My convalescence was speeded by the tonic prescribed by the doctor.*

tool *n.* utensil, implement, instrument, device *I haven't the proper tools for repairing this watch.*

top *n.* **1** peak, summit, tip, pinnacle *From the top of that mountain you can see far into the distance.* **2** cap, cover, lid *I've lost the top of the toothpaste tube.* *vb.* excel, surpass, outdo, exceed, beat, better *Ted topped his earlier performance in this week's swimming match by five seconds.* ANT. *n.* (1) bottom, base.

topic *n.* subject, issue, theme *The topic for today's discussion is 'Should children under ten be allowed to stay up till midnight?'*

topical *adj.* current, modern, contemporary; recent *Our group chooses a different topical subject for discussion each week.*

topsy-turvy *adj.* upside-down, confused, muddled; disorganized, untidy *The vandals upset the cabinets and left all the files topsy-turvy.*

torch *n.* light, lamp *Hand me that electric torch, please, so I can see what's in the back of this cabinet.*

torment *vb.* annoy, vex, pester, harass, torture, distress *Peter was tormented by the worry that he'd miss the train if he waited for the message to come through.* *n.* torture, agony, anguish, misery *I can't describe the torment I went through until I learned you were safe.*

torrent *n.* downpour, flood, deluge *When the dam cracked, a torrent of water deluged the town below.*

torrid *adj.* hot, sultry, tropical, sweltering *It was very uncomfortable in the torrid conditions near the equator.*

torture *n.* torment, anguish, misery, pain, cruelty *The soldiers used torture to make the captive tell where the guns were hidden.* *vb.* torment, hector, abuse; annoy, irritate *Stop torturing me any longer—did you pass your driving test or not?*

toss *vb.* **1** throw, pitch, hurl, cast *Larry tossed the paper into the wastepaper basket across the room.* **2** turn, stir, move, tumble *I tossed all night and couldn't have slept more than one hour.*

total *adj.* entire, whole, complete, full *The total number of students who volunteered to help clean up was six.* *n.* sum; entirety *What is the total of this column of figures?* *vb.* add *Would you please total the number of times you were late or absent?*

totter *vb.* reel, stagger, falter, teeter *There goes Mr Grundy, tottering down the street.*

touch *vb.* **1** feel, handle, finger *Please do not touch the paintings.* **2** affect, move, concern *We were all touched by the story of the orphan who had found a home.* **3** mention, refer to, treat, discuss *The speaker touched on the subject of cheating in exams and Alan looked nervous.* *n.* **1** contact; stroke *The very touch of her hand makes me tingle all over.* **2** hint, trace, suggestion *This soup needs a touch more pepper.* **3** skill, knack, ability, talent *That clock cabinet shows the touch of a master craftsman.*

touching *adj.* moving, effective, tender *The mother and child make a familiar, touching scene.*

touchy *adj.* sensitive, jumpy, nervous, short-tempered, irritable

Women's rights is a touchy subject in some countries. Don't be so touchy—I didn't mean to offend you. ANT. calm, collected.

tough *adj.* **1** strong, hard *This shoe-leather is so tough it will last for ever.* **2** leathery, inedible, sinewy *This steak is as tough as leather.* ANT. (1) weak, vulnerable. (2) tender.

tour *vb.* travel, visit *Our whole family will be touring the country this summer in our new car.* *n.* trip, excursion, voyage, journey *I once took a tour of all the sights of London.*

tourist *n.* sightseer, holiday-maker, visitor, day-tripper, traveller *Tourists provide a substantial amount of income for many European countries.*

tournament *n.* contest, match, competition *Boris is likely to win the chess tournament again this year.*

tow *vb.* pull, drag, draw, haul *How can that tiny tugboat tow that huge string of barges?*

tower *n.* spire, steeple *The tower on the parish church is in need of restoration.* *vb.* overlook, look over, soar, rise above *The new office block towers over the rest of the town centre.*

town *n.* borough, city, municipality *The nearest town is twenty miles away from where we live.*

toy *n.* plaything, game *It's time to put away your toys and come in to have dinner.* *vb.* play, trifle *Sadie was just toying with my emotions: she really loved Arthur.*

trace *n.* sign, mark, hint, suggestion, vestige *You can taste just a trace of rust in this water. I couldn't find the slightest trace of her in the entire building.* *vb.* track, hunt, pursue, follow *The detective traced the thief's movements on the night of the robbery.*

track *n.* **1** mark, sign, trail, trace *The tracks of the dog were plainly visible in the snow.* **2** trail, path, road, route, way *We went far from the beaten track to find these blueberries.* *vb.* trail, pursue, trace, hunt, follow *The police tracked the fugitive through the wilderness till they caught him.*

tract *n.* region, area, district, territory *A huge tract of land has been set aside for wildlife conservation.*

trade *n.* **1** commerce, business, dealing, traffic *Trade between the countries has become competitive.* **2** occupation, livelihood, craft, profession *Where do you think Phil learned the harness-making trade?* *vb.* barter, exchange, swap *I'll trade my bat for your football.*

tradition *n.* custom, convention, practice *It has long been a tradition in our family to celebrate birthdays with big parties.*

traditional *adj.* usual, customary, established, conventional; conservative *We sat round the fire singing traditional songs, like 'Greensleeves'.*

traffic *n.* **1** movement, flow, travel, passage *The traffic is very heavy in the rush hour.* **2** trade, business, dealings *The drugs traffic increases yearly.*

..mph *n.* conquest, victory, success *After winning the golf match, the champion had another triumph to add to his list.* *vb.* win, prevail, succeed *Justice and goodness always triumph over evil in the end, but I can't always wait till the end.* ANT. *n.* defeat, failure. *vb.* lose; fail.

..umphant *adj.* victorious, successful, conquering *The Roman legions made a triumphant entrance into the city.* ANT. defeated, beaten.

..ivial *adj.* trifling, unimportant, insignificant, petty, paltry *It is trivial to me whether you go or stay.*

..rophy *n.* prize, award, reward; medal, cup, badge *Bob won this silver trophy for singing and that gold one for stopping.*

..rouble *vb.* 1 distress, disturb, worry, concern, upset, confuse *As you can imagine, my mother was a little troubled to learn that I had failed my exam.* 2 bother, inconvenience *You needn't trouble to go to the door: I can let myself out.* *n.* 1 misfortune, difficulty, concern *Sometimes I think that our watchdog is more trouble than he's worth.* 2 pains, inconvenience, exertion, effort *Please don't go to any trouble to make anything special—beef Wellington with truffles, asparagus and pommes rissolés will be fine.*

trouble-maker *n.* rascal, mischief-maker, nuisance *Those ugly rumours about our closing down were started by that trouble-maker, Casper.*

troublesome *adj.* annoying, irritating *My new car is proving to be as troublesome as the old one.*

true *adj.* 1 correct, accurate, valid *That is a true account of what happened.* 2 genuine, real, actual, valid, legitimate *Can you prove that you are the true and rightful heir to the fortune?* 3 faithful, trusty, steady, staunch, loyal, dependable, sincere *If you were a true friend of mine, you would come to the rescue at once.*

trust *n.* 1 confidence, reliance, dependence, faith *I have always put my trust in my equipment, which is why I haven't had an accident yet.* 2 hope, faith *I shall accept your story on trust.* *vb.* rely on, have confidence in, depend on *Whenever someone earnestly says to me 'You can trust me', I don't.*

trusted *adj.* reliable, trustworthy, dependable, true, loyal, devoted, staunch *Judas, I always thought you were one of my trusted friends.* ANT. untrustworthy.

truth *n.* 1 truthfulness, correctness, veracity, accuracy; reality *The truth is not always what one sees at first glance.* 2 fact(s), the case *Please tell me the truth; what really happened?*

truthful *adj.* honest; frank, open *I wondered if Salome was being completely truthful about her relationship with John.* ANT. dishonest, lying.

try *vb.* 1 attempt, endeavour, strive *I am trying to tell you, but you keep interrupting.* 2 test, examine, analyse, investigate, prove *Let's try this new kind of washing powder.* *n.* attempt, endeavour, effort *If you give it a try, I'm sure you'll succeed.*

tragedy *n.* disaster, calamity, catastrophe, misfortune, misery *It is a tragedy when a cure is available but one cannot afford the treatment.*

tragic *adj.* sad, unfortunate, miserable, depressing, mournful, melancholy *Her tragic death at the age of twenty-nine was reported in the papers.* ANT. comic.

trail *vb.* 1 drag, draw *Phoebe came in, trailing her fur coat on the floor just to show off.* 2 pursue, track, trace, follow *The dogs trailed the fox to the woods and then lost the scent.* *n.* 1 track, smell, scent *The dogs picked up the trail of the escaped convict and began to howl.* 2 path, way *Let's follow the trail through the woods to the village.*

train *vb.* teach, guide, drill, prepare *These troops have been trained in hand-to-hand combat and are battle-ready.*

trait *n.* feature, quality, characteristic *Edward has all the traits one needs to become a compassionate doctor.*

traitor *n.* betrayer, turncoat, spy *Norman was suspected of selling secrets to the enemy and was condemned as a traitor.*

tramp *vb.* march, stamp, trample, stomp, trudge *Vickie came into the house quite angry and tramped up the stairs to her room.* *n.* vagabond, vagrant, hobo *The tramps wandered around town, wearing rags and looking forlorn.*

trample *vb.* stomp, crush, squash *The children had trampled down the newly seeded lawn.*

tranquil *adj.* peaceful, calm, undisturbed, quiet *Only the hideous laugh of the hyena broke the tranquil silence.* ANT. disturbed, upset, agitated.

transaction *n.* negotiation, deal, settlement *Their government has concluded a transaction for purchasing high-grade oil from Britain.*

transcend *vb.* go beyond, exceed, rise above *Our moral concerns transcend any mercenary thoughts others might have.*

transfer *vb.* 1 shift, move, transport *All of these boxes must be transferred to another warehouse today.* 2 assign, reassign, change *The author has transferred all his rights to the book to his wife.* *n.* change, move, shift *The transfer of ownership of the boat will be completed when we receive payment.*

transform *vb.* change, convert, turn into *The instant she kissed the prince, he was transformed into a frog.*

transient *adj.* passing, transitory, temporary *Storms and other weather phenomena are regarded as transient problems.*

translate *vb.* render, put into *Can you translate this hieroglyphic inscription into English for me?*

translation *n.* rendering, equivalent, version *My translation of Homer's works never won any prizes.*

transmit *vb.* send, dispatch, transfer, pass; broadcast *The news will be transmitted to the public as soon as it is received.*

transparent *adj.* 1 clear, limpid *If you can see everything through it, it's transparent, but if it's frosted, we call that translucent.* 2 clear, obvious, evident, plain *The meaning of this sentence is quite transparent—it can only mean one thing.* ANT. opaque.

transport *vb.* carry, transfer, move, shift *The ore is transported from the mine to the processing plant by ship.* *n.* transportation, transit, carriage *The transport systems of this country are very complex.*

trap *n.* snare, pitfall, net, deadfall *We set a trap to catch the animal that has been stealing our corn.* *vb.* ensnare, entrap, net, bag *In some places, hunters used to trap beavers for their fur.*

trauma *n.* shock; ordeal, crisis *It was a terrible trauma for the poor child to lose both parents in the same accident.*

travel *vb.* journey, voyage, cruise, roam *After travelling all over the United States, we finally returned home, exhausted.* *n.* travelling, touring *Travel to foreign countries can be very educational.*

treacherous *adj.* 1 dangerous, deceptive, misleading *The icy conditions look treacherous to me.* 2 unfaithful, false, traitorous *The colonel was found guilty of treacherous behaviour.* ANT. (2) loyal, faithful.

treachery *n.* betrayal, disloyalty, treason *Assassination of the king was an act of treachery deserving capital punishment.* ANT. loyalty, steadfastness.

tread *vb.* walk, step; trample, tramp *Tread lightly over this broken glass.* *n.* step, walk *We sneaked along with catlike tread.*

treason *n.* treachery, betrayal, disloyalty *Selling government secrets to another state is an act of treason.*

treasure *n.* riches, wealth, abundance *The pirates were said to have buried their treasure on this beach, but no one has yet found it.* *vb.* guard, prize, value *Martin told me that he treasures our friendship above anything else.*

treat *vb.* 1 handle, deal with, manage, negotiate *How do you plan to treat the problem of increased student absences?* 2 administer, attend, tend, heal *A doctor knows best how to treat the condition you complain of.* 3 approach, discuss, regard *Scientists treat UFO sightings with very little respect.* 4 indulge, pay for *May I treat you to an ice-cream cone?* *n.* 1 present, gift *Dinner tonight is to be a treat for you, so you needn't pay for anything* 2 surprise; fun, amusement *We're having a trip to the fair, as a treat for Robin's birthday.*

treatment *n.* 1 care, cure, remedy, assistance *The doctor talked with Rosemary about treatment for her asthma.* 2 handling, dealing, manner *The treatment of the subject in your essay was excellent.*

treaty *n.* pact, compact, agreement, bargain, covenant *The treaty called for Kenya to provide the coffee, Barbados the sugar, and Britain the cream.*

tremble *vb.* quiver, shake, quake, shiver, shudder *The leaves of the aspen tremble at the slightest breeze.*

tremendous *adj.* huge, enormous, gigantic, colossal, great, large *Looming above us, disappearing into the clouds, was a tremendous*

beanstalk. 1 *Informal:* excellent, fantastic; unusu *That tea was really tremendous, Mum.*

trench *n.* ditch, gully, moat, gorge *The trench surroun was filled with water for added protection.*

trend *n.* tendency, inclination, course, drift *The trena ing one's hair green and lavender is dying out.*

trendy *adj.* fashionable, chic, stylish, in vogue *Count o wear only the trendiest outfit.*

trepidation *n.* fear, anxiety, shock, dread; quaking *With we approached the border guards, seeking to get through t*

trespasser *n.* intruder, invader, encroacher *It was clear signs that trespassers who ventured on to the property would cuted.*

trial *n.* 1 test, examination, proof, analysis *The race that yesterday was just a trial to see which cars would qualify.* lawsuit, hearing, case, contest *The defendant is on trial for m* 3 ordeal, suffering, difficulty *Since her husband died, Mrs has been through a terrible trial.*

tribe *n.* clan, race *Most of the tribes of Indians living in the World are now gone.*

tribute *n.* praise, admiration, recognition, acknowledgment *We tribute today to the fallen heroes who fought to make us free.*

trick *n.* 1 deception, trickery, stratagem, wile *Throwing that peb against the window was just a trick to make the teacher look the oth way.* 2 joke, jest, prank *The children's putting salt in the sug bowl was just a trick—they meant no harm.* *vb.* dupe, fool, bam boozle, cheat, swindle, defraud *The swindlers tricked me out o £2000.*

trickle *vb.* dribble, drop, drip, seep, leak *The fuel was trickling through a small hole at the bottom of the tank.*

tricky *adj.* difficult, complicated; delicate *The situation became very tricky when we learned that the culprit was her brother-in-law.*

trifle *n.* frivolity, knickknack *Don't squander your pocket money on trifles.* *vb.* toy, dally *It is evil to trifle with other people's feelings.*

trifling *adj.* unimportant, trivial, insignificant, petty *The money I lost on that investment was trifling compared to what the banks had to write off.*

trim *vb.* 1 clip, prune, shave, cut, shear *The gardener trims the hedge about three times a year.* 2 decorate, adorn, ornament *Let's trim the Christmas tree tonight.* *adj.* neat, compact, tidy *Susan does not have what I would call a trim appearance.*

trip¹ *vb.* 1 stumble *Marla tripped over the rug and sprawled on the floor.* 2 err, bungle, blunder, slip *I tripped on the last five questions and failed the exam.*

trip² *n.* voyage, cruise, excursion, journey, tour *The fortune-teller told me that I would soon take a long trip.*

trite *adj.* commonplace, hackneyed, dull *The plot of that western is so trite—we've seen it dozens of times.*

trying *adj.* difficult, annoying, troublesome, bothersome *These hardships are proving trying for all of us.*

tube *n.* pipe, channel, conduit, hose *There is a tube connecting me to that machine over there.*

tuck (in) *vb.* 1 put in, insert; put to bed *Mother tucked the children in and kissed them goodnight.* 2 *Informal:* eat up *Here's your meal: now tuck in!*

tug *vb.* yank, pull, jerk *When I tugged at his beard, it came off in my hand!*

tumble *vb.* fall; trip, stumble *Everything came tumbling out on me when I opened the cabinet. Patrick came tumbling down the stairs and fell all in a heap.*

tumble-down *adj.* decrepit, ramshackle, dilapidated, broken-down, rickety *There's a tumble-down shack by the railway track.*

tumult *n.* to-do, ado, confusion, disturbance, commotion, disorder, uproar *There was tumult in the restaurant when a diner saw a mouse scurry across the floor.* ANT. peacefulness, tranquillity.

tune *n.* melody, song, air, strain *That's the same tune they played at our wedding party.*

tuneful *adj.* melodious, harmonious, sweet-sounding *Did Addinsell really write that tuneful melody?*

tunnel *n.* excavation, hole; shaft, passage *The prisoners dug an escape tunnel with their bare hands.*

turbulent *adj.* stormy, violent, raging, uncontrolled, restless, agitated *The sea became turbulent as we neared the whirlpool.* ANT. calm, quiet, peaceful.

turn *vb.* 1 spin, revolve, rotate *The wheel continued to turn long after the motor had stopped.* 2 reverse, change *Turn to face the wall.* 3 become, change, transform *The bitter cold turned the pond to ice overnight.* 4 send, drive *They turned me away at the door, saying I was too young.* 5 sour, spoil, ferment *The milk has turned, so you'll have to drink your coffee black.* *vb. phr.* **turn against** rebel against, defy, oppose *Why do some people turn against their friends?* **turn aside** divert, deflect *The heavy armour turned aside the spears and arrows.* **turn down** 1 lower, decrease *Please turn down the volume of that stereo.* 2 refuse, deny, reject *They turned down my application for a promotion.* **turn in** 1 deliver, offer, give *I turned in my report early this week.* 2 retire, rest *I think I'll turn in, as it's past my bedtime.* **turn into** change into, become *You can't make a frog turn into a prince by kissing it, you fool!* **turn loose** free, liberate, unchain, release *I don't want to be around when they turn that leopard loose.* **turn off** stop; close *Please turn off the machine before you leave.* **turn on** start; open *Turn on the lights.* **turn out** 1 switch off *Please turn out the lights.* 2 dismiss, discharge, evict *The landlord turned us out for not paying the rent.* **turn up** 1 appear, arrive, surface *Judy turned up late for the party.* 2 be found, come to light *The lost coins turned up in the cupboard.* 3 increase, raise *Please don't turn up the volume of the hi-fi any further.* *n.*

1 revolution, rotation, cycle, round *Let's watch the merry-go-round do one more complete turn.* **2** change, alteration, turning *Make a right turn at the corner.* **3** opportunity, chance, stint *Why can't I have a turn at shooting the gun?*

turncoat *n.* traitor, renegade *At the end of the investigation, the general himself was found to have been the turncoat.* ANT. loyalist.

tussle *vb.,n.* fight, scuffle, struggle *The ruffians tussled in the street. There was a tussle going on as to who should control the project.*

tutor *n.* teacher, instructor *Fred was doing badly in maths, so his parents paid for a tutor to help him.* *vb.* teach, instruct, coach, train, guide *I used to tutor French students when I was at college.*

twilight *n.* dusk, nightfall *We met at twilight behind the rose bush.*

twinge *n.* pang, pain *I felt a twinge of conscience for having told Evan's mother about his pinching the pie.*

twinkle *vb.* scintillate, sparkle, shine *The stars twinkled in the sky.*

twirl *vb.* spin, rotate, whirl *The villain twirled his mustachios and sniggered cruelly.*

twist *vb.* **1** intertwine, interweave, braid *These wires are so twisted I'll never get them apart.* **2** contort, distort, warp *The steel girders of the bridge were twisted out of shape by the fire. Why do you always twist everything that I say?* *n.* curve, bend, turn *The road had too many twists and turns for safety.*

twitch *vb.,n.* jerk, shudder *The dying snake lay there twitching in the sand. With a sudden twitch, the dog had released himself from the collar.*

twitter *vb.* chirp, cheep, sing *I love to awaken in the country early and hear the birds twittering.*

type *n.* **1** kind, sort, variety *What type of person would want to kill birds?* **2** sample, example, model *Is this the type of car you would like?*

typical *adj.* representative, characteristic *In the middle of the town is a typical shopping precinct.* ANT. atypical, odd.

tyranny *n.* despotism, oppression; injustice *We suffered horribly under the tyranny of the dictators.*

tyrant *n.* dictator, despot, autocrat *The tsars were terrible tyrants who had people killed on the slightest pretext.*

u

ugly *adj.* **1** unsightly, hideous, repulsive *If you want to see something really ugly, take a look at a Gila monster at the zoo.* **2** unpleasant, nasty, vicious, wicked, evil *There's an ugly rumour going around that Penny was seen going out with Charlie.*

ulterior *adj.* concealed, hidden, implied *The woman had an ulterior motive in asking me to hold her baby for a minute.* ANT. evident, revealed.

ultimate *adj.* final, last, decisive, extreme *The ultimate insult was dismissing me at the Christmas party.*

umpire *n.* referee, arbitrator, judge *After playing cricket for twenty years, Roger got a job as an umpire.* *vb.* referee, arbitrate, judge *Can we get your father to umpire the game this Saturday?*

unanimity *n.* agreement, unity, accord *The vote of 93 to 0 indicated unanimity in rejecting the proposal.*

unassuming *adj.* modest, humble, retiring *Although she has an unassuming manner you must not underestimate Janet's talents.* ANT. vain, showy, pompous, arrogant.

unattached *adj.* separate, apart; single, unmarried *There is a new club for unattached men and women.*

unaware (of) *adj.* unmindful, ignorant, oblivious *Victor seems totally unaware of what people are saying about him.* ANT. aware, informed.

unawares *adv.* unexpectedly, by surprise *Whipsteed was caught unawares and had no time to hide the incriminating evidence.*

unbalanced *adj.* deranged, mad, insane, crazy *Just because someone talks to himself that doesn't mean he's unbalanced.*

unbearable *adj.* intolerable, insufferable *The pain from the burn was almost unbearable.*

unbending *adj.* rigid, obstinate, inflexible, resolute, firm, determined, decided *The union has proved to be unbending in its pension demands.*

unbroken *adj.* continuous, complete, whole, uninterrupted *The siege of Troy continued unbroken for ten years.*

uncanny *adj.* remarkable, extraordinary, amazing *Lady Flabsheek bears an uncanny resemblance to her bloodhound.*

uncertain *adj.* unsure, doubtful, dubious, questionable, indefinite, vague *We had to ask for directions because we were uncertain of the exact location of the house.* ANT. certain, positive, unmistakable.

uncivil *adj.* rude, impolite, discourteous *The manager was most uncivil to us when we asked for room service.* ANT. polite, civil.

uncommon *adj.* rare, unusual, scarce, odd, peculiar, strange, queer, remarkable, exceptional *The man at the museum said that we had found a very uncommon variety of orchid.* ANT. usual, ordinary.

unconditional *adj.* total, absolute, complete, unqualified, unlimited *The contract calls for unconditional acceptance of the insurance requirement.* ANT. conditional, tentative.

unconscious *adj.* 1 insensible; faint, dead, out, (*slang*) out cold *The man lay unconscious on the street.* 2 unaware, unmindful *Martha seemed unconscious of the fact that she could help her mother.*

uncouth *adj.* vulgar, rude, ill-mannered, discourteous, impolite *How can you sit at table with someone who has such uncouth manners?* ANT. polite, courteous; civilized, cultivated, cultured.

under *prep.* 1 beneath, below, underneath *We crawled under the ledge of the rock and were safe till the storm stopped.* 2 following, below, in accordance with, subject to *Under the law you cannot kill other people.* ANT. (1) above, over.

undercover *adj.* secret, hidden *Bill was an undercover agent for the government.*

undergo *vb.* experience, endure, tolerate, suffer, go through *Prisoners of war often undergo terrible hardships.*

underhand *adj.* secret, sly, crafty, sneaky, stealthy, secretive *The most underhand thing he did was to tell the teacher of our plan.* ANT. open, honest, direct.

underscore *vb.* emphasize, stress *We always underscore the importance of wearing a seat belt.*

understand *vb.* 1 see, comprehend, grasp, realize *I understand what you're saying but I can't see why you'd want to squeeze oranges for a living.* 2 hear, learn *I understand that some children have been playing with fireworks.*

undertake *vb.* try, attempt, venture *The vicar said we should undertake a collection of old clothes for the poor.*

underwrite *vb.* support, guarantee, finance *I doubt that you could get any investor to underwrite such a scheme.*

undesirable *adj.* objectionable, displeasing, unwanted *We try to keep undesirable people out of our golf club.*

undoing *n.* downfall, ruin, destruction *Admitting that she had bought the murder weapon proved Natalie's undoing.*

undress *vb.* strip, divest, disrobe *Please go into the changing room to undress.*

unearth *vb.* find, discover, bring to light, dig up *Archaeologists have unearthed a 5000-year-old tomb.*

unearthly *adj.* strange, foreign, weird, eerie, supernatural, ghostly *Seeing the body rise into the air without any visible support was an unearthly experience.*

uneasy *adj.* anxious, apprehensive, worried, restless *I have been uneasy ever since the company announced new lay-offs.*

unemployed *adj.* jobless, idle, inactive, unoccupied *As robots replace people there are more and more unemployed factory workers.*

uneven *adj.* rough, rugged; irregular, variable *You need a four-wheel-*

drive vehicle to traverse such uneven terrain. Hannah's treatment of her children was very uneven.

unexpected *adj.* surprising, sudden, abrupt, startling, unforeseen *Considering the weather forecast, the rainstorm was entirely unexpected.* ANT. expected, predicted, anticipated.

unfair *adj.* unjust, partial, biased; dishonest *It was very unfair of you to change the rules in the middle of the game.* ANT. fair, objective.

unfaithful *adj.* disloyal, treacherous *The idea of Richard's being unfaithful to our cause never crossed my mind.*

unfeeling *adj.* callous, hard, unsympathetic, numb *Those unfeeling wretches trap and kill the animals purely for profit.*

unfortunate *adj.* unlucky, unhappy, sad, unsuccessful *It is most unfortunate for you that you uncovered our little plan, Holmes.* ANT. lucky.

unfriendly *adj.* hostile, antagonistic; gruff *Our neighbour has been unfriendly ever since we moved in.* ANT. friendly, kind; outgoing.

ungainly *adj.* awkward, clumsy, bungling *Everyone looks ungainly on the first day of ballet class.* ANT. dexterous.

unhappy *adj.* miserable, sad, melancholy, wretched, distressed *Are you unhappy that you have to go back to school?* ANT. happy, joyful.

unhealthy *adj.* sick, infirm, diseased, ill *Despite his having taken the cure at Montecassini, Egbert still looks unhealthy.* ANT. healthy, well.

uniform *adj.* unvarying, regular, unchanging *All laws are not uniform throughout the Common Market.* *n.* outfit, costume *Policemen wear uniforms.*

unimaginable *adj.* inconceivable, unbelievable, incredible *It is unimaginable that Dickson stole the money.*

unimportant *adj.* trivial, trifling, petty, paltry, insignificant *Once they think you guilty, it is unimportant whether you are or not.*

uninteresting *adj.* dull, boring, tiresome, tedious, dreary, monotonous *I have just completed a very uninteresting two-year course in furniture-polishing.*

union *n.* **1** combination, alliance *Father would like nothing better than a union between our two families.* **2** association, society *You cannot work here unless you are a member of the bricklayers' union.*

unique *adj.* single, sole, solitary; incomparable, unparalleled; unprecedented *Figgle missed a unique opportunity for appointment to a managerial position.* ANT. common, ordinary, commonplace.

unit *n.* entity, whole; system *Even though the building contains separate elements, the architect views it as a unit.*

unite *vb.* join, combine, connect, link, associate *The separate European countries agreed to unite to form an economic community.* ANT. divide, separate, sever.

universal *adj.* general, prevailing, prevalent, common *The universal* *feeling among the members is that you should resign.* ANT. local, regional.

universe *n.* world, cosmos, creation *In the entire universe there is no one like you.*

unjust *adj.* biased, unfair, partial *Perhaps Gwen was unjust to accuse you of taking her bracelet.* ANT. just, impartial.

unkind *adj.* unsympathetic, unfeeling, cruel, unpleasant, harsh *The head teacher said some unkind things about the English teachers in the school.*

unknown *adj.* unrecognized, unfamiliar; unexplained *Germaine always seems to have an unknown admirer who sends flowers.*

unlawful *adj.* illegal, illegitimate, illicit *It is unlawful to shoot these birds out of season.*

unlike *adj.* different, dissimilar *It would seem that we have unlike ambitions.*

unlikely *adj.* improbable, implausible *I think it highly unlikely that Edward will still arrive tonight.* ANT. likely, probable.

unlucky *see* **unfortunate.**

unmerciful *adj.* merciless, cruel, heartless, ruthless, brutal *The bully gave that little boy an unmerciful beating for no reason.*

unnecessary *adj.* needless, purposeless, pointless, superfluous *It is unnecessary to keep repeating that I made a mistake.*

unoccupied *adj.* vacant, empty, uninhabited *These houses have been unoccupied since the mines closed.*

unparalleled *adj.* unequalled, peerless, unique, rare, unmatched *In an unparalleled move, a Labour front-bencher voted with the Tories.*

unpleasant *adj.* disagreeable, offensive, obnoxious, repulsive, unpleasing *I thought I noticed an unpleasant odour when I came in.*

unqualified *adj.* 1 unfit, incompetent, incapable *Unless you can offer a year's experience, you would be unqualified for this job.* 2 absolute, unquestioned, utter *After insulting me, you can expect an unqualified 'No!' to your request for a good reference.*

unreal *adj.* imaginary, fanciful, fantastic *The reception we received when we returned home was unreal.*

unrealistic *adj.* visionary, ideal *Your plan for rebuilding the old part of the town is unrealistic because of the costs.*

unreasonable *adj.* 1 excessive, immoderate, extreme, exorbitant, inordinate *The trade unions made unreasonable demands in their wage claims.* 2 silly, thoughtless; irrational *Your unreasonable behaviour shows your immaturity.*

unreliable *adj.* undependable, untrustworthy, wavering *I told you that Winifred is unreliable and wouldn't show up.*

unrest *n.* disquiet, turmoil, trouble; tension *The entire Middle East has been marked by unrest for decades.*

unruffled *adj.* smooth, unperturbed, calm, serene, cool *Despite the press of the crowd seeking his autograph, Clive remained unruffled.*

unruly *adj.* unmanageable, disobedient, disorderly, undisciplined *The police tried to calm the unruly mob.* ANT. orderly.

unsatisfactory *adj.* displeasing, unacceptable, deficient, disappointing *The teacher handed back my paper, saying it was unsatisfactory.*

unsightly *adj.* unattractive, ugly, hideous *The county office tower in Aylesbury is the most unsightly building in England.*

unsound *adj.* **1** weak, flimsy, feeble, fragile *The foundations of the house are unsound and it will collapse in a few months.* **2** unstable, weak, diseased, sick, impaired, unhealthy *I am sorry to say that we consider your brother to be of unsound mind.* **3** faulty, invalid, false *The reasoning in your argument is unsound if you think that people will eat insects.*

unsuitable *adj.* inappropriate, unfit, improper *That lavender dress is unsuitable attire for a funeral.*

untidy *adj.* unkempt, disorderly; unorganized; sloppy, messy, slovenly *Why must you always leave your room in such untidy condition?* ANT. tidy, neat.

unusual *adj.* uncommon, exceptional, strange, remarkable, extraordinary, peculiar, queer, odd *The duckbilled platypus is, I agree, a most unusual animal.*

unwholesome *adj.* unhealthy; poisonous, dangerous *When they opened the Pharaoh's tomb an unwholesome vapour escaped, almost killing them.*

unwieldy *adj.* bulky, awkward, clumsy *These so-called portable television sets are not heavy, but they are very unwieldy.*

uphold *vb.* support, maintain, back *I uphold the right of any person to a fair trial.*

upkeep *n.* maintenance, support, sustenance *I cannot see why you feel responsible for the upkeep of your cousin's brother-in-law.*

upright *adj.* **1** erect, vertical, perpendicular *We gradually raised the flagpole till it was upright.* **2** just, honest, honourable, true *Bill is one of the most upright members of our community.* *n.* pole, support, prop, column *Slip that upright under the board while I hold it up in the air.*

uprising *n.* revolt, revolution, rebellion, mutiny *It took three days to quell the prisoners' uprising.*

uproar *n.* commotion, disturbance, tumult, disorder, noise *I couldn't hear the speaker above the uproar from the crowd.*

upset *vb.* **1** overturn, capsize, topple *The rowing boat upset in the middle of the lake and we almost drowned.* **2** disturb, agitate, fluster, bother *I was upset by the news that you were moving so far away.* *adj.* disturbed, unsettled *I had an upset stomach all night from eating a lot of chocolate.*

up-to-date *adj.* current, new, modern, latest *Count on Evelyn to be dressed in the most up-to-date fashion.*

urban *adj.* civic, municipal, city, metropolitan *The traffic problem is quite severe on the urban roads during rush hour.*

urge *vb.* **1** force, push, drive, press, prod *Unless you had urged me, I never would have run for office.* **2** plead, persuade, beg, implore *I* *urge you to finish your homework first.* **3** advise, recommend *The doctor urged that everyone stop smoking.* *n.* impulse *I suddenly got the urge to phone my sister in South America.* ANT. *vb.* dissuade, discourage.

urgent *adj.* **1** pressing, immediate *There is urgent business that prevents my mother from leaving work this week.* **2** insistent, persistent, demanding *The urgent ringing of the doorbell finally woke me, and I ran to see who it was.*

usage *n.* **1** treatment; use *This puppy has been subjected to bad usage.* **2** custom, habit, practice, convention, tradition *Usage has it that men hold doors open for women.*

use *vb.* **1** employ, utilize *I use green nail polish only on Tuesdays.* **2** exhaust, spend, expend, consume *Why use your energy to do housework?* **3** exercise, work *I use my left hand less than my right.* *n.* **1** employment, utilization *The use of certain dyes has been found unsafe for human consumption.* **2** advantage, profit, point, benefit *It's no use trying to convince you that the earth is flat.*

useful *adj.* helpful, beneficial, advantageous *If you find this old encyclopaedia useful, you may take it.*

useless *adj.* worthless, ineffective, unusable *Why don't you get rid of these useless old bicycle tyres?*

usher *n.,vb.* guide, escort *Manuel works as an usher and sees all the films for nothing. Hubert phoned to ask if he could usher me to the dance next week!!*

usual *adj.* customary, ordinary, normal, regular, habitual, accustomed, common *The usual way of attracting people's attention is by calling their name, not by throwing something at them.*

usurp *vb.* seize, lay hold of, take over, appropriate, assume *The general has usurped control from the president, using his elite guard.*

utensil *n.* tool, appliance, implement, instrument *These eating utensils, found in the dig, must be thousands of years old.*

utmost *adj.* furthest, greatest; ultimate *I shall do my utmost to see that you get a fair trial.*

utter[1] *vb.* say, speak, pronounce, express *Nicole uttered her first words at the age of nine months (and hasn't been quiet since).*

utter[2] *adj.* absolute, complete, total, unqualified *Anyone who would try to cross a motorway on foot is an utter fool.*

V

vacant *adj.* 1 unoccupied, empty; uninhabited *The flat will not be vacant till the end of the month.* 2 thoughtless, vapid, vacuous, stupid *In reply to my question, all I got was a vacant stare.* ANT. (1) filled, occupied. (2) bright, alert, intelligent.

vaccinate *vb.* inoculate, immunize *All children were vaccinated against smallpox.*

vague *adj.* uncertain, indefinite, unsure, obscure *As he gives only vague answers to my questions, I can get no information.* ANT. specific, unequivocal.

vain *adj.* 1 useless, worthless, idle, trivial, unfruitful, unsuccessful *I made a vain attempt to catch the paddle, but it had floated out of reach.* 2 proud, conceited, self-important, arrogant *Tim is a vain man who will never admit to being wrong.* ANT. (1) successful. (2) humble.

valiant *adj.* brave, bold, courageous, heroic, intrepid, dauntless, unafraid, fearless *They were valiant soldiers who died for their Queen in distant lands.* ANT. cowardly, afraid, fearful.

valid *adj.* 1 sound, logical, well-founded *Your argument is valid, but I just disagree with you.* 2 genuine, real, true, actual, authentic, trustworthy *This painted bowl is a valid example of Etruscan art.* ANT. (1) invalid, illogical. (2) fake, counterfeit.

valour *n.* bravery, boldness, courage, intrepidity, heroism, fearlessness *This medal was awarded to my father for valour on the battlefield.*

valuable *adj.* 1 important, worthy *I have valuable information that I am ready to sell to the highest bidder.* 2 costly, high-priced *This necklace is very valuable, even though you bought it at a jumble sale.* ANT. (2) worthless.

value *n.* 1 importance, worth, merit, benefit *Anyone who has had any experience has learned the value of an education.* 2 cost, price *I asked the salesman about the value of the diamond necklace.* *vb.* 1 rate, price, appraise, evaluate *This Persian carpet has been valued at more than £25,000.* 2 esteem, prize, appreciate *I value your friendship much more highly than I do the winning of the contest.*

vanish *vb.* disappear, evaporate, dissolve *The leprechaun gave a nod and vanished before my very eyes.* ANT. appear.

vanity *n.* pride, conceit, smugness *Ramona's vanity makes her spend hours before the mirror putting on make-up.* ANT. humility.

vanquish *vb.* conquer, defeat, beat, overcome, subdue *The attacking forces were finally vanquished by the freedom fighters.*

vapour *n.* mist, fog, steam; haze *The vapour rising from the soup is fogging my spectacles.*

variable *adj.* changeable, shifting, unsteady *The weather is so variable these days that you had better take an umbrella.* ANT. constant, unwavering.

variety *n.* **1** change, diversity *For variety, why not have an egg for breakfast instead of just cereal?* **2** sort, kind, form, class, type *I am not familiar with this variety of gateau, but it's delicious.*

various *adj.* several, diverse, sundry, different *We must examine the various ways in which the work can be done.*

vary *vb.* change, alter, diversify *Kathleen's moods vary from miserable to elated. Try varying your approach to see which is the most successful.*

vast *adj.* extensive, huge, enormous, immense, measureless, unlimited *We were travelling at the speed of light in the vast reaches of outer space.*

vault¹ *vb.* leap, jump, spring *The runner easily vaulted over the high wall and eluded his pursuers.*

vault² *n.* **1** tomb, sepulchre, crypt, grave, catacomb *The archaeologists unsealed the vault of the Pharaoh, who had died 3000 years before.* **2** safe, safety-deposit box *We keep our valuable papers in a vault at the bank.*

veer *vb.* swing, turn, deflect, deviate, swerve *At the corner I had to veer sharply to avoid hitting a boy on a skateboard.*

vehicle *n.* conveyance *You'd need a four-wheel-drive vehicle to travel on this road.*

veil *n.* gauze, mask, film, web *The mysterious lady wore a dark veil and we couldn't see her features.* *vb.* conceal, hide, cover *Your veiled threats don't frighten me.*

velocity *n.* speed, swiftness, quickness, rapidity *Light travels at a velocity of about 186,000 miles per second.*

vengeance *n.* revenge, retaliation *Carter was seeking vengeance for the pranks played on him by the children.*

venom *n.* **1** poison, toxin *The spitting cobra can shoot its venom into the eyes from a great distance.* **2** spite, bitterness, hate *The prisoner spoke of his accomplices with such venom that the police were afraid to release him on bail.*

vent *vb.* release, let out, discharge *Harold vented his anger on the first person he met.* *n.* opening, ventilator, hole *Can you open a vent? It's so stuffy in here.*

venture *n.* attempt, risk, chance, test *The investor wouldn't put his money in a venture like yours.* *vb.* risk, dare, gamble, hazard *I'd venture to say that we ought to leave before the fight starts. Don't try to venture out in the storm.*

verbal *adj.* spoken, oral, unwritten *We had a verbal agreement that I could visit the children once a week.* ANT. written, printed.

verbose *adj.* wordy, lengthy, long-winded, talkative *Carruthers' verbose, two-hour speech could have been delivered in five minutes.*

verdict *n.* decision, judgement, opinion, finding *The jury has returned a verdict of guilty.*

verge *n.* edge, rim, lip, margin, brim, brink *It's a good thing you reminded me—I was on the verge of telling them your secret.*

verify *vb.* confirm, prove, substantiate, affirm, corroborate *The police verified that you were home at the time of the crime.*

versatile *adj.* adaptable, all-round; many-sided *Ugolini was versatile enough to sing opera, lieder and rock 'n' roll.*

version *n.* rendering, interpretation, rendition, account *Your version of the events does not agree with the evidence.*

vertical *adj.* upright, perpendicular, erect *Harrington climbed up the vertical face of the office block.* ANT. horizontal.

very *adv.* extremely, greatly, exceedingly, considerably *This is a very bad test result. It was very good of you to come.*

vessel *n.* 1 ship, boat, craft *How many vessels pass through the Suez Canal in a year?* 2 container, receptacle, holder *Certain acids that attack glass are stored in wax vessels.*

vestige *n.* trace, hint, suggestion, token *When you have finished cleaning the floor, I don't want to find any vestige of the paint you spilled.*

veteran *n.* old hand, master; expert *Thewless is a veteran when it comes to dealing with teenagers.*

veto *n.* denial, refusal *The chairman's veto was overridden by a unanimous vote of the committee.* *vb.* deny, refuse, negate, prohibit, forbid *The college wanted to increase its staff, but the local council vetoed their decision.* ANT. *n.* approval. *vb.* approve.

vex *vb.* bother, pester, annoy, irritate, anger, plague *The teacher found James's behaviour particularly vexing.*

vibrate *vb.* tremble, shake, quake, quiver *The explosion was so intense that it caused windows five miles away to vibrate.*

vice¹ *n.* evil, wickedness, sin, corruption, depravity *Of his many vices, drinking and smoking were so mild as to be like virtues.*

vice² *adj.* deputy, subordinate; acting *The vice-chairman chairs a meeting when the chairman is away.*

vicinity *n.* neighbourhood, area, proximity; nearness *I never slept well while we lived in the vicinity of the boiler factory.*

vicious *adj.* 1 wicked, evil, bad, sinful, corrupt *Blackmail is a vicious crime.* 2 savage, dangerous, cruel *There's a vicious killer on the loose.*

victim *n.* sufferer, prey, scapegoat; target, butt; dupe, fool *A confidence man often picks elderly pensioners as his victims.*

victimize *vb.* swindle, dupe, cheat, take advantage of, deceive *People who are especially worried about the security of their savings are easily victimized.*

victor *n.* winner, champion, conqueror *The victor in the marathon was accused of having taken steroids.* ANT. loser.

victory *n.* conquest, success, triumph *Our victory at the polls is due mainly to the unpopularity of our opponents.* ANT. defeat.

view *n.* **1** sight, vision *Suddenly the figure of a huge toad came into view up the road, and we ran.* **2** vista, prospect, look *There's a lovely view of the town from this window.* **3** thought, opinion, belief, judgement, impression *Please let me have your views on the subject before tomorrow.* *vb.* see, look at, examine, regard, inspect *The entire class was invited to view the model of the city at the museum.*

viewpoint *n.* opinion, attitude, standpoint; aspect; stance *From Peter's viewpoint, an exposé might not be such a good idea.*

vigilant *adj.* watchful, alert, attentive, observant *We must remain vigilant if we are to catch the culprit.* ANT. negligent, careless.

vigorous *adj.* energetic, strong, active, forceful, powerful *With a vigorous effort we managed to reach the top of the rock.*

vigour *n.* energy, vitality, liveliness, strength *Sappersby is tackling his new responsibilities with great vigour.*

vile *adj.* **1** wicked, sinful, base, bad, wretched, evil *How could you have done such a vile thing as to feed the goldfish to the cat?* **2** offensive, objectionable, disgusting, revolting, obnoxious *Simon has some exceedingly vile habits of which failing to have a bath is the least.*

villain *n.* scoundrel, brute, rascal, rogue, scamp *As the villain was tying the heroine to the railway track the train struck them both.*

vindicate *vb.* **1** acquit, free, absolve *The statement issued by the authorities vindicated him and said that he had acted properly in the circumstances.* **2** justify, prove *His success at college vindicates my encouraging him to study further.*

vindictive *adj.* resentful, revengeful, retaliatory *Robert is so vindictive at having lost that he is taking it out on everyone.*

violate *vb.* break, infringe, transgress *If you light a cigarette in here you are violating the law.*

violent *adj.* **1** powerful, forceful, strong, forcible *A violent wind tore the sail to shreds and we were at the mercy of the waves.* **2** furious, angry, savage, fierce; passionate *My mother and father have never had a violent argument since they were married.* ANT. (1) gentle.

virgin *n.* maiden, maid *The young virgins danced around the maypole in the rites of spring.* *adj.* untouched, pure, unused, chaste *That district is virgin territory that remains to be explored.*

virile *adj.* manly, masculine, (*informal*) macho *Theo had always seemed so manly that we never guessed the truth about him.* ANT. feminine, effeminate.

virtual *adj.* potential; possible *You must be aware of the virtual danger you risk going into the Casbah at night.*

virtually *adv.* nearly, almost, practically; in effect *The role of managing director is virtually the same in both companies.*

virtue *n.* **1** goodness, morality, righteousness, honour *A man of virtue would never treat anyone badly.* **2** distinction, quality, characteristic *This machine has the virtue of never needing any oil as it has no moving parts.*

virtuous *adj.* moral, upright, upstanding, ethical *As Thea is such a virtuous young lady, I cannot believe she would do anything like that.* ANT. immoral.

visible *adj.* perceptible, apparent; evident, obvious *As the fog dispersed, the outlines of the bridge became visible.* ANT. invisible, hidden.

vision *n.* 1 sight, eyesight *The optician told me that these glasses would improve my vision.* 2 illusion, fantasy, apparition, spectre, phantom, ghost, spook *Coming down the old creaking dusty stairs was a vision of ugliness that gave me nightmares for years.* 3 farsightedness, imagination, foresight *The council had the vision, twenty years ago, to see this town as a great yachting centre.*

visit *vb.* call on, look in on, drop in on *Sometimes I visit my friends in the evenings.* *n.* appointment; call *I had a visit from your aunt last night.*

visitor *n.* guest, caller *The police surveillance team recorded that the suspect had two visitors at midnight.*

vista *n.* view, scene, aspect, prospect *From here you get a magnificent vista of the entire countryside.*

vital *adj.* essential, critical; life-and-death *I don't think that any vital organs were affected. It is vital that we get you to the hospital at once.*

vivid *adj.* clear, strong, bright *Her yellow hat stood out in vivid contrast to the surrounding black derbies.*

vocal *adj.* 1 spoken, said, oral, uttered *A vocal insult isn't ever as deeply felt as one in writing.* 2 outspoken, definite, specific *If Laura weren't so vocal in her criticism of others, she might be better liked.*

vocation *n.* career, profession, occupation, calling, employment *For what vocation does philately prepare you?*

vogue *n.* fashion, style *Short skirts are happily in vogue again this year.*

void *adj.* 1 meaningless, useless, invalid, worthless *This document is void unless both husband and wife sign it.* 2 empty, vacant, unoccupied *The light was switched on and we saw that the room was completely void.* *n.* space, emptiness *I haven't eaten since breakfast, and I feel a great void where my stomach is.* ANT. *adj.* (1) valid. (2) full.

volatile *adj.* 1 fickle, changeable, capricious *Volatile people behave in unpredictable ways?* 2 light, vaporous *Petrol is a volatile substance.* ANT. (1) constant, steady. (2) heavy, dense.

volume *n.* 1 book, work; tome *The first volume of the encyclopaedia is free.* 2 capacity, dimensions *The volume of the lorry was large enough to hold a car.* 3 quantity, mass, bulk, amount *We received a huge volume of orders for the fences.*

voluntary *adj.* spontaneous, optional, free *Voluntary gifts to the church building fund are always welcome.* ANT. compulsory, required, forced.

volunteer *vb.* come forward, offer oneself *Shirley volunteered for service in the WRNS during the Second World War.*

vomit *vb.* be sick, (*informal*) throw up *Seeing the way those children were treated was enough to make one vomit.*

vote *n.* **1** election; ballot; choice *The vote for the new parish council takes place next month.* **2** suffrage, franchise *When did women get the vote?* *vb.* elect, ballot; choose, decide *We vote for a new MP in a general election.*

vouch for *vb.phr.* guarantee, affirm, confirm *Can you vouch for the fact that Gardner was with you the entire evening?*

voucher *n.* certificate, document; receipt; slip *Present this voucher at the shop and you will receive a gift.*

vow *n.* pledge, promise, oath *I took a vow that I would get to school on time from now on.* *vb.* **1** pledge, promise, swear *The men vowed their allegiance to the new leader.* **2** declare, state, assert *Imogen vowed that she would never see Eustace again after the way he had behaved.*

voyage *n.* cruise; journey, trip, tour, excursion *We made many voyages to the Mediterranean in those days.*

vulgar *adj.* rude, crude, unrefined, coarse *I have seldom seen a home furnished in such vulgar taste.* ANT. refined.

vulnerable *adj.* defenceless, unguarded, unprotected *With all the soldiers out on manoeuvres, the fort was vulnerable to attack.*

W

wad *n.* material; stuffing, packing *Wads of cotton wool protected the fragile vase in the case.*

wage *vb.* carry on, pursue, conduct, make *The two countries waged continuous war for almost a century.* *n.* **wages.** pay, compensation, salary, rate, earnings *Your wages will be doubled because you have saved the company so much money.*

wail *vb.* moan, cry; mourn, bewail, lament *Stop that wailing, here's your teddy bear back.* *n.* moan, cry *I heard a low wail coming from the cupboard.*

wait *vb.* stay, remain, tarry, linger *Please wait a few minutes; the doctor will be right with you.* *n.* delay, postponement, pause *There will be a twenty-minute wait while the repairs are done.*

waiter *n.* steward, attendant, servant *I have been waiting an hour for the waiter to bring the bill.*

waive *vb.* forgo, renounce, relinquish *We shall be happy to waive the requirements in your case.*

wake (up) *vb.* rouse, arouse; awaken, waken *Please wake me up at six o'clock. I woke in the middle of the night and saw you near the window.* ANT. sleep, doze.

walk *vb.* amble, stroll, saunter, step, march, hike *The usher told me, 'Walk this way.'* *n.* **1** stroll, march, amble *We had a very nice walk in the garden with Grandpa.* **2** path, lane, passage; promenade *We met on the walk by the beach.*

wallow *vb.* flounder, grovel, immerse *Grundel just adored wallowing in self-pity after his arm was broken in the crash.*

wander *vb.* **1** rove, roam, ramble *This poor dog has been wandering all over the neighbourhood looking for his master.* **2** err, digress *Don't wander so much and try to keep to the point of what you're saying.*

want *vb.* desire, need, require, wish, crave *Don't you want to grow up to be a big strong man? What do you want for dinner?* *n.* need, requirement, desire *The fund has been set up for those wants that people are unable to fulfil.*

war *n.* hostilities, combat, battle *Now that we have won the war, let's see if we can win the peace.* *vb.* battle, fight *The two warring families have hated one another for three generations.*

warble *vb.* sing, trill, whistle, pipe *We used to get up very early just to hear the birds warble.*

ward *n.* **1** district, division *The town is divided into wards for elections.* **2** child, dependant, foster child, orphan *The parents and* *their ward, Joy, came to tea.* **3** room *Which ward in the hospital is Alison in?*

warden *n.* guardian, custodian, keeper, guard; jailer *You must ask the warden for permission to leave the premises.*

wardrobe *n.* **1** cupboard, closet *Michael keeps all his suits and jackets hanging in the wardrobe.* **2** clothes, clothing *Sandra will buy a completely new wardrobe for the summer.*

warehouse *n.* depot, depository; stockroom, storeroom *The books are kept in a warehouse from which they are shipped to customers.*

warlike *adj.* belligerent, bellicose, combative, pugnacious *The people in New Guinea are less warlike than before but they are still not friendly.* ANT. peaceable, peaceful.

warm *adj.* **1** heated, temperate; tepid, lukewarm *The water was warm but not hot enough for tea.* **2** eager, enthusiastic, sympathetic *The teacher was not very warm to the suggestion that we go home early.* *vb.* heat *Warm the milk before adding the chocolate.* ANT. *adj.* (1) cool, cold, brisk. (2) indifferent, cool.

warmhearted *adj.* friendly, kind, loving, kindhearted *Our neighbours gave us a warmhearted welcome when we returned from holiday.*

warmth *n.* cordiality, friendliness, geniality *Though we were strangers, we were treated with warmth by the townspeople.*

warn *vb.* caution, admonish, advise *You have been warned before not to drive so fast.*

warning *n.* caution, intimation, sign, advice *The police have been giving out warnings about parking in restricted areas.*

warp *vb.* twist, turn, bend, distort *The tabletop was badly warped by the damp in the cellar.*

warrant *n.* authorization, sanction; warranty, pledge, guarantee, assurance *The financial executive of the bank has given the broker warrants to purchase 10,000 shares.* *vb.* guarantee, declare; authorize, approve *I warrant that with his record for lateness, no one will want to hire him.*

warrior *n.* fighter, soldier, combatant *The old two warriors faced each other on the battlefield for the last time.*

wash *vb.* **1** clean, cleanse, scrub, rub, launder *The clothes and the dishes are all washed, and now I need a bath.* **2** touch, border, reach *The waves began to wash the bottom of the sea wall as the storm became more severe.*

waste *vb.* **1** squander, misspend, dissipate; spend, consume *Don't waste your money on gambling because you won't win in the long run.* **2** decay, dwindle, decrease, wear, wither *Bob has wasted away to a shadow of his former self.* *n.* **1** consumption, loss, dissipation *The waste of money last year will be difficult to make up for.* **2** rubbish, refuse; effluent *The waste from the factory is being dumped directly into the river, polluting it.* *adj.* unused, useless, extra *We take the waste paper and have it recycled.*

wasteful *adj.* extravagant, careless, reckless, prodigal, imprudent

Don't be wasteful of our precious water resources. ANT. thrifty; cautious.

watch *vb.* **1** observe, look (at), note, regard, notice *Watch the way that porpoise leaps out of the water!* **2** look after, guard, attend, tend, protect *Will you please watch the baby while I run out to buy some milk?* *n.* **1** timepiece, chronometer *No, I don't have a watch that speaks the time—I have to look at it.* **2** vigil, patrol, shift, duty *When we sailed from Bermuda, each of us took turns standing three-hour watches.* **3** guard, sentinel, sentry, watchman *The midnight watch approached us and demanded the password, which I had forgotten.*

watchful *adj.* attentive, alert, vigilant, careful, cautious, wary *When on guard duty, you must be watchful at all times.*

waterfall *n.* cataract, cascade *Please name the highest waterfall in the world.*

wave *n.* **1** undulation, ripple, breaker, whitecap, surf, sea *The waves on that coastline are very good for surfing.* **2** surge, swell, flow, tide, stream *A wave of protest followed the prime minister's announcement about imports.* *vb.* **1** flutter, stream, flap *The flag waved in the slightest breeze.* **2** gesture, signal, beckon, motion *When I saw my son coming, we both waved at each other.*

waver *vb.* **1** flicker *The light wavered and we could hardly see.* **2** hesitate, deliberate *Why do you waver over a decision as important as the one you must make?*

way *n.* **1** manner, method, approach, style, technique; fashion, mode; means, system, procedure *Which way would you suggest as the best for getting good work out of a student?* **2** road, path, trail *A narrow way leads to the stable at the back.* *n. phr.* **by the way** incidentally *By the way, did you remember to bring your walking shoes?* **by way of** through, via *You can get to Aston by way of Birmingham.* **under way** going, proceeding, moving, leaving, departing *We have to be under way before dark.*

wayward *adj.* contrary, stubborn, obstinate, headstrong, disobedient, naughty *What can the community do to help these wayward children?* ANT. obedient, submissive.

weak *adj.* **1** feeble, frail, fragile, delicate *The legs of the table are too weak to support your standing on the top.* **2** diluted, watery *This drink is a little too weak for me.* **3** undecided, irresolute, unsteady, wavering *That poor fellow is so weak that he lets his wife tell him when he's hungry and thirsty.* ANT. (1) strong, powerful.

weakling *n.* namby-pamby, sissy, milksop *Boltoff is such a weakling that he is afraid to do anything lest it offend someone.*

weakness *n.* failing, soft spot *I have a weakness for a woman's tears.* ANT. strength.

wealth *n.* **1** riches, fortune, property, means, money *The Grindles' wealth comes from a factory they own.* **2** quantity, abundance, profession *There's a wealth of mineral resources at the bottom of the sea if we could only find some economical way to get at it.*

wealthy *adj.* rich, well-to-do, prosperous, affluent *He might be wealthy now, but I remember Arthur when he was a destitute used-car dealer.* ANT. poor, destitute, impoverished, poverty-stricken.

weapon *n.* arms, armament *In that part of the city everyone carried a weapon against armed attack.*

wear *vb.* have on, be dressed in *What was she wearing when you last saw her?*

weary *adj.* **1** tired, exhausted, fatigued *I'm so weary from that hike that I could sleep for a week.* **2** bored; tiresome, tedious *Mara was just doing the same old weary tasks.* *vb.* tire, exhaust, fatigue *The same old routine, day after day, just wearies me.*

weave *vb.* plait, braid, intertwine, interlace, lace, knit *At one time these people wove blankets and rugs of intricate design.*

web *n.* cobweb, netting, net, network *The drops of dew on the spider's web look like diamonds.*

wed *vb.* marry, take; espouse *Will Sally wed the Duke?*

weep *vb.* cry, sob, lament; mourn *When that monster gets his due, no one will weep for him.*

weigh *vb.* **1** measure, balance, poise *We weighed the ingredients for the cake.* **2** consider, deliberate, ponder, study *You really have to weigh the advantages of having the extra money against working for a company like that one.*

weight *n.* **1** heaviness; pressure; mass, bulk *The weight of the suitcase on the roof rack was almost too much for the car.* **2** importance, significance, influence *Your opinion will carry a lot of weight with the other members of the committee.*

weighty *adj.* important, significant, crucial *Facing a weighty decision, Beazley finally chose the chocolate gateau instead of the éclair.*

weird *adj.* strange, peculiar, odd, unnatural, eerie *Weird things have been going on in that deserted house on the hill.*

welcome *n.* greeting, reception *We always give Dad a warm welcome when he comes home from work.* *vb.* greet, receive *There is a very attractive young lady to welcome you at the door of the restaurant.*

welfare *n.* well-being, good, prosperity *He prefers to look after his family's welfare himself, with no help from the council.*

well *adv.* **1** satisfactorily, adequately, competently *I think that Joe does his job very well.* **2** fully, completely, thoroughly *You are well rid of that unpleasant friend of yours.* **3** surely, certainly, undoubtedly *After the experience, they well know not to try doing such a thing again.* **4** personally, intimately *Of course, I know that lady very well: she's my mother.* *adj.* healthy, sound, fit, trim, robust *Are you sure you're feeling well enough to go out?*

well-behaved *adj.* polite, courteous, good *What a pleasure it is to be with such well-behaved children for a change!!* ANT. misbehaved.

well-informed *adj.* knowledgeable *It is vital for every citizen to keep well-informed about current events.* ANT. ignorant.

well-known *adj.* famous, celebrated, renowned *Claurène DuGran is a well-known lexicographer.* ANT. unknown.

wet *adj.* soaked, drenched; moist, damp, dank *I am wet to the skin from walking in the rain. In this weather, the washing stays wet for days.* *vb.* soak, drench; moisten, dampen *Don't try to wet the stamp too much, or it won't stick.* ANT. *adj.* dry, arid, parched.

whack *n.* 1 blow, strike, crack *Every time he misbehaved, his father gave him a whack.* 2 *Informal:* attempt, try *Let me have a whack at opening that jam jar.* *vb.* strike, rap, crack, slap *The man whacked his son with a stick.*

wharf *n.* dock, pier *The ship tied up at the wharf to unload.*

whine *vb.* moan, cry, whimper; complain *Stop whining about losing the cap from the toothpaste!!*

whip *vb.* thrash, beat, scourge; flog *The cruel man whipped his dog just to be mean.* *n.* scourge, cat o' nine tails, lash *The man struck the horses with his whip.*

whirl *vb.* spin, rotate, revolve, twirl, reel *Mr Cavershaw whirled Marie about the dance floor with wild abandon.*

whisper *vb.* speak softly, mutter, murmur *The girls whispered in the dormitory so that the prefects wouldn't hear them.* *n.* undertone, rustle, hum; murmur, mutter *The whispers of crickets in the grass is delightful.*

whistle *vb.* 1 trill, howl, warble *The birds' whistling in the spring is music to my ears.* 2 call, signal *The referee whistled to mark the end of the game.* *n.* 1 blast, shriek, piping *The whistle of the wind could be heard through the rigging of the ship.* 2 pipe *The old man loved to play tunes on his whistle.*

whole *adj.* 1 entire, complete, undivided, total *I can't believe that you ate that whole apple pie by yourself.* 2 unbroken, undamaged, entire, intact *If only I could make a wish and make the window I broke whole again!* ANT. (1) part, partial.

wholesome *adj.* healthy, nourishing, good, nutritious *It is important to start each day with a wholesome breakfast.*

wicked *adj.* evil, bad; sinful, immoral, ungodly, profane, blasphemous *What a wicked boy you are to have thrown a stone at the vicar!!*

wide *adj.* broad; extensive; expansive, spacious *The car is too wide to fit into my garage. The river is a mile wide at that point.* ANT. narrow, thin.

width *n.* breadth, extensiveness, wideness *The width of this cloth is 54 inches. The width of the road did not allow two cars to pass each other.*

wield *vb.* brandish, handle, flourish, manipulate *Chandler wields that duelling sword like an expert.*

wild *adj.* 1 uncontrolled, unrestrained, unruly *Some of those boys are very wild because they aren't being disciplined by their parents.* 2 primitive, savage *There was a wild animal at the zoo who they said came from far away.* 3 silly, impetuous, crazy, foolish *Going over*

Niagara Falls in a barrel is the wildest stunt I've ever heard of.
4 untamed, ferocious, undomesticated *It's against the rules to keep a wild animal as a pet in this hostel.* ANT. (1) restrained. (4) tame.

will *vb.* wish, desire *Do what you will with the sausages, but please don't ruin the eggs.* *n.* **1** decision, resolution, resoluteness, determination *Jo has a strong will, and I doubt that you'll convince her to diet.* **2** choice, volition *I have come here of my own free will.*

willing *adj.* agreeing, agreeable; energetic, eager, enthusiastic *We were able to find some willing workers who helped in picking up the storm debris.* ANT. unwilling.

wilt *vb.* droop, sag; weaken *These flowers will wilt if you don't put them in water. After a week of unbearable heat, everyone began to wilt.*

wily *adj.* sly, cunning, crafty, foxy *Wayne, that wily beggar, said he was leaving town, and then he took my girlfriend with him.*

win *vb.* **1** succeed, gain *If they win this game, we have no chance of the trophy.* **2** obtain, gain, acquire, get, earn *If you knock over all the milk bottles with this ball, you'll win a doll.* ANT. lose, forfeit; fail.

wind[1] *n.* **1** air, breeze, breath, gust, draught, flurry, puff, blow; gale, hurricane, cyclone, typhoon, tornado *A man by the name of Beaufort devised a scale for winds from calm to hurricane force.* **2** hint, suggestion, clue, rumour *We got wind of what they were planning to do, so we locked every door and window.*

wind[2] *vb.* **1** crank; coil, screw *Wind up my clock, please. Wind the tinsel round the Christmas tree.* **2** wander, meander, weave, twist *The stream winds round and round before coming to the river.*

wing *n.* **1** pinion, feathers *The spread of the albatross's wings is sometimes twelve feet.* **2** annexe *The main part of the hotel was full, so they put us up in the wing.*

wink *vb.* blink; twinkle *We could just make out the lights of the town winking in the distance.*

winsome *adj.* charming, agreeable, winning *Putting on his most winsome manner, my boss told me today that I was sacked.*

wipe *vb.* clean, dry, rub, mop *We wiped the dishes after dinner.* *vb. phr.* **wipe out** eradicate, remove, destroy *The population was almost entirely wiped out during the plague.*

wire *n.* cable, filament, line *The suspension bridge is supported by wires strung across the gorge.*

wise *adj.* **1** intelligent, sensible, reasonable, sage, judicious *You would be very wise to keep as far away as possible from that shark.* **2** learned, knowledgeable, sage; smart *A wise old man once told me that I should never fail to be loyal to someone and to some idea.* ANT. (1) foolish, foolhardy.

wish *vb.* **1** desire, want, long for, crave *I wish to have you near me always. Betty said to tell you that she wishes you all the best.* **2** bid, express, tell *Gentlemen, I wish you a good evening.* *n.* **1** desire, want, longing, craving, yearning *I hope that your wish to visit Russia* *is granted.* 2 order, command, request *In keeping with your wishes, I shall be home by ten o'clock, but I'll miss half the party.*

wit *n.* 1 humour, wittiness, drollery *Della's wit in placing the drawing pin on Vera's chair was what made everyone laugh.* 2 humorist, comedian, wag *Now, ladies and gentlemen, I have pleasure in introducing one of our greatest wits—Cosmo!*

witch *n.* sorcerer, sorceress, magician, enchanter, enchantress, warlock *By the time they discovered that the old women were not witches, they had been burnt at the stake.*

withdraw *vb.* 1 remove, retract, recall *I wish you would withdraw my nomination for being chairman.* 2 retreat, retire, depart, go; secede *When the troops saw how hopeless their position was, they decided to withdraw.* ANT. (1) place, enter. (2) advance.

withdrawn *adj.* shy, reserved, introverted, isolated *Jonathan is withdrawn today and not his usual outgoing self.*

wither *vb.* fade, dry, shrivel, decay *Without water the flowers withered and died.*

withhold *vb.* check, repress, keep back, hold back *Please withhold your questions till the end of the lecture.*

withstand *vb.* resist, oppose *It seems unlikely that the fort can withstand another attack.*

witness *n.* eyewitness, spectator, observer, onlooker *There were only two witnesses to the events that took place in that locked room.* *vb.* see, observe, watch, perceive, notice *Did you witness the defendant remove his gun from the holster?*

witty *adj.* keen, quick-witted, humorous *Winkelreed is always ready with a witty riposte.*

wizard *n.* sorcerer, magician, miracle-worker, conjuror *The wizard waved his wand and it began to rain.*

wobble *vb.* sway, rock, quake, tremble, quiver, dodder *During the earthquake all the plates wobbled on the shelves in the cabinet.*

woe *n.* grief, sadness, misery, distress, suffering, sorrow, anguish *His life as a criminal caused Jesse James's mother great woe.*

woman *n.* lady; female; girl *From the way Martyn is behaving, I'd wager there's a woman in his life.*

wonder *vb.* 1 question, conjecture *I wonder if Tim will ever make the hockey team.* 2 marvel *All the people wondered at how the escape artist could get out of his chains.* *n.* amazement, astonishment, surprise *The children watched the elephant ballet in wide-eyed wonder.*

wonderful *adj.* marvellous, extraordinary, amazing, astonishing, astounding, remarkable *We had a wonderful time at the marine museum.*

woo *vb.* court, make advances to *Kelley should get on with his work and stop trying to woo the boss.*

wood *n.* 1 log, timber; firewood, stick *Please put some more wood on the fire.* 2 woodland; forest; spinney, copse *We went for a walk in the wood.*

word *n.* term, expression; phrase, utterance *I just can't find the words to tell you how happy I am to have won the competition.* *vb.* term, express, phrase, articulate *The speech by the headmaster was very carefully worded to make sure that all the students understood.*

word-for-word *adv., adj.* literal, precise, verbatim *The telegram was translated word-for-word into English. Do you call this a word-for-word translation?*

wordy *adj.* verbose, talkative, garrulous, prolix *These wordy reports of yours, Peterson, are a thorough waste of time.*

work *n.* 1 effort, exertion, labour *It's too much work to write an essay for school three times a week.* 2 employment, occupation, job *Some people have been looking for work for more than six months.* 3 output, product; achievement, accomplishment *An enormous amount of work is turned out by this factory in the course of a week.* *vb.* 1 labour, toil *I wish you didn't have to work so hard to make a living.* 2 operate, run; function, perform *Does your old car still work as well as it did?* *vb. phr.* **work out** 1 solve, calculate *Let's work out the answer to this problem together.* 2 plan, devise *We spent the evening working out where we were going on holiday.*

workman *n.* labourer; craftsman, artisan; engineer, mechanic, operator *We shall need to hire more workmen to complete the job on time.*

world *n.* earth, globe; universe *There are more and more people in the world every day. For twenty years, that tiny island was my entire world.*

worldly *adj.* 1 earthly, secular *He lost all his worldly goods in the fire.* 2 sophisticated, urbane, suave *Women are really impressed by Noel's worldly manner.* ANT. (1) spiritual.

worry *vb.* 1 fret, bother; grieve, agonize *Don't worry about me; I'll be all right.* 2 bother, annoy, pester, disturb *Not knowing where the children are is worrying me.* *n.* anxiety, concern, uneasiness *Now that Martin is safe in bed I have one less worry.*

worsen *vb.* 1 degenerate, deteriorate *The state of morals in this country is worsening.* 2 exacerbate; increase, deepen *The cold weather worsened our problems.* ANT. improve.

worship *vb.* 1 revere, reverence, venerate, respect, glorify, honour *Each of us is to worship God.* 2 adore; idolize *All of the girls worship that new rock singer.* *n.* reverence, respect, honour *The worship of God is a very personal thing with most people.*

worth *n.* value, importance, merit *Can an expert estimate the worth of this diamond?* *adj.* deserving, meriting *I must say that I don't think that film is worth going to see.*

worthless *adj.* useless, ineffective, unprofitable, insignificant *By the time Strahan arrived with the information it was worthless.*

worthy *adj.* 1 deserving, meriting, earning *Is someone who would do such a thing worthy of our respect?* 2 good, worthwhile *I am in no doubt that you are collecting money for a worthy cause.*

wound *vb.* injure, harm, hurt, damage *Abbie came home wounded* *from the fight.* *n.* injury, damage, hurt, harm *Isaac has a wound in his leg from where he was shot by the thief he was chasing.*

wrap *vb.* cover; enclose, surround, envelop *I must spend the evening wrapping Christmas presents for the family.*

wrath *n.* anger, fury, rage *You cannot imagine Father's wrath when he found the car missing.*

wreck *vb.* ruin, damage, destroy *The car was wrecked in the accident. The discovery that there was money missing wrecked the young man's career.* *n.* destruction, ruin, devastation *The ship had struck a rock, and the wreck could now be seen, stranded on the reef.*

wrench *n.,vb.* twist, jerk, tug *I gave it a strong wrench, and the handle came off. With a sharp movement, Charlie wrenched the gun from the man's hand.*

wrestle *vb.* grapple, tussle; fight *My attackers wrestled me to the ground, stole my wallet, and fled.*

wretch *n.* scoundrel, rogue, cad, knave *Some wretch has stolen my chewing gum from under my chair.*

wretched *adj.* pitiful, miserable, sorrowful *When I returned, I found everything in wretched condition after the storm.*

wriggle *vb.* worm, twist, squirm, wiggle *I have caught you red-handed, and you cannot wriggle out of it this time!!*

wring *vb.* extract, twist *Wring out as much water as you can and it will dry quicker.*

wrinkle *n.* ridge, crease, furrow *My grandfather has many wrinkles on his face.* *vb.* crease, crumple; twist *The cloth began to wrinkle with age.*

write *vb.* record, put down; communicate *Don't rely on telling some-body—you must write it. Will you write to me when I am gone?*

writer *see* **author.**

writhe *vb.* squirm, twist *It was terrible seeing Herman writhing about in agony on the floor.*

wrong *adj.* **1** incorrect, inaccurate, false *If you had fewer wrong answers in your exam, you would have passed.* **2** bad, naughty, improper *That was the wrong thing to do, and Morris knew that he'd be punished for it.* **3** improper, inappropriate, unsuitable *You're wearing your shoes on the wrong feet, you silly boy!* **4** out of order, amiss *The thing that was wrong with my watch was that it was overwound.* *adv.* improperly, incorrectly *You've put your sweater on wrong.* *n.* **1** evil, wickedness, sin *People often re-member the wrong that a person has done rather than the right.* **2** impropriety, incorrectness *That poor fellow doesn't seem to know right from wrong.* *vb.* injure, harm, abuse, hurt *The officer was unjustly accused and he felt he had been wronged.* **ANT.** *adj.* **(1)** right, correct, accurate. **(2)** good, proper.

wry *adj.* dry, witty, droll, amusing *Flemworthy is known for his wry sense of humour.*

y

yacht *n.* boat, pleasure craft, sailing boat, cruiser *I shouldn't mind taking a yacht to cruise through the Greek islands next summer.*

yard *n.* court, square, precinct, quadrangle, enclosure; playground *The children should play in the yard where you can keep an eye on them.*

yarn *n.* 1 thread; fibre *You are using pink yarn to darn my blue socks!!* 2 *Informal:* tale, story, anecdote *The old man had many yarns he used to tell us when we sat around the stove in the workshop.*

yawn *vb.* 1 gape *If you had slept last night, you wouldn't be yawning so much today.* 2 gape, open *A huge bottomless chasm yawned before us, and Rebecca almost fell in.*

yearn *vb.* desire, want, crave, long for *On those lonely evenings, Nancy yearned for company.*

yell *vb., n.* shout, scream, roar *Don't yell at me, I'm doing the best I can. Give Bruce a yell and ask him to join us in a game of volleyball.*

yield *vb.* 1 produce, bear, supply *This year's crop will not yield as much as last year's.* 2 give way, surrender, cede, submit, give up *The strikers yielded in their demands after long negotiations.* *n.* harvest, return, fruits, produce, crop *The yield from our investment has been very poor this year. This area has a huge annual yield of strawberries.*

young *adj.* 1 youthful, immature *You are too young to see an X-rated film.* 2 undeveloped, underdeveloped *This crop is still too young to be harvested.* ANT. (1) old, mature, grown.

youth *n.* teenager; lad, youngster, child, stripling *Geoffrey takes a group of youths out on Saturdays for football and other sports.* ANT. adult, grown-up.

Z

zeal *n.* eagerness, enthusiasm, fervour, passion *Bernard's zeal in taking on any assignment earned him the gratitude of the manager.*

zealous *adj.* ardent, eager, enthusiastic *Doris is a zealous sportswoman.* ANT. indifferent, apathetic.

zenith *n.* top, acme, pinnacle *At the zenith of his career, Thridley quit and went to live on a mountain somewhere.* ANT. nadir.

zero *n.* nothing, nought *After the fall in the price of shares, Nutleigh's portfolio was worth zero.*

zest *n.* spice, relish, tang, gusto *Fiona writes with such zest about her travels that I know she is enjoying herself.*

zone *n.* area, region, district, section *The zone immediately around the plant is off limits to unauthorized personnel.*

zoo *n.* menagerie, zoological gardens *Don't you enjoy feeding the sea lions at the zoo?*

All Pan Books are available at your local bookshop or newsagent, or can be ordered direct from the publisher. Indicate the number of copies required and fill in the form below.

Send to: Macmillan General Books C.S.
                  Book Service By Post
                  PO Box 29, Douglas I-O-M
                  IM99 1BQ

or phone: 01624 675137, quoting title, author and credit card number.

or fax: 01624 670923, quoting title, author, and credit card number.

or Internet: http://www.bookpost.co.uk

Please enclose a remittance* to the value of the cover price plus 75 pence per book for post and packing. Overseas customers please allow £1.00 per copy for post and packing.

*Payment may be made in sterling by UK personal cheque, Eurocheque, postal order, sterling draft or international money order, made payable to Book Service By Post.

Alternatively by Access/Visa/MasterCard

Card No.

Expiry Date

Signature   _____

Applicable only in the UK and BFPO addresses.

While every effort is made to keep prices low, it is sometimes necessary to increase prices at short notice. Pan Books reserve the right to show on covers and charge new retail prices which may differ from those advertised in the text or elsewhere.

NAME AND ADDRESS IN BLOCK CAPITAL LETTERS PLEASE

Name _____

Address _____

_____

_____

_____

8/95

Please allow 28 days for delivery.
Please tick box if you do not wish to receive any additional information. ☐